CHINA, INDIA AND THE INTERNATIONAL ECONOMIC ORDER

With contributions by a variety of internationally distinguished scholars on international law, world trade, business law and development, this unique examination of the roles of China and India in the new world economy adopts the perspectives of international economic law and comparative law. The two countries are compared with respect to issues concerning trade and development, the World Trade Organization, international dispute settlement, regional/free trade agreements, outsourcing, international investment, foreign investment, corporate governance, competition law and policy, and law and development in general. The findings demonstrate that, though their domestic approaches to economic issues diverge, China and India adopt similar stances at the international level on many major issues, recapturing images which existed during the immediate post-colonial era. Cooperation between China and India could provide leadership in the struggle for economic development in developing countries.

MUTHUCUMARASWAMY SORNARAJAH is C. J. Koh Professor at the Faculty of Law of the National University of Singapore and the Tunku Abdul Rahman Professor of International Law at the University of Malaya at Kuala Lumpur.

JIANGYU WANG is an associate professor at the Faculty of Law of the National University of Singapore.

CHINA, INDIA AND THE INTERNATIONAL ECONOMIC ORDER

Edited by

MUTHUCUMARASWAMY SORNARAJAH

and

JIANGYU WANG

CAMBRIDGE
UNIVERSITY PRESS

CAMBRIDGE UNIVERSITY PRESS
Cambridge, New York, Melbourne, Madrid, Cape Town, Singapore,
São Paulo, Delhi, Dubai, Tokyo

Cambridge University Press
The Edinburgh Building, Cambridge CB2 8RU, UK

Published in the United States of America by Cambridge University Press, New York

www.cambridge.org
Information on this title: www.cambridge.org/9780521110570

First published 2010

Printed in the United Kingdom at the University Press, Cambridge

A catalogue record for this publication is available from the British Library

Library of Congress Cataloging-in-Publication Data

China, India, and the international economic order /
[edited by] Muthucumaraswamy Sornarajah, Jiangyu Wang.
p. cm.
Includes bibliographical references and index.
ISBN 978-0-521-11057-0
1. Foreign trade regulation–India. 2. India–Commercial policy. 3. India–Foreign economic relations–China. 4. Foreign trade regulation–China. 5. China–Commercial policy. 6. China–Foreign economic relations–India. 7. Asia–Economic integration. I. Sornarajah, M. II. Wang, Jiangyu. III. Title.
KNC842.C48 2010
343.51′087–dc22

2010008739

ISBN 978-0-521-11057-0 Hardback

CONTENTS

NOTES ON CONTRIBUTORS

DOUGLAS ARNER is a professor at the Faculty of Law of the University of Hong Kong (HKU), specialising in financial law, regulation and development. He is Director of the Asian Institute of International Financial Law (AIIFL), Faculty of Law, HKU and Director of the LLM (Corporate and Financial Law) Programme at HKU. In addition, he is the Co-Director of the HKU–Duke University Asia–America Institute in Transnational Law. Douglas has served as a consultant with, among others, the World Bank, Asian Development Bank, APEC, European Bank for Reconstruction and Development, and Development Bank of Southern Africa. Douglas holds a BA in literature, economics and political science from Drury University, a JD (cum laude) from Southern Methodist University, an LLM (with distinction) in banking and finance law from the University of London (Queen Mary College), and a Ph.D. from the University of London.

CHEN AN is a senior professor at the Law School of Xiamen University, where he served as Dean from 1987 to 1998. He is the Chairman of the Chinese Society of International Economic Law (CSIEL, a nation-wide academic society) since 1993 and an International Arbitrator designated to the International Centre for Settlement of Investment Disputes (ICSID) under the Washington Convention by the Chinese Government since 1993. A leading scholar on international economic law in China, Professor Chen is the author of numerous academic books and articles published in China and internationally.

JIANFU CHEN, BSC (CHINA), LLM (HONOURS I, SYDNEY), PH.D. (LAW, SYDNEY), is Professor of Chinese Law and Legal Globalisation and Head of School, School of Law, La Trobe University, Melbourne, Australia. He teaches international business law and international human rights. He has published more than ten books and numerous book chapters and journal articles on Chinese law, comparative law and legal globalisation. His recent work includes: *Balancing Act: Law, Policy and Politics in Globalisation and Global Trade*, ed. with G. Walker (Sydney, 2004); *Rights Protection in the Age of Global Anti-Terrorism*, ed. with Villalta-Puig and Walker (Sydney, 2007); and *Chinese Law: Context & Transformation* (Leiden/Boston, 2008).

CHEN HUIPING is an associate professor at the Law School of Xiamen University. She received her BA, MA and Ph.D. degrees in international law from Xiamen University Law School between 1986 and 1999. She has published one book in English, *OECD's Multilateral Agreement on Investment: A Chinese Perspective* (2002), authored and co-authored several books in Chinese, and published academic articles or book chapters in Chinese and international journals.

B. S. CHIMNI is Vice-Chancellor, West Bengal National University of Juridical Sciences, Kolkata, India. He has been a visiting professor at the International Center for Comparative Law and Politics, Tokyo University, a Fulbright Visiting Scholar at Harvard Law School, Visiting Fellow at Max Planck Institute for Comparative and Public International Law, Heidelberg, a visiting fellow at the Centre for Research in Arts, Social Sciences and Humanity, the University of Cambridge, and a visiting scholar at the Refugee Studies Center, York University, Canada. He was a member of the Academic Advisory Committee of the Office of the United Nations High Commissioner for Refugees from 1996–2000. In 1999 he delivered the first Barbara Harrell Bond Lecture at the Refugee Studies Centre, University of Oxford. His areas of research interest are third-world approaches to international law, international economic law and international refugee law. He is one of the General Editors of the *Asian Yearbook of International Law*.

C. L. LIM is Associate Dean for Academic Affairs and Professor of Law at the University of Hong Kong where he is also a member of the East Asia International Economic Law (EAIEL) Programme. Following a career in England as a law teacher, he served as a member of the Governing Council Secretariat of the United Nations Compensation Commission in Geneva, and as counsel to Singapore in its FTA negotiations while he was a staff member of the Singapore Attorney-General's Chambers. He has acted in an advisory and consultative capacity to various governmental agencies, non-governmental organisations, and international organisations. He gives courses in trade law and policy for the WTO and other organisations. Contact: chin.leng.lim@post.harvard.edu.

MICHAEL EWING-CHOW is an associate professor at the National University of Singapore (NUS) where he teaches world trade law and corporate law. He received an LLB (First Class) from NUS and an LLM from Harvard. Along with some colleagues, he started the first World Trade Law course at NUS. He has been a consultant to the Singapore Government as well as the World Bank and the WTO. Michael has written and published articles on trade law and investment law with a particular focus on FTAs. He has been an editor of the *Singapore Year Book of International Law*, the *Singapore Journal of International and Comparative Law* and the Singapore Law Reports (Reissue) series. He works with various NGOs and is a co-founder of aidha, an NGO which provides financial education and microfinance opportunities for domestic migrant workers and for which he was awarded a Social Entrepreneur of the Year Award.

EDRICK GAO is an associate at Baker & McKenzie, Hong Kong, where he advises on trade-related matters and tax law. He graduated from the Faculty of Law, National University of Singapore with an LLB (Second Upper). While at the National University of Singapore, he was awarded the Law Society of Singapore Book Prize, the APAA Patent Law Book Prize and was placed on the Dean's List. He was called to the Singapore Bar.

NICHOLAS CALCINA HOWSON is an assistant professor of law at the University of Michigan Law School. He practised law in Paul, Weiss, Rifkind, Wharton & Garrison LLP between 1988 and 2003. He writes and lectures widely on Chinese law topics, focusing on Chinese corporate and securities law developments. He is a member of the Council on Foreign Relations, and is a designated foreign arbitrator for the China International Economic and Trade Arbitration Commission (CIETAC). He received his JD from the Columbia Law School in 1988.

LOCKNIE HSU is an associate professor of law at the School of Law of Singapore Management University. She obtained her LLB degree from the National University of Singapore (NUS) and Masters in

Law degree from Harvard Law School. She practised as a lawyer before joining the Faculty of Law of the National University of Singapore. Her work has taken her to stints at the International Court of Arbitration of the International Chamber of Commerce, Paris, as well as at the Singapore Permanent Mission to the UN in Geneva. Her research areas include WTO law, dispute settlement and ASEAN economic integration. She has served as legal consultant to the Singapore Government, participating in a number of cross-border trade negotiations on its behalf. A member of the the Trade Law Committee of the International Law Association (London) and of the Executive Council of the Society of International Economic Law (London), she has frequently provided training in trade law for government officials.

VIKRAMADITYA S. KHANNA joined the University of Michigan Law School Faculty in 2004. He earned his SJD at Harvard Law School and has been visiting faculty at Harvard Law School, a senior research fellow at Columbia Law School, and a visiting scholar at Stanford Law School. His areas of interest include corporate law, securities fraud and regulation, corporate governance in emerging markets, corporate crime, corporate and managerial liability, and law and economics. He is a recipient of the John M. Olin Faculty Fellowship for 2002–3 and his papers have been published in the *Harvard Law Review, Boston University Law Review*, and the *Georgetown Law Journal* amongst others. He has also presented papers at Harvard Law School, Columbia University School of Law, American Law and Economics Association Annual Meeting, the National Bureau of Economic Research, Wharton Business School, Indian School of Business Hyderabad, Indian Institute of Management Bangalore, Tsinghua University Beijing, Stanford Law School and Yale Law School amongst others.

KONG QINGJIANG is currently the Dean of the Faculty of Law and Professor of International Economic Law, Zhejiang Gongshang University (previously: Hangzhou University of Commerce), China. Professor Kong's articles appear in journals such as *Journal of International Economic Law, International and Comparative Law Quarterly* and *Journal of World Trade*. He has authored three books, among which are *China and the World Trade Organization: A Legal Perspective* and *WTO, Internationalization and the Intellectual Property Rights Regime in*

China. He has also authored a few book chapters, which were published by Cambridge University Press and Oxford University Press.

DORA S. NEO is an associate professor at the National University of Singapore Faculty of Law. She was Vice-Dean (Research and Graduate Studies) from 2001–3, after which she took her sabbatical as a visiting scholar at Harvard Law School from 2003–4. She holds a first-class honours degree from the University of Oxford and an LLM from Harvard Law School, and has been called to the bar in England and Singapore. She was a consultant to the Ministry of Law in Singapore and was seconded there in 1993–4. She has researched at institutions such as the UN Commission for International Trade Law (UNCITRAL) in Vienna, Austria, presented papers in the UK, USA, Europe and Asia, was a visiting scholar at Georgetown University, Washington DC, and in 2004, was a visiting professor at the University of Aix-Marseille III, France.

PAUL LEJOT is a visiting fellow at the Asian Institute of International Financial Law, Faculty of Law, University of Hong Kong and a visiting research fellow, ICMA Centre, University of Reading.

RANDY PEERENBOOM is a professor of law at the La Trobe University, Melbourne, Australia, and Associate Fellow at the Center for Socio-Legal Studies, University of Oxford. He obtained a BA in Philosophy, MA in Chinese Religion and Ph.D. in Philosophy before obtaining a JD from Columbia Law School. In addition to serving as an expert witness on PRC legal issues, he has been a consultant to the Ford Foundation and Asian Development Bank on legal reforms and rule of law in China. He is editor-in-chief of *The Hague Journal on Rule of Law*, and general editor of the Routledge comparative law series on Asian legal systems. His recent books include *China Modernizes: Threat to the West or Model for the Rest?* (2007); *Human Rights in Asia*, ed. Peerenboom, Petersen and Chen (2006); *Asian Discourses of Rule of Law* (ed., 2004); *China's Long March toward Rule of Law* (Cambridge University Press, 2002) and the recent: *Regulation in Asia: Pushing Back on Globalization* (ed., with John Gillespie, 2009).

JULIA YA QIN is an associate professor of law at Wayne State University Law School of the United States. Professor Qin teaches international business transactions, international finance, international trade law and

Chinese law at Wayne State University Law School. Professor Qin received her LLB from Peking University, and LLM and SJD degrees from Harvard Law School. She joined the faculty of Wayne State University Law School in 2000. Before then she practised in the Hong Kong and New York offices of Cleary, Gottlieb, Steen & Hamilton, specialising in international corporate and securities transactions. Previously she clerked for the late Chief Judge Dominick DiCarlo of the United States Court of International Trade. She also taught as an adjunct professor at NYU Law School and was a research fellow at the General Agreement on Tariffs and Trade (GATT). Professor Qin has had articles published in various law journals in the areas of international trade law, public international law and Chinese law.

MUTHUCUMARASWAMY SORNARAJAH LLM (Yale) LLD (London) was Dean of the Law School of the University of Tasmania prior to joining the NUS Law School where he is the C. J. Koh Professor of Law. He was Sterling Fellow at the Yale Law School, Research Fellow at the Centre for International Law, University of Cambridge and the Max Planck Institut für Offentliches Auslandisches Recht at Heidelburg, Germany. He is Professorial Fellow at the Centre for Petroleum and Natural Resources Law at the University of Dundee, Scotland. He is Visiting Professor at the World Trade Institute of the Universities of Berne and Neuchatel, Switzerland. He is the author of *The Pursuit of Nationalized Property* (1986); *International Commercial Arbitration* (1992); *The Law of International Joint Ventures* (Longman, 1994); *The International Law on Foreign Investment* (Cambridge University Press, 1996, 2nd edn,2004) and *The Settlement of Foreign Investment Disputes* (2001). He is the Director of the UNCTAD/WTO Programme on Investment Treaties, Pretoria and New Delhi. He is a Fellow of the Australian Centre for International Commercial Arbitration and is on the Regional Panel of the Singapore International Arbitration Centre. He is an honorary member of the Indian Society of International Law.

JOEL P. TRACHTMAN is Professor of International Law at The Fletcher School of Law and Diplomacy at Tufts University. The author of over 50 scholarly publications, Professor Trachtman is a member of the Boards of the *American Journal of International Law*, the *European Journal of International Law*, the *Journal of International Economic Law* and the *Singapore Yearbook of International Law*. He has consulted for the United Nations, the OECD, APEC, the World Bank, the Organization of American States, and the US Agency for International Development. He is a member of the bar of the State of New York. From 1998 to 2001, he was Academic Dean of the Fletcher School, and during 2000 and 2001, he served as Dean ad interim. In 2002, he was Manley O. Hudson Visiting Professor of Law, and in 2004 he was Nomura Visiting Professor of International Financial Systems, at Harvard Law School. He graduated in 1980 from Harvard Law School, where he served as editor in chief of the *Harvard International Law Journal.* His undergraduate education was at the London School of Economics and Columbia College.

JIANGYU WANG (SJD and LLM, University of Pennsylvania; MJuris, Oxford; LLM, Peking University; LLB, China University of Political Science and Law) is an associate professor at the Faculty of Law of the National University of Singapore. From 2006–09, he was on secondment as an associate professor of law at the Chinese University of Hong Kong. He practised law in the Legal Department of Bank of China and Chinese and American law firms. He served as a member of the Chinese delegation at the annual conference of the United Nations Commission on International Trade Law (UNCITRAL) in 1999. He is also a Director on the Executive Board of the WTO Institute of the China Law Society, and a Fellow of the Asian Institute of International Financial Law (AIIFL), Faculty of Law, University of Hong Kong). He has also been invited expert/speaker for the International Trade Centre (UNCTAD/WTO) and United Nations Economic and Social Commission for Asia and the Pacific (UNESCAP). He recently received the Young Researcher Award 2007–08 from the Chinese University of Hong Kong in recognition of his accomplishment in research in 2006–7.

WEI WANG is an associate professor at the Law School of Fudan University, and an honorary fellow of the Asian Institute of International Financial Law (AIIFL), Faculty of Law, University of Hong Kong.

ZHANG XIAN-CHU is Professor of Law and Associate Dean of the Faculty of Law, University of Hong Kong. He specialises in commercial law, Chinese law and comparative law. Zhang Xian-Chu has been teaching both LLB and LLM courses, including business associations, PRC security and insolvency law, PRC commercial law, and cross-border legal relations. He has published extensively in both international and local journals. Zhang Xian-Chu is currently the Director of the Master of Common Law Programme, Co-Director of HKU–PekingU Legal Research Centre, and Deputy Director of the Institute of China and Global Development of the University of Hong Kong. He is an arbitrator of China International Economic and Trade Arbitration Commission (CIETAC), a trustee of the Legal Education Trust Fund of Hong Kong, a guest professor of Fudan University (Shanghai) and Shantou University (Guangdong).

PREFACE

It has never been so timely to examine the impact of the rise of China and India on the international economic order in the wake of the ongoing global economic crisis. The rapid integration of China and India into the world economy is not only lifting the living standards of over two billion people, but also shifting the global balance of power toward the East. However, the implications of this rise on the international economic and legal system have not been fully explored and many questions remain unanswered. For example, what is China's or India's attitude toward the existing international economic norms including the trading system and its dispute resolution system? What is the role of China and India in regional economic integration which may however be highly politically oriented? Further, although China and India are both on the road to economic globalisation, they seem to have adopted different domestic approaches which might have profound impact on their international behaviors.

This volume, having its origins in a highly successful international symposium of the same title organised by the Faculty of Law of the National University of Singapore in June 2006, is an attempt to address these questions. It brought together a group of distinguished scholars on international law, world trade law and law and development to conduct a unique examination of the roles of China and India in the new world economy from the perspectives of international economic law and comparative law. The two countries are compared with respect to cutting-edge issues concerning trade and development, participation in the World Trade Organization (WTO), international dispute settlement, regional/free trade agreements (RTA/FTA), outsourcing, foreign investment law, corporate governance, competition law and policy, and law and development in general. Findings of the papers demonstrate that, though their domestic approaches to economic issues diverge, China and India adopt rather similar stances at the international level on many major issues, recapturing images which existed during the immediate post-colonial era. Cooperation between China and India could provide leadership in the struggle for economic development in developing countries.

The papers presented at the symposium in Singapore have been extensively revised for publication. The editors and authors thank the National University of Singapore (NUS) for its generous financial support and the Faculty of Law, NUS, for its unreserved administrative support of this symposium. The geographic location and the determination to support academic research make the National University of Singapore an unparalleled environment to study China and India. The work fits in well with the flourishing research institutes within the University for the study of South Asia and East Asia. We are especially indebted to Dean Tan Cheng Han and other colleagues at the Faculty of Law, NUS, including especially, Teo Keang Sood and Victor Ramraj, for their encouragement from the beginning of the project. Elizabeth Chua and Daniel Tan at the Faculty of Law, NUS provided exemplary assistance in the organisation of the symposium. We must also thank three research assistants, Edrick Guo and Ng Wuay Teck of the National University of Singapore and Sean Lai of the Chinese University of Hong Kong, for their meticulous help with editing. We are grateful to editors at the Cambridge University Press for their support throughout the publication process.

Muthucumaraswamy Sornarajah
and *Jiangyu Wang*

Introduction and overview

China, India and the international economic order

MUTHUCUMARASWAMY SORNARAJAH
AND JIANGYU WANG

The rise of China and India as global economic powers has now become conventional wisdom. A recent *Financial Times* report, quoting the International Monetary Fund (IMF), observes that "the striking thing about the global economy [in 2007] is how little it relies on the U.S. as the main engine of growth. For the first time in 2007, China's rapidly expanding economy has provided the largest contribution to global growth, while half of the world's expansion over the past year has come from three countries: China, India and Russia."[1] And the implication is this phenomenon's lasting impact on the evolving international economic order. As Martin Wolf notes, "[t]he economic rise of Asia's giants is . . . the most important story of our age. It heralds the end, in the not too distant future, of as much as five centuries of domination by the Europeans and their colonial offshoots."[2]

In June 2006, an international symposium was held at the Faculty of Law, National University of Singapore, to study the resurgence of China and India as world powers from the perspective of international economic law and development. Bringing together a group of eminent scholars from Australia, China, India, Malaysia, Singapore and the United States, the project aims to approach three aspects of the China–India relationship and its impact on the international economic order, including: (1) China and India in the global economic system, especially the multilateral trade system under the umbrella of the World Trade Organization (WTO); (2) China and India within Asian regionalism; and (3) some domestic issues which concern the economic growth strategy of both China and India.

[1] C. Giles, "IMF frets over threat of turmoil and trade imbalances," *Financial Times Online*, October 18, 2007, at www.ft.com. See also IMF, *World Economic Outlook* (2007).

[2] M. Wolf, "Asia's giants take different routes," *Financial Times*, February 23, 2005, 21.

This volume reflects the views and discussions presented at this symposium. In accordance with the theme of the conference, the contributions in this volume are organized into three parts. Part I, comprising seven papers, focuses on the roles of China and India in the Doha Development Round (DDR) and the WTO system. Part II discusses the role of China and India in the regional economic integration of Asia, with a special focus on the regional trade agreements (RTAs) signed by China and India in recent years. Part III touches on some domestic legal and policy issues in the economic development of China and India. This overview offers summaries of the main points in each chapter. Needless to say, given the number of papers and the wide range of themes tackled, this overview attempts not to make a systematic analysis of each chapter. Instead, it intends to provide a synopsis of the issues explored in the various chapters of this book from the wider perspectives such as trade and development, regionalism, and law and development.

I. China and India and the global trade system

Trading nations launched the Doha Development Round in 2001, shortly after the collapse of the Seattle WTO Ministerial Conference in 1999. The Doha Round has not been blessed with success either. On the contrary, from Cancun to Hong Kong and back to Geneva, WTO talks had marched from failure to failure. Indeed, WTO Director-General Pascal Lamy, announcing the suspension of the Doha trade talks on July 24, 2006, sadly declared that "Today there are only losers."[3]

Many reasons explain why the trade talks are deadlocked. Apart from the huge gap between the United States and European Union on agricultural issues (relating mainly to agricultural market access and agricultural domestic support), two other important sets of issues are also responsible for the deadlock of the WTO negotiations, both concerning the division between the developing and developed countries with respect to trade and development in the WTO system. In this regard, the first set of issues is the non-agricultural market access modality, on which the developing and developed nations have substantially conflicting positions. The second fault line is on the so-called "development issues," which are "related to addressing the trade-related development

[3] "Talks suspended, 'Today there are only losers,'" WTO News – DDA June/July 2006 Modalities: Summary 24 July, at www.wto.org/english/news_e/news06_e/mod06_summary_24july_e.htm.

challenges faced by the least-developed countries (LDCs), and the so-called 'small, weak and vulnerable developing countries'."[4]

The WTO deadlock demonstrates that the conventional wisdom is changing, namely that powerful developed countries, leaving aside the differences among themselves, can no longer easily impose their common will upon developing countries. Significant shifts in relative economic and political power among WTO members have become a living process. A landmark example is that WTO negotiations at Cancun in 2003 collapsed after the G20, a block of developing nations established August 20, 2003 under the leadership of Brazil, China, India and South Africa, refused to negotiate the Singapore issues and requested a different negotiating position on trade in agricultural products. In fact, the G20 itself was originally created as a response of the developing countries to a common proposal released by the United States and the European Union (EU) on agricultural negotiations.

The decade of the 1990s was dominated by what writers have termed as "neo-liberalism" or "mercantilism" – an economic philosophy which stressed free market mechanisms, liberalization of the flows of capital assets, privatization and the protection of intellectual and other property rights. The drive toward liberalism was led by the United States and the financial institutions it controlled. The "Washington consensus" sought to dominate the course of global economic events.[5] Europe willingly participated in the project. The instrumental use of normative provisions to achieve neo-liberal objectives is an evident factor of the times, best represented by some of the measures adopted in the WTO.[6] A succession of economic crises in Russia, Asia and Latin America along with growing disparities in wealth within the developed world led to disillusionment with neo-liberal policies and the engines of globalization which profited from it. Disenchantment with "trickle down" economics led to vigorous protests particularly in the capitals of the developed world. A return to concerns with development of the poorer states, the

[4] Faizel Ismail, "One year since the WTO Hong Kong Ministerial Conference: Developing countries reclaim the development content of the WTO Doha Round," in Yong-Shik Lee (ed.), *Economic Development through World Trade: A Developing World Perspective* (The Netherlands: Kluwer Law International, 2007), p. 122.

[5] The term "Washington consensus" describes an assumed understanding between the White House, the World Bank and the International Monetary Fund to use their power to give effect to neo-liberal economic policies.

[6] Principally, the TRIPs instrument on intellectual property was seen as securing the interests of the large US pharmaceutical companies. The measures were dismantled by collective action by developing states in some areas.

spoliation of the environment and promotion of human rights ensured that the era of untrammeled propitiation of the forces of capital ended. The degree of concern that existed for development in the period after decolonization returned. China and India were the natural leaders of this concern with economic development. The study of their roles assumes particular significance in the light of these changing concerns.

China and India, the two largest developing countries, have a common and vital interest both in trading with each other and cooperating in the WTO to advance the trade and development agenda.[7] An important question to ask is what can the WTO do to accommodate the development needs of developing countries such as China and India? Arguments have been made to point out that the WTO may have a "development deficit" in that it has only been driven by mercantilism.[8] Hoekman notes that WTO members are now confronted with two challenges: "whether to 'save' the WTO – i.e., a multilateral trading system that is based on non-discrimination and MFN liberalization; and attaining (pursuing) national development objectives."[9]

The papers in Part I of this volume aim to examine China and India in the trade and development context from different perspectives, focusing their roles and positions in the WTO framework. In "The WTO and development policy in China and India," Joel P. Trachtman provides a comprehensive and insightful examination of the constraints that the WTO may impose on China and India as they engage in industrial policy toward development. In essence, Trachtman addresses the regulatory space, or "right to regulate," permitted under the WTO with respect to the ability of developing countries to implement development policy. The paper offers an authoritative examination of the three issues relating to trade and development in the GATT/WTO framework, namely the special and differential treatment (S&D) for developing countries, promotion of domestic liberalization and institutional reform in developing countries, and increased market access for developing country products and services in developed country markets. It also examines the four types of measures (balance of payment measures, subsidies, trade related investment measures (TRIMS), and trade related aspects of intellectual property rights (TRIPS) under the WTO law. Putting China and India in

[7] See e.g. T. N. Srinivasan, "China and India: Economic performance, competition and cooperation: An update" (2004) 15 *Journal of Asian Economics* 613, 630.

[8] Bernard Hoekman, "Doha, development and discrimination" (2007) 12(3) *Pacific Economic Review* 267.

[9] *Ibid.*, p. 269.

this analytical picture by examining the Chinese and Indian regulation for development, Trachtman points out that China and India, like many other developing countries, are not likely to achieve development through domestic protection and preferential treatment. From a legal perspective, Trachtman notes that Article XVIII, a GATT provision which might be replied upon by developing countries to obtain continent relaxation of commitments, is not helpful in practice. Distinguishing among four types of WTO obligations, Trachtman suggests, as a conclusion of the paper, the establishment of a development policy review mechanism under the auspice of the WTO (and possibly other international institutions such as the International Monetary Fund (IMF)) that could provide exceptions to developing countries for deviating from normal WTO obligations in order to implement appropriate development-motivated policies.

Also discussing the S&D issues in general and China and India in particular, Jianfu Chen argues that the current approach adopted by China and India "amounts to a fight for a lost cause and hence a fundamental re-thinking is required if China and India are to become leaders of the developing countries in ensuring a fairer and more equitable treatment for developing countries." He advances a "pro-active strategy," which would require China and India to abandon the S&D approach and to start a completely new strategy. To Chen, S&D treatment has several major problems. S&D has become a politically entangled notion that offers little value to countries that need economic assistance. Practically it is inherently unworkable as "developing countries" is an indefinable political concept. Countries that need development assistance are not necessarily those with the lowest gross national product (GNP) per capita or with the largest number of people still in poverty (such as China and India), but those lacking regulatory and institutional capacities to compete in the global market. The integrity of the WTO system is now in danger partly because of the incoherent and irrational practice of the S&D. The paper calls for the abolition of the politically charged notion of "developing countries" as well as the ineffective S&D provisions, which are to be replaced with shifts of focus to overall economic and trade capacity building. In this regard, China and India are expected to share a joint responsibility to reform the S&D system.

In their chapter forcefully titled "China–India cooperation, South–South coalition and the new international economic order," Chen An and Chen Huiping place China in the broad context of international economic order and law. Apparently arguing from a Southern perspective, they remark that the nature of China–India cooperation is one of South–South cooperation which is to be distinguished from North–South cooperation. Historically China–India cooperation was the core component of South–South cooperation which had facilitated the "first round" of the establishment of the New International Economic Order (NIEO), which both rose and fell in the 1970s. The authors, viewing the Doha Development Round in the WTO as "a new round of the establishment of the NIEO, are of the opinion that a South–South coalition based on strong China–India cooperation is the key to establishing the NIEO in the global trade system.

In "India, China and Foreign Investment," Sornarajah offers an in-depth analysis of the foreign investment policies of China and India at the global, bilateral and domestic levels. In the international arena, the joint efforts of China and India (together, of course, with other larger developing countries) successfully diffused the pressure of developed nations to codify investment liberalization discipline in the WTO. This, though it may not yet be a sign of the restoration of the days of the NIEO from a pragmatic perspective, demonstrates that "cohesion of the developing states under the leadership of China and India could bring about sufficient countervailing power to meet the demands of the developed states, including the hegemonic power, the United States." Further, given their gradualist approach in economic reform, both China and India would be averse to losing regulatory space. Further, with a comprehensive examination of the domestic investment laws and policies in China and India, including the admission of investment, privatization programmes, post-entry national treatment, performance requirements, environment protection versus property protection, corporate accountability and foreign investment protection, as well as the bilateral and regional investment treaties concluded by the two economies, the chapter concludes that the experience of China and India challenges the common liberalization assumption of neo-liberalism in that: (1) it is simply wrong to credit liberalization for the two countries' economic growth; (2) both countries have retained the power to control the flow of foreign investment; (3) it may not be accurate to describe China's success as a result combining neo-liberal economic solution with political authoritarianism; (4) India's experience suggests that the relaxation of rules on foreign investment must be addressed at the same time as the issue of poverty reduction; (5) neo-liberal prescriptions have been resisted by both states; and (6) China and India must be cautious about wholeheartedly participating in international investment dispute settlement.

In "China, India, and the law of the World Trade Organization," Julia Ya Qin attempts to assess the respective contributions of China and India to the law of the WTO with a view to gaining from a comparative perspective a better understanding on the potential impact of China on the WTO legal system. It is observed that China has played a much less significant role than India in both WTO rule-making and adjudicatory process. China's major impact on WTO law stems from the special terms of its accession, many of which depart from the basic norms and principles of the WTO law. The author suggests several factors that determine the different behavioral patterns of the two countries, including experience and legal expertise in the WTO system, calculation of economic and political interests, influence of domestic institutions, and legal culture. Significantly, the paper points out that China's relative passivity in the WTO is directly related to the elite-oriented decision-making culture, which tends to undervalue international legal process and favors instead power and diplomacy-based bilateral dealings. India, as a democracy founded on the rule of law, could however take politically strong and legally principled positions in the WTO.

In their respective contributions, Bhupinder Chimni and Locknie Hsu deal with legal topics concerning dispute settlement in the WTO and regional trade agreements. Chimni evaluates the divergent approaches to the interpretation of WTO agreements from the perspective of developing countries. He observes that the advantages of participation in the WTO dispute settlement system are also a function of the interpretative approach and method adopted by the WTO Appellate Body and panels, as the balance of rights and obligations embedded in the WTO agreements is actually decided at the interpretative moment. The chapter further concludes that the current interpretative approach, combining the textual and activist methods, favors the major trading powers and should hence be reformed from the perspective of developing countries. Hsu compares the practice of China and India in the dispute settlement in the WTO and RTAs. Although China so far has demonstrated the tendency of "dispute avoidance," Hsu finds that both China and India are poised to make valuable contributions in Dispute Settlement Understanding (DSU) reforms and in shaping dispute settlement provisions in free trade agreements.

Dora Neo conducts a comprehensive study of the roles of China and India in global outsourcing of services, focusing on the legal aspects of outsourcing under the General Agreement for Trade in Services (GATS). In particular, she examines the extent to which the provisions of GATS are conducive to promoting and regulating services outsourcing, and the implications of these findings for China and India. Her chapter offers insightful suggestions for improving the regulatory framework for world trade in services, including an update of the classification of services sectors, increased commitments by countries under GATS Mode 1, further liberalization under Modes 3 and 4 and development of rules of origin for services. Further, it suggests China and India, as outsourcing providers, conclude beneficial bilateral or regional free trade agreements with their main trading partners for offshore services in order to get round the limitations currently existing under the GATS system.

From a public international law perspective, Kong Qingjiang traces the history of China's engagement with international dispute settlement. He observes, although China used to be suspicious of judicial dissolution of disputes at the international level, it has been changing this attitude and becoming more receptive of international arbitration. Further, China's accession to the WTO, as well as its commitments to the Treaty of Amity and Cooperation in Southeast Asia and the Agreement on Dispute Settlement Mechanism with the Association of Southeast Asian Nations (ASEAN), has manifested this changing attitude.

II. China, India and regional economic integration in Asia

The chapters in Part II address the legal and policy issues relating to regional economic integration in Asia. Regional trade agreements (RTAs) are proliferating in Asia and worldwide. While Asia has jumped on the bandwagon of regionalism only recently, the current pace of development of RTA initiatives in this region is nothing but daunting. China and India, both late comers, now can be placed among the most active pursuers of RTAs.

Jiangyu Wang examines the roles of China and India in the growing regionalization development in Asia. In the process of the seemingly inevitable regional integration in Asia, China and India, given the size of their populations, as well as their central strategic position in international and regional relations, will undoubtedly play fundamentally important, and sometimes even dominating, roles. Wang notes that, in promoting Asian integration, China and India are faced with a few possible options, including bilateralism, pan-Asian free trade area, and sub-regional integration. After examining the pros and cons of each option from the perspective of small developing Asian countries, the paper concludes with offering a roadmap for Asian integration which advances, first of all, sub-regional integration in East Asia and South Asia, while simultaneously linking up the two sub-regions with bilateral free trade agreements (FTAs), amongst which the most important one should be a China–India FTA. Eventually, all the Asian FTAs will be consolidated into one pan-Asian FTA. China and India are advised to lead the region in the practice of open regionalism and deeper integration.

In Asian economic integration, the Association of Southeast Asian Nations (ASEAN) is also an important player, rhetorically even regarded as the leader of this process. Two papers authored by Michael Ewing-Chow and C. L. Lim address ASEAN-related issues. In his paper titled "The Asian Economic Community: ASEAN – A Building or Stumbling Block for China and India economic cooperation," Ewing-Chow asks how ASEAN should achieve the goal of forming the Asian Economic Community (AEC). Using the game theory to propose a normative framework, he maintains that four factors are crucial for ensuring ASEAN serves as a foundation stone of the AEC. These include clearly defined ASEAN rules and obligations, ASEAN decision-making institutions, ASEAN monitoring institutions and ASEAN enforcement institutions. The author, observing that the existing ASEAN rules and institutions do not fulfill those requirements, offers policy recommendations for improvement. Lim discusses the "China and India" phenomenon from the perspective of an eventual pan-Asian trade regime supported by the two economies. He begins his chapter by describing ASEAN's current attempt to form part of an "Asian mega jumbo-jet" with ASEAN as the fuselage, India as one wing and the Northeast Asian nations of China, Japan and South Korea as the other. However, the main focus of the chapter is on what he terms "an especially noteworthy doctrinal and legal-design innovation" under the China–ASEAN Framework Agreement's Early Harvest Programme (EHP). Lim points out two problems in this arrangement, namely it results in the misapplication of the most-favored nation (MFN) status, which would allow FTA members, the number of which is more than two, to conclude further FTAs on bilateral basis either with members or non-members of that FTA, and the further phenomenon of FTAs which do not in any event contain any significant multilateralized tariff concessions. Given that the world free trade system is based on MFN, the global impact of this novel China–ASEAN arrangement might be negative. He concludes that an arrangement of this kind between China and India might be a useful device for measuring the future impact of China and India on the legal health of the world trading system.

The last chapter in Part II, authored by Douglas Arner, Wei Wang and Paul Lejot, discusses Asian economic integration from a financial perspective. It notes that the prospect for financial cooperation and integration in East Asia is becoming generally accepted as a consensus goal of national policies. This has been driven by reasons stemming from crisis imperative, economic imperative, development imperative and political imperative. East Asian states have launched a number of concrete initiatives supporting financial cooperation and integration in areas covering trade in financial services, cooperation in monetary affairs, and development in Asian capital markets, with the assistance of institutional arrangements developed under the patronage of the Asian Development Bank. However, the essay finds that Asian economic and financial integration is still relation-oriented and lacks a developed institutional and legal framework.

III. Law and development in China and India: Domestic issues

Part III turns to some selected domestic issues in China and India from the perspective of the law and development movement, with special focuses on corporate governance and competition law issues.

Randall Peerenboom, in a chapter which provides a broad overview of the law and development in China and India, argues that the experiences of China and India are not necessarily inconsistent with the prevailing wisdom regarding the relationship between law and development. Although it is generally problematic to make direct comparisons between China and India given the enormous differences between the two giants, some possible observations would suggest that both policies and institutions matter in their economic development. With command economies from the late 1940s to the late 1970s, both countries began economic reform around 1980, although China opened its economy more rapidly than India. Both adopted a gradual approach and both followed some aspects of the Washington consensus while rejecting or modifying others. Surveys show that, to the extent that China and India are comparable in terms of institutional development, India has better judicial independence and property rights protection, but China fares better in regulation and governance. Peerenboom, however, warns that the survey results should be interpreted with caution as China's poor human rights records might have tarnished the image of the judiciary, which in practice might be largely efficient and impartial in dealing with civil and commercial cases. In contrast, India's more dependent courts, perceivably better in protecting civil and political rights, is entangled with judicial corruption and long delays. The author observes that empirical evidence might suggest that, irrespective of whether they are democratic or not, "regimes are more likely to be successful if they are market-oriented, dominated by technocrats, and relatively free from corruption, and they invest in human capital and institutional development." It remains to be seen, however, how far China and India can march even though they seem to be already on this track.

Nicholas Howson and Vikramaditya Khanna examine the development of modern corporate governance in China and India. In particular, their chapter examines the impact of "legal origins" (common law or civil) on the development of capital markets and whether the collective experiences of the two countries support the literature of global convergence in corporate law. The historical development of their stock markets does not verify that the "legal origin" account provides the best explanation. In contrast, their experiences seem to be more consistent with the politics account, which argues that political forces account for the different configuration of corporate governance structures. In terms of convergence in corporate law, the paper finds only partial evidence of convergence in law, but not in ownership or corporate structure. Given the concentrated ownership of big firms in China and India, it remains a mysterious research question why both countries have tended to adopt the Anglo-American model in reforming their corporate laws.

The last paper in this volume, authored by Zhang Xian-Chu, discusses the competition law regime in China and India. Zhang compares the development of anti-monopoly law in China and India, with a view to reflecting upon the two countries' different paths and concerns regarding modernization. Both China and India have recognized the importance of an anti-monopoly regime as crucial efficiency-enhancing institution. China now seems to be particularly enthusiastic in putting a system into practice. Further, both China and India are facing infrastructural and resources constraints in building a sound anti-monopoly regime. India, however, seems to be more active at the multilateral front, especially in the WTO's negotiations on competition policy-related issues. On domestic institutional building, China has also a lot to learn from India with respect to, in particular, the independence of the judiciary and the competition authority.

IV. Concluding remarks

This collection of essays focuses on the attitudes to international trade and investment of two emerging powers whose impact on international economic law will come to be increasingly felt. As the various contributors demonstrate, though the domestic approaches of China and India to economic issues diverge, they adopt rather similar stances at the international level, recapturing images which existed during the immediate post-colonial era. Their adoption of common policies toward the search for oil and increasing trade relations may submerge recent armed hostilities and recapture an historical age of active interaction which contributed much to mankind. If such a pattern emerges, the two countries could successfully provide leadership in the struggle for economic development. If, however, they are to emerge as competitors, the outcome would be a region divided on trade issues and partisanship toward either power. There is evidence of the latter trend as well. These are developments that need to be watched by scholars in the field and the chapters in this book provide a legal prism through which the developments could be studied.

Too optimistic a picture should not be painted as yet. Despite increasing contacts between the states, as evidenced by the visit of the Indian Prime Minister to China in the second week of January, 2008, there are many problems which still remain. China still claims the area that is Arunachal Pradesh and India claims that some 38,000 square miles on its border are occupied by Chinese forces. There is a theory that India is a part of the encirclement of China but that China too seeks the encirclement of India. These security concerns will have to be ironed out for meaningful cooperation to take place. In the light of past experience, when war broke out after a period of complacent relationship promoted by early Indian governments, there is an understandable reluctance to engage fully in close relations with China. Trade may well ensure that these feelings will take a backstage.

Exogenous factors such as the changing patterns of dominance of the international system are always relevant to the law. The existing international economic law was fashioned during the dominance of the United States when it espoused a neo-liberal vision. The dominance of the United States is now in decline and its imperial overstretch is expected to hasten that decline. The several candidates for the American presidency (2008 election) have announced their desire to move away from the neo-liberal model and the treaty systems it spawned. With the election of Obama, it could well be that there would be an adoption of protectionist policies which were announced during the campaign. The economic crisis in the United States and Europe has indicated the insufficiencies of the neo-liberal model that they along with the financial institutions advocated for the rest of the world. It is very difficult to envisage that there could be an effective propagation of this model in the future. The competing models that were instituted with success particularly in some states of East and Southeast Asia will gather greater credibility. At this time, China and India have emerged with new visions to offer. It is indeed an opportune time to initiate concerns with other visions of the international economic order. The impact of the present financial crisis on their economies is difficult to assess as yet. But, since they had not adopted policies of complete liberalization, their exposure to the economic schemes that resulted in the crisis would not be great. Yet, the fact that the traditional areas of export are undergoing turmoil would definitely require changes in policy. The study of these trends and the impact that the China and India will have on the developments of international economic law will have great significance. This book begins such a study.

References

Giles, C., "IMF frets over threat of turmoil and trade imbalances," *Financial Times Online*, October 18, 2007, at www.ft.com

Hoekman, Bernard, "Doha, development and discrimination" (2007) 12(3) *Pacific Economic Review* 267

IMF, *World Economic Outlook* (2007)

Ismail, Faizel, "One year since the WTO Hong Kong Ministerial Conference: Developing countries reclaim the development content of the WTO Doha Round," in Yong-Shik Lee (ed.), *Economic Development through World Trade: A Developing World Perspective* (The Netherlands: Kluwer Law International, 2007)

Srinivasan, T. N., "China and India: Economic performance, competition and cooperation: An update" (2004) 15 *Journal of Asian Economics* 613

"Talks suspended, 'Today there are only losers'," *WTO News* – DDA June/July 2006 Modalities: Summary 24 July, at www.wto.org/english/news_e/news06_e/mod06_summary_24july_e.htm

Wolf, M., "Asia's giants take different routes," *Financial Times*, February 23, 2005

PART I

China, India and the global trade system

1

The WTO and development policy in China and India

JOEL P. TRACHTMAN

I. Introduction

China and India are the two largest developing countries by population and Gross Domestic Product (GDP). Together they account for one third of the world's population and approximately one sixth of the world's GDP. Together, they account for half of the world's poor. They have experienced remarkable growth over the past decade. How does the (WTO) World Trade Organization figure in the further growth of China and India?

Both China and India were original members of the General Agreement on Tariffs and Trade 1947 (GATT). The government of Taiwan purported to withdraw China from the GATT after the 1949 revolution, and China famously acceded to the WTO at the end of 2001. China and India are individually and collectively an important force at the WTO. Their presence is even more critical because of their role as developing countries. However, these two countries demonstrate well that the group of developing countries is diverse, and is not always united in its interests. While China, India and a handful of other large developing countries can be expected to lead the developing country bloc, this bloc includes a good deal of diversity of interest.

To some extent, China and India are like other countries. They have domestic producers interested in protection from competition, domestic producers interested in promoting exports and domestic consumers interested in inexpensive goods. Unlike many small countries, China and

I am grateful for research suggestions and comments on earlier drafts to Steven Block, Michael Ewing-Chow, Kevin Gallagher, Julia Ya Qian, M. Sornarajah, Jiangyu Wang, and participants at the Conference on China, India and the New International Economic Order held at the National University of Singapore in June 2006, at which an earlier version of this chapter was presented. I also wish to thank Nirmalaguhan Wigneswaran for excellent research assistance. Errors are mine.

India are large enough to have terms of trade power – the power to affect prices in world markets. Standard political economy analysis suggests that domestic producers interested in protection would be able to overcome domestic consumers interested in inexpensive goods without the political intervention of domestic producers interested in promoting exports.

The WTO provides an occasion to motivate domestic producers interested in promoting exports to intervene, by providing the possibility for commitments by other states to liberalize access for their exports. This promotes liberalization and the possibility of export-led growth. Yet, the WTO also provides restrictions that are understood by some to limit the scope for industrial policy that can also induce growth. How can WTO rules be structured to limit the scope for protection by developing countries while maximizing the scope for industrial policy that promotes growth? How have WTO rules so far affected the ability of India and China to promote growth in these respects?

This essay examines the constraints that the WTO may impose on China and India as they engage in industrial policy toward development. One of the critical questions about the GATT and the WTO has been the degree to which they have constrained the "right to regulate," in particular the degree to which they have constrained the ability of developing countries to implement development policy.[1] In 2004, Dani Rodrik wrote that

> [a]lmost all successful cases of development in the last fifty years have been based on creative and often heterodox policy innovations . . . nations combined their trade policy with unorthodox policies: high levels of tariff and non-tariff barriers, public ownership of large segments of banking and industry, export subsidies, domestic content requirements, import–export linkages, patent and copyright infringements, directed credit, and restrictions on capital flows . . . [T]rade liberalization was a gradual process.[2]

Of course, the correlation of these heterodox policies with successful development would not necessarily indicate a causal relationship. Nor is there solid econometric evidence of correlation between heterodoxy and growth, or of correlation between orthodoxy and growth. Still, it is worth assessing, as a descriptive if not a normative matter, which heterodox policies are constrained by WTO law.

In Section II, I examine the main relationships between trade liberalization and poverty reduction. In Section III, I examine the ways in

[1] See, e.g., Kevin P. Gallagher (ed.), *Putting Development First: The Importance of Policy Space in the WTO and International Financial Institutions* (London: Zed Books, 2005).

[2] Dani Rodrik, 'How to make the trade regime work for development' (2004), available at http://ksghome.harvard.edu/~drodrik/How%20to%20Make%20Trade%20Work.pdf.

which WTO rules constrain the policy space available to developing countries generally. In Sections IV and V, I examine how these constraints compare with development policy in China and India. In Section VI, I examine the challenges and possible accommodations that may develop between WTO rules and development policy.

II. Trade liberalization and poverty reduction

There is a broad consensus among economists and policy-makers that liberalized trade will *generally* assist in increasing incomes in developing countries, although there is disagreement regarding the point in a state's economic history when liberalization is best.

Three issues relating to trade liberalization and development have been important since the early history of the GATT: (i) special and differential treatment for developing countries, (ii) promotion of domestic liberalization and institutional reform in developing countries, and (iii) increased market access for developing country products and services in developed country markets (as well as other developing country markets).

A. Special and differential treatment

Although it features prominently in the Doha Development Agenda, it appears that the concept of "Special and Differential Treatment" (S&D), at least as applied so far, has limited utility.[3] S&D is a complex phenomenon – some aspects of S&D are undoubtedly somewhat

[3] Paragraph 44 of the Doha Ministerial Declaration calls for a review of S&D, with a view toward making the relevant provisions more precise, effective, and operational. For a proposal to revise S&D in order to make it more favorable to poor countries, see Communication from Cuba, Dominican Republic, Honduras, India, Indonesia, Kenya, Malaysia, Pakistan, Sri Lanka, Tanzania, Uganda and Zimbabwe, *Proposal for a Framework Agreement on Special and Differential Treatment*, WT/GC/W/442, September 19, 2001. For the history of the concept of S&D, see John H. Jackson, *World Trade and the Law of the GATT: A Legal Analysis of the General Agreement on Tariffs and Trade* (Indianapolis: Bobbs-Merrill, 1969), pp. 625–71. For an analysis of the S&D principle, see Peter Lichtenbaum, "'Special treatment' vs. 'Equal participation': Striking a balance in the Doha negotiations" (2002) 17 *American University International Law Review* 1004. See also John Whalley, "Special and differential treatment in a Millennium Round" (May 1999) CSGR Working Paper 30/99, available at www2.warwick.ac.uk/fac/soc/csgr/research/workingpapers/1999/wp3099.pdf; Constantine Michalopoulos, "The role of special and differential treatment for developing countries in GATT and the World Trade Organization" (July 2000) Policy Research Working Paper 2388, available at www-wds.worldbank.org/external/default/WDSContentServer/IW3P/IB/2000/08/26/000094946_00081505321046/Rendered/PDF/multi_page.pdf.

beneficial. S&D includes several specific rules and approaches that can be placed in three categories: non-reciprocity, preferential market access, and permissive protection.[4]

First, S&D includes the concept, initially expressed in the mid-1960s, that poor countries will not be expected or requested to make reciprocal concessions in trade negotiations ("non-reciprocity").[5] This concept has clearly been honored in the breach in connection with recent negotiations with China and India, with leading industrialized countries and even WTO officials calling on them to make concessions to promote the Doha Development Agenda. After its articulation in the 1960s, this vague principle was later incorporated in Part IV of GATT.[6] However, as several commentators have noted, those who are not required to reciprocate often find coincidentally that few concessions are accorded to them – even under conditions of most-favored nation (MFN) status.[7] This is because, of course, the products of export interest to developing countries often differ from those of interest to other countries, and so are not included in the give-and-take of negotiation over concessions.

Second, S&D includes the aspiration to provide enhanced market access to developing country products. Partly because of the principle of non-reciprocity, this aspiration was often ignored. However, the area in which S&D has had its greatest effect is in connection with the Generalized System of Preferences (GSP), discussed below, which provides for reduced tariff treatment for certain developing country products.

Third, S&D includes greater permission for protection, in particular under Articles XII and XVIII of GATT,[8] relating to balance of payments. While some economists, led by Dani Rodrik, believe that protection may foster domestic industries, there is a counter-argument to the effect that protection may sustain geriatric or crony industries. Thus, the question about permission for protection is one of selectivity. Robert Hudec

[4] See Committee on Trade and Development, *Implementation of Special and Differential Treatment Provisions in the WTO Agreements and Decisions*, WT/COMTD/W/77, October 25, 2000.

[5] BISD, 13th Supp. (1965).

[6] See Robert E. Hudec, *Developing Countries in the GATT Legal System* (Aldershot, UK: Gower, 1987), p. 58.

[7] See, e.g., Constantine Michalopoulous, "Developing country strategies for the Millennium Round" (1999) 33(5) *Journal of World Trade* 1 at 25; Hudec, *Developing Countries in the GATT Legal System*, p. 46.

[8] See Chantal Thomas, "Balance-of-payments crises in the developing world: Balancing trade, finance and development in the new economic order" (2000) *American University International Law Review* 1249 at 1256.

believed that developing countries, like other countries, need the external constraints of WTO law in order to deny protection to undeserving industries.

B. *Domestic reform*

As Michael Finger has pointed out, "[p]erhaps the least development-friendly side of the Doha Declaration is its willingness to ladle out 'special and differential treatment' without a perception of where developing Members would be better off if *they themselves* observed the disciplines the negotiations aim to establish."[9] For much of the past twenty years, a consensus – part of the "Washington Consensus" – developed that poor countries would benefit from liberalization of their domestic markets. The debate about whether protection of domestic markets is good or bad for poor countries has recently been revived.[10] However, there still seem to be solid reasons for poor countries to liberalize at some point in their development path. Furthermore, there would seem to be little basis for questioning liberalization as to goods and services, such as financial and telecommunications services, that provide infrastructure for other productive activities.

C. *Market access in developed countries*

There is a strong consensus that liberalization by the wealthy states in agriculture, textiles and tropical products, even on an MFN basis, would assist growth in poor countries, although there is wide variation in view regarding the magnitude of benefit.[11] For example, exports from developing countries are limited by continuing developed country tariffs (including quotas that were tariffied in the Uruguay Round), domestic supports, and export subsidies. And indeed, market access in products of export interest to poor countries would be an important way to enhance livelihoods in those countries, although it is not unambiguous. Easier exports to wealthy countries could mean higher prices at home.

[9] J. Michael Finger, "A diplomat's economics: Development and trade perspectives on the Doha Agenda," working paper dated May 10, 2002 (emphasis in original).

[10] See Dani Rodrik and Francisco Rodríguez, "Trade policy and economic growth: A skeptic's guide to the cross-national evidence," in Ben Bernanke and Kenneth S. Rogoff (eds.), *Macroeconomics Annual 2000* (Cambridge MA: MIT Press, 2001).

[11] See Make Trade Fair, Rigged Rules and Double Standards: Trade, Globalisation and the Fight Against Poverty (2002), available at www.maketradefair.com [hereinafter, the "Oxfam Report"].

Reduction of wealthy country export subsidies on agriculture could hurt impoverished consumers in food importing states.

Tariff peaks and tariff escalation in connection with goods of export interest to poor countries has restricted market access not only in agriculture, textiles and tropical products, but also in other manufactured goods.[12] While developed country tariffs now average less than 5 percent, Hoekman points out that tariff peaks – higher tariffs – are "often concentrated in products that are of interest to developing countries."[13] Many of these apply to agricultural products, and they are often associated with tariff escalation, by which the tariffs on unprocessed products are disproportionately less than the tariffs on processed products, providing perverse incentives against manufacturing in poor countries. Tariff peaks may be a result of the principle of non-reciprocity, or may be the result of "simple political economy,"[14] and of a desire to protect the jobs of the relatively poor in rich countries.

While the GSP has provided modest benefits, it has not been applied to provide greater market access for many of the most important poor country products,[15] and the US and the EC have imposed substantial conditions on access to their GSP programs.[16] "Graduation" policies including ceilings on eligible exports have also diminished the utility of GSP. Furthermore, as developed country tariffs have decreased to an average of less than five percent, and with the formation of more free trade areas and customs unions, the preferences under the GSP have been greatly eroded, and will be further eroded in future. The magnitude of the "differential" has declined substantially. If benefits are unstable and are a wasting asset, they cannot form a sound basis for investment that would allow poor countries to actually achieve market access. Furthermore, the principle of non-reciprocity, as implemented through GSP, seems to have the effect of diminishing incentives for liberalization by beneficiary countries.[17]

[12] Paragraph 16 of the Doha Declaration calls for the reduction of tariff peaks and tariff escalation.

[13] Bernard Hoekman, "Strengthening the global trade architecture for development: The post-Doha agenda" (2002) 1 *World Trade Review* 23–45.

[14] Jagdish Bhagwati, "The poor's best hope," *The Economist*, 20 June 2002, p. 24.

[15] Paragraph 42 of the Doha Ministerial Declaration provides a commitment to the *objective* of duty-free, quota-free market access for products originating from least developed countries. If realized, this commitment could be of some importance.

[16] These conditions have been subject to challenge. See discussion below.

[17] Caglar Ozden and Eric Reinhardt, "The perversity of preferences: GSP and developing country trade policies, 1976–2000," working paper dated May 24, 2002, available at http://userwww.service.emory.edu/~erein/research/gsp2.pdf.

In 2004, the WTO Appellate Body made an important decision regarding the scope of permissible conditionality – reciprocity – that may be applied in connection with GSP programs under WTO law. The *EC-Tariff Preferences* decision examined a complaint by India against the European Union (EU) regarding the conditions under which the EC accords tariff preferences to developing countries.[18] The Appellate Body found that the requirement in the Enabling Clause for non-discriminatory treatment does not require formally identical treatment, but requires identical treatment of similarly situated beneficiaries. The distinction among beneficiaries must "respond positively" to the needs of developing countries. Thus reciprocity in the sense of developed countries extracting policy concessions in exchange for GSP treatment is sharply constrained. We may expect that the content and scope of this requirement will be tested in future litigation.

D. What happened to special and differential treatment in the Uruguay Round?

As noted above, prior to the Uruguay Round, S&D included several specific rules and approaches that can be placed in three categories: non-reciprocity, preferential market access and permissive protection.[19]

The principle of non-reciprocity was abandoned, or at least broadly modified, in the realization, as opposed to the rhetoric, of the Uruguay Round. This was partly due to a perception that S&D had not provided significant benefits in the past.[20] One may argue that non-reciprocity was abandoned in the sense that developing countries were expected to reciprocate in terms of market access in goods, and in terms of TRIPS and services. For example, in connection with the core GATT issue of tariffs, cuts were expected of developing countries at only a slightly lower level compared to those provided by developed countries.[21]

[18] WTO Appellate Body Report, European Communities—Conditions for the Granting of Tariff Preferences to Developing Countries, WT/DS246/AB/R, adopted April 20, 2004.

[19] See Note by Secretariat, Implementation of Special and Differential Treatment Provisions in the WTO Agreements and Decisions, WT/COMTD/W/77/Rev.1, September 21, 2001.

[20] See John Whalley, "Special and differential treatment in the Millennium Round" (1999) 22 *The World Economy* 1065.

[21] J. Michael Finger and L. Alan Winters, "Reciprocity in the WTO," in B. Hoekman, A. Mattoo and P. English (eds.), *Development, Trade and the WTO: A Handbook* (Washington DC: The World Bank, 2002), pp. 50, 58 and note 8.

Preferential market access was reduced in the Uruguay Round by virtue of overall reductions in tariffs on industrial goods. The reduction in the value of preferences due to MFN tariff reductions became a significant impediment in the Doha Development Agenda. Furthermore, the Uruguay Round did nothing to reduce the erosion of preferential market access through conditionality imposed with respect to preference schemes (although the *EC – Tariff Preferences* decision has subsequently constrained conditionality). This conditionality might be understood as a type of broad reciprocity.

Third, permission for protection under the balance of payments exceptions was constrained, and effectively reduced, under the Uruguay Round Understanding on Balance of Payments Provisions.

In the Uruguay Round, a new type of S&D emerged. This new S&D includes two facets: technical assistance in connection with implementation, and transition periods. For example, the Application of Sanitary and Phytosanitary Measures (SPS) Agreement, Technical Barriers to Trade (TBT) Agreement and TRIPS Agreement all contain provisions for technical assistance. These provisions have varying degrees of binding force, but none of them may be characterized as clear and unconditional obligations. Important transition period provisions include those in the TRIPS Agreement, the TRIMS Agreement, the Subsidies and Countervailing Measures (SCM) Agreement, the SPS Agreement and the TBT Agreement. At the time of this writing, all of these transition periods contained in the Uruguay Round agreements had passed, although some had been subsequently extended.

III. The WTO and the right to regulate for development

The Uruguay Round agreements did much to reduce the scope of special exceptions from GATT disciplines available to developing countries. This meant that for the first time, developing countries would have effectively binding obligations in the GATT/WTO system. The enhancement of procedures for litigation under the Dispute Settlement Understanding (DSU) meant that these obligations would be judicially applicable, while the substantive changes in the obligations meant that these obligations would actually constrain developing country measures. They therefore reduced the policy flexibility of developing countries.

The Washington Consensus continued to erode after the conclusion of the Uruguay Round.[22] In fact, something of a backlash against the Washington Consensus took place. Part of this backlash included a return to arguments for infant industry protection as a basis for export-led growth. While there seems to be wide agreement among economists that infant industry protection in developing countries is not necessarily adverse to development, there are significant questions about the choice of industries for protection, the duration and magnitude of protection and the effects of protection on reciprocal negotiations for liberalization. Importantly, even the backlash has not included a reversion to import substitution as a strategy for growth. Of course, an import substitution strategy would be aligned with maintenance of high import barriers, which would require a negotiating position of non-reciprocity if developed country import barriers are to be reduced.

The GATT 1947 obligations that developing countries incurred did not significantly restrict their development policy. As set forth above, developing countries had few obligations to liberalize, could use balance of payments exceptions to protect domestic markets and had few other obligations. This changed in the Uruguay Round, with increased tariff and other commitments, reduced access to balance of payments exceptions, greater additional obligations and stronger dispute settlement. On the other hand, while many developing countries accepted broad tariff bindings in the Uruguay Round, for many of them the commitments were well above applied rates. Therefore, the developing countries could simply move up to bound rates in order to obtain an extra measure of protection.

In this section, we focus generally on four types of measures: (i) balance of payments measures, (ii) other protection, (iii) subsidies, (iii) TRIMS and (iv) TRIPS. In Sections IV and V, we examine how the restrictions contained in WTO law might constrain possible development policies of China and India.

A. *Balance of payments measures*

During the pre-1994 GATT period, review of developing country balance of payments measures under Article XVIII lost the power to constrain

[22] See Nancy Birdsall and Augusto de la Torre, *Washington Contentious: Economic Policies for Social Equity in Latin America* (Washington DC: Carnegie, 2001); Joseph E. Stiglitz, *Globalization and its Discontents* (New York: W. W. Norton & Co., 2002).

action. Developing countries won wide discretion to determine their balance-of-payments problems, and to impose quotas in response.

The Uruguay Round Understanding on the Balance-of-Payments Provisions of the General Agreement on Tariffs and Trade 1994 (the BOP Understanding) made several changes. First, it expressed a preference for price-based measures, such as surcharges, as compared to quotas. The BOP Understanding calls on members to avoid new quotas. Second, the BOP Understanding permits the imposition of balance-of-payments measures without advance approval, but subjects them to requirements of subsequent consultations and periodic review. Importantly, the BOP Understanding affirms that WTO dispute settlement "may be invoked with respect to any matter arising from the application of restrictive import measures taken for balance-of-payment purposes." The role of dispute settlement itself was disputed in a case brought against India in 1997, discussed below. Given the inconclusive nature of most political consultations regarding balance-of-payment measures, binding dispute settlement brought the possibility of greater limitations on the freedom of action of developing countries.

The possibility of protection for balance-of-payments or infant industry protection under Article XVIII of GATT has not been viewed as significant. The member states that by 2005 had engaged in consultations within the WTO Committee on Balance-of-Payments Restrictions are Bangladesh, Bulgaria, the Czech Republic, Hungary, India, Nigeria, Pakistan, Romania, the Slovak Republic, Sri Lanka and Tunisia.

In the years after the conclusion of the Uruguay Round, there were some instances in which states asked whether the GATT-era practices relating to developing countries were really intended to end, countering clear legal text with diplomatic practice, and perhaps intent. This was the thrust of India's position in the *India – Quantitative Restrictions* case, in which India argued for continuity of the lax approach to developing country access to balance of payments exceptions that was followed under GATT. The Appellate Body in this case upheld the clear meaning of the Uruguay Round Understanding on Balance of Payments, subjecting member state claims of exceptions under Articles XII or XVIII to judicial scrutiny. Prior to the advent of the WTO, these claims were sometimes subjected to panel evaluation, but developing countries had become accustomed to undisciplined access to these exceptions.

India had been consulting with the GATT and then the WTO Committee on Balance-of-Payments Restrictions with respect to its balance of payments restrictions since 1957. The Balance of Payments Committee, of course, could only approve or disapprove by consensus. It was unable to reach consensus to approve or disapprove India's restrictions. In the GATT era, this would mean that India's restrictions were *de facto* permitted. However, after the establishment of the WTO, the United States brought a dispute settlement proceeding against India. India argued first that the BOP Committee had exclusive jurisdiction over matters of justification of balance of payments restrictions, and that therefore the panel could not consider this issue.

The original panel determined that it was competent to review the legal status of balance-of-payments measures, and the justification of these measures, to the extent necessary to address claims submitted to it within the scope of its mandate under the Dispute Settlement Understanding) (DSU).[23] The Appellate Body, examining the basic jurisdictional provisions of the DSU, and of Article XXIII of GATT 1994, agreed.[24] This reading is confirmed by footnote 1 to the Understanding on Balance-of-Payments Provisions of GATT 1994 (the "BOP Understanding"):

> The provisions of Articles XXII and XXIII of GATT 1994 as elaborated and applied by the Dispute Settlement Understanding may be invoked with respect to any matters arising from the application of restrictive import measures taken for balance-of-payment purposes.

The plain language of these provisions made India's argument for a narrow interpretation of "application of restrictive import measures" to exclude the "justification" for these measures very difficult to accept, and it was indeed rejected by the Appellate Body. The Appellate Body read the words "any" and "arising from" in footnote 1 to the BOP Understanding to evidence an intent to grant broad jurisdiction.[25] The Appellate Body rejected India's reference to the negotiating history of footnote 1, stating that there is no formal record of the negotiations, and that footnote 1 is not ambiguous.

India had argued that the panel and Appellate Body should enforce a "principle" of institutional balance, found in municipal constitutions, by creating a kind of "political question doctrine" as known in the United States (US), which would be a basis for the "judicial" organs to defer to the more "political" organs. Sometimes these types of devices are known

[23] WTO Panel Report, *India – Quantitative Restrictions on Imports of Agricultural, Textile and Industrial Products*, WT/DS90/R, April 6, 1999, para. 5.114.

[24] WTO Appellate Body Report, *India – Quantitative Restrictions on Imports of Agricultural, Textile and Industrial Products*, AB-1999–3, WT/DS90/AB/R, adopted September 22, 1999, para. 86.

[25] Appellate Body Report, *India – Quantitative Restrictions*, paras. 89–93.

as "passive virtues." The transferability of this type of principle from particular municipal settings to the WTO raises many questions, and the Appellate Body wisely avoided introducing such a principle. Indeed, it found no explicit textual basis for such a principle.

The Appellate Body saw no conflict or redundancy between the competence of the BOP Committee and the General Council and the competence of WTO panels, but considered that panels should take into account the deliberations and conclusions of these "political" bodies.[26] It concluded that the dispute settlement provisions of the WTO can be invoked with respect to any matters relating to balance-of-payments restrictions.

In subsequent Doha Round negotiations, some developing countries have called for a decision to specify that only the BOP Committee would have authority to examine the justification of balance-of-payments measures.

B. *Other protection*

WTO law generally constrains efforts at protection. However, it permits certain types of protection. These permitted types of protection include most importantly tariffs at or below bound rates (to the extent that bindings have been made). By selecting areas for higher tariff rates, states retain flexibility for industrial policy. For example, China maintains wide variation in its tariffs across products.[27] Other areas of permitted protection include contingent protection pursuant to anti-dumping, anti-subsidies and safeguard laws, and protection through standards to the extent of compliance with Article III of GATT, the TBT Agreement and the SPS Agreement. As tariffs have declined, non-tariff measures seem to increase.

C. *Subsidies*

The Uruguay Round Agreement on Subsidies and Countervailing Measures (SCM Agreement) extended the prohibition of export

[26] Appellate Body Report, *India – Quantitative Restrictions*, paras. 103–4.

[27] WTO Secretariat, *Trade Policy Review, People's Republic of China*, WT/TPR/S/161, dated February 28, 2006, p. 65, available at www.wto.org/english/tratop_e/tpr_e/tp262_e.htm (hereinafter, 2006 China TPR). "As a result of its accession negotiations, China bound 100% of its tariff, at *ad valorem* rates. In 2005, the average bound rate was 10%, 15.3% for agriculture (WTO definition) and 9.1% for non-agricultural products . . . There are considerable variations within these averages, especially in agriculture, with average rates for grains (34%), tobacco (25.4%), coffee and tea, cocoa and sugar etc. (20.2%) and beverages and spirits (20.3%) considerably higher than the overall average."

subsidies on manufactured goods to apply to developing countries, and also introduced a prohibition on import substitution subsidies: subsidies contingent upon the use of domestic over imported goods. The prohibition on import substitution subsidies had been understood to be included in Article III of GATT.

The prohibition on export subsidies does not apply to least-developed member states designated as such by the United Nations, nor to those listed in Annex VII(b) of the SCM Agreement, until the GNP per capita of such members has reached US$1,000 per annum.[28] Neither India nor China is eligible for this exception. For those developing countries that are not eligible for this exception, the SCM Agreement granted an eight-year transition period, which has now passed. Therefore, India and China are prohibited from using export subsidies on manufactured goods.

The prohibition on import substitution subsidies had no general exceptions, but only contained transition periods of eight years for least – developed countries and five years for developing countries. Therefore, all developing countries are subject to the prohibition on import substitution subsidies.

The SCM Agreement also includes the concept of "serious prejudice." Serious prejudice occurs when a subsidy (a) displaces exports or imports, (b) results in significant price undercutting, or (c) results in an increase in the subsidizing country's market share. Where subsidies cause serious prejudice, they may be subject to dispute settlement procedures, with the result that they may be required to be withdrawn or their adverse effects removed.

D. TRIMS

Within the Uruguay Round negotiations, the developed countries cut back significantly on their original demands with respect to investment liberalization, and settled for an Agreement on Trade Related Investment Measures (TRIMS) that did little more than codify restrictions that had already been found,[29] or at least considered by some to exist, in Articles III and XI of GATT. Under these provisions, investment conditions that

[28] The states listed are Bolivia, Cameroon, Congo, Côte d'Ivoire, Dominican Republic, Egypt, Ghana, Guatemala, Guyana, India, Indonesia, Kenya, Morocco, Nicaragua, Nigeria, Pakistan, Philippines, Senegal, Sri Lanka and Zimbabwe. See the UN *Least Developed Countries* available at www.un.org/special-rep/ohrlls/ldc/list.htm.

[29] *Canada – Administration of the Foreign Investment Review Act*, BISD 30S/140, 1984. The panel declined to find that export performance requirements violate GATT.

discriminate between imported and domestic goods, or that restrict imports, may be illegal. Thus, the TRIMS contains an "illustrative list" of measures inconsistent with GATT. This illustrative list includes domestic content requirements, restrictions on importation of inputs, restrictions on importation of inputs by restricting access to foreign exchange by reference to inflows attributable to the enterprise, and restrictions on exportation of products. In *Indonesia – Autos*, the panel found that local content requirements imposed in connection with favorable treatment for investment violated the TRIMS Agreement.[30]

Notably, the TRIMS does not restrict the ability of states to impose export performance requirements as a condition for investment permission.[31] Some argue that export performance requirements are a useful second-best response to alleged anti-competitive practices by multinational corporations that might otherwise restrict production for export at their developing country facilities.

E. TRIPS

The TRIPS Agreement raises a number of issues for developing countries. In this chapter, we focus on its restrictions on policy flexibility, and on the ability to provide implicit benefits to local production through appropriation of foreign-owned intellectual property. We do not focus on the absolute costs of TRIPS in terms of implementation and payment of royalties, as discussed above.

The TRIPS established requirements for harmonization of intellectual property protection, as well as minimum standards for enforcement of intellectual property rights. These provisions exceeded substantially the requirements set forth in the treaties administered by the World Intellectual Property Organization, including the Paris Convention and the Berne Convention, which contained no substantial requirements for harmonization or enforcement, and no substantial dispute settlement mechanism.

[30] *Indonesia – Certain Measures Affecting the Automobile Industry*, WT/DS54,55,59,64/R, adopted July 23, 1998.

[31] *See* Dani Rodrik, "The economics of export-performance requirements" (1987) 102 *Quarterly Journal of Economics* 633 (welfare effects of export performance requirements); Patrick Low and Arvind Subramanian, "Beyond TRIMS: A case for multilateral action on investment rules and competition policy?" in Will Martin and L. Alan Winters (eds.), *The Uruguay Round and the Developing Countries* (Cambridge University Press, 1997).

We may understand the failure to protect foreign intellectual property rights as an implicit subsidy to domestic production, and therefore as a possible means to promote growth domestically. As the most valuable intellectual property rights are owned by persons or firms based in developed countries, TRIPS denied developing countries the ability to provide these implicit subsidies at foreign expense.

IV. WTO constraint of Chinese regulation for development

In a comprehensive survey of China's performance up to 1994, Sachs and Woo (2000) conclude that China's phenomenal growth was due to its convergence to a "prototype" WTO economy.[32] In a 2001 paper, Woo finds that the "economic experimentalist" explanation for China's growth is less plausible than an explanation found in "convergence of its economic institutions to those of a typical advanced member of WTO."[33] He sees "China's . . . WTO accession . . . as an attempt by reformers to lock economic policies on to a course for further marketization and internationalization that is costly to reverse."[34] If he is correct, then WTO restrictions may not be viewed as significant impediments to Chinese development policy – in fact, just the opposite: WTO restrictions may be understood as supportive of Chinese efforts to avoid responding to claims for protection and other trade distorting benefits to domestic industry.[35]

In a 2004 paper, Rumbaugh and Blancher find that "[t]rade reforms and commitments made as part of China's accession to the [WTO] have been crucial in promoting its integration with the global trading system. These reforms, which took place over a fifteen-year period, have included substantial tariff reductions and the dismantling of most non-tariff barriers . . . Improved market access following WTO accession has also been important."[36] These authors also see benefits arising from domestic liberalization and foreign market access, and do not see threats from constraints on industrial policy. They report that "[m]any

[32] Jeffrey D. Sachs and Wing Thae Woo, "Understanding China's economic performance" (2000) 4(1) *Journal of Policy Reform.*

[33] Wing Thae Woo, "Recent claims of China's economic exceptionalism: Reflections inspired by WTO accession," working paper dated May 2001.

[34] Woo, "Recent claims of China's economic exceptionalism," 24.

[35] See Gregory C. Chow, "The impact of joining the WTO on China's economic, legal and political institutions" (2003) 8 *Pacific Economic Review* 105.

[36] Thomas Rumbaugh and Nicolas Blancher, "China: International trade and WTO accession" (March 2004) IMF Working Paper No. WP/04/36, 3.

observers have judged that a key objective of China in joining the WTO was to benefit from increased competitive pressure as an external impetus to domestic reforms. Most analyses, indeed, point to a positive net impact for China in the long run through efficiency gains and direct benefits for Chinese consumers."[37]

On the other hand, in a 1997 paper, Zhang and Long write that China used concessionary government financing and tax rates, protection, and pricing of inputs supplied by state-owned enterprises in its industrial policy.[38] Rodrik argues that certain important Chinese industries would not have developed without state support.[39]

Under China's WTO accession protocol,[40] China is permitted to maintain state trading for specified goods on both the import and export side: (i) import state trading is permitted for wheat, maize, rice, vegetable oils, sugar, tobacco, crude and processed oils, chemical fertilizers and cotton and, (ii) export state trading is permitted for tea, rice, corn, soybeans, coal, crude and processed oils, silk and unbleached silk, certain cotton products and certain tungsten and ammonium products. However, under China's accession protocol, the non-state trading enterprise share in imports of crude and processed oil must be increased annually by 15 percent for the first ten years after accession.[41]

China also agreed that purchases of goods and services by state-owned enterprises for commercial non-governmental purposes would be based on commercial considerations under WTO rules.[42] Finally, China maintains price controls or price guidance on a number of products, although China agreed not to discriminate against foreign persons in respect of their procurement of these goods.[43]

[37] Rumbaugh and Blancher, "China: International trade," 12.

[38] Xiaoji Zhang & Guoqiang Long, "China's industrial policies in the process of marketization," in Seiichi Masuyama, Donna Vandenbrink and Siow Yue Chia (eds.), *Industrial Policies in East Asia* (Singapore: Institute of Southeast Asian Studies, 1997).

[39] Dani Rodrik, "What's so special about China's exports?" (January 2006) NBER Working Paper No. 11947, available at www.nber.org/papers/w11947.

[40] World Trade Organization, *Accession of the People's Republic of China, decision of 10 November, 2001*, WT/L/432, available at www.wto.org/english/thewto_e/acc_e/completeacc_e.htm#chn (hereinafter, "Protocol of Accession").

[41] Annex 2A1. Pending conclusion of the review talks, the volume available to non-state importers on that date is to be increased annually in line with the average growth in overall imports of the product concerned over the preceding ten-year period (footnote (2), Annex 2A1 of China's Protocol of Accession).

[42] Protocol of Accession, para. 5.

[43] Protocol of Accession, para. 3.

Importantly, China's WTO accession agreement also provides for liberalization in important infrastructure services, including banking, insurance and telecommunications. Obviously, to the extent that these services are inputs to other goods or services activities, efficient infrastructure is critical to competitiveness.

So, given the liberal model of development that China seems to have chosen, its acceptance of WTO restrictions on industrial policy activities would not seem to curtail Chinese development policy.

A. *Balance of payments measures*

Given China's current balance of payments position, it seems unlikely that China would consider taking trade measures to conserve or improve its position. In fact, China has been threatened by the US if it fails to allow its currency to appreciate. Appreciation of the yuan would reduce the ability of China to continue its export-led growth. The US has threatened China with action under Article XV:4 of GATT.[44]

B. *Other protection*

Pursuant to its accession to the WTO, China has agreed to eliminate most forms of non-tariff protection. However, Stewart reports that "[i]n a number of areas, China has employed policies that effectively limit market access, impose conditions on market access, or give preferential treatment. Examples include:

- discriminatory VAT policies affecting semiconductors (issue was resolved bilaterally) and fertilizer
- failure to provide national treatment with respect to price controls on medicines and drug reimbursement
- preferential import duties and VAT treatment for certain products (particularly from Russia)
- discriminatory application of SPS measures
- disparate standards testing of foreign products compared to domestic products
- inadequate transparency regarding proposed technical regulations and conformity assessment procedures

[44] See Eric Denters, *ASIL Insight: Manipulation of Exchange Rates in International Law: The Chinese Yuan*, November 2003, available at www.asil.org/insights/insigh118.htm.

- development of unique standards for products where international standards already exist (affecting such areas as autos, telecommunications equipment, wireless local area networks, radio frequency identification tag technology, audio video coding, whiskey and other distilled spirits, and fertilizer)
- inconsistent application of the China Compulsory Certification (CCC) mark requirement and failure, so far, to accredit any foreign-invested conformity assessment enterprise capable of testing and certifying the CCC mark"[45]

Most of these examples could be subjected to WTO dispute settlement proceedings, and so China's ability to engage in industrial policy through this form of protection is at least somewhat constrained. Of course, it is not clear that this type of hidden protection, or non-tariff protection, is the best way for China to engage in protective industrial policy.

In addition, the US and the European Union (EU) commenced dispute settlement proceedings against China in 2006 in connection with its auto parts taxation measures. Essentially, China charged a tax equivalent to the tariff on complete automobiles (28%), rather than the tariff applicable to auto parts (typically 10–14%), in cases in which imported parts exceed a specified threshold. This is a clear case of Chinese industrial policy intended to promote import substitution. In July 2008, as this chapter was being concluded, the panel determined that China's measure violates Article III of GATT.

C. Subsidies

China's Eleventh Five-Year Plan does not appear to require substantial industrial subsidies to proceed. Upon accession to the WTO, China agreed to eliminate all export subsidies on manufactured goods, and otherwise took on the full range of obligations under the SCM Agreement. China abolished direct export subsidies for industrial goods in 1991. However, the US charged in 2007 that China applies a series of tax measures that reduce certain payments owed to the government in connection with exportation or manufacturing using domestic inputs, and therefore appear designed to subsidize exports of manufactured goods or to support the purchase of domestic over imported equipment

[45] Terence Stewart, "China in the WTO: Year 3: A research report prepared for the U.S.–China Economic and Security Review Commission" (January 21, 2005), available at www.uscc.gov/researchpapers/2005/05_01_21_china_inthe_wto.htm.

and certain other manufacturing inputs. This dispute was resolved before a panel was established.

China also agreed not to introduce or maintain export subsidies on agricultural products.[46] China further agreed to limit its subsidies with respect to agricultural production to 8.5 percent of the value of farm output, consistent with Article 6.4 of the Agreement on Agriculture. At the time of China's accession, its agricultural subsidies were well below this cap.

Concessionary credit terms and tax remission could constitute either domestic or export subsidies. Chinese subsidies also include: "direct transfers from the central and local government budgets to certain loss-making SOEs; subsidized loans based on a company's export performance in the automobile sector; tariff preferences for locally produced cars; subsidies for poverty alleviation and regional development; and certain tax and tariff preferences extended to special economic and other development zones and for foreign-invested enterprises."[47]

China has maintained export restrictions on products such as blast furnace coke and fluorspar. Export restrictions are generally illegal under Article XI of GATT, subject to possible exceptions under Article XI:2 and Article XX. Under its Protocol of Accession, China agreed to eliminate all export charges except those listed in Annex VI to the Protocol.[48] These export restrictions and charges tend in economic, if not legal, terms to subsidize local firms that use the restricted inputs, such as steel firms. Under WTO jurisprudence, they probably fall outside the SCM Agreement definition of "subsidy."[49] Interestingly, if the export control were applied to a state-owned firm, it might arguably be a subsidy within the definition contained in the SCM Agreement, as there would be a possible state contribution.

D. TRIMS

In the past, China has imposed conditions on foreign direct investment, in order to ensure that the investment is consistent with its economic plans. In accordance with its accession to the WTO, China agreed to

[46] Protocol of Accession, para. 12.

[47] 2006 China Trade Policy Review, citing WTO document WT/ACC/CHN/18, 6 June 2000 (Annex 5a).

[48] Protocol of Accession, para. 11.

[49] *See* WTO Panel Report, *United States – Measures Treating Export Restraints as Subsidies, WT/DS194/R*, adopted August 23, 2001 (export restraints not considered subsidies).

implement the TRIMS Agreement immediately, eliminating export and foreign exchange balancing requirements, as well as local content and required technology transfer requirements.[50] The US has objected that China's encouragement of technology transfer often amounts to a requirement, and that its officials consider export performance and local content in decision-making regarding new investment.

E. *TRIPS*

Pursuant to its accession to the WTO, China took on all of the obligations of the TRIPS Agreement. TRIPS raises the costs to domestic manufacturers of technology, and prevents China from providing an implicit subsidy to its manufacturers by allowing them to appropriate patented technology. The US has continued strenuously to question the extent of China's compliance with the obligations to enforce its intellectual property laws, and in 2007, the US brought two cases against China relating to its intellectual property protections.

V. WTO constraint of Indian regulation for development

Since independence, India has transited from a socialist, state-led economy, to one in which the private sector is recognized as the leading engine of economic growth.[51] In its Tenth Five-Year Plan, the Government of India has suggested that it needs more exports to continue growth, and that it will need to move from a defensive posture in WTO negotiations to a posture that seeks foreign markets for Indian goods and services.[52] This position should empower exporting lobbies against lobbies seeking protection for domestic production.

> Rodrik and Subramanian evaluate changes in India's growth rate: Shackled by the socialist policies and the "license-permit-quota raj" (to use C. Rajaji's memorable phrase) of the past, India used to serve as the exemplar of development strategies gone wrong. It has now become the latest poster child for efforts to unleash economic growth with a turn

[50] Protocol of Accession, para. 7.

[51] *See* "Planning Commission, Government of India, Tenth Five-Year Plan 2002–2007," available at http://planningcommission.nic.in/plans/planrel/fiveyr/welcome.html, Chapter 1, p. 7 (hereinafter, "Tenth Five-Year Plan").

[52] "Planning Commission, Government of India," pp. 12–13. See also WTO Secretariat, *Trade Policy Review, India*, WT/TPR/S/100, May 22, 2002 (hereinafter 2002 India TPR), available at www.wto.org/english/tratop_e/tpr_e/tpr_e.htm.

> toward free markets and open trade. India has yet to catch up to China's growth rates (or even to China's level of income), but thanks to its solid democratic institutions and impressive performance in information technology, the country is in the eyes of many knowledgeable observers increasingly vying with, if not displacing, China to be the country of the future.[53]

Rodrik and Subramanian argue that India's high growth rate began in 1980, preceding its liberalization in 1991. But they are interested in the question of igniting growth, and argue that India ignited growth by moving to pro-market (as opposed to pro-business) policies beginning in the 1980s. They suggest that liberalization did not contribute to igniting growth in India, because it only came after India's growth began. They find that "during the 1980s, protection through tariffs (measured in terms of effective protection) increased, and protection through quantitative restrictions (measured in terms of the coverage of these restrictions) declined only marginally."[54]

India's current five-year plan states that "[i]t is now well recognised that while industrial protection may sometimes be needed to help a particular sector, it tends to raise domestic costs and makes downstream industrial activity uncompetitive."[55] On the other hand, India has raised concerns regarding differences between permission for subsidization of agriculture in developed and developing countries.

Given India's current focus on fostering globally competitive domestic industries through openness and exports, its current policy appears generally consistent with many of the constraints imposed by WTO law.[56] In 2002, the WTO Secretariat's Trade Policy Review Mechanism report on India made the following statement: "Although the proportion of tariff lines that are bound has risen from 67% to 72.4% since the previous Review of India, the average bound rate considerably exceeds the average applied rate, thus imparting a degree of uncertainty to the tariff and providing scope for the authorities to raise applied MFN rates; indeed, tariffs were raised on some items following the recent removal of quantitative restrictions."[57]

[53] Dani Rodrik and Arvind Subramanian, "From 'Hindu growth' to productivity surge: The mystery of the Indian growth transition," (2004) IMF Working Paper WP/04/77 4, available at www.imf.org/external/pubs/ft/wp/2004/wp0477.pdf.

[54] Rodrik and Subramaniam, "From 'Hindu growth' to productivity surge," p. 19.

[55] "Tenth Five-Year Plan," p. 16.

[56] "Tenth Five-Year Plan," Chapter 4, p. 112.

[57] "2002 India TPR," part IV, p. 25.

On the other hand, the Government of India has expressed concern regarding its ability to compete in agriculture, given the relatively loose restrictions on developed country agricultural subsidies.[58]

A. *Balance of payments measures*

Pursuant to the WTO Appellate Body decision discussed above, India ended its balance of payments-based quantitative restrictions. Thus, this is an area in which WTO law constrained Indian policy.

B. *Other protection*

India maintains an import licensing regime with respect to certain vehicles. India also maintains a negative import list that prohibits importation of certain items, applies a licensing regime with respect to other items and imposes government trading monopolies with respect to certain other items. Some of these measures may violate WTO law.

C. *Subsidies*

India is generally subject to the restrictions imposed by the SCM Agreement and the Agriculture Agreement with respect to subsidies. Subsidies are an important industrial policy tool for India. The Government of India provides significant fertilizer subsidies. India provides tax holidays for certain export-oriented enterprises. Export orientation of the recipient alone would not constitute these tax holidays as prohibited export subsidies.

D. *TRIMS*

As to TRIMS, the Government of India made the following statement: "The developing countries feel the need for selective and judicious intervention of the government to support domestic industry and technology creation so as to ensure a level playing field for domestic enterprises. These developing countries also employ an appropriate mix of incentives and performance requirements for foreign investment to achieve specific developmental objectives."[59] As noted above, TRIMS

[58] "2002 India TPR," Chapter 4, pp. 122–3.

[59] "2002 India TPR," Chapter 4, p. 127.

does not impose obligations on states as to investment access, nor does it restrict export performance requirements.

After the *India – Quantitative Restrictions* case, discussed above, was decided, the US and the EU brought a complaint against India in connection with its automotive sector, relating to local content requirements and trade balancing requirements. The trade balancing requirement required foreign investors to export production of an amount equal to import licenses. The panel did not reach the TRIMS Agreement issue, but found that the Indian measures violated Articles III and XI.[60]

E. TRIPS

TRIPS raises the costs to domestic manufacturers of technology, and prevents India from providing an implicit subsidy to its manufacturers by allowing them to appropriate patented technology. The Government of India recognizes that TRIPS may raise the costs of public health measures, reducing health with a negative effect on development.

VI. Challenges and accommodation

Given that most developing countries (China, India, and a few others may be important exceptions) are unlikely to wield significant market power – to have effects on world prices – in most products, they would be unlikely to capture terms of trade benefits from protection. If they were able to select industries for protection accurately, developing countries might benefit from selective protection of infant industries until these industries become able to compete on world markets. Alice Amsden has argued that domestic "reciprocal control mechanisms," under which government support is conditioned upon the achievement of measurable goals, might allow governments to discipline domestic industries in exchange for subsidies.[61]

Like many others, Robert Hudec[62] was skeptical of the ability of developing country governments (and all other governments) to select industries to promote, and to deny protection to industries that have little hope of attaining globally competitive efficiency. He felt that

[60] WTO Panel Report, *India – Measures Affecting the Automotive Sector*, WT/DS146,175/R, panel report December 21, 2001 (appeal withdrawn), adopted 5 April 2002.

[61] Alice Amsden, *The Rise of "the Rest": Challenges to the West from Late Industrializing Economies* (Oxford University Press, 2001).

[62] Hudec, *Developing Countries in the GATT Legal System.*

selective legal obligation – tariff schedules, restrictions on quotas and other balance of payments measures, and today, services commitments – would assist developing country governments in resisting calls for protection from these hopeless industries.

One reading of Hudec's 1987 work might see it as supportive of the trade component of the Washington Consensus: the prescription to developing countries to liberalize.[63] However, this reading, while partially quite accurate, would miss an important nuance. Hudec found that even assuming that some infant industry protection or subsidization is good for developing countries, some legal commitments would also be good. The trick is in the discrimination: who discriminates, and how?

Hudec assumed that the developing country governments themselves would discriminate between good and bad protection, and would use their international legal obligations as a tool by which to bind themselves, or more accurately by which to plead to domestic lobbies that they are bound. Where commitments have been made, and where they now seem inconsistent with development goals of developing countries, what is to be done? Hudec was attracted to the GATT Article XVIII mechanism of multilateral review, and chronicled its rise and fall as an effective mechanism for discriminating between valid and invalid protection.

In connection with the Doha Development Agenda, there are important initiatives toward intensifying special and differential treatment for developing countries: for increasing the preferences available to developing countries and reducing the commitments applicable to them. Hudec's work suggested that preferences, at least as heretofore structured, would do little to help developing countries in the real world. Hudec expected these preferences to be granted with strings attached, or to develop strings over time: he did not expect the developed world to give something for nothing. While there may be greater political impetus today in developed countries to assist developing countries, it will be difficult to translate this impetus into useful preferences. Hudec also anticipated that these preferences would be granted in ways that resulted in trade diversion hurting other developing countries, rather than trade creation putting the adjustment burden on developed countries. At the 2005 Hong Kong ministerial meeting, ministers agreed to provide duty-free and quota free access for products from least developed countries.

[63] While this prescription has been criticized, and has been subject to important empirical challenge, the weight of evidence appears to support it.

This action accords with Hudec's prediction that preferential treatment would devolve into multiple tiers of preferential treatment. Finally, he understood that these preferences would be unstable, making them poor lures for investment, which is the critical factor in development.

Hoekman, Michalopoulos and Winters find that MFN liberalization of trade in goods and services that are of export interest to developing countries would be superior in global welfare terms to more selective preferences.[64] This is a critical point, and argues that developing countries should not be placated by preferences, but should demand MFN liberalization in areas where they hold actual or potential advantage. This certainly includes trade in unskilled and semi-skilled services under Mode 4 of GATS, and even more broadly suggests less reticence to put immigration on the table.

Hudec also suggested that reducing the commitments applicable to developing countries might not be helpful to their development. This is more than paternalism; it is based on a political economy perspective that understands that domestic import-competing producer interests are likely to be more influential than domestic consumer interests. Reciprocity is expected to coopt domestic export producer interests to add their voice to that of the consumers in order to counter the force of the domestic import-competing producers.

Hudec's perspective was developed with GATT market-opening obligations in mind. As suggested above, it is important to distinguish among types of obligations.

1. Category 1: goods and services liberalization. The first category, and the one on which Hudec focused his analysis, is obligations to liberalize trade in goods by removing quantitative restrictions and by reducing tariffs. Although liberalization in trade in services is different, and different service sectors might be treated differently depending on whether they are infrastructural or consumer services, many types of services liberalization can be treated as analogous to goods liberalization. Some types of services liberalization, such as Mode 4 services liberalization involving movement of natural persons to perform services, may provide substantial benefits to developing countries in particular service sectors. Other types of services liberalization, such as Mode 3 commercial presence, are akin to investment liberalization addressed in Category 4 below.

[64] Bernard Hoekman, Constantine Michalopolous, and L. Alan Winters, "Special and differential treatment in the WTO: Moving forward" (2004) 27 *The World Economy* 481.

2. Category 2: standards liberalization. The second category, implicating the "right to regulate" prudentially, is regulation of standards for manufactured goods and sanitary and phytosanitary standards for agricultural goods. This type of liberalization, in the form of disciplines on importing country product standards, is an adjunct to liberalization of explicit protection through restrictions on quotas and tariff bindings. This may assist developing countries, but it is also costly for developing countries to comply with required procedures. Furthermore, it leaves in place much of developed country product standards, which may be costly for developing country firms to meet.
3. Category 3: intellectual property rights. There is some argument that intellectual property rights protections, at least in some fields such as drugs that cure tropical diseases, might be useful to developing countries. However, it seems clear that as a whole, the increased protection of intellectual property rights required of developing countries by the TRIPS component of the Uruguay Round bargain resulted in welfare losses to developing countries. Furthermore, requirements to protect intellectual property diminish the ability of developing countries to provide implicit subsidies to local industry at the expense of foreign intellectual property holders.
4. Category 4: investment measures. While there have been initiatives to include a full panoply of requirements investment liberalization and protection within the WTO, these have not been successful. The existing rules in TRIMS are extensions of GATT obligations prohibiting requirements of local inputs and restrictions on importation of inputs as conditions for investment. Category 4 also includes investment liberalization requirements in services pursuant to Mode 3 (commercial presence) of GATS.
5. Category 5: export subsidies and import substitution subsidies. Under the WTO Agreement on Subsidies and Countervailing Measures, the GATT prohibition on export subsidies is extended to import substitution subsidies, and is applicable to developing countries (but not to least developed countries).

In economic, political and legal analysis, each of these categories should be considered separately. It complicates and muddies analysis to recognize that the Uruguay Round, like the Doha Round, is a package deal. Of course, package deals may involve trade-offs between components, such that it is unrealistic to evaluate any component individually. However, we must at least begin by analyzing the components individually, before we can synthesize an overall perspective.

It is perhaps facile to say that the main commitments in Category 1 relating to liberalization leave room for economic regulation. In connection with goods, developing countries, like other countries, make the commitments for tariff reduction that they negotiate. Their negotiation should be informed by their overall economic policy.

To what extent are developing countries making commitments that are too great – that are inconsistent with their economic growth strategy? Of course, developing countries, like other WTO members, are generally prohibited from imposing quotas under Article XI of GATT, although they may be eligible for balance of payments exceptions, as further discussed below. But quotas are a particularly wasteful form of protection, and there is little reason to protect the right to regulate through *de jure* quotas.

Hudec concluded that it would be a good thing for developing countries to accept market opening obligations of the Category 1 type. He did so on the basis that, even assuming that some protection is economically beneficial, not all protection would be beneficial. Therefore, and because governments find it difficult to resist claims for protection, developing country governments would need external support to resist the less desirable claims for protection.

According to Hudec's model, this is the critical function of GATT law. However, Hudec left unanswered several questions. First, he did not explain how commitments could be made in the first place if domestic industry lobbied for protection. Second, he did not explain why commitments would be made in the "right" sectors. Third, he did not explain why the incremental leverage against protectionism that WTO law would provide would be enough to prevail. The first two questions can be answered by appeal to the possible existence of an inconsistency in interests across time. Perhaps the protectionist interests would not yet have arisen at the time the commitments are entered into, or are at that time would not be weak enough to be the ones that would be subject to commitments.

Hudec's model also could not anticipate the significant amount of unilateral liberalization effected by developing countries since 1987. Much of this liberalization did not take place in a formal reciprocal context, although it is possible that it constituted asynchronous reciprocity, or was motivated by the desire to have a reciprocal threat to use to hold open foreign markets.

Perhaps time inconsistency explains the importance of Article XVIII to Hudec, as what we might term a "development safeguard" mechanism.[65] Article XIX of GATT, the general safeguards provision, does not provide any special privileges to developing countries. However, it does address the problem of time inconsistency where commitments give rise to unforeseen increases in imports. Article XIX itself requires compensation in another sector, although the Uruguay Round Safeguards Agreement delays the obligation to provide compensation.

Article XVIII could provide a broader tool, more easily available to developing countries, by which to obtain contingent relaxation of commitments. But Article XVIII has disappointed in a variety of ways, at various times. At some times, it has been too readily available, licensing all defections from commitments. With *carte blanche* under Article XVIII, or more broadly under Part IV of GATT, developing country commitments would mean little, either to trade partners or to domestic governments seeking arguments by which to resist domestic industries seeking protection. The purpose of Article XVIII, as envisioned in 1955 when the current version was established, is appealing today:

> The general concept of the new Article is that economic development is consistent with the objectives of the General Agreement and that the raising of the general standards of living of the underdeveloped countries which should be the result of economic development will facilitate the attainment of the objectives of the Agreement. In that sense, the new text represents a new and more positive approach to the problem of economic development and to the ways and means of reconciling the requirements of economic development with the obligations undertaken under the General Agreement regarding the conduct of commercial policy.

Article XVIII:B became the principal provision used, as it did not require prior authorization – it allows unilateral protective action. However, even Article XVIII:B has not withstood the move away from import substitution and the establishment of the WTO. Most countries that were using Article XVIII:B have now unilaterally ceased application, while India was forced to cease application through litigation.

However, in order to discriminate more accurately, in terms of economic development rather than in terms of domestic political power in the protecting country, it seems desirable to restructure and reinvigorate an Article XVIII:B-type mechanism. Ideally, such a mechanism would

[65] See the 1979 Decision on Safeguard Action for Development Purposes, 26 BISD 209–210 (1980) (providing a facility for special safeguards in order to address development needs).

provide careful and independent analysis of the justification for derogation from all WTO obligations, including but not limited to the GATT itself.[66]

At present, the WTO itself probably lacks the institutional capacity to engage in the type of detailed analysis that would be required. Under current rules and arrangements, the WTO relies to a significant extent on analysis by the IMF of balance of payments ramifications of derogations from WTO commitments under Article XVIII:B. This type of arrangement could be extended to deal more explicitly with development policy, and other organizations, such as the World Bank, could be involved.[67] The goal would be to evaluate proposed derogations to determine their consistency with the development needs of the proposing state. Under this mechanism measures consistent with development needs would be approved and accepted despite any inconsistency with other WTO obligations.

Such a mechanism could be applied wholesale to Category 1 obligations in much the same way that Article XVIII:B was intended to operate. In order for it to be useful, however, such a mechanism must apply in a way that developing countries can trust it to be available to allow appropriate derogations, and that other countries can trust it to disallow inappropriate derogations. So, it must be depoliticized and it will also take some time to develop a "jurisprudence" that would make derogations predictable. This would be a jurisprudence of development economics.

An alternative might rely on the concept of Article XVIII:C, relating to infant industries. The real development concern today is not so much balance of payments as contemplated by Article XVIII:B, as fostering the growth of industry in developing countries. For a variety of reasons, including the requirement of compensation, Article XVIII:C has only been used by Bangladesh.

Of course, the concept of Article XVIII:C is that of import substitution, at least in the sense that it is premised on the idea that by blocking imports of competing goods, a local industry may be fostered. The import substitution concept was discredited by the subsequently discredited Washington Consensus, but one might argue alternatively that

[66] See Hoekman, Michalopolous and Winters, "Special and differential treatment in the WTO" (calling for a "country-specific approach that would make implementation of new rules a function of national priorities").

[67] See J. Michael Finger, *The Doha Agenda and Development: A View from the Uruguay Round* (Manila: Asian Development Bank, 2002).

the Article XVIII:C concept is not limited to import substitution, but expects that after a period of domestic dominance the protected local industry will become capable of competing on global markets, including in an unprotected domestic market.

This concept would find some support in the Washington Consensus, but leaves unanswered three questions: (i) are protected markets or competitive markets more conducive to the growth of global competitors, (ii) how can governments select and foster domestic industries that will develop into global competitors under protection and (iii) how can protected industries be weaned from protection? It is not clear that developed country governments or international organizations have better tools with which to answer these questions than developing country governments. However, some contingent derogation mechanism – some international supervision – might be useful to constrain national governments and give them a basis on which to reject protection in some cases.

With respect to Category 2 obligations, it is not clear how much help a contingent derogation mechanism can provide. A contingent derogation mechanism can allow developing countries to apply standards without doing all of the scientific or other work necessary to justify them. However, it cannot do much to cover the costs of ensuring the compliance of developing country products with developed country standards. Here, the main problem is not the development impact of SPS Agreement constraints on developing countries, but the failure of the SPS Agreement to address the cost to developing countries of SPS measures implemented by developed countries. Agricultural exports are an important source of earnings for developing countries, and these exports can be blocked by inappropriate SPS measures. The question of proportionality might be raised: do the health benefits in the developed country importing state justify the costs of compliance imposed on the developing country exporting state? The SPS Agreement leaves much room for a developed country to impose this type of cost on developing countries, despite the "necessity" requirement of Article 2.2.

It is important to note that this type of cost pre-existed the SPS Agreement, and that the SPS Agreement did not exacerbate this cost, but provided an enhanced basis for developing countries, and others, to challenge protectionist SPS measures. The question is whether the SPS Agreement did enough to restrain the imposition of costs on developing countries. Article 9 of the SPS Agreement is an example of a rather imprecise facility that could, if applied, relieve some of this potential burden of compliance by developing country producers with developed country SPS standards. It provides for technical assistance by developed countries to developing countries to assist in compliance. It may be appropriate more specifically to require developed countries, as they implement new standards, to provide technical assistance to appropriate developing countries to ensure that compliance does not inappropriately burden the developing country suppliers of regulated goods. Articles 10.2 and 10.3 of the SPS Agreement and 12.8 of the TBT Agreement are examples of aspirational provisions intended to relieve some of this potential burden on developing countries through transition periods.

With respect to Category 3 obligations, contingent derogation may or may not be appropriate. It has become clear that derogation from the specific obligations of TRIPS will often be appropriate for developing countries, from a poverty reduction perspective. One way to legitimate and justify this derogation would be to establish a process for examination of proposed derogations. However, developing countries may view this type of incremental case-by-case derogation as too slow, unwieldy and unpredictable, while developed country constituencies may be unwilling to relinquish gains made under TRIPS. It may be more appropriate to negotiate broader, generally applicable, reduction of TRIPS obligations.

Category 4 obligations as they exist today involve only a limited range of TRIMS measures, including in particular local content requirements, but excluding export performance requirements. While local content requirements may be part of an import substitution or infant industry program, they are unlikely to be core elements of a development policy. Local content requirements imposed as a condition for investment approval act as a burden on investment, which is a critical factor in development. They also serve as a burden on domestic production, which is prevented from sourcing inputs from the most efficient supplier.[68] So, while a contingent derogation mechanism could be devised to permit certain TRIMS measures, the measures that are currently prohibited are unlikely to make a good case for derogation.

Category 5 obligations present difficult questions from a development standpoint. There is certainly wide agreement that developed country agricultural subsidies may cause harm to farmers in developing

[68] See Alexander Keck and Patrick Low, "Special and differential treatment in the WTO: Why, when and how?" (May 2004) WTO Economic Research and Statistics Division, Staff Working Paper ERSD-2004–03, available at www.wto.org/english/res_e/reser_e/ersd200403_e.htm.

countries, and while developed country agricultural subsidies may help poor farmers in some locations, and may help consumers who rely on subsidized food, one important area of reform of the WTO is reduction of developed country agricultural subsidies.

Some argue that restrictions on subsidization constrain the right of developing countries to engage in economic regulation for growth. The experience of the East Asian economies from 1960 to 2000 suggests that subsidies to promote certain types of technology and information management may be important to growth.[69] But WTO law does not generally restrict domestic subsidies, and to the extent that these subsidies are not specific to industries or groups of industries, they are not actionable. The SCM Agreement provides exceptions for least developed countries, and certain other countries, from its prohibition of export subsidies. However, from a welfare standpoint, it appears unlikely that export subsidies harm other states, while they may help the granting state. On the other hand, there may be strategic circumstances in which an export subsidy may allow producers from one country to compete effectively against producers of another (non-subsidizing) country.

The above analysis of different types of WTO obligations suggests some variations of treatment. The core perspective of these suggestions is development-favorable, with development as the primary goal of policy. However, this perspective is not necessarily deferential to developing country governments (just as it would not be deferential to developed country governments). While it responds to the African Group proposal that "notwithstanding any provisions of any WTO Agreement, [LDCs] shall not be required to implement or comply with obligations that are prejudicial to their individual development needs,"[70] it does not leave to the LDCs, or to other developing countries the unconstrained flexibility to determine what is and is not prejudicial to development needs.

It responds in a more precise and institutionally nuanced manner. In some contexts, it provides blanket exceptions, but in others it relies on specific case-based analysis and multilateral control of policy. This multilateral control is to be based not on political deliberation, but on expert analysis regarding development policy. Within the category 1 context, it recognizes that it is useful for developing countries to be able to bind themselves to liberalize. Development policy-based exceptions,

[69] Neil McCulloch, L. Alan Winters and Xavier Cirera, *Trade Liberalization and Poverty: A Handbook* (London: Centre for Economic Policy Research, 2001), p. 157.

[70] Proposal by the Africa Group, TN/CTD/W/3/REV.2.

subject to multilateral control, seem reasonable. Here, the differential treatment should be for developed countries to liberalize in the goods and services that are of export interest to developing countries.[71]

VII. Conclusion

This chapter has shown ambivalence regarding restrictions on the "right to regulate" for industrial policy under WTO law. Some restrictions may be desirable, and may be favorable, as Hudec suggested, and as Indian and Chinese policy confirm. Other restrictions may be undesirable. As Amsden and Hikino have argued, "[a]t close examination . . . the new rules of the World Trade Organization, a symbol of neoliberalism, are flexible and allow countries to continue to promote their industries under the banner of promoting science and technology. The success formula of late industrialization – allocating subsidies in exchange for monitorable, result-oriented performance standards – is still condoned."[72] It would seem useful to institute a development policy review mechanism that could provide exceptions to developing countries for appropriate development-motivated policies.

[71] Hoekman, Michalopolous and Winters, "Special and differential treatment in the WTO."

[72] Alice H. Amsden and Takashi Hikino, "The bark is worse than the bite: New WTO law and late industrialization" (2000) 570 *The Annals of the American Academy of Political and Social Science* 104.

References

Amsden, Alice, *The Rise of "the Rest": Challenges to the West from Late Industrializing Economies* (Oxford University Press, 2001)

Amsden, Alice H. and Hikino, Takashi, "The bark is worse than the bite: New WTO law and late industrialization" (2000) 570 *The Annals of the American Academy of Political and Social Science* 104

Bhagwati, Jagdish, "The poor's best hope," *The Economist*, June 20, 2002

Birdsall, Nancy and Torre, Augusto de la, *Washington Contentious: Economic Policies for Social Equity in Latin America* (Washington DC: Carnegie, 2001)

Canada: Administration of the Foreign Investment Review Act, BISD 30S/140, 1984

Chow, Gregory C., "The impact of joining the WTO on China's economic, legal and political institutions" (2003) 8 *Pacific Economic Review* 105

Committee on Trade and Development, *Implementation of Special and Differential Treatment Provisions in the WTO Agreements and Decisions*, WT/COMTD/W/77, October 25, 2000

Communication from Cuba, Dominican Republic, Honduras, India, Indonesia, Kenya, Malaysia, Pakistan, Sri Lanka, Tanzania, Uganda, and Zimbabwe, *Proposal for a Framework Agreement on Special and Differential Treatment*, WT/GC/W/442, September 19, 2001

Denters, Eric, *ASIL Insight: Manipulation of Exchange Rates in International Law: The Chinese Yuan*, November 2003, available at www.asil.org/insights/insigh118.htm

Finger, J. Michael, "A diplomat's economics: Development and trade perspectives on the Doha Agenda," working paper dated May 10, 2002

The Doha Agenda and Development: A View from the Uruguay Round (Manila: Asian Development Bank, 2002)

Finger, J. Michael and Winters, L. Alan, "Reciprocity in the WTO," in B. Hoekman, A. Mattoo and P. English (eds.), *Development, Trade and the WTO: A Handbook* (Washington DC: The World Bank, 2002)

Gallagher, Kevin P. (ed.), *Putting Development First: The Importance of Policy Space in the WTO and International Financial Institutions* (London: Zed Books, 2005)

Hoekman, Bernard, "Strengthening the global trade architecture for development: The post-Doha agenda" (2002) 1 *World Trade Review* 23–45

Hoekman, Bernard, Michalopolous, Constantine and Winters, L. Alan, "Special and differential treatment in the WTO: Moving Forward" (2004) 27 *The World Economy* 481

Hudec, Robert E., *Developing Countries in the GATT Legal System* (Aldershot, UK: Gower, 1987)

Indonesia: Certain Measures Affecting the Automobile Industry, WT/DS54,55,59,64/R, adopted July 23, 1998

Jackson, John H., *World Trade and the Law of the GATT: A Legal Analysis of the General Agreement on Tariffs and Trade* (Indianapolis: Bobbs-Merrill, 1969)

Keck, Alexander and Low, Patrick, "Special and Differential Treatment in the WTO: Why, when and how?" (May 2004) WTO Economic Research and Statistics Division, Staff Working Paper ERSD-2004–03, available at www.wto.org/english/res_e/reser_e/ersd200403_e.htm

Lichtenbaum, Peter, "'Special treatment' vs. 'Equal participation': Striking a balance in the Doha negotiations" (2002) 17 *American University International Law Review* 1004

Low, Patrick and Subramanian, Arvind, "Beyond TRIMS: A case for multilateral action on investment rules and competition policy?" in Will Martin and L. Alan Winters (eds.), *The Uruguay Round and the Developing Countries* (Cambridge University Press, 1997)

Make Trade Fair, Rigged Rules and Double Standards: Trade, Globalisation and the Fight Against Poverty (2002), available at www.maketradefair.com

McCulloch, Neil, Winters, L. Alan and Cirera, Xavier, *Trade Liberalization and Poverty: A Handbook* (London: Centre for Economic Policy Research, 2001)

Michalopoulous, Constantine, "Developing country strategies for the Millennium Round" (1999) 33(5) *Journal of World Trade* 1

"The role of special and differential treatment for developing countries in GATT and the World Trade Organization" (July 2000) Policy Research Working Paper 2388, available at www-wds.worldbank.org/external/default/WDSContentServer /IW3P/IB/2000/08/26/000094946_00081505321046/Rendered/PDF/multi_page.pdf

Ozden, Caglar and Reinhardt, Eric, "The perversity of preferences: GSP and developing country trade policies, 1976–2000," working paper dated May 24, 2002, available at http://userwww.service.emory.edu/~erein/research/gsp2.pdf

"Planning Commission, Government of India, Tenth Five-Year Plan 2002–2007," available at http://planningcommission.nic.in/plans/planrel/fiveyr/welcome.html

Rodrik, Dani, "The economics of export-performance requirements" (1987) 102 *Quarterly Journal of Economics* 633

"How to make the trade regime work for development" (2004), available at http://ksghome.harvard.edu/~drodrik/How%20to%20Make%20Trade%20Work.pdf

"What's so special about China's exports?" (January 2006) NBER Working Paper No. 11947, available at www.nber.org/papers/w11947

Rodrik, Dani and Rodríguez, Francisco, "Trade policy and economic growth: A skeptic's guide to the cross-national evidence," in Ben Bernanke and Kenneth S. Rogoff (eds.), *Macroeconomics Annual 2000* (Cambridge, MA: MIT Press, 2001)

Rodrik, Dani and Subramanian, Arvind, "From 'Hindu growth' to productivity surge: The mystery of the Indian growth transition," (2004) IMF Working Paper WP/04/77 4, available at www.imf.org/external/pubs/ft/wp/2004/wp0477.pdf

Rumbaugh, Thomas and Blancher, Nicolas, "China: International trade and WTO accession" (March 2004) IMF Working Paper No. WP/04/36, 3

Sachs, Jeffrey D. and Woo, Wing Thae, "Understanding China's economic performance" (2000) 4(1) *Journal of Policy Reform*

Stewart, Terence, "China in the WTO – Year 3: A research report prepared for the U.S.–China Economic and Security Review Commission," (January 2005), available at www.uscc.gov/researchpapers/2005/05_01_21_china_inthe_wto.htm

Stiglitz, Joseph E., *Globalization and its Discontents* (New York: W. W. Norton & Co., 2002)

Thomas, Chantal, "Balance-of-payments crises in the developing world: Balancing trade, finance and development in the new economic order" (2000) *American University International Law Review* 1249

UN, *Least Developed Countries* available at www.un.org/special-rep/ohrlls/ldc/list.htm

Whalley, John, "Special and differential treatment in a Millennium Round" (May 1999) GCSR Working Paper 30/99, available at www2.warwick.ac.uk/fac/soc/csgr/research/working papers 1999/wp3099.pdf

"Special and differential treatment in the Millennium Round" (1999) 22 *The World Economy* 1065

Woo, Wing Thae, "Recent claims of China's economic exceptionalism: Reflections inspired by WTO accession," working paper dated May 2001

World Trade Organization, *Accession of the People's Republic of China, decision of 10 November,* 2001, WT/L/432, available at www.wto.org/english/thewto_e/acc_e/completeacc_e.htm#chn (hereinafter, "Protocol of Accession")

WTO Appellate Body Report, *European Communities – Conditions for the Granting of Tariff Preferences to Developing Countries,* WT/DS246/AB/R, adopted April 20, 2004

India – Quantitative Restrictions on Imports of Agricultural, Textile and Industrial Products, AB-1999–3, WT/DS90/AB/R, adopted September 22, 1999

WTO Panel Report, *India – Measures Affecting the Automotive Sector,* WT/DS146,175/R, panel report December 21, 2001 (appeal withdrawn), adopted April 5, 2002

India – Quantitative Restrictions on Imports of Agricultural, Textile and Industrial Products, WT/DS90/R, April 6, 1999

United States – Measures Treating Export Restraints as Subsidies, WT/DS194/R, adopted August 23, 2001

WTO Secretariat, *Trade Policy Review, India,* WT/PR/S/100, May 22, 2002 (hereinafter 2002 India TPR), available at www.wto.org/english/tratop_e/tpr_e/tpr_e.htm

Trade Policy Review, People's Republic of China, WT/TPR/S/161, dated 28 February 2006, p. 65, available at www.wto.org/english/tratop_e/tpr_e/tp262_e.htm (hereinafter, 2006 China TPR)

Zhang, Xiaoji and Long, Guoqiang, "China's industrial policies in the process of marketization," in Seiichi Masuyama, Donna Vandenbrink and Siow Yue Chia (eds.), *Industrial Policies in East Asia* (Singapore: Institute of Southeast Asian Studies, 1997)

2

China, India and developing countries in the WTO

Towards a pro-active strategy

JIANFU CHEN

I. Introduction

China and India, two prominent Great Power aspirants (sometimes referred to as 'a class of two'),[1] declared jointly in 2003, and later re-affirmed repeatedly, their mutual desire in developing wider and closer cooperation in regional and international affairs and, in the context of the World Trade Organization (WTO), in enhancing their cooperation in support of the developing countries.[2]

While not under-estimating their potential for closer cooperation in broad international arenas, the realisation of such collaboration in international affairs will be hampered in the near future at least, as it has been in the last fifty years or so, by the existence of various triangle relationships, such as China–India–USA, China–India–Russia, and China–India–Pakistan,[3] the unresolved issues (e.g. Tibet, national

[1] Mark B. Baker, 'Awakening the sleeping giant: India and foreign direct investment in the 21st century' (2005) 15 *Indiana International & Comparative Law Review* 389; Sun Yuhua and Jiang Zhenglin (eds.), *Emerging Great Powers: Games and Perspective of an Historic Rise* (*Xinxing Daguo: Lishixing Jueqi de Boyi Yu Qianjing*) (Beijing: People's Press, 2004).

[2] Joint Declaration on Principles for Relations and Comprehensive Cooperation Between the Republic of India and the People's Republic of China, 23 June 2003, available at http://meaindia.nic.in/declarestatement/2003/06/23jd01.htm; Joint Statement of the Republic of India and the People's Republic of China, 11 April 2005, available at http://meaindia.nic.in/speech/2005/04/11js01.htm; and A Shared Vision for the 21st Century of the Republic of India and the People's Republic of China, 14 January 2008, available at www.pmindia.nic.in/speech_14jan2k8-1.pdf.

[3] Sandy Gordon and Stephen Henningham (eds.), *India Looks East: An Emerging Power and its Asia–Pacific Neighbours* (Canberra: The Australian National University, 1995); Gilles Boquérat and Frédéric Grare (eds.), *India, China, Russia: Intricacies of an Asian Triangle* (Singapore: Marshall Cavendish International, 2004); Bidanda M. Chengappa, *India–China Relations: Post Conflict Phase to Post Cold War Period* (New Delhi: APH Publishing Corporation, 2004); Ma Jiali, *Focus on India: An Emerging Great Power* (*Guanzhu Yindu: Jueqi Zhong de Daguo*) (Tianjin: Tianjin People's Press, 2002); B. M. Jain, *India–China*

borders and regional ambitions), and the lack of mutual trust between the two countries resulted from its twisted history of bilateral relations.[4] This complex and complicated relationship between the two Asian giants has now produced much discussion and debate on potential threat of growing powers, conflict of ambitions,[5] rivalry for domination, competition for influence, partnership for multipolarity, and cooperation for international peace and security. Much of this literature is produced by scholars in international relations, political science, general Asian studies and economics;[6] and much of the literature on Sino-Indian relations has left more questions than it has provided answers. There is a need for sharper identification of issues, clearer isolation of problems and a more active search for common ground and compromises, if we are to reach some more definite, and hopefully more promising, conclusions regarding Sino-Indian cooperation in this 'New World Order', still dominated by one single power but increasingly challenged by multiple forces.

It is the view of the present author that Sino-Indian cooperation, not rivalry, in international affairs in the context of the WTO is likely, realistic and potentially productive, if the two countries could think outside the box and beyond the current existing rules. More specifically, they need to either identify sufficient mutual interests to forge a common strategic cause or pursue a common cause in the existing WTO struggles for improvement and reform.

This chapter argues that the reform of the 'Special and Differential' (hereinafter 'S&D') treatment for developing countries is indeed such a

relations: Issues, trends and emerging scenarios, The China–India Project, Occasional Paper Series, 1, Centre of Asian Studies, University of Hong Kong, available at www.hku.hk/cas/pub/Occasional1_bmjain.pdf.

[4] B. R. Deepak, *India & China 1904–2004: A Century of Peace and Conflict* (New Delhi: Manak Publications Pvt Ltd, 2005); Zhang Mingqiu, *Sino-India Relations (1947–2003)* (*Zhongying Guangxi Yanjiu (1947–2003)*) (Beijing: Peking University, 2004); Wu Yongnian, Zhao Gangcheng and Ma Ying, *A New Focus on India's Foreign Policy in the Twenty-First Century* (*Ershiyi Shiji Yindu Waijiao Xinlun*) (Shanghai Translation Press, 2004); Jain, 'India–China relations'; Sun Shihai, 'Sino-India relationship in the 21st century', *China Daily*, 26 May 2004, available at www.chinadaily.com.cn/gb/doc/2004-05/26/content_333973.htm.

[5] Some have even talked about the 'inevitable duel' between India and China (see Warren Liu, 'India and China: Competitive or Complementary?', *China Business Infocentre*, 2 December 2005, available at www.cbiz.cn), or 'battle of supremacy' (see Jain, 'India–China relations').

[6] See Fernando, Sithara, 'Recent writings on India–China relations' (2005) 41(2) *China Report*, 173.

common cause, in which China and India share sufficient interest in getting a better and realistic deal not only for China and India, but also for economically poorer countries generally. It also argues that the current approach by China and India in this regard amounts to a fight for a lost cause and, hence, a fundamental re-thinking is required if China and India are to become leaders of the developing countries in ensuring a fairer and more equitable treatment for developing countries. To do so, China and India need to have the courage to abandon the 'S&D' approach and to initiate a completely new strategy for less developed countries in the WTO regime. In short, taking a pro-active approach, in place of the often defensive one, is called for in the Sino-Indian cooperation in the WTO.

II. China and India in the WTO: Searching for common interests

Countries cooperate for good reasons and, increasingly, for pragmatic reasons and not for ideological rhetoric. If we were only thinking about trade and economic development that would benefit both countries, there is then a short-cut to closer Sino-Indian cooperation, that is, to promote and foster bilateral economic relations.[7] Indeed, with government facilitation, bilateral trade has grown consistently over twenty per cent since 1992 (with the exception of 1998–9), with a total two-way trade growing from US$338.54 million in 1992 to US$13.6 billion in 2004 (Confederation of Indian Industry, 2005). The two countries, in 2005 (Joint Statement 2005), also committed to increase the trade volume to US$20 billion by 2008, a target that clearly has the India–US trade volume in mind,[8] and they have now committed to increase this bilateral trade from US$40 billion by the year 2010 to US$60 billion.[9] The two countries then began formal talks on an India–China Regional Trading Arrangement and agreed to establish a Joint Task Force to undertake feasibility studies on this,[10] a task that was completed by

[7] See Joint Study Group, *Report of the India–China Joint Study Group on Comprehensive Trade and Economic Cooperation*, March 2005, document on personal file.

[8] US is currently India's largest trading partner, with a trade volume stood at US$20 billion at the end of 2004. See Haider, Ziad, 'US–India–China: Giants at play', *The Indian Express*, 30 July 2005, available at http://indianexpress.com/archive/news/30/7/2005/..

[9] Satu Limaye, 'Sino-Indian relations: The four disconnects', *Policy Forum Online* 08–009A, 30 January 2008, available at www.nautilus.org/fora/security/08009Limaye.html (accessed 15 Aug 2008).

[10] Joint Statement of the Republic of India and the People's Republic of China 2005.

the end of 2007.[11] As emerging 'Great Powers', these and other measures in promoting bilateral relationships are seen as complementary to the global and strategic character of the bilateral relationship and to their currently agreed establishment of an India–China Strategic and Cooperative Partnership for Peace and Prosperity to 'jointly address global challenge and threats'.[12] However, direct cooperation in global issues is still limited, though emerging.

An important aspect for cooperation in global issues that is identified by the Joint Statement relates to cooperation in multilateral organisations and their reforms. However, no real and meaningful cooperation between two or more countries could realistically exist unless parties to the cooperation share sufficient common interests, concerns or see common benefit, current or potential, that could be derived from such cooperation. WTO is a forum that deals with practical trade issues. More importantly, WTO is meant to be a trade organisation that deals with economic and related issues, not a political one. With both countries being pre-occupied with economic development in their own respective country and in light of the economic dependency globally, WTO is naturally one of the most relevant multilateral organisations for international cooperation. Not surprisingly, the two countries have agreed to conduct a 'regular exchange of views on major international and regional issues, strengthen cooperation in the WTO and other international multilateral organisations, and to continue the consultations on other issues of common concern'. In relation to global trade, investment and development, they have agreed 'to work together to preserve stability and growth in the global economy and reduce disparities between developed and developing countries' and, thus, to promote 'the establishment of a new international political and economic order'.[13] If indeed this is what the two countries intend to do, WTO is where the focal point would be, as

[11] See 'A shared vision for the 21st century of the Republic of India and the People's Republic of China', 14 January 2008. It should be noted however, there are still major divisions among Indian government and business groups toward such an FTA arrangement until this day. Indeed, from the very beginning, India's industry sector had already expressed some strong resistance and serious concerns (see V. Sridhar, 'Free trade fears: China's proposal for a free trade agreement with India meets with resistance from Indian industry' (2005) 22(10) *Frontline (India)* 7, available at www.bilaterals.org/article-print.php3?id_article=1867), though some had offered qualified support for the FTA idea. See Arvind Panagariya, 'An India–China free trade area?' (2005), available at www.columbia.edu/~ap2231/ET/et77_April20_05.htm.

[12] Joint Statement of the Republic of India and the People's Republic of China 2005.

[13] Joint Statement of the Republic of India and the People's Republic of China 2005.

WTO is the multilateral organisation that, together with the World Bank and the IMF, defines the international politico-economic order, at least for global trade and cross-border investment. The critical question is then whether China and India share any strategic cause(s) to ensure a meaningful and long-term cooperation.

While India is a founding member of the General Agreement on Tariffs and Trade 1947 (GATT) and has enjoyed an uninterrupted membership since then, its interest in the GATT/WTO was limited until India started economic reforms towards an open and export-oriented market economy in the late 1980s and especially in the 1990s. China, on the other hand, though a founding member represented by Taiwan in the name of Republic of China, was only re-admitted to the WTO some ten years ago. In this sense, the history of their common membership in the WTO is short. However, this is not the point; the potential for their cooperation in the WTO is their commonly declared commitment to multilateralism in international affairs. Most importantly is the fact that both countries benefit tremendously in economic development and trade from an open and liberal trade regime promoted and enforced by the WTO. Politically and ideologically, both countries firmly believe that they are members of developing countries and both aspire to be the leader of and spokesman for the developing countries. As such, both countries are committed to a fair outcome in agriculture negotiations and the so-called Doha development agenda.

As two economically most powerful developing countries with rapid growth in trade, China and India do share many common concerns, problems, and interests in the WTO as well as similarity in commodity export patterns. In an excellent article, Chaisse and Chakraborty have identified many of these, including shared interests in renegotiating/restructuring WTO rules in agriculture, anti-dumping, aspects of the trade related aspects of intellectual property rights (TRIPs) agreement and the dispute settlement system.[14] For the immediate Doha Round negotiations, they share many common grounds in relation to S&D, agriculture and non-agricultural market access (NAMA). For instance, they both support the establishment of Special Products and Special Safeguard mechanisms in agricultural negotiation. On NAMA, China supports the Swiss formula provided that there is a sufficient gap between the coefficients for developed and developing countries. While

[14] Julien Chaisse and Debashis Chakraborty, 'Identifying mutual interest areas at WTO: A Sino-Indian joint perspective' (2005) 41(3) *China Report*, 267.

India rejected the proposal outright as unacceptable, it seems that India did not reject the Swiss formula *per se* but the proposed coefficient of ten for both developed and developing countries.[15] They differ, however, on some other important fronts. For instance, India seems to have taken a rather positive view on non-governmental organisations' participation in the WTO,[16] but China has not been very appreciative of this participation in the WTO or in any international organisations in general. On services, India has a strong sector which accounts for 52 per cent of its Gross Domestic Product (GDP), and a strong comparative advantage internationally in services.[17] Together with India's advantage of having a well-educated labour force fluent in English, India is keen in liberalisation of professional services trade in Modes 1 (Cross Border Supply) and 4 (Movement of Natural Persons). China on the other hand is more concerned, at the moment, with restructuring its own service industries and hence with protection of them before opening up for international competition. But importantly in searching for common interests in global trade liberalisation, China and India are not just simply competitors (low labour costs, similar line of export commodities and hungry needs for energy),[18] they are also complementary, symbolised by their complementarity in hardware and software production, and 'World Factory' (manufacturing, construction and industry in China) and 'World Office' (IT, management and financial services in India) statuses.[19] Trade liberalisation will allow each country to take its own advantages in the complementary relations, and trade disciplines will facilitate resolution of conflicts and disputes arising out of competition.

These common concerns are all important issues and worth joint pursuit by the two countries. However, aspects in anti-dumping, trade related aspects of intellectual property rights (TRIPS) and dispute settlement mechanisms are more or less *ad hoc* technical issues that could hardly foster a common strategic cause for the two countries for a long-term cooperation. While agriculture is a core concern of many developing

[15] Bo Xilai, 'Statement at the Sixth Session of Ministerial Conference', 14 December 2005; Kamal Nath, 'Kamal Nath calls for roadmap for elimination of trade destroying farm subsidies by developed countries', Hong Kong, 13 December 2005, available at http://commerce.nic.in/Feb05_release.htm; Kamal Nath, 'Minister's statement', 7 December 2005, available at http://comerce.nic.in/Dec05_release.htm.

[16] Nath, 'Kamal Nath calls'. [17] Nath, 'Minister's statement'.

[18] Sun and Jiang, *Emerging Great Powers*, pp. 243–44; Zhang, *Sino-India Relations*, pp. 231–34; Liu, 'India and China'.

[19] Deepak, *India & China*, pp. 469–74.

countries, it is clearly not in the best interests of the African and Caribbean least developed countries (LDCs) which depend on their preferential access to European markets.[20] The most vocal Korean protests in Hong Kong are not about agricultural liberalisation, but protection. Further, agriculture issues can easily be perceived by other developing countries, and indeed are, self-interest issues, as the real beneficiaries of any breakthrough are often perceived to be the large and powerful developing countries such as China, India, Brazil and some developed countries such as Australia and New Zealand.[21] As in the case of the textile industry, a substantial reduction of subsidies in agriculture in the United States (US) and the European Union (EU) may in fact harm the LDCs, which now enjoy some preferential access to the US and EU markets, and lead to fierce competition among developing countries.

On the other hand, the S&D issue or the treatment of developing countries, or issues concerning the general development agenda, is of a different nature – it is concerned with the fundamental philosophy and approach of the WTO. It is one of the most contentious issues facing the WTO.[22] Indeed, as has been rightly suggested by Hoekman, a prominent scholar on WTO and its development agenda, the medium-term viability of the WTO depends on an effective mechanism that would properly accommodate the needs of the 'developing countries'.[23]

'S&D' treatment is therefore a strategic issue. It is also an issue in which the two countries share sufficient interests and concerns. This was particularly so at the Doha Round. For instance, India demanded that the Hong Kong Conference fulfil the Development Agenda and correct the 'development deficit'. With this, India was keen to see progress on the 'S&D' negotiations. Similar views were also aired by the Chinese Minister of Commerce at the Hong Kong Conference and in many other

[20] See Peter Alford, 'EU loses to rising forces in siege of HK', available at www.theaustralian.news.com.au/printpage/0,5942,17606964,00.html.

[21] According to the World Bank, the big beneficiaries in agricultural reform will in fact be the rich subsidising countries, the big middle- and high-income farm exporters (e.g. Brazil and Australia), but the sub-Saharan Africans would be marginally worse off. See Tim Colebatch, 'Trade: postponing failure', *The Age*, 20 December 2005, available at www.theage.com.au/news/tim-colebatch/trade-postponing-failure/2005/12/19.

[22] IISD, 'Special and differential treatment' (2003) 1(13) *Doha Round Briefing Series*.

[23] B. Hoekman, 'More favourable treatment of developing countries and the Doha Development Agenda', *Trade Note*, 29 May 2003, The World Bank, www-wds.worldbank.org/servlet/WDS_IBank_Servlet?pcont=details&eid=000090341_20031010133313. See also A. Keck and P. Low, *Special and Differential Treatment in the WTO: Why, When and How?*, WTO Staff Working Paper ERSD-2004-03, available at www.wto.org/english/res_e/reser_e/ersd200403_e.htm.

occasions.[24] The result at Hong Kong was predictably disappointing, evidenced in the comments by India on the draft Hong Kong text: 'Paragraphs 17–20 of the draft text on special and differential treatment are clear evidence of this fact [serious and growing development deficit]. There has been virtually no progress in the Doha Mandate on special and differential treatment (S&D), calling for provisions to be made more effective, precise and operational. Even the five prioritised S&D proposals of the LDCs have not been agreed to'.[25] Unfortunately, this disappointment will continue, unless a radically different approach is taken in dealing with the issue. It is the view of the present author that China and India have both taken a wrong approach in following the Doha proposed solution of making S&D 'more precise and operational', as this one-size-for-all 'solution' is logically inconsistent with the diversified needs of developing countries. In fact, it is unrealistic to expect any significant breakthrough in these issues in the near future. What is required is a leadership, commensurate with their 'Great Power' leadership aspirations and their economic and trading capacities, in finding a new but realistic and practical solution; a solution that would demand a significant contribution and sacrifice from not only the developed world but also from the powerful developing countries. China and India are the ideal candidates for this leadership, if they have the political will to act so as to achieve it.

III. "S&D" treatment: A lost cause of a mutual concern at the WTO

A noble cause it might be, 'S&D' is a lost cause. I have argued elsewhere that, in the context of the WTO, the 'developing countries' problems as they are seen to be related to the WTO, are caused not only by the practices of WTO members but also by the vagueness of the notion and classification or designation of 'developing countries'.[26] Too often, the plight of LDCs is disguised by the false notion of their being 'developing

[24] Bo, 'Statement at the Sixth Session'.

[25] Indian Government, 'Draft WTO ministerial text disappointing', 1 December 2005, available at http://commerce.nic.in/Dec05_release.htm#h10.

[26] J. Chen, '"S&D" treatment for developing countries in the WTO trade regime: A false solution on a wrong footing for LDCs', in J. Chen and G. Walker, *Balancing Act: Law, Policy and Politics in Globalisation and Global Trade* (Sydney: The Federation Press, 2004), pp. 109–51; J. Chen, 'Developing Countries, "S&D" Treatment, and the Integrity of the WTO System' (2007) 1 *International Law Review* 296.

countries'.[27] The notion of 'developing countries' needs to be approached realistically so as to prioritise those objectives that are achievable in assisting the development of countries which need not only the liberalisation of international trade but also tangible and substantial assistance in trade promotion and development. The present 'S&D' mechanisms and provisions designed to deal with 'developing countries' or to address their concerns are, though sometimes inspirational, incoherent, irrational and largely inequitable.

To avoid repetition, I shall summarise below the main problems in this notion.

A. *Incoherence: Definitional problems*

The notion of 'developing countries'[28] is frequently evoked in discussions and debate in international law, international trade, international relations and international politics; its meaning is, however, assumed and has never been precisely defined in the history of GATT/WTO, though not without efforts to do so.[29] For their own purposes, some international organisations do define the notion. The United Nations Development Program (UNDP) classifies, for example, all countries other than the US, Europe, Canada, Australia, New Zealand and Japan as 'developing countries'.[30] The World Bank does so on the basis of income and further divides developing countries into low-income economies (US$755 or less per capita in 2000), lower-middle-income economies (between US$756 and US$2,995 per capita) and upper-middle-income economies (between US$2,995 and US$9,265 per capita).[31] For the purposes of WTO membership, it is a matter of self-assertion and acceptance by other WTO members, although some of the provisions of WTO agreements do attempt to provide some vague 'criteria' for enjoying certain 'S&D' treatment.[32] As of August 2008,

[27] Indeed, the word 'developing' has a positive connotation in terms of economic development that simply does not apply to many if not all LDCs.

[28] Often referred to as the 'Less-Developed Countries' in the early period of the GATT. See also *Background Document to the High Level Symposium on Trade and Development*, Geneva, 17–18 March 1999, prepared by the Development Division of WTO, available at www.wto.org, p. 5.

[29] Keck and Low, *Special and Differential Treatment*, 10.

[30] M. J. Trebilcock and R. Howse, *The Regulation of International Trade*, 2nd edn (London and New York: Routledge, 1999).

[31] Mitsuo Matsushita, Thomas Schoenbaum and Petros C. Mavroidis, *The World Trade Organization: Law, Practice, and Policy* (Oxford University Press, 2003), p. 374.

[32] Often referred to as 'special and more favourable' treatment under GATT before 1995 when the WTO was established. It should be noted that the original GATT (Art XVIII:1)

about two-thirds of the 153 WTO members have successfully declared themselves to be 'developing countries'.[33]

The practice of self-declaration and acceptance by WTO members, and its result in the actual designation of 'developing countries', is almost absurd. One has to be completely blind to think that the same set of trading rules would be equally applicable and appropriate to, say Hong Kong/Singapore and Congo/Sierra Leone (or most other African countries).[34] By all criteria, the differences in economic and social development between Hong Kong/Singapore and Congo/Sierra Leone will be much larger than those between Hong Kong/Singapore and the US (or any other 'developed countries'). However, such gaps in development among 'developing countries' have not gone unnoticed by the WTO and other international organisations. Since 1971, the UN has recognised a new category of membership, that is, the Least Developed Countries. The status of belonging to the LDCs is reviewed regularly by the UN under its criteria of having a low income (under US$750 for inclusion – a threshold lowered from US$900 after a 2006 Review), a weakness in human resources and economic vulnerability. Under the present criteria, 49 countries are included and of these thirty-three are current members of the WTO.[35] Despite the lack of any evidence of tangible benefit for being a member of the WTO, nine more LDCs are currently negotiating their accession to the WTO.[36] This further differentiation of developing countries is now partially recognised by the

contains such provisions only for those economies that 'support low standards of living and are in the early stages of development'.

33 www.wto.org.

34 Not surprisingly, the US and the EU declared, at the conclusion of the Uruguay Round, that they would not recognise such countries/regions as Hong Kong, Singapore and South Korea as 'developing countries'. See Matsushita, Schoenbaum and Mavroidis, *The World Trade Organization*, p. 375.

35 The 49 countries are Afghanistan, *Angola*, *Bangladesh*, *Benin*, Bhutan, *Burkina Faso*, *Burundi*, *Cambodia*, *Central African Republic*, *Chad*, Comoro, *Democratic Republic of Congo*, *Djibouti*, Equatorial Guinea, Eritrea, Ethiopia, *Gambia*, *Guinea*, *Guinea Bissau*, *Haiti*, Kiribati, Lao People's DR, *Lesotho*, Liberia, *Madagascar*, *Malawi*, *Maldives*, *Mali*, *Mauritania*, *Mozambique*, *Myanmar*, *Nepal*, *Niger*, *Rwanda*, Samoa, Sao Tome and Principe, *Senegal*, *Sierra Leone*, *Solomon Islands*, Somalia, Sudan, Timor-Leste, *Tanzania*, *Togo*, Tuvalu, *Uganda*, *Vanuatu*, Yemen, *Zambia* (Current members of the WTO are indicated in italics). It should be noted that until December 2007, Cape Verde was also defined as an LCD.

36 These are Afghanistan, Bhutan, Ethiopia, Laos, Samoa, Sao Tome & Principe, Sudan, Vanuatu and Yemen. See WTO website, www.wto.org. In addition, Equatorial Guinea is a WTO observer, which means that it must start negotiation for accession to the WTO within five years of being an observer.

WTO and some of its agreements. Thus, many WTO agreements now allow LDCs a more 'lenient' trading discipline and a longer period to adjust any inconsistent policies, or they are simply allowed a 'free ride'. However, WTO agreements have not been consistent in this regard. For instance, under the Agreement on Subsidies and Countervailing Measures, developing countries are divided into LDCs as designated by the UN, countries whose Gross National Product (GNP) *per capita* income is below US$1,000,[37] and other developing countries (Art. 27.2 and Annex VII). In other words, LDCs will graduate from this designation once their GNP *per capita* income reaches US$1,000, a graduation criterion that excludes other factors set out by the UN. And more often than not, LDCs will have to compete with other 'developing countries' under the 'S&D' treatment provisions.

In short, the notion of 'developing countries' is a messy one. While it encompasses countries at vastly different levels of socio-economic development and trading capacity there is only limited recognition of such differences by the UN and WTO, with no consistent, coherent and focused approach. The definitional problems are, in fact, deeply rooted in the political context in which the notion initially emerged and introduced into GATT. This political context, to be discussed below, is critical in understanding the current problems in relation to developing countries in the WTO.

B. *Inspirational: Rich rhetoric but void of practical measures under GATT*

The GATT/WTO is sometimes accused of being a club for the rich and well-off countries, but that has not been true in terms of its membership and the increasing participation of developing countries in the organisation.[38]

[37] These include Bolivia, Cameroon, Congo, Côte d'Ivoire, Dominican Republic, Egypt, Ghana, Guatemala, Guyana, Honduras, India, Indonesia, Kenya, Morocco, Nicaragua, Nigeria, Pakistan, Philippines, Senegal, Sri Lanka and Zimbabwe. Honduras was added to the list during a Special Session of the WTO in December 2000. Honduras had been left out by mistake (See ICTSD, 2000). Nepal was admitted to the WTO on 23 April 2004 and, being one of the poorest countries, should be qualified for inclusion automatically.

[38] Indeed, 11 out of the 23 original contracting parties of the GATT were developing countries. The 23 original contracting parties were Australia, Belgium, *Brazil*, *Burma*, Canada, *Ceylon*, *Chile*, (the Republic of) *China*, *Cuba*, Czechoslovakia, France, *India*, *Lebanon*, Luxembourg, Netherlands, New Zealand, Norway, *Pakistan*, *Southern Rhodesia*, *Syria*, South Africa, UK, and USA. Developing countries are indicated by italics. Further, there were 25, 68 and 76 developing countries taking part in the last three rounds of negotiations respectively (the Kennedy, Tokyo and Uruguay Rounds) (See WTO,

The membership and the increasing participation do not necessarily indicate the status of the developing countries in the organisation.

Firstly, one must not see the GATT/WTO in isolation from the other two important pillars of the Bretton Woods system, namely the World Bank and the International Monetary Fund (IMF), both of which practise a weighted vote system and hence constitutionally are indeed a 'club for the rich'.[39] Although the weighted vote system is absent from the GATT/WTO, as a matter of practice GATT/WTO generally avoided formal voting, preferring a 'consensus' approach, which means that negotiations among and between the three powers (US, EU and Japan, but sometimes with Canada as the fourth power, often referred to as the Quad) effectively set the agenda and trading policy and rules for GATT/WTO, since only a few developing countries participated actively in the core business of the GATT/WTO in negotiating market access exchange (though they did pay attention to obtaining some preferential access to industrial country markets).[40] In retrospect, it is the market access exchange, often resulting in developing countries opening their markets to developed countries, that has had a major impact on developing countries.

Secondly, the original GATT, despite its large membership of developing countries, was basically silent on the issue of developing countries as the notion itself and the North–South divide were yet to emerge. It was only after the first review session of the GATT (1954–55) that GATT allowed countries 'the economies of which can only support low standards of living and are in the early stages of development' some flexibility in modifying or withdrawing their tariff concessions and permitting some limited measures to protect a particular industry or balance-of-payments under Article XVIII.[41]

Background Document, 1999 p. 5). This has been noted in response to the frequent complaints that the GATT was a club for the rich and the powerful and disadvantages developing countries (See Jackson, *The World Trading System*, p. 319).

39 The weighted vote system simply means that the value of a vote of each member is in proportion to the actual monetary contribution to the Bank/Fund.

40 North–South Institute, *The Reality of Trade: The WTO and Developing Countries* (2003), p. 4, available at www.nsi-ins.ca/english/pdf/Reality_of_Trade.pdf.

41 Entitled 'Government assistance to economic development', but initially entitled 'Government assistance to economic development and reconstruction' and intended to provide some flexibility to all countries. See WTO, *Background Document*, p. 5. An economy supporting low standards of living is only to be judged on the basis of 'the normal condition of that economy' and an economy in the early stages of development would also include a country undergoing a process of industrialisation to correct an excessive dependence on primary production (Annex I: *Ad Article XVIII*).

Thirdly, and most importantly, the initial 'S&D' treatment accorded to developing countries under GATT was a result of the emergence of the North–South divide within the UN system in the 1960s, the deterioration of the North–South gap after a decade of the so-called export-led development strategy and the consequential demand for a New International Economic Order (NIEO).[42] It first emerged in a more political than trading context, and was seen, and still is largely seen, as a political right.[43] The 'S&D' treatment, reflected in the UNCTAD's sponsored Part IV of GATT, the 'Generalised System of Preference' (GSP), the 'Enabling Clause' and provisions in some stand-alone codes, is in fact a twin sister of the right to development and the twins consist of the main politico-economic contents of the NIEO. These 'S&D' treatment provisions are remarkably vague and fundamentally inspirational in approach,[44] technically referred to as the 'best endeavour' provisions, and legally described as 'non-mandatory and unenforceable',[45] although, like Article XVIII of the GATT, they explicitly allow some differential and preferential treatment for developing countries (still called less-developed countries). With the items important for the promotion of developing countries' export-led growth (such as textiles, light manufactures and processed agricultural products) encountering very high trade barriers in developed countries[46] and the practice of the so-called 'grey-area measures' (such as 'voluntary export restraints' (VERs) or 'orderly marketing arrangements' (OMAs)), the practical benefits of such 'S&D' treatment are clearly questionable in trading terms.[47]

C. Irrational: Liberalisation, non-discrimination, and differentiation under the WTO

The Uruguay Round of negotiations (1986–94) was not only the most ambitious round ever undertaken in the history of GATT, it was meant, like the present Doha Round, to be a development round. The reality of the Uruguay Round was that the main negotiations were conducted

[42] Trebilcock and Howse, *The Regulation of International Trade* (London and New York: Routledge, 1999), pp. 367–8.

[43] Keck and Low, *Special and Differential Treatment*, 4.

[44] WTO defines such as being in the nature of guidelines. See WTO, *Background Document*, p. 5.

[45] IISD, 'Special and Differential Treatment', p. 1; Keck and Low, *Special and Differential Treatment*, p. 4.

[46] Trebilcock and Howse, *The Regulation of International Trade*, p. 302.

[47] For detailed discussions, Chen, '"S & D" treatment'; and Chen, 'Developing countries'.

among the developed countries themselves, especially the three main powers, Japan, US and the European Community (EC), and only extended to the developing countries on a most-favoured nation (MFN) basis.[48] More importantly, GATT principles concerning developing countries only managed to be mentioned in an *ad hoc* fashion in various documents providing a few concessions for developing countries.[49] This implies that the above principles are no longer, in the language of one commentator, the 'explicit right of the developing countries (other than the least developed countries) and that it is open to the discretion of the developed countries, if they so desire, to exert pressure to obtain more commitments and concessions than are actually justified'.[50]

If anything, one can only say that the only practical treatment accorded to developing countries are those for the LDCs.[51] Nevertheless, some 145 provisions were incorporated into the various agreements (with 107 being adopted at the conclusion of the Uruguay Round, and 22 applying to least-developed country members only).[52] These have been summarised thus:

> These provisions can be classed in five main groups: provisions aimed at increasing trade opportunities through market access; provisions allowing flexibility to developing countries in rules and disciplines governing trade measures; provisions allowing longer transitional periods to developing countries; and provisions for technical assistance. Additional provisions within these five groups relate specifically to the least-developed countries.[53]

[48] M. Rom, 'Some early reflections on the Uruguay Round Agreement as seen from the viewpoint of a developing country' (1994) 28(6) *Journal of World Trade*, 5 at 6.

[49] E.g. Agreement on Technical Barriers; on Subsidies and Countervailing Measures. See Trebilcock and Howse, *The Regulation of International Trade*, p. 14. Although pre-Uruguay GATT agreements and decisions are part of the WTO package, the applicability of GATT principles (including the 'Enabling Clause') to areas other than trade in goods is questioned by some scholars. See Rom, 'Some early reflections', 7.

[50] Rom, 'Some early reflections', 8.

[51] See 'Decision on Measures in Favour of Least-Developed Countries' adopted at the Uruguay Round, and the more recent decisions to grant duty-free and quote-free treatment to the LDCs.

[52] See WTO Committee on Trade and Development, *Implementation of Special and Differential Treatment Provisions in WTO Agreements and Decisions*, WT/COMTD/W/77, 25 October 2000. Another source put the total number of S&D provisions at 155. See IISD, 'Special and differential treatment', 1.

[53] WTO, Background Document, 18.

Other than provisions on longer transitional periods as contained in individual agreements, few of the 'S&D' provisions are specific or legally enforceable. At the same time, the movement towards liberalisation, competition and non-discrimination as the fundamental underlying principles of the WTO trading regime is unmistakeable.[54] It is simply irrational to emphasise liberalisation, competition and non-discrimination while trying to provide differentiated treatment in the rules without clear qualifications. It is equally irrational to provide a one-size treatment to a greatly diversified group of members.

D. *Inequitable: The triumph of the powerful in the WTO package*

Also important in the Uruguay Round development in relation to impact on developing countries was the introduction of new subject matters for the WTO, namely the General Agreement for Trade in Services (GATS), TRIPS, trade related investment measures (TRIMS), none of which is of great benefit to less developed countries,[55] and all were the agenda items initiated by US-led Western countries, but strongly resisted by developing countries. Developing countries only agreed to include these issues either because certain concessions were made by developed countries, or through fear of being left out or simply because they had little choice but to accept.[56] In this context, the concessions made by developing countries can only be described as tremendous and as amounting to a major set-back in securing their national interests in global trade.

The end results of Uruguay thus represent:

> a change of heart and attitude from the more developed countries, returning to the basic rules of the original GATT, favouring non-discrimination and liberalisation as the fundamental tenets of the international trading system for all to be generally applicable with the minimum number of exceptions possible, the basic philosophy being that liberalisation, competition, non-intervention by government and non-discrimination are the best medicine for all – disregarding the specific circumstances and conditions in the Member countries.[57]

[54] Rom, 'Some early reflections', 7.

[55] M. Sornarajah, 'Good corporate citizenship and the conduct of multinational corporations', in Chen and Walker, *Balancing Act*, pp. 224–50.

[56] Rom, 'Some early reflections', 8–9; E. O. Awuku, 'How do the results of the Uruguay Round affect the North–South trade?' (1994) 28(6) *Journal of World Trade*, 75. See also Sornarajah, 'Good corporate citizenship'.

[57] Rom, 'Some early reflections', 7.

It is also important to point out that although (especially in the final days), developing countries had been reduced to being 'spectators on the side-lines' during the Uruguay Round negotiations,[58] some larger developing countries nevertheless contributed to the less than desirable results as they had a change of heart, believing they could achieve more individually from developed countries through concrete agreements.[59] In this context, there is little equity to talk about in relation to small and poor countries, the ones that desperately need assistance and facilitation.

E. A shared fate with the right to development

Perhaps it is time to think outside the box. In this context, the miserable failure of the UN in developing the notion of a 'right to development' may serve us as a good lesson. In fact, as mentioned above, the right to development and the 'S&D' treatment are identical twins born out of the same struggle for an NIEO.

In response to the UN NIEO Resolutions, the UN adopted two further Resolutions[60] which, first stated that the realisation of the new economic order is 'an essential element for the effective promotion of human rights and fundamental freedoms', and then emphasised that the right to development is a human right and that equality of opportunity for development is as much a prerogative of nations as of individuals within nations. Since then, the right to development has been proclaimed as a human right by virtually every single regional (except Europe) and universal human rights-related declarations, resolutions and conventions and the existence of such a right has been re-affirmed by all UN authorities include the General Assembly, the Commission on Human Rights, the Conference of Heads of State of Non-Aligned Countries, and the Assembly of Heads of State and Government of the Organisation of African Unity (now the African Union), the UN High Commissioner for Human Rights. The trouble is, no one actually knows what does the 'right to development', as a human right, mean – who has this right, against whom this right can be claimed, and how could it actually be implemented and enforced. As such and under the pressures from developing countries, the UN began

[58] Awuku, 'How do the results?', 92. [59] Rom, 'Some early reflections', 8.

[60] Resolution 32/130 (1977) and Resolution 34/46 (1979), both entitled 'Resolution on alternative approaches and ways and means within the United Nations system for improving the effective enjoyment of human rights and fundamental freedoms'.

its efforts to clarify the meaning of the 'right to development' and to work out specific and concrete measures for the actual realisation of the right to development. For this purpose, the UN first established a working group in 1981, and thereafter, various Working Groups, Intergovernmental Group of Experts, Independent Expert, and High-level Task Force have been established and many (including the UN High Commissioner for Human Rights) are still working on this admirable notion of the 'right to development', but to no avail.[61] In the end, the notion of the 'right to development' has now become everything and nothing. And if anything, it becomes increasingly a barrier to international human rights promotion and protection, as it is more often than not being used as an excuse for human rights violation and a defence against such violation – a much admirable initiative has now become a liability, if not a disgrace, for the UN.

In short, for the last thirty years or so, the UN, in response to developing countries' demands, has endeavoured to work out precise, concrete and enforceable contents of the right to development but ended with more damage to the human rights movement than enhancing it. Sounds familiar? If the Doha Declaration, the July 2004 Decision of the WTO and the Hong Kong Declaration (see discussions below) in relation to the 'S&D' treatment are any guide, the WTO is now on the same track; the brake must be applied.

[61] For those who would like to read more on the recent development in this area, the following documents might be of interest: 'The legal nature of the right to development and enhancement of its binding nature', E/CN.4/Sub.2/2004/16, 1 June 2004; 'The right to development: study on existing bilateral and multilateral programmes and policies for development partnership', E/CN.4/Sub.2/2004/15, 3 August 2004; 'Mainstreaming the right to development into international trade law and policy at the World Trade Organisation', E/CN.4/Sub.2/2004/17, 9 June 2004; 'Study on policies for development in a globalizing world: What can the human rights approach contribute?', E/CN.4/Sub.2/2004/18, 7 June 2004; 'Towards a human rights approach to development: concepts and implications', E/CN.4/Sub.2/2004/19, 10 June 2004; 'Promoting the right to development in the context of the United Nations Decade for the Elimination of Poverty' (1997–2006), E/CN.4/Sub.2/2004/13, 1 June 2004; Official reports from the Sixth Session (14–18 February 2005) of the Open-ended Working Group on the Right to Development (Commission on Human Rights) include the following: Report of the high-level task force on the implementation of the right to development, E/CN.4/2005/WG.18/2,24 January 2005; Right to Development: Report of the High Commissioner for Human Rights, E/CN.4/2005/24, 5 January 2005; Report of the Working Group on the Right to Development, E/CN.4/2005/25, 3 March 2005. All these documents are available from: http://www.ohchr.org/english/issues/development/groups/documents-6th.htm.

F. *A lost cause so far*

Although 'S&D' is seen as an important task for the Doha Round, it is not surprising at all that little agreement, other than that on LDCs, was reached at the Hong Kong Conference,[62] and thereafter, all we saw were missed deadlines by the Committee on Trade and Development, which was mandated to hold special sessions to expeditiously complete the review of all the outstanding Agreement-specific proposals and report to the General Council, with clear recommendations for a decision on S&D issues.[63] It is not unreasonable to suggest that WTO members will not be able, in the foreseeable future, to make S&D 'more precise, effective and operational' as demanded by the Doha Declaration.

[62] It is unclear, however, whether decisions in favour of LDCs will be applicable to all 50 LDCs as defined by the UNPD or only to the 32 LDC members of the WTO. Annex F to the Draft Ministerial Declaration (18 December 2005) uses the phrase 'all LDCs' in relation to duty-free and quota-free market access and 'LDC members' when dealing with commitment and concessions to be made by LDCs. This suggests that favourable treatment for LDCs will be applicable to all LDCs whether or not they are members of the WTO. However, in summing up the achievements at Hong Kong Conference, the Chair of the Conference, Hong Kong's Commerce, Industry and Technology Secretary John Tsang specifically states that '[w]e have a very solid duty-free, quota-free access for the 32 least-developed country members'. It would be very unfortunate if this favourable treatment is only applicable to the WTO's LDC members rather than to all 50 LDCs.

[63] Para. 44 of the Doha Ministerial Declaration (2001) calls for a review of all 'S&D' provisions 'with a view to strengthening them and making them more precise, effective and operational'. Para 12 of the Decision on Implementation-Related Issues and Concerns (2001) instructed the Committee on Trade and Development to

> identify those special and differential treatment provisions that are already mandatory in nature and those that are non-binding in character, to consider the legal and practical implications for developed and developing Members of converting special and differential treatment measures into mandatory provisions, to identify those that Members consider should be made mandatory, and to report to the General Council with clear recommendations for a decision [and to] examine additional ways in which special and differential treatment provisions can be made more effective, to consider ways, including improved information flows, in which developing countries, in particular the least-developed countries, . . . and to report to the General Council with clear recommendations for a decision.

Both tasks were to be completed by July 2002, and the deadline was later extended a number of times. The last deadline was July 2005 (later, extended to December 2006), and the Committee, after many special sessions, again failed to complete its mandated tasks because 'differences among Members on the best way to proceed could not be bridged'. (Report to the General Council by the Chairman of the Special Session of the Committee on Trade and Development, 29 July 2005, TN/CTD/13).

In fact, the failure at the Doha Round is almost pre-determined by the inherently contradictory demands by developing countries. For instance, at the Hong Kong Conference, the Indian Minister of Commerce pointed out that 'our problems and challenges are so manifold and our socio-economic contexts so diverse, that no single, "harmonised" development strategy can be adopted. Each country must choose the path that best suits its own genius'.[64] If this is so, one wonders how the WTO could work out a one-size-for-all 'S&D' for all developing countries. Further, while China, India and many other developing countries have strongly resisted the creation of any sub-classification of developing countries,[65] LCDs are now firmly a sub-classification. Other sub-categories, such as 'Small Economies', 'Recently-acceded Members', have also appeared in WTO programmes and declarations, many of them creations by developing countries themselves.[66]

Fundamentally, 'S&D' notion does not sit comfortably with the underlying philosophy of free trade embodied in the WTO. Indeed, despite the failure on the development agenda at the Doha Round so far, a long-term observer of the WTO, Alan Oxley has described the Hong Kong results as 'a further dumbing down of the world body's free-market mission'.[67] A realistic solution lies with the upholding of free trade as a principle and, at the same time, allowing differentiated implementation by members of the WTO. While I disagree almost entirely with the prescription for the WTO by Walden Bello, I agree with the following statement he made, '[t]he WTO may eventually suffer the fate it helped inflict on the UNCTAD:

64 Kamal Nath, 'Statement at the Sixth Session of Ministerial Conference', 14 December 2005, WT/MIN(05)/ST/17.

65 P. S. Suryanarayana, 'WTO: India, China oppose bid to divide developing countries', *The Hindu*, 13 July 2005, available at www.thehindu.com/2005.07/13/stories/2005071318661200.htm.

66 Informally, of course, there are such groups as ACP (African, Caribbean and Pacific Countries, also referred to as the G77 but consist of 56 members), African Group (41 countries), FANs (Friends of Antidumping negotiations, 11 members), FIPs (or the Five or the Quint), the G10 (9 members), the G20 (21 members), the G33 (42 members), the G90 (64 members), etc. See further nn. 78–80 below.

67 He further described India's proposal that the WTO's rules on intellectual property be revised so law on industrial property will recognise the social values of pre-industrial society as laughable. Alan Oxley, 'Anyone for global free trade deals?', *The Australian*, 19 December 2005, available at www.theaustralian.news.com.au/printpage/0,5942,17604342,00.html.

surviving but increasingly ineffective and irrelevant'.[68] If this does happen, it will not be in the best interests of any country, developed or developing.

There are good reasons, internationally and domestically, why China and India could and should cooperate to prevent the WTO suffering the same fate as UNCTAD.

IV. Towards a long-term strategy for developing countries: International considerations for China and India

At the international level, my contention is that it is now time to discard the politically charged notion of 'developing countries' and to focus on countries whose overall economic and trading capacity is inadequate for a meaningful competition in global trade. Further, it is also time to abolish the admirable yet ineffective 'S&D' provisions and transform them into enforceable commitment, not as rules of the WTO but as implementation issues, so as to maintain the coherence and integrity of the WTO regulatory regime. Thirdly, it is argued that any realisation of a just and fair treatment for 'developing countries' relies not only on the rich developed countries but also on the so-called 'developing' countries themselves, since a new approach could only be developed by consensus among all WTO members. In other words, acceptance of a new notion for differentiating WTO memberships in place of 'developing countries' will have to mean that some of the existing self-proclaimed 'developing countries' will have to lose their status of belonging to a special membership class, and that a targeted and assisted development strategy for the newly identified countries will need to be worked out.

Firstly, it is futile to think of trying to stop the process of globalisation – it is already part of our lives – yet, an 'open, export-oriented' approach does not always work for all countries. The trade-led development theory is based on the assertion or presumption that all countries have a comparative advantage in trade,[69] but the reality is that not all countries are equal and competitive because of poverty and other

[68] Walden Bello, 'There is life after Cancún', *Bangkok Post*, 21 Sept 2003, available at www.tni.org/archives/bello/cancun2.htm.

[69] See also C. Thomas, 'Poverty reduction, trade, and rights' (2003) 18 *American University International Law Review*, 1399.

underdevelopment, especially in trading capacities. We must therefore recognise that, in this age of globalisation, free market and an open economy is not necessarily the only model for development available or worth pursuing, as many economists would like us to believe.[70] In fact, many other economists have pointed out that, in terms of tariff levels and export/GDP ratio, India and China – two of the most often cited successful examples, are the least globalised countries, whereas the poorest Sub-Saharan African ones are the most globalised (with exports accounting for 30% of GDP) – being even more open than Western developed countries (19% for the OECD).[71] If anything, 'it appears that in the early 21st century it is the least globalised countries that are the best performers.'[72] Thus, the most integrated economies are ironically becoming increasingly more marginal.[73] It has been quite clear that neither trade alone nor globalisation *per se* will lead all countries to development and prosperity. Even under the comparative advantage theory, it has been pointed out that certain advantages (endowments) are more difficult to create than others (e.g. human capital) and some almost impossible to change (land ratio per capita), and thus the development path of East Asia simply will not fit the situation of Africa.[74] The economic development in South East Asia, China and India was not propelled by liberalisation of trade, but, on the contrary, it was the protected development that later led to trade.[75] In fact, in the past no countries have liberalised trade before development: not the US, UK, Germany, Japan or Taiwan.[76] Common sense would also dictate that unless an economy has a sizeable market

[70] P. Balakrishnan, 'Globalisation, growth and justice', *Economic and Political Weekly*, 26 July 2003, at 3166–67.

[71] Balakrishnan, 'Globalisation, growth and justice', 3169. Indeed, Sierra Leone, which ranked 174th out of 174 countries in the 1999 HDR, earns more from exports as a percentage of its GDP than does Hong Kong; and Guinea-Bissau (168th) is more export-oriented in this fashion than South Korea. See Thomas, 'Poverty reduction', 1409; UNDP, *Human Development Report* (1999), available at http://hdr.undp.org/reports/global/1999/en/, at 1.

[72] Balakrishnan, 'Globalisation, growth and justice', 3169.

[73] UNDP, *Human Development Report*, 2.

[74] F. Bonaglia and K. Fukasaku, *Export Diversification in Low-Income Countries: An International Challenge after Doha*, Technical Papers No. 209, OECD Development Centre, DEV/DOC, 7 June 2003, www.oecd.org/dataoecd/13/28/8322001.pdf, at 12.

[75] Balakrishnan, 'Globalisation, growth and justice', 3169; Thomas, 'Poverty reduction', 1405.

[76] L. Elliott, 'Free trade is fine in a world of equals', *The Guardian Weekly*, 11–17 September 2003, 11.

(which, comparatively, is always the case in developed countries) and it is developing at a reasonable rate, or unless the country is highly developed economically and technologically, there can be little need for trade nor indeed anything competitive to be offered for trade.[77]

Secondly, we must not only recognise that developing countries are not members of a homogeneous interest-sharing group, we must also recognise that the needs of developing countries can diametrically oppose each other. The recent formation of the G20,[78] the G90,[79] G33,[80] etc., and the formal recognition of 'small economies', 'new members' etc., simply reflects the diversity of trading interests among developing countries. Most importantly, it is not the level of economic development that determines trade competition, it is trading capacities that do. Precisely because of this, the 'S&D' regime has more often than not impacted negatively on LDCs and poorer countries because of competition among 'developing countries'. In this sense, the larger and newly industrialised developing countries have enjoyed a 'free ride' under the regime, at the expense of LDCs and other poorer countries because of the general approach to the fictional group of 'developing countries'.

[77] For detailed analyses of trade statistics and economic development, see Chen, '"S & D" treatment'; and Chen, 'Developing countries'.

[78] Initially formed as G22 (comprising Argentina, Brazil, Bolivia, Chile, Colombia, Costa Rica, Cuba, Egypt, Ecuador, El Salvador, Guatemala, India, Indonesia, Malaysia, Mexico, Pakistan, Paraguay, the Philippines, South Africa, Thailand and Venezuela) at the Cancún by developing countries concerned with agriculture issues. See Joseph A. Camilleri and George Myconos, 'WTO: The Competitive Dynamic of Globalization at Work', in Jianfu Chen and Gordon Walker (eds) *Balancing Act: Law, Policy and Politics in Globalization and Global Trade* (Leichhardt: The Federation Press, 2004), pp. 21–53 at p. 48. It is now renamed as G20 but composed of 19 members: 5 from Africa (Egypt, Nigeria, South Africa, Tanzania and Zimbabwe), 6 from Asia (China, India, Indonesia, Pakistan, Philippines and Thailand) and 8 from Latin America (Argentina, Bolivia, Brazil, Chile, Cuba, Mexico, Paraguay and Venezuela). See www.g-20.mre.gov.br/history.asp.

[79] The G90 is an umbrella body of the African Group, the least developed countries and the African, Caribbean and Pacific (ACP) Group. It is currently the largest grouping of members in the World Trade Organization. See www.twnside.org.sg/title2/gtrends16.htm.

[80] The G33, which is actually composed of 42 members concerned about food security, livelihood security and rural development needs: Antigua and Barbuda, Barbados, Belize, Benin, Botswana, China, Congo, Côte d'Ivoire, Cuba, Dominican Republic, Grenada, Guyana, Haiti, Honduras, India, Indonesia, Jamaica, Kenya, Korea, Mauritius, Madagascar, Mongolia, Mozambique, Nicaragua, Nigeria, Pakistan, Panama, Peru, Philippines, St Kitts and Nevis, St Lucia, St Vincent and the Grenadines, Senegal, Sri Lanka, Suriname, Tanzania, Trinidad and Tobago, Turkey, Uganda, Venezuela, Zambia and Zimbabwe. See www.twnside.org.sg/title2/twninfo220.htm.

Thirdly, despite the philosophical changes that occurred during the Uruguay Round, it can be said that there are no explicit GATT/WTO rules that discriminate against developing countries, but only vague and *ad hoc* rules favouring them. This perhaps explains why the 'S&D' approach *per se* has not been seriously questioned, even though the doubtful usefulness and effectiveness of these rules for developing countries has been well recognised.[81] In fact, many have concluded that 'S&D' provisions have little value for needy developing countries. Most importantly, these rules represent some 'cross-cutting' concessions and allowances to trade liberalisation, rather than exceptions to it. As such, an 'S&D' regime in fact also leads to fierce competition among developing countries, resulting in developed countries reaping the benefit of lower prices for commodities as well as for low-tech manufactured goods. Indeed, on the basis of the UN Secretary-General's report to the UN Preparatory Committee on Financing for Development, January 2001, and several other studies, the *New Internationalist* has been able to conclude that trade liberalisation would add US$141.8 billion in gains for high income countries, US$37 billion for China, US$20.6 billion for upper income Asia, but a loss of US$2.6 billion for Africa.[82] After a detailed examination of 'S&D' provisions, Keck and Low reach the following damning indictment:

> In sum, the vast majority of S&D provisions are somewhat blunt policy instruments in that they do not distinguish among developing country Members in terms of their differing development needs, access to some S&D provisions is left to the discretion of the WTO membership as a whole, and most provisions define beneficiaries in terms of an ill-specified group called developing countries.[83]

The failure of the WTO's Committee on Trade and Development in the present Doha Round to work out an effective approach to 'S&D' provisions must cast some further serious doubt over the usefulness of these provisions. For the present Round, some eighty-eight specific suggestions

[81] See, for instance, the two current major reports on reforming the WTO: *The Future of the WTO: Addressing Institutional Challenge in the New Millennium*, Report by the Consultative Board to the Director-General Supachai Panitchpakdi, The World Trade Organization, 2004 (Sutherland Report); *The Multilateral Trade Regime: Which Way Forward?*, Report of the First Warwick Commission, The University of Warwick, 2008 (Warwick Report)

[82] *New Internationalist*, Special Issue on the WTO, May 2001, at 19.

[83] Keck and Low, Special and Differential Treatment, p. 24.

have been made by developing countries,[84] and discussion on the 'S&D' treatment have evolved into a web of propositions and an astonishing array of proposals for new and improved 'S&D' provisions.[85] It is not unreasonable to suggest that WTO members will not be able, in the foreseeable future, to agree on a commonly acceptable definition of 'developing countries' – a critical notion in any effort to refine 'S&D' provisions and their enjoyment – and to make S&D 'more precise, effective and operational' as demanded by the Doha Declaration.

Despite its pro-development rhetoric, it is clear that 'S&D' treatment offers very little practical value to countries that have had difficulties in coping with the tide of globalisation and global trade. It is also clear that it fails to recognise the competing nature of the relationship among developing countries. If it makes little sense to talk about developing countries as one group in terms of international trade; it makes no sense either to talk about general 'S&D' treatment for all developing countries, not to mention the doubtful benefit of it for developing countries. Fundamentally, in international trade, it is the state and institutional capacity of a particular country in global competition that counts for the actual gaining of global trade benefits. In short, the 'S&D' treatment of the WTO, though initiated in the aspiration of a NIEO, has now become diverted into certain vague and non-binding concessions to trade liberalisation and, hence, has outlived its purpose.

Fourthly, if we agree that one size and one model do not fit all, we then must also recognise that the efforts aimed at 'developing countries' as a group make little sense as the diversity and disparity among 'developing countries' are completely ignored. In other words, efforts should instead aim at identifying countries that need assistance, not the indiscriminate special treatment for an ill defined group. I call this a 'targeted and assisted development' strategy.[86]

Finally, this 'targeted and assisted development' strategy does not lie with the design of different policies for different developing countries; the world could not afford to have any more complications in the WTO rules, at least not for the LDCs and other poor small countries, nor is the

[84] B. Hoekman, C. Michalopulos and L. A. Winters, *More Favourable and Differential Treatment of Developing Countries: Toward a New Approach in the World Trade Organisation*, World Bank Policy Research Working Paper (2003), WPS 3107, available at www-wds.worldbank.org/servlet/WDS_IBank_Servlet?pcont=details&eid=000094946_030821 04020550, at 23.

[85] Keck and Low, *Special and Differential Treatment*, p. 6.

[86] For further elaboration, see Chen, '"S & D" treatment'; and Chen, 'Developing countries'.

approach to maintain the 'S&D' treatment feasible in the complicated negotiations, as the repeated failure of the WTO's Committee on Trade and Development and its special sessions in reviewing and making recommendations for new framework on 'S&D' provisions has clearly indicated. The pressing problems with the world are not those associated with 'developing' countries, but with those in dire poverty.[87] What we need is an approach that would remove the political wrangling, accommodate the diversity of WTO membership and create effective yet realistic mechanisms for an equitable global trade regime. To do so, we need to move away from the narrow focus on the 'S&D' treatment to a broader development agenda while maintaining the integrity and coherence of the WTO regime as a whole. Specifically, we need a new approach that would encompass the following: (1) to maintain the integrity and coherence of the WTO rules, WTO should abolish the notion of 'developing countries' and remove the 'S&D' treatment provisions; (2) to accommodate the diversity of WTO membership and to recognise the needs of the countries lacking trading capacities, WTO should take a targeted and assisted development approach focusing on improving state and institutional capacity of the clearly identified countries; (3) to make the differentiated treatment effective and binding, all concessions and commitments should be negotiated during the rounds of WTO negotiation and form part of the implementation package (but not part of the general rules of the WTO) contained in Schedules of Commitment of individual countries.[88] In this way, WTO negotiations can cast away political wrangling and empty rhetoric and focus on specific trade issues and trade needs for individual countries. Finally, WTO agreements need to be tidied up to ensure the integrity and uniformity of its rules on the basis of liberalisation and non-discrimination. Such agreements then form the fundamental skeleton of the WTO structure and these agreements must maintain their relative stability rather than being subject to rounds of negotiation, hence upholding their stability, coherence and integrity.

This contention is not meant to throw away the baby with the bathwater; rather, it is to argue for re-orientation of the WTO focus towards a coherent and realistic legal framework on 'developing countries' while not undermining the fundamental philosophy of creating a

[87] Let's not forget that the great majority of the 850 million going hungry each day reside in Africa and the poorer part of Asia ('850 million go hungry despite war on poverty', *The Australian*, 26 November 2003, p. 10).

[88] For further elaboration, see Chen, '"S & D" treatment'; and Chen, 'Developing countries'.

fairer and freer global trade environment. I do not believe that the current trade regime is either free or fair, but I do believe a fairer and freer global trade system is beneficial to all nations, developed or developing, small or large.

This proposal may sound radical, but it could effectively be a simpler approach if there is a political will to do so. More importantly, it transforms the nature of dialogue from rule-making to implementation, hence significantly simplifies the global trading rules while ensuring concessions and commitments are binding and operational. It also shifts the present passive resistance by developing countries to a demand for active measures by developed countries. China and India, two countries that have benefited most from the present globalisation and liberalisation regime, have not only the capacity but also the crucial stake to take the leadership in this fundamental transformation of WTO treatment of less developed countries.

V. Towards a proactive strategy: Domestic considerations for China and India

There are also good domestic reasons for China and India to push for some radical reforms at the WTO.

The trouble with WTO negotiations is that short-term political and economic gains overwhelm negotiation agenda. This is necessarily so, as Mr Pascal Lamy, the current Director-General of the WTO, has recently pointed out that 'ministers (participating in the negotiations) often face the difficult task of explaining to national constituencies that they have gained something in negotiations, even if the negotiating process is not over'.[89] Indeed, a satisfactory outcome for agriculture is critical for the Doha Round and for many developing countries. However, as Lamy has also reminded the ministers at the Hong Kong Conference, negotiators need also to look beyond the immediate needs, think prospectively, care about the future and invest in improvement of WTO rules.[90]

While India has taken a rather active approach in WTO negotiations, especially at the Doha Round,[91] its focus is both *ad hoc* and short-term interest oriented, largely in areas of agriculture and, to a lesser extent, on

[89] Pascal Lamy, 'Opening speech at the Sixth Session of Ministerial Conference', Hong Kong, 13 December 2005, available at www.wto.org/english/news_e/sppl_e/sppl15_e.htm.

[90] Lamy, 'Opening speech'.

[91] According to Chaisse and Chakraborty, 'Identifying mutual interest areas', p. 270, India played an active role for the first time at the failed Seattle Ministerial in 1999. India has

IP and services. India's active involvement in the WTO is also indicated in its membership of the various informal groups. It is a leading member in the G20 and G33. It closely works with the African group, LDCs, and the G90. It has also co-authored and co-sponsored various proposals to the WTO with other developing countries.[92] However, as Mattoo and Subramanian have pointed out, 'India's stance in the GATT/WTO has always tended to be defensive, seeking freedom to use restrictive policies – two prongs of the so-called special and differential treatment embraced by developing countries as a whole.' It has not been clearly associated with the voices for greater and faster liberalisation of global trade.[93]

China, on the other hand, has remained a low profile member until now,[94] other than making some very general commitment to developing countries. Commenting on foreign investment and economic development, Thornhill commented that 'While the sleeping giant that was China has woken with a vengeance, India still appears to be quietly dozing in the corner'.[95] The reverse then is true regarding the role in the WTO played by India and China so far. China is aware of and becomes increasingly sensible to criticisms about its taking a low profile at the WTO. Thus the Xinhua News Agency describes the speech by the Chinese minister at the Hong Kong Conference as changing the consistently low-tune practice in the last five years, using sharp critical language, expressing a clear stand, and thus rejecting the unreasonable criticisms that China deliberately kept a low profile because it has been the largest benefit-recipient among developing countries.[96] China may not deliberately keep a low profile, but its profile in the

also been instrumental in rejecting the so-called Singapore issues, such as labour and environment standards.

92 See Nath, 'Minister's statement'.

93 See Aaditya Mattoo and Arvind Subramanian, 'India and the multilateral trading system post-Doha: Defensive or proactive?', in Aaditya Mattoo and Robert M. Stern, *India and the WTO* (Washington DC: The World Bank/Oxford University Press, 2003), pp. 327–66.

94 On the other hand, China has been very active in promoting and consolidating bilateral and regional cooperation, especially in the Asia–Pacific region. See e.g. Ho Khai Leong and Samual C. Y. Ku, *China and Southeast Asia: Global Changes and Regional Challenges* (Singapore: Institute of Southeast Asian Studies/Centre for Southeast Asian Studies, 2005) at p. 327 and Oxley, 'Anyone for global free trade deals'.

95 John Thornhill, 'China's Challenge', *Financial Times*, 12 April 2002, quoted in Mark B. Baker, '"Awakening the sleeping giant": India and foreign direct investment in the 21st century' (2005) 15 *Indiana International & Comparative Law Review* 389, 420.

96 Xinhua, 'Bo Xilai's High Profile speech: China is willing to contribute the rules of the WTO', 19 December 2005, available at http://news.xinhuanet.com/fortune/2005_12/19/content_3939771.htm.

WTO is nowhere matching its 'Great Power' status that it played in the Security Council of the UN.

On joint actions, India and China have, since 2003, jointly submitted some fourteen proposals to the WTO (three in agriculture, five to the General Council, one on investment, and five related to trade in services),[97] but all are on specific issues and none has taken a pro-active approach to address mid- to long-term strategic issues in the WTO. Neither their individual nor their joint efforts have matched their emerging 'Great Power' status or aspirations. In particular, in the pursuit of a 'fairer' outcome for developing countries, both countries seem to ignore the fundamental mission of the WTO, that is, a rule-based global order of freer trade. The two countries, in rejecting further sub-classification of developing countries, have also ignored the reality and the fact that much of the gains made for large developing countries will be at the cost of LDCs and other smaller developing countries. In this context, their legitimacy of representing the developing countries is questionable. It is also important for China and India to acknowledge that what counts in the WTO regime is not the GDP *per capita*, it is the trading capacity, largely represented by the GNP, market size and educated workforces, that matters for success in global trade and global competition.

Despite differences in political and economic systems, China and India both learnt a hard lesson of self-reliance and self-sufficiency as their national economic policies almost bankrupted the two economies by the late 1970s and early 1990s respectively. Thus, economic reform in both countries at the present can be characterised as 'open door' policy – integrating with and competing in the world.[98] By doing so, both countries have become successful stories of economic liberalisation and global integration. More crucially, both countries need further input for justifying further liberal reform to overcome WTO-related reform fatigue in China[99] and reform resistance from various vested interest groups in India.[100] At a realistic economic level, one must ask why China and India should continue their liberal reform without returns from

[97] Chaisse and Chakraborty, 'Identifying mutual interest areas'.

[98] Desai, Meghnad, 'Will India ever catch up with China?' (2005) 28(2) *Journal of South Asian Studies*, 321.

[99] See Peter Alford, 'EU loses to rising forces in siege of HK', www.theaustralian.news.com.au/printpage/0,5942,17606964,00.html.

[100] Desai, 'Will India ever catch up'; 'Democracy's drawbacks', Special Report: Reform in India, *The Economist*, 29 October 2005, 23–5.

other countries in the WTO bargain forums. In this context, neither India's nor China's approach in the WTO has been consistent with its own domestic economic reform needs. While China launched its economic reforms in 1978, its market-oriented reform started in 1992 when the Communist Party adopted a policy to establish a 'socialist market economy'. Similarly, India began its liberalisation of trading regime in the late 1970s, it only began to pull down its protection and reverse its trade protection in 1991.[101] Both benefit remarkably from these reforms and both are frequently cited as successful examples of liberal trading regimes propelling economic development and lifting people out of poverty. Both countries are likely to continue and sustain their respective economic reform towards open market and global competition. Equally importantly, both countries need external pressures, voluntarily assumed or otherwise imposed because of memberships in regional and global trade organisations, to counterbalance domestic conservative forces that argue for inward-looking protectionist policies. In this context, a defensive approach, though often justified, is not in the best interests of either.

Mattoo and Subramanian have made a very convincing case why India must take a pro-active approach in the WTO to secure its long term interest and success.[102] Their case is based on the following sound arguments. Firstly, multilateral engagement is not an end in itself; it is to serve the ends of good domestic policies. Secondly, and very crucially, a country relying on preferential treatment will never get what an equal partner would in trade negotiation, and paradoxically, a unilateral and committed reforming country will not get what it deserves either (because of the free-ride on the domestic reform efforts by trading partners). Thirdly, multilateralism is a necessary and positive constraint on government not to reverse to protection and, hence, to commitment of good policies. Fourthly, to take advantage of rule enforcement capacity in the WTO, developing countries need to take a lead in policy reforms and in guard against regionalism. Finally, it is in the interest of developing countries to multilateralise domestic liberal trading policies.[103] This line of analysis applies not only to India, but also to China.[104] Here lies a solid foundation for China and

[101] Chadha, Rajesh, Brown, K. Drusilla, Allan V. Deardorff and Robert M. Stern, 'Computational analysis of the impact on India of the Uruguay Round and the Doha Development Agenda negotiations', in Mattoo and Stern, *India and the WTO*, pp. 14–15.

[102] Mattoo and Subramanian, 'India and the multilateral trading system', 329–35.

[103] Mattoo and Subramanian, 'India and the multilateral trading system', 329–30.

[104] Indeed, China was taken as an example in their analysis.

India to cooperate at the WTO on strategic issues and to push for reform towards trade liberalisation.

It is interesting to note that Mattoo and Subramanian have only implicitly criticised the 'S&D' treatment and proceed to recommend specific pro-active measures on specific issues in the reform and negotiations of the WTO, even though they clearly question its usefulness for countries like India and China.[105] They argued that '[i]t is easy to be critical of the old obstructionist approach of developing countries that was founded on a belief in self-sufficiency and inward-looking policies. But a more complex question facing developing countries now is whether the liberal policies being pursued at home need to be multilateralised.'[106] More interestingly, they clearly see India's defensive approach as being a result of heavily relying on the S&D treatment. If this is so, neither India nor China is likely to take a more pro-active approach without seriously questioning the S&D provisions and re-positioning themselves in the WTO.

There is nothing wrong in attempting to address or making suggestions on specific issues, such as agriculture, labour movement, etc, and they are all important issues. The trouble is, the tune from India and China has been too defensive; it does not augur well with domestic reform efforts nor is it in line with their aspiration to be an emerging 'Great Power'. Most importantly, it does not contribute to the strengthening of the fundamental philosophy of the WTO, that is, freer and fairer trading.

Indeed, there will always be suspicions about the rising power of China, and India for that matter. It is also often recognised that, if China follows through its stated intention to play an important role, it could have some 'extremely positive' impact on the WTO, especially in bridging the gap between the developed and developing countries.[107] On the other hand, China is now actively encouraged by other international powers to play a greater role in international affairs and in the WTO. For instance, the US has recently redefined its policy towards China, welcomes 'confident, peaceful and prosperous China', and invites China 'to work with us [US] to shape the future international system'. On China and WTO, the US has also called on China to assume a greater role in global trade talk in line with China's growing trading powers and

[105] Mattoo and Subramanian, 'India and the multilateral trading system', 359–63.
[106] Mattoo and Subramanian, 'India and the multilateral trading system', 334.
[107] Supachai Panitchpakdin and Mark L. Clifford, *China and the WTO: Changing China, Changing World Trade* (Singapore: John Wiley & Sons (Asia) Pte Ltd, 2002), p. 192.

their corresponding responsibilities.[108] If China indeed intends to exert 'itself to push forward multilateral economic and trade relations and regional economic cooperation, to actively participate in the formulation and execution of international economic and trade rules, and to join various other countries in settling disputes and problems emerging in their cooperation, so as to promote the balanced and orderly development of the world economy', and to 'actively further trade and investment liberalisation and facilitation, remove all kinds of trade barriers, increase market access, ease restrictions on technology export, so as to establish an international multilateral trading system that is public, fair, rational, transparent, open and non-discriminatory, and construct a good trading environment conducive to orderly global economic development',[109] China must then take on not just rights but also responsibilities in the WTO. This is also true if India wants to be a new global leader.[110]

VI. Concluding remarks

A completely new approach must now be taken, if the WTO is to avoid the same mistakes as the UN in its efforts to promote the 'right to development'. In doing so, it is worthwhile highlighting once again the following. First, 'S&D' treatment is increasingly becoming a politically entangled notion that offers little value to countries that need assistance to benefit from globalisation and global trade. Secondly, the notion of 'developing countries' is a political and indefinable concept. As such, the 'S&D' treatment is inherently unworkable; any efforts to work out its 'precise, concrete and enforceable measures' are doomed to fail. Thirdly, the WTO as a body of rules must be clearly distinguished from the implementation of those rules. Fourthly, as the high-level consultative group has made clear, the integrity of the WTO regime is in danger, though not entirely but partly by the incoherent and irrational practice of the 'S&D' treatment. Fifthly, countries that need assistance to gain the benefit of global trade are not necessarily those with lower per capita GNP or with the largest number of people still in poverty – China and India are two such examples – but those lacking state and institutional

[108] 'US seeks new path to China', *The Australian*, 10–11 December 2005, p. 17 and 20.

[109] 'China's peaceful development road', a State Council White Paper issued Dec 2005, State Council Information Office.

[110] Prasenjit K. Basu, Brahma Chelleney, Parag Khanna, Sunil Khilnani, *India as a New Global Leader* (UK: The Foreign Policy Centre, 2005), available at http://fpc.org.uk/fsblob/377.pdf.

capacities in global competition. And finally, foreign aid or assistance to poorer countries, as least part of it, must be oriented – coordinated by WTO, IMF and UNDP – towards overcoming these identified difficulties in implementing WTO disciplines, gaining benefit from global trade, and earlier removal of concessions therein.[111] By so doing, we have a clear win-win situation – less developed countries are assisted towards trade liberalisation and gaining its benefit while developed countries gain further benefit in the gradual liberalisation of trade and investment regimes of the poorer countries. Most important, we can then focus on positive actions and measures from developed countries and the needs and varied difficulties of less developed countries, hence effective, operational and binding commitments from both sides.

A 'Great Power' has to take a role in global trade talks not only for its own interests or even short-term gains for a group of countries; it must take the responsibilities in ensuring justice and equity in global trade regimes such as the WTO. To do so, it might simply mean that it has to sacrifice some short-term gains in order to achieve longer term strategic interests. In this, China and India have a joint responsibility in making sure that the less developed countries, primarily the LDCs, get a fair deal in the WTO negotiations at Doha and beyond, and a fundamental reform in 'S&D' treatment is one of these strategic issues.

[111] Lack of coordination and coherence among international organisations, including aid organisations, are, of course, a well-recognised problem. See Mike Moore, *A World Without Walls: Freedom, Development, Free Trade and Global Governance* (Cambridge University Press, 2003), p. 48. This need for coordination has also been called for by the Consultative Board to the WTO Director-General. See WTO, 'The future of the WTO: Addressing institutional challenges in the new millennium', Report by the Consultative Board to the Director-General Supachai Panitchpakdi, Geneva, 2004, at 35–40. These problems are now being addressed through the 'Integrated Framework' jointly undertaken by the WTO, the World Bank, IMF, ITC (International Trade Centre), UNCTAD and UNDP, and the Aid-for-Trade initiative launched at the Hong Kong Conference.

References

'850 million go hungry despite war on poverty', *The Australian*, 26 November 2003, p. 10

Adhikari, R. and Athukorala, P.-C. (eds.), *Developing Countries in the World Trading System: The Uruguay Round and Beyond* (Cheltenham, UK: Edward Elgar Publishing Limited, 2002)

Alford, Peter, 'EU loses to rising forces in siege of HK' (2005), available at www.theaustralian.news.com.au/printpage/0,5942,17606964,00.html (accessed 19 Dec 2005)

Awuku, E. O. 'How do the results of the Uruguay Round affect the North–South trade?' (1994) 28(6) *Journal of World Trade* 75

Baker, Mark B., '"Awakening the sleeping giant": India and foreign direct investment in the 21st century' (2005) 15 *Indiana International & Comparative Law Review* 389–426

Balakrishnan, P., 'Globalisation, growth and justice' *Economic and Political Weekly*, 26 July 2003, 3166

Basu, Prasenjit K., Chelleney, Brahma, Khanna, Parag and Khilnani, Sunil, *India as a New Global Leader* (UK: The Foreign Policy Centre, 2005), available at: http://fpc.org.uk/fsblob/377.pdf (accessed 1 Feb 2006)

Bello, Walden, 'There is life after Cancún', *Bangkok Post*, 21 Sept 2003, available at www.tni.org/archives/bello/cancun2.htm (accessed 9 Dec 2005)

Bo, Xilai, Statement at the Sixth Session of Ministerial Conference, 14 December 2005

Bonaglia, F. and Fukasaku, K., *Export Diversification in Low-Income Countries: An International Challenge After Doha*, Technical Papers No. 209, OECD Development Centre, DEV/DOC (2003)07, June 2003, a pdf text is available at www.oecd.org/dataoecd/13/28/8322001.pdf

Boquérat, Gilles and Grare, Frédéric (eds.), *India, China, Russia: Intricacies of an Asian Triangle* (Singapore: Marshall Cavendish International (Singapore) Private Limited, 2004)

Camilleri, Joseph A. and Myconos, George, 'WTO: The Competitive Dynamic of Globalization at Work', in Chen and Walker (eds.), *Balancing Act*, pp. 21–53

Chadha, Rajesh, Brown, Drusilla K., Deardorff, Allan V. and Stern, Robert M., 'Computational analysis of the impact on India of the Uruguay Round and the Doha Development Agenda negotiations', in Mattoo and Stern, 13–46

Chaisse, Julien and Chakraborty, Debashis 'Identifying mutual interest areas at WTO: A Sino-Indian joint perspective' (2005) 41(3) *China Report* 267–8

Chen, J., 'Developing countries: "S&D" treatment, and the integrity of the WTO system' (2007)(1) *International Law Review* 296

'"S&D" treatment for developing countries in the WTO trade regime: A false solution on a wrong footing for LDCs'in Chen and Walker (eds.), *Balancing Act*, pp. 109–51

Chen, J. and Walker, G., *Balancing Act: Law, Policy and Politics in Globalisation and Global Trade* (Sydney: The Federation Press, 2004)

Chengappa, Bidanda M., *India–China Relations: Post Conflict Phase to Post Cold War Period* (New Delhi: APH Publishing Corporation, 2004)

Colebatch, Tim, 'Trade: postponing failure', *The Age*, 20 December 2005, available at www.theage.com.au/news/tim-colebatch/trade-postponing-failure/2005/12/19 (accessed 21 Dec 2005)

Confederation of Indian Industry, *India–China: The Road Ahead*, April 2005, available at www.indiachina.org/resources (accessed 9 Dec 2005)

Coote, B., *The Trade Trap: Poverty and the Global Commodity Markets*, 2nd edn (UK and Ireland: Oxfam, 1996)

Cutajar, M. Z. (ed.), *UNCTAD and the South–North Dialogue: The First Twenty Years* (Oxford: Pergamon Press, 1985)

Deepak, B. R., *India & China 1904–2004: A Century of Peace and Conflict* (New Delhi: Manak Publications Pvt Ltd, 2005).

Dell, S. 'The origins of UNCTAD', in M. Z. Cutajar, *UNCTAD and the South–North Dialogue: The First Twenty Years* (Oxford: Pergamon Press, 1985), pp. 10–32

'Democracy's drawbacks', Special Report *Reform in India, The Economist,* 29 October 2005, 23–5

Desai, Meghnad 'Will India ever catch up with China?' (2005) 28(2) *Journal of South Asian Studies* 321–36

Desai, Seema, 'A new India–China nexus: More than the sum of its parts', the Foreign Policy Centre, available http://fpc.org.uk/articles/334 (accessed 1 Feb 2006)

Dicke, D. C., 'Public International Law and a New International Economic Order', in P. Sarcevic and H. van Houtte, H. (eds.), *Legal Issues in International Trade* (Dordrecht: Martinus Nijhoff, 1990)

Elliott, L., 'Free trade is fine in a world of equals', *The Guardian Weekly,* 11–17 September 2003, 11

Evans, David, Kaplinsky, Raphie and Robinson, Sherman, 'The emergence of India, China and an East and South East Asia region on the world economy: A typology of drivers and impacts', *IDS Bulletin* (Oct 2005 draft), document on personal file

Fernando, Sithara, 'Recent writings on India–China relations' (2005) 41(2) *China Report* 173–82

Fritsch, P., 'Bangladesh stares into the abyss', *Far Eastern Economic Review,* 27 November 2003, 46

G20 Ministerial Declaration (19 March 2005), available at http://commerce.nic.in/wto_sub/g20/min_decln.htm (accessed 9 Dec 2005)

Gordon, Sandy and Henningham, Stephen (eds.), *India Looks East: An Emerging Power and its Asia–Pacific Neighbours* (Canberra: The Australian National University, 1995)

Gupta, K. R. (ed.), *World Trade Organisation (Successor to GATT) and India* (New Delhi: Atlantic Publishers and Distributors, 1996)

Haider, Ziad, 'US–India–China: Giants at play', *The Indian Express,* 30 July 2005, available at http://indianexpress.com/print.php?content_id=75320 (accessed 9 Dec 2005)

Hoekman, B., 'More favourable treatment of developing countries and the Doha Development Agenda', *Trade Note,* 29 May 2003, The World Bank. A pdf text is available from the World Bank website: www-wds.worldbank.org/servlet/WDS_IBank_Servlet?pcont=details&eid=000090341_ 20031010133313.

Hoekman, B., Michalopulos, C. and Winters, L. A., *More Favourable and Differential Treatment of Developing Countries: Toward a New Approach in the World Trade Organisation* (2003), World Bank Policy Research Working

Paper, WPS 3107. A pdf text is available from the World Bank website: www-wds.worldbank.org/servlet/WDS_IBank_Servlet?pcont=details&eid=000094946_03082104020550

Hoekman, B. and Özden, C., 'Trade preferences and differential treatment of developing countries: A selective survey', World Bank Policy Research Working Paper 3566 (April 2005). A pdf text is available form the World Bank website: www-wds.worldbank.org/servlet/WDS_IBank_Servlet?pcont=details&eid=000012009_20050421124442.

IISD, 'Special and differential treatment', *Doha Round Briefing Series*, vol I, no. 13 (2003)

India Economic Summit, 'India–China: A win-win partnership?', 26 November 2002, available at www.weforum.org/site/knowledgenavigator.nsf/Content/F9C32A908512976CC1.htm (accessed 9 Dec 2005)

Indian Government, 'Draft WTO ministerial text disappointing', 1 December 2005, available http://commerce.nic.in/Dec05_release.htm#h10

Jackson, J. H., *The World Trading System: Law and Policy of International Economic Relation*, 2nd edn (Cambridge MA: The MIT Press, 1997)

Jain, B. M., *India–China Relations: Issues, Trends and Emerging Scenarios*, China–India Project Occasional Paper No. 1 (2003), Centre of Asian Studies, the University of Hong Kong, available at www.hku.hk/cas/pub/Occasional1_bmjain.pdf (accessed 3 Oct 2005)

Joint Declaration, Declaration on Principles for Relations and Comprehensive Cooperation Between the Republic of India and the People's Republic of China, 23 June 2003, English version available at http://meaindia.nic.in/jdhome.htm (accessed 9 Dec 2005)

Joint Statement, Joint Statement of the Republic of India and the People's Republic of China, 11 April 2005, available at http://meaindia.nic.in/jshome.htm (accessed 9 Dec 2005)

Joint Study Group, *Report of the India–China Joint Study Group on Comprehensive Trade and Economic Cooperation*, March 2005, document on personal file

Kamath, M. V., 'India–China relations: Illusion and reality' (2003), available at www.samachar.com/features/100703-features.html (accessed 3 Oct 2005)

Keck, A. and Low, P., *Special and Differential Treatment in the WTO: Why, When and How?*, WTO Staff Working Paper ERSD-2004–03. A pdf text is available form the WTO website: www.wto.org/english/res_e/reser_e/ersd200403_e.htm

Lamy, Pascal, 'Opening speech at the Sixth Session of Ministerial Conference', Hong Kong, 13 December 2005, available at www.wto.org/english/news_e/sppl_e/sppl15_e.htm (accessed 14 Dec 2005)

Leonard, Sean, *The Dragon Awakens: China's Long March to Geneva* (London: Cameron May Ltd, 1999)

Leong, Ho Khai and Ku, Samual C. Y., *China and Southeast Asia: Global Changes and Regional Challenges* (Singapore: Institute of Southeast Asian Studies/Centre for Southeast Asian Studies (National Sun Yat-sen University, 2005)

Limaye, Satu, 'Sino-Indian relations: The four disconnects', *Policy Forum Online*, 08–009A, 30 January 2008, available at www.nautilus.org/fora/security/08009Limaye.html (accessed 15 Aug. 2008)

Liu, Warren, 'India and China: Competitive or complementary?' *China Business Infocentre*, 2 December 2005, available at www.cbiz.cn (accessed 2 Dec 2005)

MA Jiali, *Focus on India: An Emerging Great Power (Guanzhu Yindu: Jueqi Zhong de Daguo)* (Tianjin: Tianjin People's Press, 2002)

Martin, Will and Pangestu, Mari, *Options for Global Trade Reform: A View from the Asia–Pacific* (Cambridge University Press, 2003)

Matsushita, Mitsuo, Schoenbaum, Thomas and Mavroidis, Petros C., *The World Trade Organization: Law, Practice, and Policy* (Oxford University Press, 2003)

Mattoo, Aaditya and Stern, Robert M. *India and the WTO* (Washington DC: The World Bank/Oxford University Press, 2003)

Mattoo, Aaditya and Subramanian, Arvind, 'India and the multilateral trading system post-Doha: Defensive or proactive?', in Mattoo and Stern, pp. 327–66

McRae, Donald, 'Developing countries and "The future of the WTO"' (2005) 8(3) *Journal of International Economic Law* 603–610

Michalopoulos, C., 'Developing countries and the WTO', discussion paper series 2000–02. A pdf text is available at www.unu.edu/inter-linkages/doc/DiscussionP/2000_02_michalopoulos.pdf

Moore, Mike, *A World Without Walls: Freedom, Development, Free Trade and Global Governance* (Cambridge University Press, 2003)

Nath, Kamal, 'Kamal Nath calls for roadmap for elimination of trade distorting farm subsidies by developed countries', Hong Kong, 13 December 2005, available http://commerce.nic.in/Dec05_release.htm

'Minister's statement', 7 December 2005, available http://commerce.nic.in/Dec05_release.htm

'Statement at the Sixth Session of Ministerial Conference', 14 December 2005, WT/MIN(05)/ST/17

New Internationalist, Special Issue on the WTO, May 2001

Niazi, Tarique, 'China, India and the future of South Asia', *Japan Focus*, 21 August 2005, available at www.japanfocus.org/article.asp?id=371 (accessed 26 Aug 2005)

'Sino-Indian Rivalry for Pan-Asian Leadership' (2006) 6(4) *China Brief*

North–South Institute, *The Reality of Trade: The WTO and Developing Countries* (undated), p. 4. A pdf text of the document is available at www.nsi-ins.can/ensi/pdf/Reality_of_Trade.pdf

OECD Joint Group, *The Role of 'Special and Differential Treatment' at the Trade, Competition and Development Interface*, prepared by the OECD Joint Group on Trade and Competition, 2001. A pdf text is available on OECD website: www.oecd.org

Oxley, Alan, 'Anyone for global free trade deals?' *The Australian*, 19 Dec 2005, available at www.theaustralian.news.com.au/printpage/0,5942,17604342,00.html (accessed 19 Dec 2005)

'What WTO' (16 Sept 2003) *Tech Central Station* available at www2.techcentralstation.com/1051/printer.jsp?CID=1051-091603F (accessed 9 Dec 2005)

Panagariya, Arvind, 'An India–China free trade area?" (2005), available at www.columbia.edu/~ap2231/ET/et77_April20_05.htm (accessed 9 Dec 2005)

Panitchpakdi, Supachai and Clifford, Mark L., *China and the WTO: Changing China, Changing World Trade* (Singapore: John Wiley & Sons (Asia) Pte Ltd, 2002)

Picciotto, S. and Mayne, R. (eds.), *Regulating International Business: Beyond Liberalisation* (New York: St. Martin's Press, 1999)

Raghavan, Chakravarthi, *Recolonization: GATT, the Uruguay Round & the Third World* (London/New Jersey/Penang: Zed Books Ltd and Third World Network, 1990)

Ransom, D., 'If the WTO means to stay afloat it will have to lose some excess baggage' (2001) 334 *New Internationalist* 9

Robertson, A. H. and Merrills, J. G., *Human Rights in the World* (Manchester University Press, 1996)

Rom, M., 'Some early reflections on the Uruguay Round Agreement as seen from the viewpoint of a developing country' (1994) 28(6) *Journal of World Trade* 5

Sarcevic, P. and van Houtte, H. (eds.), *Legal Issues in International Trade* (Dordrecht: Martinus Nijhoff, 1990)

Schoneveld, F. R., 'The GATS – Implications and Opportunities for Trade-In-Service: The European Union View', a paper presented to the 21st International Trade Law Conference, Sydney, 17–18 October 1994

Seidi-Hohenveldem, I., *International Economic Law*, 2nd edn. (Dordrecht: Matinus Nijhoff Publishers, 1992)

Sornarajah, M., 'Good corporate citizenship and the conduct of multinational corporations', in Chen and Walker (eds.), *Balancing Act*, pp. 224–50

The International Law on Foreign Investment (Cambridge: Grotius Publications/ Cambridge University Press, 1995)

Sridhar V., 'Free trade fears: China's proposal for a free trade agreement with India meets with resistance from Indian industry' (2005: May) 22(10) *Frontline (India)* 7–20, available www.bilaterals.org/article-print.php3?id_article=1867 (accessed 9 Dec 2005)

Sun, Shihai , 'Sino-India relationship in the 21st century', *China Daily*, 26 May 2004, available at http://www.chiandaily.com.cn/gb/doc/2004-05/26/content_333973.htm (accessed 4 October 2005)

Sun, Yuhua and Jiang, Zhenglin (eds.) *Emerging Great Powers: Games and Perspective of an Historic Rise (Xinxing Daguo: Lishixing Jueqi de Boyi Yu Qianjing)* (Beijing: People's Press, 2004)

Suryanarayana, P. S., 'India, China to act in concert on WTO issues', *The Hindu*, 26 June 2003, available at www.hinduonnet.com/thehindu/2003/06/26/stories/2003062604860100.htm (accessed 9 Dec 2005)

'WTO: India, China oppose bid to divide developing countries', *The Hindu*, 13 July 2005, available at www.thehindu.com/2005.07/13/stories/2005071318661200.htm (accessed 9 Dec 2005)

Sutherland Report: *The Future of the WTO: Addressing Institutional Challenge in the New Millennium*, Report by the Consultative Board to the Director-General Supachai Panitchpakdi, The World Trade Organization, 2004

Thomas, C., 'Poverty reduction, trade, and rights' (2003) 18 *American University International Law Review* 1399

Trebilcock, M. J. and Howse, R. *The Regulation of International Trade*, 2nd edn (London and New York: Routledge, 1999)

UNCTAD, *The History of UNCTAD, 1964–1984* (New York: United Nations, 1985)

UNCTAD, *Trade and Development Report 2002*, Part II: *Developing Countries in World Trade*, available at www.unctad.org/en/docs/trade2002p2_en.pdf

UNDP, *Human Development Report* (1999), a pdf version is available at http://hdr.undp.org/reports/global/1999/en/

UNDP, *Human Development Report 2003*, a pdf text is available from the website of UNDP: http://hdr.undp.org/reports/global/2003/en/

'US seeks new path to China', *The Australian*, 10–11 December 2005, pp. 17 and 20

Warwick Report, *The Multilateral Trade Regime: Which Way Forward?*, The Report of the First Warwick Commission, The University of Warwick, 2008

Wen Jiabao, 'China India not rivals but friends', available at www.npc.gov.cn/was40/detail?record=1&channelid=20179&searchword=%20(%20%D3%A1%B6%C8+%29+and+%28+IDS%3D%27336560'%20) (accessed 9 Dec 2005)

Whalley, J., *Developing Countries and the Global Trading System*, vol. I: *Thematic Studies from a Ford Foundation Project*, vol. II: *Country Studies from a Ford Foundation Project* (London: Macmillan Press, 1989)

White Paper 2005: China's Peaceful Development Road, A State Council White Paper issued Dec 2005, State Council Information Office

Williams, M., *Third World Cooperation: The Group of 77 in UNCTAD* (London: Printer Publishers, 1991)

Wolf, Martin, 'Why is China Growing so Slowly?', *Foreign Policy* (Jan/Feb 2005), available at www.foreignpolicy.com/story/cms.php?story_id=2750 (accessed 12 December 2005)

WTO, *Background Document to the High Level Symposium on Trade and Development*, Geneva, 17–18 March 1999, prepared by the Development Division of WTO, p. 5, available at www.wto.org

'Specialand differential treatment provisions: Communication India', TN/CTD/W/6, 14 May 2002

'Specialand differential treatment provisions: Joint Communication from Cuba, Dominican Republic, Honduras, India, Indonesia, Kenya, Pakistan, Sri Lanka, Tanzania and Zimbabwe', TN/CTD/W/1, 14 May 2002

'Specialand differential treatment provisions: Joint Communication from Cuba, Dominican Republic, Egypt, Honduras, India, Indonesia, Kenya, Mauritius, Pakistan, Sri Lanka, Tanzania and Zimbabwe', TN/CTD/W/2, 14 May 2002

WTO Agriculture Background, 'Agriculture negotiation: Backgrounder, Phase 1: Developing countries', in www.wto.org/english/tratop_e/agric_e/negs_bkgrnd09_develop_e.htm

WTO Committee on Trade and Development, *Implementation of Special and Differential Treatment Provisions in WTO Agreements and Decisions*, WT/COMTD/W/77, 25 October 2000.

WTO Director-General, 'Opening Address by the Director-General to the Ministerial Conference of LDCs on Implementation of the Programme of Action for the LDCs and Combating Poverty' (2002), available from WTO website: www.wto.org/english/news_e/news02_e/speech_minist_conf_5august02_e.ht

WTO Symposium, 'Symposium on issues confronting the world trading system – summary reports by the moderators' (2001), available from WTO website: www.wto.org/english/forums_e/ngo_e/ngo-symp2001_repserv_e.htm

WTO Understanding, *Understanding the WTO: Developing Countries: Overview* (2003), available from www.wto.org/english.thewto_e/ftif_e/dev1_e.htm

WTO, 'Reclaiming Development in the WTO Doha Development Round: Submission by Argentina, Brazil, India, Indonesia, Namibia, Pakistan, the Philoppines, South Africa and Venezuela to the Committee on Trade and Development', WT/COMTD/W/145, 1 December 2005

'World trade talks collapse', *The Age*, 15 September 2003 ,internet edition, 2003

Wu, Yongnian, Zhao, Gangcheng, and Ma, Ying, *A New Focus on India's Foreign Policy in the Twenty-First Century (Ershiyi Shiji Yindu Waijiao Xinlun)* (Shanghai: Shanghai Translation Press, 2004)

Xinhua, 'Bo Xilai's High Profile speech: China is willing to contribute the rules of the WTO' (19 Dec 2005), available at http://news.xinhuanet.com/fortune/2005_12/19/content_3939771.htm (accessed 20 Dec 2005)

Yeung, May T, Perdikis, Nicholas, Kerr, William and Elgar, Edward *Regional Trading Blocs in the Global Economy* (Cheltenham, UK: Edward Elgar Publishing Limited, 1999)

Zhang, Mingqiu, *Sino-India Relations (1947–2003) (Zhongying Guangxi Yanjiu (1947–2003))* (Beijing: Peking University Press, 2004)

3

China–India cooperation, South–South coalition and the new international economic order

Focus on the Doha Round

CHEN AN AND CHEN HUIPING

I. Introduction

International economic order means the comparatively steady pattern, structure or model of international economic relations gradually formed in a specific history era. The establishment and evolution of the international economic order depends on the comparative economic, political and military power among categories of members in international society. International economic order is closely related to international economic law. International economic law is a fundamental tool to strengthen existing international economic order, and at the same time, an important means to promote and change the old international economic order and establish the new international economic order.

The development process of international economy and international economic law witnesses the continuous struggles between strong countries who are trying to maintain and enlarge their vested interests and to defend the old international economic order, and the weak countries who are striving to ensure a status of economic equality and to establish a new international economic order. These struggles are generally resolved with compromise and cooperation between the two parties. However, after a period of compromise and cooperation, new struggles arise from new interest contradictions and conflicts. This is a recurring cycle, with each recurrence raising the existing international economic order and related international economic norms to a new level or new phase. Once new international economic norms are formed and established, they can completely and effectively change the old international economic order and strongly enhance and strengthen the new international economic order.[1]

It is well known that the weak and poor Third World countries did not participate in the creation of the international economic system after the Second World War and realized few benefits from it. They wanted a complete restructuring and change in the rules of the game.[2] Therefore, the main mission of the developing countries of the South, and the core appeal of South–South cooperation since the Second World War, is to seek renewal of international law-making in order to reform the inequitable and unjustifiable old international economic order, and replace it with an equitable and reasonable new international economic order (NIEO). The first significant round of the South's endeavors to fight for the right to participate in international economic law-making (IELM) and to establish NIEO was during the 1960s and 1970s in the United Nations (UN) forum. Impressive achievements have been produced; however, during the 1980s and the mid-1990s, the struggle for NIEO lost ground. The Doha Development Round (DDR) in the WTO initiated in 2001 is regarded as the second big round for NIEO in terms of the nature and historic status of the DDR.

Ever since 1955 and during the first NIEO round, Sino-Indian cooperation – being at the centre of South–South cooperation at that time via the Bandung Conference and the Group of 77 (G77) – has played a key role and contributed to the successful adoption of the Declaration of the Establishment of the New International Economic Order, as well as the Charter of Economic Rights and Duties of States in the UN framework in the 1970s. During the present round of NIEO in the forum of the WTO, Sino-Indian cooperation is still leading the South–South coalition via the G77 and the Group of 20 (G20) in the Doha, Cancún and Hong Kong conferences, with some success.

Due to their fast economic development and the deeper cooperation between China and India, a new word was recently created, "Chindia."[3] It quickly became a fashionable word, used to describe the increasing

[1] This process can be named as spiral 6C rule, i.e., Contradiction → Conflict → Consultation → Compromise → Cooperation → Coordination → Contradiction new.

[2] Work paper. See Abdur Razzaq, "The New International Economic Order," (1991) *Barcelona Conference on the Law of the World*, 4.

[3] The word "Chindia," a combination of "China" and "India," was first created by Jairam Ramesh, Union Minister of State for Commerce and Industry of India, in his book entitled *Making Sense of Chindia: Reflections on China and India* published by India Research Press in New Delhi in 2005. See TANG Lu, "The world treats China and India as a pair"—an interview with Jairam Ramesh with regard to the rise of Chindia, *News for Reference* (Cankao Xiaoxi), May 2, 2006, p. 14.

economic cooperation between the two largest developing and adjunct Asian countries. In the past, the two countries have had a long history of friendship and cooperation in the fields of culture, politics and economy. The lone exception is the border dispute and the 1962 border war which made them geopolitical rivals and blocked further bilateral, political and economic relations for over ten years.

China started to open up to the world and carried out domestic reform from 1979. India began economic reforms in 1991, in response to a financial crisis, marking an important turning point as India started the process of trade, financial and economy-wide liberalization in earnest.[4] Now, both China and India have achieved fast economic development and will set the pace for development in the twenty-first century. It is predicted that the twenty-first century will be Asia's century. The long-standing and well-established nature of Sino-Indian relations, their complementary economic reality and the beneficial result of economic cooperation between the two countries encourage their leaders to cast aside differences in favor of reconciliation. As political and economic connections are reinforced, the strengthening economic cooperation between the two countries is drawing much of the world's attention and will have significant implications for the entire world.

From the perspective of global micro international relations, the nature of Chindia cooperation is South–South cooperation, as distinguished from South–North cooperation. Due to the key roles of both China and India in the South–South coalition, further Chindia cooperation will greatly strengthen South–South coalition and thus make greater joint contribution to the new struggle for IELM and NIEO. At the same time, other developing countries from different regions – including the least developed countries – also stand to benefit from greater Chindia cooperation.

II. Implications of Sino-Indian economic cooperation

A. The bases of current Chindia cooperation

Both China and India are adjunct countries with well-known ancient civilizations. They have maintained positive cultural, economic and political ties for over two thousand years. It is quite rare for two countries to share amicable relations for this length of time.

[4] This is a Keynote Speech to Stanford India Conference. The speaker is Acting Managing Director, International Monetary Fund. See Anne O. Krueger, "Letting the future in: India's continuing reform agenda," June 4, 2004, www.imf.org/external/np/speeches/2004/060404.htm.

Commodity exchange between China and India can be traced back to China's Han Dynasty. It was first noted by Mr. Zhang Qian, who was dispatched by the Han Emperor to the West from China (the famous Silk Way was created thereafter). In around 128 B.C., when he passed by Dayuezhi and Daxia (now the north of Afghanistan and the south of Tajikistan), he saw two Chinese commodities – gunny cloth and bamboo stick from Sichuang, China – sold there. These Chinese commodities were transported to those Middle Asia countries via India.[5] Therefore, it can be reasonably inferred that at that time there had been commodity exchange and business transactions between south-west China and India.

In ancient times, the two countries established frequent mission, business and cultural contacts. Indian medicine, mathematics, music, dancing, sugar-making method, etc. were introduced to China; by the same token, China's silk, tea, printing method, improved sugar-making method, etc. were introduced to India.[6] The long-standing friendship between the two countries is better illustrated by the well known novel *Journey to the West.* This novel recounts stories of Senior Monk Xuanzang, who overcame unimaginable difficulties on his way to India to learn Buddhism in the seventh century (Monkey King was a widely known character in the novel).

The common experience of colonization or semi-colonization and suffering from foreign imperialists in the eighteenth and ninetenth centuries increased mutual understanding as well as sympathy between the two countries. They supported each other in their anti-imperialist and anti-colonalist struggles in the first half of the twentieth century. For example, during China's war against Japan, India dispatched medical teams to the war front in China in 1938. Sacrifices like that of Indian Doctor D. S. Kotnis, who died while serving in China at the young age of 32, are highly appreciated by both countries.

India and China won national independence in 1947 and 1949, respectively, and established close relations during the 1950s. The Indian government recognized the newly founded socialist China on December 30, 1949 (less than three months after the founding of China) and established diplomatic relations with China on April 1, 1950,[7] making

[5] See "Han Dynasty history: Biographies of Zhang Qian and Li Guangli', vol. IX (Chinese Press, 1962), pp. 2689–90.

[6] ZHANG Minqiu (ed.), *Studies on Sino-India Relations* (in Chinese), (Peking University Press, 2004), p. 1. For a detailed study on the introduction of silk, printing technology and improved sugar-making method from China to India, as well as Indian literature to China, please refer to JI Xianlin, *Paper Collection on the History of Sino-India Cultural Relations* (in Chinese), (SDX Joint Publishing Company, 1982).

[7] ZHANG Minqiu (ed.), *Studies on Sino-India Relations* (in Chinese), p. 4.

India the first non-socialist country to establish diplomatic relations with China. Leaders of the two countries paid frequent visits to each other to enhance friendship and form common positions with regard to many international affairs. In 1954, China initiated the Five Principles of Peaceful Coexistence (Five Principles) (these include mutual respect for each other's territorial integrity and sovereignty, non-interference in each other's internal affairs as well as equality and mutual benefit).[8] These principles were echoed by India as guiding principles for Sino-Indian relations, as well as relations between countries with different social systems. Today, the Five Principles are recognized the world over, not only for political relations but also for economic relations.[9] The two countries maintained good relations and supported each other in international forums during the 1950s. For instance, India prevailed over all dissenting views to invite China to the 1955 Bandung Conference.[10]

Although the friendly Sino-Indian relations were blocked for over ten years, due to a border dispute and the border war in 1962, they were slowly resumed after 1976 when the two countries sent an ambassador to replace a chargé d'affaires. In 1988, Sino-Indian relations stepped into a new age when Rajiv Gandhi – India's then Prime Minister – paid a diplomatic visit to China, and the two countries reached a consensus to develop bilateral political and economic relations while seeking proper means to resolve the border dispute. From 1988 on, high government officials from the two countries have frequently paid mutual visits to maintain and strengthen Sino-Indian relations.

The temporary suspension of Sino-Indian relations in the 1960s is insignificant when compared to the two thousand years of good friendship. The long-standing and well-established Sino-Indian relations constitute a sound basis, as well as a strong safeguard, for current Chindia cooperation.

B. *The current win-win situation*

The trade and economic relations between China and India were tortuous, corresponding to their circuitous political relations: mutual aid for

8 The Five Principles are: mutual respect for sovereignty and territorial integrity, mutual non-aggression, non-interference in each other's internal affairs, equality and mutual benefit, and peaceful coexistence.

9 ZHANG Minqiu (ed.), *Studies on Sino-India Relations*, p. 10. See also "Promote the friendship between China and India and increase South–South cooperation," October 22, 1982. (This is an excerpt from a talk with a delegation from the Indian Council for Social Sciences Research.), available at www.chinaembassy.org.in/eng/zyjh/t154908.htm.

10 ZHANG Minqiu (ed.), *Studies on Sino-India Relations*, pp. 13–14.

mutual benefits in the 1950s, temporary suspension during the 1960s and mid-1970s, slow resumption in late 1970s and the 1980s, and quick increase on a steady basis from the 1990s.[11] There are several significant reasons, in addition to the long-standing and well-established Sino-Indian relations, for the prosperity both countries have enjoyed since the 1990s.

The first reason concerns economic development. China's "open-up" policy and domestic reform, which began in 1979, made China a strong country, both politically and economically, during the 1990s. India started its economic reforms in 1991, and saw a high annual GDP growth rate. These events have continued to improve economic and political prospects for both countries, who now recognize that further economic development in the context of globalization depends not only on the efforts of an individual country, but also on the economic cooperation between countries. Common interests in economy and trade, complementary economic elements as well as huge economic scales between the two countries, make close economic cooperation practical. Both countries will benefit from the other's great and unique potentials.

The second reason concerns geopolitics. In the post-Cold War era, international political situations have dramatically changed. China desires an amicable, stable and prosperous environment in Asia, in consideration of geopolitics as well as its "peaceful rise" promise. No doubt, reinforcing economic cooperation on a win-win basis with its biggest neighbor, India, can achieve the above end. India also realizes that approaching geopolitics from an "India and America versus China approach" makes no sense. Rather, reality is that China and India need each other for economic development. It should be noted that both countries are, and will continue to be, major oil importers.[12] As a result, to achieve their geopolitical ends, the two countries "fit in" readily and "chime in" easily with regard to close economic cooperation.

The third reason concerns development philosophy. Both are countries with ancient civilizations. China's philosophy is "peace is more precious"; while India's philosophy is non-violence – Gandhism. Neither will take the initiative to invade other countries or to benefit itself at the expense of others. However, both are unwilling to be subjected to

[11] ZHANG Minqiu (ed.), *Studies on Sino-India Relations*, p. 179.

[12] Jairam Ramesh, *Making Sense of Chindia: Reflections on China and India* (India Research Press, 2005).

governance by imperialism or hegemonism. In the past, they shared common interests in the struggle against colonialism or semi-colonialism; at present, they share common interests in the struggle against power and hegemonism, and in the establishment of a new international economic and political order.

Due to the aforesaid reasons, the leaders of both countries started frequent mutual visits from the beginning of 1990s that have strongly promoted bilateral political, trade and economic ties.[13] In 1996, when China's then President Jiang Zemin visited India, the two countries focused on Sino-Indian border safety and mutual trust, and decided to establish a constructive partnership of cooperation, oriented toward the twenty-first century. In May 2000, when India's President visited China, one important issue of concern was to expand trade and economic cooperation. In January 2002, China's Prime Minister Zhu Rongji visited India for the purpose of further promoting bilateral trade and economic cooperation.

In June 2003, India's Prime Minister Atal Bihari Vajpayee visited China and the countries issued their Declaration on Principles for Relations and Comprehensive Cooperation, including 10 agreements on how to cooperate in such fields as the economy, law and justice, education, ocean science, space research, etc. This agreement has declared to the world that China and India will end their border confrontation and mutual suspicion of recent times, and conduct a comprehensive cooperation to develop a constructive partnership.[14] According to the Declaration, a compact Joint Study Group (JSG), composed of officials and economists, was set up to examine the potential complementarities between the two countries in expanded trade and economic cooperation. The JSG was also charged with drawing up a program for the development of China–India trade and economic cooperation for the next five years, aimed at encouraging greater cooperation between the business communities of both sides. A Study Report on China–India Comprehensive Trade and Economic Cooperation was adopted by the two parties on March 23, 2005, in New Delhi.

In January 2005, the first strategic dialogue between the two countries was conducted in New Delhi, resulting in a decision to have close cooperation, to form the same or similar positions on issues such as

[13] ZHANG Minqiu (ed.), *Studies on Sino-India Relations*, pp. 190–3.

[14] WANG Hongwei, "A new phase of good neighborly relations between China and India," August 26, 2003, available at http://iaps.cass.cn/english/Articles/showcontent.asp?id=404.

maintaining the common interests of developing countries, promoting the democracy of international relations, and promoting South–South cooperation. In April 2005, China's Prime Minister – Mr. Wen Jiabao – paid a diplomatic visit to India, at which time both countries declared the establishment of a strategic and cooperative partnership for peace and prosperity. They also signed the five-year plan for the overall economic and trade cooperation and decided to launch a feasibility study on the free trade area between the two countries.

To further promote the friendship and economic relations between China and India, 2006 was assigned as China–India Friendship Year. A lot of trade fairs and exhibitions were held in both countries to exchange commodities, technologies, etc. In November 2006, Chinese President Hu Jintao paid a visit to India and participated in the celebrating activities for China–India Friendship Year together with Indian President Abdul Kalam. A Joint Declaration was published between the two countries. In December 2007, China and India cooperated to hold for the first time a joint anti-terrorism training for land forces in China. Then in January 2008, India's Prime Minister Manmohan Singh visited China.

The frequent visits and cooperation between the two countries promote the mutual understanding and trust with each other and are good for furthering economic cooperation.

Chindia economic cooperation involves a variety of areas such as trade, investment, coal, iron and steel, textile, IT, technology, and economic management, etc., among which trade is the focus. A recent, typical example is the cooperation in the energy area. China and India are the largest energy-consuming countries in Asia with rapid increase in the world. Both would suffer from competing with each other to obtain energy. They adopted a new strategy from competition to cooperation on the win-win basis with the Sino-Indian energy cooperation agreement, signed in January 2006.

Substantial progress has also been achieved with regard to economic cooperation. Over the past decade, Sino-Indian bilateral trade has soared, accompanying a warming political climate.[15] For instance, the annual increase of Sino-Indian trade has exceeded 30% since 1999.[16] In

[15] ZHANG Lijun, "Growing cooperation between China and South Asia", available at www.ciis.org.cn/item/2006–01–11/51216.html.

[16] "Subtle balance of the relations between China, India and America (in Chinese)," March 5, 2006, available at http://news.xinhuanet.com/world/2006–03/05/content_4259389.htm.

2004, bilateral trade volume totaled US$13.6 billion, an 80% increase over 2003.[17] In 2005, India's bilateral trade with China was US$18.71 billion, up nearly 38% from 2004. India has set a target of US$20 billion by 2008.[18] India has also become China's biggest trading partner in South Asia. It is optimistically predicted that China should emerge as India's largest trading partner, overtaking the US within a year or two, with two-way trade exceeding US$30 billion in 2007.[19] Actually, from January to November 2007, the two-way trade amounted to US$34.2 billion. Mutual investment between the two countries is also increasing. Through September 2005, India has invested 176 projects in China, with a contracted value of US$339 million and a paid-in capital of US$113 million. China has invested in19 projects in India, worth US$26.33 million.[20]

The rapid increase of investment and trade shows great potential for future development.[21] Closer Chindia economic cooperation will definitely benefit the two countries and their people in terms of greater economic strength, better living standard, etc.

C. *Implications of Chindia cooperation*

China and India are the two largest developing countries, accounting for more than one-third of the world population. The independence of the two countries in the middle of the twentieth century added to the strength of the developing countries and thus changed the balance of power in the world. They had substantial influence in international law. The Five Principles of Peaceful Co-existence jointly advocated by them are now regarded as fundamental principles in dealing with political and economic relations between countries. The strengthened, ongoing economic cooperation between them, as well as their sustained economic and social development in the twenty-first century, is vital for ensuring peace, stability and prosperity for Asia, other developing countries and the world.

[17] JIANG Yaping, "Sino-Indian relations in a new stage of comprehensive development (in Chinese)," April 8, 2005, available at www.hnby.com.cn.

[18] Paranjoy Guha Thakurta, "China could overtake US's India trade," *Asian Times online*, China Business, March 15, 2006, available at www.atimes.com/atimes/China_Business/HC15Cb06.html.

[19] Thakurta, "China could overtake US's India trade".

[20] ZHANG Lijun, "Growing cooperation between China and South Asia," available at www.ciis.org.cn/item/2006–01–11/51216.html.

[21] "China–India Joint Study Group: A Study Report on China–India Comprehensive Trade and Economic Cooperation," Chapter 1.

Some Western scholars boldly commented that the rise of China and India – also called the rise of the un-West or non-West – in the twenty-first century is a revolutionary redistribution of power internationally. The two countries will dominate the history of the rest of this century. The impact of the changes of the decline of the West and the rise of un-West will, in the longer run, have a massively important result: the transformation of the uni-polar society of states into a multi-polar system.[22] India's Prime Minister Manmohan Singh also said that, "Together, India and China could reshape the world order."[23] The rise of China and India, as well as their cooperation, was one of the hot issues at the 2006 World Economic Forum Annual Meeting in Davos, Switzerland. Sino-Indian trade and economic relations also attracted much attention in the Boao Forum for Asia Annual Meeting 2006,[24] which included a separate session on India and China – Strength in Partnership.

The above comment is not exaggerated or groundless. First, the two countries' annual gross domestic product (GDP) growth rate of about eight percent makes them the engine of the world economy. Second, the combination of the advantages of the two countries by way of economic cooperation will make them economic giants in the world. India has some long-term advantages in age distribution, political flexibility, social structure and diplomatic relationships with the West,[25] and China has advantages in cheap labor, huge markets and vast numbers of consumers. Third, if India combines its software technology with China's hardware technology, they will achieve world leadership in the global information technology industry,[26] and invent a new version of globalization, which is already negating Western hegemony by shifting wealth and power to Asia.[27] Fourth, given the vast economic potential of India and China and their big appetites for energy and other natural resources, the prospect of a more cooperative relationship has significant global implications.[28] Last but not least, China and India will jointly play an

[22] Coral Bell, "The rise and rise of the un-West," *Asia Times Online*, March 22, 2006, available at http://atimes01.atimes.com/atimes/Middle_East/HC22Ak03.html.

[23] Clyde Prestowitz, "China–India entente shifts global balance," *YaleGlobal*, April 15, 2005, available at http://yaleglobal.yale.edu/display.article?id=5578.

[24] The theme of the Boao Forum for Asia Annual Meeting 2006 is "Asia's New Opportunities."

[25] Bell, "The rise and rise of the un-West,"

[26] Prestowitz, "China–India entente shifts global balance."

[27] Prestowitz, "China–India entente shifts global balance."

[28] John Lancaster, "India, China Hoping to 'Reshape the World Order' Together," *Washington Post Foreign Service*, April 12, 2005, p. A16, available at www.washingtonpost.com/

important role again in the IELM as well as the NIEO embodied in the Doha Development Round, just as they have done with regard to the NIEO in the 1960s and 1970s. This point will be further elaborated in detail in Parts 4 and 5.

III. Chindia cooperation and South–South coalition

A. *South–South cooperation and South–North cooperation*

The South normally refers to the underdeveloped and striving developing countries while the North refers to the rich and exploitative developed countries.[29] The cooperation between the developed countries and the developing countries is called South–North cooperation, while the economic cooperation between developing countries is called South–South cooperation. The conflict or contradiction between the South and the North is called South–North contradiction.[30]

South–North contradiction and the arising struggle, conflict and confrontation between the South and the North have negative impacts on the peaceful coexistence of current international societies and the prosperity of the world economy. Over time, some world politicians with insights gradually realized that the best option to settle the South–North contradiction is to replace confrontation with dialogue and to conduct South–North cooperation. Later on, this position became an international consensus. A milestone of the consensus is the adoption of the Declaration of the Establishment of New International Economic Order (Declaration), the Program of Action on the Establishment of New International Economic Order (Program of Action), and the Charter of Economic Rights and Duties of States (Charter) in the General Assembly of the United Nations. All three instruments clearly state the importance of global cooperation, especially South–North cooperation for the purpose of global common and joint development.

The basic goal of global cooperation is to encourage structural changes in the world economy, to establish more rational and equitable

wp-dyn/articles/A43053–2005Apr11.html. See also Sir Oliver Franks, "The new international balance: Challenge to the Western world," *Saturday Review*, January, 1960.

29 Thomas W. Waelde, "A requiem for the 'New International Economic Order': The rise and fall of paradigms in international economic law," p. 2, 18 March 2000, available at http://www.dundee.ac.uk/cepmlp/journal/html/article1–2.html.

30 The South–North problem or South–North contradiction was first raised by Sir Oliver Franks, Chairman of Lloyds Bank Ltd, in "The new international balance: Challenge to the Western world," *Saturday Review*, January 16, 1960.

international economic relations and the new international economic order, and to attain wider prosperity among all countries, including a higher standard of living. Therefore, all states have the duty to contribute to the balanced expansion of the world economy, taking duly into account the close interrelationship between the well-being of the developed countries and the growth and development of the developing countries, and the fact that the prosperity of the international community as a whole depends upon the prosperity of its constituent parts.[31]

The fundamental ways and means of global cooperation is that all states are equal in jurisdiction and, as equal members of the international community, have the right to participate fully and effectively in the international decision-making process. This includes the right to find solutions for the world economic, financial and monetary problems, and to share in the benefits resulting therefrom.[32]

The key point of global cooperation is that all states should respect the sovereign equality of each state and should not attach any conditions derogating from their sovereignty. Every state should co-operate with the efforts of developing countries to accelerate their economic and social development by providing favorable external conditions and by extending active assistance to them, consistent with their developmental needs and objectives.[33] In other words, South–North cooperation is an important component of global cooperation.

In addition to South–North cooperation, the Declaration, the Program of Action, as well as the Charter stress South–South cooperation. Developing countries should take collective action and conduct collective self-reliance so as to strengthen the negotiating power of the weak and poor developing countries as a whole in the process of South–North negotiations and South–North cooperation. They will finally strive for rational and equitable interests.[34]

To sum up, both South–South cooperation and South–North cooperation are integral components of global cooperation.[35] However,

[31] See Preamble, Art. 8 and Art. 31 of Charter of Economic Rights and Duties of States.

[32] See Art. 10 of Charter of Economic Rights and Duties of States.

[33] See Preamble, Art. 17 of Charter of Economic Rights and Duties of States.

[34] See 4 (s) of Declaration of the Establishment of New International Economic Order, Part VII of the Program of Action on the Establishment of New International Economic Order, and Art. 21 and 23 of the Charter of Economic Rights and Duties of States

[35] For a detailed discussion as to South–South cooperation and South–North cooperation, please refer to CHEN An (ed.), *Jurisprudence of International Economic Law*, 3rd edn (Peking University Press, 2005), pp. 109–28.

South–South cooperation is different from South–North cooperation in terms of political basis, economic basis, and internal substance as well as practical effect.

In terms of a political basis, currently there are over 190 independent countries, over 160 of which are developing countries. They vary in terms of economic model, political system, domestic policy, and foreign relations. However, they share the historical legacy of being colonized and exploited, similar political and economic status in the world, *de facto* common interests, as well as common voice with regard to fundamental political and economic issues. All of these constitute a strong political basis for South–South cooperation.

In terms of an economic basis, developing countries have realized substantial improvement in their economic structure and have gradually strengthened their economic power. However, since gaining political independence, they are still comparatively weak and poor. They do own abundant natural resources and vast territories, and they have large populations and huge markets. The economies of these countries are complementary and mutually beneficial. All of these factors constitute sound economic bases for South–South cooperation.

Since South–South cooperation is developed on the above political and economic bases, its internal substance is completely different from that of South–North cooperation. By and large, the substance of South–North cooperation is a compromise between the exploiters and the exploited, and between the strong and the weak. It is a gradual and slow process to obtain global recognition of the existing unfair law of the jungle, created by the South–North cooperation. In contrast, South–South cooperation is the mutual aid and help between the exploited and the exploited, and between the weak and the weak, in international economic relations. It is also a joint rebellion against the existing unfair law of the jungle.

In terms of practical effect, South–South cooperation with the aforementioned internal substances dictates that it has distinct characteristics and far-reaching impact on the international society. In other words, "such cooperation conduces to the break of unequal international relations and the establishment of new international economic order. It has great strategic implications."[36]

[36] HU Yiaobang, *Comprehensive Start of a New Phase of Constructing Socialism Modernization* (Report in the 12th Representative Meeting of China's Communist Party), (Remin Press, 1982), p. 43.

The history and practice of over fifty years after the Second World War prove that the above assertion is not groundless, and that the step-by-step development of NIEO is the result of unitary cooperation and joint efforts of the Third World countries.

B. Implications of South–South cooperation

Historic experience and crucial reality make the Third World countries further realize the following points:

First, the formation of the existing international economic order or regime was primarily based on economic strength. In order to effect further and increasing change, developing countries also need strength. The struggle by these countries for NIEO cannot rely on, or wait for, grace from any country. The situation is similar to the developing countries' struggle for political independence in the past, which was forcefully created. The process of making new international economic relations depends, to large extent, on the increase of the economic strength of developing countries and the strengthening of their mutual unity and cooperation. The stronger their economic strength is, the louder their voice will be heard. Their participation in, and ability to impact decision-making on world economic affairs will be increased, as will the constraints they can put on developed countries who maintain rigid positions and arbitrary attitudes toward South–North relations. Therefore, developing countries should first empower themselves.

Second, historical lessons show that economically excessive reliance on developed countries is unfavorable to the development of the developing countries' national economy. The right and reliable way to strive for economic prosperity and enhance self-economic strength is to increase South–South cooperation, to rely on collective self-reliance, to establish independent national economies, and to reduce dependence on developed countries.

Third, South–South cooperation can pool the strength of individually scattered and economically weak Third World countries. This will create a strong international force to oppose developed countries and to, thus, raise the Third World's status in the South–North dialogue and negotiations.[37] As such, rigid and arbitrary developed countries will be forced to reform the unequal international economic relations and create a new phase for the change of old international economic order.

[37] CHEN (ed.), *Jurisprudence of International Economic Law*, pp. 116–17.

Fourth, South–South cooperation is a new type of international economic relations on the basis of mutual help and aid, learning from others' strong points to offset one's weaknesses, mutual benefits and reciprocity, as well as common progress and development. South–South cooperation, by itself, is a reflection of new international economic order. Therefore, all developing countries should especially cherish and promote the existing South–South cooperation. In the meantime, they have to admit that there certainly exist some contradictions, diversities, and differences among the South countries. These originate from colonial legacy and different situations or policies, and would become hurdles or obstacles to South–South cooperation, if not properly tackled. However, because there are no fundamental or essential conflicts of interest among the Third World countries, these conflicts and diversities can be resolved and overcome. To achieve this, Third World countries must overcome interference from the developed countries, put aside partial interests, and take into account the interests of the developing countries as a whole. Cooperation must be based on mutual understanding and accommodation as well as patient consultation. Given these facts, Third World countries could bring South–South cooperation to a new phase.

Fifth, South–South cooperation does not mean either severing the relations with the North developed countries or replacing South–North cooperation. South–South cooperation also promotes South–North negotiations, the improvement of South–North relations, the enhancing of South–North economic cooperation on the basis of equity and mutual benefit, and, finally, the realizing of general prosperity for all states.

The above international consensus on South–South cooperation surely covers and applies to the long practice of the cooperation between China and India. This is the case in the past, and should be the case now and in the future.

C. *Chindia cooperation and South–South coalition*

For developing countries, South–South cooperation should play a special role in the context of multilateralism and should be strengthened. They should have closer coordination and cooperation in order to meet the challenges arising from globalization and to promote their common interests.[38]

[38] Joint Declaration of the Heads of State and/or Government of Brazil, China, India, Mexico and South Africa, participating in the G8 Gleneagles Summit (07/07/2005), G8 Summit Joint Declaration, Press Release, available at www.brazil.org.uk/page.php?n=545.

The emerging new dynamic economies of the South, especially China and India, provide new and potential opportunities for taking South–South cooperation to a higher level of collective self-reliance through trade, investment and technological cooperation.[39] With the rise of China and India, the Third World acquires some degree of effective national consensus and reasonably efficient (though not necessarily liberal) political structures and institutions.[40]

China is keen to promote South–South cooperation and North–South dialogue. It is working hard to expand economic and trade cooperation with developing countries and has provided assistance to the best of its ability.[41] China is an important member of many international organizations and groups, including the UN, UNCTAD. With her accession to the WTO – the so-called "Economic United Nations" – in November 2001, China adds an underpinning power to South–South cooperation and the joint struggle within the WTO system.

India is also an important member of the said international organizations where it enjoys a high reputation among other developing countries. As a responsible and progressive member of the international community, India is continuing her untiring efforts to bring about a constructive dialogue between the developed and developing countries. India is convinced that cooperation and the establishment of an equitable international economic order involving structural and other changes is the only answer to the various economic ills and problems of development confronting the world today.[42]

The reconciliation and coordination of both India and China will bring the two countries together to be one voice in an international forum and thus strengthen South–South coalition.

One important reason that many international organizations, such as South Centre, G77, UNCTAD, G20, UNIDO etc., can work together for the interests of developing countries is that both China and India are key members of the organizations and act as a "bridge" among them.

[39] Paris Consensus adopted by the 39th Meeting of the Chairpersons/Coordinators of the G77, Paris, February 27–28, 2006, G-77 News Center, available at www.g77.org/newswire/index.htm.

[40] Bell, "The rise and rise of the un-West."

[41] ZHANG Zhijun, "China pursues an independent foreign policy of peace in its external relations: Speech at the 42nd Munich Conference on Security Policy," available at www.uni-kassel.de/fb5/frieden/themen/Sicherheitskonferenz/2006-zhang.html.

[42] "India: Economy, industry & trade," available at www.hcilondon.net/india-overview/economy-industry-trade/index.html.

Both China and India are also invited to participate in meetings of the organizations of developed countries. For example, the inclusion of China, India and Brazil in the G8 Summit shows the importance of developing countries. Moreover, India and Brazil are invited to participate in the Five Party Group for both developing and developed countries. This shows that the strength of developing countries is increasing more and more and that developed countries can no longer ignore or neglect the existence or demands made by developing countries when making international economic law. If the large developing countries can work together during these meetings, they will surely promote a new international economic order and redefine international economic decision-making.

The rise of China and India represents the rise of developing countries and thus can strengthen the resolve and confidence of developing countries. Some developing countries can now stand up to, or cut off their reliance on, developed countries by having diplomatic and business relations with China or India.

IV. The history of Sino-Indian cooperation in the First Round of the NIEO

A. *History of South–South cooperation*

The Bandung Conference – also named Asian-African Conference – was sponsored by India and four other countries[43] in April 1955. China was among the participating countries. At the Conference, leaders from twenty-nine countries considered problems of common interest and concern to countries of Asia and Africa. They discussed ways in which their people could achieve greater economic, cultural and political cooperation.[44] The Five Principles of Peaceful Coexistence were announced again as guiding principles to deal with inter-state relations, including international economic relations. The Conference was characterized by unity, equality and cooperation among developing countries that resulted in the formation of the "Spirit of Bandung." The Afro-Asian

[43] The other four sponsoring countries were Burma, Ceylon, Indonesia and Pakistan. twenty-four other countries including China were invited to participate in the conference.

[44] In the Conference, the developing countries decided to take "collective action," adopt "a unified approach," formulate "common policies," and consult with each other in advance with "participating countries in international forums." See "Final Communiqué of the Asian–African Conference, A. Economic Cooperation," Paras. 5, 9 &12.

states' strategic bloc formed therein was the beginning of what came to be known as the "non-aligned" movement and the "Third World."[45] It can be said that, from then on, the developing countries shaped clear strategic thought as to the nature of the South–South coalition under the circumstances of acute South–North contradictions and the sharp contrast in power between the weak South and the strong North.

B. The G77 and the first round of the NIEO

India is the original member of G77 (now it has 132 members) and plays an important role therein. After China's resumption of its membership in the United Nations and the Permanent Membership in the Security Council in 1971, it has kept in close contact with G77 (though it is not a formal member), actively supporting the Group's defense of the small and weak nations' legitimate interests, along with their justifiable demands for the renewal of international law-making and their push for regeneration of the international economic order.[46] Now many international documents mention "G-77 and China" at the same time.

The G77 is an important structure by which the developing countries carry out the South–South coalition, and it is also an important means for developing countries to renew international law-making and impel the regeneration of the old international economic order through the consolidation of otherwise dispersed powers. As the largest Third World coalition in the UN, the G77 provides the means for the developing world to articulate and promote its collective economic interests and enhance its joint negotiating capacity on all major international economic issues in the UN system. Moreover, it helps to promote economic and technical cooperation among developing countries.[47] Through this South–South coalition, impressive accomplishments have come about in international law-making, such as the establishment of the Generalized System of Preference in the GATT framework in the 1960s, and the adoption of Declaration of the Establishment of New International

[45] Matthew Quest, "The Lessons of the Bandung Conference: Reviewing Richard Wright's *The Color Curtain* 40 Years Later," available at www.spunk.org/texts/pubs/lr/sp001716/bandung.html.

[46] Clement Robes (Chair for the Group of 77 and China for 1999), "The Group of 77 and China: Current Priorities," New York, January 12, 1999, available at www.southcentre.org/southletter/s1 33/s 133–06.htm.

[47] "What is the Group of 77?," available at www.g77.org/main/main.htm.

Economic Order as well as the Charter of Economic Rights and Duties of States in the UN framework in the 1970s.

The key points of the legal principles embodied in the above instruments are as follows. First, it is confirmed that the economic sovereignty of all states is inalienable, inviolable and non-transferable. All states have full and permanent sovereignty over their natural resources and all economic activities within their territory. Second, it is confirmed that the world wealth and economic revenue should be re-allocated internationally on the principles of equity, rationality and equality, so as to limit or even eliminate the dangerous tendency that the rich get richer while the poor get poorer. Therefore, the current irrational and unfair regimes of international trade, technology transfer, taxation, financing, etc. should be completely reformed and changed. Third, it is confirmed that all states, especially developing countries, have equal rights to participation, decision-making and interest-enjoying with regard to international economic affairs. All states are equal whether they be big or small, rich or poor.

The above fundamental legal concepts and jurisprudential principles are a significant landmark in the development of the basis of the new type of international economic normative system, laying down the foundation for the later further establishment of the G20. Having been in operation for approximately thirty years, these concepts and principles won the support of peoples and were gradually developed as the *opinio juris* of the contemporary international community.[48]

C. *Joint efforts by both China and India to revive the NIEO*

From the early 1980s to the mid-1990s, South–South cooperation declined and the movement of NIEO withered. It was even contended that the NIEO had foundered,[49] or was killed and replaced with the neoliberal Washington Consensus.[50] There are five reasons for this.

First, the G77 consists of many members with different demands. It has loose rather than close institution and management. This lack of a

[48] CHEN An, *Chen's Papers on International Economic Law*, vol. I (Beijing University Press, 2005), pp. 61–9.

[49] Christina R. Sevilla, "The WTO's North–South conflict: A dangerous new (old) international economic order?," (2003) *The National Interest*, available at www.highbeam.com/library/docfree.asp?DOCID=1G1:112411727&ctrlInfo=Round19%3AMode19a%3ADocG%3AResult&ao=.

[50] Daniel W. Drezner, "The New Republic online," December 10, 2003, available at www.danieldrezner.com/policy/seventies.htm.

strong core leads to a slow response to some international affairs and acquiescence to some tricks from the developed countries.[51]

Second, G-77 does not have a permanent high-level research institution and propaganda institution and thus relevant information could not be timely collected and processed. No practical countermeasures, recommendations or suggestions could be raised in response to the agendas, issues and arguments put forward by the power countries in the international forum or during international negotiations concerning South–North dialogue.[52]

Third, the developed countries changed their strategy by moving out of the UN where developing countries have majority voting advantage to GATT/WTO, IMF, and OECD, etc. which are dominated by developed countries.[53] Accordingly, the minority of developed countries continued to control and lead the general direction of international economic affairs. Moreover, developed countries used "divide-and-rule" tactics to split and disintegrate the South–South coalition. They took advantage of the financial need of individual countries to carry out its "stick and carrot" policy to split the South so as to make these countries deviate from the originally set track and aim by G77.

Fourth, in the early 1990s, part of the Third World dissolved (collapse of the Soviet Union) as a separate, bloc-type identity.[54] Therefore, the strength of developing countries in the South–North dialogue and South–North negotiation was weakened.

Due to the above reasons, in the eight-year-long (1986–1994) GATT/WTO Uruguay Round negotiations, the developing countries failed to make collective decisions or to take joint action, and were regularly trapped in the position of inferiority in multilateral negotiations. Developed countries, especially the economic hegemonists, in contrast, could dominate in the institution of grand international trade policy and the legally binding game rules (legal rules) under the old system through the exercise of their power to manipulate the whole situation.

[51] See *Thirty Years of the Group of 77 (1964–1994), United for a Global Partnership for Development and Peace* (South Africa: South Centre Publications, 1994), pp. 9–16; See also *The Future of the Group of 77, South Centre Background Paper for the Ministerial Round Table of Group of 77* (South Africa: South Centre Publications, 1996), pp. 1–5.

[52] See *Thirty Years of the Group of 77* (1964–1994), pp. 9–16; See also *The Future of the Group of 77*, pp. 1–5.

[53] Thomas W. Waelde, "A requiem for the 'New International Economic Order': The rise and fall of paradigms in international economic law," March 18, 2000, 16, available at http://www.dundee.ac.uk/cepmlp/journal/html/article1–2.html.

[54] Waelde, "A requiem for the 'New International Economic Order'," 16.

In view of this, the developing countries reviewed and "summed up" the main deficit and lessons during that period, and started to reintegrate themselves. In 1994, they concluded the Agreement to Establish the South Centre, so as to establish an intergovernmental organization of developing countries. The main objectives of South Centre are: (1) to promote South solidarity; (2) to contribute to South-wide collaboration in promoting common interests and coordinated participation by developing countries in international forums dealing with South–South and North–South matters, as well as with other global concerns, and (3) to foster convergent views and approaches among countries of the South with respect to global economic, political and strategic issues related to evolving concepts of development, sovereignty and security, etc.[55] Gradually, the South Centre developed into a small "think tank" to give counsel and suggestion to developing countries. Both China and India are key members of the board of the South Centre.

Just as it was predicted, the (NIEO) "game" was triggered again.[56] The Doha Development Round (DDR) in the WTO initiated in the early twenty-first century is a new round of NIEO.

V. China–India cooperation and the NIEO in the twenty-first century

A. *The nature of the Doha Development Round*

The successful moving forum of IELM from the UN to the WTO by developed countries in the Uruguay Round encourages them to try their "luck" again in the WTO. The Doha Development Round (DDR) became the main forum for the new round of NIEO in the twenty-first century.

From the legal perspective, the WTO regime and its multilateral rules are important constituents of the international economic norm. Therefore, the legal nature or legal substance of the Doha Round negotiation has drawn a lot of attention as the new global negotiation model on how to improve and renovate the current WTO regime and its multilateral rules.

The G77 studied carefully in advance of the multilateral trading system and then released a declaration[57] just before the convening of

55 See "A South IGO," available at www.southcentre.org/ASouthIGO.htm.

56 Waelde, "A requiem for the 'New International Economic Order'," 22–3.

57 Declaration by the Group of 77 and China on the Fourth WTO Ministerial Conference at Doha, Qatar, October 22, 2001, available at www.g77.org/Docs/Doha.htm.

the Doha Conference in October 2001. It pointed out that there exist solemn promises in urgent need of implementation and faults in law that pose imbalance and inequity in the rights and obligations of developing countries. It also reiterated the need for full and faithful implementation of the plausible agreements and the redress of existing imbalances and inequity emanating from the Uruguay Round Agreement.[58] The suggested improvements were aimed at reforming the WTO system and its legislative deficiencies and reflected the joint appeal of the developing countries. That appeal was submitted formally to the highest WTO decision-making body, the Fourth Ministerial Conference.

These suggestions and concerns were accepted by the later adopted Fourth WTO Ministerial Conference. The Doha Declaration set forth that a new round of multilateral trade negotiations should be launched to center on the development concerns of developing countries, aimed at the necessary amelioration and renovation of the existing WTO systems and rules that were part of international economic legislation.

To further promote the alliance of developing countries in the DDR, twenty developing countries led by Brazil, India and China established the Group of 22 (it later became the Group of 20, hereinafter "G20")[59] in the final stages of the preparations for the Cancún conference. During the Cancún and Hong Kong conferences, the G20 united developing countries against the US and the EU and fought for new trade rules in compliance with the interests of the majority of the developing countries. In essence, this is a new phase of the fifty-year long complex South–North contradiction, South–South coalition and fighting for NIEO. Some commented that "the G-20 broke the monopoly over trade negotiations by the EU and the US."[60] Some even commented that G-20 could be seen as a continuation of the spirit of Bandung, a desire by Third World states to catch up with the North and effectively challenge the overwhelming power of their former colonial masters.[61]

[58] Declaration by the Group of 77 and China on the Fourth WTO Ministerial Conference at Doha, Qatar, 22 October 2001, para. 5, available at www.g77.org/Docs/Doha.htm.

[59] Originally there were 22 developing countries. It became G20 with Peru and Columbia withdrawing from the group under the pressure of the US.

[60] Walden Bello, "G-20 leaders succumb to 'divide-and-rule tactics' – NGO, South Bulletin 85," available at www.southcentre.org/info/southbulletin/bulletin85/bulletin85–06.htm.

[61] Balakrishnan Rajagopal, "A new opportunity in Cancún's failure," *YaleGlobal*, December 3, 2003, available at http://yaleglobal.yale.edu/display.article?id=2937.

B. *South–South Coalition and Chindia's promotion of the NIEO*

India and China, representing the South coalition, struggled again for the establishment of NIEO in the DDR. India supported China's accession to the WTO and signed a bilateral agreement with China for this purpose in February 2000. India played a proactive role in the deliberations at the Doha Conference and a number of concerns expressed by India were taken into account.[62] China became a formal member of the WTO in late 2001, adding to the strength of the developing countries in the WTO. At the beginning of the DDR, China contended that DDR should be conducive to the establishment of a fair, just and reasonable new international economic order.[63] China and India agreed in 2003 "to enhance cooperation at the World Trade organization, which is not only to mutual benefit but also in the broader interest of developing countries. The two sides will hold dialogues on a regular basis in this regard."[64] They also "acknowledged the importance of their respective roles in the shaping of a new international political and economic order."[65] It should be expected that India and China will be strong voices in making the Doha Round a truly development round.[66]

The G77 played a preliminary role in the launch of DDR. The G20, based on the G77 and including China, India, Brazil, Argentina and South Africa etc. is the key player of NIEO in the DDR since the G20 members own sufficient economic strength, wish to unite together and are willing to represent and fight for the weak groups.

To be specific, the G77 learned lessons from the withering of NIEO in the 1980s and 1990s, and restructured itself for the next battle. It played a preliminary and supportive role in the NEIO in the DDR by reaffirming the role of South–South cooperation and the new direction for

[62] "India: Economy, Industry & Trade," available at www.hcilondon.net/india-overview/economy-industry-trade/index.html.

[63] Statement by H. E. Minister SHI Guangsheng, Head of the Chinese Delegation, at the Fourth Ministerial Conference of the WTO, www.4english.cn/englishstudy/speechess/economy/siguangsheng.html. China reiterates the issue of NIEO and DDR several times. See Wen Jiabao, "Strengthen ASEM economic co-op", this is a speech delivered at the opening ceremony of the 6th ASEM Financial Ministers' Meeting on August 7, 2005, www.chinafair.org.cn/Chinafair2004/WebSite/English/paper/2005–8–8/p1.htm.

[64] See Declaration on Principles for Relations and Comprehensive Cooperation between China and India signed in June 2003.

[65] Declaration on Principles for Relations and Comprehensive Cooperation between China and India.

[66] China–India Joint Study Group: Report of the India–China Joint Study Group on Comprehensive Trade and Economic Cooperation, Introduction of ch. 1.

NIEO. For example, the G77stressed the ill effects of globalization, the need to establish a fairer trading system, and the right of the South to participate equitably in global decision-making in its first Havana South Summit in April 2000.[67] The theme of the first Summit was how to press the South–North dialogue to strive for both the South and the North's equitable participation in decision- and rule-making in the macro-economic working of the global economy; and how to institute an equitable, fair and reasonable new international economic order through mutual South–North beneficial co-operation.[68] This Summit marked a turning point in the developmental history of the Group of 77, symbolizing the new march of the South–South union to renew international law-making and renovate the international economic order.[69]

Before the Doha conference in 2001, the G77 raised suggestions and ascertained the direction of NIEO for the DDR. The G20, established in the final stages of the preparations for the Cancún Conference in 2003, is the key player of NIEO in the DDR. The group represents a large cross-section of the WTO membership and comprises a considerable share of the world agricultural population, production and trade. The G20 countries formulated common positions on negotiations after consultation and coordination and then submitted to the Director-General of the WTO Secretariat a joint proposal on global trade reform entitled Agriculture – Framework Proposal.[70] The G20 argued that, in order to translate the Doha Development Agenda into reality, agriculture should be fully incorporated into the rules of the multilateral trading system with a view to eliminating the distortions prevailing in agricultural trade

[67] G77's South Summit, Havana, Cuba, April 10–14, 2000, available at www.twnside.org.sg/title/havana.htm.

[68] See Declaration of the South Summit, and Havana Programme of Action, available atwww.g77.org/Docs/Declaration_G77Summit.htm and www.g77.org/Docs/ProgrammeofAction_G77Summit.htm respectively.

[69] See "South Summit in Havana to mark a "turning point" for developing countries," available at http//www.g77.org/summit/pressrelease; see also Martin Khor, "Havana Summit: A defining moment in G77 history; coordinating commission set up," *Third World Economics*, No. 232, 2000, pp. 2–3 and 12–14.

[70] Agriculture – Framework Proposal, Ministerial Conference, Fifth Session, Cancún, September 10–14, 2003, WT/MIN(03)/W/61, September 4, 2003. The joint proposal was submitted by Argentina, Brazil, Bolivia, China, Chile, Colombia, Costa Rica, Cuba, Ecuador, El Salvador, Guatemala, India, Mexico, Pakistan, Paraguay, Peru, Philippines, South Africa, Thailand and Venezuela. Thereafter, Turkey applied to join the submission of the joint proposal, and these nations were altogether called the Group of 21. Subsequently, Egypt and Nigeria joined as proposing countries on September 9, and September 30, 2003, respectively.

and production.[71] Although the Cancún conference ended in vain, its role in the development of the WTO system and the South–North dialogue should not be neglected; its influence was immense and far-reaching, demonstrating the unique status and role of the South–South coalition in the South–North dialogue and the renovation of international economic law.

As mentioned before, several decades after the Second World War, the decision-making on global trade and economy affairs and the law-making of multilateral trade regime and relevant rules are strongly led, controlled or even monopolized by the US, the EU and other economic power countries. However, during the Cancún conference, a new phenomenon arose: some developing countries united closely to be groups such as the the G20 and other groups. They clearly expressed their common position and claims toward major global trade and economic issues to be publicly against the economic powers. This new phenomenon demonstrated the will and the strength of the joint effort of developing countries, as well as, the status and role of South–South coalition in the fight for NIEO. Not long after the Cancun conference, the 132 countries of the G77 announced another joint statement stressing that they would continue to show the same unity in decision-making in the following DDR conferences. The international society has been forced to view them anew.

The Cancún conference was said to be a "political victory" for developing countries that showed unity in pressing their demands.[72] It was also commented that the Cancún conference would be remembered as one of the most consequential instances of North–South economic conflict in GATT/WTO history, fifty-six years after the inception of the GATT.[73]

After the collapse of the Cancún conference, the G20 met several times to discuss ways to fight their case on agriculture at the WTO, to exchange views and coordinate positions on how to proceed with agricultural negotiations and on how to achieve progress in the Doha Round.[74]

71 Available at http://www.cyberdyaryo.com/features/f2003_0912_02.htm.

72 Christina R. Sevilla, "The WTO's North–South conflict: A dangerous new (old) international economic order?," *The National Interest*, 2003, http://www.highbeam.com/library/docfree.asp?DOCID=1G1:112411727&ctrlInfo=Round19%3AMode19a%3ADocG%3AResult&ao=.

73 Sevilla, "The WTO's North–South conflict."

74 Examples include meetings held in October in Argentina, in December 2003 in Brasilia.

Before the Hong Kong conference, the G20 met twice to get well prepared for it. One meeting took place in September 2005 and was to consult exclusively on the common position. They raised three pillars of the agriculture negotiations which were domestic support, export competition and market access. They agreed that there must be no alternative to a bottom-up approach, as advocated by the G20.[75] The other meeting was in December 2005 and was targeted at substantive and meaningful progress in agriculture, at making positive contributions to the negotiating process by adopting a forward-looking attitude and at trying to reach ambitious results in agriculture in line with the Doha Mandate.[76]

This has transformed the Group into a driving force in these negotiations and put the developing countries – for the first time in GATT/WTO history – at the center of the decision-making process.[77] This is a small victory of NIEO for developing countries.

In addition, the G20 is actively practicing horizontal alliances, expanding the membership and power of the South–South coalition, and continues to work together with other developing countries groups. For instance, before the Hong Kong meeting, the G20 met the G33, the African Caribbean and Pacific states (ACP), the LDCs, the African Group and the Small Economies met to exchange views and decide to better coordinate their efforts in order to develop a common approach to issues of common interest, focusing on agriculture negotiations.[78] The G20 also held meetings with the Cairns Group before the Hong Kong Conference to secure the removal of distortions in international agricultural trade.[79]

C. *China and India in South–North dialogue*

In addition to conducting and promoting the communication, consultation and corresponding among the South countries and for South–South coalition, China and India also represent developing countries in actively promoting South–North dialogue with regard to the DDR, in particular with the agricultural issue. In the South–North dialogue, they

[75] Bhurban G-20 Ministerial Declaration, Bhurban, September 9–10, 2005, available at www.g-20.mre.gov.br/conteudo/statement_16122005_01.htm.

[76] G20 Ministerial Declaration, Hong Kong, December 13, 2005.

[77] G20 Ministerial Declaration, Hong Kong, December 13, 2005.

[78] Joint Statement by the Cairns Group and G20, Hong Kong, December 16, 2005, available at www.g-20.mre.gov.br/conteudo/statement_16122005_01.htm.

[79] Joint Statement by the Cairns Group and G20,

can speak for developing counties, and act as "a bridge" between the South and the North as well.

Firstly, China and India have conducted South–North dialogue by participating in meetings held by organizations of developed countries, such as the G8. Brazil, China, India, Mexico and South Africa were invited to participate in the G8 summits on several occasions, the latest one was in July 2008 in Japan. The purpose of the regular meetings between the G8 and the five developing countries is to conduct South–North dialogue and to consult on possible ways to settle global hot or difficult issues. The five countries normally hold meetings to make preparations for the G8 Dialogue in advance. Taking advantage of these opportunities, the five countries raised the DDR issues. For instance, in the G8 Gleneagles Summit 2005, they raised the issue of agriculture, which is the great concern of developing countries. China and India opined that trade-distorting domestic support for agriculture in developed countries must be substantially reduced and all forms of export subsidies must be eliminated by a date to be agreed.[80] They also reiterated that all members of the international community should work together for the reform of the current international economic system to make it stronger and more supportive of development. China and India sought assurances that developing countries would have a greater voice and suggested particular reform to the Bretton Woods Institutions.[81]

Secondly, China and India conducted South–North dialogue by attending WTO "Mini-Ministerial Green Room Meetings" that were held among selected major WTO member states to build "consensus" on critical WTO negotiations. Although the "Green Room Meetings" pattern is criticized as exclusive and non-transparent, inconsistent with WTO's transparency principle,[82] at least developing countries are involved in the

[80] Joint Declaration of the Heads of State and/or Government of Brazil, China, India, Mexico and South Africa, participating in the G8 Gleneagles Summit (July 7, 2005), G8 Summit Joint Declaration, Press Release, available at www.brazil.org.uk/page.php?n=545.

[81] Joint Declaration of the Heads of State and/or Government of Brazil, China, India, Mexico and South Africa, participating in the G8 Gleneagles Summit (July 7, 2005), G8 Summit Joint Declaration, Press Release, available at www.brazil.org.uk/page.php?n=545.

[82] For criticisms on the "Green Room Meetings," please see Raghav Narsalay, "Letter to the Indian Minister of Commerce, Mr. Arun Jaitley," February 28, 2003, Focus on the Global South-India Programme, www.focusweb.org/india/content/view/688/26/. See also "NGOs call on trade ministers to reject exclusive mini-ministerials and green room meetings in the run-up to, and at, the 5th WTO ministerial," available at www.ciel.org/Tae/WTO_5Min_112002.html; Abid Qaiyum Suleri, "WTO mini ministerial meetings:

decision-making process in the WTO. This has changed the situation so that the WTO is no longer dominated by major developed countries.

Thirdly, India and Brazil are representing the G20 in the Five Interested Parties[83] specifically established for the DDR agriculture negotiations, as well as in the G6[84] established to discuss the Doha Development Agenda and issues in the context of the Hong Kong Declaration. Both Five Interested Parties and the G6 are major players in South–North dialogue. Although it is noted that the agriculture negotiations are held only among the five countries, it is one more arbitrary step in the trend towards greater non-transparency in the WTO.[85] At least, the Five Interested Parties' negotiation pattern included Brazil and India, representing the G20 and ensuring broad and robust participation by developing countries, changing the circumstances under which the GATT/WTO core decision-making group was previously manipulated by the North. It is a small victory for the coalition of the weak. More importantly, in July 2008, China joined the US, EU, Japan, Australia, India and Brazil to form "G7". The G7 meeting was hosted by WTO chief Pascal Lamy aiming to break a stalemate between rich and poor countries over liberalizing trade in agriculture and manufacturing. It is the first time for China to take a seat in the World Trade Organization's most select negotiating group.[86] As a consequence, the developing countries have stronger power, more participation and more voice in the DDR for NIEO and their own legitimate interests.

D. NIEO progress in the DDR in the WTO

South–South cooperation, as well as South–North dialogue promoted by China and India representing developing countries, has produced

High profile decisions," available at www.sdpi.org/help/research_and_news_bulletin/jan_feb_2005/wto_mini_ministerial.htm; "NGOs call on trade ministers," available at www.ciel.org/Tae/WTO_5Min_112002.html.

[83] Five Interested Parties comprised the five key players in agriculture including the United States, the EC, Brazil, India (representing the G20) and Australia (representing the Keynes Group).

[84] The G6 includes Brazil, India, the European Union, Japan, Australia and the United States.

[85] Letter to call for end of Five Interested Parties process in Agriculture, May 6, 2005, www.oaklandinstitute.org/?q=node/view/177. This is an open letter sent to the Heads of Delegations, the Chair of the Agriculture negotiations, the Chair of the General Council and to Dr. Supachai Panitchpakdi jointly by many NGOs.

[86] WTO "G-7" includes China, http://chinabright.blogspot.com/2008/07/wto-g-7-includes-china.html, July 23, 2008.

some progress in regard to DDR and in particular with regard to the agricultural trading issue.

First, substantive progress has been made in regard to the agriculture issue. For instance, Paragraph 13 of the Doha Ministerial Declaration states the objective and task of the agriculture negotiation with DDR as, "to establish a fair and market-oriented trading system through a programme of fundamental reform . . . in order to correct and prevent restrictions and distortions in world agricultural markets." In July 2004, a framework agreement on agriculture and non-agriculture trade was concluded between developed and developing countries. The framework agreement states that developed countries should reform the three agriculture issues, that is, the elimination of export subsidies, substantial reductions in trade-distorting domestic support, and substantial improvements in market access for all products. The Hong Kong conference in December 2005 agreed that EU and other parties should ensure the parallel elimination of all forms of export subsidies on agriculture, to be completed by the end of 2013.[87] It was further agreed at the conference that all forms of export subsidies for cotton will be eliminated by developed countries in 2006,[88] and that developing countries can continue to enjoy special and differential treatment, including the flexibility to self-designate an appropriate number of tariff lines as Special Products and the right to have recourse to a Special Safeguard Mechanism.[89]

Second, developed countries gave an oral promise to conclude further agreement on agriculture in some events, though the Doha Round fails finally. For instance, at the opening ceremony of the UN World Summit on 14 September 2005, US President Bush stated that the elimination of agricultural subsidies, tariffs and other barriers that stunt the development of developing countries is key to diminishing the gaps in wealth between the poor and the wealthy nations. Therefore, WTO Members should reach agreements on the elimination of these trade barriers in the Doha Round.[90] US Trade Representative Rob Portman and EU Trade Commissioner Peter Mandelson also considered the proposal of lowering agricultural product tariffs put forward by the G20, and

[87] Para. 6 of Hong Kong Ministerial Declaration.
[88] Para. 11 of Hong Kong Ministerial Declaration.
[89] Paras. 7, 8 and 35 of Hong Kong Ministerial Declaration.
[90] See Statement of Mr. George W. Bush, President of the United States of America, 2005 "World Summit High Level Plenary Meeting," September 14, 2005, available at www.un.org/webcast/summit2005/statements.html.

admitted that they would make joint efforts to reach agreements on the reduction of agricultural trade barriers.[91]

Third, the South's appeal to have more voice in the decision-making process in the WTO has been recognized. For instance, WTO Director-General Lamy pointed out that developing countries account for over 75 percent of the WTO's membership and thus should have a central role in all trade negotiations in the WTO.[92]

All of the above progress and achievements are very limited, lack substance, and are far from what is expected. However, from the macro perspective, they represent victories achieved by developing countries in the back-and-forth process of international economic law-making, as well as the establishment of a new international economic order and thus have far-reaching implications.[93]

VI. Road ahead for the revival of the NIEO

The improvement of Sino-Indian relations and the strengthening of Chindia cooperation add to the strength of South–South cooperation and play an important role in the new round of IELM and NIEO embodied in the DDR in the WTO. However, the South can be neither satisfied with the very limited victory already made nor too optimistic as to the development of DDR and the new international economic order under the WTO framework. There is still a long way to go.

First, there exist a lot of hurdles and unsatisfactory problems in the DDR that blocked the smooth development of IELM and NIEO. (1) The North is reluctant to give much concession or compromise with the South. They try to turn the spotlight away from agriculture, where they have defensive interests, and to focus attention on areas where they have offensive interests. One example is that both the US and the EU not only refused to make substantive concessions in the agriculture negotiations, but rather made unreasonable demands on developing countries to reduce import tariff and open domestic markets to the non-

[91] See "Comprehensive Report: The Doha Round is highly likely to be finished in 2006," *Chinese Economy Report*, Issue 1276, September 17, 2005, available at www.ceh.com.cn/focus_detail.asp?id=22628.

[92] Lamy, "Trade is 'fundamental tool' in fight against poverty," October 6, 2005, available at www.wto.org/English/news_e/sppl_e/spp105_e.htm. This speech was delivered on October 6, 2005 at the session of the Trade and Development Board of UNCTAD.

[93] CHEN An, "A reflection on the South–South coalition in the last half century from the perspective of international economic law-making: From Bandung, Doha and Cancún to Hong Kong, Part III," (2006) 7(2) *The Journal of World Investment & Trade*.

agriculture products from developed countries. This is described as "giving an inch and asking not just for a foot but a mile."[94] (2) Although the negotiation patterns adopted in the DDR, including the Mini-Ministerial Green Room Meetings, Five Interested Parties as well as the G6 ministerial meetings, allow such developing countries as India and Brazil to participate and have positive significance, they are exclusive and non-transparent and thus exclude the vast number of developing countries from participating in decision-making on critical issues. Developing countries account for over 75 percent of the WTO's membership, but is represented by only one-third of the G6 countries.[95] (3) Due to the fact that some economic powers such as the US refused to make concessions on the key issues of elimination of agriculture subsidy and opening domestic markets, the short-term aim set forth by the Hong Kong conference to establish "full modalities"[96] for agriculture and non-agricultural market access (NAMA) "no later than 30 April" failed.[97] On July 24, 2006, WTO Director-General Pascal Lamy was so tired, both bodily and mentally, that he declared, "faced with this persistent impasse, I believe that the only course of action I can recommend is to suspend the negotiations across the Round as a whole."[98] On July 28, WTO General Council supported Lamy's suggestion to suspend the Doha Round.[99] The DDR was terminated until February 7, 2007 when Lamy announced a resumption of negotiations fully across the board.[100] However, the DDR collapsed in August 2008 due to failed agreement on the special safeguard mechanism on agriculture between developed and developing countries.

[94] Martin Khor, "Mood at WTO gloomy as "Ministerial Green Room" convenes, TWN Info Service on WTO and Trade Issues," November 9, 2005, available at www.twnside.org.sg/title2/twninfo296.htm.

[95] "The permanent mission of China to WTO, Ambassador Sun Zhenyu appeals to change the WTO negotiation patterns," March 17, 2006, available at http://wto.mofcom.gov.cn/aarticle/ddfg/waimao/200603/20060301704883.html.

[96] "Full modalities" include formulae for cutting subsidies and tariffs in agriculture and for cutting tariffs in NAMA, plus numbers for flexibilities such as treatment of sensitive and special products in agriculture, and for exemptions from the formula in NAMA.

[97] Martin Khor, "Deadlock persists as clock ticks on Doha talks," *SUNS* (South-North development monitor) #5985 Tuesday March 14, 2006 [email edition].

[98] Pascal Lamy, "Time out needed to review options and positions," www.wto.org/english/news_e/news06_e/tnc_dg_stat_24july06_e.htm, July 24, 2006.

[99] General Council supports suspension of trade talks at www.wto.org/english/news_e/news06_e/gc_27july06_e.htm, July 28, 2006.

[100] Lamy, "We have resumed negotiations fully across the board," www.wto.org/english/news_e/news07_e/gc_dg_stat_7feb07_e.htm, February 7, 2007.

Second, the North countries use "divide-and-rule" tactics to split and disintegrate the South–South coalition so as to stifle NIEO. (1) The US continues to carry out its "stick and carrot" policy to split the South. For instance, the G20 originally had 22 countries in the Cancún conference, however, Peru and Colombia withdrew from it under US pressure. The Chairman of the US Senate Finance Committee, Charles Grassley, warned that the behavior of Latin American countries at Cancún would influence future decisions.[101] This threatening did work to some extent. (2) The Five Interested Parties and the G6 ministerial meetings excluded China, one of the largest developing countries in the WTO, is also a sign of disintegrating South–South coalition. The formation of the Five Interested Parties is a strategy by the US and other key developed countries to bring Brazil and India – leaders of the G20 – to be a central part of the negotiations in agriculture, which was the key obstacle to any further moves at liberalization, then to accede to these countries' core demands in order to detach them from the rest of the developing countries.[102] (3) The US and other developed countries adopted a new strategy to step out of the multilateralism to focus on bilateral or regional free trade arrangements. The US Trade Representative Robert Zoellick said that the US would put its emphasis on concluding bilateral agreements with "can do" countries, implying that it would expend less effort in negotiations within the WTO.[103] In this way, the developed countries can divide and rule individual countries so as to disintegrate the South–South coalition. Moreover, this is a tactic to force the developing countries to give more concession or surrender in the DDR in multilateral trade system.

Third, the above brief historical review shows that the South–South coalition and the struggle for NIEO from Bandung Conference to Doha Round, experienced an up and down existence in different modalities. Nevertheless, they are proceeding and persevering, albeit on an uneven road. The coalition needs patience and perseverance, rather than immediate success.

Fourth, the situation of a "weak South" versus a "strong North" will continue to exist for a long period. This situation cannot be changed within a short time. However, if the individual weak and poor countries

101 Balakrishnan Rajagopal, "A new opportunity in Cancún's failure," *YaleGlobal*, December 3, 2003, http://yaleglobal.yale.edu/ display.article?id=2937.

102 Walden Bello, "G-20 leaders succumb to divide-and-rule tactics – NGO," *South Bulletin* 85, available at www.southcentre.org/info/southbulletin/ bulletin85/bulletin85–06.htm.

103 Bello, "G-20 leaders succumb to divide-and-rule tactics."

unite together as a South–South coalition, the strength of the South countries as a whole will increase and thus will gradually change the strength-unbalanced situation between the South and the North. On the other hand, the small victory achieved in the DDR by the South only means the rise of the South, not equality for the South. The South is still in a disadvantageous position.

As mentioned above, the economic power countries are trying to disintegrate and divide the South countries so as to weaken the NIEO movement. Actually, they never stop driving a wedge between China and India, the two biggest and most important countries for the South–South coalition. Some recent events by the US and Japan illustrate this.

Both the US and Japan regard rising China as their competing rivals, and regard China's rise as a strategic threat to them.[104] In addition, they are jealous of the new cooperative Sino-Indian relations and thus approach India for the purposes of containment or to "check and balance" China.[105] In recent years, US–India relations have increased, resulting in deepened cooperation in the fields of politics, trade and economy, and military affairs as well. They also intend to strengthen dialogue with regard to cooperation in non-military nuclear energy.[106] Nuclear energy, trade and economy, and strategic cooperation were the three main points of Bush's visit to India in March 2006. As a result, a nuclear energy cooperation agreement was signed, which symbolized the strategic partnership between the two countries had moved into a new era.[107]

By the same token, Japan has been trying to establish good relations with India in recent years. In November 2004, Japan and India agreed to establish a Japan–India Joint Study Group (JSG) for a Comprehensive Study to serve as a framework for reviewing their economic relationship. In April 2005, Japan's Prime Minister H. E. Mr. Junichiro Koizumi paid

[104] "Subtle balance of the relations between China, India and America," (in Chinese) March 5, 2006, available at http://news.xinhuanet.com/world/2006–03/05/content_4259389.htm.

[105] "India's Prime Minister signed the Nuclear Energy Agreement and Bush felt relieved" (in Chinese),, http://news.sohu.com/20060303/n242114833.shtml; "Subtle balance of the relations between China, India and America," (in Chinese), March 5, 2006, available at http://news.xinhuanet.com/world/2006–03/05/content_4259389.htm.

[106] "Bush's visit to India promotes US–India cooperation, *Global Times* (*Huanqiu Shibao*)," March 3, 2006, p. 6.

[107] "Three main points of Bush's visit to India: Nuclear energy, trade and economy, and strategic cooperation," March 2, 2006, available at www.chinaembassy.org.in/chn/zgbd/t237963.htm.

an official visit to India. The focus of the discussion between leaders of the two countries was on the adding of greater substance to bilateral relations and on measures to further deepen the Japan–India Global Partnership, in consideration of the new surge of change taking place in Asia.[108] Both parties directed the JSG to submit a report within a year, focusing on requirements for a comprehensive expansion of trade in goods and services, investment flows, and other areas of economic cooperation.[109] In 2006, Japan increased its loan to India, while it cut short its loan to China. India has become the largest recipient country of Japan's lending.[110] Japan intended to sign an Economic Partnership Agreement with India in the summer of 2006, and then a Free Trade Agreement in the near future.[111] One of the reasons that Japan treats India and China differently is that Japan plans to utilize India to limit China's development and influence, so as to keep its own unique position in Asia.[112]

However, Chindia cooperation will not be negatively affected by either US–India cooperation or Japan–India cooperation, which can be categorized as North–South cooperation.

First, as aforementioned, South–South cooperation is based on a strong political basis, a sound economic basis, as well as the same internal substance. Thus, it is different from North–South cooperation and cannot be easily broken. For instance, after new China was founded in 1949, India became an important strategic country in South Asia for the US. The US therefore tried hard to get closer to India by providing help and aid for the purpose of utilizing India to counter China. However, India rejected the US for the reason that they had different political positions and economic interests, and India did not want to give up its own position in exchange for economic aid from the US.[113]

108 "Japan–India partnership in a new Asian era: Strategic orientation of Japan–India global partnership," available at www.mofa.go.jp/region/asia-paci/india/partner0504.html.

109 "Japan–India Economic Partnership Agreement," available at http://aric.adb.org/regionalcooperation/integration_initiatives.asp?s=1&ss=3&iid=22&initiatives=Japan-India%20Economic%20Partnership%20Agreement.

110 "Japan's loan to India increased to the highest," *News for Reference* (Cankao Xiaoxi), April 2, 2006, p. 1.

111 "Japan's loan to India increased to the highest, *News for Reference* (Cankao Xiaoxi)."

112 "Japan cuts short its economic aid to China to a large scale, improves its relations with India to contain China," March 10, 2004, available at www.southcn.com/news/international/specialreports/zrgx/jy/japan/200412280994.htm.

113 ZHANG Minqiu (ed.), *Studies on Sino-India Relations*, p. 248.

India also rejected the offer to join the Korean War led by the US, flying the banner of the United Nations.[114]

Second, the long established friendship between China and India for over two thousand years is much more sturdy than the short forty-years' friendship between the US and India. Even in the 1960s when Sino-Indian relations were temporarily terminated over a border dispute, India did not stop its support for China to resume its UN membership.[115] The US took advantage of the bad Sino-Indian relations to approach India by providing India with economic and military help and aid,[116] for the same purpose to contain China. However, US–India relations are overshadowed by the history that the US supported Pakistan in the India–Pakistan dispute over Kashmir in the 1940s and that the US provided military aid to Pakistan in the 1950s.[117] Moreover, in 1998 when India conducted nuclear tests, both the US and Japan imposed comprehensive sanctions on India which greatly harmed their relations with India.

Third, India is clearly aware that the US is wary of India[118] even if they are developing bilateral relations, and aware that both the US and Japan are utilizing it to contain China. India is not willing to be the "echo" of the US,[119] or to be involved in the containment against China by the US and Japan that would offend China.[120] India will consider its own economic development and benefit from both Sino-Indian cooperation and US–India cooperation.

Fourth, US–India relations are not strong compared to Sino-Indian relations. India–US trade is probably one-tenth of China–US trade. India–US high-technology trade was worth just a little over one hundred million dollars, while the same trade with China was worth nearly a billion dollars.[121] The reality also shows that Sino-Indian relations

[114] ZHANG Minqiu (ed.), *Studies on Sino-India Relations*, p. 247.

[115] ZHANG Minqiu (ed.), *Studies on Sino-India Relations*, p. 29.

[116] ZHANG Minqiu (ed.), *Studies on Sino-India Relations*, p. 257.

[117] ZHANG Minqiu (ed.), *Studies on Sino-India Relations*, pp. 246, 250.

[118] "India's Prime Minister signed the Nuclear Energy Agreement and Bush felt relieved" (in Chinese).

[119] "Three main points of Bush's visit to India: Nuclear energy, trade and economy, and strategic cooperation," March 2, 2006, available at www.chinaembassy.org.in/chn/zgbd/t237963.htm.

[120] JIANG Yaping, "Focus on mutual official visits of Japan and India," *Globe Magazine*, March 30, 2006, available at http://news.sina.com.cn/w/2006–03–30/17259486761.shtml.

[121] "Present dimensions of the Indian foreign policy?" address by Foreign Secretary Mr. Shyam Saran at Shanghai Institute of International Studies, Shanghai, January 11, 2006, http://meaindia.nic.in/speech/2006/01/11ss01.htm.

have a brighter prospect than US–India relations. Moreover, "there is enough space in Asia for both China and India to rise," just as Shyam Saran – Indian Foreign Secretary – said.[122]

VII. Conclusion

History only explains the past, but it cannot guarantee the future. Generally speaking, China and India kept up a long-term good friendship in the past two thousand years. But it must be admitted that Sino-Indian relations once experienced contradictions and even military conflict. The negative impact is not yet fully eliminated. Therefore, the two countries should learn from past experience and lessons, clearly see through the complicated tactics and strategy from the developed countries, cherish the increasing Sino-Indian friendship, pay more attention to the interests of the South–South coalition rather than individual interest, and be alert to the disturbance and destruction from developed countries. Thus they would play a more important role in the NIEO movement and bring more blessings to the peoples of both China and India, for peoples of the Third World countries, and finally for all peoples of the world.

[122] "There is enough space in Asia for both China and India to rise' (in Chinese), January 12, 2006, available at http://world.people.com.cn/GB/4019715.html.

References

Bell, Coral, "The rise and rise of the un-West," *Asia Times Online*, March 22, 2006, available at http://atimes01.atimes.com/atimes/ Middle_East/HC22Ak03.html

Bello, Walden, "G-20 leaders succumb to 'divide-and-rule tactics' – NGO," South Bulletin 85, available at www.southcentre.org/ info/southbulletin/ bulletin85/bulletin85–06.htm

Bhurban G-20 Ministerial Declaration, Bhurban, September 9–10, 2005, available at www.g-20.mre.gov.br/conteudo/ statement_16122005_01.htm

"Bush's visit to India promotes US–India cooperation," *Global Times* (*Huanqiu Shibao*), March 3, 2006

Bush, George W., Statement of Mr. George W. Bush, President of the United States of America, 2005, World Summit High Level Plenary Meeting, September 14, 2005, available at www.un.org/webcast/summit2005/ statements.html

CHEN An, *Chen's Papers on International Economic Law*, vol. I (Beijing University Press, 2005)

Jurisprudence of International Economic Law, 3rd edn (Peking University Press, 2005)

"A reflection on the South–South coalition in the last half century from the perspective of international economic law-making: From Bandung, Doha and Cancún to Hong Kong, Part III," (2006) 7(2) *The Journal of World Investment & Trade*

"China–India Joint Study Group: A Study Report on China–India Comprehensive Trade and Economic Cooperation."

"Comprehensive Report: The Doha Round is highly likely to be finished in 2006," *Chinese Economy Report*, 1276, September 17, 2005, available at http://www.ceh.com.cn/focus_detail.asp?id=22628

Declaration by the Group of 77 and China on the Fourth WTO Ministerial Conference at Doha, Qatar, October 22, 2001, available at www.g77.org/Docs/Doha.htm

Declaration on Principles for Relations and Comprehensive Cooperation between China and India signed in June 2003

Drezner, Daniel W., "The New Republic Online," December 10, 2003, available at www.danieldrezner.com/policy/seventies.htm

"Final Communiqué of the Asian-African Conference, A. Economic Cooperation," paras. 5, 9 and12

Franks, Sir Oliver, "The new international balance: Challenge to the Western world," *Saturday Review*, January 1960

G77's South Summit, Havana, Cuba, April 10–14, 2000, available at http://www.twnside.org.sg/title/havana.htm.; Declaration of the South Summit, and Havana Programme of Action, available at www.g77.org/Docs/Declaration_G77Summit.htm and www.g77.org/Docs/ProgrammeofAction_G77Summit.htm respectively

"Han Dynasty History: Biographies of Zhang Qian and Li Guangli," vol. IX (Chinese Press, 1962)

HU Yaobang, *Comprehensive Start of a New Phase of Constructing Socialism Modernization (Report in the 12th Representative Meeting of China's Communist Party)* (Remin Press, 1982)

"India: Economy, Industry & Trade," available at www.hcilondon.net/india-overview/economy-industry-trade/index.html

"India's Prime Minister signed the Nuclear Energy Agreement and Bush felt relieved (in Chinese)," http://news.sohu.com/20060303/ n242114833.shtml

"Japan cuts short its economic aid to China to a large scale, improves its relations with India to contain China," March 10, 2004, available at www.southcn.com/news/international/specialreports/zrgx/ jy/japan/200412280994.htm

"Japan–India Economic Partnership Agreement," available at http://aric.adb.org/regionalcooperation/integration_initiatives.asp?s=1&ss=3&iid=22&initiatives=Japan-India%20Economic%20 Partnership%20Agreement

"Japan–India partnership in a new Asian era: Strategic orientation of Japan–India global partnership," available at www.mofa.go.jp/ region/asia-paci/india/ partner0504.html

"Japan's loan to India increased to the highest," *News for Reference* (Cankao Xiaoxi), April 2, 2006, p. 1

JI Xianlin, *Paper Collection on the History of Sino-India Cultural Relations (in Chinese)*, (SDX Joint Publishing Company, 1982)

JIANG Yaping, "Focus on mutual official visits of Japan and India," *Globe Magazine*, March 30, 2006, available at http://news.sina.com.cn/w/ 2006-03-30/17259486761.shtml

"Sino-Indian relations in a new stage of comprehensive development," (in Chinese), April 8, 2005, available at www.hnby.com.cn

Joint Declaration of the Heads of State and/or Government of Brazil, China, India, Mexico and South Africa, participating in the G8 Gleneagles Summit (July 07, 2005), G8 Summit Joint Declaration, Press Release, available at www.brazil.org.uk/page.php?n=545

Joint Statement by the Cairns Group and G20, Hong Kong, December 16, 2005, available at www.g-20.mre.gov.br/conteudo/ statement_16122005_01.htm

Khor, Martin, "Deadlock persists as clock ticks on Doha talks," *SUNS* (South–North development monitor) *#5985*, Tuesday March 14, 2006 [email edition]

"Havana Summit: A defining moment in G77 history: coordinating commission set up" (2000) 232 *Third World Economics*

"Mood at WTO gloomy as "Ministerial Green Room" convenes"*TWN Info Service on WTO and Trade Issues*, November 9, 2005, available at www.twnside.org.sg/title2/twninfo296.htm

Krueger, Anne O., "Letting the future in: India's continuing reform agenda, June 4, 2004, www.imf.org/external/np/speeches/ 2004/060404.htm

Lamy, Pascal, "Time out needed to review options and positions," www.wto.org/english/news_e/news06_e/tnc_dg_24july06_e.htm, July 24, 2006

"Trade is 'fundamental tool' in fight against poverty," October 6, 2005, available at www.wto.org/English/news_e/sppl_e/ spp105_e.htm

"We have resumed negotiations fully across the board," www.wto.org/english/news_e/news07_e/gc_dg_stat_7Feb07_e.htm, February 7, 2007

Lancaster, John, "India, China hoping to 'reshape the world order' together," *Washington Post Foreign Service*, April 12, 2005, p. A16, available at www.washingtonpost.com/wp-dyn/articles/ A43053-2005Apr11.html

Letter to call for end of Five Interested Parties process in Agriculture, May 6, 2005, www.oaklandinstitute.org/?q=node/view/177

Narsalay, Raghav, "Letter to the Indian Minister of Commerce, Mr. Arun Jaitley," February 28, 2003, Focus on the Global South-India Programme, www.focusweb.org/india/content/view/688/26/

"NGOs call on trade ministers to reject exclusive mini-ministerials and green room meetings in the run-up to, and at, the 5th WTO ministerial," available at www.ciel.org/Tae/ WTO_5Min_112002.html

Paris Consensus adopted by the 39th Meeting of the Chairpersons/ Coordinators of the G-77, Paris, February 27–28, 2006, G-77 News Center, available at www.g77.org/newswire/ index.htm

"The permanent mission of China to WTO, Ambassador Sun Zhenyu appeals to change the WTO negotiation patterns," March 17, 2006, available at http:// wto.mofcom.gov.cn/aarticle/ddfg/waimao/ 200603/20060301704883.html

Prestowitz, Clyde, "China–India entente shifts global balance," *YaleGlobal*, April 15, 2005, available at http://yaleglobal.yale.edu/ display.article?id=5578

"Promote the friendship between China and India and increase South–South cooperation," October 22, 1982. (Excerpt from a talk with a delegation from the Indian Council for Social Sciences Research.), available at www. chinaembassy.org.in/ eng/zyjh/t154908.htm

Quest, Matthew, "The lessons of the Bandung Conference: Reviewing Richard Wright's *The Color Curtain* 40 years later," available at www.spunk.org/texts/ pubs/lr/sp001716/bandung.html

Razzaq, Abdur, "The new international economic order," (1991) *Barcelona Conference on the Law of the World*

Rajagopal, Balakrishnan, "A new opportunity in Cancún's failure," *YaleGlobal*, December 3, 2003, available at http://yaleglobal.yale.edu/display.article? id=2937

Ramesh, Jairam, *Making Sense of Chindia: Reflections on China and India* (India Research Press, 2005)

Robes, Clement (Chair for the Group of 77 and China for 1999), "The Group of 77 and China: Current priorities," New York, January 12, 1999, available at www.southcentre.org/southletter/s1 33/s 133-06.htm

Sevilla, Christina R., "The WTO's North–South conflict: A dangerous new (old) international economic order?," (2003) *The National Interest*, www. highbeam.com/library/docfree.asp?DOCID=1G1:112411727&ctrlInfo= Round19%3AMode19a%3ADocG%3AResult&ao=

Saran, Shyam, "Present Dimensions of the Indian Foreign Policy?," Address by Foreign Secretary Mr. Shyam Saran at Shanghai Institute of International Studies, Shanghai, January 11, 2006, http://meaindia.nic.in/ speech/2006/ 01/11ss01.htm

SHI Guangsheng, Head of the Chinese Delegation, at the Fourth Ministerial Conference of the WTO, www.4english.cn/englishstudy/speeches/economy/ siguangsheng.html

South Centre, *The Future of the Group of 77, South Centre Background Paper for the Ministerial Round Table of Group of 77* (South Africa: South Centre Publications, 1996)

"A South IGO," available at www.southcentre.org/ASouthIGO.htm

"Subtle balance of the relations between China, India and America (in Chinese)," March 5, 2006, available at http://news.xinhuanet.com/ world/2006-03/05/content_4259389.htm

Suleri, Abid Qaiyum, "WTO mini ministerial meetings: High profile decisions," available at www.sdpi.org/help/ research_and_news_bulletin/jan_feb_2005/wto_mini_ministerial.htm

TANG Lu, "The world treats China and India as A Pair" – an interview with Jairam Ramesh with regard to the rise of Chindia, *News for Reference* (Cankao Xiaoxi), 2 May 2006

Thakurta, Paranjoy Guha, "China could overtake US's India trade," *Asian Times online*, China Business, 15 March 2006, available at www.atimes.com/atimes/China_Business/ HC15Cb06.html

"There is enough space in Asia for both China and India to rise (in Chinese), 12 January 2006, available at http://world.people.com.cn/ GB/4019715.html

Thirty Years of the Group of 77(1964–1994), United for a Global Partnership for Development and Peace (South Africa: South Centre Publications, 1994)

"Three main points of Bush's visit to India: Nuclear energy, trade and economy, and strategic cooperation," March 2, 2006, available at www.chinaembassy.org.in/chn/zgbd/t237963.htm

Waelde, Thomas W., "A requiem for the 'New International Economic Order': The rise and fall of paradigms in international economic law," March 18, 2000, available at www.dundee.ac.uk/ cepmlp/journal/html/article1-2.html

WANG Hongwei, "A new phase of good neighborly relations between China and India," August 26, 2003, available at http://iaps.cass.cn/english/Articles/showcontent.asp?id=404

WEN Jiabao, "Strengthen ASEM economic co-op," a speech delivered at the opening ceremony of the 6th ASEM Financial Ministers' Meeting on August 7, 2005, www.chinafair.org.cn/Chinafair2004/WebSite/English/paper/2005–8–8/p1.htm

"What is the Group of 77?," available at www.g77.org/main/ main.htm

ZHANG Lijun, "Growing cooperation between China and South Asia," available at www.ciis.org.cn/item/2006–01–11/51216.html

ZHANG Minqiu (ed.), *Studies on Sino-India Relations* (in Chinese) (Peking University Press, 2004)

ZHANG Zhijun, "China pursues an independent foreign policy of peace in its external relations: Speech at the 42nd Munich Conference on Security Policy," available at www.uni-kassel.de/fb5/frieden/themen/Sicherheitskonferenz/2006-zhang.html

4

India, China and foreign investment

MUTHUCUMARASWAMY SORNARAJAH

The announcement of open door policies in Asia have largely applied to foreign investment as they preceded liberalization in the area of trade. China announced its open door policy in 1979 and India set in train less stringent foreign investment controls in 1992.[1] Both events occurred well before the establishment of the World Trade Organization in 1995. To this extent, the developments as to liberalization in the area of foreign investment preceded those in international trade. The move towards free markets showed an ascendancy with the emergence of Thatcherism and Reagonomics and the fall of the Soviet Union, which removed a powerful competing model from the scene. Many factors at the time favoured liberalization of the foreign investment regime. The loans crisis arising from the circulation of petro-dollars had led to the drying up of private funds. Aid had become non existent. The states of Eastern Europe, released from Soviet hold and adopting free market economics, increased competition for the only means of private capital, the investments of multinational corporations. The situation was ripe for liberalization on a global scale. But, though individual countries did show fervour for the

[1] There are several studies on foreign investment in India and China but these are of a how to do it variety. Serious scholarly studies particularly of the law are lacking. What one finds are shallow studies produced quickly to give information to business people. For a study on India, see Aron Chaze, *India: An Investor's Guide to the Next Economic Superpower* (Singapore: John Wiley, 2006). There are a few scholarly works; see, OECD, *Investment Policy Review, China: Progress and Reform Challenges* (2003). Shan Wenhua, *The Legal Framework of EU–China Investment Relations* (Oxford, Hart Publishing, 2005); Jeffrey D. Sachs and Nirupam Bajpai, 'Foreign direct investment in India: Issues and problems 5–8' (Harvard Inst. for Int'l Dev., Discussion Paper No. 759, 2000), available at http://www2.cid.harvard.edu/india/pdfs/759.pdf. There are a few comparative articles. See Rohit Sachdev, 'Comparing the legal foundations of foreign investment in India and China' (2006) Columbia Bus. Law Rev. 167. For a general comparison, See David Smith, *The Dragon and the Elephant: China, India and the New World Order* (Profile Books, London, 2007).

adoption of the liberalization model in their foreign investment policies, at the global level, the trend towards globalization has not resulted in global rules on foreign investment. With economic crises in Asia, Russia and Argentina, there has been some rethinking on the value of liberalization of foreign investment regimes.

Despite this diminishing in the vigour of the movement towards liberalization, the support for measures to liberalize foreign investment still remains strong. It could well be that there would be further reconsideration of the policies due to the financial crisis afflicting the Western World in the last months of 2008. Overmuch exposure to the rest of the world and integration of the economy with the major economies of the world through foreign investment may not be seen as advisable. After the meeting with the Chinese Prime Minister in Beijing, the Indian Prime Minister blamed the crisis on the policies of Europe and the United States,[2] though neither China nor India showed any reluctance to integrate their economies with the developed states.

In the area of investment, both China and India have adopted inconsistent policies at the global, bilateral and domestic levels. At the global level, they have resisted the formation of multilateral principles on foreign investment. The efforts to bring the area of foreign investment under the auspices of the WTO have met with failure due largely to the opposition of India, China and other developing countries. The inclusion of investment as one of the Singapore issues was met by a joint effort headed by China, India and Brazil which finally led to the removal of that issue from further discussion in the WTO. Though there are WTO instruments which deal with limited aspects of foreign investment,[3] there has been reluctance on the part of states, both developed[4] and developing, to bring about comprehensive multilateral instruments on foreign investment. Yet, at the domestic and bilateral levels, both China and India have not been averse

[2] *The Hindu*, 26 October 2008.

[3] Principally, the Trade Related Intellectual Property Measures (TRIPs) which affect investments involving technology and the Trade Related Investment Measures (TRIMs) which deal with performance measures imposed on foreign investors. The General Agreement on Trade in Services (GATS) has provisions on delivery of services through commercial presence which is a form of foreign investment. For a critical view of the latter instrument, see Jane Kelsey, *Serving Whose Interests? The Political Economy of Trade in Services Agreements* (London: Routledge, 2008).

[4] The last effort by the Organization for Economic Cooperation and Development (OECD) was the Multilateral Agreement on Investment. It was negotiated among the OECD member countries; all developed states but failed due to dissension among them as to the content of the Agreement.

to liberalization of foreign investment rules. Both states are participants in bilateral treaty programmes.[5] Both have made free trade agreements containing investment chapters.[6] Both envisage the making of investment rules in regional treaties. Both are committed to the further liberalization of their domestic foreign investment laws. Yet, both states also retain sufficient controls over foreign investment and do not show any willingness to go all the way with liberalization.

The spectacular rise of China in economic terms has been attributed to the rapid rise of foreign investment in that country after the open door policy was announced. There had not been the same dramatic rise in India, until more recent times, which is sometimes attributed to the reluctant policies pursued in the area by India. But, it is not doubted that there has been a spurt in the growth of India as well in recent times, fuelled to a large extent, by the influx of foreign investment.[7] Various explanations are given for the disparities in the growth in foreign investment. The head start of over a decade that China had, the allegation that the Chinese figures do not reflect "round tripping" of local assets routed through Hong Kong[8] and absence of reliable statistics are given as the reasons for the dramatic Chinese spurt in influx of foreign investment. The edge of China is significantly large and cannot be accounted for by single explanations. One concern also is that there is a gross regional disparity in the distribution of foreign investment within China.[9] In India too, certain regional cities have attracted large shares of foreign investment.

Yet, the experiences of the two states are worthy of study and analysis for the reason that they will come to occupy dominant positions in the political and economic movements of the future world. The signs are that despite the previous instances of hostilities involving borders, they will cooperate to the benefit of each other.[10] The policy agreed upon

[5] India came to the practice of such treaties later than China. China has a longer track record as to these treaties and made many treaties containing weak obligations probably in the hope that they would signal a change of policy to the world. India did not have such a baggage to dispense.

[6] See, e.g., the Pakistan–China FTA and the Singapore-India FTA. Several FTAs are being negotiated by both countries.

[7] Mark B. Baker, 'Awakening the sleeping giant: India and foreign direct investment in the 21st century' (2005) 15 Indiana. Int'l & Comp. L. Rev. 389, 410–22.

[8] Nearly half of foreign investment comes from Hong Kong. The OECD countries' share is limited. OECD *Report on China*, p. 44.

[9] Guandong attracts nearly a quarter of the investments and the eastern part of China accounts for around 80% of the investments.

[10] Thus, for example, the two countries have agreed that they will not compete for the search for oil resources.

earlier to make joint bids for oil rather than compete is an indication of this cooperation.[11] Political leaders of both states have affirmed the need to cooperate. However, there is bound to be a degree of competition which is evident in the nature of the shaping of contacts with regional associations in Asia.[12] There is also the view that the closer ties that India makes with the United States are hostile to China. Equally, China's activities in Pakistan, Sri Lanka and Myanmar are said to encircle India. The possibility of cooperation of the two Asian giants and the potential for their economic conflicts make the emergence of the two giants of great significance to the rest of the world. It is necessary to identify the similarities and differences between the two states before making the study.

I. India and China: The similarities and differences

The similarities are easier to identify. Some are superficial such as the claim that there has been a reluctance to deal with foreigners in both cultures. These impressions arise from shallow observations such as that the Great Wall of China was built to exclude foreigners. Similarly, it is said that the caste system of India was a social organization that could not accommodate foreigners. Such conclusions are speculative and prejudicial. Both cultures received and benefited from foreign influences, particularly from interaction with each other in the past.[13] Other similarities have more substance. A shared colonial experience in which foreign investment and international trade were the basis of subsequent political domination of the two states is the most important of the similarities. India underwent some three centuries of British colonial rule during which period its economy was subservient to the interests of the colonial power. The role of foreign investment in the colonial era was significant. China was no different. It was not subject to colonialism but subtle controls were exercised through power. Since the Opium Wars and before, there have been forcible efforts made by European powers and the United States to open the doors of China to foreign trade and investment. With the end of the Opium Wars and treaties such as the

[11] 'A direct instance of that cooperation is the joint bid for oil in Kazakhstan,' *Straits Times*, Singapore, 9 June 2006.

[12] SAW Swee-Hock (ed.), *ASEAN–China Relations: Realities and Prospects* (ISEAS, 2005).

[13] An affectionate treatment of the historical relationship between China and India in the arts is to be found in Amartya Sen, *The Argumentative Indian* (London: Allen Lane, 2005).

Treaty of Nanjing, a system of extraterritoriality was introduced into China making the Chinese writ not applicable to European traders in the port cities. The indignity that was involved in the system could not easily be erased. Chinese international lawyers later contributed to the creation of a doctrine of unequal treaties, declaring treaties obtained through coercion, military or otherwise, invalid. A historical suspicion of foreign investment and trade, as forerunners of colonialism, is a residue of this experience which must lie hidden in the psyche of policy makers of both states. The presence of economic nationalism, which affects all states, is bound to be stronger in states which had undergone colonial experiences similar to those of India and China.

In the immediate post-colonial period, there was much cohesion between the two states. Cooperation within the non-alignment movement built strong bonds. Personal ties between the leaders of the two states were close. There was mutual admiration and shared political philosophies. Indian leaders were greatly influenced by Fabian socialism. There have always been varieties of communism present in India. Communist parties are strong enough to rule several states in the federal system of India and control the formation of central governments. State enterprises having monopoly over sectors were a feature of both economies. The aim of the state was to ensure that that welfare of the people was furthered through central economic planning. Egalitarian welfarism was a feature of policies in both states. There was, at least in the early phases, a protectionist policy adopted as to foreign trade and investment.

It has been suggested that the success of China and India have been due to liberalization of foreign investment flows. As far as China is concerned this may to some extent be demonstrable, though the controls upon entry that exist under Chinese laws are extensive and have not been dismantled to any appreciable measure despite Chinese membership of the WTO.[14] The Chinese model is distinct and should not be confused with a free market model, though supporters of the free market model strain facts to project the image that China succeeded through the adoption of market liberalization. Chinese accession to the World Trade Organization resulted in the consolidation as well as some change to the foreign investment laws but since the WTO lacked strong rules on

[14] To a large extent, what occurred in 2002 was the consolidation rather than change of the foreign investment rules. The law though neatly specified the categories of encouraged, restricted and prohibited sectors for foreign investment.

foreign investment the changes made were not substantial. In India's case, controls have always existed. Though liberal measures were introduced in 1992, much later than in China, there is disagreement as to whether it was such measures or earlier economic reforms in the 1980s that had brought about the economic progress that India has witnessed.

Besides, liberalization may have a unidirectional pull in China where the Communist Party can implement its policies without the existence of dissent except within the Party. This is not possible in India where nationalists and socialists have impeded full liberalization and the existing strong entrepreneurial groups also have collectively impeded liberalization due to the fear that such liberalization would bring competition which may affect them adversely.[15] For this reason, there is greater liberalization evident in communist ruled states of India such as West Bengal and Kerala. In these states, the provision of basic amenities to the poor combined with moves to attract foreign investment has proved successful.

But, there were significant differences as well. Foreign investment was non-existent in China. There had been nationalization of foreign investment after the Communist Revolution. This termination of foreign investment for ideological reasons had repercussions on investment. There was no basis for the accommodation of foreign investment in a state which had little by way of contract or property laws. It was only after the open door policy that China set up legal mechanisms for foreign contracts and later moved towards the protection of property. India did not abandon foreign investment after independence. Its Foreign Exchange Regulations Act (FERA) which applied to foreign investment restricted the manner in which foreign investment could be made in India through participation usually in minority shareholdings but did not seek to exclude foreign investment altogether. So, engagement with foreign investment and experience in dealing with it existed in India for a longer period. The red tape surrounding foreign investment in India at the time was heavily criticised. Yet, India had administrative machinery dealing with foreign investment in a variety of sectors. It had

[15] The dominant Indian companies, such as Tatas and Reliance Industries are capable in terms of experience and capital of competing with large Western multinationals. But, large Indian corporations would prefer to keep multinational corporations out of India. The experience in the Indian retail industry is relevant. The entry of Walmart and other Western chain stores has been resisted. But, domestically, the setting up of such chain stores by Reliance has been resisted by small retailers on the grounds that they are being driven out of business. There is Asia-wide resistance to the intrusion of foreign retailers.

not to institute rules afresh, as was the case in China, when China announced its open door policy.

There is also the problem of the so called rule of law. The existence of a rule of law in the traditional sense in China is to be severely doubted.[16] The judiciary to a large extent is still run by untrained party cadres. Protection of property as a matter of constitutional law has been debated in the last few years and there has been gradual inching towards recognition of private property. It was finally accomplished, though with reservations. Contract laws have been drafted but their administration would be what matters. A judiciary trained in the intricacies of international business is non-existent. Besides in the absence of a culture supporting the rules, it is difficult to see how the laws can operate successfully. In India on the other hand, the tradition of the common law, identifiable to at least foreign investors from the major common law countries has a vibrant existence. The court system of India, slow and clumsy though it is, does dispense justice that is acceptable to other common law jurisdictions, following the same precedents as the courts of these jurisdictions. As regards the existence of meaningful protection for property and contract, the Indian legal system does score heavily.

The comparison, however, may indicate that legal stability may not be the only determinants of rises in the rates of foreign investment. The absence of a rule of law may indeed be a help in these matters rather than an hindrance as the Chinese state, once a clear policy of liberal foreign investment regime is decided on, can implement it with a single-mindedness and without judicial scrutiny of its decisions or the dissent of opposition parties. Such single-mindedness is not possible in India where democratic processes involve discussions and protests on decisions made.

Both parties have engaged in investment treaty programmes which must be noted. But, the treaties made by China have generally been weak in that dispute settlement is restricted to disputes as to the amount of compensation for expropriation only. So far as a result, China has avoided any recourse being made to arbitration against it. But, this may change as stronger treaties are being made.[17] The stronger treaties may reflect the fact that China, being now an exporter of capital, would

[16] Randall Peerenboom, 'Let one hundred flowers bloom, one hundred schools contend: Debating rule of law in China' (2002) 23 Mich. J. Int'l L. 471; Randall Peerenboom, *China Modernizes* (New York: Oxford University Press, 2007).

[17] The China–Germany treaty made in September 2005 may indicate a change. Likewise, the Netherlands–China treaty.

seek to take advantage of the network of investment treaties. India's treaties appear to be stronger, though here again the provisions may not altogether be to the liking of foreign investors as regulatory space of the state is significantly preserved by these treaties. The investment treaty practice of the two states requires comparative examination. It is also interesting that both states have strong outward investments. They are among the largest investors in North America and Europe. It would not be long before their foreign investors use the investment treaties against the states in North America and Europe. The boot could well come to be on the unintended foot.

There are other areas which also need to be studied. The manner in which the environment has been affected has significance to both countries. India's Bhopal disaster demonstrated, as no other incident has done, the capacity for damage to the environment that a callous investor could generate. The human rights abuses that could occur, the standards of corporate responsibility that exist and the general nature of the investment protection that exists require to be studied comparatively so that lessons may be gleaned and prescriptions made as to whether there could be mutual benefit from such a study to the two states and whether they could provide examples to other states. An attempt is made to accomplish these tasks in this chapter.

II. Foreign investment and the Doha Development Round

It is a credible argument to make that the dawn of a new era of cohesion among developing countries arose during the commencement and continuation of the Doha Ministerial Meeting and particularly, with the common attitude displayed to the major 'Singapore issue'[18] of foreign investment. Developing countries had been consistently averse to the bringing about of a multilateral instrument on investment. The successive attempts at such instruments – the Abs–Shawcross Convention, the World Bank Guidelines, the OECD Multilateral Agreement on Investment – have failed, though not entirely due to the positions taken by developing countries. The attitude of developing countries, as displayed in the New International Economic Order (NIEO) and the Charter of Economic Rights and Duties of States had been to assert

[18] The Singapore issues, among them foreign investment and competition, arose as a result of the Second Ministerial Conference of the WTO held in Singapore which decided to study the possibility of extending WTO competence into these areas.

national control of foreign investment. Their project had been to universalize the Calvo doctrine which had been supported in earlier times by the Latin American states.[19] The dawn of the trend towards liberalization in the early 1990s made some commentators believe that the effort at achieving a New International Economic Order was finished. Such assessments are clouded with euphoria of the prejudiced. Movements are cyclical in international relations and a viewpoint that is based on the assertion of regulatory control cannot entirely go out of consideration and will be revived as later events have demonstrated. The effort of the developed states to make a universal investment discipline through its transference to the WTO, after the OECD's attempt had failed, met with equal failure; but before it did so, it revived efforts that were made during the time of the New International Economic Order. The developing states, led by China, India and Brazil, no doubt the larger states, insisted that if issues of protection were to be included, there should be principles formulated also on corporate conduct and responsibility. This is an idea that was associated with the New International Economic Order for one aspect of the NIEO was to bring about a binding code of conduct for transnational corporations. Whether the developing countries meant to accomplish such a discipline or whether this was a ruse used to counter an investment discipline based on protection of investment alone is a matter for conjecture but the fact is that the effort at inclusion of corporate responsibility effectively scuttled the possibility of an investment discipline and with it, the other Singapore issues. It also demonstrated that cohesion of the developing states under the leadership of China and India could bring about sufficient countervailing power to meet the demands of the developed states, including the hegemonic power in decline, the United States. One may object that this is but one swallow but it must be looked at in the context of what transpired at the Doha and Hong Kong Ministerial Meetings. There was certainly a new vigour to place the issue of development and achieve trade offs with the developed world for further liberalization.

While perhaps the restoration of the days of the New International Economic Order may yet be wishful thinking, there is a fresh willingness brought about in the face of a realization that the programme of liberalization is being jointly pushed by the richer countries to the

[19] The Calvo doctrine asserted that foreign investment was subject to the control of local laws and disputes arising from it were to be decided by local tribunals. It stood in opposition to the American view that there was an external, international minimum standard which applies to these investments.

detriment of the poorer world. The Doha development round and its continuation in Hong Kong itself is a demonstration of the awareness among developing countries that there is a need to confront the trend. Though China and India may be emerging economically, they are yet the largest countries in which people in poverty live. The flows of foreign investment have brought prosperity to a growing number in the cities but vast swathes of rural poverty still remain, posing a threat to political stability in both countries. Both states see the need to address this situation and know that internal politics does not permit the adoption of stances that are geared to advancing the interests of the elite who will profit as a result of liberalization. In the case of India, the elite themselves, being local entrepreneurs will not favour liberalization as it would mean competition for them. The booting out of the BJP government[20] in India which was more concerned with promoting foreign investment than addressing issues of poverty indicates that the achievement on one objective without addressing the other concern will not be acceptable to the Indian populace. It may appear that the ruling Congress party may have continued with excessive liberalization and stands in similar peril of losing the next elections. In the case of China, the emerging elite will pose a problem for the future. Their push for further liberalization may cause dissent both within the ruling group as well as the citizenry. It could well be that schisms could develop on this within the ruling groups, between regions and between people. The divisions which rapid liberalization of foreign investment regimes generate within societies has received extensive commentary.

Another general similarity is that both states would be averse to loosing regulatory space. China and India avoided the effects of the Asian economic crisis to a large extent because they had not engaged in liberalization of the financial sector to the same extent as the other Asian states. Both have adopted a policy of gradualism, so that time could be bought for local entities to be able to meet foreign competition. China now imposes no restrictions on international payments.[21] This incremental progress is what both states would adopt towards foreign

[20] The Bharatiya Janata Party is a nationalist party that is based on Hindu surpremacy. It campaigned on the slogan of 'India shining' indicating the wealth created through flows of foreign investment. It lost the elections to the Congress Party, which is the traditional national party of power. For a journalistic survey of the Indian scene, see

[21] Regulation on Foreign Exchange Administration (1996). See also WANG Jiangyu, 'Financial liberalization and regulation in East Asia: Lessons from financial crises and the Chinese experience of controlled liberalization' (2007) 41(1) *Journal of World Trade* 211.

investment, ensuring that they would preserve sufficient regulatory space to protect national economic interests. They are unlikely to kowtow to the mandates of neo-liberalism. 'Crossing the river by groping for the stones' is a Chinese saying that best reflects the approach adopted by both states.

The corruption of officials in both countries will also cause concern. Corruption is endemic in India. In China it is a novel phenomenon that arose with the introduction of a system that enabled the accumulation of private capital. Since corruption affects the ruling elite within China, including the officials of the Red Army, political credibility will also come to be affected. Unlike in China, the Indian public has lived with corruption among public officials as a part of daily life. Despite stringent laws against corruption in India, the problem has not reduced to any significant degree. Corruption exists from the lowest to the highest levels in India. The Indian public seems resigned to the fact.

Admission of investment

The undoubted prerogative that a state has to control alien admission is effectively employed by the two states to control entry of foreign investment. The existence of such control belies the fact that liberalization has been completely adopted in either country. Sectors of the economy still remain controlled in both countries though easier avenues of entering certain other sectors have been devised. The rapid dismantling of the admission requirements remains a feature but, with the financial crisis that is taking hold, there may be rethinking about further liberalization. Both countries have relaxed considerably the restrictions on incoming foreign investment. Initially China permitted entry only through either contractual or equity joint ventures though it has now moved to permit wholly owned enterprises. The permission of the Ministry is required for such enterprises. Permission would depend on the extent to which the investment would be in accordance with the laws of China, promote economic development and is not detrimental to Chinese sovereignty. Wholly owned enterprises are permitted on similar considerations.[22] Article 3 of the Law on Foreign Capital Enterprise reads

[22] Companies may be set up by foreigners. For the company law of China, see Kingley Ong and Colin Baxter, 'A comparative study of the fundamental elements of Chinese and English company law' (1999) 48 ICLQ 88.

> "Enterprises with foreign capital shall be established in such a manner as to help the development of China's national economy. The State may encourage the establishment of foreign capital enterprises that are export-oriented or technologically advanced."

The Law gives extensive guarantees including a guarantee against expropriation and the guarantee regarding repatriation of profits. But, such protections depend on internal laws and may seem inadequate to foreign investors.[23] The treaties that exist do not give effective protection. A further problem in China is that there does not appear to be an adequate standard of transparency in the laws. The various levels at which permissions may have to be obtained also add to the problem.

Requirements in India which preferred joint ventures have been changed, restricting the requirement to specified sectors. Licensing requirements in sectors are still retained.[24] The adage of a 'licence raj' may still apply in India but only in the restricted sectors as there is a direct route of admission provided in other sectors. In the recent budget, the Finance Minister of India announced a commitment to clear foreign investment applications in 90 days. This presumably includes clearances that are to be given at state level as well as at the central government level. The limit of the percentage of foreign shareholdings in companies has been raised in many sectors from 51 per cent to 71 per cent.

The Chinese developments in this area seem to be far more liberal than the cautious approach which India has taken. The caution that India displays is demanded by the balances it has had to make between different constituencies in the country. The Communist Parties of India which are part of the ruling coalition in India remain averse to overmuch liberalization.[25] China does not have similar constraints in devising policy in such areas. Yet, the Indian restraint is to be welcomed. It ensures that there could be a cautious, industry by industry

[23] SHAN Wenhua, 'Towards a level playing field for foreign investment in China' (2002) 3 *Journal of World Investment and Trade* 327.

[24] This is largely performed by the Reserve Bank of India under the Foreign Exchange Management Act, 1999. This enables control of acquisition of companies by foreigners as well as shareholdings in businesses to be established. An amendment provides for an automatic route for investment except in certain sectors. For manufacturing investment, licences are necessary under an old act, Industries (Development and Regulation) Act of 1951. After 1991 (the New Industrial Policy), the list of industries requiring licences has been considerably shortened. Progressively, the measures relating to entry have been reduced depending on the sector.

[25] A paradox is that in the state which it rules, the State of Bengal, is one state which has achieved spectacular success through foreign investment flows.

assessment of developments and permits the ability of the state to control developments that take place within sectors. It could well be argued that the absence of exposure of the economy to foreign integration will enable India to withstand the current financial crisis more effectively. The dominance of indigenous entrepreneurs of the economy with the ability to compete or displace foreign investors has been a feature of the Indian economy. This may not have occurred had there been a swamping of the economy by foreign investors. The Chinese liberalization is fraught with difficulties. It generates social tensions and possibly permits the round tripping of investments and other undesirable practices. The so called 'China Dream' of making a quick exit after making money fast in the market may be a phenomenon that needs to be checked in an appropriate manner. Whereas India's cautious opening up may permit such a course, the haphazard Chinese method of opening up fast may have deleterious social and economic effects in the future.[26]

The charge that is made is that the progressive relaxation of admission requirements indicates the success of neo-liberal attitudes in China and India has to be met. It is made with a certain credibility in the case of China in particular as there has been a simultaneous dismantling of welfare facilities such as medical programmes for the less privileged which had existed in China. This has not happened to any significant extent in India. Such a dismantling, it has been pointed out, could take place in a repressive state like China but not in a democratic state like India, where the progressive advancement in providing medical facilities, particularly in communist ruled states like Kerala have been spectacular.[27] An apartheid-like situation that is resulting in places like Shanghai, where workers flock from the rural areas and are treated differently by law,[28] will cause concern in the future as disparities in wealth will become spectacular. It would be difficult for governments which promise socialist equality to maintain this situation without fission. The unequal dispersal of wealth that is created as a result of foreign investment in both countries will cause concern.

[26] For India, see Aswini Ray, 'Globalization and democratic governance: The Indian experience', in Catarina Kinnvall and Kristina Jonsson (eds.), *Democratization in Asia: The Construction of Identity* (London: Routledge, 2002).

[27] Sen, *The Argumentative Indian*, 2005.

[28] These workers live in shanties and give rise to many social problems like crime. Prior to 2003, the law provided for forcible detention and removal but this law has since been repealed. Rural poverty forces people to flock to the cities in both states giving rise to many social problems.

The prospect for this situation to be dealt with in India is better because the rural poor have votes which would ensure that governments, which are protective of rural interests, are maintained in power.[29] The presence of strong communist parties will ensure that there is a check on the degree of openness that is achieved and that schisms are reduced. Thus, in the state of West Bengal, the communist government attracts foreign investment while ensuring that adequate welfare programmes are maintained with vigour. Yet, it was the recent target of protests of farmers who resented their land being taken over for industrial projects. The Communist government had to yield, despite strong-arm techniques it had used against the farmers. The extent to which the two states shift towards neo-liberalism will depend on the extent of social tensions that could arise within the states. But, the likelihood of such a shift will be unlikely in the light of the events in the West which have seen the effective passing of neo-liberal economics. Yet, it must be admitted that such social tensions would be better provided for by the democratic machinery that exists in India than the repressive mechanisms that exist in China.

In investment treaties, there is no commitment to liberalize. Liberalization treaties have been shunned by both states. China is a heavy practitioner of investment treaties, probably because it saw such treaties as a method of signalling to the rest of the world its new open door policy. But, these treaties apply only to the post-establishment phase. This is so in the case of India as well.

Privatization programmes

Privatization programmes have also afforded means of entry into many developing countries. They were symbols of liberalization as public state owned enterprises were held to be uncompetitive and neo-liberalism required that they be organized on a competitive basis through the divestment of shares into private hands, including foreign investors. This prescription was followed in many countries, particularly those in Latin America. The privatization measures have been followed by spectacular disputes in these countries many of them reaching dispute settlement tribunals.[30] China

[29] It is possible to argue that the BJP was booted out and a communist supported Congress government was instituted for this reason. The two communist parties in government as well as a group within the Congress Party ensure restraint in controlling overzealous liberalization.

[30] One spectacular instance is the Cochahamba dispute which has attracted world attention. The water monopoly vested in the state was privatized but the foreign company raised rates resulting in widespread protests. The government recovered control,

has more state enterprises than India as a result of its socialist past and the allegation has been that these have not been economically run. The pressure to privatize has been greater in China but it has been resisted on the ground that workers, many of them party cadres, would be affected. But, the pressure to privatize is still maintained. In India, the privatization measures have been heavily controlled. It is unlikely that shares will fall into foreign hands as a result. Once more, the relative transparency and political pressure that could be exerted in India will exert control over private foreign investment being in any great measure involved in the essential sectors of the economic activity that are usually reserved for control by the state.

The *Enron Case*,[31] in India, was an aberration where there was pressure exerted for the building of a power plant and supply of electricity by Enron, the US corporation which met with many difficulties. This was not a dispute involving privatization. But, it nicely illustrates the manner in which problems associated with private control of essential services could arise. The making of the contract itself involved political processes, with influence of the US government implicated. The allegations of corruption were rife. The problem, as in the case of many disputes involving power and developing countries, was that the supply of electricity and the control over prices was to be vested in the hands of the foreign investor after the project had been completed. Such situations are fraught with great difficulties, particularly if the investment capital and profits were to be realized through the tariffs imposed on the public for the supply of the commodity produced. In such circumstances, political involvement cannot be avoided and the potential for disaster is great.[32]

Post-entry national treatment

Post-entry national treatment is easily accomplished when the requirement is that the foreign investment should enter only through a locally incorporated joint venture. Though both states have considerably

resulting in a dispute being brought before ICSID under an investment treaty. *Aguas del Tunari* v *Bolivia*. The jurisdictional phase was decided. The controversy provoked discussions of the extent to which there is a right to water in human rights terms and whether privatization affects such a right. In Indonesia, the efforts at hasty privatization have been regarded as the cause of much failure and disputes. Louis T. Wells and Rafiq Ahmed, *Making Foreign Investment Safe* (New York: Oxford University Press, 2007).

31 The jurisdictional phase in the case was completed and the case was settled but there is other litigation that is contemplated on the basis of the same facts.

32 Wells and Ahmed, *Making Foreign Investment Safe* state this view largely on the basis of Indonesian experiences.

relaxed this early requirement relating to entry through joint ventures in many sectors, the requirement still continues in sectors where it is considered that the restrictions are necessary. The issue would be whether the wholly owned enterprises which are permitted entry will be granted national treatment. The entitlement to national treatment arises largely from the existence of binding treaty obligations regarding such treatment and not from national laws. Both China and India promise post-entry national treatment to foreign investors. This is not liberalization but recognizing existing ideas that an alien should be treated on the same terms as the local citizens. In India as well as in China, such a requirement does not arise from constitutional principles. The constitutional rights in the Indian constitution are promised only to its citizens which means that the rights cannot be possessed by foreign investors unless there are treaty commitments that are made. The protection of property rights is central to the discussion of the extent to which private foreign investment could be granted protection.[33]

India recognizes the individual right to property. But, as indicated, the right is confined to its citizens. It is also interpreted even in the context of the rights of the citizen in the light of broader goals of social justice, substantive equality and human dignity.[34] It is unlikely that Indian law will accept an absolute right to property.

> In the case of China, there is considerable schism whether an individual right should be recognized through amendments to the Chinese constitution when communist theory is consistent with collective rights of ownership. A commentator has noted:[35] Perhaps most importantly, economic reforms require a more predictable and accountable administration. Clearly, the ruling regime sees administrative law as a way to rationalize governance, enhance administrative efficiency, and rein in local governments. At the other end of the spectrum, rule of law responded to people's demands for greater protection of their rights and interests. As economic reforms progressed, people began to have more property and business interests to protect.

The dilemma has not been sufficiently resolved. Doctrinal purity would demand that such a departure should not be made. There have been repeated efforts at successive Communist Party plenary sessions to

[33] The importance of property rights and the extent of power it confers have been studied extensively. Laura Underkuffler, *The Idea of Property. Its Meaning and Power* (Oxford University Press, 2003).

[34] Hussainara Khatoon v State of Bihar AIR 1979 SC 1360, 1363–7.

[35] Randall Peerenbohm, 'Competing conception of the rule of law in China', in Randall Peerenbohm (ed.), *Asian Discourses on the Rule of Law*, 112 at p. 115.

discuss the inclusion of the right to property within the constitution but these have been resisted.[36] Sometimes, it is stated that what matters is not the right to property but the right to management and that this right to management can be transferred to individuals though there is no recognition of the right to property.[37] But, such a thesis ducks the issue of individual property rights as conceived by the Western experts who see the dispute in binary terms of either having the right to property or not having it. In American law there is a tendency to see the individual right to property in absolute terms.[38] It has been suggested that the thrust of the American investment treaty programme has been to impose this concept of property on its treaty partners.[39] Some American constitutional experts have gone further and asserted that American investment treaties, including the North American Free Trade Agreement (NAFTA), seek to impose notions of property that are more absolute than found in American constitutional law.[40] Eventually, the right to property has come to be recognized in China but the manner of its implementation will be fraught with difficulties.

[36] *China Daily*, 23 October 2004; The last plenary in 2006 also contained discussions on the subject.

[37] Louis Putterman, 'The right to property in China: Shifting and unbundling ownership' (1996) *Economic Reform Today.*

[38] See Justice Scalia in *Lucas* v *South Carolina Coastal Comission* (1992) 505 US. 1003, 1025–8, describing prohibition on building on the beachfront as denial of all economic valuable use 'inconsistent with the historical compact recorded in the Takings Clause that has become part of our constitutional culture'. But, see Gregory Alexander, *Commodity and Propriety: Competing Visions of Property in American Legal Thought* (University of Chicago Press, 1997) at p. 7 who pointed out that there was another American tradition that took account of public interests in land use. Also see Jennifer Nedelsky, *Private Property and the Limits of American Constitutionalism* (University of Chicago Press, 1990) on the dominant market-oriented approach to property in the United States and the need to replace it if a more democratic political order is to be created. The European and Commonwealth traditions are clearly different from the dominant American approach to property.

[39] M Sornarajah, 'The international law on foreign investment in the age of globalization' (2002) 12 *Canadian Foreign Affairs* 202 and Symposium in the same issue of the journal on this, the text of the Simon Reisman Lecture on International Trade for 2002.

[40] Vicki Bean and Joel Beauvais, 'The global fifth amendment: NAFTA's investment protection and the misguided quest for an international "regulatory takings" doctrine' (2003) 78 NYULR 30 who argue that NAFTA rulings have interpreted the expropriation provision in ways that 'significantly exceed US takings protections'. The US Congress implicitly accepted this when it enacted the Trade Promotion Authority Act of 2002 which stated that the United States should ensure that foreign investors in the United States 'are not accorded greater substantive rights' as a result of treaties negotiated by the United States. NAFTA's investment chapter was challenged in Canada on the ground that it was unconstitutional on the ground that it created greater rights of property for the foreign investor.

The cultural attitudes to property in both states do not permit such an absolute vision of property rights. The neo-liberal vision is that economic development is not possible unless there is a secure protection of the right to property. But, such protection does not exist even in the mature legal systems of the West.[41] All legal systems contain a balance that is achieved between private property rights and the interests of the state in regulating them in the public interest, which may include its taking property without the payment of compensation. The so-called regulatory taking appears to be part of most legal systems.

But, there would be efforts to drive a European vision of property rights in a sense of an absolute right to property through investment treaties. Both countries are participants in investment treaty programmes which amount to protection of property, as interference in rights that are associated with investment are protected in the treaties through the provision of international minimum standard and through the expropriation provision. Further, there is dispute settlement overseas granted as a unilateral right to the foreign investor.

It is evident that there are many visions of property. The neo-conservatives would desire to impose a uniform vision of property largely derived from the Lockean vision, which makes individual property central to constitutional principles and elevates its protection as the *raison d'être* of a state. It is unlikely that such a vision of property will be accepted in India or China which both by tradition and ideology are committed to notions of property which subject it to the public interest. In this context, a multilateral or a bilateral discipline which seeks to impose a solution based on notions of an absolute right to property will meet with failure. The approach of China and India in this respect accords generally with the views of other developing countries. The social function of property is also generally accepted in most European legal systems. It is therefore unlikely that any uniform rules based on the centrality of property protection could receive universal acceptance.

[41] David Scheiderman, 'Property rights and regulatory innovation: Comparing constitutional cultures' (2006) 4 *I-CON* 371–91. The article identifies the status of property rights as the primary legal difference between Canada and the United States. If so, the difference between Western and Asian notions of property rights must be enormous as Asian traditions are more inclined towards the communal owning of property. The Asian views were displaced during colonial times through the displacement of the traditional views by individual notions of property rights. This displacement facilitated colonialism as foreign investment and trade which were the main reasons for foreign investment depended on the recognition of individual rights to property.

Performance requirements

Performance requirements are measures which a host state imposes on a foreign investor so that it may maximize the advantages of the foreign investment. These include the requirements that a certain percentage of the production should be exported, that local materials and local labour should be employed in production and that the foreign investor should locate in identified areas. The assumption behind the adoption of the WTO Agreement on Trade Related Investment Measures (TRIMs) is that some performance requirements are distortive of international trade. This treaty prohibits performance requirements inconsistent with two main GATT obligations, i.e. article III, which establishes the obligation of national treatment, and article XI, which contains the obligation to eliminate quantitative restrictions. The Annex of the TRIMs Agreement provides an illustrative list of the kinds of performance requirements inconsistent with these two obligations.

Performance requirements were employed by virtually every industrialized state during its period of growth. Many regard the efforts to prevent the developing states from using such performance requirements as unfair in that the industrialized states are seeking to prevent the very avenues by which they reached success.[42] The restrictions that performance requirements bring about enable the host state to harness the foreign investment effectively to the development goals that it hopes to achieve. By preventing performance requirements, the developed states are not only denying developing states techniques they had used successfully to achieve development but doing so, so as to benefit themselves on the basis that international trade is distorted by such performance requirements.

One consequence of China's admission to the WTO has been that it has had to do away with performance requirements of the type that are prohibited by the Trade Related Investment Measures (TRIMs). TRIMs prohibit the use of performance requirements such as requirement to use local products or resources in manufacturing goods or the requirement to export the production. Other types of performance requirements however are not prohibited. India shows an aversion to the prohibition of performance requirements. It believes that developed states had used these requirements in the course of their development and that such an opportunity should not be denied to developing

[42] Ha-Joon Chang, *Bad Samaritans: Rich Nations, Poor Policies and the Threat to the Developing World* (London: Random House, 2007), pp. 84–103.

countries.[43] On this issue too, it is likely that China and India would adopt a similar stance, though in the case of China, TRIMs will prove to be an impediment in the way of imposing the type of requirements referred to in it. Both states have resisted the inclusion of prohibition of performance requirements in investment treaties. It is to be noted that the model investment treaties of the United States, Canada and Japan contain prohibitions on a range of performance requirements much wider than contained in TRIMs. China and India would find it difficult to accept these model treaties and make treaties on the basis of these models.

Environmental protection versus property protection

One area in which the clash between property protection and social interests has received recent elucidation in arbitral jurisprudence flowing from interpretation of investment treaties relates to the protection of the environment. A certain uniform view had developed, at least before the award in the *Methanex Arbitration*,[44] that property protection must be given priority over the interests of environmental protection. The articulation of this view is to be found in the award in *Compania del Deserello Santa Elena* v *Costa Rica*.[45] The host state had sought to rescind a project as it was thought that the building of a resort in an area that provided the habitat to the black puma, a threatened species, would harm the continued survival of that species. The arbitrators ruled that this was not a legitimate justification for the rescission of the foreign investment contract. They observed:

> Expropriatory environmental measures – no matter how laudable and beneficial to society on the whole – are, in this respect, similar to any other expropriatory measures that a state may take in order to implement its policies; where property is expropriated even for environmental purposes, whether domestic or international, a state's obligation to pay compensation remains.

[43] Ha-Joon Chang, *Kicking Away the Ladder: Development Strategy in Historical Perspective* (London:, Anthem Press, 2005) details the performance requirements used by developed countries in the past and queries the denial of their use by developing countries.

[44] In this arbitration under NAFTA, it was recognized that an interference to regulate investment in the interests of the health and safety of the community would be regarded as non-compensatable regulatory expropriation.

[45] (2003) *ICSID* Arb.

It is interesting to note that the threatened species, the black puma, was protected by the Convention on Endangered Species to which Costa Rica was a party. This disregarding of international obligations in preference to investment protection found in a bilateral or regional investment treaty has been a feature of investment arbitration. Thus in *SD Myers* v *Canada*, a NAFTA tribunal discarded the fact that Canada was in compliance with the Basle Convention on the Export of Hazardous Waste in contemplating the refusal to permit an American company engaged in disposal of toxic wastes to remove toxic wastes from Toronto for processing in its factory in Ohio. Likewise, in *Metalclad* v *Mexico*, the protection of rare cactus was held not to be a sufficient ground for violating an investment agreement. Similar views were stated in *Techmed* v *Mexico*. However, *Methanex* involved the United States, in an investment agreement which was violated by California on the ground that the banning of the manufacture of a carcinogenic substance was justified on grounds of the protection of the health of the citizens. The claimant, however, argued that it violated NAFTA provisions and was expropriatory. The Tribunal held in favour of the United States. It is unlikely that *Methanex* would be regarded as creating an exception which favours the view that takings which can be justified on environmental grounds are not compensatable.

For India and China, the course of this litigation and the general disfavour shown to environmental justifications as grounds for breaches of foreign investment agreements has consequences. Foreign investment has led to serious depletion of the environment in both countries. In India, the capacity of foreign investment to produce horrendous results was demonstrated by the Bhopal incident which led to thousands of Indian citizens being affected. These people remain inadequately compensated. The effects of the gas leak are still being felt, with many deformed births and other effects on health. The rush to liberalization has paid scant regard to the hidden costs to the environment. While economic statistics may glorify the extent of the inflows of investment as a sign of progress, the costs of environmental depletion to the people are seldom captured in such statistics. The investment flows are statistically visible. The harm to present and future generations caused by environmental pollution generated by factories and other processes that foreign investment generates are not capable of precise calculation. The extent to which dirty industries are attracted to India and China is not closely studied. It goes without saying that laxer controls in both states attract a considerable amount of dirty industries. Uncontrolled entry of such investments will continue to pose problems for both states. The presence of environmentally concerned civic societies in India will agitate against such industries but the absence of this possibility will mean an absence of such control in China.

Besides, the benefits of foreign investment are not enjoyed by the people who suffer the results of the environmental harm. The profits of the foreign investment go to the pockets of distant shareholders, both domestic and foreign. The problem of Shell in Nigeria provides a classic demonstration of this phenomenon. The oil exploitation affects the native peoples of the oil rich region but the profits accrued from such exploitation go to the central government and do not benefit the people who suffer the necessary pollution. The same situation exists in relation to foreign investment in China and India. Dirty industries migrate to India and China on the perception that environmental standards are lax in these countries. This poses real concerns. It is the perception on the basis of which Union Carbide made its plant in Bhopal and the issue is whether the law has addressed such concerns adequately.

In India, the machinery seems to be more capable of dealing with the situation than in China. Indian law does have laws in the statute book to deal with the problem but as in many states, such laws are of little use unless officials are rigorous in prosecuting. Corrupt officials turn a blind eye to the problems of the environment. But, the growth of a vigorous system of public law litigation which gives standing to any person affected by or concerned with the violation of environmental and other laws has ensured that the matter is brought before the Indian courts. This system does offer protection to those affected by environmental pollution though in the absence of government concern the adequacy of such protection is to be doubted. Yet, some avenues for redress have been created.

In China, it would appear that there is no adequate concern for environmental depletion that accompanies foreign investment. There is mounting evidence of the relationship between such environmental destruction and foreign investment in China. But the machinery for the prevention of such destruction or the deterrence for the influx of dirty industries into China seems to be inadequate.[46] Since such issues are left to local government in China and the local governments are

[46] My research student, Lu Haitian, wrote his thesis on the migration of dirty industries into China. LU Haitian, 'Migration of Dirty Industries in China', Ph.D. thesis, National University of Singapore, 2006.

more concerned with providing work to the people and attracting more foreign investment, environmental protection becomes a matter of low priority.[47]

Corporate accountability and foreign investment protection

As much as market oriented visions of property rights are central to property protection, there has been a tendency to postulate laws on investment protection without regard to the fact that multinational corporations have often done damage to their domestic economies as well as to host economies of other states through practices that are harmful. Recent scandals in the United States and Europe, involving large corporate giants like Enron and Parmalat, evidence the harm that some of these corporations have done to domestic investors as well as the domestic economies. Through corporate governance, the issue addressed has been confined largely to the avoidance of frauds perpetrated by these companies. Corporate accountability, however, is a term usually employed in connection with the activities of multinational corporations and the effect they have on the economies of host states. So far, the protection of the assets they bring into host economies is justified on the ground that flows of investment beneficial to economic development will not take place unless such protection is given. But, this neo-liberal justification does not take into account the fact that misconduct by the multinational corporations could also harm irreparably the economic interests of host states.

In developing this theme, for a variety of reasons the focus of attention has been on the environmental harm that is done through the operation of such foreign investment. Another concern on which attention has been focussed has been the violation of human rights by multinational corporations in association with the elite groups in control of the state. Both these areas have been addressed largely because of the existence of non-governmental groups in the two areas which are willing to espouse these causes. But, the possible malpractices of multinational corporations extend beyond these areas. They include corruption of public officials (an area of great concern in both India and China) and restrictive business practices such as abuse of dominant position or

[47] *Straits Times* (Singapore) 16 June 2006 reports that the State Environmental Protection Agency (SEPA) in China has only power to give instructions but not to close down polluting enterprises. It states that SEPA is to be given more powers through amendments.

tie-in practices.[48] These practices affect economic development. The employment of labour under unsatisfactory conditions, involvement in local politics and the creation of consumer tastes so as to influence the course of markets[49] are also issues that affect the local economy detrimentally. The neo-liberal thesis of foreign investment protection without addressing these issues obviously lacks merit.

Both China and India have addressed these concerns in their domestic legislation as well as in the international sphere. In the international sphere, the building up of Third World cohesion under the leadership of China and India is visible in the efforts they made together with other developing states to prevent the bringing about of an investment discipline under the WTO. The trump card played was that such a discipline should not be brought about unless it also addressed the issues of corporate accountability. While the Expert Group on Investment in the WTO was working on the possible draft of an investment discipline, India, China and Brazil together with some developing countries put up a paper in which they argued that the instrument on investment could not be confined to the issue of protection alone and should take into account the responsibility of multinational corporations for harmful acts they commit which are detrimental to the economy of host states.

The argument so advanced in the joint paper is reminiscent of the efforts to bring about a code of conduct for multinational corporations made by the now defunct United Nations Centre for Transnational Corporations. Around the same time, the United Nations Conference on Trade and Development (UNCTAD) was drafting a code on restrictive business practices of multinational corporations. The latter code seeks to address the global practices of multinational corporations which are detrimental to the developing states such as geographical restrictions of exports and the tie-in of associated products. The project was to bring an international antitrust law aimed at the practices that are detrimental to the interests of developing countries.[50] This would have been quite unlike the competition instrument contemplated in the Singapore issues which were designed to ensure a level playing field for multinational corporations which enter host states. The

[48] China now has a competition law which is widely regarded as an instrument that will be used to keep out dominant multinationals from entry into the Chinese market. In this sense, the regulation of the market may not be the main aim of the competition laws of China.

[49] These are alleged reasons for the expulsion of Coca Cola from India on an earlier occasion and agitations against Kentucky Fried Chicken.

[50] M Sornarajah, 'Towards an international antitrust law' (1984) 22 *Indian Journal of International Law* 1–31.

thrust of antitrust or competition laws which have been enacted in China and India in recent times has not been to achieve such an objective but to enhance their own economic interests.

In so acting at the international level by reviving concerns that were articulated during the period of the New International Economic Order and may have succeeded in bringing about Third World cohesion that existed on matters of foreign investment in the past. There was a revival of stances that had been taken in the past and discarded during the nineteen nineties, the period of the triumph of neo-liberalism. There was a continuous demonstration of the fact that developing countries, whatever their attitudes to foreign investment unilaterally, bilaterally and regionally, will be averse to bringing about global norms on foreign investment and entrust the application of such norms to a body like the WTO. Whether it was good strategy to address the issue of corporate accountability or whether there was a genuine belief in the proposition that protection alone cannot be the concern of an instrument on investment, the fact remains that China and India gave leadership to revive an attitude that exercised the concerns of developing states.

What of these concerns in domestic law? One has to concede that internal laws on these issues seem weak. Corruption is endemic in both countries. It may affect a non-democratic state based on principles of socialist equality more as it brings ideological positions into disrepute when leaders are seen to be corrupt and escape punishment. This will be an issue that China has to face. There are laws in India on corruption but visibly, enforcement is lacking. On issues of corporate governance there is a separate chapter in this book (see Chapter 15).

In the field of human rights, the concern of the West has been with prison labour in China and child labour in India. The extent to which sanctions could be taken in order to prevent such practices is widely discussed. There is little discussion, however, of the violations of human rights standards by multinational corporations. But, developments in this area are taking place with increasing litigation being mounted under the Alien Torts Act and through other means against parent companies of multinational corporations. None of these litigations involve events in China and India.

Bilateral and regional investment treaties

Though opposed to a multilateral treaty on foreign investments, both China and India have concluded several bilateral and regional treaties on foreign investment. China has had a more consistent and long-standing practice which commenced with its open-door policy. This practice may be as a result of using investment treaties as a device to signal that foreign investments will be protected in China unlike in the past when they were subjected to nationalization measures. The more recent treaty programme of China includes Free Trade Agreements with the Association of Southeast Asian Nations (ASEAN)[51] and one with India.[52] India has similar programmes but its bilateral treaty programme is more recent. India's push into the ASEAN region is also newer and began in 2002 with the Phnom Penh Summit of the ASEAN but India has pursued a 'look East policy' for a decade before that.[53] Both states have pursued treaties with individual states of the region. The possibility of a network of such treaties covering Asia is real. An emergence of a large region surpassing the European Union in terms of population and size is real. FTAs contain investment chapters. Once more, China and India will be the main players in the region. India's soft power in the region is immense as is China's historical contacts.[54]

China and India are not any longer passive recipients of foreign investment. They are significant exporters of capital as well. They are home to large multinational corporations.[55] They need to attract each other's investments as well as export investments into other parts of the world. As a result, their treaty practice demonstrates an ambivalent attitude. There is caution in that the surrender of sovereign control over foreign investment, a process that is inherently territorial, would mean loss of control over such investment and its subjects to the rules of the treaty regimes. This would result in the loss of regulatory space and the

[51] SHEN Danyang, 'ASEAN–China FTA: Opportunities, modalities and prospects', in SAW Swee-Hock (ed.), *ASEAN–China Relations: Realities and Prospects* (ISEAS, 2005) p. 208.

[52] The FTA with India was announced by Chinese Premier Wen Jiabao during his visit to India. 11 April 2005. As reported in *The Hindu* of the following day.

[53] There is in theory a hegemonic leader in regional groupings. China and India are bound to compete for leadership in such groupings. India seeks to do this in the South Asian Regional Cooperation grouping. It has also grouped together some South-East Asian states in BIMSTEC (Bay of Bengal Initiative for Multi-Sectoral Technical and Economic Cooperation).

[54] South East Asia is defined in terms of India and China both in terms of geography and culture. See George Coedès, *The Indianized States of South East Asia* (Honolulu: East–West Center Press, 1968).

[55] On outward investment from large multinational corporations from Brazil, Russia, India and China (referred to as the BRIC countries) see Karl Sauvant 'New Sources of FDI: The BRICs, outward FDI from Brazil, Russia, India and China' (2005) 5 *Journal of World Trade* 2005. For India, see Nagesh Kumar, *India's Emerging Multinationals* (London: Routledge, 2007).

ability to harness the foreign investment to the economic objectives of the state. At the same time, both states see the need to enter into treaties so that their outgoing investments could be subjected to regimes of protection. As a result of these mutually inconsistent objectives, there is a resulting ambivalence in the treaty practice on investment of both states.

The issue of national treatment in these treaties has vexed both states. They are unlikely to grant pre-entry national treatment which is a feature of the model treaties of the United States, Japan and Canada. Hence, conclusion of treaties with these states would be problematic.[56] As indicated earlier, the maintenance of admission controls by both China and India indicate that they will not agree to pre-entry national treatment unless at some future time, they are willing to dismantle these laws.[57]

The law applicable to foreign investment will also pose a problem for both states. The traditional standpoint in international fora has been to support the Calvo doctrine that the law applicable to the foreign investment should be the national law. The support for instruments such as the Charter for Economic Rights and Duties of States and Permanent Sovereignty over Natural Resources by both states indicates that there was or continues to be commitment to such a principle. But, the conclusion of investment treaties indicates that national laws should be displaced at least when they are inconsistent with the treaty standards or otherwise international responsibility would arise from the breach of the treaty obligations. This is a dilemma that both states face. While maintaining a stance at the multilateral level, they seek to attract foreign investment by accepting international standards at the

[56] There is a China–Japan treaty (1988) which appears to give pre-entry national treatment which is qualified heavily through subjection to considerations of 'public order, national security or sound development of the national economy'. In effect, it means not at all. Japan has concluded a recent treaty with Vietnam with pre-entry national treatment. But, in such treaties, many sectors are exempted from pre-entry national treatment.

[57] For China, further see Yu Jinsong, 'Pre-establishment national treatment of foreign investment and China's countermeasures' in Henry Gao and Donald Lewis (eds.), *China's Participation in the WTO* (London: Cameron May, 2005), p. 147. The author suggests that there is no harm in entering into pre-entry national treatment standards with other developing countries as the level of economic development would be similar. But, this presupposes a symmetric relationship which seldom exists in the field. China and India are exporters of capital vis a vis smaller developing states. China's investment treaty practice has been studied by several scholars. CHEN Huiping, in Niewenhuys (ed.), *The Multilateral Agreement on Investment* (Dordrecht: Kluwer, 2001).

bilateral or regional level. This paradox is one that applies to other developing countries as well.

There has also been no unwillingness to depart from norms accepted as a whole in the past by developing countries. This is evident from the acceptance of full market value as the compensation for expropriated property when the formula used by developing countries was that only appropriate compensation needs to be paid. There is evidence in such trends of a sacrifice of carefully built up norms of Third World international law in the adoption of such pragmatic stances that are regarded as necessary to attract foreign investment. Here, Third World cohesion seems to break down so that individual national interests could be pursued. This is an important consideration to be kept in mind. Third World cohesion is an objective to be followed only when national interests coincide with this objective.

The offensive use of investment treaties by both China and India will attract attention in the future. As Indian and Chinese multinationals invest in large numbers abroad, they will begin to use the dispute resolution provisions of investment treaties to protect their investments. The old Chinese treaties did not have strong dispute resolution provisions. They enable the subjection of disputes relating to expropriation, and even then deal only with disputes as to the manner of the calculation of damages, to overseas arbitration. But, the investment treaties signed in late 2006 with Germany and Holland have comprehensive dispute settlement provisions. This signals that China, which has become the second largest investor in Europe, is prepared to enter a new phase of thinking in terms of the protection of its own investments.

At this time too comes the news that a Chinese investor has brought a claim under a treaty against its host state. Tza Yap Shum Peru Ltd has brought a claim against Peru under the Peru–China investment treaty before the International Centre for Settlement of Investment Disputes (ICSID).[58] It is a Chinese company which had invested in the manufacture and export of fish flour in Peru. It was assessed for an amount for tax by the Peruvian government and within a short period, it is alleged, that the company's bank accounts were seized for non-payment of taxes. The allegation is that the seizure of the bank accounts paralyzed the functioning of the company and therefore amounted to arbitration. The constraints for the investor are clear. The Chinese treaties require

[58] For a report, see *Investment Treaty News*, 2 March 2007, www.iisd.org/pdf/2007/itn_mar2_2007.pdf.

the satisfaction of a six month period of negotiations. Thereafter, the older treaties permitted only disputes as to the amount of compensation to be submitted to arbitration. This is a constraint on investors who come to China. But, since the constraint is reciprocal, Chinese investors are also subject to the same restraint. So, it is necessary for the allegation to be based only on expropriation but in this particular situation, the couching of the dispute as a dispute that relates to the amount of compensation would be difficult.

The next phase of the game would be for China and India to be concerned with the protection of its own investors. In this phase, it will have to balance its concerns that regulatory space over inflowing investments would be lost as a result of overarching dispute settlement provisions with the need to protect the investments which flow out of the state into foreign countries. This would be an interesting exercise. Whether China and India would adopt stances which the Western states adopt towards developing countries is yet to be seen.

Unilateral rights of dispute settlement

The unilateral right to dispute settlement has been a feature of modern investment treaties. It is a right that has resulted in an explosion in the number of investment disputes being brought to arbitration. ICSID arbitration catapulted as a resulted of the recognition of such a right given in treaties to create jurisdiction in ICSID tribunals in *APPL* v *Sri Lanka*.[59] The consequent increase in ICSID arbitration and the expansionary interpretation of the standards in investment treaties has caused alarm to both developed and developing countries.[60] As a result, there have been reinterpretations of treaty standards.

Both China and India are parties to the ICSID Convention. China has so far managed to escape such arbitrations.[61] This is largely due to the fact that despite signing a larger number of investment treaties than

[59] (1992) ICSID Reports.

[60] M. Sornarajah, 'A coming crisis: Expansionary interpretations in investment treaty arbitrations' paper delivered at the Columbia-Sorborne Conference on Investment Treaty Arbitration, 4 April 2006 (to be published in a collection of essays on investment arbitration edited by Karl Sauvant). M. Sornarajah, 'A law for need or a law for greed? Restoring the lost law in international foreign investment law' Keynote Address at the Van Moltke Symposium at the University of Amsterdam, February 2006 (to be published in *International Agreements*).

[61] There have been investment disputes but they have been dealt with through internal domestic procedures.

India, China has carefully confined dispute settlement overseas to those disputes which involve the quantum of compensation for expropriation. This too, only after the matter had been dealt with by domestic tribunals. The position would be consistent with the NIEO documents. But, there has been a departure just last year when China made a treaty with Germany and Holland which contained a general dispute settlement provision granting prior consent to ICSID dispute settlement at the instance of the foreign investor. Such a change in treaty pattern may presage the possibility of China being a respondent state in future arbitrations.

India has had to face a series of arbitrations arising from the Dhabol Power project involving the US company, Enron. It was the problems in India that triggered off events relating to the collapse of Enron in the United States. Enron had taken the precaution of incorporating in Mauritius before investing in India thereby making it possible for it to invoke the Mauritius–India treaty. Small states such as Mauritius adopt this platform policy so that foreign investment may route itself through these small states, providing these states some advantages. This platform or gateway concept may have advantages but an important disadvantage, as India found in the Dhabol Case is that the dispute settlement provisions could be invoked. Such a concept could be used as regards China as well. It would appear that there is considerable 'round tripping' involving both states. This practice involves citizens of states incorporating in other states with favourable treaties, investing money in these corporations and then directing investments through them back to their home states. The aim is to get the protection of the investment and tax treaties. Such schemes are obviously fraudulent in that they are designed to defeat the purposes of the treaties but it would appear from decided cases that they have succeeded.[62] Unless care is taken to deal with dispute settlement, it could become a problem for states such as India and China as well as for other developing countries. There is considerable hostility being generated towards the uncontrolled exercise of discretion by arbitration tribunals to extend the law in the area and bring about an investment regime which has been variously described as an administrative law on investment[63] or as contributing to governance disciplines

[62] Tokio Tokeles v Ukraine (2004) 20 ICSID Rev. 205.

[63] Gus Van Harten and Martin Loughlin, 'Investment treaty arbitration as a species of global administrative law' (2006) 17 *European JIL* 121. Also see Gus Van Harten, *Investment Treaty Arbitration and Public Law* (London: Oxford University Press, 2007).

in the area of foreign investment. This would be to bring a multilateral body of rules on investment through the backdoor. Neither China nor India would accept such a result.

III. Conclusions

There are many views that could be stated at the conclusion of the study of the attitudes to foreign investment by China and India, the two Asian giants which have emerged with new attitudes to foreign investment. They may be tentatively stated as a series of propositions.

1. It is wrong to attribute the spurt in growth of the two economies to liberalization alone. The larger amount of investment that went into China went from Hong Kong and Taiwan into areas of China closest to these two essentially Chinese entities. Whether they are foreign investment or money circulated through these areas is uncertain. Likewise, the existing entrepreneurial class in India was given a boost through the New Industrial Policy in India and India's progress is due at least in part to the vigorous industry of Indian entrepreneurs in the new sectors of computer technology and biotechnology. Though studies by Western institutions like the OECD attribute the growth of the two states to liberalization of foreign investment regimes, this overstates the case and understates the restructuring of local industries and the impetus given to the emergence of new entrepreneurial classes through the adoption of appropriate policies. While it is an undoubted fact that foreign investment played a role, the contribution of the local entrepreneurial class should not be underestimated. If so, the case for liberalization is not overwhelming.
2. Consistent with its template based on neo-liberalism, the West believes that good things have flowed from the adoption of the template that was suggested by the institutions prescribing neo-liberal solutions. This has not been so. Neither state has abandoned its efforts at controlling the inflow of foreign investment which existed in the past though there has been relaxation of procedures to a significant extent and the elimination of controlled sectors. This is consistent with existing policy and should not be attributed to liberalization suggested from outside the two states.
3. The belief of some left wing commentators that China has adopted a neo-liberal solution while maintaining its totalitarian structure and that its success is due to this combination may not be accurate. It may be

true that the single-mindedness in adopting certain market-oriented solutions and the suppression of opposition or dealing with ensuing social problems are possible only in a state which lacks the rule of law. There is as yet no inclination on China's part to relax political control. Yet, it is far-fetched to suggest that China has adopted a neo-liberal path. Its liberalization programme has to be consistent with its socialist foundations. If it cannot be, schisms will appear in the party which would affect the progress of the programme of foreign investment-led economic development. In India's case, the existence of strong pressure groups that protect the interests of local businesses as well as strong socialist groups which are inimical to foreign investment will ensure that balances are kept.

4. The Indian experience shows that the issue of poverty must be addressed at the same time as relaxing rules on foreign investment so that more such investment flows could be attracted. The voting out of the previous government which had success with foreign investment indicates that in India, democratic processes will not permit a government to disregard the problems of the majority who are poor. Liberalization drives a wedge between the increasing poor and the diminishing elite groups which become richer. Living in gated complexes guarded against their own people is becoming a phenomenon both in India and China. The anger of the poor has to be assuaged in systems that purport to be egalitarian but promote such gross disparities in wealth. In West Bengal, meaningful measures are taken by the communist government to ensure that while attracting foreign investment, the interests of the rural poor are adequately catered for, thus ensuring that it is democratically returned to power at successive elections.
5. Neo-liberal prescriptions have been resisted by both states. The charge is made by left-wing commentators that China is successful because it is a totalitarian state which has adopted features of a market-orientated neo-liberalism. This may be a possible explanation. The explanation may explain why China is more successful in attracting foreign investment than India. But, the better explanation is that China is still committed to its socialist foundations. There are immutable foundations of policy in China and one of them is commitment to its socialist ideals. Both China and India will continue to adopt policies which they feel best ensure the achievement of their objectives. For this reason, they will ensure that there is sufficient regulatory space kept despite entering into treaty commitments for the protection of investments.

6. Care must be taken in the area of dispute settlement. Entanglement in dispute settlement processes that exist will not be in the interests of China and India. They will come out losers if they participate in them. It is best to provide adequate and effective local machinery for the settlement of foreign investment disputes. For this purpose, there is a great need to overhaul the rusty mechanism that exists in India which is slow and cumbersome, though based on principles that are understood in the West. In China, the judiciary has to become more effective and independent. The vestiges of a rule of law require to be maintained.

References

Alexander, Gregory, *Commodity and Propriety: Competing Visions of Property in American Legal Thought* (University of Chicago Press, 1997)

Baker, Mark B., 'Awakening the sleeping giant: India and foreign direct investment in the 21st century' (2005) 15 Indiana Int'l & Comp. L. Rev. 389

Bean, Vicki and Beauvais, Joel, 'The global fifth amendment: NAFTA's Investment protection and the misguided quest for an international "regulatory takings" doctrine' (2003) 78 NYULR 30

Chang, Ha-Joon, *Bad Samaritans: Rich Nations, Poor Policies and the Threat to the Developing World* (London: Random House, 2007)

Kicking Away the Ladder: Development Strategy in Historical Perspective (London: Anthem Press2005)

Chaze, Aron, *India: An Investor's Guide to the Next Economic Superpower* (Singapore: John Wiley, 2006)

CHEN Huiping, in Niewenhuys (ed.), *The Multilateral Agreement on Investment* (Dordrecht: Kluwer, 2001)

Coedès, George, *The Indianized States of South East Asia* (Honolulu: East–West Center Press, 1968)

'A direct instance of that cooperation is the joint bid for oil in Kazakhstan', *Straits Times*, Singapore, 9 June 2006

Investment Treaty News, 2 March 2007, available at http://www.iisd.org/pdf/ 2007/ itn_mar2_2007.pdf

Kelsey, Jane *Serving Whose Interests? The Political Economy of Trade in Services Agreements* (London: Routledge, 2008)

Kumar, Nagesh, *India's Emerging Multinationals* (London: Routledge, 2007)

LU Haitian, 'Migration of dirty industries in China', Ph.D. thesis, National University of Singapore, 2006

Nedelsky, Jennifer, *Private Property and the Limits of American Constitutionalism* (University of Chicago Press, 1990)

OECD, *Investment Policy Review, China: Progress and Reform Challenges* (2003)

Ong, Kingley and Baxter, Colin, 'A comparative study of the fundamental elements of Chinese and English company law' (1999) 48 ICLQ 88

Peerenboom, Randall, 'Competing conception of the rule of law in China', in Randall Peerenbohm (ed.), *Asian Discourses on the Rule of Law*, p. 112

'Let one hundred flowers bloom one hundred schools contend: Debating rule of law in China' (2002) 23 Mich. J. Int'l L. 471; Randall Peerenboom, *China Modernizes* (New York: Oxford University Press, 2007)

Putterman, Louis, 'The right to property in China: Shifting and unbundling ownership' (1996) *Economic Reform Today*

Ray, Aswini, 'Globalization and democratic governance: The Indian Experience', in Catarina Kinnvall and Kristina Jonsson (eds.), *Democratization in Asia: The Construction of Identity* (London: Routledge, 2002)

Sachdev, Rohit, 'Comparing the Legal Foundations of Foreign Investment in India and China' (2006) Columbia Bus. Law Rev. 167

Sachs, Jeffrey D. and Bajpai, Nirupam, 'Foreign direct investment in India: Issues and problems 5–8' (Harvard Inst. for Int'l Dev., Discussion Paper No. 759, 2000), available at http://www2.cid.harvard.edu/india/pdfs/759.pdf

Sauvant, Karl, 'New sources of FDI: The BRICs, outward FDI from Brazil, Russia, India and China' (2005) **5** *Journal of World Trade* 2005

SAW Swee-Hock (ed.), *ASEAN–China Relations: Realities and Prospects* (ISEAS, 2005)

Scheiderman, David, 'Property rights and regulatory innovation: Comparing constitutional cultures' (2006) 4 *I-CON*

Sen, Amartya, *The Argumentative Indian* (London: Allen Lane, 2005)

SHAN Wenhua, *The Legal Framework of EU–China Investment Relations* (Oxford, Hart Publishing, 2005)

'Towards a level playing field for foreign investment in China' (2002) **3** *Journal of World Investment and Trade* 327

SHEN Danyang, 'ASEAN–China FTA: Opportunities, modalities and prospects', in SAW Swee-Hock (ed.), *ASEAN–China Relations*

Smith, David, *The Dragon and the Elephant: China, India and the New World Order* (London: Profile Books, 2007)

Sornarajah, M., 'A coming crisis: Expansionary interpretations in investment treaty arbitrations' paper delivered at the Columbia-Sorborne Conference on Investment Treaty Arbitration, 4 April 2006

'A law for need or a law for greed? restoring the lost law in international foreign investment law' Keynote Address at the Van Moltke Symposium at the University of Amsterdam, February, 2006 (to be published in *International Agreements*)

'The international law on foreign investment in the age of globalization' (2002) 12 *Canadian Foreign Affairs* 202

'Towards an international antitrust law' (1984) *Indian Journal of International Law* 22

Underkuffler, Laura, *The Idea of Property: Its Meaning and Power* (Oxford University Press, 2003)

Van Harten, Gus, *Investment Treaty Arbitration and Public Law* (London: Oxford University Press, 2007)

Van Harten, Gus and Loughlin, Martin, 'Investment treaty arbitration as a species of global administrative law' (2006) **17** *European JIL* 121

WANG Jiangyu, 'Financial liberalization and regulation in East Asia: Lessons from financial crises and the Chinese experience of controlled liberalization' (2007) 41(1) *Journal of World Trade* 211

Wells, Louis T. and Ahmed, Rafiq, *Making Foreign Investment Safe* (New York: Oxford University Press, 2007)

YU Jinsong, 'Pre-establishment national treatment of foreign investment and China's countermeasures', in Henry Gao and Donald Lewis (eds.), *China's Participation in the WTO* (London: Cameron May, 2005)

5

China, India and WTO Law

JULIA YA QIN

I. Introduction

The establishment of the World Trade Organization (WTO) has transformed a mostly power-oriented world trading system under the General Agreement on Tariffs and Trade (GATT) into a mostly rule-oriented one. In this rule-oriented system, law, as opposed to power and diplomacy, serves as the anchor of international trade relations. The WTO claims broad jurisdiction over trade in goods, trade in services, and trade-related intellectual property rights, and its rules penetrate into the traditionally domestic regulatory space of sovereign nations more than those of any other international organization ever did. Furthermore, the WTO is equipped with a dispute settlement mechanism that features compulsory adjudication and binding decisions upon its 150-plus members. Since its inception, the WTO dispute settlement system has generated a growing body of jurisprudence that has become an important part of international law.

This article seeks to assess and compare the respective contributions of China and India to the development of WTO law. It does so by examining the practices of the two countries in the WTO rulemaking and adjudicatory processes. Although the two countries have very different backgrounds in their association with the world trading system – India has been inside the system since 1948, first as an original contracting party to the GATT and then an original member of the WTO, whereas China only acceded to the WTO in late 2001[1] – a comparison between the two can

[1] China was one of the twenty-three original contracting parties to the GATT, but never participated in GATT activities after the communist revolution in 1949. In March 1950, the ex-Chinese government then located in Taiwan withdrew China from the GATT, but the withdrawal was never recognized by Beijing. In 1986, China requested resumption of its original contracting party status in the GATT. China changed its application to accession after the establishment of the WTO. For background and analysis of the legal issues involved, see Ya Qin, 'China and GATT: Accession instead of resumption' (1993: April) 27(2) J. World Trade 77–98.

nevertheless be meaningful because of their many similarities. China and India are the two most populous countries on earth and are at a roughly comparable stage of economic development. Both are ancient civilizations with modern ambition; and both have embraced globalization and are fast rising as the new economic powers in the world.

A major purpose of this study is to gain from a comparative perspective a better understanding on the potential impact of China on the WTO system. Given that China is the largest transition economy under the rule of a communist party, its rapid rise as an economic powerhouse has caused many concerns around the world, including the fear that China may prove a disruptive force within the WTO system.[2] The result of this study shows that, contrary to such expectations, China has been mostly a 'system maintainer' rather than a 'system reformer'.[3]

An examination of WTO practices of China and India reveals that the two countries have behaved very differently in the world trade regime. While India has been one of the most active members in the WTO, China has remained rather passive in the WTO rulemaking and dispute settlement processes. As a result of its active participation, India has been able to exert much greater influence on the WTO system than China. In respect of rulemaking, India has emerged as one of the leading members in the Doha Round negotiation, which was launched by the WTO in 2001 as the forum for formulating new rules and norms in international trade. The Doha negotiation collapsed in July 2006 after the G-6 countries – the US, EU, Japan, Australia, Brazil and India – failed to bridge the differences between the developed and developing countries.[4] In the subsequent efforts to revive the Doha talks, India became one of the G-4 countries whose leadership will determine the ultimate fate of the Doha Round.[5] In contrast, China, the third largest trading nation in the world, has deliberately shunned any leadership position in the Doha

[2] See e.g., Richard Steinberg, 'Institutional implications of WTO accession for China', *Institute on Global Conflict and Cooperation, Working Papers* (February 1999) ('Predicting China's accession would cause "systems friction" in the WTO').

[3] See Margaret M. Pearson, 'China in Geneva: Lessons from the earliest years in WTO', in Alastair lain Johnston and Robert Ross (eds.), *New Directions in the Study of China's Foreign Policy* (Stanford University Press, 2006), pp. 242–75 ('Raising the question of whether China is a "system maintainer," a "system reformer," or a "revisionist power"').

[4] See 'WTO's Doha Round Talks Collapse, As G-6 ministerial ends in Acrimony', *BNA WTO Reporter*, 25 July 2006.

[5] See 'U.S. expects India to play greater role in coming months to help revive WTO talks', *BNA WTO Reporter*, 20 December 2006; 'Doha's future in doubt as G-4 talks collapse; U.S., EU blame Brazil, India', *BNA WTO Reporter*, 22 June 2007.

negotiations. In fact, China has been viewed as 'a marginal and largely silent player within the WTO', and has been repeatedly called upon to play a greater role.[6] Considering that India's share in world trade is less than one-fourth of that of China,[7] the contrast between the two countries appears even more striking.

Indeed, thus far the most significant impact of China on the world trading system remains the accession itself, which has integrated a giant economy into the liberal trading regime. As far as WTO law is concerned, however, China's influence has been limited mostly to the special terms of its accession. Unlike any other country that had previously acceded to the WTO, the accession of China was conditioned upon a large number of special terms that modify WTO rules when applied to China. These special terms either impose on China obligations that exceed the requirements of existing WTO agreements, or allow other members to deviate from WTO standards in dealing with Chinese exports. While some of these special terms are transitional with a built-in expiration, others are of unlimited duration. The making of China-specific rules represents a major departure from the fundamental WTO principle of nondiscrimination. To the extent such a departure cannot be justified by reasons consistent with WTO norms, the discriminatory terms cannot but undermine the integrity and effectiveness of the WTO legal system. Moreover, the member-specific rulemaking in the case of China set a precedent for the WTO system, which was followed, albeit to a lesser extent, in the accession of Vietnam.[8]

Although China resisted such discriminatory terms during the accession negotiations, it ultimately agreed to them. China's willingness to accept the discriminatory treatment contrasts with India's attitude towards potentially discriminatory practice. As will be discussed below, a majority of the WTO disputes brought by India involve charges of discriminatory practices, suggesting that India has been particularly vigilant about safeguarding the WTO principle of nondiscrimination.

[6] See 'A new approach to handling China', *Wall Street Journal*, 3 December 2005, at A2; 'The dragon's docile role in WTO', *Forbes*, 10 March 2006; 'Portman presses China on market access, IPR; urges China to be active in Doha talks', *BNA WTO Reporter*, 15 November 2005; 'U.S. again calls on China to play greater role in restarting WTO Trade talks', *BNA WTO Reporter*, 20 October 2006.

[7] In 2005, China's trade in goods and services totaled US$1,579 billion, whereas India's was US$338 billion. Source: WTO International trade statistics 2006, available at www.wto.org

[8] The terms of Vietnam's accession are set out in the 'Report of the Working Party on the Accession of Viet Nam', WT/ACC/VNM/48 (27 October 2006), available at www.wto.org. Vietnam's accession took effect on January 11 2007.

According to at least one commentator, the terms of China's accession were 'much more onerous than India would have ever accepted'.[9] Indeed, India even raised objection to the inclusion of some of the discriminatory terms in China's accession.[10]

A similar pattern of divergence between the two countries can be observed in WTO dispute settlement. Since its accession in December 2001, China has initiated a total of two WTO complaints and has yet to challenge specifically the discriminatory measures taken by other members against Chinese products. In the meantime, China has been sued eight times involving five sets of disputes; one of the disputes was settled before a panel was formed and the rest are currently pending.[11] When threatened with WTO litigation on several other occasions, China chose to compromise so as to prevent the launching of a formal dispute settlement proceeding. In comparison, India has been one of the top litigants in the WTO. Since the establishment of the WTO dispute settlement mechanism in 1995, India has initiated a total of 17 complaints and answered 19 complaints against it.[12] Many of the cases involving India raised important issues in WTO law and some have resulted in landmark WTO decisions.

The divergence between China and India in their WTO practices is evident. But what are the causes for such divergent behaviour? The paper identifies several major factors, including: (a) the level of experience and expertise in the WTO system; (b) the calculation of national economic and political interests; (c) domestic institutions; and (d) legal traditions and culture. While all these factors are variables, not all of them are susceptible to quick change. Given the existing differences between the two countries, therefore, it seems safe to say that, despite its growing economic clout, China is less likely to challenge the system's status quo as compared with India, and that China's impact on the WTO legal regime will remain limited at least for the foreseeable future.

The rest of the paper will proceed as follows. Section II focuses on China and WTO law. It will provide an overview of the special terms of China's accession and its post-accession practice in the WTO legal system. Section III turns to India, which will review India's role in the rulemaking and dispute settlement of the WTO and highlight some

[9] 'India–China trade relations: Not so happy a birthday', *Asia Source*, 11 December 2003, available at a website of the Asia Society www.asiasource.org/trade/seventeen.

[10] Interview with WTO Secretariat staff, Geneva, October 2003.

[11] Source: 'WTO dispute settlement – disputes by country – China', available at www.wto.org

[12] Source: 'WTO dispute settlement – disputes by country – India', available at www.wto.org

significant cases involving India. Section IV will identify and examine the major factors that are determinant of the divergent behaviour patterns of the two countries. Section V concludes.

II. China and WTO law

China submitted its application to join the GATT, the predecessor of the WTO, in 1986.[13] After an epic journey of fifteen years, China finally acceded to the WTO on 11 December 2001. During the prolonged application period, China observed the then-ongoing Uruguay Round negotiations and acquired much knowledge about the functions of the world trading system. However, most of its energy was consumed by the accession process, during which it accepted careful scrutiny by WTO members of all aspects of its domestic system relating to trade, and negotiated thousands of terms for its membership in the WTO. Hence, it was not until after the accession that China had the opportunity to engage fully in the WTO system. Nonetheless, since the special terms of China's accession modify WTO rules with respect to China trade, the impact of China on WTO law begins with these terms.

A. The China-specific rules

The terms of China's accession to the WTO are set out in the Protocol on the Accession of the People's Republic of China (the Protocol).[14] Like all other members of the WTO, China has undertaken two types of WTO legal obligations: market access obligations and rule obligations. Market access obligations are commitments of individual members to liberalize their trade in specific goods and services; as such, these obligations are country-specific and their contents vary from member to member. Rule obligations, on the other hand, are the obligations prescribed by WTO rules of conduct, which are set out in the Agreement Establishing the World Trade Organization (the WTO Agreement) and its various annexes (collectively, the WTO agreements).[15] These rules of conduct are uniform as all members should, in principle, be bound by the same set of rules. When a country accedes to the WTO, therefore, it is expected

[13] See 'History of China's accession to the WTO', in *WTO News*, Press/243, 17 September 2001, available at www.wto.org

[14] 'The Protocol on the Accession of the People's Republic of China', WT/L/432 (10 November 2001), available at www.wto.org

[15] All texts of the WTO agreements are available at www.wto.org

to make its own individual commitments on market access, but also to comply with the generally applicable WTO rules.

Unlike the case of other WTO accessions, however, the terms of China's accession include not only its market access commitments, which are extraordinarily extensive,[16] but also a large number of special rules that are applicable to China trade only.[17] These special rules can be divided into two general categories: (1) 'WTO-plus' provisions, which impose on China stricter disciplines than required by the WTO multilateral agreements; and (2) 'WTO-minus' provisions, which allow an importing member to use special protection against Chinese exports by deviating from, and lowering the standards of, WTO multilateral disciplines on trade remedies. In addition, there is another set of provisions in the Protocol that obligate China not to seek special and differential treatment of developing country Members.[18] Since the China accession protocol was made an integral part of the WTO Agreement,[19] these China-specific rules became part of WTO law, enforceable through the WTO dispute settlement mechanism.

[16] China agreed to bind all tariffs at the low statutory rates, a commitment uncommon among WTO members; its market access commitments on services were more comprehensive than most WTO members. For a comparative perspective on the scope and depth of China's market access commitments, see Nicholas R. Lardy, *Integrating China into the Global Economy* (Washington DC: Brookings Institution Press, 2002), pp. 79–80.

[17] Unlike other WTO protocols of accession, which typically include a standardized text setting out certain procedural matters and the goods and services schedules of the acceding member, the China Protocol consists of a main text of 17 sections of substantive provisions, 9 annexes (including China's goods and services schedules), and 143 paragraphs of substantive provisions incorporated by reference from the 'Report of the Working Party on the Accession of China', WT/MIN(01)/3 (10 November 2001) (WPR). Most of the 143 paragraphs so incorporated contain rule obligations of China. See *generally* Julia Ya Qin, '"WTO-Plus" obligations and their implications for the WTO legal system: An appraisal of the China Accession Protocol' (2003) 37(3) J. World Trade 483. The only other exception is Vietnam. Although Vietnam's accession protocol uses the standardized text, it incorporates by reference 70 paragraphs from the 'Report of the Working Party on the Accession of Viet Nam' that contain special rule obligations of Vietnam. See 'Report of the Working Party on the Accession of Viet Nam', para. 527.

[18] For example, China undertakes to eliminate all export subsidies upon accession, thereby foregoing the right it may otherwise enjoy under Article 27.2(b) of the Agreement on Subsidies and Countervailing Measures (the SCM Agreement), which permits developing country Members to delay such elimination till 1 January 2003. See Protocol, section 10.3. Additionally, China has undertaken not to invoke Articles 27.8, 27.9 and 27.13 of the SCM Agreement, which grant certain special treatment to developing country Members. See WPR paras. 171–4, which were incorporated into the Protocol.

[19] Protocol, section 1.2.

1. 'WTO-plus' rules

The China Protocol contains numerous 'WTO-plus' provisions, and the major ones provide legal obligations falling into the following categories:

(a) *Obligations to practice market economy.* Although WTO rules are constructed with market economy assumptions, the WTO Agreement does not prescribe any particular economic system for its members.[20] While most WTO members practise a market economy, they are not legally bound to do so under the WTO Agreement. The China Protocol, by contrast, creates certain systemic obligations that are unprecedented in WTO/GATT history. For instance, China is required to let market forces determine all domestic prices except for a few specified categories, and may not extend price controls beyond these specified categories except in exceptional circumstances and with notification to the WTO.[21] It must completely liberalize foreign trading rights,[22] and must not influence, directly or indirectly, commercial decisions on the part of state-owned or state-invested enterprises.[23] As a result of these obligations, whether China practises market economy is no longer a mere matter of domestic policy; instead, it has become a matter of WTO law.

(b) *Obligations concerning domestic governance.* China undertook a number of special commitments concerning domestic governance, including transparency, judicial review and uniform administration of law, that exceeds the requirements of the WTO agreements.[24] For instance, the Protocol requires China to provide a reasonable period for public comment on 'all laws, regulations and measures' pertaining to WTO matters before their implementation[25] and to translate all of such laws, regulations and measures into one of the three official languages of the WTO within 90 days of their

20 For example, Cuba, despite its non-market economy, is an original member of the WTO. In the prior accessions of transition economies (former centrally planned economies undergoing transformation to market economies), the acceding countries were typically required to confirm the status of their economic reforms, but none was obligated to undertake substantive obligations to practise a market economy. See Qin, '"WTO-plus" obligations and their implications for the WTO legal system: An appraisal of the China Accession Protocol', at 504.

21 See Protocol, section 9. 22 See Protocol, section 5.1.

23 See WPR, para. 46, which was incorporated into the Protocol.

24 See Qin, '"WTO-Plus" obligations', at 491–9, for more detailed discussion.

25 Protocol, section 2(C)(2). Exceptions are given to laws and regulations involving national security or publication of which would impede law enforcement.

implementation.[26] No such general obligations exist under the WTO agreements.

(c) *Obligations on foreign investment.* Existing WTO disciplines do not apply to foreign direct investment except for measures directly affecting trade in goods or services.[27] Efforts to conclude a comprehensive investment agreement within the WTO framework have failed, thanks partly to the opposition of developing countries. The China Protocol, by contrast, prescribes major investment obligations that are not part of the WTO agreements. For instance, China may not condition government approval of foreign investment projects upon the existence of competing domestic suppliers or upon any performance requirement, including transfer of technology and the conduct of research and development in China.[28] Furthermore, foreign investors and foreign-invested enterprises are entitled to national treatment with respect to all conditions affecting their production and sales in China.[29]

(d) *Obligation to eliminate export tariffs.* While lowering import tariffs is an essential part of the GATT obligations, the WTO has not imposed similar disciplines on export tariffs, although the use of quotas or quantitative restrictions on export is generally prohibited.[30] Consequently, WTO members remain free to levy tariffs on their exports, which is useful when they wish to limit exports to ensure supply for domestic production or to conserve natural resources or for any other reason. Departing from this general norm, however, the Protocol requires China to 'eliminate all taxes and charges applied to exports' except for those specifically provided in Annex 6 of the Protocol.[31] Annex 6 contains a list of eighty-four types of products with a maximum export duty rate identified for each. China promised not to raise the maximum rates except under exceptional circumstances and, if such circumstances occur, to consult with affected members prior to raising the rates.[32]

(e) *Transitional reviews.* The Protocol establishes a special transitional review mechanism to examine China's implementation of its WTO obligations.[33] Under this mechanism, China is subject to annual

[26] WPR, para. 334, which was incorporated into the Protocol.
[27] See Agreement on Trade-Related Investment Measures (TRIMS); General Agreement on Trade in Services (GATS).
[28] Protocol, section 7(3). [29] Protocol, section 3. [30] GATT, art. XI.
[31] Protocol, section 11(3). [32] Protocol, Note to Annex 6.
[33] Protocol, section 18.

reviews in the first eight years of its accession, and an additional review by the tenth year. These compliance reviews are separate from, and in addition to, trade policy reviews conducted by the WTO on all members at regular intervals.[34] No other WTO member is subject to such a special scrutiny for compliance.

2. 'WTO-minus' rules

The 'WTO-minus' provisions of the Protocol provide a set of special trade remedies that can be used against China products exclusively. Trade remedies refer to antidumping, anti-subsidy and safeguard measures used by an importing member to remedy injuries caused by imports to its domestic industries. In contrast with the 'WTO-plus' rules, which raise the bar for China in the direction of enhancing WTO disciplines, the 'WTO-minus' provisions of the Protocol lower the bar for all other WTO members by relaxing existing WTO disciplines on trade remedies when applied to Chinese products. While the China-specific provisions on antidumping and safeguards will expire after a certain period of time, those on anti-subsidy measures are of an indefinite duration.

a. Special antidumping rules The Protocol allows an importing member to treat China as a 'non-market economy' (NME) for antidumping purposes for 15 years from the date of accession.[35] This provision makes it easier for the importing member to impose antidumping duties on Chinese products. Under WTO law, dumping occurs when a product is exported at less than its normal value; and the importing country can levy an antidumping duty on an dumped product if it causes or threatens material injury to its domestic industry. The normal value of a product is generally established by referring to its domestic price in the exporting country.[36] When the exporting country is an NME, however, WTO law recognizes that 'a strict comparison with domestic prices in such a country may not always be appropriate'.[37] In practice, many importing countries, including the United States and the EU, have used the prices of like products produced in a third-country or in their own country as the base for determining the normal value of products from

[34] The WTO conducted the first trade policy review of China in 2006. See 'Trade Policy Review, Report by the Secretariat', WT/TPR/S/161 Rev.1 (28 June 2006) (TPR Report), available at www.wto.org. As the third largest trading nation, China is now subject to a trade policy review every two years.

[35] Protocol, section 15. [36] GATT art. VI:1.

[37] GATT *ad* art. VI, note 2, para. 1.

NMEs. Using this methodology generally results in affirmative determinations of dumping and higher dumping margins, since the importing country typically picks a surrogate country where the prices of like products are higher than that in the targeted NME.[38]

From the outset, WTO law has recognized the need for using NME methodologies when the exporting country 'has a complete or substantially complete monopoly of its trade and where all domestic prices are fixed by the State'.[39] This definition, however, clearly does not include a transition economy in which the state no longer has a complete monopoly of foreign trade and fixes all domestic prices. Consistent with this understanding, none of the transition economies that had acceded to the WTO before China was made subject to NME treatment in their respective protocols of accession,[40] although in practice some WTO members have continued to treat selected transition economies as NMEs without authorization of any WTO provision.[41]

The China Protocol has changed WTO law by authorizing the application of NME methodologies to the largest transition economy in the world,[42] and has thereby provided a certain legitimacy to the questionable practice of treating other transition economy members as NMEs. Despite the fact that China is required by the Protocol to adopt specific market economy practices, the importing WTO member may use NME methodologies against Chinese products until 2016, unless the Chinese producer can 'clearly show that market economy conditions prevail in the industry

[38] See Patrick A. Messerlin, 'China in the WTO: Antidumping and safeguards' (14 December 2002), Table 7 (statistics based on examination of 141 US antidumping cases (1995–1998) and 67 EC cases (1995–1997)), available at www.siteresources.worldbank.org; Chad Bown and Rachel McCulloch, 'U.S. trade policy toward China: Discrimination and its implications' (June 2005), Table 2 (showing that in 23 multi-country antidumping investigations made in the United States in 1990–2003, the mean (median) antidumping duty facing China is 177.38% (118.41%) as opposed to the mean (median) duty of 36.41% (32.23%) facing all other investigated countries), available at SSRN: //http://ssrn.com/abstract=757124.

[39] GATT *ad* art. VI, note 2, para. 1.

[40] Ten transition economy countries acceded to the WTO before China: Mongolia, Bulgaria, Kyrgyz Republic, Latvia, Estonia, Georgia, Croatia, Albania, Lithuania and Moldova. Information on the terms of their respective accessions is available at www.wto.org

[41] For example, the EU listed Mongolia, Kyrgyztan, Georgia, Albania and Moldova as non-market economies in Council Regulation (EC) No. 2238/2000 of 9 October 2000, amending Council Regulation (EC) No. 384/96 on protection against dumped imports from countries not members of the European Community.

[42] Vietnam, which acceded to the WTO on 11 January 2007, has been made subject to similar special antidumping rules as China, except that the NME treatment period for Vietnam is 12 years rather than 15 years. See 'Report of the Working Party on the Accession of Viet Nam', para. 255.

producing the product'.[43] Since the concept of 'market economy' is not defined by the WTO and the importing member has the right to determine under its own law whether China has become a 'market economy',[44] the NME provisions of the Protocol are practically non-justiciable at the WTO. As long as China is considered an NME, the importing member can easily substitute the high price in a surrogate country for the low price in China in determining the normal value of Chinese products. It should therefore come as no surprise that China has been by far the most frequently targeted country for antidumping actions.[45]

b. Special anti-subsidy rules Parallel to the special antidumping rules, the Protocol also permits an importing member to use NME methodologies to calculate Chinese subsidies. Under WTO law, a member may impose a countervailing duty on an imported product to offset foreign government subsidies received by the producer, or initiate an anti-subsidy multilateral proceeding at the WTO, if the subsidized product has caused adverse effects on its domestic industry. In general, the existence of a subsidy and the amount of the subsidy given is to be determined by reference to the marketplace benchmarks prevailing in the subsidizing country.[46] In the case of China, the Protocol authorizes members to use 'terms and conditions prevailing outside China' as the benchmarks for calculating Chinese subsidies.[47] Unlike the special antidumping rules, this authorization does not have a built-in expiration date. Consequently, a member may continue to use surrogate prices in anti-subsidy actions against China even after it must cease to do so in antidumping actions.

In addition to the NME treatment, the Protocol contains other special rules on Chinese subsidies. One such rule concerns government subsidies to state-owned enterprises (SOEs). Under WTO law, a domestic subsidy is actionable (i.e., subject to countervailing duties or WTO

[43] Protocol, section 15(a)(ii).

[44] Protocol, section 15(d). If China can establish under the national law of a WTO member that it is a market economy (or that market conditions prevail in a particular industry or sector), the NME provision of the Protocol will no longer apply (or no longer apply to that industry or sector). *Ibid.*

[45] For the period from 1995 through 2006, a total of 1,941 antidumping measures were taken by WTO members, of which 375, or nearly 20%, were against Chinese products, followed by a distant second of 136 against South Korea. Source: WTO antidumping statistics, available at www.wto.org.

[46] SCM Agreement, art. 14.

[47] Protocol, section 15(b).

multilateral proceedings) only if it is granted to a specific enterprise or industry or a specific group of enterprises or industries.[48] This rule is based on the theory that a domestic subsidy given to numerous recipients across different industries tends to have minimal effect on trade. WTO subsidy rules contain standards on how to determine whether a subsidy is specific. The China Protocol modifies such standards by adding an ownership criterion for defining specificity. It provides that government subsidies to SOEs will be viewed automatically as 'specific' if SOEs are the predominant recipients, or receive disproportionately large amounts, of such subsidies.[49] Under this criterion, SOE subsidies in China are automatically actionable regardless of whether they are granted to numerous SOE recipients across different industries. This Protocol provision is the only one within the WTO legal framework that targets state ownership for trade remedies.[50]

If the SOE-subsidy rule can be viewed as reflecting a WTO policy preference for private ownership, then another provision of the Protocol provides its antithesis. Under WTO subsidy rules, a domestic subsidy granted by a developing country member is not actionable at the WTO multilateral proceedings if the subsidy is directly linked to a privatization programme.[51] This rule is designed to encourage privatization in developing countries whose economies tend to rely on SOEs more than developed economies. The Protocol, however, explicitly precludes China from invoking this provision,[52] even though China has more SOEs than most other developing countries and has been actively engaged in privatization.

Given their indefinite duration, these special anti-subsidy rules may affect China trade for a long time to come. Although thus far China has not been subject to many countervailing investigations[53] – partly due to the fact that the United States, the largest user of countervailing measures, did not apply its countervailing law to NMEs until recently – the trend is

[48] SCM Agreement, arts. 1.2 and 2. [49] Protocol, section 10.2.

[50] For detailed discussion, see Julia Ya Qin, 'WTO regulation of subsidies to state-owned enterprises (SOEs): A critical appraisal of the China Accession Protocol' (2004) 7(4) J. Int'l Econ. Law 863.

[51] SCM Agreement, art. 27.13. The exception is subject to the conditions that the subsidy is notified to the WTO and is granted for a limited period, and that the SOE involved is eventually privatized.

[52] WPR, para. 171, which was incorporated into the Protocol.

[53] From 1995 through 2006, a total of six countervailing investigations were initiated against Chinese products, of which five were taken by Canada since 2004, and one by the US in 2006. See WTO subsidy statistics, available at http://www.wto.org.

changing. In 2007, the US reversed its longtime policy and began to launch countervailing investigations on Chinese products.[54] In addition, the United States and Mexico have brought subsidy complaints against China at the WTO dispute settlement.[55] Hence, it is merely a matter of time before members begin to utilize the special subsidy provisions of the Protocol.

c. Special safeguards The Protocol contains a set of special safeguard provisions that are separate from and in addition to the WTO safeguard mechanism. The special safeguards can be invoked against any Chinese product for 12 years from the date of China's accession till December 2013.[56]

Under the WTO safeguard mechanism, a member may temporarily 'escape' its WTO obligations and restrict the import of a particular product if there is a sudden increase in such import that causes or threatens serious injury to its domestic producers.[57] The safeguard mechanism is based on the following rationale: when imports rapidly displace domestic competing products, it can be difficult for the importing country to absorb the adjustment costs associated with the displacement; and the economic, social and political repercussions of the displacement may outweigh the economic benefits realized by the increase of imports. Through temporary restrictions on imports, safeguard measures provide the affected domestic industry a breathing space either to regain its competitiveness or to phase out its existence in an orderly fashion. Unlike antidumping and anti-subsidy measures, which are designed to remedy 'unfair trade practices' of dumping and subsidy, safeguard measures deal with import surges in 'fair' trade. The use of safeguard measures, therefore, is subject to strict WTO disciplines. A member invoking safeguards must meet the conditions set out in the WTO safeguard

[54] See Decisions of U.S. Department of Commerce in 'Coated free sheet paper from the People's Republic of China: amended preliminary affirmative countervailing duty determination', 72 Fed. Reg. 17484 (9 April 2007); 'Notice of initiation of countervailing duty investigation: Circular welded carbon quality steel pipe from the People's Republic of China', 72 Fed. Reg. 36668 (5 July 2007); 'Notice of initiation of countervailing duty investigation: Light-walled rectangular pipe and tube from the People's Republic of China', 72 Fed. Reg. 40281 (24 July 2007); and 'Laminated woven sacks from the People's Republic of China: Initiation of countervailing duty investigation', 72 Fed. Reg. 40839 (25 July 2007).

[55] See 'China – Certain Measures Granting Refunds, Reductions or Exemptions from Taxes and Other Payments', WT/DS358/1 (7 February 2007) (Request for consultations by the United States); WT/DS359/1 (28 February 2007) (Request for consultations by Mexico).

[56] Protocol, section 16.

[57] See GATT art. XIX; Agreement on Safeguards (the Safeguard Agreement), art. 2.

agreement, including the standards for import increase, serious injury, and the causal link between the import increase and the injury.[58] All safeguard measures must be applied on a nondiscriminatory basis, i.e., to all imports of the product in question, irrespective of their origin.[59] And members may not circumvent the nondiscrimination requirement by seeking voluntary export restraints (VERs) or similar arrangements.[60]

The Protocol takes a general exception to the WTO safeguard discipline. Contrary to the nondiscrimination requirement, the Protocol permits WTO members to selectively apply safeguards against products of Chinese origin. Using the concept of 'market disruption,' the Protocol set lower standards for establishing injury and its causal link with import increase. When market disruption is alleged, China is required to take VERs to remedy the situation.[61] Furthermore, the Protocol creates a novel 'trade diversion' safeguard that completely discards the injury requirement of the WTO safeguard discipline. Under this provision, a WTO member may apply safeguard measures against China if it considers there is a threat of 'significant diversions of trade into its market' as a result of another member's safeguard measures against Chinese products.[62] In other words, the member invoking the trade diversion safeguard does not need to demonstrate any injury or threat of injury to its domestic industry. Instead, so long as it believes that there may be a significant diversion of Chinese products into its market as a result of safeguard measures taken by another member, it can invoke the safeguard to restrict Chinese imports. To date, the special safeguard provisions have been used more than a dozen times.[63] It appears that more countries are poised to take advantage of these provisions.[64]

[58] See Safeguard Agreement, arts. 2, 3, 4, 5, 7.

[59] *Ibid.* art. 2.2 [60] *Ibid.* art. 11. [61] Protocol, section 16.

[62] Protocol, section 16.8.

[63] According to notifications received by the WTO, the following members have initiated more than a dozen proceedings under Section 16 of the China Protocol: United States, Canada, India, Colombia, Peru, Ecuador, Turkey and Chinese Taipei. See WTO G/SG/N/16/* documents, available at www.wto.org. In addition, EU and Poland were reported to have initiated investigations under section 16 of the China Protocol. See 'EU starts safeguard probe on China', *China Daily Online*, 21 July 2003; 'Poland signals plans to impose safeguard on Chinese footwear imports, seeks talks', *BNA WTO Reporter*, 29 January 2004.

[64] For instance, Brazil adopted administrative regulations in 2005 introducing special safeguard measures on Chinese products based on Section 16 of the Protocol. See Welber Barral and Carolina Munhos, 'The recent Brazilian regulation on safeguards against Chinese imports', available at www.brazilinfocenter.org/pdfs/november2005.pdf.

d. Special textile safeguard In addition to the special safeguards discussed above, the Protocol provides a separate safeguard that is exclusively applicable to textile and clothing products of Chinese origin. Textile trade is one of the hardest-fought areas in WTO/GATT history. For decades, it remained outside GATT disciplines and was governed instead by a global quota system under the Multifibre Arrangement (MFA). In 1995, the WTO Agreement on Textiles and Clothing (ATC) replaced the MFA, setting a 10-year transitional period to end the quota system.[65] As of 1 January 2005, textile trade became fully integrated into the WTO liberal trade regime.

The Protocol, however, provides an exception to the liberalization of textile trade. It allows a WTO member to continue to impose quotas on Chinese textiles if it 'believed' that imports of Chinese textile and apparel products 'were, due to market disruption, threatening to impede the orderly development of trade in these products'.[66] Under this provision, so long as the importing member can provide data that, in its own view, showed the existence or threat of market disruption and the role of Chinese products in that disruption, it may cap the Chinese imports in question at an annual increase of no greater than 7.5 per cent (6 per cent for wool products). The textile safeguard is valid till 31 December 2008.

The textile safeguard has already been invoked many times. Following the expiration of the global quota system at the end of 2004, Argentina, Turkey, the EU and the United States resorted to the textile safeguard against dozens of Chinese textile products, citing anticipated or actual import surges of such products.[67] China eventually entered into bilateral agreements with the United States and the EU respectively, which set limits on its exports of certain textile products to these markets for the next few years.[68]

65 The ATC established a transitional safeguard mechanism, which allowed an importing member to apply safeguard measures against a particular exporting member. The transitional safeguard mechanism expired at the end of the ten-year transitional period. See ATC, art. 6.

66 The textile safeguard is set out in WPR, para. 242, which was incorporated into the Protocol.

67 See 'Post-quota textile trade starts to take shape', *Bridges Weekly Trade News Digest*, 26 January 26 2005; 'Chinese textile exports surge; US, EU to invoke textile safeguard?' *Bridges Weekly Trade News Digest*, 6 April 2005.

68 See 'EU–China Textile Agreement', 10 June 2005, available at http://ec.europa.eu/comm/external_relations/china/intro/memo05_201.htm; Memorandum of Understanding Between the Governments of the United States of America and the People's Republic of China Concerning Trade in Textile and Apparel Products, 8 November 2005, available at www.ustr.gov

It should be noted that Chinese textile products are currently subject to the textile safeguard as well as the special safeguard rules discussed above. An importing member may choose to use safeguard measures under either mechanism, but may not apply both types of measures to the same product at the same time.[69] After expiration of the textile safeguard at the end of 2008, Chinese textile products will remain subject to the special safeguards which will not expire till December 2013.

3. Impact of the China Protocol on WTO law

The China Protocol sets forth the terms for the integration of a gigantic transition economy into the world trading system. As such, it is a historic document. But what is its impact on WTO law, given that numerous Protocol provisions deviate from the general norms of the WTO agreements?

First of all, the China Protocol broke the uniformity of WTO rules of conduct and set a precedent for country-specific rulemaking in the WTO. The uniformity of WTO rules of conduct is considered one of the major achievements in the Uruguay Round. For historical reasons, the GATT as an institution had maintained a somewhat fragmented rule structure, under which the rule obligations of its contracting parties could differ.[70] This structure, known as 'GATT à la carte,' had rendered the GATT system notoriously complex and confusing. The Uruguay Round adopted the 'single package understanding' which required WTO members to accept all WTO rules of conduct without individual reservations or country-specific exceptions.[71] The resulting uniformity

[69] WPR, para. 242(g).

[70] Under GATT, each contracting party was obligated to apply Part II of the GATT Agreement only to the fullest extent not inconsistent with its domestic legislation existing at the time of its joining the GATT. A country acceding to GATT might be subject to special terms under its protocol of accession. More significantly, a number of side agreements negotiated under GATT applied only to the contracting parties that opted to abide by them.

[71] The Plurilateral Agreements attached as Annex 4 of the WTO Agreement apply only to members that have separately accepted them. It should be noted that there have been proposals to revise the 'single package' approach so as to allow a group of WTO members to negotiate and subscribe to more advanced rules in selected areas. It should be pointed out, however, that this "side agreement" approach is fundamentally different from country-specific rulemaking in that the rules of a side agreement are generally applicable to all members that accept the rules, whereas country-specific rulemaking targets a specific member only.

of WTO rules has improved the transparency and efficacy of the multilateral disciplines, making the WTO a mostly rule-based institution, as opposed to the power-oriented GATT. The uniformity of WTO rules, however, has ended with the China Protocol. Following the precedent of China, a set of special rules has also been made for Vietnam in its accession to the WTO.[72] As a result, a significant portion of world trade is now subject to country-specific norms.

Next, the China Protocol created certain new concepts and norms that can have either positive or negative implications for the WTO system. Generally speaking, the 'WTO-plus' norms may have a positive impact on WTO law. For instance, the market economy obligations, which are the first such obligations under WTO law, provide some content for the concept of 'market economy', which is an undefined but vital notion underlying WTO disciplines. The additional obligations on transparency and other aspects of domestic governance promote the rule of law and ensure more effective implementation of WTO disciplines in China. On the other hand, the norms created by the 'WTO-minus' provisions, such as the novel 'trade diversion' safeguard, the revival of VERs, and treating a transition economy as NME for anti-dumping and countervailing purposes, may have a negative impact on WTO law because they serve to weaken the existing WTO disciplines on trade remedies.

In the final analysis, all China-specific rules of the Protocol derogate from the WTO principle of nondiscrimination, which is the cornerstone of the multilateral trading system. The WTO-minus provisions allow a member to treat China less favourably than any other member with respect to trade remedies, which directly contradicts the most-favoured-nation treatment (MFN) requirements of the WTO agreements.[73] While the WTO-plus rules do not technically violate specific MFN clauses,[74] they depart from the nondiscrimination principle by imposing on China obligations not required of any other member.

A derogation from the nondiscrimination principle may be justified if it is based on a legitimate reason, such as ensuring the effective functioning of WTO multilateral disciplines. Considering that China is the

[72] Report of the Working Party on the Accession of Viet Nam.

[73] E.g., GATT Art. I:1; Safeguard Agreement, art. 2.2.

[74] The MFN clauses of the WTO agreements generally require a member to treat all other members equally with respect to the matters specified in the clauses. See e.g., GATT Art. I:1. Since the WTO-plus obligations are that of China only, they do not give rise to the issue of how other members treat China under the MFN clauses.

largest transition economy which retains certain non-market elements that may be incompatible with market-based WTO rules, some of the special rules addressing concerns over the Chinese system, including the obligations to practice market economy and to enhance domestic rule of law, may well be justifiable. However, not all of the China-specific rules can be explained by such systemic concerns. For instance, it would be far-fetched to suggest that the transitional nature of China's economy has anything to do with its obligations to liberalize investment or to eliminate export tariffs when such obligations are not even part of WTO disciplines. Although the special trade remedy rules purportedly address adverse trade effects caused by the non-market elements of the Chinese system, their designs cannot be fully explained by that rationale. For instance, why would the need to offset adverse trade effects caused by Chinese exports warrant a trade diversion safeguard that is not based on any injury test? Why should Chinese textile products be singled out for an additional special safeguard when the textiles and clothing industry is one of the most market-oriented in China?[75] And what is the justification for treating China as an NME for countervailing purposes on a permanent basis?

Significantly, neither the Protocol, nor the accompanying Working Party Report or any other publicly available WTO document has articulated any rationale for the China-specific rules. The lack of justification for rules that derogate from the principle of nondiscrimination cannot but compromise the integrity of WTO law and undermine the credibility of the WTO as a rule-based system.

Furthermore, the China Protocol has left major gaps and inconsistencies in WTO law. Because the Protocol does not always clarify the relationship between its provisions and the WTO agreements, it is unclear how the many China-specific obligations should be interpreted in the context of WTO treaties. For example, it is uncertain whether the general exceptions under GATT and GATS should apply to the various WTO-plus obligations, such as the obligations to liberalize trading rights, to eliminate export tariffs, and to provide national treatment to all foreign investors, since the Protocol fails to specify how these

[75] China's textiles and clothing industry went through a major structural reform in the 1990s. As a result, many state-owned enterprises went bankrupt and the industry became more privatized than many other sectors. As of 2005, the industry was 87% owned by private capital and 13% owned by the state. See 'MOFCOM: China's textiles and clothing industry in the era of liberalization', available at http://eu2.mofcom.gov.cn/aarticle/chinanews/ 200509/20050900352110.html.

WTO-plus provisions relate to the basic WTO disciplines in GATT and GATS. The Protocol also contains some poorly drafted provisions that create ambiguities and inconsistencies within WTO law. A salient example is Paragraph 18 of the Working Party Report, which was incorporated into the Protocol, that requires China to 'provide the same treatment to Chinese enterprises, including foreign-funded enterprises, and foreign enterprises and individuals in China'. As worded, this obligation does not have any qualification on its scope of application, which could not have been intended by the Chinese government. Moreover, it would prevent China from granting foreign entities treatment more favourable than that accorded to its own nationals, which is not only inconsistent with the requirement of typical national treatment clauses of the WTO agreements, but also contradicts other parts of the Working Party Report.[76] When such Protocol provisions are involved in WTO disputes, as some of them already have been,[77] it would be up to the WTO tribunals to fill the gaps and to reconcile the inconsistencies. While a certain degree of 'gap filling' can be expected of any adjudication system, major gaps and inconsistencies such as these may require the WTO judiciary to create norms that do not have a clear basis in WTO treaties, a function inappropriate for the WTO dispute settlement procedure.[78]

As explained elsewhere, the reason why the *ad hoc* and unprincipled rulemaking could take place in the case of China stems from a loophole in the WTO accession regime.[79] Currently, the WTO Agreement permits a country to accede to the WTO on terms to be agreed between it and the WTO, but places no limit on the terms to be so agreed.[80] As a result, the terms of accession for a particular applicant may include not only market access commitments on trade in goods and services, but also rules of conduct specific to the applicant country. In practice, the market access terms are bilaterally negotiated between the applicant and its major trading partners. Such negotiations are necessarily driven by the

[76] For instance, Para. 17 of the Working Party Report notes that any commitment of China to provide nondiscriminatory treatment to Chinese enterprises and foreign enterprises and individuals 'would not prejudice China's rights under the GATS'. The scope of GATS national treatment clauses is subject to various limitations.

[77] See, e.g., 'China – Measures Affecting Trading Rights and Distribution Services for Certain Publications and Audiovisual Entertainment Products' (DS 363).

[78] The Dispute Settlement Understanding, art. 3.2, specifically mandates that the dispute settlement procedure may not add to or diminish the existing rights and obligations of WTO members.

[79] See Qin, '"WTO-Plus" Obligations'.

[80] WTO Agreement, art. XII.

latter's export interests on the one hand and domestic protectionist interests on the other. In the case of China, many of the special rules were demanded by the United States during its bilateral negotiations with China.[81] Although China had previously resisted any discriminatory terms at the multilateral meetings of the WTO accession working party,[82] it eventually yielded to the US demand during the bilateral negotiations.[83] The bilaterally agreed terms were subsequently adopted, almost verbatim, by the China Protocol.

B. Post-accession practice

1. Implementation of Protocol obligations

China has shown a mixed record in implementing its Protocol obligations. While it has met substantially all of its market access commitments in goods and services – a major portion of its Protocol obligations, it has not fully complied with its special rule obligations of the Protocol.[84]

With respect to the WTO-plus obligations, China has implemented some, but delayed and even resisted others. For example, China has stayed the course of its economic reform and liberalized trading rights six months ahead of the Protocol schedule.[85] On the other hand, it has failed to comply with the Protocol requirement that it publish in a designated official journal all of its laws, regulations and measures pertaining to trade before their implementation and to translate all such laws, regulations and measures into one of the three official languages of

[81] See Agreement on Market Access Between the People's Republic of China and the United States of America, 15 November 1999. Source: Office of US Trade Representative (on file with the author).

[82] See Jeffrey Gertler, 'The process of China's Accession to the World Trade Organization', in F. Abbott (ed.), *China in the World Trading System: Defining the Principles of Engagement* (The Hague; Boston: Kluwer Law International, 1998) p. 65, at p. 71.

[83] The high-handed negotiating tactics deployed by the US Trade Representative in the bilateral negotiation were widely reported. See e.g., 'To brink and back: in historic pact, U.S. opens way for China to finally join WTO', *Wall Street Journal*, 16 November 1999, at A1; 'Roller-coaster ride' to an off-again, on-again trade pact', *The Washington Post*, 16 November 1999, at A26; 'The first lady of trade: Woman in the news Charlene Barshefsky: The US trade representative was praised after China's accession to the WTO', *Financial Times (London)*, 27 November 1999, p. 11.

[84] For a comprehensive review by the WTO of China's trade law and practice in the post-accession era up to 2006, see 'Trade policy review, Report by the Secretariat'.

[85] In accordance with the Protocol requirement that China fully liberalize trading rights within three years after accession, China amended its Foreign Trade Law to implement this obligation, effective 1 July 2004.

the WTO within 90 days of their implementation.[86] This failure, however, is hardly surprising given the extraordinary burden imposed by this obligation.[87] Also, China substantially delayed its notification of government subsidies, including subsidies to SOEs, despite the specific requirement of the Protocol and repeated requests by other members.[88] The single WTO-plus obligation that China has openly resisted is the transitional review mechanism. Although it has accepted the annual exercise, China has refused to provide written answers to questions posed by other members.[89] The transitional review mechanism is perceived in China as a matter of national humiliation, and has led to highly acrimonious behaviour of the Chinese delegation.[90]

With respect to the WTO-minus rules, China has shown a tendency to rely on unilateral and bilateral means to mitigate the adverse effects of such rules. In countering the special antidumping rules, for example, China has been actively seeking recognition of its market economy status (MES) through diplomatic efforts. Thus far, it has secured MES in more than seventy countries,[91] including some of its important trading partners, such as Australia, Brazil, South Korea, the ASEAN countries and Switzerland, although similar efforts have not succeeded in the United States and the EU. The government has encouraged coordination among domestic producers in their pricing strategies and in responding to antidumping charges abroad.[92] In addition, China has aggressively pursued its own antidumping actions and has become one of the top

[86] As late as March 2006, the State Council was still instructing its ministries and local governments to notify their trade-related regulations to the Ministry of Commerce so as to enable their timely publication in the designated official journal. See 'State Council Notice concerning further implementation of the transparency provisions of the WTO Protocol on China's accession (30 March 2006), Guobanfa 2006 No. 23' (in Chinese), www.law-lib.com/law/ law_view.asp?id=154087

[87] Given the large number of laws, regulations and measures pertaining to trade issued by the Chinese central and local governments each year, it may take months for the central government to collect all relevant rules, let alone to translate them into foreign languages within 90 days. Extraordinary WTO-plus obligations such as this had little chance of being fulfilled.

[88] China did not make a full notification on subsidies as required by the Protocol until 13 April 2006. See G/SCM/N/123/CHN (April 13 2006), available at www.wto.org.

[89] See e.g., 'WTO: China's Refusal to Answer Quad Queries Shuts Down Compliance Review Session', *BNA International Trade Reporter*, 26 September 2002.

[90] See Pearson, 'China in Geneva', at pp. 250–1.

[91] Not all these countries have antidumping laws or actively use antidumping measures.

[92] See e.g., 'As China's Trade clout grows, so do price-fixing accusations', *Wall Street Journal*, 10 February 2006; Scott Kennedy, 'The price of competition: pricing policies and the struggle to define China's economic system' (2003) 49 *The China Journal* 1.

users of antidumping measures.[93] China's vigorous use of its own antidumping measures appears to be part of its response to the WTO-minus rules.

2. Rule-making in the Doha Round

China joined the WTO during the Doha Round. Also dubbed the 'development round', the Doha Round aimed at negotiating new agreements on trade liberalization and WTO disciplines, with a focus on the interests of developing country members. Although China has submitted various proposals and position papers in the negotiations[94] and has voiced its support for the developing country members on most of the issues, it has shunned taking any leadership role. When the United States approached China in 2006 with a proposal to issue a joint statement in support of the Doha agenda, China balked.[95]

Regarding market access negotiations, China has taken the position that, as a recently acceded member, it should not be asked to make substantial new concessions in the Doha Round. It has formed an alliance with a group of thirteen other recently acceded members (RAMs), calling for special treatment of RAMs in light of their relatively recent accession commitments.[96] Given that market access negotiations are driven by reciprocal bargaining, the fact that China is not prepared to make major concessions necessarily limits its role in the negotiations.

The rules negotiations in the Doha Round focus on the improvement of WTO antidumping and anti-subsidy disciplines. As the most frequently targeted country for antidumping measures and a top user of antidumping measures itself, China has a high stake in the outcomes of the negotiations. However, while China has submitted a few proposals,

[93] In the period of 2002–06, China initiated 133 antidumping investigations, after India (205) and ahead of the US (117) and the EU (116). Source: 'WTO antidumping statistics', available at www.wto.org. China's investigations targeted firms from United States, EU, Japan, South Korea, India, Russia, Taiwan and a number of other countries. For a list of China's antidumping cases as of March 1, 2005, see Scott Kennedy, 'china's porous protectionism: the changing Political Economy of Trade Policy' (2005) 120 *Political Science Quarterly* 407, 430 (Appendix).

[94] See 'WTO Trade policy review, Report by the People's Republic of China', WT/TPR/G/161 (March 17 2006), para. 67 (indicating China had submitted more than 30 proposals and position papers in the Doha negotiations).

[95] 'China balked at joint statement of support for WTO talks, US Official says', *BNA WTO Reporter*, 19 April 2006.

[96] See 'China, other new WTO members seek special terms on farm tariff, subsidy cuts', *BNA WTO Reporter*, 14 March 2007.

including a comprehensive one on the revision of antidumping rules,[97] it has generally kept a low profile in the rules negotiations. Additionally, China has declined to ally itself formally with the 'Friends of Antidumping Negotiations' (FANs), a group of Asian and Latin American countries that has taken the lead in pushing for tougher antidumping disciplines.[98]

It is also worth noting that China has been actively seeking bilateral and regional trade arrangements outside the Doha multilateral forum. It has concluded or is in the process of negotiating nine free trade agreements involving twenty-seven countries and regions.[99] These countries accounted for one-fourth of China's total trade in year 2005.[100] While bilateral and regional free trade agreements (FTAs) are permitted under the WTO, their explosive growth in recent years threatens to undermine the WTO multilateral framework. Clearly, China views FTAs favourably. With its economic clout, China is in a good position to negotiate bilateral and regional deals that serve its economic interests as well as its foreign policy goals.

3. Dispute settlement

Since its accession in 2001, China has brought two complaints, and has been sued eight times, at the WTO dispute settlement forum. In addition, it has participated as a third party in more than sixty other disputes.[101] While China has been actively involved in the dispute settlement process, it had shown a reluctance to pursue WTO litigation on its own until recently.

The first WTO complaint China brought was against the US safeguard measures on steel imports in 2002, in which it joined seven other members as co-complainants.[102] China's decision to bring claims in this

97 See 'Proposal of the People's Republic of China on the negotiation on anti-dumping', TN/RL/W66, 6 March 2003, available at www.wto.org. The four-page proposal covered twenty topics. Except for the proposed repeal of the provision permitting special rules on non-market economy, all other proposals are limited to a general position expressed in a few sentences.

98 'China urges ban on zeroing in dumping investigations as part of WTO Rules talks', *BNA WTO Reporter*, 4 May 2006.

99 They include agreements concluded with the ASEAN countries, Hong Kong and Macao, Pakistan and Chile, and ongoing negotiations with the Gulf countries, New Zealand and Australia. See 'WTO Trade policy review, Report by the People's Republic of China', paras. 77–82.

100 *Ibid.*

101 Source: 'WTO dispute cases involving China', available at www.wto.org.

102 'Appellate Body Report, United States – Definitive safeguard measures on imports of certain steel products', WT/DS248/AB/R, WT/DS249/AB/R, WT/DS251/AB/R, WT/DS252/AB/R, WT/DS253/AB/R, WT/DS254/AB/R, WT/DS258/AB/R, WT/DS259/AB/R, adopted 10 December 2003. Besides China, the other seven complainants were the EC, Japan, Brazil, Korea, New Zealand, Norway and Switzerland.

case was heavily influenced by the almost-certain outcome of the dispute and the presence of a strong team of co-complainants.[103] The second WTO complaint was filed by China individually in September 2007, challenging the US preliminary antidumping and countervailing duty determinations on imports of Chinese glossy paper.[104] As previously noted, beginning with the Chinese glossy paper case, the United States reversed its long-standing policy of not applying countervailing duty law to NMEs.[105] As a result of this reversal, the same Chinese exports to the United States can now be subject to both antidumping proceedings, in which China is treated as an NME, and countervailing duty proceedings, in which China is treated as a market economy. The Chinese government has strongly protested this shift in policy – accusing the United States of 'breaching the consensus reached by the leaders of the two countries to resolve differences through dialogue'[106] – and fought (unsuccessfully) against this policy change in a US domestic court proceeding.[107] The initial claims of China's WTO complaint, however, do not specifically raise the issue of this divergent treatment of China; rather, they charge the US application of its countervailing duty law as inconsistent with various provisions of the WTO subsidy agreement.[108] It remains to be seen, therefore, whether China will eventually raise the issue in the context of this case, and if so, whether it will challenge the treatment as discriminatory. It is also worth noting that China's filing of this complaint followed a flurry of WTO cases filed by the United States against China in early 2007, as discussed below.

To date, eight WTO complaints have been filed against China, of which five were brought by the United States, and one each by the EU, Canada, and Mexico. The eight complaints involve five sets of disputes.

[103] See Liyong Jiang, 'The WTO dispute settlement mechanism and China's participation', in Henry Gao and Donald Lewis (eds.), *China's Participation in the WTO* (London: Cameron May, 2005) p. 303, at p. 306.

[104] 'United States – Preliminary anti-dumping and countervailing duty determinations on coated free sheet paper from China, request for consultations by China', WT/DS368/1 (18 September 2007).

[105] See Decisions of US Department of Commerce in 'Coated Free Sheet Paper from the People's Republic of China: Amended Preliminary Affirmative Countervailing Duty Determination', 72 Fed. Reg. 1784 (9 April 2007).

[106] 'China hits back at new U.S. CVD duties on coated paper products', *BNA WTO Reporter*, 3 April 2007 (citing a statement of Wang Xinpei, spokesman for the Chinese Ministry of Commerce, published on the agency's website 31 March 2007).

[107] See *Government of the People's Republic of China* v. *United States*, U.S. Ct. Int'l Trade, Slip Op. 2007–50, 29 March 2007 (dismissing China's claim for lack of jurisdiction before authorities issue the final determination).

[108] *Ibid* 104.

The first case, *China – Value Added Tax*, was brought by the United States in 2004, claiming that China's policy of refunding value-added taxes to domestically produced integrated circuits discriminated against imported like products.[109] China settled the dispute before a WTO panel was established and withdrew the policy in 2005.[110]

The other seven complaints against China were brought in 2006 and 2007, and all of them are currently pending. The second dispute, *China – Automobile Parts*, involves three complaints by the EU, the United States, and Canada respectively.[111] At issue are Chinese regulations that impose a surcharge on imported automobile parts used in manufacturing vehicles for sale in China, effectively raising the tariff rate on automobile parts from 10 per cent to 25 per cent, equal to the rate for import of complete vehicles. The third dispute, *China – Subsidies*, was initiated by the United States in February 2007 and later joined by Mexico.[112] The complaints charge that China subsidizes domestic firms through various tax breaks that are WTO-illegal. The fourth and fifth disputes were brought by the United States on the same day in April 2007. The fourth, *China – Intellectual Property Rights*, claims that China's criminal law does not provide sufficient punishment for IP violations, and that its copyright law wrongfully denies protection for works under censorship review.[113] The fifth, *China – Trading Rights*, raises issue with China's implementation of its commitments on trading rights and distribution services for foreign books, magazines, films and audiovisual products, and charges among other things that, contrary to its Protocol commitments, China has continued to conduct the import of foreign cultural products through designated state-owned enterprises.[114]

[109] 'China – Value-Added Tax on integrated circuits, request for consultations by the United States', WT/DS/309/1 (23 March 2004).

[110] 'China – Value-Added Tax on integrated circuits, notification of mutually agreed solution', WT/DS309/8 (6 October 2005).

[111] 'China–Measures affecting imports of automobile parts', WT/DS339/1 (3 April 2006), 'Request for consultations by the European Communities', WT/DS340/1 (3 April 2006) 'Request for consultations by the United States', WT/DS342/1 (13 April 2006) (Request for consultations by Canada).

[112] 'China – Certain measures granting refunds, reductions or exemptions from taxes and other payments', WT/DS358/1 (7 February 2007) (Request for consultations by the United States); WT/DS359/1 (28 February 2007) (Request for consultations by Mexico).

[113] 'China – Measures affecting the protection and enforcement of intellectual property rights', WT/DS362/1 (16 April 2007) (Request for consultations by the United States).

[114] 'China – Measures affecting trading rights and distribution services for certain publications and audiovisual entertainment products', WT/DS363/1 (16 April 2007) (Request for consultations by the United States); WT/DS363/1/Add.1 (16 July 2007) (Addendum).

These pending disputes challenge important aspects of Chinese law and policies. The *Automobile Parts* case and the *Subsidies* case target tax incentives and local content requirements that China has used for decades as part of its development strategy. The IP case challenges WTO-consistency of two major pieces of Chinese legislation – the Criminal Law and the Copyright Law – and raises sensitive issues of government censorship. The *Trading Rights* case further contests government control over importation and distribution of foreign cultural products in China. These cases involve not only China's obligations under the WTO agreements, but also WTO-plus obligations prescribed by the Protocol.

In the first several years after accession, China showed a clear preference for handling trade conflicts through negotiation rather than WTO adjudication. As mentioned above, China settled the first WTO complaint against it through consultations, even though the legal issues involved were not clear-cut.[115] When threatened with WTO litigation on several occasions during this initial period, China had opted to compromise so as to avoid formal WTO complaints. For example, in 2004 China imposed an export quota on coking coal, which is used in steel production, in order to meet the rising domestic demand and to reduce pollution caused by excessive coke production. The decision met with a strong protest from the EU, whose steel industry had become reliant on Chinese coke after most of its own coke production was shut down due to pollution concerns. As the EU threatened to bring a WTO complaint, China backed down and agreed to maintain the same level of coke supply to the EU as the previous year.[116] In late 2005, when the United States threatened to initiate a WTO case against China over its antidumping decision regarding linerboard, China quickly repealed that decision.[117] Similarly, even though China accused the United States of abusing the special textile safeguard under the Protocol, it opted to

[115] For views on the background and merits of the case, see Jiang, 'The WTO dispute settlement mechanism', at pp. 307–10; Henry Gao, 'Aggressive Legalism: The East Asian Experience and Lessons for China', in Gao and Lewis (eds.), *China's Participation in the WTO*, at pp. 315, 329–334.

[116] 'EC threatens WTO suit against China unless it lifts coking-coal restrictions', *BNA WTO Reporter*, 25 May 2004; 'EC, China reach agreement on continued Chinese shipments of coking coal to Europe', *BNA WTO Reporter*, 2 June 2004. China's decision to compromise was made at the time when it was expecting an EU decision on China's market economy status. For background and analysis of this case, see Gao, 'Aggressive Legalism', at pp. 334–48.

[117] 'China lifts dumping duties on linerboard in face of US' threat of WTO proceedings', *BNA WTO Reporter*, 11 January 2006. MOFCOM announced the withdrawal of its antidumping determination without explanation. See MOFCOM Announcement

settle the differences bilaterally rather than bringing a formal complaint to the WTO.[118]

This litigation avoidance strategy began to change in 2006 when China decided not to settle the auto-parts case and went on to organize its legal defence.[119] Since then, it has also refused to settle the subsidies case,[120] and top Chinese officials have vowed to fight the IP and trading rights cases to the end.[121] The recent filing of the glossy paper case against the United States, the first case initiated by China individually, further indicates that China has become more willing to assert its interests through WTO adjudication. This shift in China's attitude may be attributable to a number of factors. First of all, the significance of the Chinese interests involved in these cases makes compromises less palatable. The several pending complaints against China, as noted above, challenge important aspects of the Chinese system, and the US antidumping and countervailing duty determinations in the Chinese paper case may set a precedent that can potentially affect Chinese exports broadly. Second, it appears that there has been a change of mentality among Chinese decision-makers. In the past they were highly concerned about losing a WTO case, regarding the loss of WTO litigation as a matter of political defeat. But over time the decision-makers seem to have realized that China cannot always avoid WTO disputes through political manoeuvres and that it needs to embrace WTO litigation as a normal way of resolving disputes. Contributing to this change of mentality is the growing confidence of Chinese trade lawyers who, through representing China as a third

[2006] No. 8, 'Terminating antidumping measures on unbleached kraft liner/linerboard', 13 February 2006, available at www.mofcom.gov.cn.

118 See 'Eu–China Textile Agreement, 10 June 2005; Memorandum of Understanding between the Governments of the United States of America and the People's Republic of China Concerning Trade in Textile and Apparel Products', 8 November 2005. See also HUANG Dongli, WTO Guize Yunyong Zhong De Fazhi: Zhongguo Fanzhipin Tebie Baozhang Cuoshi Yanjiu [Rule of Law in the Application of WTO Rules: A Study on the Special Safeguard for Chinese Textile Products], (Beijing: People's Press 2006), at pp. 12–15 (urging China to pursue WTO litigation to clarify its rights under the textile safeguard provisions rather than relying on political solutions to its alleged abuse by the US of the textile safeguard).

119 'China blocks U.S., EU, Canadian requests for WTO panel review of auto parts tariffs', *BNA WTO Reporter*, 29 September 2006.

120 'China blocks U.S., Mexican request for WTO panel on tax break subsidies', *BNA WTO Reporter*, 25 July 2007.

121 'U.S. Decision to file IPR complaints will harm relations, Chinese official says', *BNA WTO Reporter*, 26 April 2007.

party in scores of other WTO disputes, have gained much knowledge and experience in the WTO adjudication system.

It remains to be seen how the pending disputes will be resolved. To the extent that these cases raise important and novel issues in the interpretation of WTO treaties and the Protocol, how China argues its case will help to define its contribution to the development of WTO law.

C. Summary

To date, China's impact on WTO law stems primarily from the terms of its accession. Insofar as normal WTO disciplines may be insufficient in regulating trade with a giant transition economy, China's accession Protocol is expected to fill the void. However, because many special rules of the Protocol lack justification under the fundamental principles and norms of the WTO, their existence has compromised the integrity of WTO law.

In the post-accession era, China has been engaged in WTO rulemaking and adjudication, but has kept a low profile in both processes. Noticeably, it has avoided taking a leading position in the Doha negotiations, and has yet to challenge the discriminatory terms of its accession. Until recently, it had shown a preference for political solutions to trade disputes. Consequently, China's post-accession practice has not made much impact on WTO law.

III. India and WTO Law

India is an original contracting party to GATT and an original member of the WTO. As a large developing nation, India has been particularly vocal in asserting the interests of developing countries in the world trading system. Over the years, it has helped to reshape international economic law to take account of the special needs of developing countries. And it has never been shy in utilizing the GATT and WTO dispute settlement mechanisms to defend its rights and to challenge practices that it believes to be inconsistent with the rules and principles of the system. As a result, India has made significant contributions to the development of WTO law.

A. Rulemaking

India has unequivocally championed the cause of developing countries in the rulemaking of GATT and the WTO. Historically, it played a prominent role in introducing the development provisions in GATT in the early 1960s which became Part IV of the General Agreement.[122] It was actively involved in the negotiation of the Generalized System of Preferences (GSP) at the United Nations Conference on Trade and Development (UNCTAD),[123] which established the norm that developed countries should provide preferential tariff treatment to developing countries on a generalized, nonreciprocal and nondiscriminatory basis. The establishment of the GSP subsequently led to the enactment of the GATT Enabling Clause in 1979 that permanently exempts GSP programmes from the MFN requirement of GATT Article I.[124] During the Uruguay Round, India resisted the expansion of GATT disciplines to services, investment and intellectual property rights, viewing these new subjects as essentially serving the interests of developed countries at the expense of the developing world. Although unsuccessful in its overall objectives – due largely to a sea change in the attitudes of many developing countries towards freer trade in the late 1980s – India's efforts did help to limit the scope of the agreements on investment (TRIMS)[125] and intellectual property (TRIPS)[126] to their trade-related aspects.[127]

By the time the Doha Round was launched, India had undergone a major shift in its own development strategy. It had replaced its traditional policy of import substitution with a more open and outward looking policy on trade and foreign investment. This new strategy and outlook have brought vitality to the Indian economy and set the country on a fresh course of rapid economic growth.

Despite this major shift in its development strategy, India has not wavered from its historical position of championing the cause of developing countries. In fact, its newly acquired economic power has made India a more effective spokesman for the developing world. Given that the Doha Round was set out to deal with a deepening divide between the North and

122 Bhagirath Lal Das, 'India's trade negotiations: Past experience and future challenges' (1998) 35 Int'l Studies 397, 398

123 GSP was negotiated and finalized in the second conference of UNCTAD held in New Delhi in 1968 under the chairmanship of India. Das, *ibid.*

124 GATT: Decision on differential and more favourable treatment, reciprocity and fuller participation of developing countries, GATT Doc. L/4903 (28 November 1979), Basic Instrument and Selected Documents (BISD), 26th Supp. 203.

125 The Agreement on Trade-Related Investment Measures (TRIMS).

126 The Agreement on Trade-Related Aspects of Intellectual Property Rights (TRIPS).

127 See Das, 'India's trade negotiations', 399.

South,[128] it is not surprising that India should become a leader in the negotiations. Together with Brazil and South Africa, India led the initiative for the Doha Declaration on the TRIPS Agreement and Public Health[129] and sought changes to the TRIPS Agreement so as to allow exports of cheap generic drugs to developing countries that are unable to manufacture the medicines themselves. And its contribution was key to the final conclusion of the Protocol Amending the TRIPS Agreement in December 2005.[130] Across the board, India emerged as one of the G-6 countries leading the Doha negotiations.[131] It has submitted proposals on a wide range of topics concerning agriculture, non-agriculture market access, services, disputes, competition policy, trade facilitation, rules, TRIPS and special and differential treatment of developing country members.[132] After the negotiations collapsed over the differences between developed countries and the developing countries led by India and Brazil, India became one of the G-4 (along with the US, the EU and Brazil) in the efforts to revive the talks. It is no exaggeration to say that whether the Doha Round can ultimately succeed will depend to a large extent on the leadership of India.

It should also be noted that India has been a strong believer in multilateralism, and was one of the very few battlers against regionalism in trade.[133] It was not until recent years that India began to enter into regional free trade arrangements with others, mostly its neighbouring countries.[134]

[128] See Sylvia Ostry, 'The Uruguay Round North–South grand bargain: Implications for future negotiations', in Daniel M. Kennedy and James D. Southwick (eds.), *The Political Economy of International Trade Law: Essays in Honour of Robert E. Hudec* (Cambridge University Press, 2002), p. 285.

[129] WT/MIN(01)/DEC/2 (20 December 2001).

[130] WT/L/641 (8 December 2005). The amendment will take effect upon ratification by two thirds of WTO members. See Pascal Lamy, 'The WTO and the Doha Round: The way forward', Speech of WTO Director-General, New Delhi, 6 April 2006, available at www.wto.org.

[131] See 'WTO's Doha Round talks collapse, As G-6 ministerial ends in acrimony'.

[132] 'WTO Trade policy review: India, Report by the Secretariat', WT/TPR/S/182 (18 April 2007), 23.

[133] See Aaditya Mattoo and Arvind Subramanian, 'India and the multilateral trading system Post-Doha: defensive or proactive?' in Aaditya Mattoo and Robert M. Stern (eds.), *India and the WTO* (Oxford University Press, 2003) p. 327, at p. 333.

[134] For a list of India's regional trade arrangements, see 'WTO Trade Policy Review: India', at 23–28.

B. Dispute settlement

India is a frequent user of the GATT/WTO dispute settlement system.[135] It became a disputant as early as 1948[136] and filed its first complaint at the GATT in 1952.[137] After a long period of absence from the scene, India became actively engaged in GATT dispute settlement in the 1980s. During that period, it brought four complaints against Japan, the United States and the EC,[138] and answered two complaints brought against it by the United States.[139] Since the establishment of the WTO dispute settlement mechanism in 1995, India has brought seventeen complaints and served as defendant in nineteen cases, which makes India the fifth top litigant at the WTO, after the United States, the EU, Canada and Brazil.[140] In addition, India has participated in forty-nine other WTO disputes as a third party.[141]

Of the seventeen complaints brought by India, eight challenged antidumping and countervailing measures imposed by the EC, the United States, Brazil, and South Africa;[142] two against transitional

[135] For a detailed analysis of India's participation in the WTO dispute settlement system, see Ravindra Pratap, *India at the WTO Dispute Settlement System* (New Delhi: Manak Publications, 2004).

[136] 'India – Tax rebates on exports', GATT/CP.2/SR.11, BISD II/12 (24 August 1948). See Robert E. Hudec, *Enforcing International Trade Law: The Evolution of the Modern GATT Legal System* (Salem: Butterworth Legal Publishers, 1993), pp. 417–18, for a synopsis of the case.

[137] 'Pakistan – Export fees on Jute', GATT/L/41, Hudec, *Ibid.*, pp. 428–29.

[138] 'United States – Imposition of countervailing duties without injury criterion', GATT/L/5028 (Sept. 29, 1980); 'Japan – Measures on imports of leather' (initiated 11 April 1980, no GATT documents generated, see L/5623, BISD 31st Supp. 94, 108 (1985)); 'EC – Sugar regime', GATT/L/5309 (8 April 1982); 'United States – Countervailing duty procedures', GATT/SCM/20 (22 April 1982). See Hudec, *Enforcing International Trade Law*, at pp. 485; 486–7; 500–501.

[139] 'India – Import restrictions on almonds', GATT/C/M/211 (17 June 1987); 'India – Import Licenses on Almonds', GATT/C/M/211 (17 June1987). See Hudec, *Enforcing International Trade Law*, pp. 548–9.

[140] The number of cases in which the top four litigants serve as complainant and respondent respectively: US (88, 98), EC (76, 58), Canada (28, 15), Brazil (23, 14). Source: WTO dispute settlement, Disputes by country, available at www.wto.org.

[141] Source: WTO dispute settlement, Disputes by country, available at www.wto.org.

[142] 'EC – Antidumping investigations regarding unbleached cotton fabrics from India', WT/DS140/1 (3 August 1998) (EC – Cotton fabrics); 'EC – antidumping duties on imports of cotton-type bed linen from India', WT/DS141/1 (3 August 1998); 'South Africa – antidumping duties on certain pharmaceutical products from India', WT/DS168/1 (1 April 1999) (South Africa – Pharmaceuticals); 'United States – Antidumping and countervailing measures on steel plate from India', WT/DS206/1 (4 October 2000); 'United States – Continued Dumping and Subsidy Offset Act of 2000', WT/DS217/1 (21 December 2000); 'Brazil – antidumping duties on jute bags from India', WT/DS229/1

safeguard measures imposed by the US on Indian textiles;[143] two concerned preferential treatment of EC products by Poland and Turkey;[144] one on EC's differential treatment among developing countries;[145] one on rules of origin practised by the United States;[146] and the other three involved import regulations of the EC, the United States and Argentina, affecting India's exports of rice, shrimp and pharmaceuticals, respectively.[147] India was the sole complainant in all but two of the seventeen cases. Eight of the seventeen cases resulted in a final decision by a panel or the Appellate Body (AB), with India prevailing in six of them.[148] Two other cases were settled through consultations,[149] and another was terminated after the respondent withdrew the measure in question.[150]

The nineteen cases brought against India include a group of six complaints concerning quantitative restrictions (QRs),[151] two under

(9 April 2001); 'EC – Antidumping duties on certain flat rolled iron or non-alloy steel products from India', WT/DS313/1 (5 July 2004) (EC – Iron and steel); and 'United States – Customs bond directive for merchandise subject to antidumping/countervailing duties', WT/DS345/1 (12 June 2006) (US – Customs Bond).

143 'United States – Measures affecting imports of women's and girls' wool coats', WT/DS32/1 (14 March 1996) (US – Wool coats); 'United States – Measures affecting imports of woven wool shirts and blouses from India', WT/DS33/1 (13 March 1996).

144 'Poland – Import regime for automobiles', WT/DS19/1 (28 September 1995) (Poland – Automobiles); 'Turkey – Restrictions on imports of textile and clothing products', WT/DS34/1 (21 March 1996).

145 'EC – Conditions for the granting of tariff preferences to developing countries', WT/DS246/1 (3 March 2002).

146 'United States – Rules of origin for textiles and apparel products', WT/DS243/1 (11 January 2002).

147 'United States – Import prohibition of certain shrimp and shrimp products', WT/DS58/1 (8 October 1996); 'EC – Restrictions on certain import duties on rice', WT/DS134/1 (27 May 1998) (EC – Rice); 'Argentina – Measures affecting the import of pharmaceutical products', WT/DS233/1 (25 May 2001) (Argentina – Pharmaceuticals).

148 India lost in two cases: see 'Panel Report, United States – Rules of origin for textiles and apparel products', WT/DS243/R, adopted 21 July 2003 (US – Rules of Origin); and 'Panel Report, United States – Antidumping and countervailing measures on steel plate from India', WT/DS206/R, adopted 29 July 2002 (US – Steel plate).

149 'Poland – Import regime for automobiles', WT/DS19/2 (11 September 1996); 'EC – Iron and steel', WT/DS131/2 (October 27 2004).

150 'US – Wool coats', see WTO dispute settlement, DS32, at www.wto.org.

151 The six cases were initiated by the United States (DS90), Australia (DS91), Canada (DS92), New Zealand (DS93, Switzerland (DS94, and the EC (DS96). Except for the case initiated by the US, all of the other five cases were settled in 1998. The case initiated by the US resulted in an Appellate Body decision. See Appellate Body Report, 'India – Quantitative restrictions on imports of agricultural textile and industrial products', WT/DS90/AB/R, adopted 22 September 1999 (India – Quantitative restrictions).

TRIPS,[152] two on investment measures affecting the automotive sector,[153] three separate claims against India's antidumping measures,[154] and six other complaints regarding tariffs and other import and export restrictions.[155] Only five of the nineteen cases (concerning QRs, TRIPS and investment measures respectively) resulted in the final decision of a panel or the Appellate Body.

1. Significant cases

A number of disputes initiated by India have led to landmark decisions. For example, *US – Shrimp*,[156] which was brought by India, Malaysia, Pakistan and Thailand in 1996, became one of the most important cases in WTO jurisprudence.[157] In this dispute, India and other complainants challenged the US law that prohibited the import of shrimp unless the shrimp exporting country obtained a US certification that the shrimp was harvested with sea-turtle-friendly devices. The AB held that the US law fell within the purview of the environmental exception of GATT Article XX(g), but that the manner in which the law was applied constituted a means of arbitrary and unjustifiable discrimination within

[152] 'Appellate Body Report, India – Patent protection for pharmaceutical and agricultural chemical products (by US)', WT/DS50/AB/R, adopted 16 January 1998; 'Panel Report, India – Patent protection for pharmaceutical and agricultural chemical products (by EC)', WT/DS79/R, adopted 22 September 1998.

[153] 'Appellate Body Report, India–Measures affecting the automotive sector (by US and EC)', WT/DS146/AB/R, WT/DS175/AB/R, adopted 5 April 2002.

[154] 'India – Antidumping measures on imports of certain products from the European Communities', WT/DS304/1 (8 December 2003); 'India –Antidumping measures on batteries from Bangladesh', WT/DS306/1 (28 January 2004); 'India – Antidumping measures on imports of certain products from the separate customs territory of Taiwan, Penghu, Kinmen and Matsu', WT/DS318/1 (28 October 2004). None of these disputes proceeded to a panel, nor has any settlement been reported. See WTO dispute settlement, DS304, DS306, DS 318, at www.wto.org.

[155] 'India – Measures affecting export of certain commodities (by EC)', WT/DS120/1 (11 March 1998); 'India – Import restrictions (by EC)', WT/DS149/1 (28 October 1998); 'India – Measures affecting customs duties (by EC)', WT/DS150/1 (31 October 1998); and 'India – Import restrictions maintained under the export and import policy 2002–2007 (by EC)', WT/DS279/1 (23 December 2002); 'India – Measures affecting the importation and sale of wines and spirits from the EC', WT/DS352/1 (20 November 2006); 'India – Additional and extra-additional duties on imports from the United States', WT/DS360/1 (6 March 2007). None but the last two of these cases proceeded to the establishment of a panel, nor has any settlement reported. See WTO dispute settlement, DS120, DS149, DS150, DS279, at www.wto.org.

[156] 'Appellate Body Report, United States – Import prohibition of certain shrimp and shrimp products', WT/DS58/AB/R, adopted 6 November 1998.

[157] See John H. Jackson, *Sovereignty, the WTO, and the Changing Fundamentals of International Law* (Cambridge University Press, 2006), p. 188.

the meaning of the chapeau of Article XX. This decision recognized for the first time in GATT/WTO history that environmental protection is one of the objectives of the world trading system, and marked a viable path for balancing trade interests with environmental concerns within the WTO legal framework.[158]

Another landmark case brought by India is *EC – Preferences.*[159] In this case, India challenged the special GSP programme established by the European Communities for selected developing country members affected by the problems of drug production and trafficking. India claimed that the EC practice was inconsistent with the principle of nondiscrimination under the Enabling Clause. While the AB disagreed with India's view that EC may not choose to treat one group of developing countries better than another, it did find the EC's drug programme to be inconsistent with the nondiscriminatory requirement of the Enabling Clause. This case is the first in GATT/WTO history that interprets the Enabling Clause, and the decision has far-reaching implications for existing and future GSP programmes.[160]

Some other cases brought by India also resulted in significant legal decisions. One of such cases is *US – Shirts and Blouses,*[161] in which India successfully challenged the use by the United States of the transitional safeguard mechanism under the Agreement on Textiles and Clothing (ATC).[162] The AB's decision in this case articulated a clear

[158] For comments on this case, see Arthur Appleton, 'Shrimp/turtle: Untangling the nets' (1999) 2(3) J. Int'l Econ. L. 477; Steve Charnovitz, 'The Turtle-shrimp decision' (1999) 19 N. Y. L. Sch. J. In't & Comp. L. 1; Bruce Neuling, 'The shrimp-turtle case: Implications for Article XX of GATT and the trade and environment debate' (1999) 22 Loy. L. A. Int'l & Comp. L. Rev. 1.

[159] 'Appellate Body Report, European Communities – Conditions for the granting of tariff preferences to developing countries', WT/DS246/AB/R, adopted 20 April 2004 (EC – Preferences).

[160] On the implications of this case for GSP programs, see Robert Howse, 'India's WTO challenge to drug enforcement conditions in the European Community generalized system of preferences: a little known case with major repercussions for "political" conditionality in US trade policy' (2003) 4(2) Chi. J. Int'l L. 385; Robert Howse *et al.*, 'Internet roundtable: The Appellate Body's GSP decision' (2004)3(2) *World Trade Review* 239; Peter M. Gerhart and Archana Seema Kella, 'Power and preferences: Developing countries and the role of the WTO Appellate Body' (2005) 30 N. C. J. Int'l L. & Com. Reg. 515; and Gene M. Grossman and Alan O. Sykes, 'A preference for development: the law and economics of GSP' (2005) 4(1) World Trade Rev. 41.

[161] 'Appellate Body Report, United States – Measures affecting imports of woven wool shirts and blouses from India', WT/DS33/AB/R, adopted 23 May 1997 (US – Shirts and blouses).

[162] See ATC, art. 6.

principle on the burden of proof in WTO dispute settlement.[163] And its holding on the nature of the ATC transitional safeguard may be of a particular interest to China. Because such safeguard could be invoked against selected countries under the ATC, it was an exception to the MFN principle of the WTO safeguard agreement. India had argued that the transitional safeguard was an exception to WTO obligations, and consequently the party invoking the exception (in this case the United States) should have the burden of proof. The AB disagreed and held that the ATC transitional safeguard did not constitute such an exception. Instead, the AB viewed the mechanism as a 'fundamental part of the rights and obligations of WTO Members' during the ATC transitional period.[164] It described the ATC safeguard provision as 'carefully negotiated language' reflecting 'an equally carefully drawn balance of rights and obligations of Members', and held that such balance must be respected.[165] Consequently, the party claiming a violation of the provision must have the burden to prove its claim. To the extent that an analogy can be drawn between the ATC transitional safeguard and the China-specific trade remedy rules, the AB's holding may apply to the issue of burden of proof in future cases China may bring under the Protocol.

A perhaps less known case initiated by India is *US – Rules of Origin*,[166] in which India challenged certain US rules of origin for textile products as inconsistent with the WTO Agreement on the Rules of Origin (ROA). Rules of origin set criteria for determining the provenance of goods imported, which are necessary for the administration of MFN and preferential tariffs, quotas and trade remedy measures. While harmonization of rules of origin is an ongoing project at the WTO, the ROA set out the basic principles and undertakings of the members on the subject. This case is the first and only one thus far that interprets the ROA provisions. Although India lost the case, its original arguments and the resulting Panel opinion highlighted important legal and policy issues in the area.

Among the cases brought by other members against India, *India – Quantitative Restrictions* is worth special mention.[167] In this case, the United States challenged India's maintenance of quantitative restrictions on imports as unjustified by GATT Article XVIII:B, which provides

[163] See 'US – Shirts and blouses', pp. 13–15. [164] *Ibid.* at 16. [165] *Ibid.*
[166] Panel Report WT/DS243/R. [167] Appellate Body Report, WT/DS90/AB/R.

special exceptions for measures taken by developing country members for balance-of-payments (BOP) reasons. In defending its measures, India raised an important 'constitutional' issue in WTO law, namely, whether there should be a principle of 'institutional balance' between the judicial and political organs of the WTO with respect to the review of BOP measures. India argued that whether its measures were justified by BOP reasons is a matter within the exclusive competence of the political organ – the Committee on Balance-of-Payments and the General Council – rather than the dispute settlement panel.[168] Although India's argument was rejected by the AB, the issue of institutional balance within the WTO remains an important concern as the WTO evolves into a more constitutionalized institution.[169]

2. Defending the principle of non-discrimination

It is interesting to observe that a majority of the seventeen cases initiated by India involved discrimination claims. Such cases include: *US – Shrimp*,[170] which claimed arbitrary or unjustifiable discrimination under GATT Article XX; *EC – Preferences*,[171] the central claim of which was discrimination under the Enabling Clause; *US – Rules of Origin*,[172] which raised the issue of discrimination for the first time under Article 2(d) of the ROA; *Turkey –Textiles*[173] and *Poland – Automobiles*,[174] both of which involved the claim that the respondent's preferential treatment of EC products violated the MFN principle and could not be justified by the customs union exception under GATT Article XXIV; *Argentina – Pharmaceuticals*,[175] which alleged violations of both the MFN and national treatment provisions of GATT; *EC – Rice*,[176] which involved multiple claims of discrimination under Articles I, II and III of GATT and Article 2.1 of Agreement on Technical barriers to Trade (TBT); and *EC – Cotton Fabrics*,[177] *South Africa –Pharmaceuticals*,[178] *EC – Iron and*

[168] See *ibid.* paras. 80, 98.

[169] For a critique of the AB's opinion in this case, see Frieder Roessler, 'The institutional balance between the judicial and political organs of the WTO', in M. Bronckers and R. Quick (eds.), *New Direction in International Economic Law* (The Hague: Kluwer Law International, 2000), p. 325. See also Deborah Z. Cass, *The Constitutionalization of the World Trade Organization: Legacy, Democracy, and Community in the International Trading System* (Oxford University Press, 2005), pp. 109–10.

[170] See Appellate Body Report, WT/DS58/AB/R.

[171] See Appellate Body Report, WT/DS246/AB/R. [172] Panel Report, WT/DS243/R.

[173] 'Appellate Body Report, Turkey – Restrictions on imports of textile and clothing products', WT/DS34/AB/R, adopted 19 November 1999.

[174] See WT/DS19/1. [175] See WT/DS233/1. [176] WT/DS134/1.

[177] See WT/DS140/1. [178] See WT/DS168/1.

Steel,[179] and *U.S – Customs Bond*,[180] which raised the issue of nondiscriminatory application of antidumping measures under Article I of GATT and Article 9.2 of the Antidumping Agreement. In addition, *US – Shirts and Blouses*[181] and *US – Wool Coats*,[182] concerned the use of the ATC transitional safeguard invoked on a discriminatory basis.

The two landmark cases noted above, *US–Shrimp* and *EC–Preferences*, both contributed substantially to WTO jurisprudence on nondiscrimination. The case of *US–Shrimp* involved interpretation of the chapeau of GATT Article XX, which prohibits measures otherwise exemptible on policy grounds specified in Article XX if they are applied in a manner constituting 'arbitrary or unjustifiable discrimination between countries where the same conditions prevail'. This is the first case in WTO/GATT history that applied the chapeau requirement to a measure that was origin-neutral. Given the importance of GATT Article XX in WTO law, the interpretation of the chapeau requirement in this case is bound to have a major impact on the regulatory measures taken by members for non-trade concerns.[183]

India's complaint in *EC–Preferences* raised a two-prong question in WTO law: whether the Enabling Clause imposes a binding obligation of nondiscrimination on developed countries in granting preferential treatment to developing countries, and if so, whether such obligation requires the same preferential treatment be given to all developing country members. The AB answered the first prong affirmatively, thereby clarifying for the first time that GSP programmes, despite their gift-like nature, are subject to a mandatory requirement of nondiscrimination. The AB's answer to the second prong was negative. It defined the term 'nondiscriminatory' as a requirement to treat all similarly situated countries similarly. Since different developing countries may be at different stages of economic development, the donor countries may differentiate developing countries within their GSP programmes so long as the differentiation is based on objective standards.[184] This decision is particularly significant in that it has furnished a generic definition of the term 'nondiscriminatory,' signifying a new development in WTO jurisprudence on nondiscrimination.[185]

179 See WT/DS313/1. 180 See WT/DS345/1.

181 See 'Appellate Body Report, WT/DS33/AB/R. 182 See WT/DS32/1.

183 See generally Julia Ya Qin, 'Defining nondiscrimination under the law of the World Trade Organization' (2005) 23(2) Boston University Int'l Law J. 216, Pt. IV.A.

184 See 'EC – Preferences', at paras. 163, 180–9.

185 See Qin, 'Defining nondiscrimination', Pt. IV.D.

As indicated above, India brought a discrimination claim under the ROA, which led to the first judicial interpretation of the nondiscrimination obligation regarding the rules of origin. In addition, India has more than once raised the issue of nondiscriminatory application of antidumping measures under Article I of GATT and Article 9.2 of the Antidumping Agreement. Although the issue has yet to be dealt with by a WTO tribunal, India did succeed in prompting the respondent in one case to terminate the allegedly discriminatory measure in question.[186] Given that antidumping measures are often used in a *de facto* discriminatory manner, India's willingness to challenge such practice helps to enforce WTO disciplines on antidumping measures.

The number and types of discrimination claims filed by India demonstrate that India has been particularly vigilant about potential violations of the principle of nondiscrimination. In pursuing these claims, India has made significant contributions to the WTO jurisprudence on nondiscrimination.

C. *Summary*

Through active participation in multilateral trade negotiations and dispute settlement, India has made a significant impact on WTO law. With respect to rulemaking, India has been willing to challenge the status quo from the perspective of developing countries, and has substantially influenced the making of WTO rules concerning special and differential treatment of developing countries. In the current Doha Round, India has played a prominent role in advancing the development agenda, and its leadership will to a large extent determine the final outcome of the Round.

With respect to the enforcement of WTO rules, India has brought, and defended against, a wide range of claims in the WTO dispute settlement system. Cases involving India have resulted in significant WTO decisions. Through its active participation in WTO adjudication, India has contributed substantially to the clarification of many WTO rules and norms and the development of WTO jurisprudence.

[186] See 'EC – Antidumping duties on certain flat rolled iron or non-alloy steel products from India', WT/DS/313/2 (27 October 2004).

IV. Major factors determining behaviour patterns

Insofar as their impact on WTO law is concerned, the contrast between China and India is apparent. Although India's share in world trade is less than a quarter of China's, it has played a much larger role than China in the WTO system. Over the years, India's active participation in WTO rulemaking and dispute settlement has helped to shape the law of international trade. Its contributions are particularly significant with respect to WTO rules and norms concerning the interest of developing countries. In comparison, China has kept a low profile in the WTO. It has avoided taking any leadership position in the Doha negotiations and has only just begun to litigate in the WTO on its own. Thus far, the main impact of China on WTO law stems from the *ad hoc* rules of its accession, which exist largely to the detriment of the WTO legal system.

What accounts for such differences in attitude and practices between the two countries? It appears that several major factors are at play.

A. *Experience and legal expertise in the WTO system*

The WTO is a complex rule-based system. Effective participation in the WTO requires advanced knowledge and legal expertise.[187] Being an original contracting party to GATT and an original member of the WTO, India has accumulated more than fifty years' experience inside the system. The quality and expertise of India's WTO personnel is well recognized.[188] The fluency with which Indian delegates speak English, the primary working language at the WTO, also contributes to the efficacy of India's participation.[189]

[187] The increasing complexity of WTO institutions has become a real barrier to the participation of many developing countries in the system. See Sylvia Ostry, 'Trade, Development, and the Doha Development Agenda', pp. 6–7, presented at the University of Birmingham, 11–12 November 2005, www.utoronto.ca/cis/ostry/. See also J. H. H. Weiler, 'The rule of lawyers and the ethos of diplomatic reflections on the internal and external legitimacy of WTO dispute settlement' (2001) 35 J. World Trade 191 (suggesting that a consequence of the 'juridification' of the WTO is the rule of lawyers in the trade system).

[188] See Pearson, 'China in Geneva', at p. 245 (indicating the small professional staff of the Indian delegation in Geneva is regarded as highly qualified). See also Das, 'India's trade negotiations', at 402 (indicating the biggest strength of India in international trade negotiations has been its consistent adherence to certain basic objectives and its intellectual capability).

[189] I thank one of the anonymous reviewers for making this point.

By contrast, China merely began its full participation in the system in 2002. For historical reasons, China suffers from a shortage of qualified legal professionals who are also proficient in the English language. As a result, it lacks competent and experienced personnel to advise on sophisticated WTO legal matters. This deficiency in legal capacity on the part of China inevitably affected the negotiation of its accession terms. Judging from the language of the various WTO-plus and WTO-minus provisions of the Protocol, it seems obvious that at the minimum many of these provisions could have been better formulated to limit their potential adverse effects had China had quality legal advice during the negotiation.[190] The lack of experience and legal expertise continues to constrain China's ability to participate effectively in the WTO rulemaking and dispute settlement processes.[191] It might be a long time before China can catch up with India in its institutional capacity.

B. *Calculation of economic and political interests*

The divergence in economic and political interests between China and India is an important factor influencing their respective behaviour in the WTO rulemaking process. Historically, India has found its interests almost always in harmony with those of developing countries in general.[192] India's solidarity with other developing countries and its willingness to take a strong stand has been the main reason for its prominent role at the WTO.

In comparison, China's economic interests are extraordinarily diverse, which makes it undesirable for China to form coalitions with any particular interest group within the WTO.[193] Despite its rhetoric

[190] For example, the provision on the special 'trade diversion' safeguard does not even contain a definition of the concept. Instead, a loosely phrased explanation of the term is set out in a non-binding paragraph of the Working Party Report. See WPR, para. 247. For examples showing problems caused by the lack of clarity and consistency in the WTO-plus provisions, see Qin, '"WTO-Plus" Obligations', at 516.

[191] See Pearson, 'China in Geneva', at p. 245 (indicating the Chinese delegation to the WTO lacked ability to maneuver within the WTO and was overwhelmed). Although China has financial resources to hire legal expertise from developed countries, foreign counsel cannot be the solution to its full participation in WTO rulemaking and dispute settlement.

[192] Das, 'India's trade negotiations', at 400.

[193] Pearson, 'China in Geneva', at p. 254 (indicating that China has been relatively aloof from all coalitions within the WTO, and when it has joined coalitions, it does not play an active role, but rather uses its membership for image benefits).

of supporting developing countries, China's economic interests are not always in line with those of other developing nations. China's manufacturing sectors, especially its textile and clothing industry, compete directly with those of many other developing countries in exports.[194] Its ability to attract foreign direct investment is often perceived as competing with other parts of the developing world.[195] Thanks partly to the terms of its accession, China's economy is now much more liberalized than most developing countries, which makes its interest less in common with that of other developing nations in the current market accession negotiations. Moreover, China can benefit very little from the developing country status within the WTO since it has foregone in its accession most of the special treatment available to developing country members. The lack of a strong and consistent identification with the developing country group, or any other interest group in the WTO, weakens China's ability to play a leading role in the Doha negotiations. Furthermore, China is keenly aware of the concerns about the rise of its economic power shared by developed and developing countries alike. To assuage such concerns, China may find it politically desirable to keep a low profile in WTO affairs.

C. *Domestic institutions*

To a large extent, the differences in domestic institutions are responsible for the differences in WTO practices of China and India. The democratic system in India tends to ensure that its trade and WTO policies reflect a balance of various economic, political and social interests at home.[196] Even though the government decision-making process may not be totally transparent and public input may not always find its way into India's WTO policy, the democratic process and the

[194] China has strongly opposed the proposals of Turkey and certain other developing countries for new sector arrangements for textiles, accusing Turkey of trying to make China a 'scapegoat' of the sector's problem. See 'China slams Turkey proposal for WTO work program on textiles', *BNA WTO Reporter*, 18 July 2005.

[195] See e.g., Rhys Jenkins and Enrique Dussel Peters, 'The impact of China on Latin America and the Caribbean (April 2006)', at www.ids.ac.uk/ids/global/Asian-Driverpdfs/DFIDAgendaPaperIII.pdf (suggesting that China's attraction as a top destination for foreign investment has caused a decline in foreign investment to Latin American countries). But see Barry Eichengreen and Hui Tong, 'Is China's FDI coming at the expense of other countries?', NBER Working Paper 11335, available at www.nber.org (suggesting FDI in China also encourages FDI flows to other Asian countries).

[196] See 'WTO case study: Decision-making process in India: The case of the agriculture negotiations', available at www.wto.org.

free press in India ultimately provide a check on its government's handling of WTO affairs.[197]

By contrast, China's trade and WTO policies are ultimately determined by a small circle of elites with little accountability to the general public.[198] Although in an increasingly marketized society, the decision-making process in China has become much more open to public input, including business lobbying and other societal influences,[199] key decisions are still made in a top-down and nontransparent fashion. There has been a minimal check from the public on China's WTO policy and practice. Take the accession as an example. While the market access commitments were made with input from different industries through their government departments in charge,[200] the terms of the accession were not provided to the Chinese public until well after the accession had occurred.[201] Despite the fact that there was widespread dissatisfaction with the accession terms,[202] one can hardly find any published criticism in China of the government's handling of the accession.

Given the domestic political institutions in China, understanding the thinking of its leaders is crucial for understanding China's behaviour at the WTO. In the past two decades, the Chinese leaders have been following a general strategy of focusing on domestic economic development, with a foreign policy designed to secure an international

[197] According to Chimni, for example, there are six distinct perspectives on a just world order reflected in recent academic and political discourse in India, and these different perspectives are germane to understanding the response of the Indian state and people to issues relating to globalization, international law and international institutions such as the WTO. See B.S. Chimni, 'Alternative visions of just world order: Six tales from India' (2005) 46 Harv. Int'l L. J. 389. See also Das, 'India's trade negotiations', at 403–4, for a candid assessment and critique of the weakness and problems in India's handling of the Uruguay Round negotiations.

[198] For a case study on the organizational framework that governed decision-making on China's GATT/WTO negotiations, see Margaret M. Pearson, 'The case of China's accession to GATT/WTO', in David M. Lampton (ed.), *Making of Chinese Foreign and Security Policy in the Era of Reform, 1978–2000* (Stanford University Press, 2001), p. 337, at pp. 346–52 (describing the Chinese model as that of 'fragmented authoritarianism').

[199] See Pearson, *ibid.* at 351–52; Kennedy, 'China's Porous Protectionism'.

[200] See Pearson, 'The case of China's accession to GATT/WTO'.

[201] The Chinese-language version of the Protocol was not released to the public until late January of 2002, more than a month after the Protocol took effect.

[202] See Pearson, 'China in Geneva', at p. 246 (indicating that there was a domestic political backlash to WTO accession and Chinese leaders had to respond to the idea that China had been 'sold out' by the stringent concessions to which its negotiators agreed).

environment conducive to the domestic development agenda. The international aspect of the strategy reportedly comprises several elements advised by the late paramount leader Deng Xiaoping in the early 1990s: China should not be the leader of any group or seek hegemony in the world; it should stay humble and cautious, concentrating on economic development and avoiding confrontations with others; and it should no longer differentiate nations along ideological lines and should instead foster friendly relationships with all.[203] Even though Deng's advice was given when China had much less economic clout, Chinese leaders appear to have generally heeded the advice ever since.[204] Evidently, much of China's WTO practice – the acceptance of the discriminatory terms of accession, the keeping of a low profile and not forming coalitions in the Doha negotiations, and the dispute-avoidance tendency – can be explained by this line of thinking.[205] On the other hand, China's elite politics also predisposes it to rapid change in behavior. As noted above, the seemingly sudden shift in China's attitude

[203] Deng's advice was described as a strategy of *tao guang yang hui*, which is an ancient Chinese saying, literally meaning 'hide brightness and nourish obscurity'. See Michael Pillsbury, *China Debates the Future Security Environment, Prologue* (Washington DC: National Defense University Press, 2000). Deng's strategic advice was reported and discussed widely in the Chinese press. More recent articles include: Yang Chengxu, '"Tao guang yang hui, you suo zuo wei," Deng Xiaoping's thought on foreign relations', 9 August 2004, available at www.xinhuanet.com; Wang Shan Yusheng, "Rethinking China's strategy of "tao guang yang hui"', *Globe*, 8 July 2004, www.cas.cn/html/Dir/2004/07/08/4141.htm.

[204] Premier Wen Jiabao was quoted for stating in 2004 that the strategy of *tao guang yang hui* should guide China's foreign policy for at least another 100 years. See Wu Jianmin: 'Discarding"tao guang yang hui" would lead China to catastrophe', 20 Sept. 2005, available at www.people.com.cn.

[205] China's behaviour in the WTO is also largely consistent with its behaviour in the United Nations and other international organizations, where it has been regarded as a system-maintainer rather than a system-reformer. See Samuel Kim, 'China and the United Nations', in Elizabeth Economy & Michel Oksenberg (eds.), *China Joins the World: Progress and Prospects* (New York: Council on Foreign Relations Press, 1999) [hereinafter *China Joins the World*], pp. 42–89. For China's participation in multilateral international economic organizations, see Margaret M. Pearson, 'China's integration into the international trade and investment regime', in*China Joins the World*, pp. 161–205; Nicholas R. Lardy, 'China and the international financial system', in *China Joins the World*, pp. 206–30. See also Margaret M. Pearson, 'China's Track Record in the Global Economy' (2000) *The China Business Review* (January–February), p. 48. Although in recent years there have been calls for China to be more assertive on the world stage, the current leadership has not departed from the general foreign policy set by Deng. In fact, amid the growing concerns about China's rise, the leadership is emphasizing more than ever China's commitment to 'peaceful development' and to 'win-win' cooperation between China and the rest of the world.

towards WTO disputes reflects mostly a change of the mindset of its top decision-makers.[206]

D. Legal culture

The divergence in the behaviour of China and India in WTO legal processes is also attributable to their disparate legal traditions and culture. Compared to China, India has a long tradition of rule of law as law is part of its colonial heritage. The Indian legal system is based on a parliamentary democracy and an independent judiciary. Indian lawyers are trained in the same legal tradition as attorneys from the United States and other common law countries. Thanks to its mature legal culture, India is able to make sophisticated legal and policy arguments in presenting its visions of world economic order and to help shape WTO law and jurisprudence.

In comparison, China lacks a rule-of-law tradition. For historical reasons, China's legal system is still at an early stage of development and its legal profession very young. Although much progress has been made to build the system, the general level of legal consciousness remains fairly low among government elites.[207] Partly due to a weak legal culture at home, Chinese decision-makers tend to trust a relation-based approach rather than a rule-based approach in handling WTO affairs, and prefer political dialogue to WTO adjudication in resolving trade disputes. While there are signs that the perceptions of Chinese leaders are changing, it will be a long time before legal culture in China evolves to a comparable level of that in India.

V. Conclusion

The divergence in the behaviour patterns of China and India in the WTO and their respective impact on the WTO legal system is a function

[206] See 'China blocks U.S., EU, Canadian requests for WTO panel review of auto parts tariffs'; 'China blocks U.S., Mexican request for WTO panel on tax break subsidies'; 'U.S. decision to file IPR complaints will harm relations, Chinese official says'

[207] A telling example of the low level of legal consciousness in the government is the ratification of China's accession to the WTO. Instead of having the legislature ratify the accession after the signing of the accession protocol as required by the PRC Constitution, the government announced that the legislature had ratified the accession more than a year in advance of the signing of the Protocol. See LING Bing, 'WTO accession procedure may be unconstitutional', *Ming Pao Daily*, 19 November 2001 (in Chinese).

of a variety of factors. The level of experience and legal expertise in the WTO system and the calculation of national interests appear to be the direct causes of such divergence.

At a deeper level, however, the divergence reflects the differences between the two countries in their domestic institutions and legal culture. Being the world's largest democracy founded on the basis of rule of law, India is liable to take politically strong and legally principled positions at the WTO. Such positions can withstand public scrutiny at home and carry political legitimacy in the international arena. Given the maturity of its domestic legal system, India is also at ease utilizing the highly legalized WTO dispute settlement mechanism to safeguard its interests.

China's accession and post-accession practices, on the other hand, have the imprint of a weak legal culture and authoritarian institutions at home. Largely free from public scrutiny, China's WTO policies are set by the top government leaders. The wisdom of such policies is therefore at the mercy of the visions and understandings of the political elites. Generally weak in their sense of law, Chinese leaders tend to undervalue international legal processes and trust instead more power and diplomacy-based bilateral dealings. As a result, in China's accession and post-accession practices, political compromises often prevailed over legally principled positions.

Nonetheless, China will be increasingly involved in the WTO legal processes as it begins to assert and defend its interests in the WTO more actively. With the emergence of domestic interest groups from the marketplace and a growing public demand for the rule of law, the Chinese political process should become more transparent and democratized over time. And a growing legal profession in China will boost the government's capacity to handle WTO legal affairs and encourage it to adopt a more rule-oriented approach in its trade relations. Yet, only when such changes take place can China be expected to have a more significant impact on the WTO legal system.

References

Appleton, Arthur, 'Shrimp/turtle: Untangling the nets' (1999) 2(3) J. Int'l Econ. L. 477

'As China's trade clout grows, so do price-fixing accusations', *Wall Street Journal*, 10 February 2006

Barral, Welber and Munhoz, Carolina, 'The recent Brazilian regulation on safeguards against Chinese imports', available at www.brazilinfocenter.org/pdfs/november2005.pdf

Bown, Chad and Mc Culloch, Rachel, 'U.S. trade policy toward China: Discrimination and its implications' (June 2005), available at SSRN: http://ssrn.com/abstract=757124

Cass, Deborah Z., *The Constitutionalization of the World Trade Organization: Legacy, Democracy, and Community in the International Trading System* (Oxford University Press, 2005)

Charnovitz, Steve, 'The turtle-shrimp decision' (1999) 19 N. Y. L. Sch. J. Int'l & Comp. L. 1

Chimni, B. S., 'Alternative visions of just world order: Six tales from India' (2005) 46 Harv. Int'l L. J. 389

'China balked at joint statement of support for WTO talks, US Official says', *BNA WTO Reporter*, 19 April 2006

'China blocks U.S., EU, Canadian requests for WTO Panel Review of auto parts tariffs', *BNA WTO Reporter*, 29 September 2006

'China blocks U.S., Mexican request for WTO Panel on tax break subsidies', *BNA WTO Reporter*, 25 July 2007

'China hits back at new U.S. CVD duties on coated paper products', *BNA WTO Reporter*, 3 April 2007

'China lifts dumping duties on linerboard in face of US' threat of WTO proceedings', *BNA WTO Reporter*, 25 May 2004

China Joins the World see Economy, Elizabeth and Oksenberg, Michel

'China, other new WTO members seek special terms on farm tariff, subsidy cuts', *BNA WTO Reporter*, 14 March 2007

'China urges ban on zeroing in dumping investigations as part of WTO rules talks', *BNA WTO Reporter*, 4 May 2006

'Chinese textile exports surge: US, EU to invoke textile safeguard?' *Bridges Weekly Trade News Digest*, 6April 2005

Das, Bhagirath Lal, 'India's trade negotiations: Past experience and future challenges' (1998)35 *Int'l Studies*

'Doha's future in doubt as G-4 talks collapse; U.S., EU blame Brazil, India', *BNA WTO Reporter*, 22 June 2007

'The dragon's docile role in WTO', *Forbes* 10 March 2006

'EC, China reach agreement on continued Chinese Shipments of coking coal to Europe', *BNA WTO Reporter*, 2 June 2004

'EC threatens WTO suit against China unless it lifts coking-coal restrictions', *BNA WTO Reporter*, 25 May 2004

Economy, Elizabeth and Oksenberg, Michel (eds.), *China Joins the World: Progress and Prospects* (New York: Council on Foreign Relations Press, 1999)

Eichengreen, Barry and Tong, Hui, 'Is China's FDI coming at the expense of other countries?', NBER Working Paper 11335, available at www.nber.org

'EU–China Textile Agreement', 10 June 2005, available at http://ec.europa.eu/comm/external_relations/china/intro/memo05_201.htm

Gao, Henry, 'Aggressive legalism: The East Asian experience and lessons for China', in Henry Gao and Donald Lewis (eds.), *China's Participation in the WTO* (London: Cameron May, 2005)

Gerhart, Peter M. and Kella, Archana Seema, 'Power and preferences: developing countries and the role of the WTO Appellate Body' (2005) 30 N. C. J. Int'l L. & Com. Reg. 515

Gertler, Jeffrey, 'The process of China's accession to the World Trade Organization', in F. Abbott (ed.), *China in the World Trading System: Defining the Principles of Engagement* (The Hague; Boston: Kluwer Law International, 1998)

Grossman, Gene M. and Sykes, Alan O., 'A preference for development: the law and economics of GSP' (2005) 4(1) *World Trade Rev.*41

'History of China's accession to the WTO', in *WTO News*, Press/243, 17 September 2001, available at www.wto.org

Howse, Robert, 'India's WTO challenge to drug enforcement conditions in the European Community generalized system of preferences: A little known case with major repercussions for "political" conditionality in US trade policy' (2003) 4(2) Chi. J. Int'l L. 385

Howse, Robert *et al.*, 'Internet roundtable: The Appellate Body's GSP decision' (2004) 3(2) *World Trade Review* 239

HUANG Dongli, *WTO Guize Yunyong Zhong De Fazhi – Zhongguo Fanzhipin Tebie Baozhang Cuoshi Yanjiu [Rule of Law in the Application of WTO Rules – A Study on the Special Safeguard for Chinese Textile Products]* (Beijing: People's Press 2006)

Hudec, Robert E., *Enforcing International Trade Law: The Evolution of the Modern GATT Legal System* (Salem: Butterworth Legal Publishers, 1993)

'India–China trade relations: Not so happy a birthday', *Asia Source*, 11 December 2003, available at a website of the Asia Society www.asiasource.org/trade/seventeen

Jackson, John H., *Sovereignty, the WTO, and the Changing Fundamentals of International Law* (Cambridge University Press, 2006)

Jenkins, Rhys and Dussel Peters, Enrique, 'The impact of China on Latin America and the Caribbean' (April 2006), at www.ids.ac.uk/ids/global/AsianDriverpdfs/DFIDAgendaPaperIII.pdf

Kim, Samuel, 'China and the United Nations', in Economy and Oksenberg (eds.), *China Joins the World*

LING Bing, 'WTO accession procedure may be unconstitutional', *Ming Pao Daily*, 19 November 2001 (in Chinese)

Jiang, Liyong, 'The WTO dispute settlement mechanism and China's participation', in Henry Gao and Donald Lewis (eds.), *China's Participation in the WTO* (London: Cameron May, 2005), p. 303

Kennedy, Scott, 'China's porous protectionism: The changing political economy of trade policy' (2005) 120 *Political Science Quarterly* 407

'The price of competition: pricing policies and the struggle to define China's economic system' (2003) 49 *The China Journal* 1

Lardy, Nicholas R., 'China and the International Financial System', in Economy and Oksenberg (eds.), *China Joins the World*, pp. 206–30

Integrating China into the Global Economy (Washington DC: Brookings Institution Press, 2002)

Mattoo, Aaditya and Subramanian, Arvind, 'India and the multilateral trading system Post-Doha: Defensive or proactive?' in Aaditya Mattoo and Robert M. Stern (eds.), *India and the WTO* (Oxford University Press, 2003)

Memorandum of Understanding Between the Governments of the United States of American and the People's Republic of China Concerning Trade in Textile and Apparel Products, 8 November 2005, available at www.ustr.gov

Messerlin, Patrick A., 'China in the WTO: Antidumping and safeguards' (14 December 2002), available at www.siteresources.worldbank.org

'MOFCOM: China's textiles and clothing industry in the era of liberalization', available at http://eu2.mofcom.gov.cn/aarticle/ chinanews/200509/20050900352110.html

Neuling, Bruce, 'The shrimp-turtle case: Implications for Article XX of GATT and the trade and environment debate'(1999) 22 Loy. L. A. Int'l & Comp. L. Rev. 1

'A new approach to handling China', *Wall Street Journal*, 3 December 2005

Ostry, Sylvia, 'Trade, development, and the Doha Development Agenda', presented at the University of Birmingham, 11–12 November 2005, www.utoronto.ca/cis/ostry

'The Uruguay Round North–South grand bargain: Implications for future negotiations', in Daniel M. Kennedy and James D. Southwick (eds.), *The Political Economy of International Trade Law: Essays in Honour of Robert E. Hudec* (Cambridge University Press, 2002)

Pearson, Margaret M., 'China in Geneva: Lessons from the earliest years in WTO', in Alastair lain Johnston and Robert Ross (eds.), *New Directions in the Study of China's Foreign Policy* (Stanford University Press, 2006)

'China's integration into the international trade and investment regime', in Economy and Oksenberg, *China Joins the World*, pp. 161–205

'China's track record in the global economy', *The China Business Review* (2000) 48

'The case of China's accession to GATT/WTO', in David M. Lampton (ed.), *Making of Chinese Foreign and Security Policy in the Era of Reform, 1978–2000* (Stanford University Press, 2001)

Pillsbury, Michael, *China Debates the Future Security Environment, Prologue* (Washington DC: National Defense University Press, 2000)

'Portman presses China on market access, IPR; urges China to be active in Doha Talks', *BNA WTO Reporter*, 15 November 2005

'Post-quota textile trade starts to take shape', *Bridges Weekly Trade News Digest*, January 26 2005

Pratap, Ravindra, *India at the WTO Dispute Settlement System* (New Delhi: Manak Publications, 2004)

'The Protocol on the Accession of the People's Republic of China', WT/L/432 (10 November 2001), available at www.wto.org

Qin, Julia Ya, '"WTO-Plus" obligations and their implications for the WTO legal system – An Appraisal of the China accession protocol' (2003) 37(3) J. World Trade 483

'China and GATT: Accession instead of resumption' (1993: April) 27(2) J. World Trade 77–98

'Defining nondiscrimination under the law of the World Trade Organization' (2005) 23(2) Boston University Int'l Law J. 216

'WTO regulation of subsidies to state-owned enterprises (SOEs): A critical appraisal of the China accession protocol' (2004) 7(4) J. Int'l Econ. Law 863

Roessler, Frieder 'The institutional balance between the judicial and political organs of the WTO', in M. Bronckers and R. Quick (eds.), *New Direction in International Economic Law* (The Hague: Kluwer Law International, 2000)

State Council, 'State Council notice concerning further implementation of the transparency provisions of the WTO Protocol on China's accession' (30 March 2006), Guobanfa 2006 No. 23 (in Chinese), www.law-lib.com/law/law_view.asp?id=154087

Steinberg, Richard, 'Institutional implications of WTO accession for China', *Institute on Global Conflict and Cooperation, Working Papers* (February 1999)

'United States – Preliminary anti-dumping and countervailing duty determinations on coated free sheet paper from China: Request for consultations by China', WT/DS368/1 (18 September 2007)

'U.S. again calls on China to play greater role in restarting WTO trade talks', *BNA WTO Reporter*, 20 October 2006

'U.S. decision to file IPR complaints will harm relations, Chinese official says', *BNA WTO Reporter*, 26 April 2007

'U.S. expects India to play greater role in coming months to help revive WTO talks', *BNA WTO Reporter*, 20 December 2006

U.S. Trade Representative, 'To brink and back: in historic pact, U.S. opens way for China to finally join WTO', *Wall Street Journal*, 16 November 1999

U.S. Trade Representative, '"Roller-coaster ride" to an off-again, on-again trade pact', *The Washington Post*, 16 November 1999

U.S. Trade Representative, 'The first lady of trade: Woman in the news Charlene Barshefsky: The US trade representative was praised after China's accession to the WTO', *Financial Times* (London), 27 November 1999

WANG Shan Yusheng, 'Rethinking China's strategy of "Ao Guang Yang Hui"', *Globe*, 8 July 2004, www.cas.cn/html/Dir/2004/07/08/4141.htm

Weiler, J. H. H.,'The rule of lawyers and the ethos of diplomatic reflections on the internal and external legitimacy of WTO dispute settlement' (2001) 35 J. World Trade 191

WTO Agreements, Antidumping Statistics, Dispute Settlements – China, India; Subsidy Statistics; 'Trade Policy Review, Report by the Secretariat', WT/TPR/S/161 Rev.1 (28 June 2006) (TPR Report); Information on countries accessions, all available at www.wto.org

'WTO: China's refusal to answer Quad queries shuts down compliance review session', *BNA International Trade Reporter*, 26 September 2002

'WTO's Doha Round talks collapse, As G-6 ministerial ends in Acrimony', *BNA WTO Reporter*, 25 July 2006

WU Jianmin, 'Discarding "Tao Guang Yang Hui" would lead China to catastrophe':, 20 September 2005, available at www.people.com.cn

YANG Chengxu, '"Tao guang yang hui, you suo zuo wei," Deng Xiaoping "Tao guang yang hui, you suo zuo wei," Deng Xiaoping's thought on foreign relations', 9 August 2004, available at www.xinhuanet.com

6

China, India and the WTO dispute settlement system

Towards an interpretative strategy

B. S. CHIMNI

I. Introduction

The WTO established a rule-oriented dispute settlement system (DSS) to resolve disputes between member states.[1] There is today a consensus that the WTO DSS has worked well; it is seen to have worked to the advantage of both developed and developing countries.[2] Equally there is agreement that there is much room for improvement. Keeping this sentiment in view the Doha Ministerial Declaration agreed 'to negotiations on improvements and clarifications of the Dispute Settlement Understanding'. The review of DSS, yet to be concluded, has seen a large number of proposals from developing countries. Among them India has been relatively active in advancing proposals of reform of Understanding on Rules and Procedures Governing the Settlement of Disputes (DSU). It has relied on its reasonably extensive experience with the WTO DSS to advance these proposals; India has to date been complainant in 18 cases, respondent in 20 cases and a third party in 51 cases. The Indian proposals, advanced together with a number of other developing countries, have pertained to, among others, the term of appointment of Appellate Body (AB) members, litigation costs, special and differential treatment, compliance with decisions of the dispute settlement body

[1] John H. Jackson, *Sovereignty, the WTO, and Changing Fundamentals of International Law* (Cambridge University Press, 2006), pp. 134–59.

[2] 'Albeit a large number of developing countries have not made use of it; only 29 developing countries have hitherto brought a complaint before the WTO DSS' Atul Kaushik, 'Dispute settlement system at the World Trade Organization' *Economic and Political Weekly*, 12 January 2008, 26–9 at 26.

(DSB), and the issue of *amicus curiae* briefs.[3] China has had, as compared with India, a more limited experience with the WTO DSS as it acceded to WTO only in 2001; it has to date been complainant in 7 cases, respondent in 17 cases and third party in 62 cases. Its proposals for reform have been concerned with the special and differential (S&D) treatment provisions of the WTO DSU, in particular limiting the number of cases that can be filed against developing countries in a year and the defrayal of costs where a developed country has lost a case.[4]

Both China and India have not engaged, as is evident, with crucial issues such as standard of review or the doctrines of interpretation deployed by the WTO Appellate Body or Panels. A mechanical view appears to have been taken of cases 'won' or 'lost'. For instance, from the fact that India has won some cases and lost some the conclusion is reached that the DSS is working reasonably well for it and all that

[3] See WTO, Dispute Settlement Body, Special Session, TN/DS/W/47, 11 February 2003: Communication from India on behalf of Cuba, Dominican Republic, Egypt, Honduras, Jamaica and Malaysia; TN/DS/W/18, 9 October 2002: Proposals by Cuba, Honduras, India, Malaysia, Pakistan, Sri Lanka, Tanzania and Zimbabwe; TN/DS/W/19, 9 October 2002: Special and Differential Treatment for Developing Countries: Proposals by Cuba, Honduras, India, Malaysia, Pakistan, Sri Lanka, Tanzania and Zimbabwe; TN/DS/W/5, 7 May 2002: India's Questions to the European Communities and Member States on their Proposal relating to the Improvement of the DSU; TN/DS/M/32, 29 June 2006: Minutes of Meeting; TN/DS/M/30, 26 June 2006: Minutes of Meeting. JOB (04) 52, 19 May 2004: Textual Contribution to the Negotiations on the Improvement of the DSU: Non paper presented by Argentina, Brazil, Canada, India, New Zealand and Norway; JOB (05)/19, 22 February 2005: Textual Contribution to the Negotiations on the Improvement of the DSU: Non paper presented by Argentina, Brazil, Canada, India, Mexico, New Zealand and Norway and JOB (05)/19/Rev.1, 17 March 2006: Textual Contribution to the Negotiations on the Improvement of the DSU: Non paper presented by Argentina, Brazil, Canada, India, Mexico, New Zealand and Norway. For a brief review of these proposals see Thomas A. Zimmerman, 'WTO dispute settlement: General appreciation and role of India' available at http://papers.ssrn.com/sol3/papers.cfm? abstract_id=1014355 visited 11 October 2008. For a brief review of the proposals of India see 'WTO dispute settlement: General appreciation and the role of India' http://mpra.ub.uni-muenchen.de/4904/1/ MPRA_paper_4904.pdf See generally Stuart S. Malawer, 'United States–China Trade Litigation in the WTO' http://papers.ssrn.com/sol3/ papers.cfm?abstract_id=1169450.

[4] See WTO, Dispute Settlement Body, Special Session, TN/DS/W/29, 22 January 2003: Improving the Special and Differential Treatment in the Dispute Settlement Understanding: Communication from China; TN/DS/W/51, 5 March 2003: Specific Amendments to the Dispute Settlement Understanding-Drafting Inputs from China: Communication from China; TN/DS/W/51/ Rev.1, 13 March 2003: Specific Amendments to the Dispute Settlement Understanding – Drafting Inputs from China: Communication from China; and TN/DS/W/57, 19 May 2003: Responses to Questions on the Specific Input of China: Communication from China.

was needed were some marginal improvements to the system.[5] The accumulated experience of developing countries with growing WTO jurisprudence has yet to be seriously assessed by China and India to shape, what may be termed, an interpretative strategy that ensures that the balance of rights and obligations embodied in WTO agreements is not upset. This approach may be contrasted with that of the US which has made submissions to the DSB on interpretative questions in the ongoing DSU review process. If you add to this the vital fact that much of the scholarly literature on the interpretation of WTO Agreements, and commentary on AB and Panel reports, emanates from the developed world, and the increasing reference made to this academic literature, the grave implications of the abstention of developing countries on issues of interpretation becomes clear.[6]

The importance of interpretation

The neglect of interpretative issues is difficult to understand in view of: (i) the widened scope of WTO that extends to regulating intellectual property rights, trade related investment measures and trade in services; (ii) the mandatory third-party dispute resolution mechanism that has been established; (iii) the automatic adoption of panel and AB reports in view of the negative consensus principle; (iv) the fact that the question of standard of review is intimately linked to the process of interpretation;[7] (v) the grave implications that law-making or gap-filling interpretations have for rights and obligations of member states; (vi) the possibility that interpretations may bear upon ongoing or future negotiations of

[5] Kaushik sums up India's record (as of the time of writing) thus:

> India has participated in the DSM [Dispute Settlement Mechanism] 17 times as complainant, 19 times as respondent, and more than 25 times as a third party. Of the cases as complainant, India won seven, did not pursue another six, obtained mutually satisfactory solutions (MASS) in two, lost one and one case is ongoing. As defendant, out of 19 India lost five cases, got MASS in six cases, one case is suspended and one ongoing, while the rest have not been pursued by the complainants. India is one of the largest users of the DSM, and has certainly benefited from its security and predictability (Kaushik, 'Dispute settlement system at the World Trade Organization', 28).

[6] 'panels and the Appellate Body have begun actively to look for guidance in scholarly publications and to refer to the teachings of highly qualified publicists in the field of both international trade law and general public international law'. Matthias Oesch, *Standards of Review in WTO Dispute Resolution* (Oxford University Press, 2003), p. 185.

[7] Oesch, *Standards of Review in WTO Dispute Resolution*, pp. 41–2.

particular rules; (vii) the concern that the issue of institutional balance in WTO is now decided by the AB; (viii) the fact that the AB does not normally depart from its prior interpretations even though the rule of *stare decisis* does not apply to WTO reports; (ix) the problems in dealing with an AB interpretative overreach; and (x) the fact that the amendment of WTO agreements is a complex and difficult process.

Categories of indeterminacies

The role and power of interpretation is greatly enhanced in WTO DSS because of the innumerable ambiguities and gaps that characterize WTO texts. Broadly speaking, there are four categories of indeterminacies that typify WTO agreements: (i) indeterminacies relating to the determination of the object and purpose of WTO agreements; (ii) indeterminacies flowing from the ambiguities in the text itself. These include linguistic ambiguities and unanticipated gaps; (iii) indeterminacy resulting from the fact that the legal texts are couched in extremely general terms and have to be applied to a range of complex factual situations; and (iv) strategic ambiguities that are a function of a negotiation consensus to postpone closure on a particular issue.

Explaining the neglect of interpretative strategy

What therefore explains the neglect of the role and power of interpretation of the WTO Dispute Settlement Body (DSB)? There are several factors that can be mentioned by way of explanation: (i) the absence of expertise in international trade law, in particular WTO law. It has meant that developing country governments do not carefully study WTO Panel and AB reports, in particular when they are not directly involved in the case; (ii) the sheer volume of WTO jurisprudence being produced, making it difficult to carry out an assessment; in the first ten years WTO Panels and AB are estimated to have generated nearly 27, 000 pages of WTO jurisprudence;[8] (iii) the general lack of a sophisticated understanding of

[8] Gregory Shaffer, 'Weaknesses and proposed improvements to the WTO dispute settlement system: An economic and market-oriented view', May 2005 http://wage.wisc.edu/uploads/ WTO%20Conference/shaffer%20paper-weaknesses-short.pdf at p. 2 reports:

> WTO members filed 330 complaints in just over ten years (from January 1995-April 2005). Just to read through and understand the growing WTO case law is an immense task, including for specialized academics. While panel decisions under the GATT typically averaged around a dozen pages,

international law rules relating to interpretation both within the relevant government agencies and in the legal academia; (iv) the ensuing myth that WTO Panels and AB merely interpret the agreements and do not add or subtract from the obligations undertaken; (v) a lack of appreciation of the significance of some central issues such as the standard of review applicable in deciding disputes; and (vi) the superficial view, as noted earlier, that the WTO DSS is working well for all WTO member states and therefore all that is necessary is to introduce some improvements in the existing system to meet the concerns of developing countries.

The result is a *lack of systematic engagement with approaches and methodology of interpretations* beyond protesting particular interpretations linked with an individual case.[9] The failure to do so can prove expensive as the balance of rights and obligations embodied in WTO agreements, it deserves emphasis, do not come pre-interpreted. It may be mentioned here that in only 24 per cent of the cases initiated by the developing countries (in contrast to 72 per cent when initiated by developed countries) are appealed.[10] While there may be many reasons for this situation, at least one reason is the lack of full appreciation of issues of law and legal interpretation in the Panel Reports that form the sole basis of AB jurisdiction.

Scheme of the chapter

If China and India have to ensure that the balance of rights and obligations in WTO agreements is not undermined it is imperative that

under the WTO they range from 100–500 pages. While the GATT produced an average of 86 pages of panel findings per year from 1986–1995, the WTO produced 693 pages of panel findings in 1999. If one counts the entire judicial reports and not just the sections on 'findings', then, in 2000, there were 6,008 pages of WTO panel decisions, which mounts to 7,251 pages when one includes Appellate Body and arbitration decisions concerning implementation periods, compliance measures, and sanctions. The Consultative Board to the WTO Director General reported in December 2004 that the first '81 cases for which reports are adopted, and reports whose adoption is pending, amount to more than 27,000 pages of jurisprudence'.

[9] In the words of Qureshi, 'the Doha agenda, along with the contribution of developing members thus far, has been mainly concerned with the actual interpretation of particular provisions, including S&D provisions, rather than with the fundamental and underlying process of interpretation that will facilitate the attainment of the development objective on a permanent basis'. Asif Qureshi, *Interpreting WTO Agreements: Problems and Perspectives* (Cambridge University Press, 2006), p. 158.

[10] Kaushik, 'Dispute settlement system at the World Trade Organization', 27.

both countries frame a strategy of interpretation. The central aim of this chapter is to identify possible elements of such an interpretative strategy. It proceeds as follows. Section II refers to different provisions relating to interpretation of WTO agreements and looks at the defenders and critics of the textual approach allegedly followed by WTO Panels and AB. In this context it also reviews the views of the US contained in its submission to the ongoing review of the DSU to contend that the interpretations of the WTO Panels and AB should not be looked at from a neat and contrasting textual versus activist/gap-filling standpoints. The interpretative process is a complex act that cannot be captured by any either/or formula. It underlines the need for a close scrutiny of the interpretative strategy of the WTO Panels and AB to ensure that the concerns and rights of developing countries are not ignored. Section III briefly examines three landmark cases in which India has been involved to underline the significance of having an interpretative strategy. Section IV identifies the key elements that should form part of an interpretative strategy that countries like China and India should articulate as a way of defending their crucial trade interests. Section V contains some final reflections.

II. Different interpretation perspectives and strategies

Provisions relating to interpretation

Several provisions in the WTO agreements deal with the question of their interpretation. The key provision is of course Article 3.2 of the Understanding on Rules and Procedures Governing the Settlement of Disputes (DSU). It states:

> The dispute settlement system of the WTO is a central element in providing security and predictability to the multilateral trading system. The Members recognize that it serves to preserve the rights and obligations of Members under the covered agreements, and to clarify the existing provisions of those agreements in accordance with customary rules of interpretation of public international law. Recommendations and rulings of the DSB cannot add to or diminish the rights and obligations provided in the covered agreements.

It is generally agreed that the words 'customary rules of interpretation' is a reference to Articles 31 and 32 of the Vienna Convention on the Law of

Treaties (VCLT).[11] There are other provisions relating to the interpretation of WTO agreements. Article XVI (1) of the Agreement establishing the World Trade Organization notes:

> Except as otherwise provided under this Agreement or the Multilateral Trade Agreements, the WTO shall be guided by the decisions, procedures and customary practices followed by the CONTRACTING PARTIES to GATT 1947 and the bodies established in the framework of GATT 1947.

This clause 'helps maintain continuity between the jurisprudence and practice of the GATT, and that of the new WTO'.[12] Article IX of the

[11] The two articles of the Vienna Convention read as follows:

> Article 31
> General rule of interpretation

1. A treaty shall be interpreted in good faith in accordance with the ordinary meaning to be given to the terms of the treaty in their context and in the light of its object and purpose.
2. The context for the purpose of the interpretation of a treaty shall comprise, in addition to the text, including its preamble and annexes:
   (a) any agreement relating to the treaty which was made between all the parties in connection with the conclusion of the treaty;
   (b) any instrument which was made by one or more parties in connection with the conclusion of the treaty and accepted by the other parties as an instrument related to the treaty.
3. There shall be taken into account, together with the context:
   (a) any subsequent agreement between the parties regarding the interpretation of the treaty or the application of its provisions;
   (b) any subsequent practice in the application of the treaty which establishes the agreement of the parties regarding its interpretation;
   (c) any relevant rules of international law applicable in the relations between the parties.
4. A special meaning shall be given to a term if it is established that the parties so intended.

> Article 32
> Supplementary means of interpretation
> Recourse may be had to supplementary means of interpretation, including the preparatory work of the treaty and the circumstances of its conclusion, in order to confirm the meaning resulting from the application of article 31, or to determine the meaning when the interpretation according to article 31:

(a) leaves the meaning ambiguous or obscure; or
(b) leads to a result which is manifestly absurd or unreasonable.

[12] John H. Jackson, 'International law status of WTO dispute settlement reports: Obligation to comply or option to 'buy out'?' (2004) 98 *American Journal of International Law* 109–23 at 112.

agreement provides for the adoption of authoritative interpretations: 'The Ministerial Conference and the General Council shall have the exclusive authority to adopt interpretations of this Agreement and of the Multilateral Trade Agreements'. However, given the fact that the decision to adopt an interpretation must be taken by a three-fourths majority vote this authority is unlikely to be used. Finally there is Article 17 (6) (ii) of the Agreement on Implementation of Article VI of the General Agreement on Tariffs and Trade 1994 that provides for a different standard of review from that applicable to other covered agreements in anti-dumping cases. It reads:

> the panel shall interpret the relevant provisions of the Agreement in accordance with customary rules of interpretation of public international law. Where the panel finds that a relevant provision of the Agreement admits of more than one permissible interpretation, the panel shall find the authorities' measure to be in conformity with the Agreement if it rests upon one of those permissible interpretations.

This clause officially recognizes, as will be discussed later, that a text can yield two permissible interpretations, seriously undermining a textual approach.

The textual approach: Defending AB

The application of Articles 31 and 32 of VCLT is generally seen as implementing a textual approach and the work of WTO AB is judged by that standard. The WTO AB has articulated the textual approach embodied in VCLT in the *US Shrimp* case thus:

> A treaty interpreter must begin with, and focus upon, the text of the particular provision to be interpreted. It is in the words constituting that provision, read in their context, that the object and purpose of the states parties to the treaty must first be sought.[13]

Based on this self-representation of WTO AB its record has been stoutly defended by scholars like Jackson and former AB member Bacchus. Jackson is effusive in his praise of the WTO AB:

[13] Appellate Body Report on *US – Shrimp*, para. 114. See also Panel Reports on *US – Section 301 Trade Act*, para. 7.22; *India – Patents (US)*, para. 7.18; *US – Underwear*, para. 7.18; Appellate Body Report on *Argentina – Footwear (EC)*, para. 91. The AB in *Japan – Alcoholic Beverages II* stated:

> Article 31 of the *Vienna Convention* provides that the words of the treaty form the foundation for the interpretative process: 'interpretation must be based above all upon the text of the treaty' (p. 11).

> The Appellate Body has brought a sense of rigor and deep analysis that goes well beyond the jurisprudence that developed during the more than three [sic] decades of the GATT, and indeed, may go beyond the record of any international law tribunal known to history.[14]

Likewise, Bacchus suggests that any criticism of the AB is either self-serving or ill founded or is advanced by those who may be well intentioned but are echoing baseless criticisms.[15] In his view the WTO AB is doing nothing other than to implement the textual approach contained in VCLT:

> in fulfilling its task of treaty interpretation, and in thereby fulfilling its responsibilities to the Members of the WTO, the Appellate Body is left with the words of the treaty, and with the clear mandate of the Members of the WTO to use a textual approach to treaty interpretation that focuses above all on the words of the treaty. The Members of the WTO have given the Appellate Body absolutely no discretion as to *whether* to use this approach to treaty interpretation. Furthermore, the Members of the WTO have given the Members of the Appellate Body absolutely no discretion as to *when* to use this approach. Those who see 'overreaching' in some of the rulings of the Appellate Body tend to overlook this lack of 'quasi-judicial' discretion in treaty interpretation in WTO dispute settlement.[16]

Three critiques of the textual approach

At least three types of critique of the textual approach are discernible in the literature. These may be termed the representation, development and sceptical critiques.

The representative critique calls upon the AB to reach out to a wider constituency. Picciotto thus argues that the AB has embraced a debilitating formalism because it sees itself as being accountable only to states that have established and delegated powers to it.[17] This formalism is problematic as it 'tends to exclude debate about the values involved in

[14] Cited in James Bacchus, 'Appellators: The quest for the meaning of *and/or*', www.worldtradelaw.net/articles/bacchusappellators.pdf p. 3.

[15] *Ibid.*

[16] Bacchus, 'Appellators', p. 8. See also Jackson, *Sovereignty, the WTO, and Changing Fundamentals of International Law*, p. 166.

[17] According to him the formalist approach sees AB 'as requiring only the application of the rules in the texts according to their clear and natural meaning. A formalist approach deploys a closed epistemology, based on an objectivism which treats the abstract concepts in the texts through an instrumental rationality, resulting in decisions expressed in legalistic terms'. Sol Picciotto, 'The WTO's Appellate Body: Legal formalism as a legitimation of global governance' School of Public Policy Working Paper Series: ISSN 1479–9472 Working Paper 14, January 2005, p. 3. www.ucl.ac.uk/spp/download/publications/spp-wp-14.pdf.

the interpretive choices made by the adjudicator, which would entail acceptance of a more extended and direct accountability to a broader political constituency, rather than through national governments. It is also technicist (taking its specialist part for the whole), since its closed rationality excludes reflexive dialogue with those outside its closed epistemological sphere'.[18] What Picciotto wants the AB to do is to 'find a language to justify its decisions which could persuade a constituency far beyond trade officials and insiders'.[19] According to Picciotto:

> the AB is caught on the horns of an institutional dilemma. It feels restrained from expressing in more open terms the policy considerations which underpin its interpretations, for fear of usurping the political legitimacy of the governments to which it is primarily accountable. They in turn are motivated by a reluctance not so much to concede power as to admit to their domestic constituencies how much power has already been transferred to supranational instances such as the AB.[20]

The Picciotto critique however does not take into account the fact that the AB has reached out to a wider constituency in certain cases (for example, the *Shrimp Turtle* and *EC–Hormones* cases) but only when this constituency is located in the developed countries. In these cases the WTO AB has referred to a range of issues including constraints imposed on representative democracies, consumer anxiety etc.[21] In order to do so it has adopted a particular mix of text and context to formulate interpretations

[18] *Ibid.* [19] *Ibid.*, p. 5

[20] Picciotto, 'The WTO's Appellate Body: Legal formalism as a legitimation of global governance', p. 16.

[21] In *EC – Hormones* case, for example, AB showed its willingness to descend into the social world in order 'to determine whether an SPS measure is *sufficiently supported or reasonably warranted* by the risk assessment'. In its view:

> It is essential to bear in mind that the risk that is to be evaluated in a risk assessment under Article 5.1 is not only risk ascertainable in a science laboratory operating under strictly controlled conditions, but also risk in human societies as they actually exist, in other words, the actual potential for *adverse effects on human health in the real world where people live and work and die.*
>
> WT/DS26/AB/R and WT/DS48/AB/R, 16 January 1998: EC Measures concerning meat and meat products: Report of the Appellate Body para 187. Further, the AB noted the 'depth and extent of the anxieties experienced' and 'the intense concern of consumers' within the EC. The AB Report reveals, as Perez has noted, 'surprising sensitivity to public anxieties regarding ecological risks, and adopts a broad concept of the concept of risk' which represents an important step forward in the attempt to integrate trade and environment objectives. It thus created 'a legal link' between the level of public anxiety and conformity to WTO rules,

that appeal to the wider constituency. In short, while the AB may be committed to a theoretical formalism, in practice it adopts an eclectic pragmatism that allows it to reach out to constituencies that wield power.

A second critique of the textual approach, advanced by Qureshi, seeks to inject (from the perspective of developing countries) an explicitly development perspective in the interpretative process. He laments the fact that the 'development dimension in the interpretation of WTO Agreements has hitherto been neither sufficiently articulated nor coherently structured in the architecture of international trade agreements'.[22] Qureshi urges an umbrella interpretative principle of development since the 'the development dimension has a legitimate claim for being inculcated in the very apparatus of interpretation of the WTO agreements'.[23] The claim, he contends, can be supported by innumerable provisions of WTO agreements: ranging from the Preamble of the Marrakesh Agreement to the Ministerial Declaration launching the Doha Round negotiations. He rejects the textual approach and contends that such an approach is supported by states that stand to benefit from it. On the other hand the teleological (development) approach is advanced by those states that wish to secure long-term objectives of the WTO agreements.[24] The teleological (development) dimension comes into play in the interpretative process in the following contexts:

> Factoring in the development dimension objectives; factoring the condition of development into the interpretation and application of the WTO Agreements; factoring in the special characteristics of development; factoring good governance into the process of interpretation; factoring in relevant rules of international law that facilitate development; factoring in the appropriate approach to interpreting S&D terms; factoring in the textual approach *in rein*; factoring in the rehabilitation of the teleological approach for the development dimension.[25]

endowing the civil society with the power to confer legitimacy on governmental regulatory measures. Oren Perez, 'Reconstructing science: the *Hormone* conflict between the EU and the United States' (1998) 1 *European Foreign Affairs Review*, 563–82 at 563 and 572.

[22] Qureshi, *Interpreting WTO Agreements: Problems and Perspectives*, p. 116.

[23] *Ibid.*, p. 229.

[24] 'those whose gains in the WTO system will materialize more in the long term (the long-term winners) will emphasize the objects and purposes of the agreement [i.e., *the teleological approach*], which facilitates future gains'. *Ibid.*, p. 117.

[25] *Ibid.*, p. 119.

Bacchus squarely rejects the proposed teleological approach, and more specifically the economic analysis of interpretation, in no uncertain terms:

> Some have suggested as well that the Appellate Body should engage in purposive treaty interpretation by making 'teleological' decisions according to what the Members of the Appellate Body themselves think *ought* to be the meaning of the text of the WTO treaty based on what *they* see personally, and according to their own individual preferences and predilections, as the treaty's purpose. But if the Appellate Body took that approach, then it surely *would* be 'overreaching'.[26]

While Bacchus is dogmatic in his understanding of the approach of WTO AB, Qureshi does not like Picciotto recognize that what the WTO AB is unwilling to adopt is not a non-textual approach in general but the teleological (development) approach that he is suggesting. This becomes clear not only from US proposals but from the record of the WTO AB.

The sceptical approach: The US proposals

The political membership of WTO does not accept the Bacchus contention that all the WTO AB is doing is to follow a textual approach. In its submission to the ongoing review of the DSU the US has sought to remind the WTO AB that it should practise what it preaches. It critiques the record of WTO Panels and AB, albeit indirectly, by reminding the DSB of the following. First, that 'WTO adjudicative bodies must take care that interpretive approach they may use results neither in supplementing nor in reducing the rights and obligations of Members under the covered agreements'.[27] Second, it reminds the AB that because negotiations 'entail a number of compromises', 'the text of the covered agreements is the best representation of the expectations of WTO Members'.[28] Third, it cautions that:

> when interpreting a provision of a covered agreement, while other provisions of the covered agreements may serve as useful context, it is not possible to deduce from the existence of certain provisions that WTO Members have agreed on a particular underlying policy and that this

[26] Bacchus, 'Appellators', p. 7.

[27] WTO, TN/DS/W/82/Add.1, 25 October 2005, Negotiations on Improvements and Clarifications of the Dispute Settlement Understanding: Further Contribution of the United States on Improving Flexibility and Member Control in WTO Dispute Settlement Communication from the United States, Addendum, p. 1.

[28] *Ibid.*

> policy may be used as a guideline to interpret other provisions. In other words, it is not appropriate to extrapolate from the fact that Members have agreed to move in a particular direction in one provision and conclude that therefore Members must have intended another provision to move equally in the same direction. It often may be possible to reach agreement only on one particular obligation or discipline while being unable to reach agreement on any obligation or discipline even in a related area.[29]

Fourth, US notes that sometimes the ambiguity in the text 'is deliberate'. It must be remembered that 'constructive ambiguity can serve as a placeholder marking an area where negotiators accept that it may be appropriate to agree on disciplines but where further negotiation is necessary before those disciplines can be specified'.[30] The US identifies two kinds of unacceptable gap filling:

> *First* would be to read into the text of a covered agreement an obligation or right that is not present in the text, for example by extrapolating from a different provision.
>
> *Second* would be to resolve ambiguity in the text of a covered agreement in a manner that supplements or diminishes rights and obligations under the covered agreement.[31]

The US emphasizes that 'the function of WTO adjudicative bodies is to resolve disputes over obligations undertaken, not to substitute for negotiators and re-write, reduce or supplement the agreed text'.[32] The US goes on to make the point that 'prior reports of WTO adjudicative bodies are not covered agreements. They do not themselves represent agreed text. Accordingly, it is not appropriate to treat or interpret a prior report as though it is agreement text or to use a prior report to add to or diminish rights and obligations under a covered agreement'.[33] Fifth, the US submits that 'WTO Members have agreed that the WTO dispute settlement system is not to add to or diminish the rights and obligations under the covered agreements. They have not agreed to delegate to WTO adjudicative bodies the task of filling in gaps in the covered agreements'.[34] Sixth, an area of concern that the US had earlier noted was 'situations in which legal concepts outside the WTO texts have been applied in a WTO dispute settlement proceeding, including asserted principles of international law other than customary international law rules of interpretation'.[35] The US had underlined the need

[29] *Ibid.*, pp. 1–2 [30] *Ibid.*, p. 2. [31] *Ibid.* [32] *Ibid.* [33] *Ibid.*, p. 3. [34] *Ibid.*
[35] WTO, TN/DS/W/82, 24 October 2005, Negotiations on Improvements and Clarifications of the Dispute Settlement Understanding: Further Contribution of the United

for respecting 'limitations on the use of public international law in WTO dispute settlement':

> Recognizing that international dispute settlement fora vary regarding the breadth of their adjudicatory authority, WTO dispute settlement under the DSU is focused on the adjudication of rights and obligations under specified agreements. These 'covered agreements' are listed in Appendix 1 of the DSU. While other international law might properly play a role in WTO dispute settlement fora, it is not the function of WTO dispute settlement to adjudicate rights and obligations beyond those in the covered agreements.[36]

To meet the concerns outlined the US has suggested an interim review stage for the AB as well. It has recommended that provision be made for 'a mechanism for parties, after review of the interim report, to delete by mutual agreement findings in the report that are not necessary or helpful to resolving the dispute, thus continuing to allow the parties to retain control over the terms of reference'.[37] Further it has indicated that provision be made 'for some form of "partial adoption" procedure, where the DSB would decline to adopt certain parts of reports while still allowing the parties to secure the DSB recommendations and rulings necessary to help resolve the dispute'.[38]

In March 2006 the US advanced further proposals 'on improving the flexibility and members control in WTO Dispute Settlement'.[39] It reiterated that 'the purpose of the system is not to produce reports or to 'make law', but rather to help Members resolve trade disputes among them'.[40] This represents a departure from the view that security and predictability of the multilateral trading system can be enhanced through producing coherent jurisprudence. It is in many ways a return to the idea of a 'diplomatic' approach to be found in GATT. The US specifically proposed that the WTO adjudicative bodies 'avoid making findings that are not aimed at resolving the dispute'. Second, it reminded the adjudicative bodies that they 'are not permitted to render authoritative interpretations of the covered agreements'.[41] It also emphasized that the 'order of analysis followed by WTO adjudicative bodies should respect the

States on Improving Flexibility and Member Control in WTO Dispute Settlement: Communication from the United States.

36 *Ibid.*, p. 6. 37 *Ibid.*, p. 3. 38 *Ibid.*

39 WTO TN/DS/W/82/Add.2, 17 March 2006: Negotiations on Improvements and Clarifications of the Dispute Settlement Understanding: Further Contribution of the United States on Improving Flexibility and Member Control in WTO Dispute Settlement.

40 *Ibid.*, p. 1. 41 *Ibid.*

function assigned to those bodies. In particular, the order of analysis should respect the fact that findings need to relate to "measures affecting the operation of any covered agreement" taken by a Member'.[42] It had in mind two situations:

> WTO dispute settlement is not concerned in a dispute with a measure of a Member that expired prior to the date of the request for consultations by another Member in that dispute or that otherwise does not exist as of the date of the request for consultations.

The question whether a measure does x is a factual question because at that point it is not a question of the interpretation of a provision of a covered agreement or of whether a provision applies to the measure.[43]

What explains the US approach and the recommendations in its submissions, especially because arguably the developed countries have gained most where WTO Panels and AB have departed from a 'strict' textual approach or the manner in which they have dealt with the relationship between WTO law and public international law (PIL)?[44] First, it may have been adopted to reassure the US Congress that US sovereignty and negotiating positions will not be compromised. Second, it seeks to sustain the myth that the task of the AB is to remain faithful to the textual approach and the activist reports represent a departure from it. Third, it is advanced to rule out possible damaging activism on the part of the AB. That is to say, the US is sending a message to the AB that *gap filling will be acceptable only if it does not harm the interests of the United States.*

From the perspective of developing countries the concrete proposals that should not be accepted are the proposal for an interim review in AB proceedings or the proposal for partial adoption of a report by the DSB. Their acceptance will only allow the US to exercise even greater influence over the WTO DSS. But most importantly, developing countries like China and India must advance their views on the interpretative record of WTO AB, something that is completely absent at the moment. Before proceeding to identify the possible elements that can constitute an interpretative strategy derived from such analysis some further reflection is called for on whether WTO Panels and AB have adopted a textual approach.

[42] *Ibid.*, p. 2 [43] *Ibid.*

[44] See Section III for brief analysis of three cases that would evidence this contention.

Textual or non-textual approach

While Bacchus answers the question in the affirmative, Steinberg notes that there is sufficient evidence that the AB has engaged in 'expansive lawmaking through interpretation'.[45] It is our argument that from a developing country perspective the problem may be that the AB does not adhere to either a textual or a law making approach. In this context it may at first be pointed out that there is no consensus on whether VCLT endorses the textual approach. According to McLachlan: 'The Convention eschews taking a fixed stand on any of the great doctrinal debates on interpretation, save that it is firmly focused on objective reference points rather than the chimera of the intentions of the parties. Thus it adopts both an ordinary meaning and a purposive approach.'[46]

Second, the law making approach can be legitimized through the use of several legal strategies. Steinberg mentions four: First, 'the interpretation of a particular provision may be skewed by favoring one of the three elements [ordinary meaning, context and object and purpose] in Article 31 of the Vienna Convention over others'.[47] Second, 'insofar as "object and purpose" is considered, it may represent a tendency to assume incorrectly that the WTO agreements favor liberalization instead of a contractual balance between liberal and nonliberal purposes'.[48] This is possible because there are three options here: (i) the reference to the

[45] Richard Steinberg, 'Institutional implications of WTO accession for China', *Institute on Global Conflict and Cooperation, Working Papers* (February 1999) p. 248. Steinberg explains the meaning of 'activism' in this regard:

> 'Activism' is a term subject to alternative definitions and normative assessments, but debates over WTO activism usually concern Appellate Body holdings that domestic measures contravene WTO obligations, or the Appellate Body's fidelity to some posited, deduced, or constructed intent of those who negotiated a substantive provision of a WTO agreement. Most of those characterizing WTO dispute settlement as 'activist' do so pejoratively, and some have suggested that this activism might warrant an extreme policy response, such as threatening unilateral US withdrawal from the WTO.

[46] Campbell McLachlan, 'The principle of systemic integration and Article 31 (3) (c) of the Vienna Convention' (2005) 54 *International and Comparative Law Quarterly*, 279–320 at 291. It is not possible here to examine the scheme of interpretation incorporated in VCLT. Broadly speaking, we occupy the middle ground between radical indeterminacy and radical objectivism. For the linguistic and philosophical basis of this position see B. S. Chimni, *International Law and World Order: A Critique of Contemporary Approaches* (Delhi: Sage Publications Pvt. Ltd, 1993), pp. 83–105, 271–283.

[47] Steinberg, 'Institutional implications of WTO accession for China', p. 261.

[48] *Ibid*., p. 262.

object and purpose is to the treaty as a whole (e.g., Agreement establishing the World Trade Organization); (ii) the reference is to the object and purpose of the treaty in which the provision that is being interpreted appears (viz., the DSU or GATT 1994); and (iii) the object and purpose of the particular provision (e.g. Article XX of the GATT 1994 Text).[49] Third, 'some commentators favor using Article 3.2 of the WTO DSU to import substantive non-WTO international law into WTO law in an effort to unify international law'.[50] It is contended that 'WTO law is not a secluded island but part of the territorial domain of international law. The WTO, important as it may be, must thus be put in perspective. For public international law at large, this approach pleads for the unity of international law, not its fragmentation'.[51] This view introduces an element of indeterminacy even in the objectives and provisions of the WTO DSS that can be used by the WTO AB to offer different interpretations in different cases. Fourth, 'some propose interpreting WTO agreements creatively to accommodate a wide range of values and environmental change'.[52]

Third, the text has to be applied to complex facts that may themselves invite varying assessment of the text. Thus the AB in the *Japan – Alcohol Beverages* case observed:

[49] In the *EC – Customs Classification of Frozen Boneless Chicken Cuts* the AB observed:

> It is well accepted that the use of the singular word 'its' preceding the term 'object and purpose' in Article31(1) of the *Vienna Convention* indicates that the term refers to the treaty as a whole; had the term 'object and purpose' been preceded by the word 'their', the use of the plural would have indicated a reference to particular 'treaty terms'. Thus, the term 'its object and purpose' makes it clear that the starting point for ascertaining 'object and purpose' is the treaty itself, in its entirety. At the same time, we do not believe that Article31(1) excludes taking into account the object and purpose of particular treaty terms, if doing so assists the interpreter in determining the treaty's object and purpose on the whole. We do not see why it would be necessary to divorce a treaty's object and purpose from the object and purpose of specific treaty provisions, or *vice versa*. To the extent that one can speak of the 'object and purpose of a treaty provision', it will be informed by, and will be in consonance with, the object and purpose of the entire treaty of which it is but a component'.

[50] Steinberg, 'Institutional implications of WTO accession for China', p. 262.

[51] Joost Pauwelyn, *Conflict of Norms of Public International Law: How WTO Law Relates to Other Rules of International Law* (Cambridge University Press, 2003), p. xi.

[52] *Ibid.*

> WTO rules *are not so rigid or so inflexible* as not to leave room for reasoned judgments in confronting the *endless and ever-changing ebb and flow of real facts in real cases in the real world*. They will serve the multilateral trading system best if they are interpreted with that in mind. In that way, we will achieve the 'security and predictability' sought for the multilateral trading system by the Members of the WTO through the establishment of the dispute settlement system.[53]

Thus, the appreciation of 'real facts in real cases in the real world' creates space for activist interpretations in the guise of not being 'rigid or so inflexible'. It introduces a subjective element in the interpretation of WTO agreements.

Finally, the manner in which the subjective element plays itself out depends on which gap is being filled with what outcomes, especially if it involves the interests of powerful trading states. Steinberg offers two overlapping reasons for this move. First, 'a pattern of judicial lawmaking that opens foreign markets for EC or U.S. export-oriented producers may foster support for the Appellate Body'.[54] Second, 'judicial lawmaking that fundamentally shifted the balance of WTO rights and responsibilities against the interests of both the European Communities and the United States might prompt their cooperative action'.[55]

It equally deserves mention that where the AB does *not* want to adopt the activist approach given political sensitivities involved there are equally available what Hudec calls 'avoidance techniques' that 'include use of doctrines like "judicial economy," "nonjusticiability," *in dubio mitius*, and *non liquet* to avoid making a decision'. Use of such techniques for politically sensitive issues should, according to Hudec, 'diminish the probability of severe political correction'.[56] But the question is politically sensitive for whom? The AB has not been a reluctant activist where trade environment relationship is concerned or on issues relating to institutional balance in so far as these have been politically sensitive issues for developing countries. Thus when you speak of political sensitivity it is always the political sensitivity of the developed countries. To put it differently, the WTO AB, despite its ostensible commitment to a textual approach, has sufficient interpretative flexibility available with which it shapes its interpretative strategy.

[53] Appellate Body Report on *Japan – Alcoholic Beverages II*, p. 31. [54] *Ibid*., p. 268.
[55] Steinberg, 'Institutional implications of WTO accession for China', p. 265.
[56] Steinberg, 'Institutional implications of WTO accession for China', p. 269.

III. Three cases: The strategic importance of interpretation

This becomes clear even from a cursory analysis of three cases in which India has been involved viz., the *India–Quantitative Restrictions* case, the *Shrimp Turtle* case and the *EC Preferences* case. These cases are considered here only in the limited context of highlighting the significance of the moment of interpretation in the WTO scheme of things.

The India–Quantitative Restrictions *case*

Jackson has noted that 'the choices by a juridical body for an international institution created by a treaty, as to what techniques will be used to interpret the treaty, can have profound effects on the "allocation of power," both vertical and horizontal'.[57] There is no better illustration of this proposition than the *India–Quantitative Restrictions* case in which a central issue was that of institutional balance or the doctrine of separation of powers in WTO between the executive and the judicial bodies. The WTO AB described the Indian contention as follows:

> . . . India argues that there is a principle of institutional balance which requires panels, in determining the scope of their competence, to take into account the competence conferred upon other organs of the WTO. According to India, the drafters of the WTO Agreement created a complex institutional structure under which various bodies are empowered to take binding decisions on related matters. These bodies must cooperate to achieve the objectives of the WTO, and can only do so if each exercises its competence with due regard to the competence of all other bodies. In order to preserve a proper institutional balance between the judicial and the political organs of the WTO with regard to matters relating to the balance of payments restrictions, review of the justification of such matters must be left to the relevant political organs, i.e., the BOP [Balance of Payments] Committee and the General Council. In light of the powers attributed to these organs under Article XVIII: 12 of the GATT 1994 and the BOP Understanding, panels should, according to India, refrain from reviewing the justification of balance-of-payments measures under Article XVIII:B (Para 98).

The AB rejected the contention of India that there was a principle of institutional balance in WTO, albeit on the basis of the specific facts of the case. Consequently even if the AB position were to be accepted in this case the larger question of institutional balance is far from being

[57] Jackson, *Sovereignty, the WTO, and Changing Fundamentals of International Law*, p. 182.

exhausted.[58] For as Qureshi has argued, the AB itself recognized that the judicial function was not 'unlimited'.[59] It should not therefore be left to be determined on a case-by-case basis. Roessler rightly argues that:

> The adoption of the DSU led to a clear separation between the judicial and political organs determining the legality of trade measures. The now independent judicial organs should . . . refrain from using their interpretive power to confer decision-making authority upon themselves that the Members of the WTO have explicitly assigned to bodies composed of the Members.[60]

The Roessler objection is supported by the eminent trade economist Bhagwati who writes that 'I have some sympathy for Frieder Roessler's view that the dispute settlement panels and the appellate court must defer somewhat more to the political process instead of making law in controversial matters'.[61]

The Shrimp Turtle *case*

The *Shrimp Turtle* case has been described by Jackson as 'the most important 'constitutional' case in all of WTO jurisprudence so far'.[62] It dealt with a range of issues including the critical issue of whether

[58] Qureshi notes that 'the principle of institutional balance has a function in the interpretative process concerned with the determination of the limits of competence of the various organs of the WTO' (Qureshi, *Interpreting WTO Agreements: Problems and Perspectives*, p. 66).

[59] Qureshi notes the elements in AB Report from which a principle of institutional balance can be discerned. These are:

1. recognition that different organs have different functions – that is, that the BOP [Balance of Payments] Committee and Panels have different functions;
2. recognition that judicial findings need to be without prejudice to the role of political organs – that is, panel findings need to be without prejudice to the role of the BOP Committee and the General Council;
3. recognition that the judicial organ cannot substitute itself for the political organ –that is, the finding that 'panels can review the justification of balance-of-payments measures' is not tantamount to the Panel substituting itself for the BOP Committee;
4. recognition that the judicial organs cannot ignore the determinations of the political organs – that is, Panels should not ignore the decisions of the BOP Committee and the General Council.

Qureshi, Interpreting WTO Agreements: Problems and Perspectives, p. 66.

[60] Cited by Steve Charnovitz, 'Judicial independence in the World Trade Organization', p. 14. www.worldtradelaw.net/articles/charnovitzjudicial.pdf

[61] *Ibid.*

[62] Jackson, *Sovereignty, the WTO, and Changing Fundamentals of International Law*, p. 161.

unilateral measures to implement environmental protection measures were permissible.[63] The AB answered the latter in the affirmative, albeit attaching certain pre-conditions that needed to be satisfied. It was an entirely unanticipated development so far as developing countries were concerned. It was of serious concern because unilateral measures could have protectionist aims and translate into non-tariff barriers against the exports of developing countries. Especially because, as Jackson notes, the AB:

> seems actually to have entertained what is called in GATT and WTO jurisprudence a process and production method (PPM) . . . The worry, clearly, is that of the 'slippery slope', which could lead to a whole variety of governmental claims for exceptions for PPMs, including even a demand that imported products carry the same regulatory burdens and wage levels at the production phase as those of the importing country (which could result in a dramatic undermining of comparative advantage and trade liberalization).[64]

Another controversial interpretative move of the AB was in the context of Panel accepting unsolicited *amicus curiae* briefs. As is well known, the AB rejected the Panel view that non-requested information could not be accepted from non-governmental sources. The AB distinguished between a legal right to make a submission before a WTO tribunal and what a tribunal was authorized to do under the DSU. While the legal right to make a submission only vested with WTO members, Article 13 of the DSU entitled 'Right to Seek Information' gave, in the view of WTO AB, ample authority to a Panel to '"seek" information and technical advice from "any individual or body" it may consider appropriate, or from "any relevant source"'.[65] That right was subsequently confirmed in further disputes, 'causing outrage among many developing country Members who feared undue interference from NGOs'.[66]

[63] B. S. Chimni, 'WTO and environment: The *Shrimp–Turtle* and *EC–Hormone* cases', *Economic and Political Weekly*, 13 May 2000, 1752–61; 'WTO and environment: The legitimization of unilateral trade sanctions', *Economic and Political Weekly* 12–18 January 2002, 133–40; Jackson, *Sovereignty, the WTO, and Changing Fundamentals of International Law*, p. 189.

[64] Jackson, *Sovereignty, the WTO, and Changing Fundamentals of International Law*, pp. 190–1.

[65] WT/DS58/AB/R, 12 October, 1998: United States – Import Prohibition of Certain Shrimp and Shrimp Products: Report of the Appellate Body para 104.

[66] Thomas A Zimmerman, 'WTO dispute settlement at ten: Evolution, experiences, and evaluation' (2005) 60 *Aussenwirtschaft: The Swiss Review of International Economic Relations*, 27–61 at 42–3.

The reasons for feeling exasperated with this interpretation of AB are not far to seek.[67] First, apart from the fact that the text of Article 13 is clear in the matter, the negotiating history appears to show that the idea of allowing NGOs access to the dispute settlement process had already been proposed but rejected. Second, the likely beneficiaries of the AB ruling would be those with capacity in terms of human and material resources. These entities would mainly come from the developed world. Third, the AB decision would create an 'impossible burden' for any developing member who may wish to comment on or respond to the *amicus* briefs. If a number of briefs are received, it could mean a large number of texts to go through and legal arguments to be responded to in a few days time. Perhaps in response to the concerns of the developing world the AB has, as Zimmerman notes, 'de facto developed a very pragmatic approach'.[68] But the fact that the AB adopted a number of interpretations of WTO agreements that were novel and departed from prior understanding of Member States shows that it is far from adhering to a textual approach stressing the significance of the moment of interpretation in terms of determining the balance of rights and obligations.

The EC Preferences *case*

The *EC Preferences* case,[69] according to Shaffer and Apea, represented 'a lawyer's paradise of ambiguous legal provisions interpreted by judicial bodies in a case having significant political and institutional implications'.[70] It dealt with S&DT principle. India had contended that 'by

[67] This section relies heavily on B. S.Chimni, 'WTO, democracy and development: A view from the South' (2006) 40 *Journal of World Trade*, 5–36.

[68] Zimmerman, 'WTO dispute settlement at ten', 50–1:

> On the one hand, the Appellate Body displays a general openness towards the acceptance of *amicus curiae* briefs. On the other hand, it does not appear to accord decisive weight to these submissions in its decisions – at least not explicitly. This approach gives adjudicating bodies a maximum of flexibility while it respects the concerns of Members who are against such briefs.

[69] European Communities – Conditions for the Granting of Tariff Preferences to Developing Countries: Report of the Appellate Body WT/DS246/AB/R 7 April 2004 (*EC Preferences* case)

[70] See Gregory Shaffer and Yvonne Apea, 'Institutional choice in the GSP case: Who decides the conditions for trade preferences? The law and politics of rights', www.worldtradelaw.net/articles.htm#shaffer, p. 12.

consenting to the adoption of the Enabling Clause, developing countries did not "relinquish [] their MFN rights [under Article I of the GATT 1994] as between themselves, thus permitting developed countries to discriminate between them'.[71]

In this case the AB reversed the Panel's findings that (i) 'the term "non-discriminatory" in footnote 3 [to paragraph 2 (a) of the Enabling Clause] requires that identical tariff preferences under the GSP schemes be provided to all developing countries without differentiation, except for the implementation of a priori limitations';[72] and (ii) 'the term "developing countries" in paragraph 2 (a) [of the Enabling Clause] should be interpreted to mean *all* developing countries, with the exception that where developed countries are implementing *a priori* limitations, "developing countries" may mean *less than all* developing countries'.[73]

In order to do so AB had to look at the context of Para 2 (a) of the Enabling Clause and at 'the object and purpose of the WTO Agreement and the Enabling Clause' as the application of the ordinary meaning rule to the word 'discriminate' pointed 'in conflicting directions with respect to the propriety of according differential treatment'.[74] The AB *inter alia* concluded that 'the term "developing countries" in paragraph 2 (a) does not prohibit preference-granting countries from according different tariff preferences to different sub-categories of GSP beneficiaries'.[75] The importance of AB report is that special incentive arrangements could be validated provided they met certain conditions and were justified under the relevant WTO rules. Shaffer and Apea write that

> while the initial purpose of the GSP was to create a general system to advance the interests of developing countries as a whole, the proliferation of specialized preference regimes with unilaterally-determined conditions has placed developing countries in a less-advantageous negotiating situation.[76]

Furthermore, 'it is a US and EC political process that makes the determinations. In practice, this process will be subject to considerable biases. For example, the United States withdrew GSP benefits in the 1980s on labor protection grounds from Nicaragua (governed by the Sandinistas)

[71] *EC Preferences* case, above n. 69, para. 150.
[72] European Communities – Conditions for the Granting of Tariff Preferences to Developing Countries: Report of the Appellate Body WT/DS246/AB/R 7 April 2004, para. 190 (e).
[73] *Ibid.* [74] *Ibid.*, p. 152. [75] *Ibid.*, para. 175.
[76] Shaffer and Apea, 'Institutional choice', p. 19.

and not from El Salvador or Guatemala, actions that appeared targeted to advance the Reagan administration's foreign policy goals rather than labor protection'.[77] Likewise, in the past, 'GSP conditionality was used as "a key lever" to press recalcitrant developing countries to agree to the inclusion of the TRIPS Agreement into the new WTO system in 1995.[78] Finally, open-ended GSP schemes would 'undermine the certainty of WTO trading rules for developing country traders in their most important foreign markets. The United States, for example, decides on the allocation of GSP benefits at least annually.[79]

The significance of the interpretations advanced by the AB for developing countries in all the three cases, apparently arrived at through a textual approach, hardly need be stressed. These decisions have by all accounts upset the balance of rights and obligations contained in WTO agreements to the disadvantage of developing countries.

IV. Towards an interpretative strategy: Some elements

What should in the circumstances be the interpretative strategy of countries like China and India, or for that matter developing countries? In our view the interpretative strategy can consist of the following elements: (1) an exhaustive analysis of WTO jurisprudence followed by submission of considered views to the DSB; (2) devising an appropriate interpretative approach to negotiations; (3) demanding the application of National Deference Principle on S&DT basis; (4) clarifying the relationship between WTO law and public international law; (5) ensuring selection of AB members not biased against developing countries; and (6) promoting quality academic scholarship. Each of these may briefly be considered in turn.

Analyse the jurisprudence of WTO AB

If China and India (along with other developing countries) wish to shape a global trade order that protects their interests they clearly need to participate actively in the debate on issues relating to the interpretation of WTO agreements. The framework of interpretation is not simply a matter of concern with reference to specific disputes but also crucial to the framing and faithful implementation of the legal and

[77] *Ibid.*, p. 20. [78] *Ibid.*, p. 22. [79] *Ibid.*

institutional framework of WTO. It calls for an in depth analysis of WTO jurisprudence, especially the implications of the more contentious interpretations advanced by WTO Panels and AB. It is no accident that the US is actively involved in thinking through a suitable interpretative strategy that helps defend its trade interests. There is the clear realization that in the final analysis it is the interpretations of WTO Panels and AB that decide the content of rights and obligations under WTO Agreements.

At a practical level China and India need to set up working groups at the national, bilateral and multilateral levels (with other key developing countries like Brazil and Malaysia) to closely examine the interpretations advanced by WTO Panels and AB. This exercise should immediately begin at least at the national level leading to submissions on the subject to the DSU review process so as to be able to influence its outcome. For such a move to take place the bureaucracy that deals with WTO issues needs to be sensitized to the significance of framing a strategy of interpretation. Towards this end the national working group should consist of international trade law experts from the academia, law firms and industry.

Devise interpretative strategy for negotiations

The lessons learnt from the analysis of WTO jurisprudence should be used to inform the negotiations strategy of developing countries. As key countries in any WTO negotiations China and India have a particular responsibility in this regard. Learning from how WTO Panels and AB approach and interpret agreements there is a need to build into future texts (for example, to be adopted in the Doha Round negotiations) provisions that safeguard the interests of developing countries when a dispute arises. Thus, for instance, the Preamble to an agreement should not be treated lightly as it can often be invoked in the context of understanding the object and purposes of a particular agreement. Likewise, as Qureshi notes, 'the agreement should be drafted in such a way that sufficient flexibility is built in to promote development'.[80] Finally, developing countries 'should ensure the creation of a paper trail showing an adequate history of development-friendly interpretation'.[81]

[80] Qureshi, *Interpreting WTO Agreements: Problems and Perspectives*, p. 137.
[81] *Ibid.*

Argue for adoption of the national deference principle

WTO Panels and AB are today interpreting WTO agreements without effectively taking into account the concerns of developing countries. For instance, according to one observer the 'S&DT provisions in the DSU are virtually dead letter'.[82] Consider this:

> Article 12.11 requires an explicit indication of the form in which account was taken of the S&DT of developing countries. Of the five cases in which it was invoked (*Mexico–taxes on soft drinks*, *US–Byrd*, *US–safeguards*, *Brazil–aircraft* and *India–quota restrictions*, it was actually applied only in the India-quota restrictions case as the subject matter itself (Article XVIII, GATT) was a S&DT provision.[83]

It is important for China and India along with other developing countries to insist that the S&DT provisions of the WTO DSU be adhered to.

But a more significant way of ensuring that the particular needs of developing countries are taken cognizance of is to propose that the national deference principle, as contained in Article 17 (6) (ii) of the Agreement on Anti-Dumping, be applied on an S&DT basis to all disputes involving developing countries. Since developing countries are forced to accede to a package of complex trade agreements through the 'single undertaking' formula, it is only appropriate that some flexibility be permitted to them in the enforcement of their obligations to protect their developmental interests. The adoption of a national deference principle will create this interpretative space and allow developing countries to pass implementing legislation in light of their developmental concerns. It is often argued that 17 (6) (ii) does not in any case permit more than one permissible interpretation since such application can only yield one correct interpretation. As Oesch observes: 'In essence, it is incompatible with customary rules of interpretation for an interpreter to arrive at more than one correct interpretative conclusion . . . the second sentence of Article 17.6 (ii) can never come into play, simply because the correct application of the VCLT never leaves an interpreter to choose among a range of permissible interpretations'.[84] But Jackson aptly describes this view as 'naïve'.[85] He notes that 'we have many

[82] Kaushik, 'Dispute settlement system at the World Trade Organization', p. 27.

[83] *Ibid.*

[84] Oesch, *Standards of Review in WTO Dispute Resolution*, p. 94.

[85] Jackson, *Sovereignty, the WTO, and Changing Fundamentals of International Law*, p. 171. Qureshi likewise terms such a view 'dogmatic'. Qureshi, *Interpreting WTO Agreements: Problems and Perspectives*, p. 217.

manifestations of courts being split (five to four, three to two, or two to one) regarding interpretations, and that could be taken as evidence of the existence of more than one permissible or, at least, more than one reasonable (and reasonable might mean permissible) interpretation'.[86]

The ongoing review of the WTO DSU provides a unique opportunity to affirm the national deference principle in the context of disputes of developing countries.[87] It is worth noting that the possibility of universalizing the national deference principle was kept open by a ministerial decision while adopting the Final Act of the Uruguay Round of Trade Negotiations.[88] The suggestion here is, it bears repetition, to universalize the application of the national deference principle only with respect to developing countries. While it is true that at present this proposition, even when not applied as S&DT treatment, 'has not been accepted by any member of the WTO' there are advocates of such position in many governments.[89] The reason for the absence of wider acceptance among developing countries is that not many developing countries have understood its meaning and implications. Here China and India can undertake a counterfactual exercise to show how some critical cases could have been differently decided if the national deference principle would have been applied. This empirical exercise is crucial to persuading its own officials and other developing country governments of the usefulness of such a move.

[86] *Ibid.*

[87] Zimmerman, 'WTO dispute settlement at ten', 40:

> DSU review started already in 1997. However, it could not be concluded so far as several deadlines lapsed without tangible achievements. The last deadline missed so-far had been set for May 2004. As part of the so-called 'July package' adopted on 1 August 2004, the mandate to continue the negotiations has been renewed, however, without a new deadline being set.

For a brief review of ongoing negotiations see Zimmerman, 'WTO dispute settlement at ten', 46 ff.

[88] The Results of the Uruguay Round of Multilateral Trade Negotiations (Geneva: WTO, 1994), p. 453. The Ministers decided:

> The standard of review in paragraph 6 of Article 17 of the Agreement on Implementation of Article VI of GATT 1994 shall be reviewed after a period of three years with a view to considering the question of whether it is capable of general application.

See also Jackson, *Sovereignty, the WTO, and Changing Fundamentals of International Law*, p. 169.

[89] *Ibid.*

Clarify the relationship between WTO law and PIL

An important issue that bears on how WTO agreements are interpreted is the relationship between WTO law and PIL. Broadly speaking there are two schools of thought: a first school proposes a unified perspective and the second school opposes it on the ground that it will, by drawing in obligations from 'outside', upset the balance of rights and obligations contained in the WTO agreements, especially against the interests of developing countries. A key question is 'how far the process of interpretation may be used to determine the relationship between the obligations in any particular treaty and other, potentially conflicting, obligations in other parts of international law'.[90] The tension is 'between the jurisdictional constraints upon the scope of the tribunal's competence and interpretation of the law to be applied'.[91] Mclaghlan comes up with rules for the application of the idea of 'systemic integration'. The questions to be answered are the weights to be attached to external sources and to the text of the agreement in dispute.[92] The AB in *US Gasoline* case noted that the general rule of interpretation set out in VCLT 'reflects a measure of recognition that the *General Agreement* [GATT] is not to be read in clinical isolation from public international law'.[93] The problems arise beyond recognition of a minimal interface between WTO law and PIL. The critics of the unified approach point out that the fragmentation of international law is not a problem as it simply reflects the unwillingness of states to undertake at present a certain set of obligations. The critics see enforcing unity as 'a mistaken quest'.[94] For instance Trachtman observes that 'it seems quite incorrect to say that WTO law is generally trumped by international environmental, human rights, or labor agreements'.[95] The significant point is that the question of the relationship of WTO law with PIL offers much interpretative flexibility to WTO Panels and AB. It belies the assertion of a textual approach by the AB. The *Shrimp Turtle* case in which the AB accepted

[90] McLachlan, 'The principle of systemic integration and Article 31 (3) (c) of the Vienna Convention', 285.

[91] *Ibid.*, 288. [92] *Ibid.*, 310.

[93] Appellate Body Report on *US – Gasoline*, p. 17. See also Appellate Body Reports on *India – Patents (US)*, para. 46; *Japan – Alcoholic Beverages II*, pp. 10–12; and *US – DRAMs*, para. 6.13.

[94] Joel P. Trachtman, Book Review of Joost Pauwelyn, *Conflict of Norms of Public International Law: How WTO Law Relates to Other Rules of International Law* (2004) 98 *American Journal of International Law* 855.

[95] *Ibid.*, at 860.

the validity of unilateral measures to enforce environmental protection and discussed the issue of PPMs brings out the dangers of accepting a unified approach. The developing countries therefore urgently need to put forth their understanding on the basis of a comprehensive analysis of the relevant WTO jurisprudence.

Encourage production of academic scholarship

It has been repeatedly noted that widespread ambiguities characterize WTO agreements. The interpretative gaps that arise are today filled with the aid of scholarship produced in the developed world. The international trade law scholarship that emanates from there frames legal issues in specific ways or advances interpretations of texts that further the cause of developed country interests and values.[96] These scholarly interpretations often find their way into the Panel and AB reports[97] Thus, for instance, the interpretation of the Enabling Clause in the *EC Preferences* case was dominated by an interpretive community of predominantly North American and European scholars publishing on the internet or in the major trade law journals that are read by WTO judicial decision-makers.[98] This literature is said to have influenced the interpretations of the AB in the *EC Preferences* case.

The scholarship deficit that characterizes international trade law can only be bridged through the production and dissemination of quality scholarship from the developing world.[99] For this to happen its industry and universities must invest in the research of WTO law so as to be in a position to seriously contest understandings and interpretations that

[96] In debates in first world law journals the standpoint of developing countries is rarely taken into account. To give one example, in a symposium on 'The Boundaries of the WTO' in the *American Journal of International Law* no representative of the developing country or scholar was invited to write. In his reactions to the contributions to the Symposium Jackson regretted 'the absence of certain important viewpoints . . . particularly the absence of a developing, or least-developed, country' John Jackson, 'Afterword: The question of linkage' (2002) 96 *American Journal of International Law* 118. Likewise Bhagwati noted that 'almost none of the papers come to terms with the important North–South divide'. Jagdish Bhagwati, 'Afterword: The question of linkage' (2002) 96 *American Journal of International Law* 126.

[97] Shaffer and Apea, 'Institutional Choice', p. 12

[98] *Ibid.*

[99] 'given that publicists play an important role in shedding light on interpretations of international law, it is important to encourage and promote legal scholarship and publications that are development oriented'. Qureshi, *Interpreting WTO Agreements: Problems and Perspectives*, p. 137.

only further the interests of the developed world. There is a need in this respect to establish specialized institutes, launch trade law journals and create Internet sites. It would be helpful in this regard if developing countries take the conscious decision to involve its academia in disputes before the WTO DSS. For practical experience with the working of the DSS will help in advancing proposals to strengthen the position of developing countries in the WTO DSS.

Ensure careful selection of AB members

Since interpretation plays such a key role in defining the balance of rights and obligations of member states there needs to be a great deal of attention paid to the appointment of AB members. At present the US and the EU have in the words of Steinberg 'a unilateral veto' over the selection of AB members, and 'a candidate's approach to judicial decision making figures prominently in those members' decisions on whether to block a candidacy'.[100] Developing countries should equally block candidates that are biased against their interests. The interpretative record of candidates for appointment to AB should be scrutinized to see if there is any such bias. In order for their intervention to be effective key developing countries like Brazil, China and India must collectively agree on the candidates that it would support. Since the bureaucracy in developing countries has control over the process leading to the support of one or other candidate ensuring transparency in the selection process will prevent its favored candidates from being appointed as AB members.

V. Conclusion

Shaffer has ably summed up the advantages of greater participation in WTO DSS:

> First . . . WTO legal decisions affect specific economic outcomes . . . Second . . . WTO jurisprudence shapes the interpretation, application, and social perceptions of the 'law' over time, and thus affects future bargaining positions in light of these understandings . . . third . . . WTO law affects bilateral and domestic political bargaining in the shadow of a potential case without any formal complaint being filed.[101]

[100] Steinberg, 'Institutional implications of WTO accession for China', p. 249.

[101] Shaffer, 'Weaknesses and proposed improvements to the WTO Dispute Settlement System: an economic and market-oriented view', pp. 12–13.

This chapter has argued that the role and power of interpretations and the approach and method to interpretations adopted by the WTO AB and panels has not received adequate attention of policy makers in China and India, and developing countries as a whole. This is unfortunate as it is the interpretative moment that decides the balance of rights and obligations embedded in the WTO agreements. It is in this context that it has been concluded that the debate of a textual versus a law-making or gap-filling approach is a contrived one, positing a false dichotomy that does not capture the actual practice of WTO adjudicative bodies. For all interpretative approaches combine the textual and activist approaches in some measure. The claim that it is the textual approach that prevails is difficult to accept. Indeed, Article 17 (6) (ii) of the Agreement on Anti-dumping concedes that legal texts yield alternative permissible interpretations. An analysis of *India-Quantitative Restrictions*, *Shrimp Turtle* and the *EC Preferences* cases confirms that WTO Panels and AB have used permissible interpretations to favor major trading powers calling for a clearer and sharp focus on framing an interpretative strategy from the perspective of developing countries. This strategy should minimally consist of the following elements: examining on a continuous basis WTO jurisprudence and making appropriate submissions to DSB, using lessons learnt to devise an interpretative strategy for negotiations, propose the application of national deference principle to developing countries on S&DT basis, clarify the relationship between WTO law and PIL, pay greater attention to the appointment of AB members and invest resources in the production and dissemination of international trade law scholarship.

References

'Appellate Body Report on *US – Shrimp*, para. 114. See also Panel Reports on *US – Section 301 Trade Act*, para. 7.22; *India – Patents (US)*, para. 7.18; *US – Underwear*, para. 7.18; Appellate Body Report on *Argentina – Footwear (EC)*, para. 91

Bacchus, James, 'Appellators: The quest for the meaning of *and/or*', www.worldtradelaw.net/articles/bacchusappellators.pdf

Bhagwati, Jagdish, 'Afterword: The question of linkage'(2002) 96 *American Journal of International Law* 126

Charnovitz, Steve, 'Judicial independence in the World Trade Organization', www. www.worldtradelaw.net/articles/ charnovitzjudicial.pdf

Chimni, B. S., *International Law and World Order: A Critique of Contemporary Approaches* (Delhi: Sage Publications Pvt. Ltd, 1993)

'WTO, democracy and development: A view from the South' (2006) 40 *Journal of World Trade*

'WTO and environment: The legitimization of unilateral trade sanctions', *Economic and Political Weekly* 12–18 January 2002

'WTO and environment: The *Shrimp–Turtle* and *EC–Hormone* cases', *Economic and Political Weekly*, 13 May 2000

Jackson, John H., 'Afterword: The question of linkage'(2002) 96 *American Journal of International Law* 118

'International law status of WTO dispute settlement reports: Obligation to comply or option to 'buy out'?'(2004) 98 *American Journal of International Law*

Sovereignty, the WTO, and Changing Fundamentals of International Law (Cambridge University Press, 2006)

Kaushik, Atul, 'Dispute settlement system at the World Trade Organization' *Economic and Political Weekly*, 12 January 2008

Malawer, Stuart S., 'United States–China trade litigation in the WTO' http://papers.ssrn.com/sol3/papers.cfm?abstract_id=1169450

McLachlan, Campbell, 'The principle of systemic integration and article 31 (3) (c) of the Vienna Convention' (2005) 54 *International and Comparative Law Quarterly*

Oesch, Matthias, *Standards of Review in WTO Dispute Resolution* (Oxford University Press, 2003)

Pauwelyn, Joost, *Conflict of Norms of Public International Law: How WTO Law Relates to Other Rules of International Law* (Cambridge University Press, 2003)

Perez, Oren, 'Reconstructing science: the The *Hormone* conflict between the EU and the United States' (1998) 1 *European Foreign Affairs Review*

Picciotto, Sol, 'The WTO's Appellate Body: Legal formalism as a legitimation of global governance', School of Public Policy Working Paper Series: ISSN 1479–9472 Working Paper 14, January 2005, http://www.www.ucl.ac.uk/spp/download/publications/spp-wp-14.pdf

Qureshi, Asif, *Interpreting WTO Agreements: Problems and Perspectives* (Cambridge University Press, 2006)

Shaffer, Gregory, 'Weaknesses and proposed improvements to the WTO Dispute Settlement System: an An economic and market-oriented view', May 2005 http://wage.wisc.edu/uploads/WTO%20Conference/ shaffer%20paper-weaknesses-short.pdf

Shaffer, Gregory and Apea, Yvonne, 'Institutional choice in the GSP case: Who decides the conditions for trade preferences? The law and politics of rights', http://www.www.worldtradelaw.net/articles.htm#shaffer

Steinberg, Richard, 'Institutional implications of WTO accession for China', Institute on Global Conflict and Cooperation, Working Papers (February 1999)

Trachtman, Joel P., Book Review of Joost Pauwelyn, *Conflict of Norms of Public International Law: How WTO Law Relates to Other Rules of International Law*(2004) 98 *American Journal of International Law*

Zimmerman, Thomas A., 'WTO dispute settlement: General appreciation and role of India' available at http://papers.ssrn.com/sol3/ papers.cfm?abstract_id=1014355 visited 11 October 2008

'WTO dispute settlement at Tenten: Evolution, experiences, and evaluation' (2005) 60 *Aussenwirtschaft: The Swiss Review of International Economic Relations*

7

China, India and dispute settlement in the WTO and RTAs

LOCKNIE HSU

> You should respect each other and refrain from disputes; you should not, like water and oil, repel each other, but should, like milk and water, mingle together.
> – Buddha
> (Johannes P. Schade, *Encyclopedia of World Religions* (Foreign Media Group, Inc., 2006))

I. Introduction

India's population is approximately 1.1 billion while that of China is approximately 1.3 billion.[1] Together, they comprise more than a third of the world's population and a formidable economic pair in the developing world.

China and India share several characteristics. Both have great ancient civilizations of rich and long-standing cultures. Parts of their populations share common religious traditions. In the international arena, China and India together forged the Five Principles of Peaceful Coexistence in the 1950s, which still strongly influence developing state relations today.[2] However, the two also diverge in many ways.

Unlike India, China is emerging from its chrysalis of a centrally planned economy and transforming into a 'socialist market economy'. As part of this transformation, its legal system, belonging to the civil law tradition, has been undergoing massive changes in recent years – many of which are a result of its entering the World Trade Organization (WTO). In terms of rule of law, China has a greater challenge in

[1] World Bank country profile data, 2004, for India (http://devdata.worldbank.org/external/CPProfile.asp?PTYPE=CP&CCODE=IND) and China (http://devdata.worldbank.org/external/CPProfile.asp?CCODE=CHN&PTYPE=CP) respectively.

[2] The Principles are found in the 'Agreement Between the People's Republic of China and the Republic of India on Trade and Intercourse Between Tibet Region of China and India', signed on 29 April 1954.

overcoming perceptions about the strength and soundness of its legal system and adherence to the rule of law.[3] Enormous changes have been made to China's legal system in the wake of WTO membership. Some of these changes are of watershed significance, for they spell departures from prior tradition and practice.

By contrast, India is an established parliamentary democracy, heavily influenced in its law, economics and civil service systems by British presence which dates back to as early as the eighteenth century. The English influence has led to Indian law being of the common law tradition. Breaking away from colonial rule, India became a republic in 1947, the same year that the GATT was signed. Post-Independence, India has seen a vast change in economic wealth from the 1950s where it was a poor, agrarian economy, to the present rapid-growth, IT-driven economy. Although India has had a market-oriented economy much earlier than China, significant liberalization came about during the 1990s. This was a period that saw rapid deregulation, dismantling of state monopolies and privatization. Unlike China's concentrated and large-scale reforms, India's reforms have been described as 'piecemeal and incremental'.[4]

In terms of WTO dispute settlement, China is, by virtue of its accession in late 2001, a relative newcomer to the system. It has, however, already participated as a complainant in seven cases, and as a third party in at least sixty-five WTO disputes.[5] India, on the other hand, has been a founding GATT member prior to formation of the WTO, and has played a part in GATT activities from an early date. As a founding member of the WTO as well, India has had more time and experience in the use of the WTO dispute settlement system. India has, for instance, successfully challenged laws and practices of other members including countries larger and wealthier than itself. In addition, India has also found itself a respondent, challenged under the WTO system.

[3] Numerous commentaries have discussed the rule of law in China after the Mao era and the legal reforms which China has been undertaking. See, for instance, Stanley B. Lubman, *Bird in a Cage: Legal Reform in China After Mao* (Stanford University Press, 1999); Kong Qingjiang, 'Enforcement of WTO agreements in China', in Deborah Z. Cass, Brett G. Williams and George Barker (eds.), *China and the World Trading System: Entering the New Millennium* (New York: Cambridge University Press, 2003), pp. 148–9; Alice E. S. Tay and Hamish Redd, 'China: Trade, law and human rights', in Cass, Williams and Barker (eds.), *China and the World Trading System*, pp. 163–5.

[4] Arvind Panagariya, 'India's economic reforms: What has been done? What remains to be done?', ADB ERD Policy Brief Series, No. 2, 2001, www.adb.org/Documents/EDRC/Policy_Briefs/PB002.pdf.

[5] See www.wto.org/English/thewto_e/countries_e/china_e.htm#disputes.

Despite the differences, there are many new points of convergence emerging for China and India. Both enjoy WTO membership. As a result, both have submitted to the jurisdiction of the WTO dispute settlement system. They may be both foes (should a dispute arise between them) and allies (in joint action against other members) within this system. Looking for instance at the future of the WTO dispute settlement system, China and India together can provide a strong voice in proposing improvements to the Understanding on Rules and Procedures Governing the Settlement of Disputes (DSU) system, especially with respect to developing member interests.

Apart from sharing the WTO arena and increasing roles in world trade, both China and India are increasingly becoming parties to regional trade agreements (RTAs). These agreements contain binding commitments. China, for instance, has entered a free trade agreement with the ten members of the Association of Southeast Asian Nations (ASEAN), while negotiations are underway for an agreement between ASEAN and India. Both China and India are also parties to bilateral trade agreements. For example, China has signed agreements with Hong Kong, Chile and Thailand, and is negotiating others, while India has signed an agreement with Singapore. As these agreements usually also carry their own dispute settlement systems, both China and India therefore have access to, as well as face challenges under, these other systems should disputes arise under those agreements.

II. Multilateral commitments

The long process of negotiations leading up to China's accession to the WTO in 2001 culminated in a legally binding set of commitments by China vis-à-vis each of the other members. If the accession had been a simple agreement to fulfil WTO treaties existing at the time, China would have stood in a very similar situation to other existing members – like India, which was a founding member bound by the agreements concluded at the Uruguay Round of negotiations. This is, however, not the case for China. The accession commitments exceed those made by founding members of WTO, leading to the view that China's commitments are 'WTO-plus'.[6]

What implications do these commitments have for China, in terms of dispute settlement risks? It is submitted that four factors increase China's legal risks in WTO dispute settlement.

[6] See, for instance, Julia Ya Qin, '"WTO-plus" obligations and their implications for the World Trade Organization legal system' (2003) 37 (3) *Journal of World Trade* 483.

First, China's legal obligations found in the Protocol of Accession and the Working Party Report exceed those of, say, a founding member of the WTO. Unlike India, which entered into the same agreements as other founding members, China accepted a number of additional commitments through its Protocol of Accession and the related Working Party Report. Such commitments expose China to a greater risk of challenge, in view of the number of additional obligations. While not all such commitments can be discussed here, a few are highlighted as illustrations.

For instance, general WTO membership already imposes requirements of transparency and uniform application of laws at various levels of government by each member. China, however, has specifically made additional commitments in this respect. In its Protocol of Accession, China committed to ensuring the uniformity of application and compliance with WTO of central and local laws and regulations. Given the concern over difficulties arising from divergences in central and sub-central government decision-making, this is no mean promise and opens China to allegations of violations of WTO agreement as well as liability under the Protocol and Working Party Report.[7] The United States, for one, has already raised concerns over the lack of uniformity in transparency compliance at various levels of government in China and it is not inconceivable that this may form the basis of a complaint in future.[8] In fact, a dispute relating to a such obligations has already come before a WTO panel.[9]

Another commitment by China relates to the regulation of state-owned enterprises. This is found in Articles 6 and 10.2 of the Protocol, as well as paragraphs 208 to 217 of the Working Party Report. Clearly, the obligations there surpass those found in the GATT.[10]

Commitments such as the above illustrate the additional risk undertaken by China of being brought to WTO dispute settlement, should any violation at any level of government be shown.

[7] See, for instance, the remarks of Kong, 'Enforcement of WTO agreements', 148–50. See also concerns raised by members of the Working Party for China's accession, at paras. 69 and 71.

[8] USTR Report on China's Compliance and National Trade Estimates Report 2006, www.ustr.gov/assets/Document_Library/Reports_Publications/2006/2006_NTE_Report/asset_ upload_file684_9235.pdf at 158–59.

[9] The United States, Canada and the European Communities have succeeded in a complaint in WTO panel proceedings in respect of China's taxes on automobile parts. See www.wto.org/english/tratop_e/dispu_e/cases_e/ds342_e.htm, text accompanying note 27.

[10] Provisions on state trading enterprises can be found in Article XVII GATT 1994, and the Understanding on the Interpretation of Article XVII of GATT 1994.

Secondly, the additional obligations have not so far been interpreted or applied by the WTO dispute settlement machinery. Several of these contain text which differ from that in existing WTO agreements, or contain new rules. An example of such new rules vis-à-vis China – already examined elsewhere – is the provisions regarding price comparability in anti-dumping found in the Protocol.[11] Such new treaty language as regards China's commitments has no counterpart in existing WTO agreements (and thus no interpretations in WTO case law). While one would expect any interpretation of such language to be carried out in accordance with the principles in the Vienna Convention on the Law of Treaties, there remains a considerable amount of uncertainty as to how such interpretation will play out.[12]

Thirdly, despite diligent, ongoing reforms, China's governmental system comprising the National People's Congress, State Council, local people's congresses, provincial, city and county governments still makes it a challenge to ensure that all of these fully comply with WTO obligations. As a member of WTO, China is obliged to ensure this. In addition, China specifically committed to such multi-level compliance in Article 2 of the Protocol and Working Party Report paragraph 73 which includes Special Economic Zones. For a large country with several sub-levels of government, each step in decision-making, interpretation and implementation in relation to WTO obligations carries an added risk of non-compliance. Even though existing provisions of GATT 1994 and other agreements do contain requirements of compliance at all sub-levels,[13] the additional commitments in this area by China coupled with its complex layers of bureaucracy bring added risks of challenge.

Fourthly, China's low-cost labour translates into relatively cheaper goods, and these continue to be viewed with suspicion with a view to dumping allegations. In goods of interest to China's trading partners, such as shoes, bags and furniture, the risk of antidumping allegations is particularly high.[14] Domestic disquiet regarding China's economic-rise – often seen as taking place at the domestic constituents' expense in

[11] See Michael Lennard, 'China's Accession Protocol and Anti-dumping' in Cass, Williams and Barker (eds.), *China and the World Trading* System, pp. 393–99.

[12] On applicability of the Vienna Convention on the Law of Treaties to China's Protocol of Accession, see Lennard, 'China's Accession Protocol'.

[13] See, for instance, GATT 1994 Art. XXIV:12; GATS Art. I:3; SPS Agreement Art. 13 and the DSU Art. 22.9.

[14] See, for instance, comments in February 2006 by Peter Mandelson, the EU Trade Commissioner, http://ec.europa.eu/comm/trade/issues/respectrules/anti_dumping/pr230206_en.htm. See also www.euractiv.com/en/trade/china-eu-trade-issues-pile/article-153226.

other WTO countries – may exacerbate this risk. Strong lobby and interest groups in these countries may make it more urgent for their governments to be seen to be dealing with 'the China problem', by taking it to the WTO.

Apart from the above factors particularly pertinent to China, a legal risk which exists for all WTO members is the possibility of facing a non-violation complaint. Article XXIII:1(b) of GATT permits such complaints (through its words, '*whether or not* [a measure] conflicts with the provisions of this Agreement', emphasis added). While the use of this provision has been extremely limited, it remains a potential source of disputes especially where no particular measure may be identified as having violated WTO agreements. In the first WTO case brought under this provision, *Japan – Measures Affecting Consumer Photographic Film and Paper*, the complaint failed.[15] The panel stated that the remedy in Article XXIII:1(b) 'should be approached with caution and should remain an exceptional remedy'.[16] This sentiment was echoed in another case where the complaint arose, in *European Communities – Measures Affecting Asbestos and Asbestos-containing Products*.[17] In particular, the WTO panel in *Korea – Government Procurement* was prepared to recognize that treaty negotiations can lead to the formation of legitimate expectations – a notion which arises specifically in relation to non-violation complaints – which may be nullified or impaired in a non-violation situation.[18] Notwithstanding the failed attempts to use this complaint and the caveat on it, therefore, it does not mean that a future complaint cannot be raised, or succeed.

III. WTO disputes and China

A. *Dispute avoidance*

WTO disputes may be viewed from a 'defensive' view and an 'offensive' view. On the 'defensive' side, a member should be vigilant and aware of its ongoing obligation under the WTO Agreement to ensure continual

[15] WT/DS44/R, panel report, adopted 22 April 1998. For an overview of such complaints and provisions on them in recent free trade agreements, see Hsu, 'Non-violation complaints:World Trade Organization issues and recent free trade agreements'(2005) 39 (2) *Journal of World Trade* 205.

[16] WT/DS44/R, panel report, para. 10.37.

[17] WT/DS135/AB/R, adopted 5 April 2001, para. 186.

[18] WT/DS163/R, panel report, adopted 19 June, 2000, para. 7.100. On the evidence, the panel found that the US had, however, not discharged its burden; see paras. 7.93–7.126.

compliance.[19] In addition, a member can take certain precautions for dispute avoidance, to reduce the likelihood of a dispute either occurring, escalating, or leading to defeat if it went to a panel or the Appellate Body. On the 'offensive' side, each country should seek to ensure that that the interests of their companies are protected in other members, in the treatment of their goods, services and investments. If any violation is found, the country of the aggrieved company may take the matter up at the WTO; whether it ever proceeds beyond consultations would dependent on factors such as the nature of the dispute, action or inaction by the country complained against and the interests at stake. Even if a matter does not proceed to a full panel proceeding, members have to be aware of possible action that they may need to take up at the WTO.

In China, institutions already exist to provide 'early warning' systems in areas such as antidumping and safeguard remedy measures imposed by other countries as a defensive measure.[20] Such systems can help alert the government as to potential complaints that may need to be raised, and the need to gather evidence for such a case. Besides providing an early heads-up on potential disputes, such systems can also help members clarify matters, with a view to possible settlement and avoidance of full-blown WTO dispute proceedings having to be brought.

In terms of dispute avoidance, China also needs to ensure continuing and consistent adherence to rule of law particularly in its treatment of foreign investments and products and services, continuing commitment to transparency and compliance at all levels in accordance with GATT Article XXIV:12.

Two developments in the WTO system, namely increased levels of legalization, and an increase in the number of transparency-related obligations are imposing a profound change on China as a WTO member and have required China to undertake a major revamp of its laws, regulations, procedures and institutions. To head off any allegations of violation of such obligations, China enacted new laws, including the Legislation Law (2000), the Administrative Permission Law (2003), and the Regulations on Procedures for the Formulation of Administrative Permission (2002). The comprehensive scope and language show the People's Republic of China (PRC) government's

[19] Article XVI:4 of the WTO Agreement states: 'Each Member shall ensure the conformity of its laws, regulations and administrative procedures with its obligations as provided in the annexed Agreements'.

[20] For instance, the Shanghai WTO Affairs Consultation Center has such an early-warning system. See its website at www.sccwto.net.

intention to meet obligations of transparency in lawmaking and adherence to the rule of law.

Another aspect of dispute avoidance relates to the availability of information and strength of bargaining power based on such information. While countries such as the United States keep close watch over China's compliance with obligations in the WTO agreements, China's accession commitments and commitments to the US, made in bilateral fora such as in the US–India Joint Commission on Commerce and Trade (JCCT),[21] China has so far not – at least not publicly – kept an equivalent, meticulous record and plan of action to ensure other countries' compliance.

In addition, China is subject to special annual trade policy reviews for the first eight years after accession, and a final review in the tenth year.[22] These reviews provide an opportunity for other members to seek clarification and explanation from China on her laws, regulations and practices, especially if they are new. Through such reviews, potential disputes may surface, be defused or accelerate into a full-fledged trade dispute that makes it way to a panel. As a 'defensive' move to prevent disputes from crystallizing, China can use these reviews as opportunities to provide clarification and updating of its progress in compliance.

China's many bilateral negotiation and dialogue channels with major trade partners, can also serve as dispute avoidance instruments.[23]

Further, on the 'defensive' side, China has so far not had any case proceed against it before a panel (although one case is pending). The first case initiated against China in the WTO was that of *China – Value-Added Tax on Integrated Circuits*.[24] The United States complained against the value-added tax (VAT) on integrated circuits (ICs) imposed

[21] The United States conducts a number of reviews on Chinese laws, regulations and policies. These include those by United States Trade Representative (USTR), such as the recent 'Top-to-Bottom' Review on US–India Trade Relations (February 2006), the 2005 Report to Congress on China's WTO Compliance (11 December 2005), and those under the 'Special 301' review on intellectual property rights (April 2005).

[22] Article 18.4 of the Protocol of Accession.

[23] For instance, China has trade dialogues with the US on various levels, including the JCCT, the US–India Joint Economic Committee, the Joint Liaison Group, the US–India Economic Development and Reform Dialogue, and the Joint Committee on Cooperation in Agriculture (see US–India Trade Relations Top-to-Bottom Review, www.ustr.gov/assets/Document_Library/Reports_Publications/2006/asset_upload_file921_8938.pdf at 21). With the EC, there is the EU-China Summit, the EC-China Joint Committee, meetings of the Economic and Trade Working Group, the Trade Policy Dialogue, a joint study process on areas on the Doha negotiation agenda, and sectoral dialogues (see http://ec.europa.eu/comm/external_relations/china/intro/sect.htm).

[24] WT/DS309.

by China on imported ICs. Like imported ICs, sale of domestically produced or designed ICs were subject to a 17 per cent VAT. The complaint alleged, however, that unlike other imported ICs, the ICs produced in, or designed in China but produced elsewhere, enjoyed a partial VAT refund which amounted to less favorable treatment for imported ICs. This dispute was eventually settled, with China agreeing to revoke or eliminate the measures complained about.

In 2005, disputes over textile quotas with the United States and the European Union (EU) were averted through bilateral negotiations. The negotiations led to agreements with both trade partners.[25]

More recently, the United States Trade Representative's office (USTR) announced that another potential WTO complaint had been averted in relation to Kraft linerboard from the United States. China had dropped an antidumping order on the goods after negotiations and an announcement by the United States of its intention to initiate WTO proceedings.[26]

In September 2006, the United States, European Communities (EC) and Canada initiated WTO panel proceedings against China, and the panel delivered its report in July 2008.[27] This is the first case in which China's compliance with obligations under the Protocol of Accession and Working Party report has been formally called into question in the WTO dispute settlement arena.[28]

On the 'offensive' side, China has already participated as a complainant in seven cases. In the first such case, China brought the complaint against the US in *US – Steel Safeguards*[29] as a co-complainant with several other countries, barely three months after its accession to the WTO. It is clearly not averse to making use of the system. The first case in which China participated as a complainant in the WTO dispute settlement system was when China submitted the request for consultations in March 2002 – just three months after it formally joined

[25] Agreement with the EU was reached in June 2005 (see http://ec.europa.eu/comm/external_relations/china/intro/memo05_201.htm) while agreement with the US was reached in November 2005.

[26] USTR website at www.ustr.gov/Document_Library/Press_Releases/2006/January/China_Terminates_Antidumping_Duty_Order_on_Kraft_Linerboard.html.

[27] WT/DS339/R, WT/DS340/R, WT/DS342/R, panel report circulated 18 July 2008; see www.wto.org/english/tratop_e/dispu_e/cases_e/ds342_e.htm. The complaint also raises provisions of the GATT 1994, TRIMS, SCM and Rules of Origin agreements.

[28] See 'Canada's request for consultations with China dated 13 April 2006', www.dfait-maeci.gc.ca/tna-nac/documents/Canada-AutomibileParts130405.pdf. Australia, the EC, Japan, Mexico and the US have joined the request for consultations by Canada.

[29] United States – Definitive Safeguard Measures on Imports of Certain Steel Products, WT/DS252.

the WTO. This shows that China is not averse to using the WTO system where the interests concerned are important enough.

B. *Examples of disputes*

There are some flashpoints which have led to other disputes in the WTO with major WTO partners, including those in the areas of international property rights (IPRs), valuation of the Chinese yuan and under the transitional safeguard mechanism which China agreed to under its Protocol of Accession. For now, potential disputes with the United States and the EU in the area of textiles and footwear appear to have been diffused through bilateral agreements.[30]

In 2005, the United States placed China on its Priority Watch List under its so-called 'Special 301' provisions.[31] Subsequently, it formally launched a complaint in 2007 in the WTO system over China's enforcement of IPR laws.[32] In 2007, the United States also launched a complaint against China in respect of trading rights and distribution services of certain publications and audiovisual entertainment products.[33]

On the issue of China's currency exchange rate, there have been at least two US Bills put forward to provide for action to be taken by the United States against countries found to engage in 'currency manipulation' (as defined in those Bills) in the WTO.[34] Whether an actual complaint will be lodged at the WTO remains to be seen.

In February 2006, the USTR prepared a 'top-to-bottom' review of US–India trade relations. Some possible flashpoints can be found in the review. Transparency is an issue which crops up repeatedly in that review and in the USTR Report to Congress of China's compliance in 2006. Another relates to China's restriction on distribution of imported books, newspapers and magazines in China by foreign businesses. The restriction, found in the Administrative Measures on the Subscription of

[30] With the US, China signed the Memorandum of Understanding Between the Governments of the United States of America and the People's Republic of China Concerning Trade in Textile and Apparel Products) on 5 November 2005, while with the EU, China signed the EU–China Textile Agreement on 10 June 2005. See www.ustr.gov/assets/Document_Library/Reports_Publications/2006/2006_Trade_Policy_Agenda/asset_upload_file922_9075.pdf, p. 237, and http://europa.eu.int/comm/external_relations/china/intro/memo05_201.htm respectively.

[31] 'Special 301' refers to IPR enforcement provisions under the US' 1974 Trade Act, which requires the USTR to monitor and take action against countries identified has having weak IPR protection.

[32] See WT/DT362/R.

[33] *Ibid.* [34] See CRS Issue Brief for Congress, p. 16.

Imported Publications issued in 2004,[35] appeared to limit distribution of such imports to Chinese state-owned enterprises.

IV. WTO disputes and India

India's experience with the WTO and its predecessor agreement, the GATT, is of longer standing than that of China.

Up to April 2010, India had filed eighteen complaints, acted as respondent in twenty complaints and as third party in fifty-one cases.[36] India has scored several successes in the complaints it lodged. In particular, it has succeeded in challenging systemic aspects of foreign regimes, leading to a chain of further challenges of such aspects by other complaining members. Some of the more significant or recent disputes are mentioned here.

A. *As complainant*

US – Shirts and Blouses[37] was the first complaint that India brought under the WTO's dispute settlement system. The complaint brought India into its first direct trade dispute with the United States. The dispute arose from a transitional safeguard measure imposed by the United States under the Agreement on Textiles and Clothing. Most notably, this case has been cited for its pronouncements on the allocation of burden of proof in a WTO dispute proceeding.

In *EC – Bedlinen*[38] India successfully challenged the EU's practice of 'zeroing' in its calculation of antidumping margins. This in turn has encouraged Canada to challenge 'zeroing' by the United States in the *US – Final Dumping Determination on Softwood Lumber from Canada,*[39] and further challenges of the practice by the EC.[40] India was also one of the complainants in the very important decision, *US – Shrimps.*[41]

In *Turkey – Textiles,*[42] India successfully challenged Turkey's measures in preparation for joining the customs union of the EU. India also succeeded

[35] See www.fdi.gov.cn/resupload/epdf/e03894.pdf: under the Decree, only 'imported publication management entities' may distribute imported publications.
[36] See www.wto.org/english/thewto_e/countries_e/india_e.htm.
[37] WT/DS33/AB/R, Appellate Body report adopted 23 May 1997.
[38] WT/DS/141/AB/R, Appellate Body report adopted 12 March 2001.
[39] WT/DS/294/AB/RW, Appellate Body report, adopted 1 September 2006.
[40] US – Laws, Regulations and Methodology for Calculating Dumping Margins ('Zeroing'), WT/DS294/AB/R, Appellate Body report, adopted 9 May 2006.
[41] WT/DS58/AB/R, Appellate Body report, adopted 6 November 1998.
[42] WT/DS34/AB/R, Appellate Body report, adopted 19 November 1999.

against the United States as a complainant in the *US – India Steel Plate* case[43] and as co-complainant in the *US – Byrd Amendment* case.[44]

Other significant successes of India as complainant include *EC – Tariff Preferences*, where India successfully challenged the preferential tariff arrangements offered by the EC to certain drug-exporting countries under its so-called Drug Arrangements, and *US – Customs Bond Directive for Merchandise Subject to Anti-dumping/Countervailing Duties*.[45]

In *US – Rules of Origin for Textiles and Apparel Products*, India did not succeed in its challenge of the US regulations on rules of origin applicable to textile products.[46]

B. *As respondent*

India has acted as respondent in several disputes at the WTO, such as the case where its balance-of-payments measures were challenged, *India – Quantitative Restrictions on Imports of Agricultural, Textile and Industrial Products*.[47] In *India – Automobiles*, India's regulations relating to local content and trade balancing in respect of automobiles were successfully challenged by the EC and United States.[48] In *India – Protection of Pharmaceutical Patents*, the United States successfully challenged India's patent system under the TRIPS Agreement, arguing that the failure to provide a transitional 'mailbox' system for registration of patents was a violation of the agreement of Article 70.8 of the agreement. As a result, India has amended its patent legislation to take into account this challenge, among other things.[49] Bangladesh's complaint against India in *India – Antidumping Measure on Batteries* from Bangladesh was the first complaint ever lodged at the WTO by a least-developed country. That dispute has been resolved by a mutually satisfactory solution.[50]

[43] WT/DS206/R, panel reported 29 July 2002.

[44] WT/DS217/AB/R, WT/DS234/AB/R, Appellate Body reports adopted 27 January 2003.

[45] Respectively, WT/DS246/AB/R, Appellate Body report, adopted 20 April 2004, and WT/DS345/R, panel report circulated 1 August 2008.

[46] WT/DS243/R, panel report adopted 21 July 2003.

[47] WT/DS90/AB/R, Appellate Body report, adopted 22 September 1999.

[48] WT/DS146/R and WT/DS175/R, adopted 5 April 2002 (the appeal was withdrawn).

[49] WT/DS50/AB/R, Appellate Body report, adopted 16 January 1998. The Indian Patents (Amendment) Act was enacted in 2005 and includes amendments dealing with patent registration as well as biopiracy; No. 15 of 2005. See www.patentoffice.nic.in/ipr/patent/patent_2005.pdf.

[50] DS306. See www.wto.org/english/tratop_e/dispu_e/cases_e/ds306_e.htm.

V. Antidumping disputes

In terms of the antidumping regime in WTO, both China and India have been making use of antidumping procedures. As at 31 December 2005, China was maintaining definitive duties on products from nineteen WTO members, while India was maintaining measures against products from thirty WTO members.[51] As against products from each other, for just the period of 1 July–31 December 2005, India had initiated antidumping cases against no fewer than twenty-five products from China – the largest number against any of its WTO partners (as compared with eight products from the United States being targeted in the period) – while in the same period, China had initiated such action against one product from India.[52] As against other partners, products from Japan faced the highest number of actions by China, while products from the EU and its constituent states faced the most actions by India. At the same time, for the period in question, India notified the highest number of new final measures applied, after the EU.[53] While these actions may not culminate in dispute settlement actions, and although the number of antidumping actions as a whole has declined,[54] they do indicate the frequent resort by both countries to use of antidumping mechanisms to check imported goods and potential for disputes to be brought to the DSU system.

VI. Special and differential treatment provisions

Before mentioning the special and differential provisions in WTO dispute settlement which are available to both China and India as developing country members, it should be noted that the rules-based DSU system enables both countries to both challenge and defend themselves against other WTO members, big or small. The playing field is more level now

[51] See, respectively, Semi-Annual Report under Article 16.4 of the Anti-dumping Agreement by China to the WTO Committee on Antidumping Practices, G/ADP/N/139/CHN, 17 March 2006, at 8–9, and similar Report by India to the same Committee, G/ADP/N/130/IND, 8 May 2006, at 7–10 (counting actions against various groups of EU members as one action against one member for this purpose).

[52] See previous note.

[53] WTO press release 2006, www.wto.org/english/news_e/pres06_e/pr441_e.htm.

[54] See WTO press releases for 2005 and 2006, respectively www.wto.org/english/news_e/pres05_e/pr406_e.htm and www.wto.org/english/news_e/pres06_e/pr441_e.htm, and more recently, www.wto.org/english/news_e/pres08_e/pr535_e.htm (where the Secretariat reported that the member reporting the most initiations and imposition of new measures in the second half of 2007 was India, while China was the most frequent subject for investigations and of new measures during the same period).

than in the days of GATT, through removal of the 'veto' that used to be possible. Instead of permitting a country that has lost a challenge to block adoption – as was possible pre-WTO – the rule is now one of 'reverse consensus'. Unless all members choose not to adopt a panel or Appellate Body report, such a report will be adopted. The consensus process has been reversed in favour of the 'winning' country. Therefore, whether China or India (or any other developing country) is pitted against a richer and politically powerful opponent in dispute settlement, the rules of the DSU apply strictly. Any weakness in dispute settlement remains in either the flaws or incompleteness of the DSU rules, and not in an unequal access to a law-based outcome. For instance, criticisms remain of the implementation and retaliation processes of the DSU but these processes apply to all WTO disputes, whether brought by China, India or other members.

As a WTO member, China would be able to take advantage of special and differential treatment (SDT) provisions in WTO agreements insofar as China has not agreed to forego any of these in its Protocol of Accession and the Working Party Report. In dispute settlement in particular, there are provisions that specifically address developing countries' concerns, ranging from panel composition (Article 8.10 DSU) to assistance (Article 27.2 DSU).

Similarly, India, as a developing country member, would be able to avail herself of special and differential treatment provisions in WTO agreements.

However, there has been dissatisfaction among developing countries – including China and India – over the SDT provisions in the WTO agreements. A number of proposals have been submitted to strengthen these provisions, some relating to the role of dispute settlement in this respect. Some of these are discussed in Section VIII.B below.

VII. China and India: Regional and other dispute settlement

A. *Dispute settlement systems in free trade agreements*

a) ASEAN–China Framework Agreement and Dispute Settlement Agreement

In 2002, China signed a Framework Agreement with the ten nations in ASEAN to establish an ASEAN–China FTA[55] (the ASEAN–China Framework Agreement). Article 11 of the Framework Agreement envisaged the

[55] Framework Agreement on Comprehensive Economic Co-operation Between the Association of South East Asian Nations and the People's Republic of China, signed on 4 November 2002 and in force with effect from 1 July 2003.

establishment of a dispute settlement mechanism and procedures 'for the purposes' of the Agreement. In 2004, such a mechanism was set up through the Agreement on Dispute Settlement Mechanism of the Framework Agreement on Comprehensive Economic Co-operation Between the Association of Southeast Asian Nations and the People's Republic of China (China–ASEAN DSM Agreement).[56]

The China–ASEAN DSM Agreement is important. It establishes a dispute settlement system modeled after the WTO's dispute settlement system. This in itself is not startling, as many regional trade agreements are, too.[57] However, the significance for China is that it represents a willingness to submit to a rule-based system. It indicates yet another commitment by China to the rule of law in settling trade disputes under the ASEAN–China Framework Agreement.

In particular, it is an acknowledgment of China's submission to rules of international law which may be applicable in relations with fellow signatories. Article 8.3(b) of the China–ASEAN DSM provides that the arbitration tribunal established to resolve a dispute 'shall make its decision in accordance with the Framework Agreement and the rules of international law applicable between the parties to the dispute'.[58]

Extending this observation in two areas: it means firstly that China is willing to submit to scrutiny of an arbitration tribunal its government measures at all levels. This is because Article 2.4 of the China–ASEAN DSM Agreement states that it may be invoked with respect to measures of 'central, regional or local governments or authorities'.

Secondly, Article 1(b) of the ASEAN–China Framework Agreement states as an objective, the intention to 'further liberalise and promote trade in goods and services *as well as create a transparent, liberal and facilitative investment regime*' (emphasis added). While the Agreement itself does not contain any express obligation relating to transparency, if the eventual Free Trade Agreement that is being negotiated does, then issues of transparency may also form the subject-matter of dispute settlement in future.

[56] Signed on 29 November 2004, in force with effect from 1 January 2005.

[57] See, for instance, the ASEAN Protocol on Enhanced Dispute Settlement Mechanism, signed on 29 November 2004, in force with effect from the same date, www.aseansec.org/16754.htm.

[58] This provision appears to be partially based on the language found in Article 31.3(c) of the Vienna Convention on the Law of Treaties (VCLT), relating to examination of a treaty's context. The VCLT provision states: '3. There shall be taken into account, together with the context: . . . (c) any relevant rules of international law applicable in the relations between the parties'.

A final noteworthy point in relation to the China–ASEAN DSM Agreement is its express exclusion of non-violation complaints[59] and implicit exclusion of 'situation' complaints.[60] Article XXIII of GATT provides for both these types of complaints.[61] While the 'situation' complaint has not posed a practical problem in the GATT and WTO systems, the non-violation complaint has been a subject of discussion and criticism.[62]

Articles 4 and 10.3 of the China–ASEAN DSM Agreement retain the concept of 'nullification or impairment' found in Article XXIII of GATT 1994. If an arbitration tribunal is called upon in future to interpret this phrase, it is conceivable that WTO/GATT jurisprudence on the same phrase will have some bearing. Even though there is no formal hierarchy governing decisions made by WTO and other trade dispute tribunals, a common practice of referring to WTO interpretations has been observed. For instance, the North American Free Trade Agreement (NAFTA) and the International Centre for Settlement of Investment Disputes (ICSID) tribunals, interpreting language similar to that in a WTO agreement, have often made references to WTO interpretations as a guide, while recognizing that other provisions in the treaties being interpreted may differ from those in WTO agreements.[63]

[59] Footnote 1 to Article 4.1 states: 'Non-violation disputes are not permitted under this Agreement'.

[60] By the wording of Art. 4.1:

1. A party complained against shall accord due consideration and adequate opportunity for consultations regarding a request for consultations made by a complaining party with respect to any matter affecting the implementation or application of the Framework Agreement whereby:
   (a) any benefit accruing to the complaining party directly or indirectly under the Framework Agreement is being nullified or impaired; or
   (b) the attainment of any objective of the Framework Agreement is being impeded, as a result of the failure of the party complained against to carry out its obligations under the Framework Agreement.

[61] For a detailed discussion of non-violation complaints especially in relation to regional trading agreements, see Hsu, 'Non-violation Complaints'.

[62] See, for instance, Frieder Roessler, 'the concept of nullification and impairment in the legal system of the World Trade Organization', in E.-U. Petersmann (ed.), *International Trade Law and the GATT/WTO Dispute Settlement System* (The Hague: Kluwer Law International, 1997), vol. XI, ch. 2; Thomas Cottier and Krista N. Schefer, 'Non-violation complaints in WTO/GATT dispute settlement: Past, present and future', in M. Bronckers and R. Quick (eds.), *New Directions in International Economic Law, Essays in Honour of John H. Jackson* (The Hague: Kluwer Law International, 2000), ch. 4.

[63] For example, in the NAFTA dispute in *Cross-Border Trucking Services*, the arbitration panel referred to WTO jurisprudence for 'guidance' on the interpretation of the phrase

b) China–Thailand and China–Chile bilateral free trade agreements

The China–Chile agreement, signed on 18 November 2005, is the first bilateral FTA signed between China and a Latin American country. At the time of writing, the texts were unavailable to the writer.

c) Closer Economic Partnership Agreement (CEPA)

The Closer Economic Partnership Agreement (CEPA) contains no elaborate dispute settlement mechanism. Instead, Article 18 provides for resolution of disputes through a Joint Steering Committee comprising senior representatives or officials designated by each side, whose decisions are to be by consensus.[64] Further provision is made for problems in interpretation or implementation to be resolved 'through consultation in the spirit of friendship and cooperation'.

d) ASEAN–India

This agreement is currently under negotiation.

e) South Asian Free Trade Area, South Asia Free Trade Agreement (SAFTA), South Asian Association for Regional Co-operation (SAARC), SAARC Preferential Trading Arrangement (SAPTA)

The South Asian Free Trade Area Agreement was signed in 2004 by the People's Republic of Bangladesh, the Kingdom of Bhutan, the Republic of India, the Republic of Maldives, the Kingdom of Nepal, the Islamic Republic of Pakistan and the Democratic Socialist Republic of Sri Lanka. The dispute settlement provisions are found in Article 20 of the Agreement. It contains a relatively simple mechanism comprising consultations, followed by reference of the dispute to a Committee of Experts. The Committee is to make 'recommendations'. A peer review by a 'specialist' from a Contracting State not party to the dispute may be made to the Committee. Appeals may be made from the Committee's recommendations to the SAFTA Ministerial Council. Failure to implement recommendations may lead to a withdrawal of concessions.

'in like circumstances' – Secretariat File No. USA-MEX-98–2008–01, Final Report of the Panel, 6 February 2001, paras. 251 and 260–270.

[64] Article 18.3(3) and 18.5. Under Article 10.5, it is stated that the Committee of Experts shall act as the Dispute Settlement Body under the agreement.

f) Bay of Bengal Initiative for MultiSectoral Technical and Economic Cooperation (BIMSTEC)

In 1997, Bangladesh, India, Sri Lanka and Thailand agreed to form the Bangladesh–India–Sri Lanka–Thailand Economic Co-operation (BISTEC) trade plan. Later that year, Myanmar joined the group, forming BIMSTEC. In 2004, Bhutan and Nepal joined the group, and a framework agreement including these countries was negotiated. Article 9 of that agreement calls for establishment of a dispute settlement mechanism by December 2005.[65] At the time of writing, documentation on the BIMSTEC dispute settlement mechanism, agreed in December 2005, was unavailable to this writer.

g) Comprehensive Economic Cooperation Agreement (CECA)

Like many other free trade agreements, the Comprehensive Economic Cooperation Agreement between the Republic of India and the Republic of Singapore contains both a general dispute settlement system (in Chapter 15) and an investment dispute settlement system (in Chapter 6). Separate arbitration procedures are provided in these. Chapter 9, which deals with Movement of Natural Persons, contains a rather unusual provision in the form of Article 9.12. That provision requires a number of prerequisites before any dispute may be brought under the Chapter 15 system in respect of refusals of temporary entry under Chapter 9. One of these prerequisites is that a 'pattern of practice' must be shown. For disputes other than those under Chapter 15, such a pattern does not need to be first established.

h) Other examples of FTAs

India–Sri Lanka FTA This agreement, signed in 1998, contains a relatively rudimentary dispute settlement clause in Article XIII, comprising mainly a process of amicable settlement followed by arbitration.[66]

India–Bhutan FTA This agreement, signed in 1995, contains a consultation clause and no substantial dispute settlement clause.[67]

[65] See www.bimstec.org.
[66] Text available at http://commerce.nic.in/ilfta.htm#art13.
[67] See Article X. Text available at www.commerce.nic.in/bhutan.doc.

India–MERCOSUR Preferential Trade Agreement and Agreement on South Asian Free Trade Area The India–MERCOSUR Preferential Trade Agreement contains a separate dispute settlement chapter and provides for a combination of 'direct negotiations', and action by a Joint Committee as well as a committee of experts to resolve disputes.[68] Article 20 of the Agreement on South Asian Free Trade Area (SAFTA)[69] also refers to a Committee of Experts, from which there is an appeal to the SAFTA Ministerial Committee (SMC). In the former agreement, Article 2.6 is of interest, as it stipulates that disputes arising in connection with antidumping and countervailing measures shall be exclusively submitted to the WTO under the DSU. This is to be contrasted with the general position for other disputes in Articles 2. 2 and 2.4, for which the parties may select whether to submit to the FTA mechanism, or to the WTO DSU mechanism.

B. Choice of dispute systems in agreements

Apart from preferential trade agreements, both China and India are parties to several bilateral investment treaties (BITs) with their trading partners. Typically BITs would carry their own dispute settlement systems, usually providing for a combination of methods of resolution. Disputes arising out of BITs may, for instance, be resolved by international arbitration. A recent example was the arbitration action brought against India by the US. The US Government initiated state-to-state arbitration proceedings on behalf of OPIC (its trade insurance body) against the Government of India in respect of a power project in Dabhol, India, for a claim of US$300–400 million.[70] That dispute has now been settled.

Several important international investment disputes offer insight for dispute settlement. Two recent issues stand out in particular. The first relates to the current debate on linkage of most-favoured nation (MFN) provisions to dispute settlement provisions within a regional trade agreement. The second relates to the role of precedent in such disputes. This issue arises mainly because of the lack of a clear hierarchy among

[68] Text of the dispute settlement chapter available at www.commerce.nic.in/flac/Annex-V%20DSP_mercosur_pta.pdf.

[69] Parties are members of the South Asian Association for Regional Cooperation (SAARC), comprising Bangladesh, Bhutan, India, Maldives, Nepal, Pakistan and Sri Lanka. See www.infopak.gov.pk/saarc/safta.htm.

[70] See USTR National Trade Estimates Report on India (2005), www.ustr.gov/assets/Document_Library/Reports_Publications/2005/2005_NTE_Report/asset_upload_file383_7446.pdf, at 273.

such decisions, and indeed, vis-à-vis other international disputes such as those in the WTO.

The MFN dispute settlement issue received international attention after the decision by an ICSID arbitration tribunal in *Emilio Agustín Maffezini* v *The Kingdom of Spain*. In that case, Mr Maffezini, an Argentine national, brought a claim in arbitration against Spain for treatment received from Spanish entities by his investment in the Spanish area of Galicia. The claim was brought before an ICSID tribunal. It was based on provisions firstly, on a bilateral investment treaty (BIT) between Argentina and Spain, and secondly, on the MFN provision in that BIT, to invoke dispute settlement provisions in a separate BIT between Chile and Spain. The claimant sought essentially to rely on more favourable dispute settlement provisions (as opposed to substantive ones) from the Chile–Spain BIT, rather than those in the Argentina–Spain BIT. He took this route to try to avoid the requirement in Article X of the Argentina–Spain BIT to first have the matter heard in Spanish courts. The Article permitted international arbitration only if the matter was not first settled within eighteen months of such court proceedings. The ICSID tribunal permitted the claimant to rely on the MFN clause, and hence international arbitration could proceed.

The *Maffezini* decision has since sparked off similar arguments in subsequent cases.[71] A more recent ICSID decision on this subject is *Plama Consortium Ltd* v *Republic of Bulgaria*, where the tribunal markedly shows a much more restrained attitude towards the linkage of MFN and dispute settlement provisions.[72]

Chinese and Indian negotiators should note the implications of the *Maffezini* decision, as well as its progeny, to avoid any surprise in relation to choice of dispute settlement systems in any trade or investment agreements under negotiation.

C. *A lack of hierarchy in precedents*

If one examines the decisions emanating from the various tribunals of NAFTA and ICSID, to name just two, one comes quickly to the conclusion that there is no clear hierarchy among such decisions. There is no

[71] See, for instance, *Siemens A.G.* v *The Argentine Republic*, ICSID Case No. ARB/02/8, and *Salini Costruttori S.p.A. and Italstrade S.p.A.* v *The Hashemite Kingdom of Jordan*, ICSID Case No. ARB/02/13, Decision on Jurisdiction. For a fuller discussion of the *Maffezini* and related cases, see Hsu, 'MFN and dispute settlement:When the twain meet' (2006) 7 (1) *Journal of World Investment and Trade* 25.

[72] ICSID Case No. ARB/03/24.

rule of binding precedent as such. However, as a matter of practice, tribunals frequently refer to prior decisions for guidance (or in disagreement) – possibly as a matter of practicality, or as some have argued, because there is pressure to ensure that there is not too much divergence.[73] Therefore, it probably makes good sense for the governments of China and India to stay abreast of interpretative developments (particularly where there is very similar language between texts) in the WTO and in other international tribunals.

VIII. Contribution of China and India to WTO dispute settlement

A. *Panelists and members of the Appellate Body*

There have so far been one panelist and one Appellate Body member from China (excluding Hong Kong). (Notably, the immediate past President of the International Court of Justice is from China.) There have, on the other hand, been at least seven panelists from India. On the Appellate Body, one member has been from India.

It is surely not for lack of talent or competence that China has not been represented as such; perhaps the qualified persons need to raise their international profiles in order to be recognized and called upon for these roles. In the second decade of WTO life, perhaps one can expect to see more panelists from China.

A related challenge for developing countries is to continually build up a core of persons with international reputations of legal competence and impartiality.[74] If there are disputes in less prominent fora, they can serve as panelists to gain experience. Many Chinese arbitrators already serve in China International Economic and Trade Arbitration Commission (CIETAC) dispute; those with WTO knowledge can benefit from such exposure at the WTO and RTA levels of dispute settlement. International prominence of their legal scholarship

[73] See, for instance, T. W. Wälde, 'Investment arbitration under the energy charter treaty: An overview of key issues' (2004) 1 (2) *Transnational Dispute Management*, available at www.transnational-dispute-management.com/samples/freearticles/tv1–2-article224b.htm. For a more extensive discussion of the relationship between WTO principles and free trade agreement tribunal decisions, see Hsu, 'Applicability of WTO law in regional trade agreements: Identifying the links', in Lorand Bartels and Federico Ortino (eds.), *Regional Trade Agreements and the WTO Legal System* (Oxford University Press, 2006).

[74] The difficulties faced by developing countries in the formation of panels were raised by Thailand and Indonesia at the WTO, TN/DS/W/61.

and a high level of proficiency in at least one WTO language would also increase opportunities for appointment.

Another challenge is to foster legal independence and encourage the building of domestic legal expertise. Resources are required for developing world-class advocates to argue their own disputes instead of permanent and sole reliance on foreign counsel. This, however, has to be accompanied by a willingness to invest in and create opportunities for training and exposure. A related task facing WTO members – particularly developing members – is the ability to ensure monitoring of case developments, to ensure that they keep abreast of the latest interpretations, and analysis of implications. This is a challenge that Chinese and Indian policy-makers, legislators, and academics must keep up, both for dispute avoidance, as well as for the most effective use of the WTO dispute settlement system.

B. *Negotiations on reform in the Doha Round*

China has submitted several proposals for reforming the WTO's DSU system. Two proposals stand out for discussion.

First, China has suggested that where a dispute involves a developed-country complainant and a developing-country respondent, the developed country should first of all exercise restraint in bringing a case, and secondly, *not bring more than two cases in a calendar year* to the WTO Dispute Settlement Body.[75] This is an attempt to limit the annual exposure of developing-country members to dispute settlement. Such a limitation would help developing-country governments cope better with handling WTO disputes, presumably by conserving resources to concentrate on a limited number of disputes, and to have time to gain knowledge and expertise in handling such disputes. Indeed, China's explanation for this proposal is as follows:

> The initiation to propose this article is inspired by the provisions in the WTO Agreements to grant S&D treatment to developing-country Members. As pointed out by China in its previous proposal, the lack of human and financial resources as well as capacities and experiences of developing-country Members results in *de facto* imbalance in the participation in the dispute settlement mechanism. However, in contrast to

[75] Communications from China in TN/DS/W/29, TN/DS/W/51 and TN/DS/W/51.Rev, and Communication from China, 'Responses to Questions on the Specific Input of China', TN/DS/W/57, 19 May 2003. See also China's elaboration of its proposals in TN/DS/W/57.

> other covered agreements, most S&D treatments in the DSU are reflected through a best endeavor approach, which is insufficient to address this imbalance.[76]

Although China is a relative newcomer to the WTO dispute settlement system, it has already participated as a third party in an impressive sixty-five disputes since accession in 2001, as mentioned. The exposure to other members' disputes provides a good source of training in both the substantive and procedural rules and practices of the WTO. While there is merit in arguing for a limitation in the *number* of cases that can be brought in a given period against developing countries, it may be questioned whether such a limitation to two disputes per year may firstly be too arbitrary, and secondly, too restrictive on the rights and interests of developed countries. A developing country may abuse the situation because it knows its 'quota' of disputes has been used for a year and may proceed to enact or maintain non-compliant measures for the time that it enjoys this immunity against action. China needs to address and balance this concern against genuine cases of nullification and impairment of a developed country's rights under the WTO agreements which require resolution under the DSU's normal time-frame.

Secondly, China has proposed that, in such disputes, where the developing country is found not to have violated its obligations under the WTO Agreements, its legal costs should be borne by the developed-country member initiating the dispute settlement proceedings.[77] Indeed, legal costs form an important and legitimate concern, particularly for developing countries which have to rely on foreign law firms for advice and representation. Although the Advisory Centre on WTO Law (ACWL) exists to assist developing-country members of the WTO in dispute settlement proceedings, representation is subject to membership. While Hong Kong is a member of the ACWL, China is not.[78] A non-member may obtain legal advice on a non-priority basis from the ACWL. By contrast, India has availed herself of the services of the ACWL as a member.[79]

While no specific method of calculation of such costs was put forward by China in her proposal, one suggestion made has been to establish a trust fund administered by the Secretariat, to meet such legal costs.[80]

[76] TN/DS/W/57. [77] TN/DS/W/57.
[78] See the ACWL's website, www.acwl.ch/e/members/members_e.aspx.
[79] See the cases in which ACWL represented India, www.acwl.ch/e/dispute/wto_e.aspx.
[80] TN/DS/W/57, p. 3.

In the China–ASEAN Dispute Settlement Mechanism – presumably because between China and predominantly developing countries no such compensation provision was included. On the contrary, Article 15 of that Agreement provides for parties to bear their own arbitrators' and legal costs, and to share the costs of the arbitral tribunal chair and expenses related to conduct of the proceedings. The ASEAN Protocol on Enhanced Dispute Settlement Mechanism, which applies to disputes arising from economic agreements between ASEAN members – such as the ASEAN Free Trade Agreement (AFTA) – does provide for a Dispute Settlement Mechanism Fund but it is for meeting expenses of panels, the Appellate Body and the related expenses of the ASEAN Secretariat.[81] It does not serve the function suggested by China for a DSU trust fund.

India, on the other hand, is party to a proposal to establish an umbrella or framework agreement on SDT.[82] The proposal seeks to have WTO members elaborate on provisions to more fully reflect SDT principles and objectives. One of the elements of such a framework agreement is to make SDT 'mandatory and legally binding through the dispute settlement system of the WTO (including notification requirements and inclusion of these commitments in country schedules)'.[83] This reflects the desire to be able to use the DSU system to enforce SDT commitments. The proposal does not set out details such as how any violation established by a DSU panel, if not remedied, may be enforced. If the existing retaliation system is used, a host of issues could arise as to the efficacy and practicability of such retaliatory measures by a developing country member against a developed country member. If the 'losing' country chooses to continue its violation, how effective would a suspension of concessions be for the 'winning' country? Such a system may therefore require a re-examination of the implementation of recommendations as well.[84]

Finally, India is also party to proposals in the current round of negotiations to amend the DSU.[85] Of interest is the proposal to exclude

81 ASEAN Protocol on Enhanced Dispute Settlement Mechanism, art. 17.

82 Communication from Cuba, Dominican Republic, Honduras, India, Indonesia, Kenya, Malaysia, Pakistan, Sri Lanka, Tanzania, Uganda and Zimbabwe, WT/GC/W/442.

83 Communication from Cuba, Dominican Republic, Honduras, India, Indonesia, Kenya, Malaysia, Pakistan, Sri Lanka, Tanzania, Uganda and Zimbabwe, para. 15.

84 Indeed, India is party to proposals to amend the retaliation provisions: see TN/DS/W/47 (proposal to add Article 22.3*bis*) and TN/DS/W/19, on Suspension of Concessions and other Obligations.

85 See Communication from India on behalf of Cuba, Dominican Republic, Egypt, Honduras, Jamaica and Malaysia, TN/DS/W/47.

acceptance of unsolicited information by a panel and the Appellate Body.[86] At the same time, the proposal calls for provision of any Secretariat documents, notes and information given to a panel, to be made available promptly to the parties of the dispute.[87]

The proposal also seeks to deal with litigation costs, by requiring award of such costs to a developing country where its dispute does not end in a finding against it. The proposal seeks an award of litigation costs of US$500,000 or actual expenses, whichever is higher.[88]

IX. Conclusion

With China and India in the WTO, one can expect certain trends particularly with respect to dispute settlement. Three such possible trends include the following.

Firstly, one can expect continuing participation by China and India in the use of the DSU system. Secondly, new paradigms in regional provisions could emerge such as the exclusion of non-violation complaints (e.g. in the China–ASEAN agreement). Judging from existing FTAs, there is no single template for dispute settlement systems, although a preference for a DSU-like system (in that there is a panel process, recommendations and retaliation) does appear in several agreements. Thirdly, China and India can make valuable contributions in DSU reforms. Indeed, both countries have submitted interesting proposals for the current round of negotiations.

The influence of these two economic giants within the WTO is inevitable. It remains to be seen precisely how they will exert that influence in the next decade of the Organization's work, particularly in relation to the DSU system. At the same time, as a parallel development, they will play a part in shaping dispute settlement provisions in free trade agreements which they negotiate with trade partners.

[86] Communication from India on behalf of Cuba, Dominican Republic, Egypt, Honduras, Jamaica and Malaysia, proposals to add footnotes to Articles 13 and 17.6 of the DSU. This follows a number of disputes in which the panels and the Appellate Body accepted unsolicited *amicus curiae* briefs. See for instance, *US – Shrimp*, WT/DS58/AB/R, *US – Bismuth Steel*, WT/DS138/AB/R and *EC – Asbestos*, WT/DS135/AB/R. See also Negotiations on the Dispute Settlement Understanding, Proposals on DSU by Cuba, Honduras, India, Malaysia, Pakistan, Sri Lanka, Tanzania and Zimbabwe, TN/DS/W/18, Part III.

[87] TN/DS/W/47, proposal to amend para. 10 of Appendix 3 of the DSU.

[88] TN/DS/W/47, proposal to add Article 3*bis*.

References

Cass, Deborah Z., Williams, Brett G. and Barker, George (eds.), *China and the World Trading System: Enetring the New Millennium* (New York: Cambridge University Press 2003)

Cottier, Thomas, and Schefer, Krista N., 'Non-violation complaints in WTO/GATT dispute settlement: Past, present and future', in M. Bronckers and R. Quick (eds.), *New Directions in International Economic Law, Essays in Honour of John H. Jackson* (The Hague: Kluwer Law International, 2000)

Hsu, Locknie, 'Applicability of WTO law in regional trade agreements: identifying the links', in Lorand Bartels and Federico Ortino (eds.), *Regional Trade Agreements and the WTO Legal System* (Oxford University Press, 2006)

'MFN and dispute settlement:When the twain meet' (2006) 7(1) *Journal of World Investment and Trade* 25

'Non-violation complaints:World Trade Organization issues and recent free trade agreements'(2005) 39(2) *Journal of World Trade* 205

Lennard, Michael, 'China's Accession Protocol and Anti-dumping', in Cass, Williams and Barker (eds.), *China and the World Trading System*

Lubman, Stanley B., *Bird in a Cage: Legal Reform in China After Mao* (Stanford University Press, 1999)

Panagariya, Arvind, 'India's economic reforms: What has been done? What remains to be done?', ADB ERD Policy Brief Series, No. 2, 2001, www.adb.org/Documents/EDRC/Policy_Briefs/PB002.pdf

Qin, Julia Ya, '"WTO-plus" obligations and their implications for the World Trade Organization legal system' (2003) 37(3) *Journal of World Trade* 483

Qingjiang, Kong, 'Enforcement of WTO Agreements in China', in Cass, Williams Barker (eds.), *China and the World Trading System*

Roessler, Frieder, 'The concept of nullification and impairment in the legal system of the World Trade Organization', in E.-U. Petersmann (ed.), *International Trade Law and the GATT/WTO Dispute Settlement System* (The Hague: Kluwer Law International, 1997), vol. XI, ch. 2

Tay, Alice E. S. and Redd, Hamish, 'China: Trade, law and human rights', in Cass, Williams and Barker (eds.), *China and the World Trading System*

US–India Trade Relations Top-to-Bottom Review, www.ustr.gov/assets/Document_Library/Reports_Publications/2006/asset_upload_file921_8938.pdf

USTR National Trade Estimates Report on India (2005), www.ustr.gov/assets/Document_Library/Reports_Publications/2005/2005_NTE_Report/asset_upload_file383_7446.pdf

USTR Report on China's Compliance and National Trade Estimates Report 2006, www.ustr.gov/assets/Document_Library/Reports_Publications/2006/2006_NTE_Report/asset_upload_file684_9235.pdf

Wälde, T.W., 'Investment arbitration under the Energy Charter Treaty: An overview of key issues' (2004) 1(2) *Transnational Dispute Management* available at www.transnational-dispute-management.com/samples/freearticles/tv1–2-article224b.htm

World Bank country profile data, 2004, for China (http://devdata.worldbank.org/external/CPProfile.asp?CCODE=CHN&PTYPE=CP)

World Bank country profile data, 2004, for India (http://devdata.worldbank.org/external/CPProfile.asp?PTYPE=CP&CCODE=IND)

WTO – Dispute Settlement: Archive list of Panel and Appellate Body reports, available at www.wto.org

8

China, India and global outsourcing of services under GATS

DORA S. NEO

In recent years, China and India have often been mentioned together in the context of their phenomenal economic growth and their combined potential to shift the centre of world influence to Asia. Both countries also come to mind as leading suppliers of outsourced services to developed countries such as the USA, a trend which has generated international attention and controversy amongst policy makers, scholars and analysts.

This chapter will focus on the legal aspects of outsourcing under the General Agreement for Trade in Services (GATS). After an introduction to outsourcing and the role of China and India in the outsourcing of services, the chapter will examine to what extent the provisions of GATS are conducive to promoting and regulating the global outsourcing of services, and the implications of these findings for China and India. Matters that will be considered include the existing level of liberalisation of trade in outsourced services; protectionist measures to curb offshore outsourcing; the importance of rules of origin particularly in free trade agreements (FTAs); and options for liberalisation of trade in offshored services in the future.

I. Outsourcing

1. *What is outsourcing?*

Much international attention has been focused on the outsourcing phenomena, but it must be noted that various writers and speakers might not necessarily be referring to the same thing when they refer to 'outsourcing'. On a general level, outsourcing is 'the act of transferring some of a company's recurring interval activities and decision rights to outside providers, as set out in a contract'.[1] More specifically however, outsourcing can be further divided into sub-categories.

Outsourced activities can be transferred to four possible types of suppliers:[2]

(i) an affiliated firm in the home economy (captive onshore outsourcing);
(ii) a non-affiliated firm in the home economy (non-captive onshore outsourcing);
(iii) an affiliated firm abroad (captive offshoring); and
(iv) a non-affiliated firm abroad (non-captive offshoring).

There is no consensus regarding the precise terminology for each variant of outsourcing,[3] but the term 'offshoring' is a commonly accepted way to refer to outsourcing that takes place internationally, i.e., types (iii) and (iv) in the list above.

The outsourced product could either be goods or services. In the early days, outsourcing referred typically to a situation where firms purchased the physical components necessary for the manufacture of their final product instead of making these components themselves. An example might be a motor company that purchases seat covers to install in the cars it manufactures. With global outsourcing of physical production having become commonly accepted practice in the manufacturing industry, the international spotlight has now shifted to services. Indeed, the global outsourcing of services has grown at a rate that might have been unimaginable just ten years ago. This development has been fuelled by the possibility of delivering large amounts of information across international boundaries quickly and accurately as a result of advances in electronic information and communications technology. These advancements mean that software development for a Japanese company located in Tokyo can conveniently be carried out in Beijing, China,[4] and a CT scan taken at the radiology department of a hospital in Texas, USA,

[1] Maurice F. Graever II, 'Strategic outsourcing', in *A Structural Approach To Outsourcing Decisions and Initiatives* (New York: American Management Association, 1999).

[2] See generally WTO, *World Trade Report 2004*, Section III. Thematic Essays, C. Offshoring Services: Recent developments and prospects, available at www.wto.org/english/res_e/booksp_e/anrep_e/world_trade_report04_e.pdf.

[3] For instance, the OECD refers to captive onshore outsourcing as internal domestic supply, and captive offshoring as internal offshoring. See *OECD Information Technology Outlook 2004*, Chapter 2, 'Globalisation of the ICT sectors and international sourcing of ICT enabled services', Paris, OECD.

[4] Interesting case studies on the offshoring of IT services to China are available at the website of Shinetech Software Inc at www.shinetechchina.com/softwave/case_study/e_commerce_website.htm.

can be read and analysed within minutes by a well-qualified radiologist in Bangalore, India.[5]

This chapter will concentrate on the outsourcing of services to non-affiliated firms abroad in an arm's-length supply of services, with the supplier and buyer remaining in their respective countries, ie, non-captive offshoring.[6] Unless the context requires otherwise, references to outsourcing and offshoring in this chapter are directed at the supply of services and not goods. Although captive offshoring (where a buyer of services establishes a business in a foreign country in order to supply the home company with services) is a common phenomenon, it will generally not be covered in this chapter as it raises issues of foreign investment rather than issues specific to the phenomenon of offshore outsourcing.[7]

As discussed later in this chapter, it is important to note the precise sub-category of services outsourcing that is being referred to, as this would affect the applicability of GATS as well as its specific provisions.

2. *Introduction to Global Outsourcing*

Companies that outsource part of their operations potentially stand to gain in terms of greater profitability and greater efficiency. By relying on outside service providers to carry out its non-core activities, a company frees itself to focus on its core business. Further, specialisation also enables the service provider to do the job more cheaply than the company would have been able to do itself. These advantages, theoretically available from any form of outsourcing, are dramatically magnified when services are outsourced to a foreign country with a well qualified workforce, and where labour and operating costs are a fraction of what they are at home.[8]

The first services to be outsourced overseas were relatively straightforward services such as data processing and call centre services. However, offshoring now potentially covers a wide range of services of varying complexities and involving different industries. These are usually

[5] For an example, see 'Outsourcing radiology to India – how does it work?' available at www.outsource2india.com/why_india/articles/radiology-information.asp.

[6] Indeed, some influential trade economists have expressed the view that the current global outsourcing debate should be focused on this type of outsourcing. See Jagdish Bhagwati, Arvind Panagariya and T. N. Srinivasan, 'The muddles over outsourcing' (2004) 18 (4) *Journal of Economic Perspectives* 93–114.

[7] Bhagwati, Panagariya and Srinivasan, 'The muddles over outsourcing'.

[8] There are, of course, limits to offshoring and pitfalls to guard against such as possible language barriers, the difficulty of managerial control, lack of local knowledge, negative impact on staff morale and possible disruption in supply.

discussed under two main headings, business process outsourcing (BPO) and information technology (IT) services, with the possibility of an overlap between the two.[9] IT outsourcing covers computer related services such as IT support services, software development, web hosting, internet content preparation and data warehousing. Business process outsourcing, on the other hand, involves the contracting of a specific business task to a third party service provider who undertakes to completely manage, deliver and operate the relevant business process or function. These include back office processes (such as data entry, data processing, payroll administration and inventory control), customer interaction services (such as airline and hotel reservations, customer services helpline, membership management and telemarketing) and other professional services (such as accounting services and human resource services). Whilst BPO services traditionally involved the performance of well-specified tasks in a structured rule-based manner, a less structured, more specialised form of BPO has now emerged. Referred to as 'knowledge process outsourcing' (KPO), it targets high-end knowledge-based tasks such as intellectual property research for patent applications, legal services, medical services, animation and design, training and consultancy and R&D in pharmaceuticals and biotechnology.[10]

Advantageous as offshoring might be for the individual company that buys services from abroad, from a broader perspective, economists are not unanimous about its global benefits. By and large, offshoring is lauded as being consistent with the principles of free trade, and a phenomenon which, by the economic laws of comparative advantage, would lead to overall gains in economic growth, both for the outsourcing country as well as the country supplying the outsourced services. The theory is that even if there might initially be temporary job losses in the outsourcing country, other high-value jobs will arise as a result, for

[9] The wide range of services offered by offshore suppliers across various industries can be seen by visiting the internet pages of organisations such as NASSCOM (India's National Association of Software and Service Companies), or the internet service pages of leading offshoring service suppliers such as Tata Consultancy Services, Wipro Technologies, Infosys Technologies, eFunds Corporation and IBM Daksh services. See also Aadityah Mattoo and Sacha Wunsch-Vincent, 'Pre-empting protectionism in services: The GATS and outsourcing' (2004) 7 *Journal of International Economic Law* 765.

[10] See, for example, the study by Evalueserve, a business research firm active in KPO: 'The next big opportunity, Moving up the value chain, From BPO to KPO' available at www.evalueserve.com/home.asp. Offshore KPO was recognised by Forrester Research in 2005 as an emerging trend in 'Offshore knowledge process outsourcing emerges' available at www.forrester.com/Research/Document/Excerpt/0,7211,37661,00.html.

instance, of the development of new jobs and products, or of insourcing, which is the reverse process when others from abroad buy services produced by the country concerned.[11] However, distinguished economist Paul Samuelson has cautioned that increased technical progress abroad as a result of offshoring might lead to a permanent shift in comparative advantage from the buying country to the supplying country so as to induce permanent lost per capita income in the former.[12]

3. *Patterns of global outsourcing and the position of China and India*

Offshoring of services covers such a wide variety of nations, activities and industries that is difficult to put a number on this. It is notoriously difficult to obtain accurate and current figures on the total global value of services offshoring. Official statistics are not tailored to adequately record such offshoring activities and most of the information available on services offshoring is based on private surveys and anecdotal evidence. The WTO's *World Trade Report 2004* relied heavily on two of the most promiment studies undertaken on the size of services offshoring in recent years.[13] One was an OECD report[14] which put the value of offshored IT and business process services around the region of US$32 billion in 2001 (representing 12.3% of the global market of the outsourcing of such services, estimated at close to US$260 billion). Significantly, the OECD report estimated that two-thirds of offshoring was captive offshoring. Also mentioned was a McKinsey report[15] which identified the USA as the major importer of offshored IT and business process services.[16] According to McKinsey, US companies accounted for about

[11] For a detailed analysis of the positive effects of offshoring, see generally Bhagwati, Panagariya and Srinivasan, 'The muddles over outsourcing'.

[12] Paul A. Samuelson, 'Where Ricardo and Mill rebut and confirm arguments of mainstream economists supporting globalization' (2004) 18 *Journal of Economic Perspectives* 135–46. Samuelson's model has been criticised by Arvind Panagariya. See 'Why the recent Samuelson article is not about offshore outsourcing' available at www.Columbia.edu/~ap2231/.

[13] See WTO, *World Trade Report 2004*, Section III. Thematic Essays, C. Offshoring Services: Recent developments and prospects.

[14] See *OECD Information Technology Outlook 2004*, Chapter 2, Globalisation of the ICT sectors and international sourcing of ICT enabled services (Paris: OECD). This report is published once every two years.

[15] McKinsey Global Institute, *Offshoring: Is it a win-win game?* (McKinsey Global Institute, 2003).

[16] To put things in perspective, balance of payment figures for the USA show that offshoring is not a one-way phenomenon, as the USA in fact exports more services than it

70 per cent of the global offshoring market and offshored US$26 billion of IT and business process services to 12 major suppliers in 2001, implying a global value of at least US$35 billion for offshoring of such services in 2001.[17] Based on these reports, the WTO estimated that global figures for offshored IT and business process services would have been in the region of US$40 to US$45 billion in 2003.

India is by far the largest supplier of offshore services. A NASSCOM–McKinsey report published in December 2005 estimated that India accounted for 65 per cent of the global industry in offshore IT and 45 per cent of the global market for business process offshoring.[18]

NASSCOM figures on the IT and IT-enabled services sector, show that total services and software revenues were US$12.9 in FY 2004 and

imports. WTO *Report 2004,* Section III. Thematic Essays, C. Offshoring Services: Recent developments and prospects at p. 280. Global growth consulting company Frost & Sullivan have identified USA, Japan, Germany, UK and France as the largest exporters of IT jobs, i.e., the largest IT offshoring consumers. They found that in 2004, a total of 826,540 IT jobs were expected to be exported by France, Germany, Hong Kong, Japan, the United Kingdom and the United States to lower cost countries, amounting to a combined value of US$51.6 billion, with the US and Japan slated to emerge as the top two exporters of IT jobs in 2004. Of the low cost countries examined by Frost & Sullivan (including India, China, Brazil, Mexico, Malaysia, Poland, Romania and Russia), India emerged as the single largest recipient of IT job imports, followed by China. See www.prnewswire.co.uk/cgi/news/release?id=135558

[17] McKinsey's figure of US$35 billion for all offshored IT and business process outsourcing in 2001 exceeds the OECD estimates of US$32 billion. Such discrepancies reflect how difficult it is to gauge the size of offshore services activities. As mentioned in the text, official statistics are not tailored to adequately record offshoring activities. Although balance of payments statistics of service imports is sometimes used to measure offshore service activities, this method is far from ideal. For instance, not all service imports result from offshore service activities, detailed sectoral recording of services trade is not always available at the national level, and even where they are available, might not be adequate to capture IT and business process services. Even where statistics or estimates of outsourcing exist, these might not be broken down to reflect to reflect the offshore portion as distinct from the domestic portion, nor might the figures for goods be separated from those for figures. And even where offshoring statistics are compiled, these are often in relation to specific industries or countries. Comparison of estimates provided by different countries or from different sources is difficult as each study might have taken into account different sub-sectors under the same broad heading. Surveys of IT and business process offshoring (the subject of the global services outsourcing survey by the OECD and McKinsey mentioned in the text), are the widest category of offshoring for which figures are available, but even these cannot provide an exhaustive list of all global offshoring.

[18] See NASSCOM–McKinsey, NASSCOM–McKinsey Report 2005 – *Extending India's Leadership in the Global IT and BPO Industries* (2005). NASSCOM is the National Association of Software and Service Companies, a body that represents the software industry in India.

US$17.7 in FY 2005, with an estimate of US$23.4 in FY 2006.[19] The figures for China are less comprehensive, but in spring 2005, McKinsey estimated that China's IT services and BPO offshore business was worth US$6.8 billion.[20] Although the offshoring industry is more developed in India than it is in China, the general perception is that China has much potential as an offshoring destination. It has been ranked second only to India in various studies. For example, India and China were ranked first and second respectively in A. T. Kearney's *Global Services Location Index 2005*,[21] a study which assessed the attractiveness of 40 countries as locations for offshoring of service activities such as IT and business processes. Similarly, in survey results released in early 2006 by the UK's Chartered Institute of Personnel and Development on offshoring and the role of HR professionals in the process, India emerged as the most popular overseas destination, followed by China.[22]

II. Services offshoring and GATS

Given that 153 countries in the world are members of the WTO and are correspondingly bound by General Agreement for Trade in Services (GATS), this agreement has potentially the greatest influence on the growth of services offshoring. The question is whether such potential can in fact be realised.

1. The GATS framework

GATS seeks to promote the liberalisation of trade in services by guaranteeing members access to each other's markets, and non-discriminatory

[19] The various IT related sectors included in computing these figures were IT services, IT enabled business process outsourcing, engineering services and R & D and software products. Full details of the Indian IT offshoring industry available at www.mckinsey.com/clientservice/bto/pointofview/outsourcing.asp

[20] McKinsey on IT, 'Can China Compete in Global IT Outsourcing?'(2005). Available at www.mckinsey.com/clientservice/bto/pointofview/outsourcing.asp.

[21] Available at www.atkearney.com/shared_res/pdf/GSLI_Figures.pdf. The criteria used to arrive at the rankings were organised under three broad categories with varying weights: financial structure (40%), people skills and availability (30%) and business environment (30%). In A. T. Kearney's 2004 report, the rankings of India and China also first and second respectively. 3rd to 10th position in the 2005 report went to Malaysia, Philippines, Singapore, Thailand, Czech Republic, Chile, Canada and Brazil respectively. For general information on the offshoring industry in India and China see neoIT's research paper 'Mapping Offshore Markets' available at www.neoit.com/pdfs/whitepapers/Mapping-Offshore-Markets.pdf.

[22] See www.cipd.co.uk/NR/rdonlyres/B3CC9F18–261E-4C70–882F-74884F80E476/0/offshoringhr0106.pdf.

treatment under the principles of national treatment and most-favoured nation treatment. As WTO Members have agreed to apply the principle of progressive liberalisation under GATS, these guarantees are not absolute, but are subject to the commitments made by individual countries in their GATS Schedule of Commitments.

There are three core obligations under GATS: market access (MA), national treatment (NT) and most-favoured nation treatment (MFN). The MFN obligation is couched as a general obligation, meaning that it applies to all members and to all services.[23] It requires each Member to accord 'to services and service suppliers of any other Member treatment no less favourable than it accords to like services and services suppliers of another country'.[24] However, a country can list exemptions in its Schedule that will allow it to give more favourable treatment to certain countries in respect of services specified in the list.[25] Unlike the MFN obligation, the MA and NT obligations are specific obligations which apply only to the modes of supply and the service sectors that Members have specified in their individual GATS Schedules.[26] Where a Member has undertaken MA commitments, it is obliged (subject to the terms of its schedule) not to maintain measures that would interfere with market access, such as limitations on the number of service suppliers or the total value of

[23] Another important general principle under GATS is that of transparency (Art. III), to enable traders doing business in foreign countries to know what rules and regulations they face.

[24] GATS Art. II.

[25] GATS Art. II.2. Many WTO Members have taken advantage of this provision to subject their Art. II commitments to certain exemptions. The rules for these exemptions are set out in a separate annex to the GATS. Apart from the exemptions specified in Members' schedules, the only other possible exemption to the MFN principle under GATS is in relation to countries that are members of regional trading agreements under GATS Art. V.

[26] The Guidelines for the Scheduling of Specific Commitments under the GATS (Document S/L/92), adopted by the WTO Council for Trade in Services on 23 March 2001, explains the inter-relation of the three obligations: A Member taking a national treatment or a market access commitment in a sector must accord the stated minimum standard of treatment specified in its schedule to all other Members. The MFN obligation requires that the most favourable treatment actually accorded in all sectors, whether the subject of a commitment or not, must also be accorded to all other Members. Where an MFN exemption has been granted for a measure, a Member is free to deviate from its Article II obligations, but not from its Article XVI and Article XVII commitments. Therefore, in such cases, a Member may accord treatment in that sector more favourable than the minimum standard to some Members, as long as all other Members receive at least that minimum standard of market access and national treatment appearing in its schedule.

service transactions.[27] NT commitments require a Member (subject to its Schedule) to accord to services and service suppliers of any other Member, in respect of all measures affecting the supply of services, treatment no less favourable than that which it accords to its own like services and service suppliers.[28] However, Members have the option of listing limitations in their Schedule that will enable them to maintain measures that are contrary to the principles of MA and NT.

Because of the structure of GATS, it is impossible to assess, without looking at a Member's Schedule, whether its GATS commitments in relation to MA and NT are conducive to the development of offshore outsourcing. There are countless permutations and each Member is permitted to commit as much or as little as it wishes under GATS. In order to have a favourable effect on offshore outsourcing, commitments to MA and NT must have been made in relation to the modes of supply and the service sectors that are particularly applicable to the offshoring industry. These matters are discussed in the next section.

2. *GATS schedules and offshore outsourcing issues*

(a) The four modes of supply

GATS applies to measures by Members which affect trade in services. Trade in services is defined as the supply of services (a) from the territory of one Member into the territory of any other Member; (b) in the territory of one Member to the service consumer of any other Member; (c) by a service supplier of one Member, through commercial presence in

[27] GATS Art. XVI. The full list of prohibited measures is as follows: (a) limitations on the number of service suppliers whether in the form of numerical quotas, monopolies, exclusive service suppliers or the requirements of an economic needs test; (b) limitations on the total value of service transactions or assets in the form of numerical quotas or the requirement of an economic needs test; (c) limitations on the total number of service operations or on the total quantity of service output expressed in terms of designated numerical units in the form of quotas or the requirement of an economic needs test; (d) limitations on the total number of natural persons that may be employed in a particular service sector or that a service supplier may employ and who are necessary for, and directly related to, the supply of a specific service in the form of numerical quotas or the requirement of an economic needs test; (e) measures which restrict or require specific types of legal entity or joint venture through which a service supplier may supply a service; and (f) limitations on the participation of foreign capital in terms of maximum percentage limit on foreign shareholding or the total value of individual or aggregate foreign investment. Under footnote 9, subparagraph 2(c) does not cover measures of a Member which limit inputs for the supply of services.

[28] GATS Art. XVII.

the territory of any other Member; (d) by a service supplier of one Member, through presence of natural persons of a Member in the territory of any other Member.[29] These four modes of supply are commonly referred to respectively as cross border supply (Mode 1), consumption abroad (Mode 1), commercial presence (Mode 3) and presence of natural persons (Mode 4), and this abbreviated terminology will be used in this chapter.

It is commonly thought that Mode 1 is the mode most relevant to offshoring, as this typically involves the supply of services from the supplier's country to the buyer's country, where only the service crosses international borders and neither the supplier or buyer needs to do so. An offshore service provider intending to supply services into the territory of a WTO Member will therefore be in an advantageous position if the Member has made Mode 1 commitments in the relevant sectors.

One question that has arisen in relation to the electronic supply of some services (for instance a consumer in country X buys architectural plans over the internet from a supplier in country Y) is whether such supply might fall under Mode 2, consumption abroad. Whilst under the traditional analysis, Mode 2 envisaged the service consumer from one country being present in another country and consuming the service in the foreign country (for example, tourism), in the context of cyberspace, some services may be consumed abroad in the territory of another WTO Member even though the consuming entity remains in its own country, and it is unclear whether such supply would take place under Mode 1 or Mode 2. For convenience, this chapter will generally refer to Mode 1 as the relevant mode, always with the unspoken caveat that Mode 2 might also prove to be relevant to the online supply of services.

Studies have shown that existing GATS commitments made by WTO Members under Mode 1 and Mode 2 are different, with a generally higher rate of commitment for Mode 2 than Mode 1.[30] This was probably because at the time the commitments were made, countries did not feel that they could do much to regulate Mode 2 supply, which took place outside their borders. If a Member has fully committed to a certain service sector under Mode 2 but not Mode 1, classifying the supply of e-services as Mode 2 might mean that the Member would have

[29] GATS Art. I.1 and I.2.

[30] See L Altinger. and A. Enders, 'The scope and depth of GATS commitments' (1996) 19 (3) *The World Economy* 307, 320. See also OECD Working Party of the Trade Committee, 'Electronic commerce – Existing GATS commitments for online supply of services', Document TD/TC/WP(99)37/FINAL (2000).

inadvertently given up the right to regulate the e-supply of that service because it had made the Mode 2 before e-services became common.[31] Given the practical importance of whether the supply of e-services falls under Mode 1 or Mode 2, it is a pity that the question has been left unanswered despite being considered under the WTO Work Programme on E-commerce.[32]

Modes 3 and 4, although less prominent in any discussion of offshoring, could be relevant. Although the focus of this chapter is non-captive offshoring, it must be pointed out that Mode 3 is important in captive-offshoring, where a buyer from country X establishes a commercial presence in country Y to take advantage of lower operating and labour costs. Liberalisation of Mode 3 could therefore affect buyers from developed countries who might wish to set up their own offshore supply centres in lower cost countries. It could also be of interest to suppliers from low cost countries that follow their multi-national clients abroad to other low cost countries in order to provide them with outsourcing services, as has been seen in the case of Indian companies moving into China and vice versa. Mode 4, involving supply by the presence of natural persons in the territory of the consumer, although not directly relevant to offshoring, could sometimes be significant. For instance, an offshore service supplier may need to send its employees for training at

[31] Emad Tinawi and Judson Berkey, 'E-services and the WTO: Inadequacy of the GATS classification framework' in the background documentation for the October 1999 OECD Forum on Electronic Commerce available at www.oecd.org/dataoecd/12/60/2092597.pdf

[32] The Council for Trade in Services in its Interim Report to the General Council on its Work Program on E-Commerce summarised the position thus: 'while discussion will continue on all of the issues so far considered, Members agreed that some issues would require substantial further study before their implications could be properly understood'. One of the unresolved issues related to clarification of the distinction between Mode 1 (cross border) and Mode 2 (consumption abroad) in situations where a service is being delivered electronically. Issues on which a common understanding appeared to be emerging included the following: (a) The electronic delivery of services falls within the scope of the GATS, since the Agreement applies to all services regardless of the means by which they are delivered, and electronic delivery can take place under any of the four modes of supply. Measures affecting the electronic delivery of services are measures affecting trade in services and would therefore be covered by GATS obligations. (b) The technological neutrality of the Agreement would also mean that electronic supply of services is permitted by specific commitments unless the schedule states otherwise. (c) All GATS provisions, whether relating to general obligations (e.g. MFN, transparency, domestic regulation, competition, payments and transfer, etc.) or specific commitments (Market Access, National Treatment or Additional Commitments), are applicable to the supply of services through electronic means. See document S/C/W/8 (31 March 1999) available at www.wto.org/english/tratop_e/serv_e/cbt_course_e/c6s5p2_e.htm

the client's business premises in the country where the client is based, and an inability to do so could be a setback that prevents the offshoring arrangement from working optimally.

(b) Service sectors and GATS commitments

(i) Classification of services Most Members have, according to GATS guidelines, scheduled their MA and NT commitments relating to various service sectors on the basis of the Secretariat's Services Sectoral Classification List, often referred to as W/120.[33] Each sector contained in the Secretariat's list identified by the corresponding Central Product Classification (CPC) number.[34] There are twelve broad sectors: (1) business services; (2) communication services; (3) construction and related engineering services; (4) distribution services; (5) educational services; (6) environmental services; (7) financial services; (8) health related and social services; (9) tourism and travel related services; (10) recreational, cultural and sporting services; (11) transport services and (12) other services not included elsewhere. These broad sectors are further divided into sub-sectors.[35] Members can choose to make commitments relating to some of the twelve sectors only and not others; and within any chosen sector, they can decide to commit to some sub-sectors only and not others.

The positive-list approach of GATS means that unless a Member specifically lists a service sector or sub-sector in its Schedule, it makes no commitments in relation to that sector. An important question is therefore whether the structure of the W/120 and the CPC facilitate the making of commitments in the service sectors and sub-sectors which are most relevant to the offshoring industry. Many common IT and BPO

[33] Document MTN.GNS/W/120, (dated 10 July 1991).

[34] The version of the CPC used as a reference for W/120 is the provisional CPC of 1991. References in this paper to the CPC refer to this version, unless otherwise stated. Statistical Papers Series M No. 77, Provisional Central Product Classification, Department of International Economic and Social Affairs, Statistical Office of the United Nations, New York, 1991.

[35] For instance, business services are divided into sub-sectors A to F: professional services; computer and related services; research and development services; real estate services; rental/leasing services without operators; and other business services. Each of these sub-sectors are further sub-classified, for example, 'other business services' is further divided into sub-sectors (a) to (t), starting with advertising services and ending with the catch-all residual category of business services, 'others'. Similarly, the CPC classification system also consists of various levels, starting from sections, through to divisions, groups, classes and sub-classes. The classification numbers get progressively more detailed, from a single digit number for sections to five digit numbers for sub-classes.

services might fit piecemeal into a combination of various existing W/120 sectors, for instance, under certain professional services (e.g. the accounting, legal and architectural sub-sectors), or some of the sub-classifications under the education sectors (e.g. adult education), telecommunication services (e.g. online data processing), as well as the computer and related services and other business services sectors. However, offshoring includes such a wide range of service activities that some of these are not comfortably covered by the current W/120 classifications. Mattoo and Wunsch-Vincent have pointed out that certain key support services such as payroll services and call centre activities are not captured.[36] The closest existing classification that might fit a call centre is the sub-category of telephone answering services, but this classification is inadequate for capturing the full range of services that a call centre might provide, such as technical support, telephone bookings for hotels and travel, taking orders for products, providing or soliciting information and carrying out surveys.

As technological advancement has enabled the supply of new and advanced services, it is important that WTO Members should reach a clear understanding on the scope of the computer and related services sector in W/120 (CPC 84).[37] One issue is the possibility of overlapping sectors. For example, web-hosting and application service providers (ASPs) might be seen to fall within computer related services but possibly also within telecommunication services. Such overlap is particularly problematic where a WTO Member's GATS commitment for each of the relevant sectors is not the same.[38] Another problem is the fact that the sub-sectors under computer related services might not expressly cover more elaborate computer and related services such as systems integration and web hosting, which are in fact merely combinations of four sub-sectors already covered under CPC 84, i.e., consultancy services related to the installation of computer hardware; software implementation services; data processing services and database services. Such potential ambiguities would be avoided if the scope of CPC 84 were clarified.

[36] Mattoo and Wunsch-Vincent, 'Pre-empting protectionism in services'. The authors also identify medical transcription services, insurance claims adjudication and web-enabled technical support services for electronic equipment as common offshored services that are missing from the W/120 classification.

[37] This proposal was in fact made by the EC in 2002. See Council for Trade in Services – Special Session, Communication from the European Communities and Their Member States, GATS 2000: Computer and Related Services (CPC 84), Addendum, S/CSS/W/34/Add.1 (15 July 2002).

[38] Mattoo and Wunsch-Vincent, 'Pre-empting protectionism in services', 778.

Further, computer technology is often inextricably linked with the electronic supply of other core services such as banking or education, and it becomes important to distinguish the core service from the underlying technology. If a bank obtains software services from a supplier, this would fall under the classification computer and related services, but when the bank supplies its banking services electronically to its customer, this would fall under the financial services classification.[39]

It should be noted that even under the current structure of the CPC, it is possible for a Member to commit to service sub-sectors which are not specifically mentioned in the list. This is because the CPC is designed to provide exhaustively for all services. Any service that is not expressly listed in the CPC can be fitted into the residual 'other' sub-classification. For instance, a Member who wishes to liberalise the supply of call centre services could inscribe a commitment under the 'other' classification of the sub-category 'other business services', which in turn falls under the broad category 'business services', and accompany this with a detailed definition of the scope of the service covered. However, there is clearly very little incentive for any Member to do this. Moreover, if a Member makes a commitment in the lowest level 'other' category without specifying any further details, this could be read to mean that the Member is making a commitment in relation to all other business services, current and future, which do not otherwise fall within any of the other sub-headings, a position that would probably be too broad for the comfort of most Members.

A case which illustrates the possible unintended consequences of making a GATS commitment in a particular sector is the case of *United States – Measures Affecting the Cross-border Supply of Gambling and Betting Services* (*US Gambling* case).[40] Antigua and Barbuda brought a case before the WTO Dispute Settlement Body challenging several US state and federal laws that prohibited the cross border delivery of gambling services. This case is an extremely significant one for GATS generally, and it raises some important issues which are beyond the scope of the present discussion. One question raised in the case that is especially pertinent here was whether gambling services were covered by the GATS obligations undertaken by the USA, which had made GATS commitments in respect of 'other recreational services (except

[39] See Council for Trade in Services – Special Session, Communication from the European Communities and Their Member States, GATS 2000.

[40] Appellate Report WTO Doc.WT/DS285/AB/R, modifying Panel Report WT/DS285/R.

sporting)'.[41] The Appellate Body interpreted this to include a commitment to gambling. Their view was that 'sporting' did not include gambling and betting services, and these services were therefore not excluded by virtue of the exclusion of sporting in the Schedule. In reaching this conclusion, the Appellate Body looked at two documents, 'W/120' and '1993 Scheduling Guidelines', and treated them as *travaux préparatoires* that could be used for interpretative purposes under Article 32 of the Vienna Convention on the Law of Treaties where the ordinary meaning of a treaty provision was ambiguous. The Appellate Body found that the CPC class that corresponded with 'sporting services' (9641) did not include gambling and betting services, as these were included in another heading. In the light of this, the Appellate Body felt that it was reasonable to assume that the parties would, absent a clear intention to the contrary, have expected the sector to have the same coverage as the corresponding W/120 sector.[42] The decision in *US Gambling* highlights the importance for WTO Members to be vigilant when scheduling commitments in the 'other' subcategories to avoid over-commitment. As it would in most cases be too late for Members to modify their GATS Schedule after the *US Gambling* decision, they will have to bear the consequences of their earlier scheduling decisions, and take care not to violate their GATS obligations. In the context of offshoring, *US Gambling* also confirms (if at all confirmation is required) that a Member's GATS commitments apply also to the electronic supply of the services. However, the Appellate Body did not have to decide whether offshoring falls under Mode 1 or Mode 2 as the US commitment to 'other reacreational services (except sporting)' was the same for both Modes.

(ii) GATS commitments relating to offshoring The problems posed by the structure of W/120 and the weakness of the positive list approach are

[41] Another important issue in this case was whether the USA had breached its market access commitments under Article XVI of GATS, This depended on whether a measure that prohibited online gambling could be viewed as a quantitative restriction. The Appellate Body felt that the US prohibition against one, several or all means of delivery across borders amounted to a zero quota which fell within quantitative restrictions within the meaning of Article XVI:2(a) of GATS on market access. As to whether the USA was entitled to rely on the exception provided in Article XIV of GATS for measures necessary to protect public morals, the Appellate Body found that the measures were necessary, but that the exception did not apply as the USA failed to show that the prohibitions embodied in the measures were applied to both foreign and domestic service suppliers of remote betting services for horse racing.

[42] See Appellate Body Report WTO Doc.WT/DS285/AB/R especially at paras 195, 201, 204 and 208.

exacerbated by the fact that the current level of commitments made by WTO Members' under GATS is not as favourable to offshoring as it could potentially be. In a useful and detailed study, Mattoo and Wunsch-Vincent found in the year 2000 that in sectors that are specially relevant to offshoring, commitments to Mode 1 had been made by more than half the WTO members only in relation to professional services, financial services and other business services, but these were often only partial commitments. They also found that the number of Members who had made commitments in other sectors which could be subject to electronic transactions such as audio-visual services, education services, health services and recreation services was even more limited.[43] The prognosis for the future is not any better. Although the ongoing GATS negotiations present an opportunity for WTO Members to broaden their commitment to business support services, an analysis of the publicly available initial offers made by eight industrialised countries in 2003 showed that they did not generally improve their existing GATS Schedules for business process and support services.[44]

2. *Options for greater trade in offshore services*

(a) GATS

There are various possibilities for facilitating greater trade in offshore services under GATS that range from the modest to the ambitious.

(i) Negative-list approach The most effective way of promoting freer trade in offshore services under GATS would be to convert the 'positive-list' to a 'negative-list', an approach which is increasingly being used in free trade agreements.[45] The current positive list structure of GATS poses a built-in obstacle to the liberalisation of trade in services as Schedules of Members are static rather than dynamic. Commitments are locked-in once they are scheduled and new services will have to be separately scheduled unless they fall within an existing sector that has already been committed. Adopting a negative-list approach will result not just in the liberalisation of service sectors and modes related to

[43] Mattoo and Wunsch-Vincent, 'Pre-empting protectionism in services', 780–2.

[44] *Ibid.*, 782–5.

[45] One of the earliest examples of the negative list approach can be found in the North American Free Trade Agreement (NAFTA). More recent examples include more recent free trade agreements entered into between the US and countries such as Chile, Singapore, Australia and Morocco.

offshoring, but to an overall liberalisation of global trade in services. Under this approach, all sectors are open for trade unless they are specifically excluded, usually in an annex of non-conforming measures. The negative list approach forces countries to concentrate on identifying the sectors which they do not wish to liberalise, and is potentially more liberal than the positive list approach as there will be no restrictions to trade in the service sectors that are not specifically mentioned in the annex. However, the most effective approach might not be realistic in the multilateral context as many WTO Members would regard this as being contrary to the progressive liberalisation philosophy agreed upon under GATS.

(ii) Horizontal commitments for Modes 1 and 2 over all sectors A less unrealistic but nevertheless ambitious proposal focuses on Modes 1 and 2 (which are most relevant for offshoring), and suggests that WTO Members could be asked to provide market access and national treatment for a wide range of service sectors in relation to services supplied under these two modes. This could be done by having Members make horizontal commitments for Modes 1 and 2 that will apply to all service sectors, and allowing a closed list of pre-defined exempted services for which no commitments are undertaken.[46] This is a clever suggestion that, in relation to Modes 1 and 2, has the same liberalising effect as the negative list approach, but without the untidiness of individually selected exclusions, and without departing from the format of the GATS Schedule that WTO Members have agreed upon and are familiar with. Currently, Members have made more commitments under Modes 1 and 2 than under the other two modes, so a consensus for this approach might seem achievable, especially if the countries that already take a *de facto* liberal approach agree to lock in their positions by making a formal commitment. However, such an approach would still be a quantum leap from the state of GATS negotiations as they now stand.

(iii) Model schedule A more moderate approach towards improving the GATS environment for the offshoring of services would be to have

[46] Mattoo and Wunsch-Vincent, 'Pre-empting protectionism in services', 789–3. The authors suggest that financial services and transport services could be excluded from the commitments, as these sectors potentially involve additional factors such as the movement of capital, goods and people, and might have far-reaching consequences which would have to be further investigated.

WTO Members make specific commitments according to a formula or model schedule.[47] This is more efficient and could lead to many more commitments being made than under the time consuming and incremental bilateral request-and-offer procedure adopted under the ongoing GATS negotiations which started in 2000. Such an approach might dovetail well with the system of plurilateral negotiations that started after the WTO Hong Kong Ministerial meeting in December 2005.[48] For instance, groups of countries with similar interests in developing their offshore services could get together to present requests to their partners in the form of a formula or model schedule. The challenge would be convincing trading partners to accept the sectors listed in the model schedule. Whilst developing countries that are active in supplying offshore services in IT and business processes would want to include these services in the model schedule, an important question would be what these countries would have to concede in exchange for such commitments from their partners.

(iv) Change in classification system If even model schedules prove too contentious, the least that can be done for offshoring in the future might be to propose a change in the GATS classification system. Although the CPC has been revised twice since GATS was signed, the model that continues to be used by WTO Members as a basis for their GATS Schedule continues to be the 1991 provisional CPC.[49] These revisions took place in 1998 (CPC1.0) and 2002 (CPC 1.1), and the latest version

[47] *Ibid.*, 786–8.

[48] See WTO news item, 'Plurilateral negotiations in services start', 28 February 2006 available at www.wto.org/english/news_e/news06_e/serv_28feb06_e.htm. In this new report, the WTO envisaged that sectors and modes of supply in which plurilateral requests were likely to be submitted would include, but not be limited to, telecommunications, distribution, environmental, financial, audio-visual, maritime, logistics, energy and Mode 4. Amongst WTO Members, Canada, for instance, reported in the International Trade Canada website in April 2006 that it was participating in plurilateral requests in relation to services of special export interest to the country, i.e., financial services; telecommunications services; computer and related services; environmental services; energy services; construction services; architectural, engineering and integrated engineering services; legal services, and maritime transport services. See www.dfait-maeci.gc.ca/tna-nac/TS/plurilateral-en.asp. There appears to have been no publicity about any plurilateral requests by WTO Members focusing on services that are commonly offshored which, by their nature, would have to straddle several broad sectors.

[49] The WTO's '*Guidelines for the Scheduling of Specific Commitments under GATS*' adopted by the Council for Trade in Services on 23 March 2001 (Document S/L/92, 28 March 2001) continues to refer to the W/120, which has CPC numbers based on the

better reflects the new services that have developed recently.[50] Two examples of common offshore services which are not provided for under the W/120, payroll services and call centre services, were identified earlier in this chapter. These are covered under CPC 1.1 which has a separate category for 'support services' (CPC 85). 'Telephone call centre services' (CPC 85931) are included under this sector. The explanatory note to CPC 85931 states that it includes taking orders for clients by telephone, soliciting contribution or provided information for clients by telephone and telemarketing. Payroll services do not have a separate CPC number but would fall under 'other support services n.e.c.' (CPC 85990). The explanatory note to CPC 85990 lists many included activities, including payroll services, and also a limited number of service subclasses which are excluded.[51] Regardless of whether there is a consensus amongst WTO Members to change the convention of classifying GATS Schedules according to the 1991 CPC numbering scheme, individual Members could choose to reference their revised commitments to the CPC 1.1 instead.

(b) Free trade agreements

To complement GATS, suppliers of offshore services such as China and India could seek greater access to the markets of their foreign customers by way of free trade agreements. This might enable them to obtain commitments from their targeted trading partners that the latter may not be willing to grant to all WTO Members under GATS. Apart from the possibility of bilateral agreements yielding commitments in a larger number of sectors, there is also a greater possibility of seeking trade liberalisation for services based on a negative list approach. Of course, the negative list is a double-edged sword as it requires all parties to consider carefully the sectors that they would like to exclude from free trade, and a country cannot reap the benefits of such an agreement without itself being ready to open up its service markets. In this

provisional CPC of 1991. The various versions of the CPC are available online at the UN website http://unstats.un.org/unsd/cr/registry/regct.asp?Lg=1.

[50] A more updated version, CPC 2.0, is being finalised, and will take into account developments such as those related to information and communication technologies. See http://unstats.un.org/unsd/cr/registry/regcst.asp?Cl=25.

[51] The position in relation to payroll services in CPC 1.1 is much better than under the 1991 CPC, but it is still not completely satisfactory, as making a commitment under CPC 85990 (other support services n.e.c.) would include committing not just to payroll services, but to all other services that could conceivably fall under this heading, of which the explanatory note already expressly lists eighteen.

connection, the USA, currently the largest consumer of offshore services, has shown a preference for using the negative list approach in its recent free trade agreements, for example in its agreements with Chile, Singapore, Australia and Morocco.

3. *Protectionist sentiments and GATS*

Protectionist sentiments in service importing countries have been stoked as workers in these countries lose their jobs to workers in lower cost destinations, especially India, because of offshore outsourcing of services. Although calls for governments to act against offshoring have gone largely unheeded in countries like the United Kingdom, the position in the USA has been quite different. The year leading up to the November 2004 US Presidential elections saw more than 200 state bills to restrict outsourcing, tabled by politicians out to score points with American voters appalled by the loss of US jobs.[52] Of these, only five became law in 2004. Although international media attention on such legislation has waned somewhat, political interest in sponsoring such bills remains high. In the 2005–6 sessions, 190 bills were introduced in state legislatures to restrict or report on outsourcing. Of these seven were passed restricting outsourcing, and three to establish commissions or study outsourcing. In 2006, two state bills were passed.[53] In contrast to the activity at state legislatures, at the federal level, law makers have been less zealous in introducing and passing anti-outsourcing legislation.[54]

Proposed state and federal anti-outsourcing legislation fall into a few main categories, most of which are reflected in the limited number of successful statutes. The most stringent approach seeks to establish a ban on outsourcing. This is reflected in the New Jersey state law that imposes an outright ban on outsourcing by preventing state contract work from being performed outside the USA.[55] At the federal level, there have been various bills proposing a partial ban limiting the number of projects or situations wherein federal contract work can be done overseas, but only a few of these have become law. Another legislative model requires

[52] Stuart Anderson, 'Outsourcing attacks not over', *National Review* 11 Feb 2005 available at www.nfap.com/researchactivities/studies/NationalReview021105.pdf

[53] 'Anti outsourcing efforts down but not out', NFAP Policy Brief, April 2007, available at www.nfap.com/pdf/0407OutsourcingBrief.pdf

[54] These are discussed at Beverley Earle, Gerald A. Madek and Christina Madek: 'A finger in the dike? An examination of the efficacy of state and federal attempts to use law to stem outsourcing' (2007) 28 *Northwestern Journal of International Law & Business* 89.

[55] [2005] N.J. Laws 494.

contractors to disclose where the work will be done, or call centre operators to identify their location and, in some cases, to switch calls back to the USA if requested to do so. Other legislative approaches include those curtailing outsourcing by preferring local in-state and in-country goods and services; by preventing the disclosure of sensitive information to non-nationals, and through subsidy incentives. Sometimes, there is no need for the law to step in, as the weight of public opinion could be enough to change behaviour. This was seen in New Jersey in 2003, where even before any anti-offshoring law was passed, the state government adjusted its contract with a call centre to avoid using Indian workers and to place more workers in New Jersey.[56] As this was a call centre for state unemployment services, it would have been ironical for the state to be seen sending even the lowest level jobs offshore, even if 'saving' American jobs cost more than the original amount under the contract.

It has been argued that far from being positive measures to create jobs, the proposed bills and existing statutes to restrict outsourcing possibly violate the US Constitution, risk trade retaliation and increase budget costs.[57] An assessment of the legality of the US anti-outsourcing legislation under US law is beyond the scope of this chapter,[58] and the discussion here will be confined to GATS-related issues.

To assess the legality of anti-outsourcing legislation under GATS, the first stage of enquiry would be the GATS Schedule of the Member that is proposing to enact the legislation, as there is no prohibition on legislation that limits market access or national treatment for uncommitted sectors and activities.

In this connection, it should be noted that even if a Member has made commitments in a particular sector, for example, architectural services or insurance services, this does not mean that offshore computer related services (like website design) or business process services (like database services, payroll services or call centre services) supplied to an architectural or insurance company would necessarily qualify for protection under GATS, as a distinction is made between the final service and the inputs to that service. This is best summarised by the WTO's Guidelines for the Scheduling of Specific Commitments under GATS, which states: 'It is understood that market access and national treatment commitments apply only to the sectors or sub-sectors inscribed in the schedule.

[56] Anderson, 'Outsourcing attacks not over'. [57] *Ibid.*

[58] For a full discussion of these issues, see Earle, Madek, and Madek: 'A finger in the dike?'.

They do not imply a right for the supplier of a committed service to supply uncommitted services which are inputs to the committed service'.[59] Such a position has been criticised for having 'far reaching implications with respect to the value of existing free trade commitments applicable to the trade in services',[60] but it seems justifiable. If a country has made no GATS commitment in relation to call centre services, for example, it is difficult to see why it should be bound to allow call centre activities for certain industries, like insurance, where there is a broad sectoral commitment, and not other sectors. The sectoral commitments are in relation to insurance and should be regarded as being relevant only for the supply of a service that is properly regarded as an insurance service. If other support services are intended to be liberalised, these should be separately scheduled.

As far as potential US legislation restricting offshoring of call centre activities is concerned, the earlier discussion on the current sectoral coverage of the W/120 and the 1991 CPC is relevant. Given that there is no classification specifically for call centres, it is not surprising that the US has made no commitment towards liberalising call centre services under its current GATS Schedule. The situation has not changed with its revised offer under the ongoing GATS negotiations.[61]

One recurring feature of the US legislative attempts is that the bills seek to restrict offshoring largely in government contracts. This

[59] *Guidelines for the Scheduling of Specific Commitments under the GATS* (Document S/L/92). See also footnote 9 to GATS Article XVI (2)(c). Article XVI(2)(c) provides that in sectors where market access commitments are taken, the measures which a Member shall not maintain or adopt are defined as '(c) limitations on the total number of service operations or on the total quantity of service output expressed in terms of designated numerical units in the form of quotas or the requirement of an economics needs test'. Footnote 9 provides: 'Subparagraph 2(c) does not cover measures of a Member which limit inputs for the supply of services'. Although the WTO Guidelines seems to take an expansive interpretation of this requirement to cover all market access and national treatment obligations, it must be noted that footnote 9 only applies to the specific market access subcategory listed in GATS Art. XVI(2)(c). Such a qualification is not elsewhere mentioned in the text of GATS.

[60] Mattoo and Wunsch-Vincent, 'Pre-empting protectionism in services', 778. These authors suggest that as the broad definition of 'supply of a service' under GATS Art. XXVIII(b) explicitly includes the production, distribution, marketing, sale and delivery of a service, if a commitment is made on a certain 'final' service such as financial services, it should include all operational processes (for example, payroll and billing) to support this service. See also Karen Lapid, 'Outsourcing and offshoring under the General Agreement on Trade in Services' (2006) 40 *Journal of World Trade* 341.

[61] WTO Council for Trade in Services Special Session, *United States Revised Services Offer*, Document TN/S/O/USA/Rev.1 received on 31 May 2005.

potentially avoids any conflicts with GATS, as the market access, national treatment and most-favoured nation obligations do not apply to services purchased by governmental agencies or for governmental purposes.[62] However, such legislation might cause the USA to breach its obligations under the plurilateral Agreement on Government Procurement to which it is a party together with some 40 WTO Members (including the 27 EC Member States). Under this agreement, products and suppliers of signatories shall receive MFN and national treatment in competing for government procurement contracts that are covered by the agreement.[63] China is a party to this agreement and protected by it. However, India is not, and therefore has no legal right to complain about US laws restricting offshoring in government contracts.

IV. 'Services and service suppliers' and the origin of services

Under the terms of GATS, market access, national treatment and most-favoured nation protection is given to 'services and service suppliers of any other Member'.[64] Assuming that a Member has made relevant commitments under its Schedule, there are therefore two elements that will decide whether a service or service provider qualifies for protection under GATS: the service must be a service of a Member, or the service supplier must be a service supplier of a Member. These requirements are akin to the rules of origin for goods which are an important part of the GATT regime, but have largely been ignored in the context of services.

1. 'Service of a Member'

Under GATS Article XXVII (f), 'service of a Member' is defined as services which are supplied from or in the territory of that other Member, or in the case of services which are supplied through commercial presence or by presence of natural persons, by service suppliers of that other Member. Although no modes of supply are expressly mentioned in this definition, it seems clear that the four modes of supply are being referred to in turn: Services from the territory of the other Member refers to Mode 1, services supplied in the territory of the other Member refers to Mode 2, and services supplied

[62] GATS Art. XIII. [63] Agreement on Government Procurement Art. III.
[64] See GATS Arts. II, XVI and XVII.

through commercial presence or by presence of natural persons refer to Modes 3 and 4 respectively.

An examination of the details is important. It shows that in relation to Modes 1 and 2, the relevant consideration is geographical: the services must be supplied from or in the territory of the other member. The focus is on where the service comes from rather than who is supplying it. This would mean that it could be possible for a service that is supplied by a national of a non-WTO member country under Modes 1 and 2 to be protected under GATS as long as the service is supplied from or in the territory of a WTO member country. However, whether a case is in fact brought to the WTO in the event of a contravention will depend on whether the Member from or in whose territory the relevant service is being supplied takes the initiative to begin such an action. It might not have much incentive to do so if the service supplier concerned is not one of its nationals. Where a service is supplied under Modes 3 and 4, it would be a 'service of a Member' if it is supplied by a service supplier of that other Member. This aspect of the protection given to the services of a Member overlaps with the general protection given to service suppliers of a Member under the market access, national treatment and most-favoured nation provisions of GATS. Because of the wide definition of 'service of a Member', this automatically includes services provided by service suppliers of that Member. The question of when a supplier would be regarded as a service supplier of a Member is considered in the next section.

2. *'Service suppliers of a Member'*

Read together, the various definitions in GATS Article XXVII together indicate that a 'service supplier of a Member' is either (i) a natural person who lives in the territory of that Member or any other Member and is a national or permanent resident of that Member; or (ii) a legal entity constituted or otherwise organised under the law of that Member and engaged in substantive business operations in the territory of that Member or any other Member,[65] or (iii) in the case of Mode 3 services supplied through commercial presence, the supplier must be an entity that is owned or controlled by natural or juridical persons of that Member.[66]

[65] See GATS Arts. XXVII (g), (j), (k), (l) and (m).

[66] Under GATS Art. XXVII (n), a juridical person is 'owned' by persons of a Member if more than 50 per cent of the equity interest in it is beneficially owned by persons of that Member, and 'controlled' by persons of a Member if such persons have the power to name a majority of its directors or otherwise to legally direct its actions.

Protection under GATS for service suppliers of a Member is expressed as independent from that for services of a Member. This might seem to indicate that a service supplier of a Member would be protected even if the service itself is not a service of that Member because it is not supplied from or in the territory of that member. However, it should not be assumed that all service suppliers of a Member would be protected regardless of the geographical origin of the service. This is because Members are allowed to deny the benefits of GATS to the supply of a service if the service is supplied from or in the territory of a non-Member.[67]

The criteria of 'services of a Member' and 'service suppliers of a Member' work in parallel and nuances of their interplay can be quite complex. Table 8.1 illustrates the inter-relationship in diagrammatic form.

3. *Application of GATS rules to offshoring scenarios*

In a typical Mode 1 offshoring transaction, a company in the USA imports services from a BPO supplier located in China. If the USA has made relevant GATS commitments for this service, the transaction will be protected because the service is a 'service of a Member', being supplied to the USA from a WTO Member country, China. If the enterprise that is supplying this service is properly constituted under Chinese law, the transaction would qualify for protection also by virtue of the fact that it concerns a 'service supplier of a Member', i.e., China. As there is no requirement in Mode 1 apart from the geographical origin of the service, this could mean that the protection could be given to an enterprise that is supplying the service from China to the USA even if it is not constituted under Chinese law nor owned or controlled by Chinese nationals or entities (assuming the operation of such an enterprise in China is possible under the domestic law).[68] Either way, this would

[67] GATS Art. XXVII (a).

[68] In any case, as the definition of 'juridical person' is a wide one, 'juridical person of a member' is likely to be interpreted to have a correspondingly wide meaning, so as to encompass all forms of doing business in a particular territory. GATS Art. XXVIII(l) provides that 'juridical person' means any legal entity duly constituted or otherwise organised under applicable law, whether for profit or otherwise, and whether privately owned or governmentally owned, including any corporation, trust, partnership, joint venture, sole proprietorship or association. GATS Art. XXVIII(m) provides that 'juridical person of another Member' means, inter alia, a juridical person which is constituted or otherwise organised under the law of that other Member, and is engaged in substantive business operations in the territory of that Member or any other Member.

Table 8.1 *The inter-relationship between 'services of a Member' and 'service suppliers of a Member'*

Scenario:

Assume Country A (*'A'*) is a WTO member that has made the relevant GATS commitments in its schedule for the service sectors and modes of supply in question. Country B (*'B'*) and Country C (*'C'*) are WTO members but Country Z (*'Z'*) is not. For Modes 1 and 2 assume that the service is supplied to *A* or to a service consumer of *A*.

Question:

If *A* does not fulfil its GATS obligations in each of the listed situations, does *B* have rights against *A* under the WTO system? (The rights of *C*, if any, are not considered.)

Legend:

Yes(a): B has rights against A as the service is a 'service of *B*'

Yes(b): B has rights against A as the service supplier is a 'service supplier of *B*'

	Service supplied from or in *B* (Modes 1 & 2)	Service supplied from or in *C* (Modes 1 & 2)	Service supplied from or in *Z* (Modes 1 & 2)	Service supplied by commercial presence in *A* (Mode 3)	Service supplied by presence of natural person in *A* (Mode 4)
Service supplied by natural person who is					
– national or permanent resident of *B* & resides in *B* or any other WTO member	Yes (a+b)	Yes (b)	No	NA	Yes (a+b)
– national or permanent resident of *B* & resides in non-WTO member	Yes (a)	No	No	NA	No
– non-national or permanent resident of *B*	Yes (a)	No	No	NA	No

Service supplied by juridical person that is					
– constituted under the law of *B* and engaged in substantive business operations in *B* or any other WTO member	Yes (a+b)	Yes (b)	No	Yes (a+b)	NA
– constituted under law of *B*, but not engaged in substantive business operations in *B* or any other WTO member	Yes (a)	No	No	No	NA
– owned or controlled by natural or juridical persons of *B*	Yes (a)	No	No	Yes (b)	NA
– not constituted under the law of *B* and not owned or controlled by natural or judicial persons of B	Yes (a)	No	No	No	NA

have positive implications for foreign investment in China. If instead of GATS, the agreement concerned is a free trade agreement to which China is a party, the effect might be even more dramatic. Assuming that this FTA has the same rules relating to protection of 'services of a Member' and 'service suppliers of a Member' as GATS does, a foreign enterprise that manages to supply the service from China could enjoy the benefits under this FTA despite not being a party to it. However, depending on the constitution and ownership of such an enterprise, the benefits that it might obtain could be dependent on the Chinese government being willing to enforce China's rights under the FTA on behalf of a service supplier that is not its national.

The operation of the rules can be further illustrated by another example. Assume this time that a company constituted under Indian law exports services to the USA from various low cost locations around the world. Assuming that the USA has made the relevant GATS commitments, this company will be protected under GATS if it is a 'service supplier of a Member', in this case, India. All that is required under Mode 1 is that this company be constituted under the law of India, and engaged in substantive business operations in India, or in the territory of any other WTO Member. If this requirement is satisfied, there is no restriction as to the countries from which this company might supply services to the USA, except that services cannot be supplied from a non-WTO Member country. This could be advantageous for Indian companies as it enables them to set up offshoring centres in other countries which are WTO Members without having to incorporate a local company (assuming that this is permitted under the laws of the host country), and still enjoy the protection of GATS. And if the Indian company were to incorporate a subsidiary in another WTO Member country, such as China, from which it supplies services to the USA, this subsidiary would also be protected as a service supplier of China, even if it is still owned or controlled by Indian nationals. Transposed to a situation where we assume that India and the USA have a bilateral FTA with the same rules of origin as GATS, however, the situation would be more limiting in the sense that an Indian company supplying services to the USA from another country will not be covered under the FTA as the services would be supplied from the territory of a non-member. However, as far as companies incorporated in India are concerned, these would be regarded as Indian service suppliers that are entitled to the benefits of the FTA, and this would have the positive implications on foreign investment discussed above. There are built in controls against abuse, as the company must have substantive business interests in India in order to qualify as an Indian service supplier. A non-party to the FTA is therefore prevented from setting up a shell company in India for the sole purpose of free riding on the benefits of its FTA with the USA.

4. *'Services and service suppliers of a Member' under FTAs*

Although the previous discussion referred to and analysed hypothetical FTAs that contained the same rules of origin for services and service suppliers as under GATS, the reality is that FTAs vary in form and content. Each FTA must therefore be carefully scrutinised in order to determine how it would affect offshore outsourcing patterns. A few specific examples will be considered here. The services chapter of the FTA between India and Singapore, known formally as the Comprehensive Economic Co-operation Agreement between the Republic of India and the Republic of Singapore (CECA), takes an approach that is very close to the GATS model. Supply of services under the CECA is divided into the same four modes as GATS, and the market access and national treatment obligations are in relation to 'service and service suppliers of the other Party'. Much of the analysis above would therefore apply to the CECA. But there are differences. For instance, the definition of juridical person of the other Party is defined as a juridical person which is constituted or otherwise organised under the law of the other party, but unlike in GATS, there is no requirement that it be engaged in substantive business operations in the territory of that Party. The definition of a natural person of a Party is also more relaxed under the CECA than under GATS, as this person merely has to be a national or permanent resident under the laws of that Party, but need not reside in the territory of that Party. It would appear that it is easier to qualify as a service supplier of India or Singapore under the CECA than as a service supplier of a Member country under GATS.

An FTA that takes a different approach from GATS is the North American Free Trade Agreement (NAFTA) between USA, Canada and Mexico. This agreement is a prominent example of the negative list approach, where trade in all services is liberalised except for non-conforming measures which are listed in a schedule. Under NAFTA, only three modes of supply, roughly corresponding the GATS Modes 1, 2 and 4, are covered under the services chapter, whilst the equivalent of Mode 3 is covered under the investment chapter. Unlike GATS, there is no emphasis on the distinction between the various modes of supply in the schedule. Also unlike GATS, which applies to both services as well as service suppliers of a Member, market access and national treatment protection under NAFTA is given only to a 'service provider' of the other Party.[69] This means that under NAFTA, a service would qualify for protection not by virtue of whether it was supplied from or in the territory of another Party, but by virtue of the characteristics of the service provider. In order to be a service provider of a Party, the service provider must be an enterprise constituted or organised under the law of a Party, or a natural person who is a national or a permanent resident of a Party. Taking the example of a business located in Mexico and supplying offshore services to a company in the USA, the fact that the service is supplied from Mexico to the USA does not mean it qualifies for protection under NAFTA. It would qualify only if the provider of the service were a Mexican national or a Mexican enterprise.[70] So if the service is being supplied from Mexico to the USA by a non-Mexican person or a foreign company that is not constituted in Mexico, the market access and national treatment obligations under NAFTA would not apply. Even in the case of a company that is constituted in Mexico, if it is owned or controlled by the nationals of a non-Party and has no substantial business activities in the territory of a NAFTA Party, it is not entitled to NAFTA benefits.[71]

[69] At first glance, this also seems to be the approach taken under the US–Singapore Free Trade Agreement (US–SFTA), where market access and national treatment must be given to 'service suppliers of the other Party'. However footnote 8–1 to Art. 8.1.8 states that the Parties understand that for purposes of Articles 8.3, 8.4, and 8.5 of this Agreement, 'service suppliers' has the same meaning as 'services and service suppliers' as used in GATS Articles II, XVI, and XVII. The implications of this could be important, as the earlier analysis shows that there is a real difference between protecting the services of a Member and protecting the service suppliers of a Member. Apart from this difference, the US–SFTA takes a very similar approach as NAFTA towards establishing who are the service suppliers of the other Party who would qualify for the benefits under the agreement.

[70] NAFTA Arts. 201.1 and 1213.

[71] See NAFTA Art. 1211.1. A company that is properly constituted under the laws of a Party can also be denied benefits under NAFTA if the other Party can show, for instance that the service is being provided by an enterprise owned or controlled by nationals of a non-Party, and (i) the denying Party does not maintain diplomatic relations with the non-Party, or (ii) the denying Party adopts or maintains measures with respect to the non-Party that prohibit transactions with the enterprise or that would be violated or circumvented if the benefits of this Chapter were accorded to the enterprise. Similar provisions exist in the Investment Chapter which applies to investments that correspond to GATS Mode 3. See NAFTA Art. 1113.

5. *Rules of origin in complex situations*

The foregoing discussion was directed at the question of whether a service or a service supplier qualifies for protection under an agreement that liberalises trade in services between member countries. It contemplated the most straightforward situation relating to offshore outsourcing, where a complete service is being supplied wholly from one country to another. As the discussion showed, even in that simple situation, it is important to have a clear definition of the qualifying services and service providers under GATS as well as other trade agreements.

The situation becomes more complex when the provision of a service from one country to another involves inputs from service suppliers who are from other countries, ie, there are two layers of offshoring, one of the final service, and the other of the components that make up the final service. In such cases, the existence of advanced rules of origin are even more vital, particularly in a bilateral or regional free trade agreement where, unlike GATS which applies to all WTO members, there are only a few member countries that can take advantage of the benefits of the agreement. For instance, a US internet education provider which supplies educational services to consumers in Canada may in turn obtain data processing services from a supplier in China, and website development and human resource services from India. The question would then be whether the education services being supplied from USA to Canada still qualify as services of the USA under GATS, NAFTA, or any other trade agreement to which USA and Canada might both be parties.

Rules of origin are a very important part of the regulatory regime relating to trade in goods, where it is common for various components of the final product to have come from different countries. These rules help to determine the source of supply for a specific product, and are necessary as trade policies discriminate between exporting countries.[72] In contrast, it has been observed that there is no evidence that rules of origin were of any particular concern to the Group of Negotiations on Services or that the rules were the subject of any particular debate in the

[72] Such discrimination can be preferential (e.g. lower tariffs for products from developing countries or partners under free trade agreements) or non-preferential (e.g. countervailing duties, safeguard measures). Rules of origin also help distinguish between products of domestic origin and those of foreign origin. See also Bernard Hoekman, 'Rules of Origin for Goods and Services, Conceptual Issues and Economic Considerations' (1993) 27 (4) *Journal of World Trade* 81, 82–3.

context of drafting and negotiating the GATS.[73] Indeed, no rules of origin appear to have been crafted for services apart from the requirements discussed earlier of requiring either the service or the service supplier to be a service or service supplier of a party to the relevant trade agreement. As GATS was finalised at a time when cross border supply of services was limited to a few types of transactions, and face to face contact between service suppliers and service consumers was the norm, this is not surprising. Now that situation has changed, it is necessary to examine the issue and formulate appropriate rules of origin for services if necessary.

Even in relation to goods, there are no universally agreed rules of origin that apply worldwide, and each WTO Member has its own rules based on the broad principles set out in the Agreement on Rules of Origin, which requires for instance, that the rules be transparent and applied in a consistent and impartial manner.[74] Most customs administrations around the world apply rules that decide the origin of goods according to where the product underwent its last substantial transformation.[75] Alternative means to decide whether a product qualifies on this basis include change in customs heading (where a product has been sufficiently changed in a particular country to move its customs classification from one heading to another) and the percentage criterion (which determines how much value was added to the product in that country).[76]

It is difficult to apply the substantial transformation criteria used for goods to determine the origin of services, as 'most trade services will be "substantial transformations" of whatever inputs are used, simply because the service will not have existed before it was sold'.[77] Bernard Hoekman suggests that a nationality based origin rule for services such as the location of incorporation is perhaps the simplest and most transparent procedure to determine the origin of service suppliers.[78] If this is the case, it would appear that not much more needs to be done, as GATS already uses a nationality test of origin, discussed earlier when considering the meaning of 'service supplier of a Member'. These rules

[73] Aly K. Abu-Akeel, 'Definition of trade in services under the GATS: Legal Implications' (1999) 32 *George Washington Journal of International Law and Economics* 189, 204.

[74] The Agreement on Rules of Origin set out a work programme to establish new harmonised rules which has not been completed at the time of writing.

[75] WTO Secretariat, *Guide to the Uruguay Round Agreement* (The Hague: Kluwer Law International, 1999), p. 118.

[76] *Ibid.* [77] Hoekman, 'Rules of origin for goods and services', 89. [78] *Ibid.*

can be stated with precision and where desired, combined with other criteria such as country of residence and control or ownership. Such criteria might be most advantageous to the growth of outsourcing. In the example of the internet education provider constituted under the laws of the USA and supplying educational services via the internet from USA to Canada, rules of origin based on nationality of the supplier would lead to the conclusion that the USA is the country of origin for the educational service, even if supporting service activities like HR and data processing might have been done in countries other than the USA. Such a rule of origin would enable US companies to use offshore service suppliers without sacrificing their benefits under trade agreements to which the USA is a party but the countries supplying it with offshore services are not, a result that would be beneficial for countries like China and India.

Aly Abu-Akeel argues, however, that adopting a rule of origin for services that is based on the nationality of the service supplier is not compatible with the underlying economic rationale of mandating rules of origin unless the supplier is the actual provider of the services.[79] Where this is not the case, any rule of origin for services has to look beyond the nationality of the legal supplier to the sources of the actual inputs into the traded services. Abu-Akeel postulates a 'substantial input' rule of origin for services, which is comparable to the 'substantial transformation' rule for goods, where in order for substantial input to be attributed to a particular country it must be provided not only from that member's territory but also by its own residents.[80] The challenge in applying such a rule would be to determine what amount of input would qualify as substantial, and also to distinguish the various inputs in order to isolate the input provided by the country in question. It is likely that a substantial input rule would involve a determination of how much value was added to the service in a particular country. In an ideal world, this would be the fairest and most acceptable way of determining the country of origin for services. However, in practical terms, the lack of visibility of the service production process might make it difficult to determine accurately how much value was added at a particular location.[81]

The problems with formulating a workable rule of origin for services based on substantial input or value added might lead to the conclusion

[79] Abu-Akeel, 'Definition of trade in services under the GATS', 206. [80] *Ibid.*, 207.

[81] See Hoekman, 'Rules of origin for goods and services', 89.

that the most convenient position to take is that the value chain of service inputs should be ignored for the purposes of determining the origin of the final service. If the final service that is being supplied is an educational service, it might be reasonable to say that we need not take into account the fact that the HR and data processing services that contributed to provision of the educational service were in fact supplied in another country, as these support services are different and independent services from the final service. This would be consistent with the position taken under GATS and discussed earlier, that commitment made by a Member to a particular service sector does not necessarily imply that the supplier of the committed service may supply uncommitted services which are inputs to the committed service.[82] In other situations, however, it might be difficult to ignore the service inputs that were provided by an offshore supplier. Assume that there is an FTA between Country A and Country B under which Country B makes commitments in the medical services sector, that a hospital in Country B sends X-rays to be read in a hospital in Country A, and further that the hospital in Country A in turn outsources the reading of these X rays to another hospital in Country C. Should it be irrelevant that much of the work for the services provided by the hospital in Country A to the hospital in Country B is in fact done by a hospital in Country C? If the answer is that such a high degree of input from another country should be relevant, then a rule must be formulated to distinguish the situation where inputs from other countries are irrelevant from one where they are.

Abu-Akeel is of the view that 'calling a producer-based rule a rule of origin will be a contradiction in terms. It will amount to having no rule of origin at all to govern international trade in services'.[83] This is probably an overstatement, but it captures very well the underlying philosophical problem with looking at service suppliers and not the components of the service itself. Nevertheless, one should not dismiss the nationality rule, as the alternatives are difficult to implement in practice and it could be the best choice in the circumstances. Regardless of the result that might be reached, the formulation of rules of origin for services is a matter that should be discussed in greater detail at an

[82] See WTO *Guidelines for the Scheduling of Specific Commitments under the GATS* (Document S/L/92) and footnote 9 to GATS Article XVI (2)(c).

[83] Abu-Akeel, 'Definition of trade in services under the GATS', 207.

international level now that technology allows various components of a service to be sourced from all over the world.

III. Conclusion

The great potential of China and India to continue growing as offshore outsourcing providers rests largely on their own international comparative advantage. This can be enhanced by various developments in relation to GATS and the regulation of world trade in services. Some of the current limitations under GATS apply not just to offshore outsourcing but are inherent in the GATS system itself, and if progressive liberalisation carries on at a steady pace in the future, the offshoring industry should reap corresponding benefits. Specific matters which would be helpful to the offshore outsourcing industry include an update of the classification of sectors under GATS; a clarification on whether the supply of some electronic services takes place under Mode 1 or Mode 2; increased commitments by countries under Mode 1 (and possibly Mode 2) across sectors for activities specially relevant to offshore outsourcing; and to a lesser extent, further liberalisation under Modes 3 and 4. Development of suitable rules of origin for services would also be important, although whether these benefit or disadvantage suppliers of offshored services like China and India would depend on the content of the rules and on trading patterns. In addition, China and India, as outsourcing providers, could seek to conclude beneficial bilateral or regional free trade agreements with their main trading partners for offshore services in order to get round the limitations currently existing under the GATS system.

References

Abu-Akeel, Aly K, 'Definition of trade in services under the GATS: Legal implications' (1999) 32 *George Washington Journal of International Law and Economics* 189

A. T. Kearney, *Global Services Location Index* (2005) www.atkearney.com/shared_res/pdf/GSLI_Figures.pdf

Altinger, L. and Enders, A., 'The scope and depth of GATS commitments' (1996) 19(3) *The World Economy* 307

Anderson, Stuart, 'Outsourcing attacks not over', *National Review*, 11 February 2005 available at www.nfap.com/researchactivities/studies/NationalReview 021105.pdf

Bhagwati, Jagdish, Panagariya, Arvind and Srinivasan, T. N. 'The muddles over outsourcing' (2004) 18(4) *Journal of Economic Perspectives*

Chartered Institute of Personnel and Development, *Offshoring and the Role of HR*, Survey report (January 2006), available at http://www.cipd.co.uk/NR/rdonlyres/B3CC9F18–261E-4C70–882F-74884F80E476/0/offshoringhr0106.pdf

Earle, Beverley, Madek, Gerald A., Madek, Christina, 'A finger in the dike? An examination of the efficacy of state and federal attempts to use law to stem outsourcing' (2007) 28 *Northwestern Journal of International Law & Business* 89

Evalueserve, 'The next big opportunity, Moving up the value chain, From BPO to KPO' available at www.evalueserve.com/home.asp

Forrester Research, 'Offshore knowledge process outsourcing emerges' www.-forrester.com/Research/Document/Excerpt/0,7211,37661,00.html

Hoekman, Bernard, 'Rules of origin for goods and services: Conceptual issues and economic considerations'(1993) 27(4) *Journal of World Trade* 81

Graever II, Maurice F., 'Strategic outsourcing', in *A Structural Approach to Outsourcing Decisions and Initiatives* (New York: American Management Association, 1999)

Lapid, Karen, 'Outsourcing and offshoring under the General Agreement on Trade in Services' (2006) 40 *Journal of World Trade* 341

Mattoo, Aadityah and Wunsch-Vincent, Sacha, 'Pre-empting protectionism in services: The GATS and outsourcing' (2004) 7 *Journal of International Economic Law* 765

McKinsey Global Institute, *Offshoring: Is it a win-win game?* (McKinsey Global Institute, 2003)

McKinsey on IT, 'Can China compete in global IT outsourcing?' (2005), available at www.mckinsey.com/clientservice/bto/pointofview/outsourcing.asp

NASSCOM–McKinsey Report 2005 – *Extending India's leadership in the global IT and BPO industries* (2005)

National Foundation for American Policy, 'Anti-outsourcing efforts down but not out', NFAP Policy Brief April 2007, available at www.nfap.com/pdf/0407OutsourcingBrief.pdf

'Privacy concerns and global sourcing restrictions', NFAP Policy Brief, March 2006

NeoIT, 'Mapping offshore markets', available at www.neoit.com/pdfs/whitepapers/Mapping-Offshore-Markets.pdf

OECD Information Technology Outlook 2004

OECD Working Party of the Trade Committee, 'Electronic commerce – Existing GATS commitments for online supply of services', Document TD/TC/WP(99)37/FINAL (2001)

'Outsourcing radiology to India – how does it work?' available at www.outsource2india.com/why_india/articles/radiology-information.asp

Panagariya, Arvind, 'Why the recent Samuelson Article is not about offshore outsourcing' available at www.Columbia.edu/~ap2231/

Samuelson, Paul A., 'Where Ricardo and Mill rebut and confirm arguments of mainstream economists supporting globalization' (2004) 18 *Journal of Economic Perspectives* 135–46

Tinawi, Emad and Berkey, Judson, 'E-services and the WTO: Inadequacy of the GATS classification framework', in the background documentation for the October 1999 OECD Forum on Electronic Commerce available at www.oecd.org/dataoecd/12/60/2092597.pdf

United Nations, Statistical Office, Department of International Economic and Social Affairs, *Provisional Central Product Classification*, Statistical Papers Series M No. 77 (New York: Statistical Office of the United Nations, 1991), available at http://unstats.un.org/unsd/cr/registry/regct.asp?Lg=1.

WTO, *Guidelines for the Scheduling of Specific Commitments under the GATS* (Document S/L/92)

WTO, *World Trade Report 2004*, available at www.wto.org/english/res_e/booksp_e/anrep_e/world_trade_report04_e.pdfWTO Council for Trade in Services Special Session, *United States Revised Services Offer*, Document TN/S/O/USA/Rev.1 received on 31 May 2005

WTO news item, 'Plurilateral negotiations in services start', 28 February 2006 available at www.wto.org/english/news_e/news06_e/serv_28feb06_e.htm

WTO Secretariat, *Guide to the Uruguay Round Agreement* (The Hague: Kluwer Law International, 1999)

9

International dispute settlement

The Chinese approach and practice, and their implications

KONG QINGJIANG

International disputes are often blights to international relations between disputing nations. It is especially true if the disputes, which relate to the vital interests such as sovereignty of states and international peace and security, are not settled in a reasonable manner. The hanging disputes will not only impact on the relations of disputing parties, but also have a bearing on the interests of the region concerned or the whole world. Against this backdrop, it goes without saying how important the dispute settlement mechanism is vis-à-vis dispute settlement. This becomes more prominent when the bilateral relationship between the disputing parties is fragile and intense. Settlement of disputes plays an important role when both parties intend to maintain their relationship at a certain level. In other words, the function of the dispute settlement mechanism is simply to maintain the relationship between the disputing parties.

The past thirty years since China opened its doors to the outside world witnessed constant disputes between China and other countries (especially the United States), ranging from territorial disputes, to political disputes and to trade disputes. As the nation rises as an emerging economic giant, a resurgence of nationalism across the globe and muscle-flexing by China can be expected, and thus more disputes are likely to occur between the country and the rest of the world.[1] As a party

[1] The reasons are: Firstly, disputes are an integral part of international relations. China has come out of self-absorption to embrace globalization, and participated in all sorts of international intercourses in width and depth. The nation is eager to be respected as a big power while pursuing its interests. In the meantime, other countries (even the United States) begin to envisage a threat from the new intruder. Against this background, the occurrence of disputes is sometimes unavoidable. Secondly, China's ideology and political system, which somewhat displace the nation, will inevitably conflict with the Western

to international disputes that related to the territorial integrity, sovereignty and other vital interests of the nation, China was often seen to be hostile to any judicial solution and to have demonstrated a strong preference for political solution (especially through means of consultation and negotiation which rule out the possibility of any third party involvement). With the increasing integration of the country due to globalization, China has accepted more and more juridical solutions, especially international arbitration, as the means of international dispute settlement. China's accession to the World Trade Organization (WTO), and its commitments to the "Treaty of Amity and Cooperation in Southeast Asia" and the "Agreement on Dispute Settlement Mechanism" with the Association of Southeast Asian Nations (ASEAN) have evidenced the nation's willingness to subject herself to the jurisdiction of the international dispute settlement mechanisms, which are similar to the traditional judicial means. This signifies that the Chinese practice of settling international disputes, to which China is a party, has undergone a significant change. Moreover, the new approach to international dispute settlement may provide predictability or stability to a potential trade development and political situation in the region. In view of the above, the chapter is to examine the Chinese approach to, and its practice of, the settlement of international disputes, to which China herself is a party.

I. An overview of international dispute settlement mechanisms

Means to dispute settlement are classified by traditional international law as mandatory means and non-mandatory means. The mandatory means refer to those by which a disputing party takes coercive measures to have the other party act to obviate the occasion of the dispute, or to force the other party to accept the designed solution to the dispute. The mandatory means include restoration, revenge, pacific blockade and intervention.[2] The non-mandatory means refer to a settlement of international disputes in a peaceful manner. Dispute settlement has a direct effect on international interests. Undoubtedly, therefore, the best approach to settle disputes efficiently and to prevent international relations from getting worse is that in which all disputing parties can settle

polity, which can be best described as a free market economy and liberal democracy. For example, conflicts on China's human rights issue arise therefrom.

[2] The warfare and other forms of use of force were recognized as mandatory means to dispute settlement before the Second World War.

their disputes in a peaceful way, i.e. on the basis of mutual respect and in the spirit of goodwill. Settling international disputes peacefully is not only accepted as one of the fundamental principles of contemporary international law,[3] but also adopted by all nations and international organizations in their practices. As a result, dispute settlement mechanisms that facilitate the peaceful settlement of disputes came into existence gradually.

In the theories of international law, there are two peaceful approaches to dispute settlement: the political approach and the juridical approach. The former includes consultation and negotiation,[4] good offices, conciliation, inquiry and mediation. All the means are applicable to all types of international disputes.[5] The latter means an approach by which disputes are resolved by an institution that has independent jurisdictions. In this sense, both judicial litigation and international arbitration belong to the category.

II. The Chinese approach to peaceful settlement of international disputes

On the settlement of international disputes, the Chinese government has expressed many times on various occasions since the founding of the People's Republic of China that international disputes should be resolved through peaceful consultation.[6]

The Chinese government holds that to settle international disputes peacefully is a fundamental principle of international law. In a world whose members are getting more and more interdependent, only by

[3] The Charter of the United Nations, other important decisions and declarations of the United Nations, charters of certain regional international organizations and some regional treaties specifically require the members or contracting states to settle any dispute among themselves peacefully.

[4] Strictly speaking, consultation is a form of negotiation. Professor J. G. Merrills examined consultation as a means to dispute settlement in the first chapter, "Negotiation," of his book J. G. Merrills, *International Dispute Settlement*, 3rd edn (Cambridge University Press, 1998), pp. 1–8.

[5] Jian-ming Cao, Hong-jun Zhou and Hu-hua Wang (eds.), *Public International Law* (Beijing: Law Press, 1998), pp. 627–9.

[6] Premier Zhou announced the position of the Chinese government in his speech on the Indo-China question at the Geneva Conference in 1954, that the disputes among Asian countries be settled by means of peaceful consultations, rather than by use of force or threat of use of force. In the Asia–Africa Conference in April 1955, Premier Zhou pointed out that with the guarantee of the Five Principles of Peaceful Co-existence, one had no reason to believe that international disputes cannot be settled.

co-existing peacefully and behaving in a friendly manner toward each other, can all the states achieve common development and prosperity. In principle, international disputes should be settled in accordance with the principles of the Charter of the United Nations, and also should not contravene the fundamental principles of international relations; only in this way can it be ensured that the settlement of international disputes be peaceful and reasonable. Moreover, making use of the good offices, arbitration or mediation committee under the United Nations should facilitate the distribution of labor and coordination among the General Assembly, the Security Council and the Secretary General, and should also be instrumental in the checking and balancing of their obligations under the Charter of the United Nations with regard to the maintenance of international peace and security.[7] International disputes, be they political or juridical in nature, could lead to international conflicts or the worsening thereof, or even trigger a war and thus endanger world peace, if they are not resolved peacefully. Peaceful settlement of international disputes has the function of reducing war risks and maintaining world peace. The Charter of the United Nations, Article 2, recognizes the peaceful settlement of international disputes as a principle and outlaws non-peaceful solutions to international disputes. As a principle of international law, the peaceful settlement of international disputes carries weight nowadays under such a turbulent and tense international situation.[8]

By arguing that international disputes should be settled peacefully in accordance with the principles embodied in the Charter of the United Nations and the principles for international relations, China actually implies that while seeking a political solution to an international dispute, a state should attach great importance to the following: to respect the sovereignty and territorial integrity of all states in the world; not to resort to the use of force or threat of the use of force; and not to accept the outcome resulting from the use of force or threat of the use of force.[9]

China also considers that disputes of whatsoever nature among sovereign states should be resolved through dialogue, because it is not only

[7] "Liu Li-yang's speech on the peaceful settlement of international disputes at the Sixth Committee of the United Nations General Assembly" (1998) *Chinese Yearbook of International Law* 700.

[8] "Li Huan-ting's speech on the peaceful settlement of international disputes at the 40th meeting in the Sixth Committee of the United Nations General Assembly" (1986) *Chinese Yearbook of International Law* 610.

[9] *Ibid.*

helpful for all disputing parties to get a closer understanding of each other, to clarify the facts and resolve contradictions, but it can also avoid bringing tragedies to the people of all disputing parties. Dialogue is a proper approach to the peaceful resolution of international disputes.[10] Apparently, the dialogue approach that China advocates is equivalent to consultation and negotiation, which is an important approach to political settlement of international disputes.

It is noteworthy that China stands for a strong United Nations role in the prevention of conflicts. She further also holds that a political solution to international disputes cannot be replaced by the United Nations peacekeeping activities. China strongly opposes excessive use of force in peacekeeping activities, and emphasizes that the principles such as respect for national sovereignty and non-interference in each other's internal affairs should be observed in peacekeeping activities.[11] China believes that on the one hand, the role of the United Nations in the prevention of conflicts and maintenance of international peace and security should be strengthened; on the other hand, the procedure of conflict prevention should be regulated strictly in accordance with the relevant rules of the Charter of the United Nations. For example, as for the issue of strengthening the Secretary General's role in conflict prevention, the rules of the Charter of the United Nations regarding the interrelations among all the agencies concerned should also be observed so as to keep a balance and coordination.[12]

Here what needs attention is that peaceful settlement of international disputes is allowed to appear in the form of both a political solution and a juridical solution in international law. The well-established position of China in this regard, however, only means the former, which encompasses mediation, conciliation and negotiation. In other words, China has her own understanding of the peaceful settlement of international disputes. Up to now, China has never, no matter whether as a third party or one of the permanent members of the Security Council of the United Nations, required or urged the disputing parties to resolve their disputes by juridical means.

[10] "Wang Hou-li's speech on the Report of the Special Political Committee of the Charter of the United Nations at the 41st Meeting in the Sixth Committee of the United Nations General Assembly" (1988) *Chinese Yearbook of International Law* 827.

[11] En-zhao Liu, *The United Nations Peacekeeping Activities* (Beijing: Law Press, 1999), pp. 252–4.

[12] "Wang Hou-li's speech," p. 827.

III. The practice of China on the settlement of international disputes to which she is a party

Compared to the general approach of China to international dispute settlement, the Chinese practice on the settlement of international disputes, to which she is a party, is more intriguing.

A. The practice of China on political solutions to international disputes

1. Negotiation and consultation

Negotiation and consultation are the means to international dispute settlement to which China is strongly attached. They are also always visible in her practices of international dispute settlement. Meanwhile, in China's diplomacy, a lot of issues of vital importance to China and those rooted in history were settled through direct negotiations and consultations between the Chinese government and governments of other countries concerned:

Questions around territorial and boundary disputes between China and her neighboring countries gave rise to most controversies. China had such controversies with India, Pakistan, Myanmar and Russia,[13] and has the territory disputes over Diaoyu Island with Japan and over Spratley Islands with Vietnam, the Philippines, Malaysia and Brunei. The Chinese practices show that China has unexceptionally tried to solve all these territorial and boundary disputes by way of negotiation and consultation. An apparent instance is: China opposes resolving the dispute over Spratley Islands via arbitration, which is to be hosted by any third party.[14] With the negotiation and consultation approach, the Chinese government has settled the boundary disputes with Russia, Pakistan and Myanmar. In 1960, as a result of a diplomatic negotiation between the Chinese government and the government of the Union of Myanmar, an agreement was signed on border issues, which led to the resolution of the first territorial dispute between China and other countries.[15] Subsequently, the boundary disputes between China and some other neighboring countries, such as Pakistan and Nepal, were respectively settled through negotiations or consultations; by means of negotiation, China

[13] Hai-shan Liu, *International Law* (Beijing: Law Press, 1992), pp. 201–12.

[14] Lian-qin Fang, Jin-zhi Liu and Bing-yuan Wang, *Post-War History of International Relations* (Peking University Press, 1996), pp. 1059–65.

[15] Tie-ya Wang, *International Law* (Beijing: Law Press, 1995), p. 610.

and Russia (previously the Soviet Union) reached an agreement on the eastern part of the Sino-Soviet border in 1991, an agreement on the western part of the Sino-Russian border in 1994, and a supplementary agreement on the eastern part of the Sino-Russian border in 2005. And these agreements put an end to the taunting border disputes between the two neighboring powers on the whole. Almost at the same time, China signed border demarcation agreements respectively with Kazakhstan, Kirghizstan and Tajikistan on the basis of negotiation and consultation.[16] Also, by way of negotiation, China successfully signed a land boundary treaty with Vietnam in 1999 and, an agreement on the demarcation of the Gulf of Tonkin territorial sea between the two neighboring countries in 2000.

It was by means of negotiation that China settled other disputes relating to its sovereignty, such as the question of Hong Kong and the question of Macao.[17] Since 1983, after twenty-two rounds of deliberate and patient negotiation, an agreement was finally reached between the United Kingdom and China on the handover of Hong Kong to China, i.e. the "Joint Declaration of the Government of the United Kingdom of Great Britain and Northern Ireland and the Government of the People's Republic of China on the Question of Hong Kong." The successful resolution of the question of Hong Kong by means of negotiation set up a model for the resolution of the question of Macao. In 1985, as the Chinese premier and the premier of Portugal had friendly consultations on the question of Macao, both parties agreed to start negotiation in Beijing in 1986. After four rounds of negotiations from 1986 to 1987, the "Joint Declaration of the Government of the People's Republic of China and the Government of the Republic of Portugal on the Question of Macao" was reached in Beijing.

In addition to territorial and boundary disputes and the disputes relating to the sovereignty and vital interests of China, China has also tried to resolve, by means of negotiation, other international disputes that are of great political or economic importance. For example, quite a few disputes between China and relevant parties of great political implications, such as the non-proliferation of nuclear weapons, were settled by way of negotiations and consultations.[18] In the past decade, disputes often arise between China and the United States concerning intellectual

[16] Shou-yuan Li, *International Relations and China's Diplomacy* (Beijing: Beijing Broadcasting Institute Press, 1999), p. 173.

[17] Fang, Liu and Wang, *Post-War History*, p. 1026.

[18] Li, *International Relations and China's Diplomacy*, p. 282.

property, trade in textiles, etc, and sometimes they escalated to such a point that both parties were about to take trade retaliatory measures against each other. Interestingly, by means of negotiation, an understanding could always be finally reached before an imminent trade war broke out.[19] When the bombing of the Chinese embassy in Yugoslavia triggered widespread anger among the Chinese people and an anguished diplomatic accusation from the Chinese government in 1999, China did not give up negotiating with the United States and a mutually acceptable consensus ended the dangerous diplomatic row.[20] Such is the case with China in dealing with the Southeast Asian countries: in 2002, China and the ASEAN signed the Declaration on the Conduct of Parties in the South China Sea, which signified that China, as well as the ASEAN, is willing to commit herself to the stability and peace in the South China Sea rim, and to settle, by peaceful means, disputes between herself and any other country. At the China–ASEAN Summit in Bali, Indonesia (October 2003), China formally became a member of the "Treaty of Amity and Cooperation in Southeast Asia," which requires that all the signatory states settle the disputes among themselves by means of friendly negotiations, and demands that in the event that no solution is reached through direct negotiations, a High Council comprising a Representative at ministerial level from each of the Contracting Parties take cognizance of the dispute or the situation and recommend to the disputing parties appropriate means of settlement such as good offices, mediation, inquiry or conciliation.[21]

2. Good offices and conciliation

China has not attempted to resolve international disputes through good offices; but she has been found to employ conciliation as a means to resolve the disputes between China and other countries: After the border skirmish broke out between India and China in 1962, six African-Asian countries put forward a proposal with a view to mediating the conflict. The Chinese government declared the acceptance of the proposal in principle as the basis for the commencement of direct negotiations between China and India. In consequence of India's requirement that China accept the proposal unconditionally, the mediation effort ended in failure. On the settlement of the disputes relating to the territorial

[19] Fang, Liu and Wang, *Post-War History*, pp. 948–58.

[20] Li, *International Relations and China's Diplomacy*, p. 149.

[21] Treaty of Amity and Cooperation in Southeast Asia, arts. 13 and 15.

integrity and national sovereignty or other vital interests of China, China apparently opposes any conciliation and mediations by a third party. For instance, China refused the United States' intervention in the question of Taiwan and the dispute around the Spratley Islands.[22] So far, China has not been found to have resolved a dispute, to which China herself is a party, by means of inquiry and mediation.[23]

But China has been found to have contributed to the settlement of international disputes as a mediator. In order to find a peaceful solution to the Cambodia issue, for example, China took an active part in the large-scale United Nations-led collective mediation, which resulted in a solution to the question which had lasted for thirteen years.[24]

B. The practices of China on the juridical solution to international disputes

China has been keen on resolving international disputes by diplomatic means – negotiation and consultation, but she is quite cautious towards the two juridical means – international arbitration and judicial solution. The reason for this is China's reluctance to be sued at the international forum – be it international court or international arbitration. More or less, this reflects the fact that China does not trust the international judicature, or at least she has a sense of estrangement. The Western international lawyers blame this all on the historical sense of humiliation of China.[25]

1. International arbitration

In all the treaties and agreements – except some foreign trade agreements – that China had signed before the 1980s, there were no arbitration clauses. China made reservations, if permitted, to almost all the arbitration clauses in the multilateral treaties and international conventions – that China signed, acceded to or ratified. After the border skirmish

[22] Amidst the tension across the Taiwan Straits in the late 1990s, China also turned down the offer of Lee Kuan-yew, the then Senior Minister of Singapore, to conciliate the dispute by taking advantage of his good relations with both sides of the Taiwan Straits.

[23] Wang, *International Law*, p. 611.

[24] Liu Ming, *International Intervention and National Sovereignty* (Chengdu: Sichuan People's Publishing House, 2000), pp. 191–2.

[25] For example: J. A. Cohen and H. Chiu, *People's China and International Law* (Princeton Publishing Press, 1974) and Shao-chun Leng and Hungdah Chiu (eds.), *Law in Chinese Foreign Policy: Communist China and Selected Problems of International Law* (Dobbs Ferry, NY: Oceana Publications, 1972).

between India and China broke out in 1962, the Indian government suggested that both parties "accept sort of international arbitration under the auspices of one person or a people who was or were nominated or accepted by both parties" so as to render "a ruling which is binding on both governments." But the Chinese government rejected the proposal on the ground that "border disputes are such vital questions relating to national sovereignty that they can only be settled through direct negotiations between both parties, and any other approaches, such as international arbitration, are not acceptable."[26]

In the later 1980s, China changed her attitude toward arbitration as a means to international dispute settlement. When she signed, acceded to or ratified international conventions, China began to make no reservations to arbitration provisions therein. Noteworthily, these conventions are none other than those concerned with economic, trade, technology, transportation, aviation, environment, health care, and other professional and technical cooperation.[27] While acceding to some conventions of a political nature, China still made reservations to arbitration clauses therein.[28] Meanwhile, arbitration clauses and dispute settlement clauses in general (including arbitration) were seen in treaties and agreements on bilateral trade investment technology cooperation and cultural exchange to which China was a party. For example, according to the "Agreement between the United States of America and the People's Republic of China on Investment Insurance" and its accompanying "Exchange Notes," article 6, if the dispute cannot be resolved through

[26] Wang, *International Law*, p. 611.

[27] In 1988, China acceded to the "Convention Establishing the Multilateral Investment Guarantee Agency," which requires that the disputes between a contracting state and the organization be settled by means of negotiation, mediation or arbitration. When she ratified the "Convention on the Settlement of Investment Disputes between States and Nationals of Other States" in 1992, China agreed to submit to the ICSID Center the disputes between herself and nationals of any other contracting states concerning expropriation and compensation. When she ratified the "United Nations Convention to Combat Desertification in Those Countries Experiencing Serious Drought and/or Desertification, Particularly in Africa" in 1996, the "Convention of the International Telecommunications Union, the International Telecommunications Convention" in 1997. While acceding to or ratifying these conventions, China did not make reservations to the arbitration clauses therein.

[28] When she acceded to the "Convention on the Prevention and Punishment of Crime Against International Protected Persons Including Diplomatic Persons" in 1987, China made reservations to the arbitration provisions therein; again, when she acceded to the "Vienna Convention on the Law of Treaties" in 1997, a reservation was made to Article 66, which requires the parties to resolve disputes by means of judicial solution or arbitration.

negotiation, the government of either party may submit an arbitration application. Similar provisions are incorporated in the bilateral investment agreements between China and other countries, such as France, the United Kingdom, the Netherlands and Canada. However, the bilateral treaties on extradition or on judicial assistance, which China signed, contain no provisions concerning dispute settlement by arbitration, but clauses for dispute settlement by diplomatic methods or negotiation and consultation.[29]

At the same time, the Chinese government began to take an active part in the activities of the Permanent Court of Arbitration (PCA). In 1993, China appointed four arbitrators to the PCA.

2. Judicial solution

Based on the principle that all sovereignties are equal and independent, the Chinese government insists that without the consent of a country, any other country or international organization has no power to exercise the jurisdiction over the national sovereignty. Thus in 1972, soon after the resumption of her seat in the United Nations, the People's Republic of China announced that the statement, which the former Republic of China made to accept the compulsory jurisdiction of the International Court of Justice (ICJ), ceased to be effective. China has signed with other countries no special agreements that mandate disputes be submitted to the ICJ. International conventions that China acceded to or ratified, contained no clauses, by which contracting parties shall resolve the disputes between them by referring disputes to the ICJ; even if such clauses do exist in those conventions, China makes reservations to the clauses without exception. As a matter of fact, China refuses to subject herself to the jurisdiction of the ICJ.

As the role of the ICJ and other international adjudicatory bodies in the peaceful settlements of international disputes have been gradually recognized, and as the relationship between China and the ICJ became closer, China's attitude towards settling international disputes by the ICJ has undergone a change: China became more open with such provisions

[29] The "Extradition Treaty between the People's Republic of China and the Kingdom of Thailand," art. 19; The "Treaty on the Civil and Commercial Legal Assistance between the People's Republic of China and the Kingdom of Spain," art. 28; The "Treaty Concerning Judicial Assistance in Criminal Procedures between the People's Republic of China with Canada," art. 32, and other judicial assistance treaties between China and Greece, the Republic of Korea, Singapore, the United States respectively have such similar provisions.

when she acceded to or ratified international conventions. Where conventions are concerned with economic, trade, aviation, environment and other professional activities, China tends not to make reservations to such clauses mandating the use of the ICJ and other international adjudicatory bodies by disputing contracting parties.[30] China acceded to the "United Nations Convention on the Law of the Sea" in 1998. Part XV of the Convention requires that State Parties to the Convention settle any dispute between them concerning the interpretation or application of the Convention by peaceful means in accordance with article 2, paragraph 3, of the "Charter of the United Nations" and shall seek a solution by the means indicated in article 33, paragraph 1, of the Charter. Where, however, no settlement has been reached, article 286 of the Convention stipulates that the dispute be submitted at the request of any party to the dispute to a court or tribunal having jurisdiction in this regard.[31] It is noted that China has so far referred no relevant dispute to the International Court of Justice or the International Tribunal for the Law of the Sea for a solution. The Convention also has an optional compulsory jurisdiction provision (article 287), which provides: "while signing, ratifying or acceding to this Convention or at any time thereafter, a state shall be free to choose, by means of a written declaration," the International Tribunal for the Law of the Sea, the International Court of Justice, an arbitral tribunal and a special arbitral tribunal for the settlement of disputes concerning the interpretation or application of this Convention. China has not yet made such a declaration.

IV. The impact of China's accession to the WTO on her approach to international dispute settlement

The WTO established a powerful dispute settlement mechanism to monitor members' regulation of international trade, the aim of which is to provide the multilateral trading system with safety and predictability.

[30] For example: when China signed and ratified the "Convention on the Production, Stockpiling and Use of Chemical Weapons and on Their Destruction," she did not make a reservation to article 14, a dispute settlement provision which provides that disputes be submitted to the ICJ on the condition that all the disputing parties agree to it.

[31] Article 287 of the Convention defines those courts or tribunals as: (a) The International Tribunal for the Law of the Sea (established in accordance with Annex VI of the Convention) including the Seabed Disputes Chamber; (b) The International Court of Justice; (c) An arbitral tribunal constituted in accordance with Annex VII of the Convention; (d) A special arbitral tribunal constituted in accordance with Annex VIII for one or more of the categories of disputes specified therein.

This mechanism is governed by the "Rules and Procedures on Dispute Settlement Understanding" (hereinafter referred to as Understanding), which itself is an integral part of a package agreement of the WTO. The systemized and normative provisions of the Understanding far exceed those embodied in the General Agreement on Tariffs and Trade (GATT). Institutionally, the WTO dispute settlement mechanism is based upon an international organization which has an international juridical personality. Moreover, a new body called the Dispute Settlement Body (DSB), which is an *alter ego* of the General Council of the WTO, was created to operate the mechanism. The DSB has compulsory jurisdiction on trade disputes between WTO members and has its own rules of operation. It can establish a panel of experts to handle the dispute if one party to a trade dispute requests so, adopt the reports of the Panel, supervise the implementation of the recommendation and approve the compensation measures, if required. The report of the Panel or the report of the Appellate Body (AB, a standing body of the WTO), comes into effect automatically, unless it is not adopted by the DSB with consensus, which in fact is impractical.

The procedure called "negative consensus" is the most prominent feature of the dispute settlement mechanism of the WTO. According to the "negative consensus" principle, if any party to a trade dispute requests, the Panel is to be set up automatically. Unless one party or both to the dispute appeals to the AB, the Panel report will come into effect. In case of appeal, the AB will evaluate the legal matters which relate to the Panel report.[32] Once the report of the AB is made available, the DSB shall adopt it with the "negative consensus" principle, and then the AB report comes into effect.

The DSB is also responsible for the proper implementation of its "recommendations."[33] The party whose trade measures have been found not to be in compliance with WTO rules should modify or repeal the measures concerned. If the party fails to implement the "recommendations," which form part of the adopted report, compensation may be imposed on the party or the concessions that the other parties made under the WTO agreement may be withdrawn.[34] Therefore, as far as trade disputes among the WTO members are concerned, the dispute settlement mechanism of the WTO is no more than an international court.

[32] Understanding, Art. 17, para. 6.

[33] Understanding, Art. 21.

[34] Understanding, Art. 22.

China has been a member of the WTO since 11 December 2001. By acceding to this global trade system, China has accepted the jurisdiction of the dispute settlement mechanism of the WTO. This means that China's approach to the settlement of disputes in the trade area has undergone a significant change.

Not long after China's accession to the WTO, China's attitude towards the WTO dispute settlement mechanism was tested. The United States imposed safeguard measures against steel imports from China, the European Union and other countries. After a few rounds of consultation failed, the European Union brought the dispute to the DSB of the WTO. China joined the process. This was the first time that China had resorted to an international institution for a solution to a dispute to which she was a party.

The dispute with the United States concerning steel safeguard measures has been the only one that China referred to the DSB. However, it is intriguing to note that she was reluctant when it was brought to the DSB. In two other cases, China was subjected to the DSB in 2004 for its policy on tax rebate for integrated circuits exports and in 2006 for duties on auto parts imports. In the semiconductor case, when China received the notification that the United States had requested the DSB to establish a panel, she was unhappy because she had not been given adequate opportunity for consultation.[35] As a matter of fact, upon China's insistence, the two parties reached a solution even prior to the initiation of the panel process.

V. The impact of the ACFTA dispute settlement mechanism on the Chinese approach to dispute settlement

China seems eager to establish preferential access to fast expanding regional markets through legally binding commitments. An example is the formation of the proposed ASEAN–China Free Trade Area (ACFTA). In November 2002, the leaders of China and the ASEAN member countries signed the "Framework Agreement on Comprehensive Economic Cooperation," which provides for an ACFTA by the year 2010 for Brunei Darulassam, China, Indonesia, Malaysia, the Philippines, Singapore and Thailand, and by 2015 for the newer ASEAN member countries,

[35] According to Sun Zhenyu, China's permanent representative to the WTO, the US side filed the complaint while the two sides were still in talks. China felt regret over this and could not understand the US decision. "U.S. launches WTO complaint against China," *China Daily*, March 19, 2004.

Cambodia, Laos, Myanmar and Vietnam. ASEAN and China have signed the "Trade in Goods Agreement," and the "Dispute Settlement Mechanism Agreement" at the ASEAN–China summit in November 2004 in Vientiane, as part of the implementation of the Framework Agreement.

It is not difficult to find that the international legal framework for dispute settlement in the ACFTA "Agreement on Dispute Settlement Mechanism," is certainly among the most intricate and elaborate rules that bind China in relation to dispute settlement.

Although the ACFTA Agreement does not prejudice any right of China, as well as other parties to have recourse to dispute settlement procedures available under any other treaty to which they are parties,[36] the ACFTA Dispute Settlement Mechanism amounts to an enhanced international dispute settlement mechanism available to China. Moreover, her commitment to this enhanced dispute settlement mechanism consolidated China's new approach to the settlement of disputes, at least in the trade area.

VI. Concluding remarks

As a party to international disputes concerning territorial integrity, sovereignty and other vital interests of the nation, China was often seen to be hostile to any judicial solution and to have demonstrated a strong preference for political solution (especially through means of consultation and negotiation which rule out the possibility of any third party involvement). With the increasing integration of the country through globalization, China could now afford to follow a less stringent attitude toward the other disputants to which she is a party and pursue a more balanced policy towards the rest of the world. Accordingly, China has accepted more and more juridical solutions, especially international arbitration, as the means to the settlement of international disputes to which she is a party.

China's accession to the WTO, and its commitments to the "Treaty of Amity and Cooperation in Southeast Asia" and "Agreement on Dispute Settlement Mechanism" with the ASEAN have evidenced the nation's commitment to subject herself to the jurisdiction of the international dispute settlement mechanisms, which are similar to the traditional

[36] The ACFTA Agreement on Dispute Settlement Mechanism, art. 2(5).

judicial means. This signifies that the Chinese practice of settling international disputes, to which China is a party, has undergone a significant change.

The WTO and the ACFTA legal regimes govern the settlement of disputes between China and its trade partners in the region. Unlike uncertain, less formal cooperation, the rules of dispute settlement provide the only predictability or stability to a potential investment or trade-development situation. It marks a brand new approach of China to international dispute settlement. Moreover, the new approach to international dispute settlement may provide the only predictability or stability to a potential trade development and political situation between China and its trade partners in the region.

References

Cao, Jian-ming, Zhou, Hong-jun and Wang, Hu-hua (eds.), *Public International Law* (Beijing: Law Press, 1998)

Cohen, J. A. and Chiu, H., *People's China and International Law* (Princeton Publishing Press, 1974)

Fang, Lian-qin, Liu, Jin-zhi and Wang, Bing-yuan, *Post-War History of International Relations* (Beijing: Peking University Press, 1996)

Lee, Shuang-yuan and Huang, Hui-kang, *International Law* (Wuhan: Zhongnan University of Technology Press, 2000)

Leng, Shao-chun and Chiu, Hungdah (eds.), *Law in Chinese Foreign Policy: Communist China and Selected Problems of International Law* (Dobbs Ferry, NY: Oceana Publications, 1972)

Li, Shou-yuan, *International Relations and China's Diplomacy* (Beijing: Beijing Broadcasting Institute Press, 1999)

LIU Ming, *International Intervention and National Sovereignty* (Chengdu: Sichuan People's Publishing House, 2000)

Merrills, J. G., *International Dispute Settlement*, 3rd edn (Cambridge University Press, 1998)

"U.S. launches WTO complaint against China," *China Daily*, March 19, 2004

Wang, Tie-ya, *International Law* (Beijing: Law Press, 1995)

PART II

China, India and regional economic integration in Asia

10

The role of China and India in Asian regionalism

JIANGYU WANG

I. Introduction to regional economic integration and regionalism

A. The conceptual definitions

Regionalism, regionalization, regional economic integration, regional economic cooperation, regional trade agreements, free trade agreements . . ., terms like these appear frequently in newspapers, academic articles and official documents when international trade, investment or finance is concerned. In essence, they all refer to one phenomenon: the cross-border preferential economic initiatives undertaken by national governments or private sectors at regional or bilateral level, as opposed to multilateral initiatives which are conducted on non-discrimination basis under the auspice of the World Trade Organization (WTO).[1]

Although these terms can be understood loosely and used interchangeably, it is important and useful to distinguish one term from another conceptually. Winters, when discussing the regionalism v. multilateralism debate, defines regionalism 'loosely as any policy designed to reduce trade barriers between a subset of countries regardless of whether those countries are actually contiguous or even close to each other'.[2] According to Lamberte, regionalism shall refer to 'formal economic cooperation and economic arrangements of a group of countries aimed at facilitating or enhancing regional integration'.[3] Regionalism is to be distinguished from regionalization, which is 'market-driven integration, spurred by unilateral reforms in individual economies within a particular region'.[4]

[1] L. Alan Winters, *Regionalism versus Multilateralism*, World Bank Policy Research Working Paper No. 1687 (Washington DC: World Bank, 1996).

[2] *Ibid.*, pp. 2–3.

[3] Mario B. Lamberte, 'An overview of economic cooperation and cooperation in Asia', in Asia Development Bank, *Asian Economic Cooperation and Intergration: Progress, Prospects and Challenges* (Manila: Asian Development Bank, 2005), p. 4.

[4] *Ibid.*

Literally, regionalization also refers to the actions of building regionalism through public and/or official efforts. According to the Dictionary of Trade Policy terms developed by the WTO, regionalism is described as 'actions by governments to liberalize or facilitate trade on regional basis, sometimes through free-trade areas or customs unions'.[5] Following these inspirations, economic regionalism can be roughly understood as (a) formal economic cooperative measures (b) undertaken by governments (c) to facilitate regional economic integration (d) which however is not necessarily confined to a geographical region. Put differently, regionalism can now be broadly characterized as the tendency towards the creation of preferential trade arrangements between a number of countries located in the same or even different regions, which discriminate against third countries.

This naturally leads to the definition of economic integration. Bela Balassa, in his seminal work *The Theory of Economic Integration*, defines economic integration as a process and a state of affairs: 'Regarded as a process, it encompasses measures designed to abolish discrimination between economic units belonging to different national states; viewed as a state of affairs, it can be represented by the absence of various forms of discrimination between national economies'.[6] Balassa further explains the different forms of integration:

> Economic integration . . . can take several forms that represent varying degrees of integration. There are free-trade area, a customs union, a common market, an economic union, and complete economic integration. In a free-trade area, tariffs (and quantitative restrictions) between the participating countries are abolished, but each country retains its own tariff against nonmembers. Establishing a customs union involves, besides the suppression of discrimination in the field of commodity movements within the union, the equalization of tariffs in trade with nonmember countries. A higher form of economic integration is attained in a common market, where not only trade restrictions but also restrictions on factor movements are abolished. An economic union, as distinct from a common market, combines the suppression of restrictions on commodity and factor movements with some degree of harmonization of national economic policies, in order to remove discrimination that was due to disparities in these policies. Finally, total economic integration presupposes the unification of monetary, fiscal, social, and

[5] WTO Secretariat,'Scope of RTAs', available at www.wto.org/english/ tratop_e/region_e/scope_rta_e.htm (visited 27 April 2006).

[6] Bela Balassa, *The Theory of Economic Integration* (Homewood, IL: Richard D. Irwin Inc., 1961), p. 1.

> countercyclical policies and requires the setting-up of a supra-national authority whose decisions are binding for the member states.[7]

Since its introduction, the Balassa-stages approach has been indispensable for an understanding of both the literature and practice of economic integration. The usage of this approach is widespread and the terms contained therein for describing the different degrees of integration, especially the free-trade area and customs union, have hence come into fairly standard usage. It is nonetheless important to note that, in light of the later theoretical and practical development of regionalism, the Balassa-stages approach should be amended and clarified in order to provide a more precise analytical framework for economic integration. For example, it should be understood that the Balassa-stages are presented sequentially for analytical purpose, and hence the sequence is not to be followed rigidly.[8] Economic integration in Europe, for instance, started directly with a customs union instead of a free-trade area. Balassa's distinction between common market and economic union also presents a conceptual problem. The European Union's experience shows that integration beyond customs union is difficult to define and conceptualize, and in this sense Balassa's third and fourth stages (common market and economic union) should be taken together.[9] Furthermore, it is probably not necessary – and useful as well – to define the final stage as 'total economic integration' with a supranational authority. It is more realistic to 'envisage several partial "unions" beyond the economic union, such as a tax union, a social union, a monetary union and a political union'.[10] Whether these sub-unions will work together towards a unitary state, as Balassa's final stage implies, is currently beyond the theoretical studies as well as the practice of economic integration.

In both the literature and legal instruments of economic integration, the term 'single market' is becoming increasingly popular. The Single European Act of 1987 formally created a Single Market in Europe that came into operation on 1 July 1987. In the 2003 Declaration of ASEAN Concord II (Bali Concord II), the heads of ASEAN countries adopted the goal that the 'ASEAN Economic Community shall establish ASEAN as a single market and production base'.[11]

[7] *Ibid.*, p. 2.

[8] Jacques Pelkmans, *European Integration: Methods and Economic Analysis*, 2nd edn (London: Financial Times/Prentice Hall, 2001), p. 7.

[9] *Ibid.* [10] *Ibid.*

[11] Text of the Bali Concord II is available at www.aseansec.org/15159.htm (visited 28 April 2006).

Apparently, a single market is more than a common market, but how much more is an interesting question. The Single European Act describes it as 'an area without internal frontiers in which the free movement of goods, persons, services and capital is ensured'. Criticizing that this definition is imprecise,[12] Lloyd defines a single market 'as one in which the Law of One Price must hold in all goods, services and factor markets', which means that 'there should be a single price in the regionwide market for every tradable commodity and factor, expressing all prices in a common currency and adjusting for the real costs of moving goods or factors between locations'.[13] In essence, a single market requires not only the elimination of border measures and full national treatment of beyond-the-border measures applying to imports, but also harmonization of rules and procedures across participating states. 'Hence, a single market is synonymous with complete economic integration of the area'.[14] However, without becoming a unitary state, how complete the market can be remains a question beyond the reach of this chapter.

Regionalism, as noted above, can be a cross-region phenomenon. For analytical purpose, it is useful to define regional economic integration as a dynamic process encompassing integration of economies within a geographic region. Hence in this chapter, 'regional economic integration in Asia', 'Asian regionalism' or 'East Asian regionalism', or other similar terms, are all used to refer to the integration activities in the particular Asian region concerned.

Economic integration is conducted through trade agreements. It is important to define the concepts of 'regional trade agreements' (RTAs) and 'free trade agreements'(FTAs) which are to be used frequently in this chapter. Following the usage of the WTO, this chapter does not distinguish between regional trade agreements or free trade agreements, as, '[i]n the WTO context . . . RTAs may be agreements concluded between countries not necessarily belonging to the same geographical region'.[15] Also no distinction is made between bilateral trade agreements concluded between two parties and those agreements between more than two parties. They are instead all referred to as regional trade agreements

[12] Peter J. Lloyd, 'What is a single market? An application to the case of ASEAN' (2005) 22 (3) *ASEAN Economic Bulletin* 251–65, 252.

[13] *Ibid.*, 254.

[14] Peter J. Lloyd and Penny Smith, *Global Economic Challenges to Asean Integration and Competitiveness: A Prospective Look*, REPSF Project 03/006a (2004)(prepared for the ASEAN Secretariat). Available at http://www.ausaid.gov.au/publications/pdf/global_econ_challenge.pdf (visited 02 January 2010), p. 11.

[15] Bali Concord II.

or free trade agreements, with the two terms used interchangeably in this chapter.[16] However, to the extent that RTAs also cover agreements between countries in different regions, Asian RTAs are used to mean those arrangements between countries in Asia.

Economic integration may be conducted through different approaches, each of which however also represents a different degree of integration. Machlup distinguishes between three approaches in this regard. First, there is *sectoral* integration, which is used to mean integration which is '(i) limited to particular industries or sectors of the economy or economies concerned; (ii) gradual, proceeding successively from sector to sector'. Second, *functional* integration refers to integration which is '(i) gradual, proceeding successively from sector to sector; (ii) by means of price incentives operating in a free market'. In its first sense, functional is identical to the second sense of sectoral integration. However, the latter is more inclined to be used as distinct from general across-the-board integration. The last one is *institutional* integration, used to mean integration which is 'by means of adaptations of national or international institutions (in the widest sense of the word, for example monetary practices and arrangements)'.[17] In the regionalism literature, the second sense of institutional has been more customary.

Sectoral and/or functional integration is often characterized as 'market-driven' integration whilst institutional integration is known as 'policy-driven' . It is observed that regional economic integration in Europe under the auspices of the European Union (EU) corresponds more to the policy-driven model of institutional integration as, in Europe, 'the origins of integration have been institutional in nature, and the development of institutions has been prominent throughout the process'.[18] In contrast, integration in East Asia has been market-driven. Although the existing institutions in this region are fairly weak

[16] Jagdish Bhagwati has suggested the use of 'preferential trade agreements' instead of free trade agreements and customs unions because the latter two phrases can mislead the public to equate them with nonpreferential free trade. See Jagdish Bhagwati, Pravin Krishna and Arvind Panagariya, *Trading Blocs: Alternative Approaches to Analyzing Preferential Trade Agreements* (Cambridge, MA: MIT Press, 1999), p. 33.

[17] F. Machlup, 'Economic integration', in Miroslav N. Jovanovic (ed.), *International Economic Integration: Critical Perspectives on the World Economy*, Volume I: *Theory and Measurement* (London and New York: Routledge, 1998), pp. 119–49, at p. 142.

[18] Eisuke Sakakibara and Sharon Yamakawa, 'Market-driven regional integration in East Asia', in Julie McKay, Maria Oliva Armengol and Georges Pineau (eds.), *Regional Economic Integration in a Global Framework*, G-20 Workshop organized jointly by the People's Bank of China and the European Central Bank, 22–23 September 2004, Beijing, China (Frankfurt: European Central Bank, 2005), pp. 35–78, at p. 35.

and ineffective, '[i]ntra-industry trade in parts and components and foreign direct investment – conducted by corporations and encouraged by significant liberalization – have been and continue to be the key driving forces of the established production-sharing system, of the evolution of these cross-border networks and of the fostering of regional cooperation and integration'.[19] As will be discussed below, China is a major player in this production-sharing regime and plays a key role in shaping the market-driven integration in Asia.

It is, however, over-simplistic to characterize any of the two integration model as entirely market-driven or policy-driven. The role of the market forces in European integration should never be underestimated. For instance, in the sense that the extent of regionalization is commonly measured by the share of intra-regional trade in total trade, intra-regional trade in Western Europe (EU-15) had exceeded 50 per cent long before the Single Market was formed in 1992.[20] On the other hand, national governments in Asia, through intergovernmental cooperation, have been playing a significant role in the integration process, albeit Asian supranational institutions have not yet developed.

Lastly, it is fundamentally important to stress that, although regional integration requires substantial political will to cooperate, it does not necessarily include the political commitment to political integration or political union. In other words, 'aspirations for political union are not a necessary precondition for building regional institutions that foster economic integration'.[21] This is of course the experience of Europe, but it would be highly relevant in the Asian context as political integration in Asia is almost unattainable in the foreseeable future.

[19] Julie McKay, Maria Oliva Armengol and Georges Pineau (eds.), *Regional Economic Integration in a Global Framework*, G-20 Workshop organized jointly by the People's Bank of China and the European Central Bank, 22–23 September 2004, Beijing, China (Frankfurt: European Central Bank, 2005), p. 12. Available at www.ecb.int/pub/pdf/other/regionaleconintegrationglobalframework2005en.pdf (visited 2 May 2006).

[20] ADB , *Asian Development Bank Outlook 2006* (Manila: Asian Development Bank, 2006), p. 272.

[21] C. Randall Henning, 'Regional economic integration and institution building', in Julie McKay, Maria Oliva Armengol and Georges Pineau (eds.), *Regional Economic Integration in a Global Framework*, , G-20 Workshop organized jointly by the People's Bank of China and the European Central Bank, 22–23 September 2004, Beijing, China (Frankfurt: European Central Bank, 2005), pp. 79–100, at p. 79.

B. The regionalism v. multilateralism debate in the Asian context

1. Economic impact of RTAs: Trade creating or trade diverting?

Regionalism, practised mainly through RTAs/FTAs at this stage, is questioned by conventional economic theory for its benefits to both the contracting parties and the third countries outside the agreements. Using the words of Jacob Viner in his pioneering analysis of the economics of customs unions, the question is about the economic costs and/or benefits of a RTA '(a) for each of the [RTA participating] countries taken separately; (b) for the two combined; (c) for the outside world; and (d) for the world as a whole'.[22]

The analytical framework of the economics of RTAs is still based on the key concepts of trade creation and trade diversion introduced by Viner. Trade creation takes place when, as a result of the removal of tariffs on intra-area trade, domestic production of a product is displaced by imports from another member of the RTA whose comparative advantage enables it to produce the goods at a lower cost. The preferential tariff rate established by a RTA might also cause trade diversion, defined as a shift of production away from a lower-cost producer outside the RTA to a higher-cost source of supply within it.[23]

Both the economic literature and empirical studies of the impact of RTAs lead to notoriously ambiguous results. With regard to the trade stimulating effects of RTAs on the participating members, the findings generally suggest that RTAs have a positive welfare consequence on the members.[24] This is because regional cooperation in the RTAs 'offers one route to overcome the disadvantages of smallness, by pooling resources or combining markets'.[25] RTAs can first of all foster competition in an enlarged market, and as such they can increase efficiency of domestic firms which have to face greater competition brought about by the entry of foreign competitors in previously trade-protected sectors. There are also market-size effects associated with RTAs, in the sense that the combined size of the consumer base and the suppliers can offer significant

[22] J. Viner, 'The economics of customs unions' (1950), in Miroslav N. Jovanovic (ed.), *International Economic Integration: Critical Perspectives on the World Economy*, vol. I: *Theory and Measurement* (London and New York: Routledge, 1998), pp. 168–83, p. 169.

[23] *Ibid.*, p. 170.

[24] ADB (Asia Development Bank), *Asian Development Outlook 2002* (Manila: Asian Development Bank, 2002), p. 176; World Bank, *Global Economic Prospects 2005* (Washington DC: The World Bank, 2005), pp. 57–65.

[25] World Bank, *Trade Blocs* (Oxford University Press, 2000), pp. 30–1.

scale effects. Further, RTA membership can make the participating countries more attractive to foreign direct investment (FDI) as foreign investors will be induced to invest in the integrated market.[26]

Trade-diversion of RTAs is an issue that economists and policy-makers have long studied and debated. In this regard, Viner's seminal contribution was in showing that the formation of a RTA is not necessarily welfare-improving. As Bhagwati puts it, this serves to 'destroy the common fallacy that a preferential move towards (total) free trade was necessarily welfare improving and thus to demonstrate that all preferential paths to (total) free trade were not monotonic in welfare'.[27] However, the voluminous literature generated thereafter does not offer conclusive evidence as to whether, in any particular RTA or all the RTAs overall, trade creation will exceed trade diversion or *vice versa*.[28] For instance, regarding the enlargement of the European Union (to include Greece, Portugal and Spain), the study of Bayoumi and Eichengreen finds no evidence of trade diversion, while another study by Wei and Frankel discovers 'massive trade diversion'.[29] Not surprisingly, former US Treasury Secretary Lawrence Summers, who is also a distinguished economist, offered the opinion that '[t]rade diverting regional arrangements may be desirable despite their trade diverting effects', and concluded that he found 'it surprising that this issue is taken so seriously – in most other situations, economists laugh off second best considerations and focus on direct impacts'.[30]

A very recent staff study of the International Monetary Fund (IMF), using a widely adopted gravity model, suggests that Asian RTAs have not led to trade diversion as the rapid trade growth among members for RTAs was not associated with any decrease in trade with nonmembers.[31] Further, compared to RTAs in other regions of the world, the study

[26] ADB, *Asian Development Outlook 2002*, pp. 175–6.

[27] Jagdish N. Bhagwati, *The World Trading System at Risk* (Hemel Hempstead: Harvester Wheatsheaf, 1991), p. 59.

[28] Jiangyu Wang, 'China's regional trade agreements: The law, geopolitics, and impact on the multilateral trading system' (2004) 8 *Singapore Year Book of International Law* 119, 143.

[29] World Bank, *Global Economic Propspects 2005*, p. 61.

[30] Lawrence H. Summers, 'Regionalism and world trading system', in *Policy Implications of Trade and Currency Zones* (Kansas City: Federal Reserve Bank, 1991), pp. 295–301, at p. 299. Available at www.kansascityfed.org/publicat/Sympos/1991/SYM91.HTM (visited 25 April 2006).

[31] IMF (International Monetary Fund), *Asia and Pacific Regional Economic Outlook* (Washington DC: International Monetary Fund, 2006), p. 75. Available at www.imf.org/external/pubs/ft/reo/2006/eng/01/areo0506.htm (visited 8 May 2006).

suggests that 'the members of RTAs in Asia – especially ASEAN – showed a higher degree of openness with nonmembers than other RTA countries outside the region do'.[32] According to the IMF study, the fact that RTAs in Asia have been more trade-creating than other RTAs to date can be explained by another fact, which is that 'regional trade integration in Asia followed a long period of unilateral liberalization during the 1980s and 1990s'.[33] This is in line with the economic theory that, to avoid the asymmetric distribution of the gains and losses of integration between regional members, the best solution is to lower the external trade barriers.[34]

2. WTO constraints on RTAs

A RTA must comply with WTO rules if any of its contracting parties is a WTO Member. However, any RTA, because it incurs preferential treatments between only its members, is, by definition, a violation of the principle of non-discrimination of the WTO, embodied in the most-favoured-nation clause in WTO Agreements such as the General Agreement on Tariffs and Trade (GATT) and the General Agreement on Trade in Services (GATS). The draftsmen of the GATT and WTO were well aware of this and therefore created several safe habours to accommodate RTAs. Under the current WTO regime, RTAs are subject to three sets of rules. The first is Article XXIV of GATT 1947 which, as clarified in the *Understanding on the Interpretation of Article XXIV* of the GATT 1994, provides for the formation and operation of customs unions and FTAs on trade in goods. The so-called '*Enabling Clause*', formally called the *Decision on Differential and More Favorable Treatment, Reciprocity and Fuller Participation of Developing Countries* passed by the GATT Council in 1979,[35] permits preferential trade arrangements in trade in goods between developing country members. Finally,

[32] *Ibid.*, p. 76. [33] *Ibid.*, p. 77.

[34] Hoekman and Schiff suggest three reasons why a RTA should lower external trade barriers: '(a) to generate classical gains from trade; (b) to lessen the chances that trade diversion will occur; and (c) to reduce income transfers between member countries resulting from the [RTA] and the tensions that can arise from such transfer'. See Bernard Hoekman and Maurice Schiff, 'Benefiting from regional integration', in Bernard Hoekman, Aaditya Mattoo and Philip English (eds.), *Development, Trade, and the WTO: A Handbook* (Washington D.C.: World Bank, 2002), pp. 548–58 at p. 552.

[35] The Decision on Differential and More Favorable Treatment, Reciprocity and Fuller Participation of Developing Countries, (1979), GATT Doc. L/4903 [hereinafter the Enabling Clause].

Article V of GATS, entitled 'Economic Integration', governs the formation of RTAs in the area of trade in services.[36]

Are the above rules effective in terms of judging the WTO-consistency of any RTA? It is noted that 'RTAs are generally WTO-consistent', albeit 'this is because the requirements of Article XXIV and the Enabling Clause and GATS are very weak and have never been enforced'.[37] This statement reveals the poverty of the WTO rules in containing regionalism, despite the WTO's view that it is an adversary of the multilateral trading system. Regarding whether RTAs can comply with WTO Rules, one commentator observes:

> Theoretically, the answer is yes. After all, if a country is a Member of the WTO, the obligation to comply with the rules of the multilateral trading system is mandatory. However, a more useful answer is probably 'no', because of the reasons implied in the above analysis. To summarize, firstly, the WTO rules on the introduction of RTAs are troublesomely ambiguous and cannot be followed in an operational way. It is the inadequacy of the WTO rules that is principally to blame, as opposed to Members' non-compliance (if any). Secondly, the nature of the WTO as a consensus-based institution prevents it from strengthening the enforcement of the existing rules. Roughly starting with the examination of the EEC, which was given up in early GATT days due to a clash of political interests, and was never picked up again. Although the reason behind the failure of enforcement is the divergent interpretations of WTO rules by Members, the real implication seems to be that almost no RTA can ever be declared unlawful under the current WTO regime and that the process of CRTA examination can, in practice, be ignored.
>
> Experience shows that, to comply literally with GATT/WTO rules governing RTAs, Members involved in RTAs need only to notify the agreements to the WTO in a timely fashion either before or after their taking effect. Until the WTO substantially revises its rules governing regional economic integration, there is no imminent need for RTA members to worry about compliance with the substantive WTO requirements. In this sense, since China has already notified the WTO of its RTAs, it can be assumed that those RTAs are to be deemed compatible by the WTO unless the WTO can render adverse reports and recommendations.[38]

[36] Marrakesh Agreement Establishing the World Trade Organization, 15 April 1994, 1867 UNTS 3 at Annex 1B, art. V [hereinafter WTO Agreement].

[37] Peter Lloyd, 'Implications for the multilateral trading system of the new preferential trading arrangements in the Asia Pacific Region' (2002), paper presented at the PECC Trade Forum) November 2002, available at www.pecc.org.

[38] Jiangyu,Wang, 'China's regional trade agreements', 138.

3. The systemic problems

The explosive proliferation of RTAs is constructing an extreme network of different trading rules. The existence of several hundred regional agreements has meant overlapping members for many countries, some of which are parties to dozens of agreements.[39]

However, the fear of Asian RTAs being detrimental to the interest of trading nations has caused the ADB, an enthusiastic promoter of Asian regionalism, to point out that

> [T]he proliferation of a large number of bilateral FTAs can lead to the 'Asian noodle bowl effect' highlighted by [ADB] President Kuroda following Professor Bhagwati's initial observation. There can be harmful effects caused by multiple rules of origin arising from overlapping agreements among members of different FTAs. Complex rules increase administrative and business costs, particularly for small and medium enterprises which have limited capacity to deal with them. Furthermore, if they have large transactions costs, such rules can deter foreign investment and trade.[40]

The complex rules and procedures for trade related policies in RTAs have also caused the grave concern of the private sector. In a trade conference of the United Nations Economic and Social Commission for Asia and the Pacific (ESCAP), a Hong Kong businessman pointed out the troublesome consequences for the global production system created by RTAs:

> I am deeply concerned that the proliferation of bilateral agreements is forcing businesses to sub-optimize. Imagine the situation facing the supply chain manager. You have thousands of products in tens of countries, and hundreds of factories. In structuring the supply chain, every country of origin and every bilateral has to be tacked on as an additional consideration. With each new bilateral, the considerations related to 'rules of origin' multiply and become more complex . . . Even larger companies have a hard time keeping the track. For small firms, it is impossible. That is why the multilateral system is so important. It defines rules of universal application. It is necessary to understand only one guiding set of rules.[41]

[39] Singapore, for example, has concluded 11 FTAs and are in the process of negotiating 15 more. See Singapore's FTA Network at www.iesingapore.gov.sg/wps/portal/FTA. The EU has concluded over 30 preferential trade agreements, and the U.S. has over 20.

[40] Liqun Jin, 'Issues and challenges in designing free trade agreements in Asia – welcome remarks by Liqun Jin, Vice-President, Operation 1, Asian Development Bank, at the Brainstorming on Free Trade Agreements' (20 March 2006), available at www.adb.org/Documents/Speeches/2006/ms2006016.asp (visited 16 April 2006).

[41] Victor Fung, 'Luncheon Address by Mr Victor Fung, Chairman, Li & Fung Group Ltd, On business perceptions and expectations regarding the WTO Doha negotiations' in United Nations Economic and Social Commission for Asia and the Pacific, *Delivering on*

He further observes,

> From a business standpoint, the question in instructing the supply chain should not be how to qualify for favourable 'rules of origin' treatment. Instead, the question should be 'what is the optimal way to create a product?' I should do this in the most cost-effective way for the final consumer. That is the only thing about which I should be worried. Why should I worry about where is the point of 'substantive transformation'? Why should I worry about it occurring in any particular location in order to qualify for duty-free treatment? The whole world should do it based on economics.[42]

It is however politically unrealistic to expect the trading nations to call a stop to the proliferation of RTAs, especially in light of the domino effect of regionalism, whereby countries participate in bilateral or regional trade arrangements to avoid marginalization as more and more countries become members of – in many situations more than one – RTAs.[43] Further, the formation of rules of origin and other rules or procedures in a RTA is influenced by many factors, including, significantly, the interest of domestic producers to expect exclusive protection from those rules that may help to prevent competition from foreign exporters. It is important to bear in mind that, for many domestic interests, the philosophy of trade is not yet 'the freer, the better'.

In the global context, the burgeoning number of RTAs has been continuing the trend to add greatly to the complexity of international trade and to the costs of trade. Realistically, it is impossible to avert the problems entirely, as, by definition, RTAs have different rules and systems. A more practical solution might lie in synthesizing RTAs with the multilateral, namely the WTO, system, including the harmonization of rules and convergence of procedures and standards. The general idea is that, under the guidance of the principles of the WTO, Asian RTAs should adopt common rules and procedures to the maximum extent, and conduct most-favored-nation (MFN) based liberalization whenever possible.

the WTO Round: A High-level Government–Business Dialogue (New York: United Nations Publications, 2006) (papers and statements presented at the Conference on Delivering on the WTO Round: A High-Level Government–Business Dialogue for Development, organized by ESCAP in collaboration with the International Trade Centre, UNCTAD/WTO and Government of Macao, China, Macao, China, 4–6 October 2005).

42 Fung, 'Luncheon Address'.

43 Regarding the domino effect of regionalism, see e.g., Richard Baldwin, *A Domino Theory of Regionalism*, NBER Working Paper No. 4465 (Cambridge, MA: National Bureau of Economic Research, September 1993).

4. Concluding remarks: Making regionalism complementary to multilateralism

There is little doubt that multilateral liberalization is still the best approach to international trade and development. Without challenging this, regionalists argue that regionalism is the second-best approach for liberalization, especially given the frustration caused by the slow and halting pace of multilateral trade negotiations conducted under the auspices of the WTO.

The fact that WTO constraints on RTAs are ineffective does not entail that RTAs should be WTO-inconsistent. On the contrary, efforts should be made to ensure that RTAs are 'building blocks' rather than 'stumbling blocks' to the goal of multilateral freeing of trade.[44] In this regard, the following recommendations are made:

(a) RTA members should reduce external trade barriers while participating in regional initiatives. Both theory and empirical evidence suggest that the lower the external trade barriers, the lesser the possibility of trade diversion exists.
(b) Solving the systemic problem represented by the 'spaghetti bowl' is a rather urgent problem for global RTAs. The complex rules of origin, used beyond what is necessary to prevent trade deflection or the transshipment of goods from third countries through a member for the purpose of obtaining preferential RTA tariffs, have indeed been evolving towards protectionism. While it is unrealistic to abolish the rules of origin in RTAs, it is highly advisable to harmonize them, although the process is bound to be difficult. At the minimum, in the interest of regional integration, Asian countries, while negotiating RTAs, should reach an informal common understanding on adopting the same or similar rules of origin.
(c) Apart from rules of origin, other trade institutions, including national policies, should also be harmonized or coordinated at the regional level to further economic integration, provided that the harmonization is beneficial. This would involve domestic competition policies, product standards, regulatory regimes, investment laws, services rules, environmental polices, and so on.[45] Policymakers

[44] Jagdish Bhagwati, Pravin Krishna and Arvind Panagariya (eds.), *Trading Blocs: Alternative Approaches to Analying Preferential Trade Agreements* (Cambridge, MA: MIT Press, 1999), p. 36.

[45] Robert Z. Lawrence, *Regionalism, Multilateralism, and Deeper Integration* (Washington DC: The Brookings Institution, 1996), p. 17.

should however be careful about this as, in some situations, 'there are good reasons for diversity in domestic policies across nations and that harmonization is . . . not a welfare-enhancing proposition'.[46] Further, harmonization on the wrong policy can be only counterproductive, if not disastrous.[47]

(d) In any event, a RTA should be WTO-plus and should adopt the common trade rules already established by the WTO.

(e) Open regionalism is an integral part to the success of RTAs which are building blocks. 'Open regionalism' is defined as with the following characteristics: (1) open membership, with membership extended to nonmembers on a mutually reciprocal basis; (2) commitment of members to lower external trade barriers while trade is liberalized internally on an MFN basis; (3) encouragement of unilateral liberalization by members to other members or nonmembers.[48] Although Asian countries are encouraged to conduct unilateral liberalization in any event, it is however doubtful that, in the interests of Asian economic integration, an Asian FTA or East Asian Economic Community should extend its membership to countries outside the region.

II. Regional economic integration in Asia and the role of China and India

A. *Regional economic integration in Asia*

The rise of Asia is no longer an idea – it has become a sustaining reality. *Asian Development Outlook 2006*, the flagship publication of the Asian Development Bank (ADB), notes that developing Asia (excluding Japan) had expanded its export almost tenfold from 1984 to 2004, while world exports grew just fivefold over the same period. Developing Asia's share of world exports doubled over the past two decades, reaching 21.3% by 2004.[49] Asia not only expanded its share globally, but it also increased the intraregional trade share. In 2004, intraregional trade in developing

[46] Arvind Panagaria, 'The regionalism debate: An overview' (1999) 22 (4) *World Economy* 477–512, 506.

[47] Lawrence, *Regionalism, Multilateralism, and Deeper Integration*, p. 33.

[48] C. Fred Bergsten, *Open Regionalism*, Working Paper 97–3 (Washington DC: Institute for International Economics, 1997). Available at www.iie.com/publications/wp/wp.cfm?researchID=152 (last visited 8 May 2006).

[49] ADB (Asian Development Bank), *Asian Development Outlook 2006* (Manila, Asian Development Bank , 2006), p. 269.

Asia accounted for 44% of the region's total trade, jumped from just 21.6% in 1980. Needless to say, this magnitude of intraregional trade has given lofty hopes for pushing further economic integration in Asia, ideally (or idealistically) towards an Asian free trade area or something more (such as an Asian Monetary Union).[50]

Although there is already rather large intraregional trade in Asia, a recent ADB study shows there is still plenty of room for Asian countries to gain from further regional economic integration in Asia.[51] Using the new Global Trade Analysis Project (version 6) database with a dynamic global model, the study concludes, among others,

(i) *Trade within the Asian region is far from reaching its potential*, and policies that facilitate integration and more efficient regional trade accelerate growth and expand its basis, especially for lower-income Asia.
(ii) Tariff barriers are only part of the challenge to further economic integration and trade expansion in the region . . . A deeper and more inclusive Asian Free Trade Area can achieve for its members larger benefits than what would arise from global trade liberalization along [WTO] lines.
(iii) The economies of the [ASEAN] have the most to gain (in domestic terms) from Asian economic integration, provided that this happens in a relatively uniform way.

Apparently, this study suggests that a RTA aiming at a deeply integrated Asia would bring substantial benefits to Asian countries regardless of whether the multilateral trading system ever delivers results.[52]

[50] See Haruhiko Kuroda, 'New visions and models for economic cooperation', speech by Haruhiko Kuroda, President of Asian Development Bank, at the Plenary Session II of the Annual Conference of the Boao Forum of Asia, 22–23 April 2006, Boao, Hainan. Available at www.adb.org/Documents/Speeches/2006/ms2006025.asp (visited 1 June 2006). In his speech the ADB President envisages a vision of Asia 'free of poverty – diverse yet united, well integrated within itself and with the global economy, and contributing profoundly to the ongoing progress of humankind'. He further remarks that, 'Some skeptics may call this vision of deeply integrated Asia a pipe dream. Some say the disparities are too wide, the political divides too deep. But strong bridges for a united Asia, open to the world, are already being built'.

[51] David Roland-Holst, Jean-Pierre Verbieft, and Fan Zhai, 'Growth and trade horizon for Asia: Long-term forecasts for regional integration' (2005) 25 (2) *Asian Development Review* 76–107.

[52] See also Haruhiko Kuroda, 'New dynamics, new opportunities: Toward deeper Asian economic integration', speech by Haruhiko Kuroda, President, Asian Development Bank, at the 31st ASEAN–Japan Business Meeting, 24 November 2005, Bangkok, Thailand.

The fast growth of Asian trade and accelerated regional integration was in substantial measure due to locomotive economic performance of East Asia. If Japan is included, intraregional trade makes up 54% in East Asia. The President of the ADB has remarked that this is 'higher than the 46% intraregional trade in the NAFTA region and is very much comparable to intraregional trade in the European Union before the 1992 Maastricht treaty'.[53]

ADB observes that there is a trade-FDI nexus in Asia which, understood as the mutual reinforcement between trade and FDI, is a strong boost to regional economic integration in this area. FDI to Asian developing countries from more developed economies (Japan; Korea; Taiwan, China; Hong Kong, China) has helped shape totally new Asian production networks, in which cross-border production sharing is featured with a high and rising degree of intraregional trade in parts and components that are produced and assembled into final goods within Asia.[54]

Apart from trade investment, Asian economic integration has also been seen in monetary and financial cooperation, and sub-regional cooperation in infrastructure. As Kawai notes, in East Asia, '[m]arket-driven financial integration has also been underway as a result of the increased deregulation of the financial system, opening of financial services to foreign institutions, and liberalization of the capital account'.[55] Regional financial cooperation, through the Chiang Mai Initiative (CMI), the ASEAN+3 economic surveillance process, and the Asian Bond Markets Initiative, has been taking firm root in Asia. Although these efforts are being mainly undertaken in East Asia, South Asian countries have also started regional policy dialogue on financial cooperation.[56]

Sub-regional cooperation on infrastructure is a key part of the economic integration process in Asia. Roland-Holst, Verbiest and Zhai observe that 'if trade within the Asian region can be made more efficient,

Available at www.adb.org/Documents/Speeches/2005/ms2005084.asp (visited 29 April 2006).

53 Haruhiko Kuroda, 'Towards a borderless Asia: A perspective on Asian Economic Integration', speech by Haruhiko Kuroda, president of the Asian Development Bank, at the Emerging Markets Forum, 10 December 2005, Oxford), available at www.adb.org/Documents/Speeches/2005/ms2005088.asp (visited 29 April 2006).

54 ADB, *Asian Development Outlook 2006*, p. 272.

55 Masahiro Kawai, 'East Asian economic regionalism: Progress and challenges' (2005) 16 *Journal of Asia Economics* 29–55, 34.

56 Kuroda, 'Towards a borderless Asia'.

even by small continuing improvements in reducing distribution costs, the gains would be much greater than those resulting from tariff or other trade policy reform'.[57] In this regard, connecting Asian countries through roads, ports, bridges, power and telecommunications networks is fundamentally important for another wave of income and growth and employment creation in Asia. One of the remarkable achievements in this regard is the Greater Mekong Subregion Program (GMS). Involving Cambodia, China, Laos, Myanmar, Thailand and Vietnam, the GMS has achieved international recognition with regard to the development of infrastructure to enable the development and sharing of the resource base, and promotes the freer flow of goods and people in the sub-region.[58]

B. The economic role of China and India in Asia economic integration

China's rapid and massive rise as an economic power is generating enormous impact on the global and regional economy. In terms of regional integration, China is playing the leading role in two aspects. First, China's import capacity has created the new basis for Asian regional growth: internal demand.[59] With many Asian economies' exports to China rising by double-digit percentage over the recent years, that country has consolidated its position as the leading market for Asian traders. In 2003, China replaced Japan as the third largest importer in world merchandise trade and the biggest Asian market for both Asian and EU exporters. The result is that Asian countries are becoming less dependent on the North American and European markets, and more on the Chinese market,[60] although increasing Chinese demand for raw

[57] Roland-Holst, Verbiest and Zhai, 'Growth and trade horizon for Asia', 77.

[58] For details of the GMS see the 'GMS economic cooperation strategy and program (RCSP)', available at www.adb.org/Documents/CSPs/GMS/2004/default.asp (visited 29 April 2006).

[59] Roland-Holst, Verbiest and Zhai, 'Growth and trade horizon for Asia', 78.

[60] From 2000–4, China had doubled its share in the imports and exports of a number of Asian economies. Over the same period, although Asia's exports to North America and Europe continued to increase by 20% and 24%, respectively, the share of North America in Asia's exports went down to 22.3% from a higher figure, while the share of Europe remained unchanged at 17.5%. See WTO, *International Trade Statistics 2005* (2005), 15, available at www.wto.org/English/res_e/statis_e/its2005_e/its2005_e.pdf (visited 27 May 2007).

materials has been regarded as an important factor in reversing the long-term downward trend in the prices of non-oil commodities.[61]

A second profound impact of China's rise on Asian economic integration is that China is the major factor in shaping the new division of labour in Asia, largely as a result of the trade-FDI nexus mentioned previously. As an UNCTAD report observes,

> Deeper production-sharing practices within the [East Asia] region have contributed substantially to the rise of intraregional trade flows. In particular, China's emergence as a major production site for labor-intensive stages of production and assembly has exerted a huge impact on such flows, both within Asia and between Asia and the rest of the world. Goods that were previously processed and exported by other Asian countries are now finalized in China for export. This phenomenon explains, in large part, the increasing bilateral trade imbalances between China and its major trading partners; China has recorded growing trade surpluses with North America and Europe, while widening its trade deficit with the rest of Asia.[62]

Compared with China, India as a trader is much less significant. China's economy is 2.7 times larger than that of India's, and the annual foreign direct investment received by China is more than ten times as large. China's share in world merchandise trade is roughly six times that of India's. Needless to say, India, unlike China, is not yet an important enough market for Asian traders. However, there are two developments in India's foreign trade which deserve special attention. First, India's merchandise trade has experienced strong growth in recent years. Its merchandise exports grew 33% and 19% in 2004 and 2005 respectively, and imports rose even more at the rate of 37% and 35% respectively.[63] India's merchandise trade with East Asian economies more than doubled from US$13 billion in 1997–8 to about US$27 billion in 2003–4. In fact, India expanded its trade with all East Asian countries except Japan over the same period.

A UN report reveals that, although India is still far from having manufacturing-driven growth that has characterized the other rapidly growing Asian economies,[64] the 'structure of India's merchandise trade

[61] UNDPPO, *World Economic Situataion and Prospects 2005*, pp. 28–9.

[62] UNCTAD (United Nations Conference on Trade and Development), *Trade and Development Report, 2004* (Geneva: United Nations, 2004), p. 46.

[63] WTO, *International Trade Statistics 2005* (Geneva: WTO, 2005).

[64] UNCTAD, *Trade and Development Report 2005* (Geneva: United Nations, 2005), pp. 42–3, p. 69.

is likely to follow a sequence of changes similar to that of China, but with a lag of one or two decades', provided 'the role of industrialization in India's further economic ascent is similar to that in the other fast growing Asian economies'.[65]

Secondly, the recent growth of India's services trade is almost unparalleled. The growth rate for services exports and imports were 66% and 53% in 2004, and 76% and 73% in 2005.[66] In about five years since 2001, India moved from the nineteenth to the tenth position in the ranking of the largest traders of commercial services in the world. If such rapid growth is sustained, India is likely to overtake several countries, including China, in services trade in a few years. No other major trading nation was able to have such a remarkable growth in services trade in the past few decades.

As UNCTAD 2005 observes, given 'the large size of the Chinese and Indian economies, and their specific patterns of demand, changes in the two countries' level and structure and demand will tend to have a much larger impact on the composition of world trade than those of Japan and the Republic of Korea during the economic ascent'.[67] China and India, with sustained rapid growth and rising living standards, will certainly play dominant roles in the economic integration process in Asia.

III. Regional trade arrangements in which China and India participate

Regional trade agreements (RTAs) are proliferating in Asia and worldwide. At the global level, almost every WTO Member is now a party to one or more RTAs. While Asia has jumped on the bandwagon of regionalism only recently, the current pace of development of RTA initiatives in this region is nothing but daunting. The Asian Development Bank (ADB) observes in its most recent report on Asian economic development that, by 2005, a total of thirty-six RTAs involving its Asian members have been formally notified to the World Trade Organization (WTO), with a much bigger number of agreements are under negotiation.[68] The ADB has disclosed that '[i]n East Asia alone there are currently sixteen FTAs under implementation, close to twenty-two under negotiation, and more than a dozen others proposed. Practically

65 *Ibid.*, p. 43.
66 WTO, 'World Trade 2005, Prospects for 2006', Press/437, 11 April 2006.
67 UNCTAD, *Trade and Development Report 2005*, pp. 42–3.
68 ADB, *Asian Development Outlook 2006*, p. 276.

every East Asian economy has at least one bilateral agreement with its Asian neighbours in place and many have several overlapping accords'.[69] Although China and India jumped onto the bandwagon only recently, they can now be placed among the most active pursuers of RTAs. The regional initiatives of China and India are examined in the following subsections.

A. *China's regional trade initiatives*

1. The CEPAs with Hong Kong and Macau

Although China was a late comer to regionalism, seemingly it firmly believes that 'a regional economic integration process consistent with WTO rules would not only promote regional but also worldwide liberalization by achieving further tariff reduction and broader market access for services and investment'.[70] China has been involved in over fifteen regional trade arrangements. The Mainland and Hong Kong Closer Economic Partnership Arrangement (China–HK CEPA), signed in June 2003, marked the start of China's regional initiative, which was followed immediately by the signing of the China–Macau CEPA three and half months later.[71] The CEPAs contain substantial unilateral concessions from China to the two former Western colonies in merchandise and commercial services trade, and investment. Under the China–HK CEPA, China agreed to slash tariffs on imported goods of Hong Kong origin in stages, with full elimination of all tariffs no later than 1 January 2006. The CEPA rules of origin, which are relatively liberal, feature a 30 per cent value-added of Hong Kong's local content. In the area of trade in services, the mainland offers preferential treatment to Hong Kong and Macau service suppliers in twenty-seven service areas, effectively granting business in these two economies the first-mover advantage.

[69] Jin, Liqun, 'Issues and challenges in designing free trade agreements in Asia – Welcome remarks by Liqun Jin, Vice-President, Operation 1, Asian Development Bank, at the Brainstorming on Free Trade Agreements' (20 March 2006), available at www.adb.org/Documents/Speeches/2006/ms2006016.asp (visited 16 April 2006).

[70] WTO, 'Trade policy review: People's Republic of China –Report by the Secretariat', WTO Document No.: WT/TPR/S/161, 28 February 2006, p. 45.

[71] In the China–HK CEPA, two supplements to CEPA, called CEPA II and CEPA III, were signed on 27 October 2004 and 18 October 2005 respectively. See the main website of CEPA at www.tid.gov.hk/english/cepa/index.html (visited 19 May 2006).

2. China–ASEAN free trade agreement

Considering that Hong Kong and Macau are two special administrative regions under Chinese sovereignty, ostensibly the two CEPAs are less regarded as RTAs. Among China's regional trade agreements, one of the most influential is the proposed ASEAN–China Free Trade Agreement (ACFTA). Almost coming as a surprise to his counterparts in the ASEAN countries, Chinese Premier Zhu Rongji proposed at the China–ASEAN Summit of November 2000 forming a 'free trade agreement' between China and ASEAN. In November 2002, Chinese and ASEAN leaders signed the Framework Agreement on Comprehensive Economic Co-operation (hereinafter the Framework Agreement), which lays the groundwork for the eventual formation of a free trade agreement by the year 2010 for China and the six older members of ASEAN (ASEAN 6, including Brunei Darussalam, Indonesia, Malaysia, the Philippines, Singapore and Thailand), and by 2015 for the newer ASEAN Member States (the CLMV countries including Cambodia, Laos, Myanmar and Vietnam).[72] The Framework Agreement was amended by a Protocol on 6 October 2003 by the contracting parties at their annual summit in Bali (hereinafter the Protocol).[73] With the conclusion of a series of substantive agreements on trade in goods, services, dispute settlement mechanism and investment from 2004 to 2009, a fully fledged FTA will be formed in 2010.

The Framework Agreement establishes only preliminary measures for trade liberalization between China and ASEAN countries as well as agendas for further negotiations. The eleven countries have committed in the Framework Agreement to strengthen cooperation and to 'progressively liberalize and promote trade in goods and services as well as create a transparent, liberal and facilitative investment regime'.[74] This suggests that the proposed ACFTA will cover trade in goods and services, as well as, trade and investment facilitation.

The ACFTA Framework Agreement is known for its rather innovative Early Harvest Programme (EHP), under which the parties agreed to cut tariffs on certain products before the onset of the formal FTA. In brief, eight categories of agricultural products and dozens of specific

[72] Jiangyu Wang, 'China's regional trade agreements', 124. The text of the Framework Agreement is available at the ASEAN Secretariat's official website at www.aseansec.org/13196.htm (visited 31 March 2006).

[73] The text of the Protocol is available at the ASEAN Secretariat's official website at www.aseansec.org/15157.htm (visited 31 March 2006).

[74] The Framework Agreement, art. 1(b).

manufactured goods would be liberalized ahead of the planned establishment of the free trade area. A key element of the EHP is that China has also given unilateral concessions to ASEAN Members who feel they would not benefit as much from the EHP.[75] This is because, for ASEAN's exports to China, all the products in Chapters 1–8 of the Harmonized System (HS) are covered for preferential tariff rates, while for exports to ASEAN countries, not all of the products in Chapters 1–8 are covered. ASEAN countries are allowed to come up with exclusion lists indicating the items for which they would not grant tariff concessions to Chinese goods. In essence, the EHP 'allows ASEAN products to be exported to China at significant concessionary rates so that ASEAN countries can actually benefit from the benefits of a free trade agreement even before the agreement itself is finalized'.[76]

The Trade in Goods (TIG) Agreement represents the important, second, phase of strategy to form ACFTA. From July 2005, China and the 'ASEAN 6' have begun to reduce tariffs of commodities trade. On 20 July 2005, tariffs on more than 7,000 items, accounting for over 90 per cent of all goods traded between China and ASEAN 6, were slashed to 5 per cent or less.

The Dispute Settlement Mechanism (DSM) Agreement represents another landmark achievement in China–ASEAN bilateral trade relations. It provides, first of all, a formal, institutional, design for solving trade and investment disputes between China and an ASEAN Member State. The significance of this agreement lies in its establishment of a rule-based setting for the resolution of economic disputes between the nations concerned, without which the governments are likely to resort to unilateral and retaliatory measures if they feel – sometimes rightly – that the multilateral trading system like the WTO does not provide for efficient and fair dispute settlement methods.

3. Other signed RTAs

The Asia–Pacific Trade Agreement (APTA), known as the Bangkok Agreement between 1975 and 2005, is the first preferential trading arrangement among developing countries in the Asia–Pacific region, developed under the auspices of the United Nations Economic and Social Commission for Asia and the Pacific (ESCAP). China joined the agreement in 2001, and started offering concessions from 2002. Presently, 749

[75] Annex 2 of the Framework Agreement.

[76] 'ASEAN, China launch first stage of free-trade plan', *AFP*, 7 October 2003 (on file).

tariff lines carry lower rates than the MFN rates committed under the WTO, mostly involving textile products. The significance of the APTA does not lie in the almost ignorable tariff concessions, given that the overall average applied tariff rate is 9.5 per cent under the APTA compared with an MFN rate of 9.7 per cent.[77] APTA is important symbolically for two reasons: (1) it provides a mechanism for giving special and differential treatment to the least developed countries; (2) it serves as a platform to link sub-regional RTAs. In an area where the development stages of countries are diverse, regional economic integration must involve compensation to the lesser developed members through special and preferential treatment. In this regard, the APTA mechanism provides a useful example to study. Further, APTA is the only agreement that currently links South Asia and East Asia, the two most dynamic sub-regions both of which are core parts of Asia.[78] As such, it may serve an important role in consolidating the various sub-regional agreements in Asia.

China signed an FTA with Chile on 18 November 2005, which eliminates immediately 74% of Chile's tariffs, and 63% of China's tariffs within two years. By 2015, 97% of both countries' tariffs are to be eliminated.[79] With Pakistan, China concluded an FTA Early Harvest Agreement on 5 April 2006, under which bilateral tariffs on certain products are to be gradually slashed and eventually eliminated between 1 January 2006 and 1 January.[80] This was followed by the China–New Zealand Free Trade Agreement, signed in April 2008, which was, however, China's first FTA with a developed country. It is also a comprehensive FTA, covering broad and deep concessions from both countries. In addition, it has a robust dispute settlement mechanism. It is also China's first FTA that contains a binding Environment Cooperation Agreement and a binding Memorandum of Understanding on Labour Cooperation. Another FTA with an advanced country, the China–Singapore FTA, was signed in October 2008. It is another comprehensive FTA China signed with its Asian neighbours. The most recent comprehensive FTA China signed was an agreement with Peru in April 2009.

[77] WTO, 'Trade policy review: People's Republic of China – Report by the Secretariat', p. 47.

[78] Tiziana Bonapace and Mia Mikic, 'Multilateralizing regionalism: Towards an integrated and outward-oriented Asia–Pacific economic area' , in *Delivering on the WTO Round: A High-level Government–Business Dialogue*, Studies in Trade and Investment 56 (United Nations Economic and Social Commission for Asia and the Pacific, 2005), pp. 85–110, at p. 96.

[79] WTO, 'Trade policy review: People's Republic of China – Report by the Secretariat', p. 49.

[80] *Ibid.*, pp. 49–50.

4. FTA negotiations with Australia and potential agreements with other nations

In China's pursuit of regionalism, the negotiations with New Zealand and Australia deserve special attention. For one reason, New Zealand and Australia are two developed, OECD economies. More significantly, the contents of the negotiations are rather comprehensive, heralding the coming of the final agreements which will bring about broader and deeper economic integration.

China and Australia signed the initial Trade and Economic Framework Agreement in October 2003. It sets out areas of strategic cooperation in areas including energy and mining, textiles, agriculture, industrial products, IT, services, investment, intellectual property rights, and others. A joint feasibility for a China–Australia FTA by the two governments was completed in March 2005, concluding that the FTA will bring tremendous benefits to both countries. Formal negotiations targeting such an agreement were commenced on 18 April 2005.[81] Negotiations for an FTA between China and New Zealand were started even earlier, in December 2004, following the conclusion of the China–New Zealand Trade and Economic Cooperation Framework on 28 May 2004, covering a broad range of economic areas, and a joint feasibility study completed in November 2004.[82]

In addition, China has initiated negotiations on bilateral FTAs with the Southern African Customs Union (SACU) and the Gulf Cooperation Council (GCC). It has started feasibility studies on bilateral FTAs with India and Iceland.

B. *India's regional trade initiatives*

1. India's involvement in regional integration in South Asia: SAARC/SAPTA/SAFTA/BIMSTEC

India is also a member of APTA but this section will focus on India's trade agreements in South Asia. India is the founding member of the South Asian Association for Regional Cooperation (SAARC), which comprises all South Asian countries with the exception of Afghanistan.[83]

[81] Further information is available at www.dfat.gov.au/geo/china/fta/ (visited 19 May 2006).

[82] Further information is available at www.mfat.govt.nz/Trade-and-Economic-Relations/0–Trade-archive/0–Trade-agreements/China/0-jointstudyreportindex.php (visited 27 May 2007).

[83] SAARC members hence include Bangladesh, Bhutan, India, Maldives, Nepal, Pakistan and Sri Lanka.

SAARC members signed the South Asian Preferential Trade Arrangement (SAPTA) in April 1993, with the view to creating the South Asian Free Trade Area (SAFTA). As a framework merely for the exchange of tariff concessions through product-by-product or positive-listing approach, the progress of SAPTA in terms of tariff liberalization has been rather slow. For instance, intra-SAARC trade rose slightly from 2.42 per cent in 1990 to 4.7 per cent in 2003, much of which was, however, attributed to unilateral, bilateral and multilateral (WTO) liberalization, rather than to SAPTA.[84]

SAFTA was signed into a regional trade agreement by all members of SAARC at the Twelfth SAARC Submit in January 2004, and came into force from 1 January 2006. Under Rule 7 of the phased tariff liberalization programme, in 2 years, tariffs of India, Pakistan and Sri Lanka will be slashed to 20% in 2 years, while Bangladesh, Bhutan, Maldives and Nepal (as Least Developed Countries) will reduce tariffs to 30%. In 5 to 8 years, the contracting parties will bring tariffs down to 0–5%. SAFTA includes also measures not covered by SAPTA, such as harmonization of standards, mutual recognition of tests and accreditation of testing laboratories, trade facilitation measures such as simplification and harmonization of customs clearance, import licensing, registration and banking procedures, and removal of intra-SAARC investment barriers.

The Bay of Bengal Initiative for Multi-Sectoral Technical and Economic Cooperation, an association known as BIMSTEC, groups together Bangladesh, Bhutan, India, Myanmar, Nepal, Sri Lanka and Thailand. In the first BIMSTEC Summit in July 2004, the leaders adopted a Declaration calling for the establishment of a free trade area covering trade in goods, services, and investment, as well as mutual recognition of standards, customs cooperation, business migration, among others. For India, BIMSTEC is highly politically motivated, as it 'resolves the problem of slow movement in South Asian cooperation by eliminating Pakistan and including Myanmar and Thailand'.[85] BIMSTEC is nevertheless instrumental for regional economic integration in Asia as it serves as a formal link between South Asia and Southeast Asia.

[84] Jayanta Roy, 'South Asian regional trade agreements: Perspectives, issues and options', paper presented at the International Trade Roundtable 'The WTO at 10 Years – The Regional Challenge to Multilateralism', Brussels, Belgium, 27 June 2005. Available at http://mba.tuck.dartmouth.edu/cib/news/itr_2005_pdf/Roy.pdf (visited 20 May 2006).

[85] Roy, 'South Asian regional trade agreements'.

2. India–ASEAN FTA

Propelled by the ASEAN–China FTA initiative, India and ASEAN signed a Framework Agreement on Comprehensive Economic Cooperation (CECA) on 8 October 2003, which commits the parties to working towards an ASEAN–India Regional Trade and Investment Area as a long-term objective. The India–ASEAN CECA includes a small list of exchange of tariff concessions. Like the ASEAN–China FTA, it also has an Early Harvest Programme (EHP) as a confidence building measure. However, due to disagreement on rules of origin as well as protectionist pressure from domestic industry in India, the EHP could not be implemented.[86]

One of the political aspects of the India–ASEAN CECA is India's ambition to compete with China for influence in Southeast Asia. As stated by Jayanta Roy, the Principle Advisor to the Confederation of Indian Industry, '[u]nlike China, India is not competing with [ASEAN] economies in trade and FDI. An agreement with India will also give ASEAN countries a chance to reduce their excessive dependence on China as a trading partner'.[87]

3. India's other bilateral FTA initiatives

India has signed a number of FTAs with its Asian neighbours. The India–Sri Lanka FTA, signed in December 1998, is one of India's earliest bilateral trade arrangements. India and Singapore signed a Comprehensive Economic Cooperation Agreement in July 2005, under which trade in goods, services, investment protection, standards and technical regulation, and other areas of economic and regulatory cooperation are addressed. A Framework Agreement for establishing Free Trade between India and Thailand was signed in October 2003. In addition, India is negotiating FTAs or jointly exploring the possibilities of FTAs with China, Malaysia, Indonesia, Korea, Mauritius, Chile, SACU, GCC and MERCOSUR (the Common Market of South America).

IV. Asian economic integration: Choices for China and India

A. *Different types of regionalism*

In addition to unilateral and multilateral liberalization, both China and India have intensified their regional initiatives. Countries have good

[86] See Government of India, Ministry of Commerce and Industry, 'India's current engagements in RTAs' (2006), available at http://commerce.nic.in/india_rta_main.htm (visited 20 May 2006), and Amita Batra, 'Micro pains, macro gains', *Financial Express*, 20 May 2006, available at www.financialexpress.com/fe_full_story.php?content_id=127689 (visited 22 May 2006).

[87] Roy, 'South Asian regional trade agreements'.

reasons to espouse regionalism, as previously noted, which encompass both political and economic aspects. However, this is not to say that they should abuse their regional options. In a world where economic interdependence is rapidly increasing, trading nations, while pursuing their national interest, must also consider their long-term interest by factoring regional, global, and even other countries' national interests into consideration.

As the above analyses demonstrate, China and India are crucial players in the regional economic integration process in Asia. It also seems that both countries are actively pursuing regionalism, mainly in the form of bilateral FTAs. In promoting regional economic integration in Asia, China and India are faced with the following possible options:

- Bilateralism
- Pan-Asian FTA
- Sub-regional integration in East Asia and South Asia respectively, with the two sub-regions linked through ASEAN–India FTA and China–India FTA

This section discusses the various options, with a view to evaluating their different degrees of suitability for promoting regional economic integration in Asia.

B. *Hub-and-spokes bilateralism*

Both China and India are now obsessively negotiating and signing bilateral FTAs. The number of RTAs in which India is a party exceeds that of China. However, almost all India's RTAs involve only 'shallow' integration, in the sense that there has been neither substantial tariff reduction nor broad coverage of issues in those RTAs. They nevertheless should be paid attention, not only because of India's recently demonstrated obsession with regional arrangements, but also because of the need for finding an answer to the question of whether India can serve a leading role or hub in South Asian integration, which is obviously an important part of regional economic integration in Asia.

The bilateral initiatives of China and India are driven by both economic and political factors, including the so-called 'domino effect' or 'fear of exclusion'.[88] The pursuit of bilateralism, if taken to its extreme, can lead to a hub-and-spoke situation. As the World Bank observes, in

[88] Baldwin, *A Domino Theory of Regionalism.*

the hub-and-spoke pattern, 'the largest markets sign individual agreements with a wide range of peripheral countries among which market access remains restricted'.[89] However, such a system 'can marginalize the spokes, where market access conditions are usually less advantageous than in the hub, which enjoys improved access to all of the spokes'.[90] In a region which accommodates several large economies, overlapping hub-and-spoke configurations tend to emerge. In the worst scenario, hubs have multiple FTAs with smaller spokes, but the spokes do not liberalize between themselves. This will not only create multiple layers of discrimination through exclusive trade preferences and complex rules of origin, but also place the spokes at a disadvantage as foreign investment tends to move to the hubs in order to gain more market access.

Using a global 'computable general equilibrium' model (GEMAT) to trace the numerical impact of trade globalism, regionalism and bilateralism, ADB finds that, if two hub-and-spoke configurations in Asia are stimulated, namely the 'China hub' and the 'ASEAN hub',

> Compared to the Asian free trade scenario that extends MFN status to countries outside Asia, the Asian hub-and-spoke scenario generates somewhere between one fifth and one quarter of the global gains. Within developing Asia [excluding Japan], hub-and-spoke systems are inferior to regional free trade and to multilateral liberalization initiatives. A [China] hub generates just over half the benefits of Asian free trade for Asian developing countries, and an ASEAN hub, which implicitly entails the removal of more trade distortions, about 70% of the benefits.[91]

However, in pursuing trade bilateralism, the hub economies – in the ADB model which are China and ASEAN – gain larger benefits. For instance, China's welfare gain from a regional hub position is almost four times that from pan-Asian free trade, and ASEAN as well is better off by becoming a hub than under the Asian free trade scenario.

India is not treated as a hub in the ADB report, presumably because of its foreign trade and investment is not comparable to that of China or ASEAN. According to the conventional hub-and-spoke theory, India, as the largest economy in South Asia, will benefit from a sub-regional hub position in that area. India however will lose 0.24 per cent of its GDP in the 'China hub' system, and its GDP will negligibly increase 0.08 per cent in the 'ASEAN hub' system.[92] Put simply, India has little or nothing to gain if other big economies such as China and ASEAN are placed in the position of hubs.

[89] World Bank, *Global Economic Prospects 2005*, p. 40.
[90] ADB, *Asian Development Outlook 2006*, p. 281. [91] *Ibid.*, p. 288. [92] *Ibid.*

C. *Asian free trade or Asian Economic Community*

The ADB report, consistent with the findings of Roland-Holst, Verbiest and Zhai,[93] offers the conclusion that the 'estimated benefits from free trade in Asia (with the extension of MFN to the rest of the world) are nearly as large as those from global free trade.[94] Further, there will be no trade diversion as 'no country or global region loses under the assumption of Asian free trade'.[95] This finding is reaffirmed by the IMF, as discussed above.[96] This is because, for most Asian developing countries, the bulk of gains from global free trade will still originate from trade liberalization in Asia. However, given China's foreign trade structure (i.e. its strong trading links with non-Asian markets), its gains from Asian free trade are less than half those from global trade liberalization. India's gain from pan-Asian free trade is 1.15 per cent expansion in its GDP, slightly higher than the projected benefits from global trade liberalization.[97] Furthermore, in spite of overall gains, ADB suggests that 'Asian free trade could lead to a significant deterioration in the terms of trade for Asia's two mammoth economies, the PRC and India'.[98] This is because these two nations now mainly trade with non-Asian countries, while the increased demand for goods produced in other parts of the world would not be compensated by increase in the demand for their exports outside Asia, thus creating raised import prices relative to export prices.

India has been advocating an Asian Economic Community for years. As the Indian Prime Minister has enthusiastically indicated, 'we envision an Asian Economic Community, which encompasses ASEAN, China, Japan, Korea and India . . . This community of nations would constitute an 'arc of advantage', across which there would be large-scale movement of people, capital, ideals and creativity'.[99] The basic idea is to bring the major blocs in East and South Asia, including Japan, ASEAN, China, India and Korea, which are collectively called the JACIK economies, to create an FTA or Asian Economic Community.[100] This community, with

[93] Roland-Holst, Verbiest and Zhai, 'Growth and trade horizon for Asia'.
[94] ADB, *Asian Development Outlook 2006*, p. 286.
[95] *Ibid.* [96] IMF, *Asia and Pacific Regional Economic Outlook.*
[97] ADB, *Asian Development Outlook 2006*, p. 287. [98] *Ibid.*
[99] 'Indian Prime Minister Manmohan Singh's speech at the Third India–ASEAN Business Summit', 21 October 2004, available at http://pmindia.nic.in/speech/content.asp?id=35 (visited 30 May 2006).
[100] Sachin Chaturvedi, John Humphrey, Nagesh Kumar and Hubert Schmitz, 'Asian economic integration: Dynamics and impacts', paper prepared for the Seventh Annual

a combined population of 3 billion, gross national income (GNI) of US $16 trillion, total exports of US$1.66 trillion, and foreign exchange reserves of US$1.6 trillion (in 2003), will be the largest trade bloc in the world. This FTA-based community will eventually force other Asian economies to join, thus eliminating the noodle-bowl problems.

D. *An East Asia bloc and a South Asian bloc linked with bilateral FTAs: A more viable route for Asian economic integration*

East Asian economies have developed strong economic interdependence and integration with the global economy through external liberalization and internal, market-driven, reforms. In recent decades, their independence is further strengthened by the newly developed Asian division of labour system centred on China which is on top of the vertical trade in East Asia. In addition to trade and FDI, East Asia economic integration is also linked by financial and macroeconomic interdependence.[101]

Economically, East Asian economic integration, via the creation of an East Asian trade bloc, is a viable option confirmed by numerous studies.[102] Gilbert, Scollay and Bora, using the methods of both the computable general equilibrium (CGE) and gravity models, credibly show that East Asian economies are natural trading partners and hence integration agreements tend to be building blocks in moves to achieve free trade in the Asia–Pacific region.[103] Specifically, it is argued that East Asian integration would be based on arrangements in which Northeast Asian economies would necessarily form the core. As such, the proposed Japan–Korea and China–Japan–Korea FTAs, plus the proposed ASEAN+3 FTA which serves as the link between Northeast Asia and Southeast Asia, are therefore essential elements in the construction of an East Asia FTA. With regard to the welfare-enhancing effects of the relevant FTAs, Gilbert, Scollay and Bora find:

Global Development, workshop on Asian and Other Drivers of Global Change, St Petersburg, 18–19 January 2006. Available: www.ids.ac.uk/ids/global/AsianDriverpdfs/Chatur-Humph-Schmitz-Kumar.pdf (last visited 28 May 2006).

101 Kawai, 'East Asian economic regionalism'.

102 See, e.g., Kawai, 'East Asian economic regionalism'; Suthiphand Chirathivat, 'East Asia FTA: Economic modalities, prospects and further implications' (2004) 15 *Journal of Asian Economics* 889–910; Jong-Wha Lee and Innwon Park, 'Free trade areas in East Asia: Discriminatory or non-discriminatory?' (2005) 28 (1) *World Economy* 21–48; and John Gilbert, Robert Scollay and Bijit Bora, 'New regional trading developments in the Asia–Pacific Region', in Shahid Yusuf, M. Anjum Altaf and Kaoru Nabeshima (eds.), *Global Change and East Asian Policy Initiatives* (Washington DC: World Bank, 2004), pp. 121–90.

103 Gilbert, Scollay and Bora, 'New regional trading developments in the Asia–Pacific region'.

> A Japan–Korea FTA produces relatively weak benefits for the two participating economies (0.3 percent of GDP for Korea and close to zero effect for Japan). The widespread negative effects on nonparticipants are negligible when expressed as a percentage of initial GDP, reaching 0.1 percent of GDP only in the case of Vietnam.
>
> Including China in the proposed arrangement significantly improves the welfare outcome for Korea and Japan, to 0.7 percent and 0.1 percent of GDP, respectively. In China's case, however, the welfare gain is negligible . . . With the inclusion of China in the FTA, the negative effects on nonmembers start to appear significant, particularly for Taiwan, China, and for the ASEAN economies, which compete directly with China in many markets.
>
> The negative welfare effects on the ASEAN economies are converted into positive effects . . . if the proposal is expanded into an ASEAN+3 FTA, comprising the 10 ASEAN economies plus China, Japan, and Korea. Proportionately to GDP, the ASEAN economies and Korea are the biggest gainers from this arrangement, although for Korea there is only a marginal improvement in the welfare outcome relative to the outcome from the China–Japan–Korea FTA. In comparison with the latter arrangement, Japan enjoys a slightly larger welfare gain, although as a percentage of GDP, the gain is still small. . .[T]he welfare effect on China is negligible, although very slightly inferior to that from the China–Japan–Korea FTA.[104]

In the case of South Asia, it has been pointed out that enhanced regional cooperation, including regional integration, is an imperative if the countries in the region 'are to strengthen their competitive position, both individually and as a group, so as to attract foreign private capital from outside and even within the region to widen and diversify their production base'.[105] Because the trade barriers between South Asian countries are traditionally high, trade liberalization through FTA or custom union would substantially increase intra-regional trade and foreign investment. According to one study, the FTA approach (i.e. SAFTA), if removing all intra-regional tariff barriers, would lead to gross domestic product (GDP) growth, trade expansion, and welfare gains for all South Asian countries, although the extent of benefits vary among the members. For instance, Sri Lanka would benefit the most from free trade in the region, with real GDP expanded by two percent. India and Bangladesh have lesser gains (0.8% and 0.3% GDP expansion respectively), while

[104] *Ibid.*, p. 140.

[105] RIS (Research and Information System for the Non-Aligned and Other Developing Countries), *South Asia Development and Cooperation Report 2004* (New Delhi: RIS, 2004), p. 48.

the rest of the South Asian countries are projected to gain 0.9% in real GDP.[106] India's lesser gains in GDP growth can be compensated by benefits obtained in other aspects, as, for instance, 'India appears to enjoy a positive contribution from terms of trade movements towards increased welfare gains in comparison to the other FTA members'.[107] If South Asia opts to achieve regional integration via a customs union, the benefits are strikingly much more significant.[108] Needless to say, given the political economy in this region, a customs union is nearly impossible in the near future, although a preliminary FTA (SAFTA) has already been instituted.

A possible route for Asian economic integration is that East Asia and South Asia progress to achieve sub-regional integration respectively, while developing bilateral FTAs between countries in these two sub-regions simultaneously.

E. *Concluding analysis: Which Asian regionalism is acceptable to China, India and other Asian economies?*

As discussed above, the benefits from regionalism cannot be taken for granted. Countries have no incentives – not to mention obligations – to pursue regional economic integration unless immediate or long-term gains outweigh the costs.

As the preceding section shows, neither China nor India is among the largest economic beneficiaries of regional economic integration in Asia. Economically, China gains the most from a system of bilateral FTAs in which it is a hub.[109] According to the stimulation results in ADB, China's welfare gains are projected to be 0.41% of its 2025 baseline GDP from a PRC-hub regime, 0.22% of the same GDP from global trade liberalization, and only 0.11% of it from Asian free trade.[110] Even in the scenario of China–Japan–Korea FTA or ASEAN+3, China's welfare gains are at best 'negligible'. That is to say, for China, the gains from pan-Asian free trade (Asian regionalism) are less than half those from global free trade (multilateralism), and only a quarter of those from bilateral FTAs (China regionalism). China also does not gain much from East Asian regionalism according to Gilbert, Scollay and Bora.[111] Presumably, if

[106] Mahinda Siriwardana, 'Trade liberalisation in South Asia: Free trade area or customs union?' (2003) 26 (3) *Journal of South Asian Studies* 309–29, 318.

[107] *Ibid.*, 321. [108] *Ibid.*, 319–27. [109] See §IV.2 above.

[110] ADB, *Asian Development Outlook 2006*.

[111] Gilbert, Scollay and Bora, 'New regional trading developments in the Asia–Pacific region', pp. 121–90. See §IV.4 above.

India is put in a regional hub position, its incomes would rise much faster than that from other channels. Hence there is an apparent question: Why would a country such as China or India pursue a regionwide RTA such as an Asian FTA, or an East Asian FTA, or an Asian Economic Community?

India might have a stronger incentive for an Asian Economic Community, as India will relatively gain more benfits from a pan-Asian free trade arrangement. However, it is not easy to convince China to sincerely endorse such an idea. It seems that the Chinese practice of RTAs has been following both Chinese regionalism (centred on a China-hub) and multilateralism. This can be seen from China's active pursuit of WTO accession as well as the sheer number of bilateral RTAs it has concluded and is negotiating. In Asia only, it is exploring bilateral arrangements with important economies such as ASEAN, Korea, Japan, India and Pakistan. It has not demonstrated strong interest in regional economic integration in Asia, be it an Asian Economic Community or Asian FTA. To the extent that East Asian economic cooperation is concerned, China's Prime Minister Wen Jiabao has warned that the cooperation should not be 'close, exclusive and directed against any particular country', indicating that 'China takes the position that in pursuing regional cooperation, it is imperative to be open minded and promote open regionalism so as to achieve progress for all countries and development in all regions'.[112] This type of open regionalism, as almost all other countries, including currently non-Asian countries such as US, EU, Russia, and arguably Australia and New Zealand, are equally welcomed and treated, will cause Asian regionalism to lose its distinctive identity and eventually the momentum to development into full regional economic integration. This practice, featuring the parallels of multilateralism and Chinese bilateralism, is generally in line with China's economic interests, and is presumably not against its interests in other aspects.

Obviously the gains and costs have both economic and political dimensions. Whalley observes that trading nations have a wide range of considerations when they seek to negotiate RTAs.[113] Apart from the traditional trade gains, countries might want to strengthen domestic

[112] 'East Asia cooperation should be transparent, open: Chinese Premier', *People's Daily Online*, 14 December 2005, available at http://english.people.com.cn/200512/14/eng20051214_227982.html (visited 30 May 2006).

[113] John Whalley, 'Why do countries seek regional trade agreements?' in Jeffrey A. Frankel (ed.), *The Regionalization of the World Economy* (University of Chicago Press, 1998), p. 63.

policy reform, as is the case of the Mexican negotiating position on the North American Free Trade Agreement (NAFTA). The underlying philosophy is that 'a regional trade treaty can underpin domestic policy reform and make it more secure; that is, by binding the country to the masthead of an international trade treaty, any future reversal of domestic policy reform becomes more difficult to implement'.[114] They might also pursue RTAs for the purpose of increasing multilateral bargaining power with third countries by negotiating a preferential agreement, as in the case of the European Community or MERCOSUR.[115] RTAs might also be used to make access to the larger economy's market more secure for the smaller economy. This was the obvious purpose of Canada in forming the Canada–US Free Trade Agreement.[116] A further country objective is the formation of strategic linkage with trading partners in a RTA, which can help underpin security arrangements among the participating countries. The strategic objective was the central theme in early European integration which was aimed at preventing a fresh outbreak of European war by bringing Germany and France together through a trade agreement.[117] Finally, the objective could be using regional agreements for tactical purposes of achieving multilateral negotiating objectives. For example, in the Uruguay Round of GATT negotiations, 'it was widely thought that it was to the U.S.'s advantage to have regional trade negotiations underway, so that in dealing with recalcitrant multilateral negotiating partners, the United States could threaten to actually play the bilateral card, and engage in active discussions with prospective regional partners'.[118]

Needless to say, not all the objectives will appear at once in a country's negotiation of a RTA. One or two objectives might be dominant in some cases, while in others multiple objectives exist.[119] Either way, it is often the case that non-economic, strategic, objectives quite rightly occupy the central place in RTA negotiations.

Furthermore, although countries are not required to practise altruism in the international trade arena, big trading powers, as their policy would have tremendous impact on other countries, are expected to factor not only their national interests, but also regional and global interests, into their policy-making. China and India, as the two most dynamic trading nations, shoulder such a responsibility.

[114] *Ibid.*, p. 71. [115] *Ibid.*, p. 72. [116] *Ibid.*, pp. 72–3.
[117] *Ibid.*, p. 73. [118] *Ibid.*, p. 74. [119] *Ibid.*, p. 71.

But does this responsibility translate into an obligation not to pursue (self-interest oriented) bilateralism? Is it not right that China or India can maximize its national interests by mainly focusing on bilateralism and, while possible, multilateralism? Obviously, China could achieve its economic and strategic goals through signing bilateral FTAs with its Asian neighbours.[120]

For the following reasons, it is submitted that China and India should pursue regionalism on a broader basis – namely involving more Asian countries with fewer agreements – instead of focusing on hub-and-spoke regionalism:

1. Both China and India, and undoubtedly all Asian economies, have a long-term interest in broader liberalization on a multilateral basis which will lead to greater net benefits for all trading nations. In fact, China's projected gains from bilateralism and India's projected gains from pan-Asian free trade are also based on the assumption that multilateral trade liberalization, which might move at an unsatisfactorily slow pace, nevertheless, does not stop. As China and India – and especially China at this stage – are heavily dependent on non-Asian markets such as North America and Europe (both of which are unlikely to sign FTAs with China and India in the foreseeable future), global trade liberalization is actually crucial to their trade and economic growth. Therefore, countries like China and India should make sure that their regionalism should supplement multilateralism when the latter progress slowly, but it should not stand in the way of global free trade. In this sense, bilateralism, featuring a hub-and-spoke system of FTAs, is more likely to harm the multilateral trading system in the long run as they are more likely to become stumbling blocks for global free trade. In contrast, as the above sections show, an Asian FTA, East Asian FTA, and South Asian FTA, are more likely to be building blocks with more trade creating effects.
2. The many bilateral FTAs signed by the hubs, be it China, India or ASEAN, contribute greatly to the complexity of trading rules and to the potential costs of trade. In essence, systemic problems such as the 'spaghetti bowl phenomenon' should not be overlooked. By creating a large number of (overlapping) bilateral FTAs, the hubs also create problems for the multilateral trading system. When the problems backfire, it might hurt the hubs' long-term interest in global free trade. As such, it is in the interests of the hubs, in this case they are

[120] Jiangyu Wang, 'China's regional trade agreements', 129.

China and India, to minimize the number of RTAs by consolidating them into a regional one encompassing more countries.

3. China's and India's fast growing trade frictions with non-Asian countries have generated the need for the two Asian giants to explore other markets. This is especially urgent for China, as its astronomical trade surpluses with the United States and EU have led to enormous protectionist pressure in the latter two trading powers. Building an alternative, integrated, market in Asia through Asian regional economic integration can strengthen the negotiating positions of all Asian countries, most significantly China and India, with respect to their trade relations with the US and EU.

Additionally, both China and India have political and security interests in a more integrated, economically interdependent Asia. Using the ASEAN–China FTA as an example: although it is believed that the long-term benefit of the ACFTA will be enormous to both sides, it is also observed by commentators that 'China's [RTA] approach, as a strategic movement, must be viewed in a larger context that embraces both economic and geopolitical considerations, with the latter playing a relatively more important role at this stage'.[121] Specifically, 'China's worldwide [RTA] movement, which has primarily engaged its Asian neighbours at this stage, is aimed at expanding its political influence through peaceful economic exchange and cooperation.'[122] On the part of ASEAN, China's proactive pursuit of a regional trade pact offers a 'win-win' opportunity which ASEAN cannot afford to reject, as remarked by ASEAN's spokesman: 'there is no other way [for ASEAN] to deal with China but to engage it in regional process. China is important as a neighbour politically, in terms of security and is also important as an emerging economic power'.[123]

[121] *Ibid.*, 129. See also, Gungwu Wang, 'China and Southeast Asia: Changes in strategic perceptions', in Khai Leong Ho and Samuel C. Y. Ku (eds.), *China and Southeast Asia: Global Changes and Regional Challenges* (Singapore: Institute of Southeast Asian Studies, 2005), pp. 3–14; Vincent Wang, 'The logic of China–ASEAN FTA: Economic statecraft of "peaceful ascendancy"', in Khai Leong Ho and Samuel C. Y. Ku (eds.), *China and Southeast Asia: Global Changes and Regional Challenges* (Singapore: Institute of Southeast Asian Studies, 2005) and Alice D. Ba, 'The politics and economics of "East Asia" in ASEAN–China relations', in Khai Leong Ho and Samuel C. Y. Ku (eds.), *China and Southeast Asia: Global Changes and Regional Challenges* (Singapore: Institute of Southeast Asian Studies, 2005).

[122] Jiangyu Wang, 'China's regional trade agreements', 132.

[123] Isaqani de Castro, 'China snuggles up to Southeast Asia', *Asia Times*, 7 October 2003, available at www.atimes.com.

Especially in recent years, China has been gesturing, with also many concrete measures, to allay the fears of its neighbours about the growing Chinese economic and military power. China has emphasized that its major objective, evidentially at this stage, is to seek a friendly international and regional environment to facilitate its economic development endeavour.[124] But for China's small neighbours, they would more likely be reassured if the bilateral relation with China were contained in a multilateral and, if possible, regional framework.[125] Consequently, if China is to succeed in its 'good neighbour' policy, it has to help create a regional economic architecture to support it. The same logic can also be applied to China's bilateral relations with other Asian countries, even including Japan.

India is also located in a region (South Asia) where political relations are tense and distrust between countries is strong. India and Pakistan have a long-standing hostility towards each other. Serious political differences also exist between India and other smaller South Asian countries, which are strengthened by the rigid positions of political and military leaders towards each other in this area. There is in addition a fear of Indian dominance in bilateral relations. Like China, India has also a crucial task of introducing a regional framework which is open to other regions as well as to the multilateral system in order to create a harmonious regional setting for its economic development.

In brief, although the economic gains from regionalism are not necessarily larger than bilateralism (based on a China-hub or India-hub), leading Asian giants like China and India do have a long-term interest in regional economic integration in Asia if non-economic objectives are taken into consideration of policy-making. As to the type of regionalism to be adopted, it is submitted that the best route for the realization of Asian integration is sub-regional integration in East Asia and South Asia, while linking the two by bilateral FTAs. The next section, as concluding remarks, will analyze this approach and put forward policy recommendations for China and India on Asian economic integration.

V. Policy recommendations

China and India are among the most important economies in Asia. Since the 1997 Asian financial crisis, regional trade in Asia is becoming

[124] 'Chinese premier delivers speech at East Asia Summit Leaders Dialogue', *People's Daily Online*, 13 December 2005, available at http://english.people.com.cn/200512/12/eng20051212_227412.html (visited 30 May 2006).

[125] Gungwu Wang, 'China and Southeast Asia', p. 10.

increasingly integrated, particularly with China, since China's rise as both a production network and a final export market for the region has been a key factor in boosting intra-Asian trade and investment. China and India are also active participants in the growing regional economic cooperation initiatives, including bilateral and regional trade agreements as well as Asian cooperative measures in the areas of finance and investment.

China and India, together with other Asian countries, share the imperative to promote regional economic integration in this continent. Given the size of their economy and the central location of their development in international politics and economy, China and India should take the lead in this endeavour. The scope of gains from Asian regionalism can be formidable if it is realized through well-designed RTAs which complement the unilateral and multilateral liberalization approach and anchor domestic reform programmes to increase efficiency and improve competitiveness. In light of the above, the following policy recommendations regarding Asian economic integration are made, with a special focus on the role of China and India.

A. The routes for Asian economic integration: East Asian FTA + South Asian FTA + others = Asian free trade

While it is unlikely that the trend of bilateral initiatives in Asia will stop, it is wise for the region as a whole to have coordinated regionalization policy. As noted above, the hubs and spokes systems, while inducing larger benefits for the hubs, may damage the spokes by discrimination in other spoke markets. Hubs and spokes regimes not only add layers of discrimination in the region, but also lead to greater resistance to multilateral liberalization. This is not in the long-run interest of the economies which have potential to be – or already are – hubs, including China, India, Japan and ASEAN, as all of them are still heavily dependent on markets outside Asia.

A pan-Asian free trade area or an Asian economic community is unlikely to be achieved or even seriously discussed. Asia is no more than a geographic concept, sharing no common heritage between the sub-regions. However, countries in each sub-region, including East Asia, South Asia, Central Asia, share not only geographic contiguity but also common cultural, social and economic characteristics. Furthermore, the numerous sub-regional initiatives have demonstrated that the countries involved are preparing for economic and financial integration at the sub-regional level. It is hence submitted that East Asia and South Asia should strive to realize their sub-regional integration respectively, while linking the two sub-regions with bilateral integration agreements between individual countries.

Economic integration in East Asia should aim at creating an East-Asia wide FTA (EAFTA) comprising ASEAN, China, Japan and Korea. East Asia is now in a better position to achieve integration ahead of other sub-regions, because its intra-regional trade had reached 55 per cent in 2004. There has also been a rapid rise in intra-regional investment flows, shaping a visible trade-investment nexus.[126] As discussed in the previous section, various studies conclude that an EAFTA offers visible and meaningful benefits to all participating countries while generating little trade diversion. Although China does not gain as much as other East Asian countries do, it does, however, have a long-term, strategic, interest in this arrangement. For one instance, China would profit from cost advantages of input imports from the regional partners in the EAFTA community, which will make the Chinese products more competitive in third markets. Being placed in an integrated regional market could also strengthen China's negotiating position *vis-à-vis* other global trading powers.

Despite its possession of enormous physical resources and 22 per cent of global population, South Asia is the least integrated economic region of the world. The largest economy accounting for 70 per cent of the total sub-regional GDP, India should take the lead in South Asia integration under the auspices of SAFTA. Although business in this area believes that intra-regional trade will be tripled in five years if South Asia regional integration is facilitated, especially in the areas of trade, traffic and transport, integration in this sub-region has been hampered by long-standing political hostility and a protectionist mentality.[127] However, as a business leader of Pakistan remarks, '[i]f USA could allow MFN status to China whom it considered archenemy for five decades and Russia and USA having long standing conflicts in social, political and

[126] Haruhiko Kuroda, 'New visions and models for economic cooperation', speech by Haruhiko Kuroda, President of Asian Development Bank, at the Plenary Session II of the Annual Conference of the Boao Forum of Asia, 22–23 April 2006, Boao, Hainan. Available at www.adb.org/Documents/Speeches/2006/ms2006025.asp (visited 1 June 2006).

[127] Khalid Amin, 'South Asia regional integration: Pakistan country note', prepared for the World Bank/International Monetary Fund 2004 Annual Meetings, Programme of Seminars, 1 October 2004. Washington DC. Available at http://siteresources.worldbank.org/INTSOUTHASIA/Resources/Pakistan-Final.pdf (1 June 2006).

economic fields could become allies, what is restraining the countries of South Asia from economic integration?.[128] Furthermore, South Asia countries, most importantly India, should conduct significant reduction in tariff and non-tariff barriers. India is one of the most protected major markets in the world, with a high level of tariff and non-tariff protection for its domestic industry. India's vibrant economic growth in recent decades, mainly as a result of trade and investment liberalization, is, however, a strong proof that liberalization, not protection, is the engine for economic growth.

The two sub-regions should not pursue integration separated and isolated from each other. Rather, the two, before the time is right to consolidate them into one, will be connected by bilateral arrangements between countries in the two regions. Most notably, India is negotiating an FTA with ASEAN and has concluded the FTA with Singapore. China and Pakistan have signed an early harvest agreement and have started negotiating a comprehensive FTA. More link-ups between the two sides should be encouraged provided that they follow the guidelines discussed below and serve as building blocks for global trade.

If an Asian Economic Community is formed by consolidating the East Asian FTA and SAFTA, other Asian countries will be compelled to join it. Eventually, pan-Asian will be accomplished through these routes.

B. *Establishing a China–India FTA to link up the two sub-regions*

In terms of using bilateral FTAs to link East Asia and South Asia, a China–India FTA will be most helpful in this regard. China–India trade is one of the most rapid growing bilateral trade relationships in the world. During 1995–2003, the average annul growth of merchandise trade between the two was 26.4 per cent, a figure higher than each country's growth rate with other trading partners. In 2003, the growth rate of bilateral services trade was 125.5 per cent. Still, the low share of the two countries in each other's foreign trade suggests an enormous potential for trade expansion.[129]

Arvind Panagaria, a distinguished economist who has generally been 'critical of the discriminatory trade blocs not just because such arrangements fragment the global trading system but also because they often

[128] *Ibid.*, p. 16.

[129] India–China Joint Study Group, 'Report of the India–China Joint Study Group on comprehensive trade and economic cooperation', 23 March 2005, p. 20. Available at http://meaindia.nic.in/treatiesagreement/2005/11ta1104200504.pdf (visited 1 June 2006).

hurt economic efficiency within the countries forging the arrangements', nevertheless favours an India–China FTA.[130] Panagaria has beautifully stated the following reasons to support a Sino-Indian deal in the interests of both Asian economic integration and global free trade, as well as China's and India's national competitiveness:

> The case for an India–China FTA is based principally on its strategic value. During the last decade, with the creation of the NAFTA, several expansions of the EU and a host of smaller FTAs in Latin America, Asia has suffered from a diversion of these regions' trade away from it. One response to this trade diversion for Asia would be to move towards a bloc of its own. Such a bloc may give Asia the necessary leverage to pry open the NAFTA and EU blocs to outsiders through multilateral liberalization.
>
> If one accepts this argument, an India–China FTA is probably the best starting point for such an Asian bloc. For example, as an alternative, even if India and China both make good on their respective framework agreements with the members of the Association of Southeast Asian Nations (ASEAN) to forge FTAs with them, an effective Asian bloc will not form without these two countries signing an FTA agreement with each other. On the other hand, if India and China signed an agreement, chances are much higher that the remaining countries in Asia will rush to sign agreements with them. Presently, the ASEAN is driving the integration process in Asia but with the emergence of India and China as major economic powerhouses and the relative stagnation faced by the most populous ASEAN country, Indonesia, its ability to serve as the engine of the Asian integration has substantially diminished.
>
> An India–China FTA also has the advantage that it will help promote an alternative FTA template that focuses on trade integration rather than non-trade subjects including labor standards, intellectual property rights and even restrictions on the use of capital controls. These subjects are integral parts of the US FTA template that the US may eventually want to turn into the WTO template. An Asian bloc that relies on a 'trade only' template will be an effective instrument of countering the US template in the future WTO negotiations.
>
> Internally, India can surely benefit from cooperation with China in shaping its labor-intensive industry. In particular, direct competition with China may help push some of the key reforms necessary to stimulate the expansion of the labor-intensive industry. With the wages in China now rising, the time for India could not be more opportune for moving in a big way into such labor-intensive sectors as apparel, footwear and toys. Likewise, China could gain from increased interaction with India in the information technology sector.

[130] Arvind Panagaria, 'An India–China free trade area?', *The Economic Times*, 20 April 2005. Available at www.columbia.edu/~ap2231/ET/et77_April20_05.htm (visited 1 June 2006).

C. *China and India should lead Asia to practice open regionalism (with Asian identity)*

China and India, as well as some of their Asian neighbours, all have a crucial interest in global trade liberalization, partly because their exports mainly go to markets outside Asia. In this sense, Asian regionalism is merely adopted as the 'second-best' strategy due to the stalemate in the multilateral trade negotiations. The best framework for harvesting sustainable benefits from liberalization is still the global framework, while regional arrangements represent the middle ground in the framework spectrum. Nevertheless, in the current situation of world trade, there seems to be no alternative to totally replace regionalism for trading nations.

It is widely recognized that Asian regionalism must be, first of all, 'open regionalism'. There is, however, no fixed definition of what constitutes open regionalism.[131] Difficult questions will be raised if open regionalism must mean, as some commentators suggest, open membership, which means that any country, be it geographically located in the region or not, can join on the same terms. This opens the possibility that a RTA can eventually encompass the entire world and hence – at least theoretically – lead to multilateral liberalization.[132] This will render the concept of Asian economic integration senseless (or make it become global economic integration) as it is, by definition, economic integration in Asia, which is pursued for the very reason that global integration is halted by the slow negotiations at the multilateral level. As such, it is inconceivable that membership of a regional arrangement is 'open' for all countries of the world. More often, the membership of a regional integration group is strictly confined to a given geographic area.[133]

The openness of regional groupings, in a more practical way, should lie in their willingness to extend intra-regional concessions and preferential treatment to nonmembers. As such, Wei and Frankel define open regionalism concisely as 'external liberalization by trade blocs, that is, the reduction in barriers on imports from nonmember countries that is undertaken when member countries liberalize the trade among themselves'.[134] This is not to say that all the concessions and privileges must

[131] See section I on the general definition of open regionalism.
[132] Panagaria, 'The regionalism debate', 503.
[133] Chirathivat, 'East Asia FTA', 906.
[134] Shang-jin Wei and Jeffrey A. Frankel. 'Open regionalism in a world of continental trade blocs' (1998) 45 (3) *IMF Staff Papers* 440–53, 441.

be offered to nonmembers on an MFN basis – this would probably cause the regional integration arrangement to lose its regional nature. As Wei and Frankel point out, the 'degree of liberalization on imports from nonmembers need not be as high as that from member countries'.[135]

Therefore, the World Bank encourages developing countries to adopt a three-pronged strategy that integrates unilateral, regional and multilateral liberalization initiatives.[136] The success of Asian emerging economies, including East Asia economies and India, is to a large extent attributed to the unilateral government reform programmes. In the practice of open regionalism, Asian countries are encouraged to liberalize their trade and investment barriers unilaterally to the maximum extent possible in order to improve their competitiveness and reduce poverty, as well as to avoid trade diversion effects. Although not an obligation embodied in the regional integration agreement, they are free to extend its regional liberalization to nonmembers on a mutually reciprocal or even unconditional basis. Further, Asian countries participating in the integration process should take this as an opportunity to consolidate their diverse views and form consensus to push the multilateral trade negotiations.

D. Deeper integration

It has been advocated that the new wave of regionalism should practise 'deep integration' as opposed to 'shallow integration'. In the scenario of shallow integration, mainly trade in goods is liberalized among members. Deep integration goes beyond trade, involving investment, services, product standards and technical regulations, competition policy, and even environmental and labour standards, among others. In short, deep integration may induce welfare gains for participating countries by lowering the costs of production and improving efficiency in general, and for outside countries by avoiding trade diversion through stimulating trade.[137]

Regional agreements in Asia are increasingly comprehensive in scope, going beyond reduction/elimination of tariff and tariff barriers. In the Asian context, deep integration should be achieved through investment liberalization, financial cooperation and trade facilitation

[135] *Ibid.* [136] World Bank, *Global Economic Prospects 2005*, p. 147.
[137] Lawrence, *Regionalism, Multilateralism, and Deeper Integration*, pp. 28–33.

Asian countries either heavily rely on foreign investment for economic development or aspire to attract foreign investment. Hence Lee and Park observe that 'the movement of East Asian countries towards RTAs has been motivated by facilitating investment and providing a more flexible environment for the operation of multinational firms'.[138] In most Asian FTAs, investment commitments are centred on national treatment and/or MFN treatment for foreign investors alongside rules on expropriation, compensation and repatriation of earning. Countries have also committed to create a liberal and competitive environment for investment, as well as improve transparency in their legal system.[139] Frankly, in China's and India's regional initiatives, the investment commitments are rather general, with little detail to guide the practice. If Asian countries wish to continue to draw investment from each other and from outside the region, they should make efforts to liberalize their investment regime, relax restrictions on foreign ownership, remove discriminative performance requirements, and allow impartial dispute settlement procedures. It is important to stress, however, that these countries should manage to strike a balance between investment liberalization and promotion of competitiveness of domestic industries.

Services trade is another important area that facilitates deep integration. Unfortunately, Asian integration in services trade is very shallow. SAFTA does not even have a service dimension. In East Asia, although ASEAN's FTA initiatives, including ASEAN–China, ASEAN–India, ASEAN–Japan and ASEAN–Korea, commit the parties to conducting GATS-plus liberalization, it is questionable that the voluntary nature of the commitment will lead to significant progress.[140] Again, China and India, with growing comparative advantage in certain services sectors, should take the lead in regional services liberalization. Initial opening at the regional level may help create an economy of scale, nurturing efficient and competitive domestic and regional firms which can stand up to competition from outside the region, and provide opportunities for learning-by-doing. Further, as some commentators correctly note, 'regulatory co-operation, such as harmonization and mutual recognition

[138] Lee and Park, 'Free trade areas in East Asia', p. 41.

[139] O. G. Dayaratna Banda and John Whalley, *Beyond Goods and Services: Competition Policy, Investment, Mutual Recognition, Movement of Person, and Broader Operation Provisions of Recent FTAs Involving ASEAN Countries*, NBER Working Paper 11232 (Cambridge, MA: National Bureau of Economic Research, 2003), pp. 15–17.

[140] Tubagus Feridhanusetyawan, *Preferential Trade Agreements in the Asia–Pacific*, IMF Working Paper WP/05/149 (Washington DC: International Monetary Fund, 2005), p. 24.

of domestic regulations in financial, professional and a range of other services, may be more feasible in a regional context'.[141] Needless to say, the building of a strong and flexible regulatory framework, which ensures fair competition, and regulates and remedies market failures, should accompany the whole liberalization process.

A danger in regional agreement is that countries will tend to avoid making tough liberalization decisions by excluding whole sectors from preferential arrangements. This can happen to both merchandise trade (especially the agricultural sector) and services. For instance, the Japan–Singapore FTA totally excludes the agricultural sector. Although it is widely recognized that reduction of trade barriers in agriculture is particularly important for poverty reduction, with which tremendous gains can be conferred on the poor households of the less developed countries in this region. For most of the major economies in Asia, including ASEAN, Japan, Korea and India, agriculture is still viewed as a sensitive sector placed outside the liberalization agenda. In this regard, China's commitment to a regime of low protection in agriculture demonstrates that the country is taking the lead on some issues relating to regional liberalization. China's WTO commitments in agriculture are already impressive, and its stance towards agricultural trade at regional level warrants further attention. Under the Early Harvest Programme of the ASEAN–China FTA framework agreement, China undertakes to grant unilateral concessions to agricultural products (Chapters 1–8 of the HS Code) of ASEAN countries provided that the latter also commit some degree of agricultural liberalization. It is remarked that 'China's binding to low tariff levels as part of its agricultural policy therefore offers scope for the liberalization of agriculture in a regional setting, which could set in place a favourable political dynamic for more open agricultural sectors through East Asia'.[142] One would question the effectiveness of this approach as the Chinese method is to 'induce' – with the imposition of no compulsory obligations – trading partners to liberalize by offering unilateral concessions. The fact that this approach cannot readily deliver reciprocal commitments implies that it may have a limited potential as a vehicle for trade liberalization. Without a more formal and institutionalized approach,

[141] Kathie Krumm and Homi Kharas, *East Asia Integrates: A Trade Policy Agenda for Shared Growth* (Washington DC: World Bank; Oxford University Press, 2004), p. xxxii.

[142] Homi Kharas, 'Trade and economic integration in the Asia Pacific Region', in OECD (ed.), *Regional Integration in the Asia Pacific: Issues and Prospects* (Paris: Organization for Economic Co-operation and Development, 2005), pp. 103–35, at p. 107.

the liberalization process in sensitive sectors such as agriculture and financial sector can be unsatisfactorily slow.

E. 'Common guidelines' or 'best practice' for bilateral FTAs

As analysed above, regional integration in Asia will have to be achieved through a web of regional and bilateral free trade agreements. Every agreement adds to the layers of discrimination and worsens the systemic problems of regionalism. For example, regarding rules of origin alone, a survey of several RTAs in Asia demonstrates that the 'spaghetti bowl' effect is apparent. For instance, under the Singapore-Australia FTA, the general rule of a specified threshold of local value content is either 30% or 50%. In the Japan-Singapore FTA, each product has one corresponding specific rule of origin, although a significant portion of the rules require 60% of local content. Such a world of complex clauses governing rules of origin, criticized the President of the Asian Development Bank, 'could create a bureaucratic tangle that might put individual companies off trading together'.[143]

It is suggested that, to cure the systemic problems and facilitate deeper integration, East Asian and South Asian countries should establish an institution to develop common standards and best practice to guide the regional FTAs. This body, with the participation of all interested Asian countries and under the auspices of a regional forum such as the East Asia Summit or ASEAN+3 cooperation, should produce a set of guidelines and principles for Asian FTAs, with a view to ensuring that the regional FTAs lead to integration rather than fragmentation of trading relations in Asia. It is highly possible that bilateral and sub-regional arrangements, if designed with measures incorporated to mitigate distortions and inefficiencies, can deepen regional economic integration and even 'present additional opportunities to those currently accommodated within the multilateral framework'

The suggested guidelines for sub-regional and bilateral trade agreements in Asia should include the following which is nevertheless not an exhaustive list:

- Asian FTAs should be, at least, WTO-consistent. This not only refers to compliance with GATT Article XXIV and GATS Article V. The bottom line is that every FTA should be WTO-plus. Further, they must follow,

[143] David Pilling, 'ADB chief hits out at "noodle bowl" trade', *Financial Times* (Asia), 2 February 2006, p. 1.

to the widest extent, the principles, terminologies, concepts and rules embodied in the WTO, although they are encouraged to develop liberalization-oriented rules for areas not covered by the WTO.

- Deeper integration and comprehensiveness in Asian FTAs. Numerous studies show that agreements with deeper and broader integration can lead to larger trade and income effects. WTO disciplines also require regional FTAs to eliminate barriers to trade and investment between the parties, including tariffs and non-tariff restrictions in goods, services and investment. Furthermore, given Asia's relative backwardness in infrastructure, comprehensive cooperation in trade facilitation should be the focus of any FTA in this region.
- Asian FTAs should adopt liberal, or at least nonrestrictive, rules of origin. The best solution is to have an Asia-wide set of rules of origin. If this is not possible, the rules of origin in Asian FTAs should at least be transparent, clear, and consistent, and have 'transparent and consistent implementing regulations (e.g. accounting practices, paperwork for certification of origin) that are chosen at the minimum level needed to prevent trade deflection'.[144] As the bottom line, they should not serve as a trade policy mechanism for protecting 'sensitive sectors' or special interest. In brief, a set of Asian 'best practice guidelines' for rules of origin can be an invaluable contribution to Asian economic integration.
- 'Clear and simple codes that guide technical barriers to trade, such as product standards and phytosanitary standards to protect public health and safety (based on the WTO agreements on standards). Likewise, agreements that cover environmental and labour standards should embrace the rights of partners to establish and implement their own laws and regulations in conformity with existing international obligations in the areas of environmental protection and labour rights and conditions'.[145]
- Harmonization of regulatory standards may or may not be required in Asian FTAs, depending on the readiness of the participating economies. Countries are encouraged to adopt international standards provided that all parties have the capacity to implement it. Mutual recognition is also encouraged. However, it is important to realize that, given Asian countries' diverse backgrounds, regional cooperation in standards can be very difficult. The best starting point is that all members of the FTA should maintain an open and transparent

[144] ADB, *Asian Development Outlook 2006*, p. 290. [145] *Ibid.*

system, with standards published and easily accessible to the business and the public.

- Dispute settlement procedures should be established in Asian FTAs to promote legalism in trade relations. Disputes should be resolved, first, through amicable consultations. If bilateral consultations do not offer solutions, then an independent third party should be established to resolve the disputes in an impartial, expeditious manner, and its decisions should be fully implemented. Mediation should be allowed in the whole process of dispute resolution. Further, the parties should avoid duplication with the WTO dispute settlement mechanism where appropriate.

VI. Conclusion

Asian economic integration is caused and pushed by the painful experience from the Asian financial crisis, the delay in global trade negotiations of the Doha Round, concern for the rise of the giant Chinese and Indian economies, as well as some strategic and political considerations. It is a 'second-best' approach which Asian countries unfortunately have to follow. In the process of regional economic integration, China and India, given the size of their population, as well as their central strategic position in international and regional relations, will inevitably play fundamentally important, if not entirely dominating, roles. This chapter suggests that regional economic integration in Asia should first of all realize sub-regional integration in East Asia and Southeast Asia, while linking up these two sub-regions with bilateral FTAs, among which the most important one should be a China–India FTA. Eventually, all the FTAs will be consolidated into one pan-Asian FTA. China and India must take the lead in promoting Asian economic integration. They are advised to lead the region to practise open regionalism (with however Asian identity) and conduct deeper integration. Lastly, it is suggested that Asian countries should, at this stage, establish an institution to develop common principles and guidelines for the sub-regional and bilateral FTAs.

References

ADB (Asian Development Bank), *Asian Development Outlook 2006* (Manila: Asian Development Bank, 2006)

Asian Development Outlook 2002 (Manila: Asian Development Bank, 2002)

Amin, Khalid, 'South Asia regional integration: Pakistan country note'. Prepared for the World Bank/International Monetary Fund 2004 Annual Meetings, Program of Seminars, 1 October 2004. Washington D.C. Available at http://siteresources.worldbank.org/INTSOUTHASIA/Resources/Pakistan-Final.pdf (1 June 2006)

Antkiewicz, Agata and Whalley, John, 'China's New Regional Trade Agreements' (2005) **28**(10) *Journal of World Trade* 1539–57

Asher, Mukul G. and Sen, Rahul, *India–East Asia Integration: A Win-win for Asia*, RIS Discussion Paper RIS-DP # 91/2005 (New Delhi: Research and Information System for the Non-Aligned and other Developing Countries, 2005). Available at www.ris.org.in/dp91_pap.pdf (last visited 2 May 2006)

Ba, Alice D., 'The politics and economics of "East Asia" in ASEAN–China relations', in Khai Leong Ho and Samuel C. Y. Ku (eds.), *China and Southeast Asia: Global Changes and Regional Challenges* (Singapore: Institute of Southeast Asian Studies, 2005)

Balassa, Bela, *The Theory of Economic Integration* (Homewood, IL: Richard D. Irwin Inc., 1961)

Baldwin, Richard E., 'Asian regionalism: Promises and pitfalls' (2002). Paper presented at the conference 'Prospects for Economic Cooperation in East Asia', Seoul, 27 September 2002 organized by KIEP. Published in Choong Yong Ahn, Richard E. Baldwin and Inkyo Cheong (eds.), *East Asian Economic Regionalism: Feasibilities and Challenges* (Dordrecht:Springer, 2005). Available at http://hei.unige.ch/~baldwin/PapersBooks/KIEP_paper_conf_version.pdf (visited 20 May 2006)

'*A Domino Theory of Regionalism*, Working Paper No. 4465 (Cambridge, MA: National Bureau of Economic Research, September 1993)

'Managing the noodle bowl: The fragility of East Asian regionalism', CEPR Discussion Paper No. 5561 (Centre for Economic Policy Research, 2006). Available at www.cepr.org/pubs/dps/DP5561.asp (last visited 22 May 2006)

Banda, O. G. Dayaratna and Whalley, John, *Beyond Goods and Services: Competition Policy, Investment, Mutual Recognition, Movement of Person, and Broader Operation Provisions of Recent FTAs Involving ASEAN Countries*, NBER Working Paper 11232. Cambridge, MA: National Bureau of Economic Research, 2005)

Batra, Amita, 'Micro pains, macro gains', *Financial Express*, 20 May 2006, available at www.financialexpress.com/fe_full_story.php?content_id=127689 (visited 22 May 2006)

Bergsten, C. Fred, *Open Regionalism*, Working Paper 97–3. (Washington DC: Institute for International Economics, 1999). Available at www.iie.com/publications/wp/wp.cfm?ResearchID=152 (last visited 8 May 2006)

Bhagwati, Jagdish, *The World Trading System at Risk* (Hemel Hempstead: Harvester Wheatsheaf, 1991)

Bhagwati, Jagdish, Pravin Krishna and Arvind Panagariya (eds.), *Trading Blocs: Alternative Approaches to Analyzing Preferential Trade Agreements* (Cambridge, MA: MIT Press, 1999)

Bonapace, Tiziana and Mikic, Mia, 'Multilateralizing regionalism: Towards an integrated and outward-oriented Asia–Pacific economic area', in *Delivering on the WTO Round: A High-level Government-Business Dialogue*, Studies in Trade and Investment 56 (United Nations Economic and Social Commission for Asia and the Pacific, 2005), pp. 85–110

Castro, Isaqani de, 'China snuggles up to Southeast Asia', *Asia Times*, 7 October 2003, available at www.atimes.com

Chaturvedi, Sachin, Humphrey, John, Kumar, Nagesh and Schmitz, Hubert, 'Asian economic integration: Dynamics and impacts', paper prepared for the Seventh Annual Global Development, workshop on *Asian and Other Drivers of Global Change*, St Petersburg, 18–19 January 2006. Available at: www.ids.ac.uk/ids/global/AsianDriverpdfs/Chatur-Humph-Schmitz-Kumar.pdf (last visited 28 May 2006)

Chirathivat, Suthiphand, 'East Asia FTA: Economic modalities, prospects and further implications' (2004) **15** *Journal of Asian Economics* 889–910

EIU (Economist Intelligence Unit), *Country Report: China* (London: The Economist Intelligence Unit, 2006)

Country Report: India (London: The Economist Intelligence Unit, 2006)

ESCAP (United Nations Economic and Social Commission for Asia and the Pacific), *Facts about the Bangkok Agreement (Asia–Pacific Trade Agreement): Informal Information Note* (Bangkok: ESCAP, 2005)

Feridhanusetyawan, Tubagus, *Preferential Trade Agreements in the Asia–Pacific* IMF Working Paper WP/05/149 (Washington DC: International Monetary Fund, 2005)

Fung, Victor, 'Luncheon Address by Mr Victor Fung, Chairman, Li & Fung Group Ltd, On business perceptions and expectations regarding the WTO Doha negotiations' in United Nations Economic and Social Commission for Asia and the Pacific, *Delivering on the WTO Round: A High-level Government–Business Dialogue* (New York: United Nations Publications, 2006) (papers and statements presented at the Conference on Delivering on the WTO Round: A High-Level Government-Business Dialogue for Development, organized by ESCAP in collaboration with the International Trade Centre, UNCTAD/WTO and Government of Macao, China, Macao, China, 4–6 October 2005).

Gilbert, John, Scollay, Robert and Bora, Bijit, 'New regional trading developments in the Asia–Pacific region', in Shahid Yusuf, M. Anjum Altaf and Kaoru Nabeshima (eds.), *Global Change and East Asian Policy Initiatives* (Washington DC: World Bank, 2004), pp. 121–90

Government of India, Ministry of Commerce and Industry, *India's Current Engagements in RTAs* (2006), available at http://commerce.nic.in/india_rta_main.htm (visited 20 May 2006)

Henning, C. Randall, 'Regional economic integration and institution building', in Julie McKay, Maria Oliva Armengol and Georges Pineau (eds.), *Regional Economic Integration in a Global Framework*, G-20 Workshop organized jointly by the People's Bank of China and the European Central Bank, 22–23 September 2004, Beijing, China (Frankfurt: European Central Bank, 2005), pp. 79–100

Hoekman, Bernard and Schiff, Maurice , 'Benefiting from regional integration', in Bernard Hoekman, Aaditya Mattoo and Philip English (eds.), *Development, Trade, and the WTO: A Handbook* (Washington DC: World Bank, 2002), pp. 548–58

Hufbauer, Gary Clyde and Wong, Yee, *Prospects for Regional Free Trade in Asia*, Working Paper 05–12 (Washington DC: Institute for International Economics, 2005). Available at www.iie.com

IMF (International Monetary Fund), *Asia and Pacific Regional Economic Outlook* (Washington DC: International Monetary Fund, 2006). Available at www.imf.org/external/pubs/ft/reo/2006/eng/01/areo0506.htm (visited 8 May 2006)

India–China Joint Study Group, 'Report of the India–China Joint Study Group on comprehensive trade and economic cooperation', 23 March 2005. Available at http://meaindia.nic.in/treatiesagreement/2005/11ta1104200504.pdf (visited 1 June 2006)

Jin, Liqun, 'Issues and challenges in designing free trade agreements in Asia – Welcome remarks by Liqun Jin, Vice-President, Operation 1, Asian Development Bank, at the Brainstorming on Free Trade Agreements' (20 March 2006), available at www.adb.org/Documents/Speeches/2006/ms2006016.asp (visited 16 April 2006)

Kawai, Masahiro, 'East Asian economic regionalism: Progress and challenges' (2005) **16** *Journal of Asia Economics* 29–55

Kharas, Homi, 'Trade and economic integration in the Asia Pacific Region', in OECD (ed.), *Regional Integration in the Asia Pacific: Issues and Prospects* (Paris: Organization for Economic Co-operation and Development, 2005), pp. 103–35

Krumm, Kathie and Kharas, Homi, *East Asia Integrates: A Trade Policy Agenda for Shared Growth* (Washington DC: World Bank; Oxford University Press, 2004)

Kuroda, Haruhiko, 'New dynamics, new opportunities: Toward deeper Asian economic integration', speech by Haruhiko Kuroda, President, Asian Development Bank, at the 31st ASEAN–Japan Business Meeting, 24 November 2005, Bangkok, Thailand. Available at www.adb.org/Documents/Speeches/2005/ms2005084.asp (visited 29 April 2006)

'New visions and models for economic cooperation', speech by Haruhiko Kuroda, President of Asian Development Bank, at the Plenary Session II of the Annual Conference of the Boao Forum of Asia, 22–23 April 2006, Boao,

Hainan. Available at www.adb.org/Documents/Speeches/2006/ms2006025.asp (visited 1 June 2006)

'Towards a borderless Asia: A perspective on Asian economic integration', speech by Haruhiko Kuroda, President, Asian Development Bank, at The Emerging Markets Forum, 10 December 2005, Oxford. Available at www.adb.org/Documents/Speeches/2005/ms2005088.asp (visited 29 April 2006)

Lamberte, Mario B., 'An overview of economic cooperation and integration in Asia', in Asian Development Bank, *Asian Economic Cooperation and Integration: Progress, Prospects, and Challenges* (Manila: Asian Development Bank, 2005)

Lawrence, Robert Z., *Regionalism, Multilateralism, and Deeper Integration* (Washington DC: The Brookings Institution, 1996).

Lee, Jong-Wha and Park, Innwon, 'Free trade areas in East Asia: Discriminatory or non-discriminatory?' (2005) **28** (1) *World Economy* 21–48

Lloyd, Peter, 'Implications for the multilateral trading system of the new preferential trading arrangements in the Asia Pacific Region', paper presented at the PECC Trade Forum) November 2002 available at www.pecc.org

'What is a single market? An application to the case of ASEAN' (2005) **22**(3) *ASEAN Economic Bulletin* 251–65

Lloyd, Peter J. and Smith, Penny, *Global Economic Challenges to ASEAN Integration and Competitiveness: A Prospective Look*, REPSF Project 03/006a (2004) (prepared for the ASEAN Secretariat). Available at www.ausaid.gov.au/publications/pdf/global_econ_challenge.pdf (visited 02 January 2010) (visited 02 January 2010)

Machlup, F., 'Economic integration', in Miroslav N. Jovanovic (ed.), *International Economic Integration: Critical Perspectives on the World Economy*, Volume I: *Theory and Measurement* (London and New York: Routledge, 1998), pp. 119–49

McKay, Julie, Armengol, Maria Oliva and Pineau, Georges (eds.), *Regional Economic Integration in a Global Framework*, G-20 Workshop organized joint by the People's Bank of China and the European Central Bank, 22–23 September 2004, Beijing, China (Frankfurt: European Central Bank, 2005). Available at www.ecb.int/pub/pdf/other/regionaleconintegrationglobalframework2005en.pdf (visited 2 May 2006)

Mehta, Rajesh and Narayanan, S., *India's Regional Trading Agreements*, Discussion paper (UNDP Regional Centre in Colombo, 2005). Available at www.undprcc.lk/web_trade/tradegeneva/10RTA/India%20RTA%20paper.pdf (visited 20 May 2006)

Panagaria, Arvind, 'An India–China free trade area?', *The Economic Times*, 20 April 2005. Available at www.columbia.edu/~ap2231/ET/et77_April20_05.htm (visited 1 June 2006)

'The regionalism debate: An overview' (1999) **22** (4) *World Economy* 477–512

Pelkmans, Jacques, *European Integration: Methods and Economic Analysis*, 2nd edn (London: Financial Times / Prentice Hall, 2001)

Pilling, David, 'ADB chief hits out at "noodle bowl" trade', *Financial Times* (Asia), 2 February 2006.

RIS (Research and Information System for the Non-Aligned and Other Developing Countries), *South Asia Development and Cooperation Report 2004* (New Delhi: RIS, 2004)

Roland-Holst, David, Verbieft, Jean-Pierre and Zhai, Fan, 'Growth and trade horizon for Asia: Long-term forecasts for regional integration' (2005) **25** (2) *Asian Development Review* 76–107

Roy, Jayanta, 'South Asian regional trade agreements: Perspectives, issues and options', paper presented at the International Trade Roundtable *The WTO at 10 Years – The Regional Challenge to Multilateralism*, Brussels, Belgium, 27 June 2005. Available at http://mba.tuck.dartmouth.edu/cib/news/itr_2005_pdf/Roy.pdf (visited 20 May 2006)

Sakakibara, Eisuke and Yamakawa, Sharon, 'Market-driven regional integration in East Asia', in Julie McKay, Maria Oliva Armengol and Georges Pineau (eds.), *Regional Economic Integration in a Global Framework*, G-20 Workshop organized jointly by the People's Bank of China and the European Central Bank, 22–23 September 2004, Beijing, China (Frankfurt: European Central Bank, 2005), pp. 35–78

Siriwardana, Mahinda, 'Trade liberalisation in South Asia: Free trade area or customs union?' (2003) **26** (3) *Journal of South Asian Studies* 309–29

Summers, Lawrence H., 'Regionalism and world trading system', in *Policy Implications of Trade and Currency Zones* (Kansas City: Federal Reserve Bank, 1991), pp. 295–301. Available at www.kansascityfed.org/publicat/Sympos/1991/SYM91.HTM (visited 25 April 2006)

UNCTAD (United Nations Conference on Trade and Development), *Trade and Development Report*, 2004 (Geneva: United Nations, 2004)

Trade and Development Report, 2005 (Geneva: United Nations, 2005)

UNDPPO (United Nations Development Policy and Planning Office), *World Economic Situation and Prospects 2005* (Geneva: United Nations, 2005)

World Economic Situation and Prospects 2006 (Geneva: United Nations, 2006)

UNDP-RCC (UNDP Regional Centre in Colombo), *The Grate Maze – Regional and Bilateral Free Trade Agreements in Asia: Trends, Characteristics and Implications for Human Development*, Discussion Paper (2005). Available at www.undprcc.lk/web_trade/publications/Policy%20Paper%20Book%203.pdf (visited 20 May 2006)

Viner, J. 1950. 'The economics of customs unions', in Miroslav N. Jovanovic (ed.), *International Economic Integration; Critical Perspectives on the World Economy*, Volume I: *Theory and Measurement* (London and New York: Routledge, 1998), pp. 168–83

Wacziarg, Romain, 'India in the world trading system', in T. N. Srinivasan and Irena Asmundson (eds.), *India after a Decade of Economic Reforms* (Stanford University Press, 2005). Available www.stanford.edu/~wacziarg/downloads/indiatrade.pdf (visited 20 May 2006)

Wang, Jiangyu, 'China's regional trade agreements: The law, geopolitics, and impact on the multilateral trading system' (2004) **8** *Singapore Year Book of International Law* 119

'The international legal personality of ASEAN and the legal nature of the China–ASEAN FTA', in John Wong, Zou Keyuan and Zeng Huaqun (eds.), *China–ASEAN Relations: Economic and Legal Dimensions* (Singapore: World Scientific, 2006)

Wang, Gungwu, 'China and Southeast Asia: Changes in strategic perceptions', in Khai Leong Ho and Samuel C. Y. Ku (eds.), *China and Southeast Asia: Global Changes and Regional Challenges* (Singapore: Institute of Southeast Asian Studies, 2005)

Wang, Vincent, 'The logic of China–ASEAN FTA: Economic statecraft of "peaceful ascendancy"', in Khai Leong Ho and Samuel C. Y. Ku (eds.), *China and Southeast Asia: Global Changes and Regional Challenges* (Singapore: Institute of Southeast Asian Studies, 2005).

Wei, Shang-jin and Frankel, Jeffrey A., 'Open regionalism in a world of continental trade blocs' (1998) **45** (3) *IMF Staff Papers* 440–53

Whalley, John, 'Why do countries seek regional trade agreements?' in Jeffrey A. Frankel (ed.), *The Regionalization of the World Economy* (University of Chicago Press, 1998), pp. 63–89

Winters, L. Alan, *Regionalism versus Multilateralism*, World Bank Policy Research Working Paper 1687 (Washington DC: The World Bank, 1996)

World Bank, *China Quarterly Update – February* 2006 (Beijing: World Bank Office)

Global Economic Prospects 2005 (Washington DC: The World Bank, 2005)

Trade Blocs (Oxford: Oxford University Press, 2000)

WTO (World Trade Organization), *International Trade Statistics 2004* (2004)

International Trade Statistics 2005 (2005)

Regionalism and the World Trading System (Geneva: World Trade Organization, 1995)

'Trade policy review: India. Report by the Secretariat' (2002), WTO Document No.: WT/TPR/S/100

'Trade policy review: People's Republic of China – Report by the Secretariat', WTO Document No.: WT/TPR/S/161, 28 February 2006

'World Trade 2005, Prospects for 2006', Press/437, 11 April 2006

11

The Asian Economic Community

ASEAN – A building or a stumbling block for China and India economic cooperation

MICHAEL EWING-CHOW AND EDRICK GAO

I. Introduction

The rise of China and India, two economic superpowers (if not quite yet military superpowers), almost simultaneously is perhaps unprecedented in history and this presents both opportunities and challenges. While the likelihood of actual military conflict has been somewhat limited by norms against the use of force since the Second World War, proxies for actual military conflict are often found as the trade skirmishes fought between the US, Japan and the EU have illustrated.

However, China and India have ostensibly chosen to pursue development strategies based on cooperation rather than competition. China has assured the Asian region that it will stay on the path of peaceful development and it is actively engaging other nations to work towards win-win partnerships. In particular, China has, along with Japan and South Korea, been working with ASEAN in the ASEAN+3 process. India has also embraced a policy that encourages regional cooperation. At the first East Asia Summit (EAS) held in Kuala Lumpur on 14 December 2005, the Indian Prime Minister, Manmohan Singh, outlined his vision of an emerging Asian Economic Community (AEC) as including ASEAN, India and China. He also envisioned a Pan Asian Free Trade Agreement which, together with many other free trade agreements (FTAs) being negotiated in the region, would form the building blocks of the eventual AEC. ASEAN is already in the process of negotiating FTAs with both China and India and has already concluded Framework Agreements (FAs) for these FTAs.

Indeed, with significant progress on the Doha Round of the World Trade Organisation (WTO) looking increasingly difficult, it is likely that progress on trade liberalisation, at least for the near future, will be largely driven by such FTAs. It is therefore important to explore how such regional economic cooperation could be developed. In particular, with ASEAN being central to both China's and India's conception of a regional economic community (whether it is China's more limited ASEAN+3 East Asian Economic Community (EAEC) or India's more encompassing, AEC) the present structure of ASEAN itself should be examined as to its suitability as an integral part for such a regional endeavour. With the need to manage the emergence of two economic superpowers and the importance of regional trade liberalisation as a viable second best alternative to the WTO's multilateral process, the question that must be asked of ASEAN is whether it will be a building block of the AEC or whether it will be a stumbling block for economic cooperation between China and India.

A. *Towards closer economic cooperation*

While only established in 1967, ASEAN's recent emphasis on economic cooperation has intensified over the years and this has already tested its internal processes. Since 1992, ASEAN has formulated numerous agreements which promote greater economic cooperation. These plans include the ASEAN Free Trade Area,[1] the ASEAN Framework Agreement on Services (AFAS), the ASEAN Investment Area,[2] the ASEAN Vision 2020, the Hanoi Plan of Action and the proposal in October 2003 to progress towards an ASEAN Economic Community (ASEAN EC) by 2020.[3]

It is interesting to note that such recent emphasis on economic cooperation was initially prompted by the increasingly competitive environment in Asia particularly by China and India. ASEAN states feared that Southeast Asia would be overtaken by the emerging economies of China and India and foreign direct investment inflows (FDI) would be diverted from ASEAN. ASEAN members hoped that an

[1] Framework Agreement on Enhancing ASEAN Economic Cooperation, Singapore, 28 January 1992. [AFTA]

[2] Framework Agreement on the ASEAN Investment Area, Makati, Philippines, 7 October 1998. [AIA]

[3] Declaration of ASEAN Concord II (Bali Concord II), Bali, Indonesia, 7 October 2003. [AEC]

integrated ASEAN with a market of over 500 million people would retain the region's attractiveness as a foreign direct investment (FDI) destination and revitalise production networks in the region.[4]

With such increasing cooperation, academics such as Acharya,[5] Rüland[6] and Wanadi[7] have argued that ASEAN's integration should be rules-based and supported by formal and institutionalised mechanisms for cooperation. They criticise ASEAN's current institutional framework and warn that the continued failure to establish formalised institutions would impede economic cooperation.

Recent economic data, however, suggest that the growth of China and India is not necessarily a zero-sum game for ASEAN. During the period 1990–2002, both China and Southeast Asia increased their share of global merchandise exports.[8] Despite the increase in China's trade surplus with the United States and its FDI inflows, Southeast Asian economies have gained a larger share of global exports as they have increasingly become part of the supply chain of industrial components and raw materials that China needs for its export-led growth. From 2003 to 2004, FDI into ASEAN grew by 20.4%, surpassing flows into China (13.2%) and slightly below the amount going to India (27.9%).[9] While it is likely that some trade and FDI diversion from ASEAN has occurred, an explanation for this aggregate win-win situation is that production networks in Asia are highly integrated and with manufacturing across different locations and by a high level of trade in intermediate inputs.[10] In addition, China and India should not be seen only as factories churning out low-cost goods and services but also as rapidly growing markets, with

[4] Denis Hew, 'Introduction: Roadmap to an ASEAN Economic Community', in Denis Hew (ed.), *Roadmap to an ASEAN Economic Community* (Singapore: ISEAS Publications, 2005) at 4.

[5] Amitav Acharya, 'Realism, institutionalism and the Asian economic crisis' (1999) 21(1) *Contemporary Southeast Asia* 1 at 19.

[6] J. Rüland, 'ASEAN and the Asian crisis: Theoretical implications and practical consequences for Southeast Asian regionalism' (2000) 13(3) *The Pacific Review* 421 at 444.

[7] Jusuf Wanandi, 'ASEAN's challenges for its future', *The PacNet Newsletter* (22 January 1999), online: Columbia International Affairs Online, available at www.ciaonet.org/pbei/csis/pac99/waj01/.

[8] Manu Bhaskaran, *The Economic Impact of China and India on Southeast Asia, Southeast Asian Affairs* (ISEAS, 2005).

[9] Raymond Lim, 'Creating a globally connected Asian community, finance and development' (2006) 43(2) *Finance and Development*, 'Point of View'.

[10] *Ibid.*

a demand proportional to their populations for goods and services produced in Asia and elsewhere.[11]

All of this has made it even more attractive for ASEAN, China and India to seek regional economic cooperation. While ASEAN is also currently negotiating other economic partnerships with Japan, South Korea and the closer economic partnership countries of Australia and New Zealand, it is nonetheless China and India who will shape the development of regional economic cooperation. Whether ASEAN will be the lynchpin for this development will depend on whether ASEAN itself can continue to drive the current initiatives forward.

B. Objectives of this chapter

In light of these developments in Asia, the main objective of this chapter is to provide suggestions on how ASEAN should achieve the goal of forming the AEC.

Section II will use game theory to propose that certain legal rules and institutions should exist in ASEAN as a foundation stone of the AEC. Such a proposal will be reached by examining the applicability of game theory to economic cooperation and by the identification of the obstacles preventing the formation of the AEC. The relationship between these rules and institutions will also be discussed.

Section III will focus on the first requirement of clearly defined rules and obligations. It will examine the current rules within ASEAN and argue that ASEAN does not fulfil this requirement. Suggestions will be provided on the possible reforms to achieve this requirement.

Section IV will examine the requirement of having a decision-making institution. It will examine the various decision-making bodies within ASEAN and demonstrate how these bodies do not fulfil the second requirement. Suggestions on the possible reforms to this area will be made.

Section V will examine whether ASEAN fulfils the requirement of a monitoring institution and provides suggestions on possible reforms.

Section VI will examine the requirement of having an enforcement institution. It will argue that the current enforcement institutions in ASEAN do not fulfil this requirement. Suggestions on the

[11] *Ibid.*

various reforms to achieve an effective ASEAN enforcement institution will be proposed.

Finally, section VII will examine the structure of the Framework Agreements (FAs) of both ASEAN–China FTA (ACFTA) and ASEAN–India FTA (AIFTA) to assess whether they have similar inherent weaknesses and will apply the preceding analysis to recommend structural changes to facilitate the formation and implementation of an AEC.

II. Game theory and institutions

This section examines the relevance of game theory to economic cooperation. Using game theory, it analyses the obstacles to economic cooperation and proposes that four rules and institutions are required in order to achieve the AEC.

A. *Prisoners' dilemma and economic cooperation*

Game theorists identify the Prisoners' Dilemma problem as an obstacle to cooperation.[12] The Prisoners' Dilemma problem involves two players – player A and player B. Applying the paradigm of the Prisoners' Dilemma problem to trade liberalisation, if both players cooperate by opening their economies to each other, the net gain is maximised and if both players choose to defect by not opening their economies, the net loss is maximised.

However, if player A cooperates while player B defects, player A would be placed in a worse situation compared to the scenario where both players do not cooperate as player A would have opened its economy to player B while not having equal access to player B's economy. In contrast, player B would be placed in a better situation compared to the scenario when both players cooperate as player B would have greater access to player A's economy while protecting its domestic industries. The converse situation where player B cooperates and player A defects would have similar results with player A having maximum gain and player B having maximum loss. As a result, each player would have equal incentives to cooperate or to defect.[13]

[12] Zakir Hafez, *The Dimensions of Regional Trade Integration in Southeast Asia* (New York: Transnational Publishers, 2004) at 245.
[13] *Ibid.*

Game theorists note that in international cooperation, each state would choose the dominant strategy of defecting while hoping that the other states would cooperate as such a strategy would result in the highest individual payoff for each. Unfortunately, both states eventually end up being worse off. Game theorists note that the dilemma persists even if cooperation is achieved because both states continue to have strong incentives to defect.[14]

There are several reasons why a state would choose to defect by closing its economy while expecting other states to open their markets. These reasons include protecting domestic infant industries, protecting jobs and the protection of national sovereignty. These reasons for defection are evident in the trade lixberalisation process in ASEAN as members frequently resort to long exclusion lists and only include non-trading goods under the inclusion list for tariff reduction purposes.[15]

B. *Use of rules and institutions to facilitate cooperation*

Game theory suggests that in order to facilitate cooperation, rational players would create institutions to systematically implement strategies that increase the likelihood of sustained cooperation over time. By creating institutions that affect payoff structures in a predictable manner, players who are choosing strategies would be more likely to cooperate.[16] These facilitative institutions include monitoring institutions and enforcement institutions that have power to punish players who defect.[17] Such institutions adjust payoffs either by rewarding cooperators or punishing defectors and thus increase the incentive for cooperation.[18]

However, a prerequisite of such institutions is the existence of clear rules and obligations of the game. Such rules and obligations form the basis of such cooperation. Monitoring institutions and enforcement institutions are only important when there are rules and obligations to monitor and enforce. Hence, clear rules and obligations are essential to economic cooperation.

In addition, Frischmann has argued that in addition to clearly defined rules and obligations, monitoring institutions and enforcement institution, states should create institutions directed not only at detecting defection and altering payoffs in the event of defection but

[14] *Ibid.* at 246. [15] *Ibid.*

[16] Brett Frischmann, 'A dynamic institutional theory of international law' (2003) 51 Buff. L. Rev. 679 at 721.

[17] *Ibid.* at 719. [18] *Ibid.* at 721.

decision-making institutions which allow the adjustment of the rules of the game.[19] Frischmann contends that the games being played by states evolve in response to exogenous events which are independent of players' performance and chosen strategies. He argues that exogenous events, such as a significant change in economic or political conditions, would affect the stability of the game by altering the payoff structure.[20] Hence, states should create decision-making institutions to reduce uncertainty and transaction costs associated with such events by allowing such institutions to adjust commitments in future iterations.[21]

In summary, following the preceding analysis, four factors are crucial to ensure that players will choose a strategy which promotes cooperation. These factors are required in order to achieve the AEC. First, there should be clearly defined rules and obligations which allow players to be aware of the parameters of the game. Second, there should be decision-making institutions which allow the adjustment of the rules of the game in response to exogenous events. Third, there should be monitoring institutions which monitor and implement the rules and obligations. Finally, there should be enforcement institutions which deter defection by enforcing the rules and obligations of the game.

The following sections examine whether ASEAN's institutional framework satisfies each of these four requirements. Reforms will be recommended to bring ASEAN's institutional framework in line with these four requirements.

III. Rules and obligations

Rules and obligations are required to form an AEC as they set the parameters of the game such that members know exactly how they are expected to act. Such rules and obligations should be in clearly enforceable forms. Otherwise, there would be nothing an enforcement institution could enforce. This section examines ASEAN's current rules and contends that ASEAN itself does not satisfy this requirement. Also, suggestions on possible reforms that may be undertaken will be made.

A. ASEAN's current rules and obligations

ASEAN's current rules and obligations are contained in a variety of documents such as ASEAN Free Trade Area (AFTA), ASEAN Framework

[19] *Ibid.* at 722. [20] *Ibid.* [21] *Ibid.*

Agreement on Services (AFAS), ASEAN Investment Area (AIA), the ASEAN Vision 2020, the Hanoi Plan of Action and the Bali Concord II.

The AFTA focuses on the gradual reduction of intra-ASEAN tariffs under the Common Effective Preferential Tariff Scheme.[22] The AFAS focuses on services liberalisation. In addition, the AIA focuses on functional cooperation and investment facilitation programmes, awareness-raising measures and investment liberalisation. The AIA is made up of a mixture of declarations of intent, pledges and national and collective commitments.[23]

The ASEAN Vision 2020, the Hanoi Plan of Action and the Bali Concord II are focused on achieving free flow of goods, services, investment and a freer flow of capital in ASEAN by 2020 via the AEC.[24]

B. Problems with ASEAN's current rules and obligations

1. Unclear provisions regarding the applicability of ASEAN's rules and ASEAN's lack of legal personality

Currently there are no clear provisions on the applicability of ASEAN's rules to member states. Such ambiguity affects cooperation because member states do not know clearly how they are obligated to carry out ASEAN's rules.

This ambiguity is worsened by ASEAN's lack of legal personality.[25] Even if the relationship between ASEAN's rules and domestic laws is clearly stated, if ASEAN does not have legal status, it would indirectly cause member states to perceive ASEAN's rules as of lower status. This is because if ASEAN as an entity has only a quasi-legal status, it is possible that members would not perceive the legal rules of such an entity as binding.

Therefore, these two factors result in the lack of clear rules and obligation in ASEAN.

[22] Agreement on the Common Effective Preferential Tariff Scheme for the ASEAN Free Trade Area, Singapore, 28 January 1992. [CEPT]

[23] Chia Siow Yue, 'ASEAN–China Free Trade Area', online: Hong Kong Institute of Economic and Business Strategies, available at www.hiebs.hku.hk/aep/Chia.pdf at 3.

[24] *Ibid.*

[25] Rodolfo Severino, 'Framing the ASEAN charter: An ISEAS perspective', in Rodolfo Severino (ed.), *Framing the ASEAN Charter: An ISEAS Perspective* (Singapore: ISEAS Publications, 2005) at 6.

2. Loopholes in ASEAN's agreements

Currently, there are loopholes in some of ASEAN's agreements. For example, the Agreement on the Common Effective Preferential Tariff (CEPT) Scheme for the ASEAN Free Trade Area (AFTA) provides loopholes which allow countries to withdraw tariff concessions which they are obligated to make. This is evident in the 2003 Protocol Regarding the Implementation of the CEPT Scheme Temporary Exclusion List (CEPT Protocol) which states that it seeks to provide flexibility for members.[26]

These regulations undermine the CEPT because they allow ASEAN members to withdraw tariff commitments which have already been agreed upon under the liberalisation scheme. Also, as ASEAN had already enacted another CEPT amendment – the 1999 Protocol on the Special Arrangement for Sensitive and Highly Sensitive Products (Sensitive Protocol) – the CEPT already allows ASEAN members flexibility to backtrack from their commitments on sensitive products. In addition, as only the products under the CEPT Inclusion List are subject to liberalisation, it should be noted that specific tariff lines can be kept out of the Inclusion List interminably.

While flexibility is required for any relationship to work, as a result of these loopholes, there are effectively no real rules or obligations which ASEAN members are bound to in relation to ASEAN's internal tariff reduction. Indeed, the very genesis of the CEPT Protocol was as a retrospective legitimisation of Malaysia's withdrawal in 2002 of automobiles, and completely knocked down automobile kits from the AFTA tariff reductions it had previously agreed upon. All of this has shown that ASEAN members can backtrack from their commitments on scheduled tariff liberalisation at no great political or economic cost.[27]

3. Certain ASEAN rules and obligations are too broad

Currently, certain ASEAN rules and obligations are too broad. Academics have observed that some of these rules and obligations such as those in the Hanoi Plan of Action appear to be more philosophical than directly enforceable.[28]

[26] Marcus Hund, 'From "neighbourhood watch group" to community? The case of ASEAN institutions and the pooling of sovereignty' (2002) 56(1) *Australian Journal of International Affairs* 99 at 103.

[27] *Ibid.* at 104.

[28] Simon S. C. Tay, 'Institutions and processes: Dilemmas and possibilities', in Simon S. C. Tay, Jesus P. Estanislao and Hadi Soesastro (ed.), *Reinventing ASEAN* (Singapore: Institute of Southeast Asian Studies, 2001) at 265.

Therefore, in light of such deficiencies, ASEAN does not fulfil the first requirement of the elements needed to achieve the AEC. Therefore, reforms should be made such that ASEAN has clear rules and obligations.

C. *Reforms which will allow ASEAN to have clear rules and obligations*

1. Clarification of ASEAN's legal personality

ASEAN should be established as a juridical personality and legal entity.[29] While this will not have a direct effect of creating clear rules and obligations in ASEAN, such a reform will elevate the status of ASEAN as an entity. Such an elevation in status should give rise to a stronger sense of obligation among ASEAN members in relation to ASEAN's rules.

2. Clarification of the applicability of ASEAN's rules and obligations on ASEAN members

There is a need to clarify the applicability of ASEAN's rules and obligations on ASEAN members. ASEAN members need to know the applicability of such rules in order to know how they are obligated to comply. In this regard, some characteristics of the European Union (EU) could be examined. Such a reference to the EU is appropriate because with the exception of the EU, few countries have attempted plans which are as ambitious as the AEC.[30] However, due regard will be given to the differing circumstances of the EU and ASEAN.

Like the EU, the rules in ASEAN could be split into directives and regulations. A regulation should be binding in its entirety and have direct applicability. Such provisions are self-executing and confer rights and obligations on member states without further legislative participation.[31]

In contrast, a directive is only binding in its objectives. Member states have some leeway in its introduction and the manner in which it is introduced in their countries.[32]

[29] Locknie Hsu, 'Towards an ASEAN charter: Some thoughts from the legal perspective', in Rodolfo Severino (ed.), *Framing the ASEAN Charter: An ISEAS Perspective* (Singapore: ISEAS Publications, 2005) at 47.

[30] N. Akraseanee and J. Arunanondchai, 'Institutional reforms to achieve ASEAN market integration' in Sharon Siddique and Sree Kumar (ed.), *The 2nd ASEAN Reader* (Singapore: Institute of Southeast Asian Studies, 2003) at 509.

[31] Hilaire Barnett, *Constitutional & Administrative Law*, 3rd edn (Sydney: Cavendish Publishing Limited, 2000) at 322.

[32] *Ibid.*

Hence, with a clear definition of such rules and obligations, ASEAN members will have clear ideas of the applicability of ASEAN's rules and obligations on them.

3. Consolidation of existing rules and obligations

The existing rules and obligations in ASEAN should be consolidated and clarified. Using the classification scheme proposed above, the existing rules and obligations should be divided in directives and regulations. Once the effect of the existing rules and obligations are clarified, ASEAN members would be expected to follow them.

4. Removal of loopholes

The loopholes of the AFTA should be addressed. For example, the different exclusion lists should be phased out because they render the rules and obligations ineffective.

In summary, the existing rules and obligations in ASEAN are not sufficiently clear. Thus, the reforms proposed could be adopted in order to achieve the requirement of clear rules and obligations. If ASEAN internally cannot create clear rules and obligations, then the creation of clear rules for an AEC with the two economic giants of China and India will be even more difficult.

IV. Decision-making institutions

Decision-making institutions are the second of four requirements which, having reference to game theory, are important for achieving the AEC. As such institutions are meant to promote cooperation in ASEAN, there should be a significant neutral element representing ASEAN's community interests – an honest broker, if you will.

This section reviews the current institutions within ASEAN to see if the requirement of a decision-making institution is satisfied. Reforms will be suggested on how ASEAN should evolve into an effective decision-making institution.

A. ASEAN's current decision-making structure

Currently, the decisions in ASEAN are made up by a number of ministerial meetings, senior officials meetings and to a certain extent the ASEAN Secretariat and the Secretary-General.[33]

[33] Paul J Davidson, *ASEAN: The Evolving Legal Framework for Economic Cooperation* (Singapore: Times International Publishing, 2002) at 21.

1. ASEAN Heads of Government Meeting

The ASEAN Heads of Government Meeting (AHGM) is the supreme decision-making authority in ASEAN which is in charge of laying the direction and initiatives for ASEAN activities. This meeting comprises the heads of the member states.[34]

2. Ministerial meetings

The various ministerial meetings are second in hierarchy to the AHGM. The two most prominent ministerial meetings are the Annual Ministerial Meeting (AMM) and the ASEAN Economic Ministers Meeting (AEMM).[35]

The AMM comprises the Foreign Ministers of member states. The main functions of the AMM are (i) the coordination of the policies of different ASEAN working units, (ii) the formulation of policy guidelines, (iii) the review of all decisions and (iv) handing down the approved policies and programmes to the various bodies.[36]

The AEMM is tasked to handle all aspects of ASEAN economic cooperation.[37]

In addition, there are other meetings among Ministers of specific sectors of economic cooperation and among Ministers of non-economic areas.

3. Meetings of senior officials

In addition to the variety of ministerial meetings, the meetings of various senior officials of ASEAN members are also part of the decision-making structure. These meetings include (i) the Senior Officials Meeting which is in charge of political matters, (ii) the Senior Economic Officials Meeting (SEOM) which is in charge of economic matters and (iii) other Senior Officials Meetings in other areas such as environment.[38]

4. ASEAN Secretariat and the Secretary-General of ASEAN

The ASEAN Secretariat is the central administrative organ of ASEAN. It has a variety of functions. In relation to decision-making, the ASEAN Secretariat is theoretically supposed to have the right to initiate certain ASEAN matters.[39]

The ASEAN Secretariat is headed by the Secretary-General of ASEAN who is appointed based on merit for a renewable period of five years by

[34] *Ibid.* [35] *Ibid.* at 23. [36] *Ibid.*
[37] *Ibid.* [38] *Ibid.* [39] *Ibid.* at 37.

the ASEAN Heads of Government. The Secretary-General is accorded ministerial status and like the ASEAN Secretariat is theoretically given some decision-making powers in the form of initiating measures in relation to ASEAN activities.[40]

B. *Problems with ASEAN's current decision-making structure*

1. Lack of clear objectives of cooperation

The clarity of the objectives of cooperation is important to the effectiveness of a decision-making institution in an indirect way. In order for the decision-making institution to make rules to help in the development of ASEAN cooperation, the decision-making institution must know what ASEAN is planning to advance towards. The institution will only be able to make useful decisions when there is a clear end goal.

However, ASEAN's current objectives of cooperation are scattered in numerous documents. Critics note that such objectives are too broad to provide clear guidance for decision-making.[41] An example of such ambiguity can be found in the proposal to achieve the ASEAN EC by 2020. Critics note that the end goal of the ASEAN EC is not clearly defined conceptually. These critics observe that the end goal could be a FTA-plus arrangement, a customs union or even a common market. These critics further observe that the ASEAN EC project is losing momentum due to such ambiguity.[42]

2. Problems with the structure of existing decision-making bodies

(a) Lack of clear division of decision-making powers between the current decision-making bodies ASEAN has been criticised for the lack of an integrated decision-making structure. Current decision-making powers are too fragmented as numerous bodies exercise such powers.[43] In addition, the power and jurisdiction of the numerous ministerial meetings are unclear. For example, although the AHGM is

[40] *Ibid.* at 26.

[41] Rodolfo Severino, 'Framing the ASEAN charter: An ISEAS perspective'.

[42] Denis Hew, 'Towards an ASEAN charter: Regional economic integration' in Rodolfo Severino (ed.), *Framing the ASEAN Charter: An ISEAS Perspective* (Singapore: ISEAS Publications, 2005) at 38.

[43] Muthiah Alagappa, 'Institutional framework recommendations for change', in Sharon Siddique and Sree Kumar (eds.), *The 2nd ASEAN Reader* (Singapore: Institute of Southeast Asian Studies, 2003) at 23.

supposed to be the highest decision-making body, it has no specific role in the management of ASEAN cooperation apart from providing political direction. Moreover, there is a lack of coordination between the two other key decision-making organs of ASEAN – the AMM and the AEMM.[44]

Such a lack of clear delineation of power and jurisdiction of the various decision-making bodies leads to an absence of an effective decision-making institution in ASEAN.

(b) Dominant emphasis on national interests and national representation Currently, there is a dominant emphasis on national interests and national representation in the decision-making structure. This is evident from the fact that most of the decision-making bodies are made up of the national representatives of the ASEAN member states. There are no decision-making bodies which represent ASEAN's community interest.[45]

This is unlike the EU which has several supranational institutions in particular, the European Presidency and Commission, which could act as honest brokers. While the EU is a completely different creature from ASEAN and care must be taken when comparing the two entities, rational choice institutionalism and game theory suggest that supranational institutions with informational and procedural resources to set negotiation agendas and to prepare the ground for decision-making, alleviate the risk of negotiation failure by acting as honest brokers.[46]

Moreover, the only arguably supranational body in ASEAN, the ASEAN Secretariat, suffers from some deficiencies. Critics note that the home-based staff system adopted in staffing the ASEAN Secretariat places emphasis on national representation and this affects the ability of the ASEAN Secretariat to represent ASEAN's community interest effectively. In addition, the ASEAN Secretariat is chronically understaffed and underfinanced. The ASEAN Secretariat employs around 100 staff in contrast to the 500 million people represented by ASEAN.[47] Hence, the Secretariat does not have the capacity or the potential to assume a supranational role in ASEAN and has been relegated to a subordinate position in relation to decision-making.

[44] *Ibid.* [45] *Ibid.*

[46] See Jonas Tallberg, 'The power of the Presidency: Brokerage, efficiency and distribution in EU negotiations' (2004) 42(5) *Journal of Common Market Studies* 999–1002.

[47] Agreement on the Common Effective Preferential Tariff Scheme for the ASEAN Free Trade Area, Singapore at 115.

As a result of the dominant emphasis on national interests and national representation in ASEAN, there is a lack of an effective decision-making institution to promote regional integration. As discussed in a preceding section, as decision-making institutions are meant to promote cooperation in ASEAN, there should be a significant neutral element representing ASEAN's community interests.

(c) **Low frequency of meetings among key decision-making organs** In addition, the key decision-making organs in ASEAN only function periodically. For example, the AMM and the AEMM only take place twice a year on average and the AHGM only takes place once a year informally. Such infrequent meetings have led to excessively long durations to process major programmes.[48]

(d) **Method of making decisions – Problems with the ASEAN way** The current method of making decisions in ASEAN is characterised by the ASEAN Way. The ASEAN Way of making decisions emphasises the requirement of consensus on all issues. Critics note that this method of decision-making is inefficient because even when a proposal would benefit ASEAN's community interest, such a proposal can be struck down by a sole dissenting member.[49]

Therefore, in light of such inadequacies, ASEAN does not fulfil the second requirement needed to achieve the AEC. Hence, reforms should be made to enable ASEAN to fulfil this requirement.

C. *Reforms to create effective decision-making institutions*

1. Setting the objectives and guidelines for cooperation (two elements)

There are two main elements which are important to provide guidance to decision-making institutions.

First, the end goal of the regional integration should be clearly defined. Academics have suggested that the ultimate goal of should be a common market which would require the elimination of all barriers to

[48] Davidson, *ASEAN: The Evolving Legal Framework for Economic Cooperation*.

[49] Hadi Soesastro, 'ASEAN in 2030: The long view', in Simon S.C. Tay, Jesus P. Estanislao and Hadi Soesastro (eds.), *Reinventing ASEAN* (Singapore: Institute of Southeast Asian Studies, 2001) at 281.

trade in goods among members. Members should also be required to adopt a common external tariff. In addition, there should be free movement of goods, services, people and capital within the AEC.[50]

However, as any potential AEC currently would inevitably include countries with significantly different levels of economic development, a common market is unlikely to be achieved. Like the EU, movement towards a common market should be in phases. It has been suggested that ASEAN should lead the way with the first phase being an AFTA-Plus arrangement by 2020.[51] Such an AFTA-Plus arrangement would require the elimination of barriers to trade in goods between members and freer movement of goods, services, investments, capital and labour. The second phase would be to achieve a customs union by 2030. In addition to the progress under the first phase, a customs union would require a common external tariff to be set up which members would apply to trade with non-members. The third phase would require the establishment of an common market by 2050.

Regardless of whether these phases and deadlines are achievable, clear goals such as these will allow a decision-making institution to formulate rules which are consistent with a plan.

Second, another guideline which should direct the decision-making institution to the development gaps between the more developed ASEAN–6 countries[52], the CLMV,[53] China and India. Such a guideline to decision-making is important in order to avoid the creation of a multi-tiered AEC. Therefore, any decision-making institutions should make special consideration for the less developed countries by measures such as providing special timelines for the performance of their commitments.[54] This has been already an informal guideline adopted within ASEAN for the CLMV countries which should be expanded to the AEC.

2. New Roles of decision-making institutions

The following sub-sections (1)–(5) will describe a possible restructuring of the decision-making bodies in ASEAN if ASEAN is to be a building block of the AEC. Significant reference will be made to the EU in order

[50] Denis Hew, '*De facto* Economic Integration in East Asia', online: Korean Institute for International Economic Policy, available at www.kiep.go.kr/inc/download.asp?fnm=(2005–09–05–065003433279927)%20Denis%20Hew.pdf at 11.

[51] Davidson, *ASEAN: The Evolving Legal Framework for Economic Cooperation* at 39.

[52] These countries are Singapore, Malaysia, Indonesia, Brunei, Thailand and the Philippines.

[53] These countries are Cambodia, Laos, Myanmar and Vietnam.

[54] Hund, 'From "Neighbourhood Watch Group" to Community', at 50.

to formulate such institutions. As mentioned previously, such a reference is made because with the exception of the EU, few countries have attempted the ambitious plan considered by ASEAN. Hence, despite the differing circumstances of the EU and ASEAN, the EU could provide important indications on how to achieve the AEC.

(a) **Role of the ASEAN heads of government** The AHGM should be institutionalised and have its functions clearly defined in a legally binding document such as an ASEAN Charter. It is proposed that this meeting should have the main function of providing general political guidance and impetus. In this way, the AHGM would be in charge of setting the agenda for cooperation within ASEAN.

(b) **Role of the ministerial meetings** The various ministerial meetings should be institutionalised and form the ASEAN Council of Ministers. The ASEAN Council of Ministers would consolidate all the various ministerial meetings such as the AMM and the AEM. Different groups of ministers would meet under the ASEAN Council of Ministers depending on the agenda. The areas of responsibility of each group of ministers should be clearly defined in a legally binding document such as an ASEAN Charter. Such responsibility should not overlap in order to prevent a conflict among the areas of responsibility.

For example, the functions of the Economic Ministers could include: (i) the advancement of ASEAN's economic cooperation, (ii) the formulation of proposals promoting the integration of the regional economy, (iii) the handling of ASEAN's relations with non-ASEAN members on economic matters, and (iv) the coordination of ASEAN positions in international economic forums.[55]

Within these clearly defined areas of responsibility, the ASEAN Council of Ministers would have two main functions. The first function would be to refine the broad agendas set by the ASEAN Heads of Government. The second function would be to approve the legislations proposed by the ASEAN Secretariat.[56]

(c) **Role of senior officials and technical committees** The current senior officials meetings and the various technical committees should be reorganised as committees providing a supporting role to enable the

[55] Frischmann, 'A dynamic institutional theory of international law', at 21.
[56] The reformed function of the ASEAN Secretariat will be discussed later.

Council of Ministers to fulfil its dual functions. Such committees should provide the necessary assistance such as carrying out research, surveys and other matters which the Council of Ministers require to refine the agendas for cooperation and to decide whether to adopt the proposed legislations.

(d) Role of the ASEAN Secretariat and the Secretary-General Both the ASEAN Secretariat and the Secretary-General should have stronger powers. Under the new decision-making structure, the main function of the ASEAN Secretariat, which is headed by the Secretary-General, should be to formulate legislative proposals. This function should be clearly defined in a legally binding document. In carrying out its function, the ASEAN Secretariat and the Secretary-General should seek to further ASEAN's community interests. In this respect, the ASEAN Secretariat would be similar to the European Commission.[57]

In order to ensure that the ASEAN Secretariat is able to take on such a supranational function, there are two important considerations. First, the members of the ASEAN Secretariat should be independent. Second, the ASEAN Secretariat should have adequate resources such as sufficient manpower and sufficient funding.

In order to ensure the independence of the ASEAN Secretariat, its staff should be recruited competitively from the citizens of ASEAN states based on merit. In addition, the staff of the ASEAN Secretariat should not hold positions in the governments of member states.

Furthermore, in order to meet the demands of such an important role, the ASEAN Secretariat should be given adequate funding. Various methods can be used to achieve this. The ASEAN Secretariat could be given the right to propose an annual budget to finance its needs. Such a proposal would have to be approved by the AGHM.

Such a reform of the ASEAN Secretariat is admittedly a controversial suggestion. However, as discussed previously, a significant neutral element representing ASEAN's community interests should be present in the decision-making structure. Among the various decision-making institutions, the ASEAN Secretariat is least influenced by the governments of ASEAN members. Thus, this makes it a natural candidate to fulfil the requirement of a neutral decision-making institution.

[57] J. Peterson and M. Shackleton, *The Institutions of the European Union* (New York: Oxford University Press, 2002) at 152.

In addition, at the current time, the ASEAN Secretariat is already supposed to initiate matters that promote cooperation in ASEAN. The additional function of proposing legislations could be seen as giving substance to its current theoretical role.

(e) **Relationship between the different institutions** According to this proposed model, decision-making in ASEAN should proceed as follows. The AHGM would suggest broad agendas for cooperation. Thereafter, the Council of Ministers would refine these broad agendas by providing clearer guidelines. Using these guidelines, the ASEAN Secretariat would come up with legislative proposals. These legislative proposals would then be submitted to the Council of Ministers for approval. Thereafter, the Council of Ministers would decide whether to adopt these legislative proposals. These decision-making institutions should meet regularly in order to ensure efficient rates of decision-making.

In this model, there is sufficient balance between national representation and the representation of ASEAN's community interest.

3. New methods of making decisions

(a) **The '2+X' principle** The '2+X' principle is an alternative to the ASEAN Way of making decisions. This principle was first suggested at the Bali Summit. This principle allows two member countries to integrate specific sectors first.[58] Hence ASEAN members who are keen to expedite economic integration could use this principle. Other ASEAN members would then join when they are ready. However, academics note that such an approach could alienate the less developed ASEAN member countries such as the CLMV as more developed ASEAN members would move ahead. These academics also worry that the bilateral nature of this process could lead to a *fait accompli* where the third '+X'country may be bound to whatever had been agreed by the first two countries.[59] Such problems could impede economic cooperation.

In light of these problems, the following method of making decisions would be more appropriate.

(b) **Five categories of decisions** Another alternative to the ASEAN Way would be to make distinctions between five types of issues.

[58] Davidson, *ASEAN: The Evolving Legal Framework for Economic Cooperation*, at 38.

[59] Tallberg, 'The power of the Presidency: Brokerage, Efficiency and Distribution in EU negotiations', at 10.

These five types of issues would be subject to different rules of decision-making.[60]

Severino suggests that the five types of issues should be: (i) matters fundamental to ASEAN such as amendments to fundamental ASEAN documents, the admission of members and the appointment of the Secretary-General; (ii) matters that involve the suspension of members or the imposition of sanctions; (iii) matters involving economic arrangements and agreements dealing with transnational problems; (iv) matters relating to administrative and budgetary issues and (v) procedural matters.[61]

Severino suggests that type (i) issues should be decided by the AHGM and would require unanimity. In addition, type (ii) issues should also require unanimity but without the participation of the member state that is the subject of the proposed suspension or sanction. Type (iii) issues should be decided based on a simple majority by the ministerial bodies concerned. Type (iv) and type (v) issues should be subject to the decisions by the Council of Foreign Ministers. The same requirement should apply to matters under (v).[62]

Such a method of decision-making would be more efficient compared to requiring consensus for all matters. As issues differ in importance, it is logical that the requirements to make decisions should vary in accordance to the importance of the issues. This method of decision-making would lead to a more effective decision-making institution.

In summary, the current decision-making bodies in ASEAN do not work well enough to undertake the role envisaged by game theory. Such a situation would affect the progress towards the AEC. Thus, the reforms proposed could be adopted in order to achieve the requirement of an effective decision-making institution.

V. Monitoring institutions

Monitoring institutions are the third of four requirements which, having reference to game theory, are important for promoting cooperation between member states. The main functions of such institutions are to monitor the actions of the players in order to ensure that players do not defect and to implement the rules and obligations of the game like, if one expands on the metaphor of the Prisoner's Dilemma, a police force.

[60] Frischmann, 'A dynamic institutional theory of international law', at 26.
[61] *Ibid.* [62] *Ibid.* at 27.

Since monitoring institutions are intended to prevent the players from defecting, it is necessary for these institutions to have a strong neutral element representing ASEAN's community interests. Allowing a monitoring institution to be dominated by the representatives of member states is tantamount to asking a player to prevent himself/herself from defecting.

This section examines the organisations which currently perform such functions in ASEAN and identify the problems affecting such organisations. Suggestions regarding the reforms which will ensure effective monitoring institutions in ASEAN will be provided.

A. *ASEAN's current monitoring organisations*

1. ASEAN Secretariat and the Secretary-General

The ASEAN Secretariat's and Secretary-General's functions of initiating ASEAN activities have already been described in relation to ASEAN's decision-making structures. However, in addition to those functions, the ASEAN Secretariat and the Secretary-General have the additional duties of implementing and monitoring ASEAN's rules and obligations. For example, the ASEAN Secretariat has a Bureau of Functional Cooperation which is in charge of monitoring, coordinating and implementing the Actions Plans for Science and Technology, Environment and Culture and Information.[63]

2. AFTA Council

The AFTA Council is tasked to supervise, monitor and coordinate the implementation of the CEPT. It comprises ministerial-level members from member states and the Secretary-General and is appointed by the AEMM.[64]

3. AIA Council

The AIA Council is tasked with monitoring and implementing the AIA. The AIA Council is established by the AEMM and comprises the ministers responsible for investment and the ASEAN Secretary-General.[65]

63 Akraseanee and Arunanondchai, 'Institutional reforms to achieve ASEAN market integration', at 25.

64 Agreement on the Common Effective Preferential Tariff Scheme for the ASEAN Free Trade Area at 103.

65 *Ibid* at 106.

B. *Problems with ASEAN's current monitoring organisations*

1. Weaknesses of the ASEAN Secretariat and the Secretary-General

The weaknesses of the ASEAN Secretariat described previous also affects its effectiveness as a monitoring body. These weaknesses include the lack of manpower, lack of funds and the subordinate role of the ASEAN Secretariat. Also, the home-based staff policy adopted in staffing the ASEAN Secretariat affects the ability of the ASEAN Secretariat to represent ASEAN's community interests effectively.

2. Dominant emphasis on national interests and national representation in the AFTA Council and the AIA Council

The criticisms made against the AFTA Council and the AIA Council regarding their effectiveness as monitoring institutions are similar. Critics note that the AFTA Council and the AIA Council are not independent bodies overseeing the unconditional implementation of the CEPT and the AIA respectively. As these councils are made up of the ministers of ASEAN states, they are merely the extended arm of the national governments of these states.[66]

As discussed previously, a strong neutral element representing ASEAN's community interests is essential for an effective monitoring institution. Based on the function required of a monitoring institution, according to game theory, the AFTA Council and the AIA Council are ineffective monitoring institutions. This is due to the domination of representatives of member states in these councils and the absence of a neutral element representing ASEAN's community interests.

Therefore, in light of such deficiencies, ASEAN does not fulfil the third factor needed to progress towards the AEC. Hence, reforms should be made.

C. *Reforms to create effective monitoring institutions*

Since an important requirement of an effective monitoring institution is independence from the players, all monitoring functions should be carried out by the ASEAN Secretariat. The various Councils and organisations in charge of the monitoring and implementation of ASEAN rules and obligations should be centralised with the ASEAN Secretariat.

[66] *Ibid.*

Within the ASEAN Secretariat, different committees may be formed and be in charge of a specific area of cooperation. For example, an investment committee will be in charge of the monitoring and implementation of the rules and obligations in relation to investment cooperation.

In addition, the staff of the ASEAN Secretariat should be independent in order to have a sufficient representation of ASEAN's community interests. Thus, the staff of the ASEAN Secretariat should be recruited from citizens of ASEAN states based on merit. In addition, the staff should not be allowed to hold positions in the governments of ASEAN members.

In summary, the monitoring bodies in ASEAN do not work well enough to undertake the role envisaged by game theory. Thus, the reforms proposed could be adopted in order to achieve the requirement of an effective monitoring institution. Such reforms are necessary to progress towards the AEC.

VI. Enforcement institutions

An enforcement institution is the fourth institution required for economic cooperation from a game theoretical perspective. Its main function is to deter players from defecting by imposing penalties which would nullify the payoffs the defector would obtain by defecting. In addition, an enforcement institution should be neutral and represent the community interest acting as an impartial adjudicator. As an enforcement institution is meant to punish defectors, allowing the dominance of representatives of the member states would be tantamount to asking a defector to play a role in punishing himself/herself.

This section reviews the current institutions within ASEAN to see if the current arrangements in ASEAN satisfy the requirement of an effective enforcement institution. Reforms will be suggested on how ASEAN should achieve an effective enforcement institution.

A. ASEAN's current enforcement mechanism

ASEAN's current enforcement mechanism is the ASEAN Protocol on Enhanced Dispute Settlement Mechanism (DSM).[67] The DSM covers

[67] ASEAN Protocol on Enhanced Dispute Settlement Mechanism, Vientiane, 29 November 2004 [DSM].

economic agreements and is used to resolve disputes between ASEAN members. The DSM is administered by the SEOM.[68]

The DSM encourages the use of consultations, conciliation or mediation to solve disputes. The dispute will only be raised with the SEOM when consultations do not resolve the dispute. Thereafter, the SEOM is required to establish a panel unless the SEOM decides by consensus not to establish a panel.[69]

After the panel has made a report, the SEOM has to adopt the report unless the SEOM decides by consensus against such adoption or a party to the dispute appeals.[70]

Appeals from panel cases are decided by an Appellate Body. Such a body is established by the ASEAN Economic Ministers. The Appellate Body is appointed for a four-year term and comprises people with various expertise.

The SEOM is required to adopt an Appellate Body report unless the SEOM decides by consensus not to do so.[71]

Where a member is found to be acting inconsistently with an agreement, such a member is required to bring their actions into conformity with that agreement. Failure to do so would lead to various penalties such as compensation and suspension of concessions.[72]

B. Problems with ASEAN's current enforcement mechanism

1. Weak mechanisms to implement rulings

Critics note that the DSM's lack of sufficient regulations to implement the rulings of the panel report or Appellate Body report renders the mechanism meaningless.[73]

Currently, when a member state does not comply with ASEAN's rules and obligations, that member faces no punitive measures. All that is required is for a defecting member to enter into negotiations with the party that invoked the DSM with a view to developing mutually acceptable compensation. However, such compensation is merely voluntary and the defector cannot be forced to provide compensation.[74]

[68] Article 1 of the DSM.
[69] Article 5 of the DSM.
[70] Article 9 of the DSM.
[71] Article 12 of the DSM.
[72] Article 14 of the DSM.
[73] Agreement on the Common Effective Preferential Tariff Scheme for the ASEAN Free Trade Area at 108.
[74] Article 14 of the DSM.

When the defector does not provide acceptable compensation, the most severe consequence would be for the complaining party to suspend its obligations to the defector. While this is a common element of international dispute settlement particularly in the trade area where similar processes can be found in FTAs and even the WTO, it may be that the DSM is not entirely suitable for the creation of an economic community.

By solely relying on the self-help remedy of suspension of obligations, all that would happen is at best the reversion to the *status quo* in that area of cooperation and at worst a race to the bottom in other areas.[75] In addition, while the suspension of obligations may act as a deterrent when members of somewhat equal economic strengths are involved as in the case of ASEAN, if such a system were to be implemented for the AEC with the incorporation of economic giants like China and India, the disparity in economic strengths may render the remedy unfeasible for the smaller economies since any suspension of obligations may well affect the smaller economies much more than the larger ones. An alternative enforcement remedy may be found in the power of the European Court of Justice (ECJ) to impose a financial penalty for failure by a member state to comply with a judgment of the ECJ.[76]

Thus, at present, since the DSM cannot mandate financial compensation, it does not reduce the payoffs obtained by the defector through defection. As a result, the DSM fails to adequately reduce the incentives for member states to defect.

2. Political influence in the DSM

Critics note that the DSM is still influenced by the political realm.[77] This is evident from the influence of the SEOM and the ASEAN Economic Ministers in the DSM. For example, the SEOM which comprises senior officials of the governments of member states has the significant role of administering the DSM.[78]

As discussed in a preceding section, allowing political influence in the DSM would be tantamount to asking a defector to play a role in

[75] For an analysis of a similar problem faced within the WTO, see Marco Bronckers and Naboth van den Broek, 'Financial Compensation in the WTO: Improving the Remedies of WTO Dispute Settlement' (2005) *Journal of International Economic Law* 101–26.

[76] See Article 228 of the Treaty establishing the European Community (consolidated text) *Official Journal* C 325 of 24 December 2002.

[77] Hew, 'Introduction: Roadmap to an ASEAN economic community', at 3.

[78] Article 1 of the DSM.

punishing himself/herself. Hence, the influence of the political realm renders the DSM ineffective.

C. *Reforms to create effective monitoring institutions*

1. Moving the DSM from the political realm

There are two possible ways to move the DSM from the political realm. The first way, which was recommended by the Institute of Southeast Asian Studies (ISEAS) Study, would be to establish a high-level judicial body to enforce the DSM. Such a judicial body would comprise judges from every ASEAN member. The second way, which was recommended by the McKinsey Study, would be to establish a Dispute Settlement Bureau within the ASEAN Secretariat to enforce the DSM.[79]

Both these methods would reduce the political influence on the DSM as a judicial body and the ASEAN Secretariat are not dominated by government-related personnel. However, a high-level judicial body might be more appropriate. As it has been suggested that the ASEAN Secretariat should be in charge of legislative proposals and the monitoring of compliance to ASEAN's rules, the exercise of judicial powers by a different institution would ensure separation of powers. Allowing the ASEAN Secretariat to have too much power could lead to the abuse of power.

2. Strong mechanisms to implement rulings

There are several methods of enforcing the rulings of the enforcement institution. These mechanisms are important as they reduce the incentive to defect by reducing the payoffs from defection.

(a) Coordinated suspension of concessions The enforcement institution could enlist the help of other countries to suspend concessions to the defector. Such a wider scale of suspension of concessions would be a more severe penalty and would reduce the payoffs from defecting to a greater extend compared to a solitary withdrawal of concessions. However, the costs of coordinating such suspension on a wide scale could be too high to make such an option feasible.[80]

[79] Hadi Soesastro, 'ASEAN economic community: Concepts, costs, and benefits', in Denis Hew (ed.), *Roadmap to an ASEAN Economic Community* (Singapore: ISEAS Publications, 2005) at 28.

[80] Hund, 'From "neighbourhood watch group" to community?', at 510.

(b) Monetary compensation Alternatively, penalties in the form of monetary compensation could be required from the defecting state. The quantum of such compensation should be determined by the enforcement institution. The parties to the dispute should not be allowed to negotiate the quantum.

Academics have referred to the ECJ's approach in relation to the question of how to enforce the enforcement institution's orders of compensation. These academics suggest that the preliminary reference procedure under the ECJ could be adopted in ASEAN.[81] The significance of the preliminary reference procedure is the coordination between the ECJ and the national courts of member states. Under this procedure, a ruling of the ECJ is binding on all the courts of the member states faced with the same issue. While a national government might be tempted to defy a ruling of an international tribunal, it would usually not dare to defy its own courts.[82]

Therefore, using this approach, certain rulings of the ASEAN enforcement institutions could be binding on the domestic courts of the defecting states. In this way, defecting states would have greater incentives to pay such monetary compensation. Hence, this would lead to a decrease in the incentive to defect.

In summary, the enforcement mechanisms in ASEAN are not sufficiently effective. Thus, the reforms proposed could be adopted in order to achieve the requirement of an effective enforcement institution.

VII. ASEAN–China FTA (ACFTA) and ASEAN–India FTA (AIFTA)

Before the Asian financial crisis of 1997–8, apart from AFTA, there was no other regional trade agreement initiative by ASEAN. But this crisis highlighted the vulnerability of the entire Southeast region to both externally generated economic dislocation and also to subsequent political intervention from international financial institutions. The rise of China and India in the aftermath of the Asian crisis added urgency to this recognition by ASEAN members of the need for regional economic integration. As ASEAN sought to engage other regional economies, China and India also recognised the need for them to engage ASEAN for access to the natural resources and potential FDI from ASEAN.

In 2001 at the ASEAN–China Summit in Brunei, China put forward the proposal to establish an FTA within a decade. On 5 November 2002,

[81] *Ibid.* [82] *Ibid* at 125.

ASEAN and China signed the Framework Agreement (FA) on Comprehensive Economic Cooperation between ASEAN and China which will serve as a roadmap for the future ACFTA. Negotiations have started on trade in goods, services and investments in the hope that by January 2010, an ACFTA would be realised with the ASEAN-6 and by 2015, all the other ASEAN countries.

A year after the ASEAN–China Summit in Brunei, in November 2002, at the first ASEAN–India Summit at Phnom Penh, ASEAN and India agreed to negotiate towards an FTA. The Framework Agreement (FA) to Enhance ASEAN–India Trade and Economic Co-operation towards an FTA covering goods, services and investment, was signed on 8 October 2003 by the leaders at the Bali Summit. Under the FA, the AIFTA would be realised with the ASEAN-6 by 31 December 2011 with the remaining ASEAN countries included in the AIFTA by 2016.

Both of these initiatives are likely to be the foundations of any AEC which includes ASEAN as a building block.

A. ACFTA, AIFTA and the WTO

With the exception of Vietnam and Laos, all the parties to the FAs are members of the WTO. The fundamental principle of the WTO as expressed in Article I of the General Agreement on Trade and Tariffs (GATT) is that any concessions offered by any member of the WTO to any other member of the WTO must be accorded to all other members of the WTO (MFN). However, Article XXIV of the GATT allows the formation of an FTA, or to use the WTO nomenclature, a Regional Trade Agreement (RTA), with preferential tariff concessions for FTA members, subject to certain conditions.

Article XXIV requires that any FTA has to result in greater trade liberalisation among the countries to the FTA without raising barriers on trade with the other WTO members who are not members of the FTA. In other words, WTO members who are not included in the FTA should not find trade with the FTA members any more restrictive than before the FTA was set up. Article XXIV also provides that duties and other trade barriers should be reduced or removed on 'substantially all the trade' in the region. The term 'substantially all the trade' is less than clear and has yet to be interpreted.

Regardless of the applicability of Article XXIV, all parties to the FAs of ACFTA and AIFTA are all either developing or least-developed countries (LDCs). For those that are WTO members, this enables them to invoke the Enabling Clause allowing preferential regional trade among developing countries without the stricter limitations imposed by Article XXIV. In particular paragraph 2(c) of the Enabling Clause provides for the removal of the 'substantially all the trade' requirement while allowing for preferential tariff concessions between developing economies.

Thus, despite concerns that FTAs may in general cause trade diversion, both the ACFTA and AIFTA should be consistent with the obligations of their WTO members.

B. Common features of the ACFTA and AIFTA

Both FAs of the FTAs have identical objectives such as the strengthening and enhancing of economic, trade and investment cooperation, the progressive liberalisation of trade in goods and services, the exploration of new areas for closer economic co-operation, the facilitation of the more effective economic integration of the newer ASEAN members and the bridging of the development gaps among the parties.[83]

Article 3 of both the FAs provides for the reduction and eventual elimination of tariffs on the basis of a two track approach – a Normal Track and Sensitive Track. Under the ACFTA tariff for the products that are listed under the Normal Track will be gradually reduced and eventually eliminated in accordance with specified schedules and rates from 1 January 2005 to 2010 or 2015 (2010 for original ASEAN members and 2015 for the rest). Under the AIFTA this period is from 1 January 2006 to 2011 and 2016.[84] But the number of products listed in the Sensitive Track shall be subject to a maximum ceiling which is to be mutually agreed among the Parties and will be reduced in accordance with mutually agreed end rates and end dates.

Article 4 of both the FAs provides that all the parties expressly agree to enter into negotiations to progressively liberalise trade in services on a preferential basis with substantial sectoral coverage. However, there is no specific provision as to the extent of liberalisation mentioned in either of the FAs.

Article 5 of both the FAs expresses the willingness to promote investments and to create a liberal, facilitative, transparent and competitive

[83] Article 1 of the FAs of ACFTA and AIFTA.

[84] In response to some concerns expressed by the Philippines it was also agreed that India and the Philippines will eliminate tariffs for each other on a reciprocal basis only by 2016.

investment regime. Here again the identification and scope of the liberalisation of the sectors is left for future negotiations.

Article 9 provides that both China and India will extend its WTO MFN rates to all the non-WTO ASEAN members (currently Vietnam and Laos) immediately upon the signing of the FAs.

Both FTAs of ACFTA and AIFTA also provide for an Early Harvest Programme (EHP). Under the ACFTA this programme allows the reduction of tariffs on certain agricultural products before the onset of the FTA. The EHP was initially a proposal by China to cover mainly agricultural goods and was initially proposed as a unilateral concession by China. However, China eventually tied EHP to reciprocity but also agreed to extend concessions on 130 specific manufactured goods to Brunei and Singapore being non-agricultural exporting countries. AIFTA's EHP provides for exchange of tariff concessions and elimination of tariffs on an agreed common list of items based on full reciprocity between India and the ASEAN-6 within three years and for the CLMV in six years. A significant aspect of the EHP is that, by allowing the members of the EHP access to certain markets via preferential tariffs not currently available to other WTO members, it gives the members a 'first mover' advantage.

C. *Impact of ACFTA and AIFTA*

It is anticipated that the establishment of ACFTA will create an economic region with 1.7 billion consumers, regional gross domestic product (GDP) of about US$2 trillion and total trade estimated at US$1.23 trillion.[85] The removal of trade barriers between ASEAN and China will indeed lower costs of production through economies of scale, increase intra-regional trade and increase economic efficiency. Simulations conducted using the Global Trade Analysis Project (GTAP) suggest that an ACFTA will increase ASEAN's exports to China by 48% and China's exports to ASEAN by 55.1% and could potentially increase ASEAN's GDP by 0.9% or by US$5.4 billion while China's real GDP could expand by 0.3% or by US$2.2 billion.[86] As an indication of the success of the EHP, as of December 2004, ASEAN agricultural exports to China increased by 38.7% year-on-year and China's agricultural exports to ASEAN also increasing by 33.9% reaching US$270 million.[87]

[85] See ASEAN Secretariat, *Towards a Single Economic Space* (2003).
[86] *Ibid.*
[87] Ministry of Trade and Industry, Singapore, Information Paper on China–ASEAN Free Trade Area (ACFTA) available at http://app.fta.gov.sg/data/fta/file/ACFTA_Info_Kit.pdf.

In comparison, the AIFTA will have a combined consumer base of 1.5 billion and a GDP of US$1.5 trillion.[88] While official economic analysis has not yet been published, ASEAN and India are aiming to increase two-way trade to US$15 billion by 2005 and to US$30 billion by 2007.[89]

The ACFTA and AIFTA despite all their potential benefits, will face significant challenges to their creation and implementation. Particularly, in dealing with removal of barriers in trade in services, the parties would have to tackle the very sensitive issue of the freer flow of labour. While some countries may not be immediately unsympathetic to the freer movement of professional and skilled labour, many may not be so keen on opening up their labour markets to less skilled labour due to concerns of unmanageable movements and potential social problems caused by a massive influx of foreign labour from larger and less developed neighbours.

In addition, India has also been historically very much a protectionist country with very high tariff rates. Indeed, the Indian record for the implementation of FTAs has been far less than convincing as is evident from the follow up of its Indo-Thai FTA and Comprehensive Economic Cooperation Agreement with Singapore. The reason for this slow progress is perhaps due to the fact that Indian industry is not yet sure about its competitive efficiency and many sectors do not want competition on their home turf which is still protected to a great extent. Already due to a difference of opinion on Rules of Origin, the AIFTA's EHP, agreed under the FA, while scheduled for implementation by November 2004, has not yet been implemented.

ASEAN itself will face internal challenges that will need to be overcome. The CLMV will have to look for alternative ways of financing government spending instead of relying on tariffs and some ASEAN countries may also face severe competition in the shorter term from cheaper Chinese goods, especially electronics, footwear, apparel and textiles, and the outsourcing of some services to India.

Finally, the devil will be in the details. To achieve any real benefit from the FTAs, customs procedures of the parties will have to be simplified, product standards harmonized, transport and communication networks strengthened, rule of law, transparency and governance improved, and

88 Seema Gaur, 'ASEAN India ties entering a new phase', *ISEAS Viewpoints* (8 October 2003).

89 *Ibid.*

labour productivity raised. All these efforts would require strong political commitment and appropriate institutions.

D. ACFTA, AIFTA and the AEC

Apart from obvious problems with negotiation and implementation challenges, historical distrust and external pressures may also add to the difficulties of the FTAs and the proposed AEC. China and India share the mutual wariness of two great nations with a common border. Sino-Japanese relations continues to be strained by memories of the Japanese invasion and occupation of China in the last century. Finally, Western powers, the US in particular, have concerns about China's rise as a superpower. The US has already tried to limit China's direct engagement with the region by emphasising the Asia Pacific Economic Cooperation (APEC) forum. All of these concerns make ASEAN, as a relatively neutral party, at present the only viable building block for the AEC.

Nonetheless, ASEAN, as highlighted above, faces its own internal institutional problems. To reiterate, it lacks (i) clearly defined rules and obligations, (ii) effective decision-making institutions, (iii) sufficient monitoring institutions, and (iv) enforcement institutions. Some of these problems have been replicated in some form in the FAs to the FTAs.

1. Rules and obligations

Like the CEPT's Inclusion and Sensitive Lists, the The FAs provide for two different tracks – the Normal and the Sensitive Track – for tariff reduction. While as highlighted above, the Normal Track provides for clear deadlines for tariff reduction, the Sensitive Track leaves the difficult negotiating to be determined at a future date. This ASEAN penchant for postponing difficult decisions and thereby leaving the rules less than clear will make it difficult to develop those rules later. While there is much to be said for a gradual phasing in of new initiatives, without clear obligations, politicians may be tempted to cater for local interests in priority over further trade liberalisation and include most of the difficult tariff reductions in the Sensitive Track. However, one advantage the FAs have over AFTA is the absence of a loophole like the CEPT to allow parties to backtrack from previously agreed upon concessions. It is hoped that such a loophole will be avoided in the final FTAs.

2. Decision-making institutions

The FAs envisage a negotiation modality under Article 12 for the establishment of a Trade Negotiation Committee (TNC) with the ASEAN Secretariat and the relevant trade ministries in China and India providing the necessary secretarial support. The TNC will report direct to the AEM and the relevant trade minister through the joint meetings of the SOEM and the trade ministries of China and India. While this structure was inevitable given the lack of an existing supranational institution incorporating the countries that could act as a forum for the negotiations, the lack of an honest broker to alleviate potential negotiation failures will add to the already considerable challenges.

While the negotiations should ostensibly be between ASEAN and China and ASEAN and India, in reality, as unlike the EU, there is no common ASEAN trade policy, negotiations are conducted to some extent bilaterally between the ASEAN members individually and China particularly on sectoral concessions. As this is the case, there is a possibility for the ASEAN Secretariat to play a bigger role in 'neutral' agenda setting and ground work preparation. However, as the ASEAN Secretariat has limited resources, it is hoped that the recognition of the stakes involved in these FTAs and the potential AEC, that resources will be particularly allocated towards such efforts.

It is, however, interesting to note that ASEAN, having learnt some of the lessons from its own economic cooperation efforts, has tried to incorporate where possible clear goals and deadlines so as help the TNC formulate rules which are consistent those goals. Also incorporated into the FAs are guidelines that direct the TNC to the development gaps between countries by making special consideration for the less developed countries by measures such as providing different timelines for the performance of their commitments.

3. Monitoring institutions

There is no mention in the FAs of any monitoring institutions though the Article 16 of the Agreement on Trade in Goods of the Framework Agreement on Comprehensive Economic Co-operation between ASEAN and the People's Republic of China (ACFTA Trade in Goods Agreement) does provide that pending the establishment of a more permanent body, the ASEAN Secretariat, will act as the institution to monitor the implementation of the ACFTA Trade in Goods Agreement. This is an interesting development which illustrates to some extent the perception by China of the 'neutrality' of the ASEAN Secretariat. As the AIFTA TNC has yet to conclude negotiations on goods, it remains to be seen whether a similar provision will be included in the AIFTA. It is suggested that some of the measures recommended above to promote the independence and capacity of the ASEAN Secretariat as a monitoring institution should be implemented to enhance its role as a monitoring institution. In the absence of such measures being implemented, it is hoped that if a permanent body to monitor the ACFTA and AIFTA is created, that the structure should focus on the need to ensure that that body is sufficiently independent and has the freedom and resources to ensure that it has sufficient capacity.

4. Enforcement institutions

Article 11 of both FAs provide for the establishment of formal dispute settlement procedures within one year of the entry into force of the FAs. China has already entered into an Agreement on Dispute Settlement Mechanism of the Framework Agreement on Comprehensive Economic Co-operation Between ASEAN and the People's Republic of China (ACFTA DSM) which entered into force on 1 January 2005 which was actually more than one year from the date of the entry into force of the FA of ACFTA being 1 July 2003. The FA of AIFTA entered into force on 1 July 2004 and to date no DSM has yet been agreed upon by the parties. It should be noted that Article 11 also provides vaguely that pending the establishment of the formal dispute settlement procedures and mechanisms, any disputes concerning the interpretation, implementation or application should be settled amicably by consultations and/or mediation.

The ACFTA DSM largely mirrors the ASEAN DSM substantively save for the addition of some procedural details and some differences in the dispute settlement timetable. However, in the absence of an institution like the SEOM in ASEAN to establish a tribunal, the ACFTA DSM resorts to the often used arbitral procedure of allowing each party to appoint its own respective arbitrator with the chair left to mutual agreement. If mutual agreement is not reached, then the ACFTA DSM provides for the chair to be named by an external neutral party such as the Director-General of the WTO (provided that the D-G is not a national of either party) or the President of the International Court of Justice (ICJ) where one of the parties to the dispute is not a WTO member.[90] This is a disappointing second best option as it hardly

[90] Article 7 ACFTA DSM.

provides for a enforcement institution which is perceived to be impartial and as the arbitral tribunal is only established on an *ad hoc* basis, it fails to give the institution any continuity. It is hoped that as more steps are taken towards the AEC, a more permanent and independent institution could be established to act as an adjudicator and enforcer of the rules.

It is also disappointing to note that the ACFTA DSM also does not provide for mandatory compensation in the absence of implementation. Article 13 of the ACFTA DSM still provides that compensation should be voluntary and if there is a failure to agree upon the compensation, the complaining party may request the original tribunal to assess the appropriate level of suspension of concessions. As suggested above this is a less preferred enforcement mechanism to the ECJ's ability to award compulsory financial compensation particularly when dealing with disputes between parties of unequal economic strengths.

VIII. Conclusion

This chapter has suggested that from the perspectives of game theory, these four elements are crucial to successful economic cooperation and will probably be required in order to achieve the AEC. However, the review of ASEAN's current institutional framework shows that these four elements are currently less than adequately provided for in ASEAN and as a result could also be potentially lacking in the ACFTA and AIFTA.

While there are certain organisations in ASEAN which attempt to fulfil these four elements, most of these attempts have been less than effective. Therefore, in order for ASEAN to act as a building block of the AEC, the reforms proposed in this paper should be considered. However, as these reforms require fundamental changes to the current institutional framework, ASEAN members will have to find the political will to undertake these proposed reforms. While the four elements are essential to the formation of the AEC, these will not be able to substitute a lack of political will to implement them.

Before ASEAN can be a building block of an AEC incorporating China and India, ASEAN will have to first address these issues. Regardless of whether the AEC proceeds down towards either of Lamy's 'happy family' or 'good neighbours' options,[91] ASEAN must first fix its own

[91] See Speech by Pascal Lamy, 'Europe and Asia: Old partners with a new agenda', Asia-Europe Foundation, Singapore, 15 February 2002 available at http://ec.europa.eu/comm/archives/commission_1999_2004/lamy/speeches_articles/spla95_en.htm.

house. A failure by ASEAN to do so will lead instead to ASEAN diverting valuable trade negotiating resources and efforts towards less than effective FTAs thus acting as a stumbling block for economic cooperation between China and India rather than an honest broker and a building block for greater regional cooperation.

IX. Postscript

Soon after the finalising of this chapter, the ASEAN Charter[92] was signed on 20 November 2007 at the 13th ASEAN Summit in Singapore. The ASEAN members also issued a Declaration on the ASEAN Economic Community[93] which adopted the AEC Blueprint[94] for the implementation of the AEC by 2015. The Declaration states that '[t]he AEC Blueprint will transform ASEAN into a single market and production base, a highly competitive economic region, a region of equitable economic development, and a region fully integrated into the global economy'.[95]

However, while the ASEAN Charter and the AEC Blueprint have been adopted many of the problems highlighted above have yet to be completely resolved. First, the ASEAN Charter will only become effective on the 30th day after the tenth instrument of ratification is submitted to the ASEAN Secretary-General.[96] This means that every one of the ten members of ASEAN must ratify the ASEAN Charter. Myanmar[97] has

[92] ASEAN Charter available at www.aseansec.org/ASEAN-Charter.pdf.

[93] Declaration on the ASEAN Economic Community available at www.aseansec.org/21081.htm.

[94] AEC Blueprint available at www.aseansec.org/21083.pdf.

[95] Declaration on the ASEAN Economic Community, paragraph 1.

[96] Article 47.4 of the ASEAN Charter.

[97] In 1989, the military government officially changed the English version of the country's name from Burma to Myanmar, along with changes to the English versions of many place names in the country, such as its former capital city from Rangoon to Yangon. The official name of the country in the Burmese language, Myanmar, did not change. The renaming proved to be politically controversial. As the military government was not legitimately elected, some governments such as the US have contended that it did not have the authority to officially change the name in English and have continued to use the name Burma instead. The EU uses the term Burma/Myanmar. For the purposes of this chapter the official name Myanmar will be used solely as a convenience without any political connotations. For an analysis of the human rights situation in Myanmar and its impact on ASEAN, see Michael Ewing-Chow, 'First do no harm: Myanmar trade sanctions and human rights' (2007) 5(2) *Northwestern Journal of International Human Rights*, available at www.law.northwestern.edu/journals/jihr/v5/n2/1/Ewing-Chow.pdf.

been the latest member to do so on 21 July 2008 but to date, Indonesia, the Philippines and Thailand all have yet ratify the ASEAN Charter because they believe that Myanmar should first provide firmer commitments to democracy.[98] It is difficult to see how Myanmar may be persuaded to do so when all other efforts have met with little success.

Second, quite apart from the ratification issue, the ASEAN Charter itself is still vague about many of the issues raised above. While the ASEAN Charter does take the important step of conferring legal personality to ASEAN,[99] it does not sufficiently address the problems of decision making, monitoring and enforcement for ASEAN.

While the ASEAN Charter does envisage that a committee of Permanent Representatives will be appointed to ASEAN with the rank of Ambassador based in Jakarta,[100] that committee will not be the primary decision-making body. Instead, the ASEAN Summit will continue to be the main forum for decision making[101] and decisions at all levels will continue to be made by consultation and consensus.[102]

Also, while the ASEAN Secretary-General and the ASEAN Secretariat have been given greater responsibility to monitor compliance and facilitate the implementation of the AEC,[103] the budget for the ASEAN Secretariat remains very tight. In the Financial Year 2007/08, the ASEAN Secretariat was given US$9.05 million with each Member State contributing equally US$905,000 to the budget.[104] This insistence on equal contributions will continue to keep the ASEAN Secretariat budget tight as some of the ASEAN members may find it more difficult to increase their contributions.

In the area of enforcement of ASEAN disciplines, the ASEAN Charter does provide that where specific ASEAN instruments provide for a dispute settlement mechanism, disputes would be resolved with reference to that mechanism.[105] In particular, disputes concerning the interpretation or application of ASEAN economic agreements would be settled in accordance with the ASEAN Protocol on Enhanced Dispute Settlement Mechanism,[106] which provides for a negative consensus rule

[98] 'Burma ratifies ASEAN Charter', 22 July 2008 *The Australian*, available at www.theaustralian.news.com.au/story/0,25197,24056268–2703,00.html.

[99] Article 3 of the ASEAN Charter.

[100] Article 12 of the ASEAN Charter.

[101] Article 7 of the ASEAN Charter.

[102] Article 20 of the ASEAN Charter.

[103] Articles 11 and 27 of the ASEAN Charter.

[104] ASEAN Secretariat, Media Release: ASEAN Leaders Sign ASEAN Charter, Singapore, 20 November 2007, available at www.aseansec.org/21085.htm.

[105] Article 24.1 of the ASEAN Charter.

[106] Article 24.3 of the ASEAN Charter.

for the adoption of any report.[107] While these provisions do provide more certainty for enforcement, where there are no pre-existing dispute settlement mechanisms, the ASEAN Charter suggests that 'appropriate dispute settlement mechanisms, including arbitration, shall be established'.[108] What those mechanisms will be and how they will be established remains to be seen. In addition, the ASEAN Charter also anticipates that if disputes remain unresolved, the dispute shall be referred to the ASEAN Summit for its decision, which will mean that the 'ASEAN Way' rule that decisions be made by consultation and consensus will be the guiding principle.[109] How this impacts on the right of an ASEAN member to compensation and suspension of concessions against another ASEAN member if a measure is not brought into conformity with a report is not entirely clear. The ASEAN Protocol on Enhanced Dispute Settlement Mechanism does provide for such a right subject to authorization from the SEOM.[110] If the SEOM is obliged to continue to make decisions in the 'ASEAN Way', while reports may be adopted by negative consensus, the enforcement of such reports will be more problematic.

Nonetheless, while beset with some areas that will need to be addressed as ASEAN evolves, the ASEAN Charter does provide for some hope that ASEAN may be able to become a cornerstone for Asian economic cooperation. It hoped that this is not the final legal chapter for ASEAN but rather a step in the development of a more effective regional entity.

[107] Articles 9.2 and 12.13 of the ASEAN Protocol on Enhanced Dispute Settlement Mechanism available at www.aseansec.org/16754.htm.
[108] Article 25 of the ASEAN Charter.
[109] Article 26 read with Article 20 of the ASEAN Charter.
[110] Article 16 of the ASEAN Protocol on Enhanced Dispute Settlement Mechanism.

References

Acharya, Amitav, 'Realism, institutionalism and the Asian economic crisis' (1999) 21(1) *Contemporary Southeast Asia* 1

Agreement on the Common Effective Preferential Tariff Scheme for the ASEAN Free Trade Area, Singapore, 28 January 1992

Alagappa, Muthiah, 'Institutional framework recommendations for change', in Sharon Siddique and Sree Kumar (eds.), *The 2nd ASEAN Reader* (Singapore: Institute of Southeast Asian Studies, 2003)

Akraseanee, N. and Arunanondchai, J., 'Institutional reforms to achieve ASEAN market integration', in Sharon Siddique and Sree Kumar (eds.), *The 2nd ASEAN Reader* (Singapore: Institute of Southeast Asian Studies, 2003)

Article 228 of the Treaty establishing the European Community (consolidated text) Official Journal C 325 of 24 December 2002

ASEAN Protocol on Enhanced Dispute Settlement Mechanism, Vientiane, 29 November 2004 [DSM]

Barnett, Hilaire, *Constitutional & Administrative Law 3rd edn* (Sydney: Cavendish Publishing Limited, 2000)

Bhaskaran, Manu, *The Economic Impact of China and India on Southeast Asia, Southeast Asian Affairs* (ISEAS, 2005)

Bronckers, Marco and van den Broek, Naboth, 'Financial Compensation in the WTO: Improving the Remedies of WTO Dispute Settlement' (2005) *Journal of International Economic Law*

'Burma ratifies ASEAN Charter', 22 July 2008 *The Australian*, available at www.theaustralian.news.com.au/story/0,25197,24056268–2703,00.html\

Davidson, Paul J., *ASEAN: The Evolving Legal Framework for Economic Cooperation* (Singapore: Times International Publishing, 2002)

Ewing-Chow, Michael, 'First do no harm: Myanmar trade sanctions and human rights (2007) **5**(2) *Northwestern Journal of International Human Rights*, available at www.law.northwestern.edu/journals/jihr/v5/n2/1/Ewing-Chow.pdf

Frischmann, Brett, 'A dynamic institutional theory of international law' (2003) 51 Buff. L. Rev. 679

Gaur, Seema, 'ASEAN India ties entering a new phase', *ISEAS Viewpoints* (8 October 2003)

Hafez, Zakir, *The Dimensions of Regional Trade Integration in Southeast Asia* (New York: Transnational Publishers, 2004)

Hew, Denis, '*De facto* economic integration in East Asia', online: Korean Institutefor International Economic Policy, available at www.kiep.go.kr/inc/download.asp?fnm=(2005–09–05–065003433279927)%20Denis%20Hew.pdf

'Introduction: Roadmap to an ASEAN Economic Community'in Denis Hew, ed., *Roadmap to an ASEAN Economic Community* (Singapore: ISEAS Publications, 2005)

'Towards an ASEAN Charter: Regional economic integration'in Rodolfo Severino, ed., *Framing the ASEAN Charter: An ISEAS Perspective* (Singapore: ISEAS Publications, 2005)

Hund, Marcus, 'From "neighbourhood watch group" to community? The case of ASEAN institutions and the pooling of sovereignty' (2002) 56(1) *Australian Journal of International Affairs* 99

Lamy, Pascal, 'Europe and Asia: Old partners with a new agenda, Asia—Europe foundation', Singapore, 15 February 2002, available at http://ec.europa.eu/comm/archives/commission_1999_2004/lamy/speeches_articles/spla95_en.htm

Lim, Raymond, 'Creating a globally connected Asian community, finance and development'(2006) 43(2) *Finance and Development*, 'Point of View'

Locknie Hsu, 'Towards an ASEAN Charter: Some Thoughts from the Legal Perspective' in Rodolfo Severino, ed., *Framing the ASEAN Charter: An ISEAS Perspective* (Singapore: ISEAS Publications, 2005)

Ministry of Trade and Industry, Singapore, Information Paper on China–ASEAN Free Trade Area (ACFTA) available at http://app.fta.gov.sg/data/fta/file/ACFTA_Info_Kit.pdf

Peterson, J. and Shackleton, M., *The Institutions of the European Union* (New York: Oxford University Press, 2002)

Rüland, J., 'ASEAN and the Asian crisis: Theoretical implications and practical consequences for Southeast Asian regionalism' (2000) 13(3) *The Pacific Review* 421

Severino, Rodolfo, 'Framing the ASEAN Charter: An ISEAS Perspective' in Rodolfo Severino (ed.), *Framing the ASEAN Charter: An ISEAS Perspective* (Singapore: ISEAS Publications, 2005)

Soesastro, Hadi, 'ASEAN Economic Community: Concepts, costs, and benefits' in Denis Hew (ed.), *Roadmap to an ASEAN Economic Community* (Singapore: ISEAS Publications, 2005)

'ASEAN in 2030: The long view'in Simon S. C. Tay, Jesus P. Estanislao and Hadi Soesastro (ed.), *Reinventing ASEAN* (Singapore: Institute of Southeast Asian Studies, 2001)

Tallberg, Jonas, 'The power of the Presidency: Brokerage, efficiency and distribution in EU negotiations' (2004) 42(5) *Journal of Common Market Studies*

Tay, Simon S. C., 'Institutions and processes: Dilemmas and possibilities', in Simon S. C. Tay, Jesus P. Estanislao and Hadi Soesastro (eds.), *Reinventing ASEAN* (Singapore: Institute of Southeast Asian Studies, 2001)

Wanandi, Jusuf, 'ASEAN's challenges for its future', *The PacNet Newsletter* (22 January 1999), online: Columbia International Affairs Online, available at www.ciaonet.org/pbei/csis/pac99/waj01/

Yue, Chia Siow, 'ASEAN–China free trade area', online: Hong Kong Institute of Economic and Business Strategies, available at www.hiebs.hku.hk/aep/Chia.pdf

12

The China–ASEAN tariff acceleration clause

C. L. LIM

I. Introduction

India–China trade in the near future is likely to take place against the backdrop of an emerging, uncertain network of Asian Free Trade Agreements (FTAs). This chapter takes a look at the contemporary history of regional trade negotiations. It traces the influence of a third party; namely, ASEAN's efforts to build links to the rest of Asia through a complex network of FTAs. That influence suggests a disturbing possibility – the exportation of a tariff acceleration device developed during the ASEAN–China negotiations to the rest of Asia. The ASEAN–China FTA contains a tariff acceleration clause and similar devices which would allow separate bilateral deals between China and the individual ASEAN nations to be cut beneath the larger umbrella of the China–ASEAN FTA.

These devices are significant because ASEAN has become something of a common medium for India and the 'Plus 3' nations to join in the build-up of a regional network of Asia-wide FTAs. In the near to medium term, the Plus 3 are unlikely to have bilateral agreements between themselves. There is no evidence that China, Japan and South Korea will be aiming for FTAs between themselves anytime soon. Instead, they appear content to trade with each other on preferential terms *through* their individual FTAs with ASEAN and the ASEAN nations instead. If these become as heavily bilateralized as the China–ASEAN FTA, the result could be an 'MFN black hole' in intra-Asian trade liberalization.

This chapter therefore focuses not on the issue of China–India trade itself, but on the structure of China–ASEAN trade liberalization and the potential entry of India into an emerging network of ASEAN plus 3 FTAs (i.e. ASEAN's FTA negotiations with China, Japan and

Support received from HKU's Seed Funding Programme for Basic Research is hereby gratefully acknowledged.

South Korea).[1] For the sake of completeness, Section II of this chapter will first describe ASEAN's attempt to build an ASEAN Economic Community (AEC) within itself. That treatment is merely prefatory to Section III which deals with ASEAN's current attempt to locate itself at the centre of a network of FTAs with India to the West, and China, Japan and Korea to the East. Section IV explains how, and why this could lead to the problem mentioned at the outset – MFN erosion in the emergence of a complex network of FTAs governing Asian trade liberalization. A central assumption which this chapter calls into question is the idea that broader regional FTAs are necessarily more beneficial than a 'spaghetti', or 'Asian noodle bowl', of overlapping, bilateral FTAs.[2] The principal argument in this chapter is that trade regionalism in Asia could still amount to no more than 'bilateralism multiplied'.

II. A short history of ASEAN trade liberalization

The first phase of Asian trade liberalization which forms the regional backdrop for near to medium-term China–India trade liberalization has occurred largely within ASEAN. The following is a short account of ASEAN liberalization from 1992 to the present day. Readers who are already familiar with that account may wish to skip this part and to proceed directly to Section III, below.

A. From the 1992 inception of AFTA to the 1998 Hanoi Action Plan

An ASEAN Free Trade Area (AFTA) was initiated in 1992 through a Framework Agreement incorporating a 'Common Effective Preferential Trading Scheme' (or CEPT for short).[3] According to the 1992 CEPT

[1] For the history of the 'ASEAN plus 3' process, see Rodolfo C. Severino, *Southeast Asia in Search of an ASEAN Community* (Singapore: ISEAS, 2006)

[2] *Cf.* Fred Bergsten, 'Plan B for world trade: Go Regional', *Financial Times* (London), 15 August 2006; Robert Scollay, 'Prospects for linking preferential trade agreements in the Asia–Pacific Region', in Charles E. Morrison and Eduardo Pedrosa (eds.), *An APEC Trade Agenda? The Political Economy of a Free Trade Area of the Asia–Pacific* (Singapore: ISEAS, 2007), 164.

[3] Framework Agreement on Enhancing ASEAN Economic Cooperation, Singapore, 28 January 1992; Agreement on the Common Effective Preferential Tariff Scheme for the ASEAN Free Trade Area, Singapore, 28 January 1992.

Agreement, the six original ASEAN member states agreed to eliminate quantitative restrictions (QRs) and other non-tariff barriers (NTBs), and to reduce tariff rates on intra-ASEAN trade in goods to 0–5% within 15 years, beginning 1 January 1993. This rule would apply to goods meeting a 40% ASEAN content requirement.[4]

AFTA took one year to negotiate before signature in 1992. It precedes both NAFTA and the WTO Agreements. During the course of the ten-year period from its inception to the Hanoi Plan of Action in 2001, the targets originally set for the achievement of the 0–5% tariff target for the original ASEAN 6 were shifted twice, from the original date of 2008 (i.e. 15 years from the inception of AFTA) to 2003 in 1994 and again, from 2003 to 2002 in 1998 during the Sixth Summit in Hanoi.[5] The Hanoi Action Plan also saw the emergence of the term 'ASEAN Economic Integration', based on an open regionalist model. This was in part due to the strong trade links between individual ASEAN members and countries outside ASEAN.[6] Notwithstanding AFTA, individual ASEAN nations would continue to pursue a 'multi-track' approach by negotiating and concluding FTAs with trading nations outside ASEAN. Finally, the Hanoi Action Plan also set the target dates for achieving the 0–5% range for Vietnam (2006), Laos and Myanmar (2008), and Cambodia (2010).[7]

B. *The ASEAN Economic Community*

The Hanoi Plan was followed-up in 2003 with the Declaration of ASEAN Concord II of 7 October 2003 (commonly referred to as the 'Second Bali Concord').

Paragraph 1 of the declaratory part (hereafter, the 'Bali II Declaration') was a watershed in the evolution of ASEAN economic

[4] So far as the current figures are concerned, more than 99% of the items on an 'inclusion list' of goods for the original six members have been brought down to the 0–5% range. As for the newer members (Cambodia, Laos, Myanmar and Vietnam), 66% of almost 80% of the total products which have been moved into their inclusion lists are already within that range. See the website of the ASEAN secretariat at www.aseansec.org.

[5] LOK Hwee Chong, Christopher H. Lim and Ng Lyn (eds.), *A Guide to Free Trade in ASEAN*, Singapore Yearbook of International Law 2007 (National University of Singapore), para. 10–100.

[6] Speech by Mr ONG Keng Yong, ASEAN Secretary-General, 22 March 2003, Ballroom of the Regent Hotel, Singapore (on file).

[7] See also the website of the US–ASEAN Business Council at www.us-asean.org.

integration.[8] Declaring the establishment of an 'ASEAN Community',[9] it adds that:[10]

> An ASEAN Community shall be established comprising three pillars, namely political and security cooperation, economic cooperation, and socio-cultural cooperation that are closely intertwined and mutually reinforcing for the purpose of ensuring durable peace, stability and shared prosperity in the region. . .

Paragraph 2 states that:[11]

> ASEAN shall continue its efforts to ensure closer and mutually beneficial integration among its member states and among their peoples, and to promote regional peace and stability, security, development and prosperity with a view to realizing an ASEAN Community that is open, dynamic and resilient. . .

The notion of an 'open' ASEAN Community is elaborated upon in paragraph 7:[12]

> ASEAN is committed to deepening and broadening its internal economic integration and linkages with the world economy to realize an ASEAN Economic Community through a bold, pragmatic and unified strategy.

C. The 'Framework'

The Bali II Declaration goes on to adopt a 'framework to achieve a dynamic, cohesive, resilient and integrated ASEAN Community' – hereafter, the 'Bali Framework'. It states that:[13]

> The ASEAN Economic Community is the realisation of the end-goal of economic integration as outlined in the ASEAN Vision 2020, to create a stable, prosperous and highly competitive ASEAN economic region in which there is a free flow of goods, services, investment and a freer flow

[8] Declaration of ASEAN Concord II (Bali Concord II), 7 October 2002 (hereafter, 'Bali Concord II Declaration').

[9] References to an ASEAN Economic Community had also been made earlier. During the Thirty-Sixth ASEAN (Foreign) Ministers' meeting in Phnom Penh, the Ministers issued a joint communiqué 'reaffirmed the need to move deeper economic integration towards an ASEAN economic community'; Joint Communiqué of the Thirty-Sixth ASEAN Ministerial Meeting, Phnom Penh, 16–17 June 2003, para. 8.

[10] Bali Concord II Declaration, para. 1.

[11] *Ibid.*, para. 2.

[12] *Ibid.*, para. 7. See further, Severino, *Southeast Asia in Search of an ASEAN Community*, 256.

[13] 'Bali Framework' of the Declaration of ASEAN Concord II, para. 1, Part B.

> of capital, equitable economic development and reduced poverty and socio-economic disparities in year 2020.

The Community would employ 'clear timelines' to 'deepen and broaden economic integration efforts'.[14] Paragraph 3 of the Bali Framework adds that the Community itself 'shall establish ASEAN as a *single market* and production base'.[15]

Because the economic divide between ASEAN's older and newer members poses a problem in this regard, paragraph 4 states that:

> The ASEAN Economic Community shall ensure that deepening and broadening integration of ASEAN shall be accompanied by technical and development cooperation in order to address the development divide and accelerate the economic integration of Cambodia, Lao PDR, Myanmar and Viet Nam . . . so that the benefits of ASEAN integration are shared and enable all ASEAN Member Countries to move forward in a unified manner.

Thailand, Singapore and Malaysia then lobbied to move the target date for achieving the AEC forward to 2015 at the 2006 ASEAN Summit in Cebu.[16]

D. *From AFTA to the ASEAN Economic Community*

While Hanoi was about completing the AFTA, at Bali the ASEAN members raised their expectations to an ASEAN Community, including an ASEAN Economic Community.[17] While we should think things and not words, as Oliver Wendell Holmes once said, ASEAN has described the Economic Community in terms of the creation of a 'single market' and 'single production base' with a 'free movement of goods, services and capital'. As one ASEAN Prime Minister put it, echoing paragraph 3 of the Bali II Framework:[18]

[14] *Ibid.*, para. 2. [15] *Ibid.*, para. 3.

[16] En-Lai Yeoh, 'Southeast Asia speeds single market plan', *Associated Press*, 22 August 2006 (on file).

[17] Severino, *Southeast Asia in Search of an ASEAN Community*, 342–52. See further, Denis Hew (ed.), *Brick by Brick: The Building of an ASEAN Economic Community* (Singapore: ISEAS, 2007).

[18] Keynote Address by Prime Minister GOH Chok Tong at the ASEAN Business and Investment Summit, 6 October 2003, Bali, Indonesia, available at the ASEAN Secretariat website www.aseansec.org. It was the Singapore Prime Minister who had proposed the creation of an economic community at the ASEAN Summit in Phnom Penh in 2002. See further, Severino, *Southeast Asia in Search of an ASEAN Community*, 342.

> [T]he need for ASEAN to press on with economic integration remains as urgent as ever, if not more so. We must push towards an ASEAN Economic Community: a single production base and a single market, with free movement of goods, services and capital. This is the only way to make sure we remain competitive in the face of growing regional and bilateral FTAs, post-Cancun.

In short, a 'common market' not a customs union. Since then ASEAN has adopted an ASEAN Charter, aimed at improving its institutional and decision-making processes.[19] However, there has been a parallel development since the early 1990s. ASEAN has also looked to China, Japan, South Korea, India and beyond. It is this wider ambition which has also become the engine of pan-Asian trade liberalization in recent years.

III. The emerging structure of Asian preferential trade

A. *The 'mega jumbo-jet' metaphor*

ASEAN has since then aimed to move in ever-widening circles, encompassing other parts of Asia within ASEAN's vision of the benefits of having an open, liberal trading system. The following statement captures a part of that aspiration:[20]

> Strategically positioned between China and India is Southeast Asia. We are a significant market of half a billion people – equivalent to the whole of Europe . . . That is not all. ASEAN is also jointly and individually negotiating Free Trade Agreements with China, India, Japan and South Korea. So the economies of Asia are being integrated too. By 2025, it will be a different Asia, more integrated and less divided.
>
> . . .
>
> I like to think of new Asia as a mega jumbo jet that is being constructed. Northeast Asia, comprising China, Japan and South Korea, forms one wing with a powerful engine. India, the second wing, will also have a powerful engine. The Southeast Asian countries form the fuselage. Even if we lack a powerful engine for growth among the 10 countries, we will be lifted by the two wings.

[19] Charter of the Association of Southeast Asian Nations, 20 November 2007. See further, Mely Caballero-Anthony, 'The ASEAN Charter', in Daljit Singh and Tin Maung Maung Than (eds.), *Southeast Asian Affairs 2008* (Singapore: ISEAS, 2008), 71.

[20] 'Global City of Opportunity', Keynote Address by Senior Minister GOH Chok Tong of the Republic of Singapore at the Singapore Conference, 15 March 2005, Singapore Government Press Release, 15 March 2005.

B. *In trading terms*

Currently, two-thirds of the goods coverage of the six original ASEAN members under the CEPT has been liberalized multilaterally under the GATT following intra-ASEAN liberalization. One third has not. According to one commentator, the aim is to minimize the risk of trade diversion. This can be done by minimizing the difference between intra- and extra-ASEAN tariff rates.[21] While the International Monetary Fund (IMF) finds no evidence of FTAs causing trade diversion in Asia, the explanation lies in Asia's 'higher'openness towards non-members as the result of two decades of unilateral concessions during the 1980s and 1990s.[22] Notwithstanding debate on how well the GATT-born method of trade negotiations serves global trade liberalization,[23] how much of trade liberalization in Asia today is likely to consist of intra-Asian multilateralized concessions?

C. *'Exporting' ASEAN's internal trade preference structure*

A recent survey of the Asia–Pacific region as a whole suggests that different devices are being employed, that there is a spectrum of

[21] Jayant Menon, 'Building blocks or stumbling blocks?: The GMS and AFTA in Asia', (2007) 24(2) *ASEAN Economic Bulletin* 254–66, 259. According to Jacob Viner, trade diversion is shown by a shift in production from a lower-cost producer outside the FTA to a higher-cost producer within and an FTA is efficiency and welfare reducing if it results in more trade diversion than trade creation; Nigel Grimwade, *International Trade Policy* (London: Routledge, 1996), 237–8. Jacob Viner in his *Customs Union Issue* (Washington DC: Carnegie Endowment for International Peace, 1950) is therefore credited with having exploded the myth that preferential trade agreements are necessarily efficiency and welfare improving. See further Carnegie Endowment Study Group on International Trade, *Reflections on Regionalism* (Washington DC: Carnegie Endowment for International Peace, 1997), 11–18. On the legal side, this is now linked to calls for tighter WTO disciplines as a result. The literature is voluminous, but see (e.g.) John McMillan, 'Does regional integration foster open trade? Economic theory and GATT's Article XXIV', in Kym Anderson and Richard Blackhurst (eds.), *Regional Integration and the Global Trading System* (New York: St Martin's Press, 1993) 292, 297; Jagdish Bhagwati, 'Preferential trade agreements: The wrong road' (1995–6) 27 *Law & Policy in International Business* 865; Colin B. Picker, 'Regional trade agreements versus the WTO: A proposal for reform of Article XXIV to counter this institutional threat' (2005) 26 *University of Pennsylvania Journal of International Economic Law* 267, 270.

[22] International Monetary Fund, *Asia and Pacific Regional Economic Outlook* (Washington DC: International Monetary Fund, Inc., 2006), available on the Fund's website at www.imf.org.

[23] See (e.g.) Andreas F. Lowenfeld, *International Economic Law* (Oxford University Press, 2002), 45–67.

creativity, in dealing with the pace and comprehensiveness of preferential trading arrangements. Long transition periods are only one option. While differential transition periods are employed in ASEAN as part of a 'two-track approach' in dealing (generally speaking) with the original ASEAN 6 members and the newer 'CMLV' members (Cambodia, Myanmar, Lao P.D.R. and Vietnam), another major feature which is not *solely* concerned with the integration of the lesser developed economies of ASEAN is the use of 'exclusion' and 'sensitive' lists.[24] Exclusion list products are excluded 'temporarily', while sensitive list products would not require total tariff elimination as opposed to tariff reduction above zero per cent *ad valorem*.[25] Such 'variable geometry' has also been exported to ASEAN's treaties with the 'Plus 3' nations. Scollay observes that this approach has also been adopted in the China–ASEAN FTA (discussed further, below):[26]

> [W]here each member has designated a large number of products as 'sensitive products'. There is a rather low correlation between the products listed as 'sensitive' by each ACFTA member.

The same structure applies to the ASEAN–Korea Trade in Goods Agreement.[27] Put simply, ASEAN's member nations have entered into preferential trading between themselves while still grappling with sharp differences in their economic structures, and ASEAN as a whole has

[24] Agreement on the Common Effective Preferential Tariff Scheme for the ASEAN Free Trade Area, Singapore, 28 January 1992, Articles 2(3), 3; Protocol to Amend the Agreement on the CEPT Scheme for AFTA, 15 December 1995 (on the phasing in of products on the temporary exclusion list); Protocol on the Special Arrangement for Sensitive and Highly Sensitive Products, 30 September 1999 (i.e. all such products to be moved to the 'inclusion list' by 2010 for 'ASEAN 6'); Protocol Regarding the Implementation of the CEPT Scheme Temporary Exclusion List, 22–25 November 2000 (flexibility in phasing in products on the temporary exclusion list). See also Protocol to Amend the Agreement on the CEPT Scheme for AFTA for the Elimination of Import Duties, 31 January 2003 (tariff elimination on all products in the inclusion list by 2010 for 'ASEAN 6').

[25] Protocol on the Special Arrangement for Sensitive and Highly Sensitive Products, 30 September 1999, Article 3(d) (flexibility for highly sensitive products, but tariffs not to exceed 20%).

[26] Scollay, 'Prospects for linking preferential trade agreements in the Asia–Pacific Region', 175. See further, Agreement on Trade in Goods of the Framework Agreement on Comprehensive Economic Co-operation between ASEAN and the People's Republic of China, Vientiane, 29 November 2004, Article 3(2)(a) and (b).

[27] Agreement on Trade in Goods under the Framework Agreement on Comprehensive Economic Cooperation among the Governments of the Member Countries of the Association of Southeast Asian Nations and the Republic of Korea, 24 August 2006, Article 3(2).

sought FTAs with the 'Plus 3' nations at the same time. This, as we will discuss further below, has led to creative treaty devices which, if they are allowed to spread unchecked, suggests some cause for concern about the design of Asian trade preferentialism more generally. One principal reason has to do with the fact that China, Japan, Korea and thus far, India too, appear to prefer to *trade through a network of FTAs with ASEAN* than to have FTAs between themselves.[28]

D. *The China–ASEAN 'dialectic'*

At the ASEAN Economic Ministers' (AEM) meeting in Chiengmai in October 2000, the secretariat proposed economic integration amongst the 'ASEAN Plus 3' nations (ASEAN, Japan, China and South Korea). Following the absence of a consensus amongst ASEAN members, the Chair proposed a study of the feasibility of FTAs with individual Plus 3 members instead. This was accepted; the secretariat tabled the proposal during ASEAN's meeting in Chiengmai with the Ministers of Japan, China and South Korea.

The following month, Chinese Premier, Zhu Rongji proposed an ASEAN–China FTA joint study at the ASEAN–China Leaders' meeting in Singapore. Similarly, an AEM-(Japanese) Ministry of International Trade and Industry (MITI) meeting in Hanoi in September 2001 established an Expert Group to commence study on a Closer Economic Partnership Agreement (CEP) with Japan. The group met several times prior to the AEM–METI (Ministry of Economy, Trade and Industry) meeting in Bandar Seri Begawan in September 2002 at which both the AEM and METI recommended commencing negotiations on a framework agreement.[29] That recommendation was in turn accepted during the ASEAN–Japan Leaders' meeting in Cambodia in November 2002. Hatakeyama Noboru has put it memorably where he observed that:[30]

> [T]he stimulus caused by the Japan–Singapore Economic Partnership Agreement (JSEPA) towards FTAs in the Asian region has led to the reaction on the part of China, which has invited another action by Japan . . . [and Hegel would have called this] . . . a dialectical development.

[28] See Severino, *Southeast Asia in Search of an ASEAN Community*, 264.

[29] The MITI was in charge of industrial policies in Japan. In 2001, it was replaced by the newly created METI.

[30] Hatakeyama Noboru, 'A short history of Japan's movement to FTAs (Part 3)' (2003: March/April) 22 *Journal of Japanese Trade & Industry*, 42.

Today, the China–ASEAN Framework Agreement is complemented by the Trade in Goods Agreement[31] which has in turn been supplemented by two additional protocols in 2006. A Trade in Services Agreement was signed on 14 January 2007. It is anticipated that the entire ASEAN–China FTA will have been concluded by 2010 with the ASEAN 6 (i.e. the original six members of ASEAN), and by 2015 with all of ASEAN.[32]

While China has been a late-comer to the 'FTA game',[33] its FTA with ASEAN is the most advanced and comprehensive regional trade structure in Asia at the present time. It is anticipated that by 2010, the average customs duty for goods will be between 0–5% covering a population of 1.7 billion people, 40% of the world's foreign exchange reserves and 10% of world GDP.[34]

E. ASEAN–Japan

Japan adopted a different strategy. While ASEAN–Japan negotiations were only launched in 2005, Japan had successfully conducted bilateral FTAs with Singapore, Malaysia, Philippines and Thailand ahead of the Japan–ASEAN Comprehensive Economic Partnership Agreement (EPA) with ASEAN which was signed in April 2008.[35] The Japanese negotiation strategy however is well captured in the following remarks by Hatakeyama Noboru:[36]

> Japan has been engaged in studying a possible EPA with ASEAN on the one hand, and similar mechanisms with the Philippines or Thailand on the other . . . Japan has started exploring both regional and bilateral

[31] Agreement on Trade in Goods of the Framework Agreement on Comprehensive Economic Co-operation Between ASEAN and the People's Republic of China, Vientiane, 29 November 2004.

[32] Framework Agreement on Comprehensive Economic Cooperation between ASEAN and the People's Republic of China, Phnom Penh, 5 November 2002.

[33] See Henry Gao, 'The RTA strategy of China', in *The New International Architecture in Trade and Investment: Current Status and Implications*, APEC Human Resources Working Group Capacity Building Network (Singapore: APEC Secretariat, 2007), 33.

[34] 'Sino-ASEAN FTA Nears Final Stage', *China Business Weekly* (Beijing), 26 October 2004, available at www.bilaterals.org.

[35] Agreement on Comprehensive Economic Partnership among Japan and Member States of the Association of Southeast Asian Nations, April 2008.

[36] Noboru, 'A Short History of Japan's Movement to FTAs (Part 3)', 42–43. See also Shujiro Urata, 'Japan's FTA strategy and a free trade area of the Asia–Pacific', in Morrison and Pedrosa (eds.), *An APEC Trade Agenda? The Political Economy of a Free Trade Area of the Asia–Pacific* (Singapore: ISEAS, 2007), 99.

> approaches . . . Which approach would be better? Ideally speaking, a regional approach. First of all . . . ASEAN countries may blame Japan for trying to split ASEAN. In addition, in the case of a bilateral approach, Japan should have as many as 10 EPAs . . . Trading houses would then be stifled by the vast quantities of documents . . . However, realistically speaking, if Japan takes a regional approach alone – studying or negotiating just with ASEAN as a whole, an ASEAN country can have the veto power against it . . . I think Japan will inevitably need to take a double track approach.

F. ASEAN–Korea

Korea, partly because of its concerns with agriculture, has been slower than China and Japan in its response to the spread of regional FTAs.[37] This was ironic. It was South Korean President Kim Dae-Jung who had proposed an East Asian Vision Group which subsequently proposed the establishment of an East Asia Free Trade Area comprising ASEAN, China, Japan and South Korea.[38]

Earlier in 2002 Korea had concluded an FTA with Chile. That was a cautious first step. Following President Kim's visit to Japan in 1998, there was also some movement, at least at the level of officials, towards a Korea–Japan FTA.[39] While there has been no real development on that, an ASEAN–Korea Trade in Goods Agreement has been in force since June 2007.[40] In November 2004, the ASEAN Economic Ministers+Republic of Korea (AEM—ROK) Summit had:[41]

> agreed that (i) negotiations for the AKFTA commence in 2005 and be concluded within 2 years, (ii) that ASEAN-6 and Korea eliminate tariffs for 80% of all products by 2009, as a key milestone in the realisation of the AKFTA.

[37] Dukgeun Ahn, '"Korea's FTA Policy," WTO and East Asia: New perspectives' in *The New International Architecture*, 49.

[38] *Ibid.*, 43; also Severino, *Southeast Asia in Search of an ASEAN Community*, 267–8.

[39] See Won-Mog Choi, 'Regional economic integration in East Asia: Prospect and jurisprudence' (2003) 6 *Journal of International Economic Law* 49, 53–54 (also stressing the agriculture issue for South Korea).

[40] Agreement on Trade in Goods under the Framework Agreement on Comprehensive Economic Cooperation among the Governments of the Member Countries of the Association of Southeast Asian Nations and the Republic of Korea, 24 August 2006.

[41] See the ASEAN–Korea FTA (AKFTA) section on the Singapore Government FTA website, available at www.app.fta.gov.sg.

This was followed by a Framework Agreement which was signed in December 2005,[42] and the Trade in Goods Agreement.

G. *India*

Thus, instead of an East Asian FTA what we see is a network of FTAs between ASEAN and the 'Plus 3' nations – China, Japan and Korea. The picture with India is virtually the same amidst a more general proliferation of RTAs in the Asian region.[43] There is no China–India deal, and indeed no India–Japan or Korea–India FTA. Instead India is nearing completion in its negotiations with ASEAN, coming hot on the heels of the ASEAN Agreements with the 'Plus 3' nations.

While the popular imagination today is captivated by the potential of both China and India, ASEAN's focus in previous decades has been on China. There are modern historical roots to this. The position China took in relation to the Vietnamese invasion of Cambodia impressed itself on the strategic imagination of the Cold War members of ASEAN. India's Treaty of Friendship and Cooperation with the Soviet Union in 1971 also played a part in distancing India from ASEAN. For all ASEAN's talk of non-alignment during the Cold War years, the coalescence of ASEAN through its opposition to the Soviet-sponsored Vietnamese invasion was the glue which held ASEAN together as an organization. It was China which therefore became the focus of ASEAN's preoccupation from the Sino-Soviet conflict to the US–India rapprochement. After that, US–India–USSR relations continued to be a major preoccupation throughout the 1970s, as was the case with US–India–Japan relations throughout the 1980s.[44] India's significance as a partner is therefore relatively new, and this reorientation forms the background to ASEAN's current FTA negotiations with India. On India's part, New Delhi has also recognized a similar need to link up with East Asia since the early 1990s.[45]

[42] Framework Agreement on Comprehensive Economic Cooperation among the Governments of the Member Countries of the Association of Southeast Asian Nations and the Republic of Korea, Kuala Lumpur, 13 December 2005.

[43] Rahul Sen, 'New regionalism in Asia: A comparative analysis of emerging regional and bilateral trading agreements involving ASEAN, China and India' (2006) 40 *Journal of World Trade* 554.

[44] See (e.g.) 'Speech by Mr GOH Chok Tong, Senior Minister at the Official Launch of the Institute of South Asian Studies, ISAS, 27 January 2005', *Singapore Government Press Release*, 27 January 2005.

[45] Severino, *Southeast Asia in Search of an ASEAN Community*, 290.

A Framework Agreement to Enhance ASEAN–India Trade and Economic Cooperation was signed on 8 October 2003, and the target date for an ASEAN–India FTA (AIFTA) with the ASEAN 6 is currently 2011 and 2016 for ASEAN 10.[46] Recent reports suggest that the sticking point to current negotiations has to do with concessions sought from Indonesia in particular and better market access, generally, from the rest of ASEAN.[47]

IV. The China–ASEAN tariff acceleration clause

The greatest success has been with the China–ASEAN FTA. Yet its treaty design features could have broader implications for Asian trade regionalism.

A. *Two senses of open regionalism*

The ASEAN FTA policies which we have discussed above may be used to illustrate, and to test, the oft-heard claim today of 'MFN erosion' and the decline of multilateral trade liberalization more broadly.[48]

Actual trade diversion has never been conclusively proven one way or the other.[49] Nonetheless, classical economic theory supports open, not closed regionalism. One view is that open-regionalism should mean something more than the extension of membership to non-members. The concept has at least two senses, according to Fred Bergsten. First, it should include a commitment to continue reducing barriers to non-member countries while liberalizing internally on an MFN basis', as well as a 'willingness to extend . . . regional liberalization to nonmembers

[46] Singapore Government FTA website available at www.app.fta.gov.sg.

[47] 'India–ASEAN FTA hinges on Indonesia, market access', *Economic Times* (Haryana, India), 21 March 2008.

[48] Viewing the spread of liberalization through multilateralised concessions as an overriding aim involves a distinct set of assumptions. For a seminal treatment of the MFN clause from the perspective of public choice theory (protecting concessions against future erosion *versus* the free-rider problem), see Warren F. Schwartz and Alan O. Sykes, 'The economics of the most favored nation clause', in Jagdeep S. Bhandari and Alan O. Sykes (eds.), *Economic Dimensions in International Law* (Cambridge University Press, 1997) 43, 43–53, 58–65.

[49] Jiangyu Wang, 'China's regional trade agreements: The law, geopolitics, and impact on the multilateral trading system' (2004) 8 *Singapore Year Book of International Law* 119, 143. See also World Bank, *Global Economic Prospects 2005* (Washington DC. The World Bank, 2005), 61, also cited in Wang, 'The role of China and India in Asian regionalism', chapter 10 in this volume.

on a mutually reciprocal basis'.[50] In short, the first sense of open regionalism is about preventing MFN erosion.[51] On the other hand, the second sense of open regionalism involves 'recognition that any individual APEC member can unilaterally extend its APEC liberalization to nonmembers on a conditional or unconditional basis'.[52]

Open regionalism is understood largely in the second sense in the regional treaty behaviour of the ASEAN 'Plus 3' nations. If we should simply replace the reference to 'APEC' with the 'ASEAN Plus 3 nations', we will find open-regionalism in that second sense. Following China's FTA with Chile in 2005, it has negotiated FTAs with New Zealand, Pakistan, the Gulf Cooperation Council, Australia and Iceland. The China–Pakistan FTA was concluded in November 2006 and the China–New Zealand FTA was concluded in April 2008. Japan has on-going Economic Partnership Agreement (EPA) negotiations with Switzerland, India, the Gulf Cooperation Council and Australia whereas Korea concluded its FTA with the European Free Trade Area (EFTA) in November 2006 and signed KORUS with the United States in 2007. ASEAN itself is negotiating with the European Union which has also started negotiations with India and South Korea.[53]

Bergsten's first sense has been neglected instead. We can call it the 'obligation' to multilateralize trade concessions. Creating an FTA MFN exception is one thing, permitting members of the same FTA to form further bilateral deals *solely* between themselves is another.[54]

Article XXIV: 4 of the GATT-WTO states that: 'The contracting parties recognize the desirability of increasing freedom of trade by the development, through voluntary agreements, of closer integration between the economies of the countries parties to such agreements.'

[50] Fred C. Bergsten, *Open Regionalism*, Working Paper 97–3 (Washington D.C.: Institute for International Economics, 1997), available online at the Institute's website, available at www.iie.com. Bergsten's recommendations were directed at the Asia–Pacific Economic Cooperation (APEC) organization, but he argues that they should also apply to other FTAs; *ibid.* His recommendation draws on the work of the APEC Eminent Persons' Group (EPG) from 1993–5; see *ibid.*

[51] See further Thomas Cottier, 'The erosion of non-discrimination: Stern warning without true remedies' (2005) 8 *Journal of International Economic Law* 595, 599.

[52] *Ibid.*

[53] Razeen Sally, 'Looking East: The European Union's new FTA negotiations in Asia', Jan Tumlir Policy Essay No. 03, 2007.

[54] See also the Protocol to Amend the Framework Agreement on Comprehensive Economic Co-operation Between the Association of South East Asian Nations and the People's Republic of China, 6 October 2003, available at the ASEAN Secretariat website, available at www.asean.org.

So that, at least, is the spirit of WTO permissiveness in relation to the formation of FTAs.[55] Viewed in this way, multi-party, regional FTA partners negotiating further bilateral and plurilateral agreements between themselves runs against one important sense in which we might use the term 'open regionalism' – namely, the need to liberalize 'internally', between the regional FTA partners themselves, on an MFN basis.

B. 'The tariff acceleration problem'

Under the China–ASEAN FTA's Early Harvest Programme (EHP), tariff concessions by the parties were originally intended for immediate realization. So far, so good. The EHP covers agricultural products falling under Chapters 1–8 of the HS System and applies to those products falling outside the China–ASEAN Trade in Goods Agreement of 2004.[56] However, controversy arose over the possibility of free-riding where country A's concessions are immediately realized by all other members under the MFN clause without sufficient concessions in exchange. In a sense, this was a negotiating breakdown or failure since a pre-condition would have been the similar inclusion of products in the EHP schemes of the beneficiaries. However, the Philippines and China failed to establish an EHP scheme altogether while others feared competition from Thai farmers. Malaysia broke away and proposed an innovative clause that would allow it to negotiate bilaterally with China in return for Chinese concessions.[57] Thus, the China–ASEAN-type tariff acceleration agreement was born by way of an amendment to the ASEAN–China Framework Agreement on Comprehensive Economic Cooperation.[58] Article 6(3)(b)(i) states that while (1) 'A Party may accelerate its tariff reduction and/or elimination under this Article in relation to the rest of the parties on a unilateral basis':

[55] On the 'teleological' significance of Article XXIV:4 as a general principle, see further, Sungjoon Cho, 'Breaking the barrier between regionalism and multilateralism: A new perspective on trade regionalism' (2001) 42 *Harvard International Law Journal* 419, 439; Mitsuo Matsushita, 'Legal aspects of free trade agreements: In the context of Article XXIV of the GATT 1994', in Mitsuo Matsushita and Dukgeun Ahn, *WTO and East Asia: New Perspectives* (London: Cameron May, 2004), 497, 501.

[56] China–ASEAN Trade in Goods Agreement, Article 3.

[57] See Wang, 'China's regional trade agreements', 126.

[58] 'The Protocol to Amend the Framework Agreement on Comprehensive Economic Co-operation Between the Association of South East Asian Nations and the People's Republic of China', 6 October 2003, Article 2.

(2) One or more ASEAN Member States may also conduct negotiations and enter into a bilateral or plurilateral acceleration arrangement with China to accelerate their tariff reduction and/or elimination under this Article.

That the other members can subsequently accede to these 'bilateral or plurilateral acceleration arrangements' may not provide much comfort.[59]

In addition, Article 4 of the 2003 Protocol Amending the China–ASEAN Framework Agreement inserts a new Article 12A in the Framework Agreement:[60]

> Nothing in this Agreement shall prevent or prohibit any individual ASEAN Member State from entering into any bilateral or plurilateral agreement with China and/or the rest of the ASEAN Member States relating to trade in goods, trade in services, investment, and/or other areas of economic co-operation outside the ambit of this Agreement. The provisions of this Agreement shall not apply to any such bilateral or plurilateral agreement.

Thus, while China and ASEAN envisage an FTA between the two entities, other full-blown FTAs (as opposed to 'bilateral or plurilateral tariff acceleration arrangements') have been concluded or are currently being negotiated between the ASEAN members and between China and individual ASEAN members. AFTA is of course the clearest example of the need for Article 12A's 'notwithstanding clause'. Article 12A preserves AFTA's treaty rights and duties against the fresh obligations undertaken in the China–ASEAN Framework Agreement. But it also allows other bilateral FTAs to be negotiated between the ASEAN members, and between China and these individual members.

China has yet to conclude an FTA with individual ASEAN members, unlike Japan which, as we have observed, has concluded agreements with Singapore, Malaysia, the Philippines and Thailand. Likewise, India which is set to conclude a deal with ASEAN has FTAs with Singapore and Thailand whereas Korea has an FTA with Singapore.

It must be observed, however, that the freedom to negotiate further bilateral or plurilateral FTAs solely *between* the members of a broad, regional multi-party FTA is different from the freedom to negotiate FTAs with trading nations outside the broad, regional FTA (i.e. Bergsten's second sense of open regionalism, above). The latter is a device to restrict the negative effects of preferential trading arrangements whereas the former is about having further 'FTAs within FTAs'.

[59] *Ibid.*, Article 2. [60] *Ibid.*, Article 4.

C. *WTO disciplines*

Agreements like the China–ASEAN FTA may be so expansive in their geographical reach that at some point they compete directly with the WTO. Indeed, their rules may be substantially similar to those of the WTO. This makes it all the more significant that cardinal rules, such as MFN treatment, should not be abandoned so easily. The China–ASEAN Framework Agreement's tariff acceleration clause under Article 6(3)(b)(i) allows China or an ASEAN member to avoid multilateralizing concessions under the Framework Agreement's Early Harvest Programme. The new Article 12A allows the same effect to be achieved. Such clauses are largely unproblematic under WTO law where the FTA is notified under the Enabling Clause. Amongst other things, the Enabling Clause does not contain a 'substantially all trade' requirement.[61] But what if this practice were to spread in the current build-up of Asian FTAs, or even more broadly in the FTA practice of WTO members, to those preferential agreements which cannot be notified under the Enabling Clause?[62] What would GATT Article XXIV have to say?

There was until recently only a rudimentary notification requirement under Article XXIV:7 (the 'prompt notification' procedure).[63] But Article XXIV also requires the Committee on Regional Trade Agreements to apply the 'not on the whole higher or more restrictive' and 'substantially all trade' standards under Articles XXIV:5(b) and XXIV:8(b).[64] The Framework Agreement would therefore have to fulfill the

[61] Presently, the ASEAN Agreements would seek to rely on the Enabling Clause. See *Decision on Differential and More Favourable Treatment, Reciprocity and Fuller Participation of Developing Countries*; B.I.S.D. (265h Supp.) 203–5 (1980). The ASEAN–China FTA and AFTA were both notified to the WTO under the Enabling Clause. There remains the question of the exact legal relationship between Article XXIV (especially, Article XXIV: 4) and the Enabling Clause.

[62] As of 1 March 2007, the only Asian FTAs which have been notified under the Enabling Clause as opposed to GATT Article XXIV have been AFTA (notified, 1992), the China–ASEAN FTA (notified, 2004), the India–Sri Lanka FTA (notified, 2001) and the FTA between Thailand and Laos (notified, 1991).

[63] For the new transparency mechanism, see WTO, General Council, Transparency Mechanism for Regional Trade Agreements – decision of 14 December 2006, WTO Doc. WT/L/671, 18 December 2006. For the background proposal leading to the new mechanism, see WTO, negotiating Group on Rules, Submission on Regional Trade Agreements – Chile, WTO Doc. TN/RL/W/16, 10 July 2002.

[64] C. L. Lim, 'Free trade agreements in Asia: Some common legal problems', in Yasuhei Taniguchi, Alan Yanovich and Jan Bohanes (eds.), *The WTO in the Twenty-First Century: Dispute Settlement, Negotiations and Regionalism in Asia* (Cambridge University Press/ WTO: 2007), 434, 438–439.

'substantially all trade' requirement for intra-FTA trade under GATT Article XXIV:8,[65] even if it fulfills GATT Article XXIV:5's requirement that 'duties and other regulations of commerce' applying to non-FTA members should be 'not on the whole higher or more restrictive'.

Doctrinally this presents interesting questions which are not yet fully resolved. Does the China–ASEAN tariff acceleration clause cover substantially all trade? In one sense, that is a factual or quantitative question.[66] For example, Australia has complained in Geneva that some FTAs 'backload an unreasonable amount of liberalization commitments towards the end of their implementation period'.[67] But it is at least arguably not purely a question of fact alone. The Appellate Body in the *Turkey–Textiles* case considered that the provision should include both quantitative and qualitative aspects.[68] What is especially noteworthy is that the European Communities has recently proposed that the solution must lie in the clarification of WTO legal disciplines.[69]

Could it also be argued that the 'substantially all trade' requirement does not apply because a tariff acceleration agreement is only an 'interim agreement' within the meaning of Article XXIV:5? The 'substantially all trade' requirement under Article XXIV:8 applies only to a final, full-blown FTA. The principal discipline which applies to an interim agreement is a surveillance mechanism under Article XXIV:5(c) whereby a 'plan or schedule for the formation of . . . [the FTA] . . . within a

[65] Similar concerns have been expressed in respect of intra-ASEAN trade treaty behaviour in Rahul Sen, *Free Trade Agreements in Southeast Asia* (Singapore: ISEAS, 2004), 88.

[66] See Patrick F.J. Macrory, Arthur E. Appleton and Michael G. Plummer: *The World Trade Organization: Legal, Economic and Political Analysis*, vol. II (New York: Springer, 2005), 227 arguing that the provision refers only to 'a certain percentage of trade'. This is also the European Communities' position in Geneva, citing a requirement of 80% of trade; The European Economic Community: Reports Adopted on 29 November 1957, L/778, GATT B.I.S.D. (6th Supp.) § D para. 30 (1958). Another view is that it would be inappropriate to fix a general figure; *ibid.* The European Free Trade Association has proposed a figure of 90% instead; European Free Trade Association, 4 June 1960, GATT B.I.S.D. (9th Supp.) (1961), para. 48. See also WTO, Committee on Regional Trade Agreements, Communications from Australia, WT/REG/W/22/Add.1, 24 April 1998. For criticism, see Cho, 'Breaking the barrier between regionalism and multilateralism', 443. *Cf. Turkey – Restrictions on Imports of Textile and Clothing Products*, AB-1999–5, report of the Appellate Body, 22 October 1999, WT/DS34/AB/R, 99–4546, para. 48.

[67] Currently, Australia proposes that 70% of tariff lines should be liberalized at point of entry; TN/RL/W/180, Negotiation group on Rules, Submission on RTAs by Australia, 13 May 2005, para. 7.

[68] *Turkey – Restrictions on Imports of Textile and Clothing Products*, para. 49.

[69] Submission Regional Trade Agreements by the European Communities and their Member States, Negotiating Group on Rules, World Trade Organization, TN/RL/W/14, 9 July 2002.

reasonable period of time' should be given. If other WTO members consider that an FTA that fulfills both the 'substantially all trade' and 'not higher or more restrictive' requirements would not result within such a reasonable period, they can then certainly make their recommendations known.[70]

It appears that, as a matter of positive law, neither the Enabling Clause nor Article XXIV is currently sufficient to deal with MFN erosion under devices such as the China–ASEAN tariff acceleration-type clause. But the issue is not that a China–ASEAN-type clause is legally justifiable under the Enabling Clause and GATT Article XXIV. The question is whether it should be.

D. Not different from NAFTA? The origins of the China–ASEAN tariff acceleration clause

Tibor Mende once wrote:[71]

> For about a thousand years after Buddhism brought China and India into contact, pilgrims and scholars journeyed between the two countries bringing new doctrines and new ideas. They traveled overland and by sea, and as messengers of two great civilizations they exercised a powerful influence on the thought of the South-East Asian peoples through whose lands they passed.

Today, a new idea emerges in the shadows of Asia's complex preferential trading arrangements – the multi-party regional FTA *sans* MFN. Perhaps it is not truly different from resort to tariff acceleration elsewhere – such as under NAFTA's Article 302. In the case of NAFTA, tariff acceleration may be trilateral (i.e. between all three parties) or bilateral, in which case it would raise substantially similar questions as the China-ASEAN tariff acceleration clause.[72] The China–ASEAN clause in this sense mimics NAFTA Article 302. In the case of NAFTA, this design feature had resulted from negotiations on Canada's

[70] Wang concurs with Jackson that this would require that the other members agree on the set of recommendations to be made, and that this requirement therefore operates as a presumption in favour of the validity of notified agreements; Wang, 'China's regional trade agreements', 137; citing John H. Jackson, *The Jurisprudence of GATT and the WTO: Insights on Treaty Law and Economic Relations* (Cambridge University Press, 2000), 104.

[71] Tibor Mende, *South-East Asia Between Two Worlds* (London: Turnstile Press, 1955), 316.

[72] North-American Free Trade Agreement, 17 December 1992, Article 302. Article 302 is essentially a 'successor' clause to the (bilateral) tariff reduction accelerator clause in Article 401.5 of the Canada-United States Free Trade Agreement, 2 January 1988.

refusal to proceed with comprehensive liberalization and the elimination of agricultural marketing boards. But from Montreal onwards the ministers had decided on two separate bilateral agreements on agriculture and the negotiations proceeded on three separate fronts – between Mexico and Canada, Canada and the United States, and Mexico and the United States.[73] It was the by-product of a wrinkle during the negotiations stage.

However, the China–ASEAN Framework Agreement's tariff acceleration clause under Article 6(3)(b)(i) has somewhat different origins. Its true predecessor is probably Article 4 of ASEAN's 1992 CEPT Agreement which established ASEAN's own FTA. Article 4 dealt with arrangements for the reduction of ASEAN tariffs above the 20% mark,[74] as well as reduction arrangements for tariffs already at or below the 20% mark as of 1 January 1993.[75] As for the latter, the terms of Article 4(1)(c) of the CEPT Agreement are strikingly similar to Article 6(3)(b)(i) of the subsequent China–ASEAN Framework Agreement. Article 4(1)(c) states that:

> Two or more Member States may enter into arrangements for tariff reduction to 0–5% on specific products at an accelerated pace to be announced at the start of the programme.

But the philosophy underlying Article 4(1) (c) extends beyond that provision. Article 4(2) requires tariffs to be at 20% or lower before a product may enjoy the concessions given by another ASEAN member under the CEPT Agreement for the same product.[76] That philosophy is, in a word, reciprocity; the very antithesis of unconditional MFN treatment, the very hallmark of GATT.[77]

[73] Maxwell A. Cameron and Brian W. Tomlin, *The Making of NAFTA: How the Deal was Done* (Ithaca, NY: Cornell University Press, 2000), 147. See further Hermann von Bertrab, *Negotiating NAFTA: A Mexican Envoy's Account* (Westport, CT: Praeger and the Centre for Strategic & International Studies, 1997), 53.

[74] Agreement on the Common Effective Preferential Tariff Scheme for the ASEAN Free Trade Area, Singapore, 28 January 1992, Article 4(1) (a), (b). Tariffs would be reduced to the 20% mark over 5–8 years, followed by a formula for further reductions over 7 years.

[75] *Ibid.*, Article 4(1)(c).

[76] *Ibid.*, Article 4(2) states that: 'Subject to Articles 4(1)(b) and 4(1)(c)' which deal respectively, as we have seen, with arrangements for further reductions below the 20% mark and tariffs already at that mark as of 1 January 1993 'products which reach, or are at tariff rates of 20% or below, shall automatically enjoy the concessions'.

[77] See further, Arnold Duncan McNair, *The Law of Treaties* (Oxford: Clarendon, 1961), 274–6 for the distinction between conditional and unconditional MFN treatment.

We should however distinguish between two senses of the word 'reciprocity' which is often loosely used. First, there is the situation, sometimes described as conditional MFN treatment, where concessions given by country A on an MFN basis for a certain product depends upon a condition being fulfilled, such as achievement of at least a 20% tariff mark for the same product by countries B and C. The second situation is where there is no MFN treatment at all – country A and country C may agree on preferences which are not extended to a third country, B. Whereas Article 4(2) is about the former sense of reciprocity, Article 4(1) (c) is reciprocity in the latter sense. It was, in all probability, the blueprint for the tariff acceleration clause under Article 6(3) (b)(i) of the China–ASEAN Framework Agreement.

While it was confined to ASEAN, the tariff acceleration clause was contained. If it spreads to the rest of Asia and beyond, it would be contrary to the basis of the GATT and the WTO. More importantly, the idea which we mentioned at the outset – that a patchwork of bilateral FTAs will in due course converge, more beneficially, into larger, regional trade regimes – needs to be revisited and the question should be asked if precedents such as the tariff acceleration clause might detract from some of the optimism implied in that view.[78]

V. Conclusion

The WTO has sound legal and policy reasons to regulate FTAs to ensure the achievement of the general aspiration of greater global trade liberalization. If WTO members wish to enjoy the MFN-exemption under GATT Article XXIV in the case of FTAs with broad geographical coverage, can they say that individual FTAs once constituted should become an MFN 'no man's land' under the GATT because of Article XXIV, and under the FTA because the FTA contains no MFN obligation? Against this, the GATT–WTO MFN clause has always served as something of a world-wide 'trade accelerator'.[79] So what does it mean today for an indeterminate number of countries being smaller than the number of

[78] Bergsten, 'Plan B for world trade: Go regional', Scollay, 'Prospects for linking preferential trade agreements in the Asia–Pacific region'.

[79] See e.g. Kenneth W. Dam, *Cordell Hull, the Reciprocal Trade Agreement Act and the WTO*, John M. Olin Law & Economics Working Paper No. 228 (2nd series) (Chicago: Law School, University of Chicago, 2004), 6.

WTO members and the total number of trading nations to disapply the unconditional MFN doctrine altogether?

The good news is that the China–ASEAN precedent has not been followed in Article 6 of the Korea–ASEAN Goods Agreement. Article 6(2) states that:[80]

> Nothing in this Agreement shall preclude any Party from negotiating and entering into arrangements to accelerate the implementation of concessions made under this Agreement or to incorporate new goods into such concessions, provided that such arrangements are mutually agreed upon *and applied to all the other Parties.*

It resembles Article 10 of the China–ASEAN Goods Agreement instead.[81] The two agreements – the Goods Agreement and the Framework Agreement – cover different product lists.[82] While the latter covers Chapters 1–8 of the Harmonized System (HS) the former covers some 7,000 products – almost the entirety of Chapters 9–97 of the HS instead.[83]

At present, the only other completed agreement between ASEAN and a 'Plus 3' nation is the Japan–ASEAN Economic Partnership Agreement. As we have observed, Japan's negotiation strategy has been to secure individual FTAs with a range of major ASEAN nations prior to the

[80] Agreement on Trade in Goods under the Framework Agreement on Comprehensive Economic Cooperation among the Governments of the Member Countries of the Association of Southeast Asian Nations and the Republic of Korea, 24 August 2006, Article 6(2) (my emphasis).

[81] Article 10 states: 'Nothing in this Agreement shall preclude the Parties from negotiating and entering into arrangements to accelerate the implementation of commitments made under this Agreement, provided that such arrangements are mutually agreed to and implemented by all the Parties'; Agreement on Trade in Goods of the Framework Agreement on Comprehensive Economic Co-operation between ASEAN and the People's Republic of China, Vientienne, 29 November 2004.

[82] Article 3 of the Goods Agreement states that: 'The tariff reduction or elimination programme of the Parties shall require the applied MFN tariff rates on listed tariff lines to be gradually reduced and where applicable, eliminated, in accordance with this Article', before stating that 'The tariff lines which are subject to the tariff reduction or elimination programme under this Agreement shall include all tariff lines not covered by the Early Harvest Programme under Article 6 of the Framework Agreement'; *ibid.*

[83] Tariff reduction or elimination takes place under a 'Normal Track' and a 'Sensitive Track' which in turn is divided further into a 'Sensitive List' and a 'Highly Sensitive List' of products; *Ibid.*, Article 3(2) (a) & (b). See further, Hong Kong Trade Development Council, *China–ASEAN Free Trade Area and Implications for Hong Kong as a Trade Hub* (Hong Kong Trade Development Council: 2006), note 16. Here, the separate difficulty which we have already alluded to (in our discussion of Scollay's views, above) is that there is little convergence in what ASEAN members consider to be sensitive products.

conclusion of the Japan–ASEAN EPA. Should there be no serious effort to multilateralize the concessions in Japan's individual full-blown FTAs with ASEAN members under the new Japan–ASEAN EPA, the problem of intra-regional FTA MFN erosion would be a real one. It is the same problem as that under Article 12A of the China–ASEAN Framework Agreement. That it is not technically the same as the tariff acceleration clause under Article 6(3)(b)(i) of the China–ASEAN Framework Agreement would be poor consolation indeed.

It might be hoped that the India–ASEAN negotiations will, when concluded, adopt the Korea–ASEAN model and eschew use of the China–ASEAN tariff acceleration precedent; that eventually the China–ASEAN tariff acceleration clause and similar MFN erosion devices will prove in Asia to be no more than a negotiating anomaly resulting from the unique negotiating history of that agreement. This would be especially important if what we are witnessing today is truly the beginning of a broader Asian trade regionalism which in time will replace various, smaller bilateral FTAs.[84] It is too early to tell, but we would be poorer off if what remains, at the end of the day, is a complex system of countless bilateral and plurilateral FTAs masquerading as one or more broad, regional FTAs.

[84] For the benefits of larger groupings, see (e.g.) Bergsten, 'Plan B for world trade: Go regional'; *contra* Sungjoon Cho, '"Plan B" is Always Inferior to "Plan A"', *Financial Times* (London), 22 August 2006. For the need for 'convergence' in the Asia–Pacific, see Scollay, 'Prospects for Linking Preferential Trade Agreements in the Asia–Pacific Region', generally.

References

Agreement on Comprehensive Economic Partnership among Japan and Member States of the Association of Southeast Asian Nations, April 2008

Agreement on the Common Effective Preferential Tariff Scheme for the ASEAN Free Trade Area, Singapore, 28 January 1992

Agreement on Trade in Goods of the Framework Agreement on Comprehensive Economic Co-operation Between ASEAN and the People's Republic of China, Vientiane, 29 November 2004

Agreement on Trade in Goods under the Framework Agreement on Comprehensive Economic Cooperation among the Governments of the Member Countries of the Association of Southeast Asian Nations and the Republic of Korea, 24 August 2006

Ahn, Dukgeun, ''Korea's FTA policy', WTO and East Asia: New perspectives', in *The New International Architecture*

Bergsten, Fred, 'Plan B for World Trade: Go Regional', *Financial Times* (London), 15 August 2006

Open Regionalism, Working Paper 97–3 (Washington DC: Institute for International Economics, 1997), available online at the Institute's website, available at www.iie.com

Bertrab, Hermann von, *Negotiating NAFTA: A Mexican Envoy's Account* (Westport, CT: Praeger and the Centre for Strategic & International Studies, 1997)

Bhagwati, Jagdish, 'Preferential trade agreements: The wrong road' (1995–6) 27 *Law & Policy in International Business* 865

Caballero-Anthony, Mely, 'The ASEAN Charter', in Daljit Singh and Tin Maung Maung Than (eds.), *Southeast Asian Affairs 2008* (Singapore: ISEAS, 2008)

Cameron, Maxwell A. and Tomlin, Brian W., *The Making of NAFTA: How the Deal was Done* (Ithaca, NY: Cornell University Press, 2000)

Carnegie Endowment Study Group on International Trade, *Reflections on Regionalism* (Washington DC: Carnegie Endowment for International Peace, 1997)

Charter of the Association of Southeast Asian Nations, 20 November 2007

Choi, Won-Mog, 'Regional economic integration in East Asia: Prospect and jurisprudence' (2003) 6 *Journal of International Economic Law* 49

Cho, Sungjoon, 'Breaking the barrier between regionalism and multilateralism: A new perspective on trade regionalism' (2001) 42 *Harvard International Law Journal* 419

'"Plan B" is always inferior to "Plan A"' *Financial Times* (London), 22 August 2006

Cottier, Thomas, 'The erosion of non-discrimination: Stern warning without true remedies' (2005) 8 *Journal of International Economic Law* 595

Dam, Kenneth W., *Cordell Hull, the Reciprocal Trade Agreement Act and the WTO*, John M. Olin Law & Economics Working Paper No. 228 (2nd series) (Chicago: Law School, University of Chicago, 2004)

Declaration of ASEAN Concord II (Bali Concord II), 7 October 2002 (hereafter, 'Bali Concord II Declaration')

Framework Agreement on Comprehensive Economic Cooperation among the Governments of the Member Countries of the Association of Southeast Asian Nations and the Republic of Korea, Kuala Lumpur, 13 December 2005

Framework Agreement on Comprehensive Economic Cooperation between ASEAN and the People's Republic of China, Phnom Penh, 5 November 2002

Framework Agreement on Enhancing ASEAN Economic Cooperation, Singapore, 28 January 1992; Agreement on the Common Effective Preferential Tariff Scheme for the ASEAN Free Trade Area, Singapore, 28 January 1992

Gao, Henry, 'The RTA strategy of China', in *The New International Architecture in Trade and Investment: Current Status and Implications*, APEC Human Resources Working Group Capacity Building Network (Singapore: APEC Secretariat, 2007)

GOH Chok Tong, 'Global city of opportunity', Keynote Address by Senior Minister Goh Chok Tong of the Republic of Singapore at the Singapore Conference, 15 March 2005, Singapore Government Press Release, 15 March 2005

Keynote Address by Prime Minister Goh Chok Tong at the ASEAN Business and Investment Summit, 6 October 2003, Bali, Indonesia, available at the ASEAN Secretariat website www.aseansec.org

'Speech by Mr. Goh Chok Tong, Senior Minister at the Official Launch of the Institute of South Asian Studies, ISAS, 27 January 2005', *Singapore Government Press Release*, 27 January 2005

Grimwade, Nigel, *International Trade Policy* (London: Routledge, 1996)

Hew, Denis (ed.), *Brick by Brick: The Building of an ASEAN Economic Community* (Singapore: ISEAS, 2007)

Hong Kong Trade Development Council, *China–ASEAN Free Trade Area and Implications for Hong Kong as a Trade Hub* (Hong Kong Trade Development Council: 2006)

'India–ASEAN FTA hinges on Indonesia, market access', *Economic Times* (Haryana, India), 21 March 2008

International Monetary Fund, *Asia and Pacific Regional Economic Outlook* (Washington DC: International Monetary Fund, Inc., 2006), available on the Fund's website at www.imf.org

Jackson, John H., *The Jurisprudence of GATT and the WTO: Insights on Treaty Law and Economic Relations* (Cambridge University Press, 2000)

Lim, C. L., 'Free trade agreements in Asia: Some common legal problems', in Yasuhei Taniguchi, Alan Yanovich and Jan Bohanes (eds.), *The WTO in the Twenty-First Century: Dispute Settlement, Negotiations and Regionalism in Asia* (Cambridge University Press/WTO, 2007)

LOK Hwee Chong, Lim, Christopher H. and Lyn, Ng (eds.), *A Guide to Free Trade in ASEAN.* Singapore Year Book of International Law 2007 (National University of Singapore)

Lowenfeld, Andreas F., *International Economic Law* (Oxford University Press, 2002)

Macrory, Patrick F. J., Appleton, Arthur E. and Plummer, Michael G., *The World Trade Organization: Legal, Economic and Political Analysis*, vol. II (New York: Springer, 2005)

Matsushita, Mitsuo, 'Legal aspects of free trade agreements: In the context of Article XXIV of the GATT 1994', in Mitsuo Matsushita and Dukgeun Ahn, *WTO and East Asia: New Perspectives* (London: Cameron May, 2004)

McMillan, John, 'Does regional integration foster open trade? Economic theory and GATT's Article XXIV' in Kym Anderson and Richard Blackhurst (eds.), *Regional Integration and the Global Trading System* (New York: St Martin's Press, 1993)

McNair, Arnold Duncan, *The Law of Treaties* (Oxford: Clarendon, 1961)

Mende, Tibor, *South-East Asia Between Two Worlds* (London: Turnstile Press, 1955)

Menon, Jayant, 'Building blocks or stumbling blocks?: The GMS and AFTA in Asia' (2007) 24(2) *ASEAN Economic Bulletin* 254–66

Noboru, Hatakeyama, 'A short history of Japan's movement to FTAs (Part 3)' (2003: March/April) 22 *Journal of Japanese Trade & Industry*

ONG Keng Yong, Speech by Mr Ong Keng Yong, ASEAN Secretary-General, 22 March 2003, Ballroom of the Regent Hotel, Singapore (on file)

Picker, Colin B., 'Regional trade agreements versus the WTO: A proposal for reform of Article XXIV to counter this institutional threat' (2005) 26 *University of Pennsylvania Journal of International Economic Law* 267

Protocol on the Special Arrangement for Sensitive and Highly Sensitive Products, 30 September 1999

Protocol Regarding the Implementation of the CEPT Scheme Temporary Exclusion List, 22–25 November 2000

Protocol to Amend the Agreement on the CEPT Scheme for AFTA, 15 December 1995

Protocol to Amend the Agreement on the CEPT Scheme for AFTA for the Elimination of Import Duties, 31 January 2003

Protocol to Amend the Framework Agreement on Comprehensive Economic Co-operation Between the Association of South East Asian Nations and the People's Republic of China, 6 October 2003

Sally, Razeen, 'Looking East: The European Union's new FTA negotiations in Asia', Jan Tumlir Policy Essay No. 03, 2007

Schwartz, Warren F. and Sykes, Alan O., 'The economics of the most favored nation clause', in Jagdeep S. Bhandari and Alan O. Sykes (eds.), *Economic Dimensions in International Law* (Cambridge University Press, 1997)

Scollay, Robert, 'Prospects for linking preferential trade agreements in the Asia–Pacific region', in Charles E. Morrison and Eduardo Pedrosa (eds.), *An APEC Trade Agenda? The Political Economy of a Free Trade Area of the Asia–Pacific* (Singapore: ISEAS, 2007)

Sen, Rahul, *Free Trade Agreements in Southeast Asia* (Singapore: ISEAS, 2004)

'New regionalism in Asia: A comparative analysis of emerging regional and bilateral trading agreements involving ASEAN, China and India' (2006) 40 *Journal of World Trade* 554

Severino, Rodolfo C., *Southeast Asia in Search of an ASEAN Community* (Singapore: ISEAS, 2006)

Singapore Government FTA website available at www.app.fta.gov.sg

'Sino-ASEAN FTA nears final stage', *China Business Weekly* (Beijing), 26 October 2004, available at www.bilaterals.org

Urata, Shujiro, 'Japan's FTA strategy and a free trade area of the Asia–Pacific', in Morrison and Pedrosa (eds.), *An APEC Trade Agenda? The Political Economy of a Free Trade Area of the Asia–Pacific* (Singapore: ISEAS, 2007)

Viner, Jacob, *Customs Union Issue* (Washington DC: Carnegie Endowment for International Peace, 1950)

Wang, Jiangyu, 'China's regional trade agreements: The law, geopolitics, and impact on the multilateral trading system' (2004) 8 *Singapore Year Book of International Law* 119

World Bank, *Global Economic Prospects 2005* (Washington DC: The World Bank, 2005)

Yeoh, En-Lai, 'Southeast Asia speeds single market plan', Associated Press, 22 August 2006 (on file)

13

Financial cooperation and integration in East Asia

DOUGLAS W. ARNER, WEI WANG AND PAUL LEJOT

I. Introduction

This chapter discusses the efforts being made in East Asia towards financial integration, and the prospects for it becoming generally accepted as a consensus goal of national policies. At present, financial integration in East Asia is largely a discussion topic for national officials in regional gatherings, both formal and bilateral and the subject of research, rather than a planned objective or even a limited agreed direction of policy. At the same time, several separate motives and common external forces have caused an increase in discussion of prospects for financial cooperation and integration in East Asia, and greater cooperation among national interests that traditionally compete in economic, financial and trade objectives. This has made the possibility of an agreement on financial integration as a deliberate objective more tangible than before.

This chapter begins with a discussion of the reasons underlying discussions relating to East Asian financial cooperation and integration (section II). It then reviews progress to date in a number of areas, of which the most significant are initiatives involving regional economic cooperation and Asian bond market development (section III). In looking to possible future developments, it is useful to compare the experience to date of the most successful regional financial integration initiative, that of the European Union (EU) (section IV). The chapter concludes with a discussion of possible implications for governance in the region and a number of recommendations for future consideration, based on these underlying rationales, current progress and experience in Europe (section V).

II. Rationale for East Asian financial cooperation and integration

In addition to issues of general economic cooperation and integration in East Asia, financial cooperation and integration are taking an increasingly significant place in regional discussions and initiatives. There are a number of reasons for this, which can be assessed as: (1) the crisis imperative; (2) the economic imperative; (3) the development imperative; and (4) the political imperative.

A. *The crisis imperative*

The Asian financial crisis of 1997–8 had a significant and continuing impact on both East Asian national economies and East Asian policymakers and academics. The crisis revealed a number of weaknesses in the financial systems of individual economies, and highlighted increasing economic and financial interlinkages within the region.

In relation to the former, the crisis has resulted in significant economic and financial reforms in individual economies in efforts to both recover from and to prevent similar situations from occurring in future. These reforms have typically increased the role of markets within individual economies and in some respects reduced the role of government control within individual economies. The reform process has therefore in many cases increased the role of economic and financial markets and actors within the region, thereby supporting a continued increase in trade and financial transactions. At the same time, state influence in financial market operation has persisted, seen most notably in the effects of international currency management.

In addition, the crisis highlighted interlinkages and cross-vulnerabilities across the region. It also caused many policymakers to believe that the existing international arrangements for addressing economic problems were inappropriate to East Asia's needs. At the time of the Asian financial crisis, this resulted initially in a number of developments. First, when faced with initial problems, individual countries (for example, Thailand) first sought assistance not from multilateral economic and financial institutions (the IMF and World Bank) but rather from East Asian economic powers (Japan), before turning for assistance to the US and finally the IMF. Unfortunately, at the time, there were no formal arrangements in place in East Asia to deal with these issues, which at the preference of the US were considered within the remit of the IMF. This fracture led to discussions within East Asia over the need for regional arrangements to address similar problems in future, both regionally (mainly through Japanese proposals for an Asian Monetary Fund, or AMF) and bilaterally (through agreements between individual economies to provide future mutual support and assistance). At the time, the US was strongly against proposals for an AMF and in the context of fighting the fires of crisis, the idea was dropped from public discussions. Nonetheless, discussions between East Asian policymakers continued (and continue to this day) to focus on the prevention of future crises, specific needs of the regional economy and individual economies, and on mechanisms to avoid the repetition of the crisis and the ensuing need for international assistance (from the IMF and the US, especially) in addressing any future crisis.

As a result, the Asian financial crisis continues to drive discussions and initiatives regarding East Asian financial cooperation and integration. Fears over a recurrence of a similar shock have also led to a sustained precautionary element within national economic policy formation, most clearly manifested in the widespread accumulation of international reserves.

B. The economic imperative

While the Asian financial crisis highlighted East Asian economic and financial vulnerabilities, it importantly also increased awareness of regional economic and financial interlinkages. Trade between East Asian economies now constitutes a very significant portion of total trade flows of the individual economies. While an important element of these trade flows may eventually be destined for re-export to North America or Europe, at the same time, this is noticeably less so than a decade ago. Today, economic interlinkages and increasing economic integration are more of a reality in East Asia than at any period since the seventeenth century (before which, Asia and especially East Asia were economically interlinked and integrated to a certain extent).

Partly as a result of increased trade within the region, cross-border investment has also increased. Greater trade and investment have also increased the need for financial development, for example through cross-border trade finance, fundraising for direct investments (including both formative capital investment and increasingly interest in corporate acquisitions and privatisation) and of related treasury and cash management needs of businesses across the region. The needs for finance related to economic integration have served to highlight a wide range of impediments to finance in the region as well as initiatives designed to address such impediments and thereby support economic and financial development both in individual economies and across East Asia.

C. *The development imperative*

A key aspect of many discussions and initiatives related to East Asian financial cooperation in recent years has been the goal of using financial resources generated within the region to support East Asia's economic development. This stands separately from promoting economic development through the prevention and resolution of crises and enabling regional economic integration.

This line focuses on two high-profile elements. First, East Asian central banks (including the Bank of Japan) have built up substantial international reserves since 2000 (currently over US$2,600 billion). These were initially accumulated in order to help prevent a repeat of the sudden devaluations and related problems of the Asian financial crisis. As the economies in the region have recovered, the rate of accumulation increased as a result of efforts to maintain competitive exchange rates, especially in relation to the US dollar (to which the currencies of essentially all the economies in the region are formally or informally linked, and which was itself depreciating in real terms). Today, these accumulated foreign exchange reserves (managed by central banks, though often with more government input than would be found in Europe or North America) are to a great extent invested in US dollar assets, particularly US government and federal agency bonds.

East Asian economies are both secure in their view that they possess sufficient foreign exchange reserves to both meet transactional needs as well as to serve as adequate protection against any possible future currency volatility. As a result, East Asian policymakers (as well as the public and business) are increasingly expressing the view that these accumulated reserves should not be used to support the US government, currency and economy, but rather at least some portion should be devoted to supporting East Asian currencies and economic development.

In addition to sizeable foreign exchange reserves, East Asian economies have generally been characterized by historically high rates of savings relative to national income compared to most OECD members, resulting in significant liquidity in banks and financial markets throughout the region. East Asian savers have tended to keep most of their savings in bank deposits, thus making possible the type of state-directed or -encouraged lending prevalent prior to the Asian financial crisis as well as the eventual misinvestment of those funds. It is not known to what extent high sustained levels of saving represent volition within domestic economies, given that provident schemes are generally underdeveloped and other forms of non-bank financial intermediation have traditionally been far less substantial. As part of the crisis and development imperatives, East Asian economies hope to diversify their financial systems away from their previous bank–government dominated structures to more balanced market-based systems.

The development imperative thus focuses on the use of both domestic foreign exchange reserves and private savings to support economic development in East Asia.

D. The political imperative

From a political standpoint, the region's competitive economic position *vis-à-vis* especially the US and the EU is an important rationale underlying discussions and initiatives supporting East Asian financial cooperation and integration, in addition to the various considerations highlighted thus far. While in many ways the US is viewed as the preeminent economic model in the region, East Asian policymakers have also realized that the EU has had some not inconsiderable success in forming an economic counterbalance to the US and that efforts within Europe to promote economic and financial integration have been substantially successful. Similarly, the re-emergence of the economies of China and India has also highlighted the benefits of economic and financial agglomeration for smaller economies in the region, not only as a means of compensating for the political-economic weight of the US and the EU but also to counterbalance the region's emerging dominant economic powers. This last factor is especially important as a spur to efforts within the Association of South East Asian Nations (ASEAN), and has increased interest in ASEAN as a possible counterbalance to the economies of Japan, China and India.

III. Financial integration and development initiatives in East Asia

On the basis of these varying rationales, East Asian policymakers have begun a number of concrete initiatives supporting financial cooperation and integration. As a general matter, the most significant of these fall into three categories: trade arrangements including aspects of financial services ('trade in financial services') (section A); cooperation in monetary affairs (section B); and cooperation and integration in finance, focusing to date primarily on Asian bond market development (section C). In addition to these, the Japanese policy framework outlining strategies for financial cooperation and integration in the region also includes taxation (to be addressed through a web of first bilateral and eventually regional tax treaties – beyond the scope of the present discussion). Finally, these various initiatives to some extent have been and may increasingly be supported by various regional institutional arrangements, of which the roles of Asian Development Bank (ADB) and ASEAN are perhaps the most significant to date (section D). With the exclusion of taxation, this framework of analysis is not dissimilar from that which underlies the present international financial architecture (IMF – monetary affairs, World Bank – finance for development, WTO – trade, including trade in financial services).

In looking at these various initiatives and arrangements in the context of their underlying rationales discussed in the previous section, it is clear that certain approaches have been taken in the context of regional and international economic and political circumstances (domestic, regional and external). Of these, perhaps the most interesting is the use of varying approaches (domestic, regional, external) in the context of different initiatives to achieve differing purposes.

In this context, at the outset, there are often discussions and frequently disagreements regarding whether the focus of Asian financial development initiatives should be on domestic or regional finance. Often, external influences (US, IMF, World Bank) focus on development of domestic financial markets in the region as the primary goal. The suggestion is that Asia will achieve the greatest benefits in terms of economic development and crisis prevention by focusing efforts on reforming and liberalizing the domestic financial systems of individual economies. Those supporting this line often suggest at a second level that there is no need to focus on regional finance (cross-border within the region). On the other side (primarily East Asian government officials), arguments are made that the problems being addressed (regional financial contagion, for instance) are rather issues of cross-border regional interest and must be dealt with by the region on a regional basis. Those supporting this line often agree that domestic financial reform and liberalization is also a reasonable idea.

The result of these philosophical differences (and they are indeed often philosophical) is that initiatives tend to develop in the context of the forum of least resistance: for example, ASEAN or ASEAN+3 (which both exclude the US) tends to be the focus for initiatives that the US will oppose (regional financial development), while the Asia Pacific

Economic Cooperation Forum (APEC) (which includes the US) tends to be the focus for policy proposals that the US will support (domestic financial development within the region).

The contention here is that both these approaches (domestic and regional development) are important and significant in the context of the several rationales discussed above. At the same time, both can be mutually reinforcing: this is addressed in the final section of the chapter.

A. *Trade in financial services*

In relation to trade in financial services, developments to date have to some extent been limited; however, given recent increases in commitment to regional trade and economic arrangements, there is the distinct possibility of more concrete developments, though probably at a slow pace (as has generally been the case with trade in financial services elsewhere). This section thus focuses on the institutional framework for Asian economic cooperation, the focus of pillar two of the proposed Asian Economic Community (AEC). Specifically, this section addresses the following: (1) the background to Asian economic cooperation, with a focus on financial services liberalization; (2) the current structure of the ASEAN Free Trade Area (AFTA); and (3) the international framework addressing financial services liberalization and its implications for the creation of an Asian financial services market.

1. East Asian economic cooperation: Background

Asian economic cooperation has taken a number of forms, with those of ASEAN and ASEAN+3 being most concrete and influential in the area of trade in financial services.

ASEAN was founded in 1967. It has a hierarchical structure with an annual summit, periodic ministerial meetings, and a series of standing and specially convened committees. In general, ASEAN historically was not been overly successful in the economic area, though its greater success in the political field may have created a positive image as a cooperative body. However, following the Asian financial crisis, the success of European and North American economic regionalism, and the economic re-emergence of China, it has begun to take a more significant role in economic regionalism. Nonetheless, diversity in developmental stages and economic structure continues to hinder smooth and effective cooperation in ASEAN economies, and especially with the expanded grouping '+3' of China, Japan and South Korea.

In December 1995, the ASEAN Heads of Government declared that:

> ASEAN shall move towards greater economic integration by building on existing economic cooperation activities, initiating new areas of cooperation, and promoting closer cooperation in international fora.

In line with this decision, in March 1997, the first ASEAN Finance Ministers Meeting was held to further ASEAN cooperation in the area of finance. The ASEAN finance ministers emphasized the importance of concrete and pragmatic cooperation in the area of finance as a part of the building block to realize ASEAN's goal of greater economic integration. One important achievement of the meeting is the Ministerial Understanding on ASEAN Cooperation in Finance,[1] which provides a framework to enhance cooperation within the existing institutional arrangement in several areas of finance which include banking and finance, financial and capital markets, customs matters, insurance matters, taxation, and human resource development in the area of finance.[2] Detailed activities include exchanging views on macroeconomic policies, improving transparency, encouraging regular meetings among policy makers and regulators, promoting public–private sector linkages in the area of finance, etc.[3] The Ministerial Understanding on ASEAN Cooperation in Finance also adopted a consensus mechanism for decision making,[4] through regular ASEAN Finance Minister meetings (AFMM), supported by the ASEAN Senior Finance Officials Meeting (ASFOM), all of which are assisted by the ASEAN Secretariat.

2. AFTA

The member states of ASEAN reached the Framework Agreement on Enhancing ASEAN Economic Cooperation,[5] during the fourth ASEAN Summit Meeting held in Singapore in 1992. As one aspect, the ASEAN Free Trade Area (AFTA) was established, which is only one part of an entire economic cooperation system centred on ASEAN.

The Framework Agreement on Enhancing ASEAN Economic Cooperation, signed in 1992 as signalling the establishment of the AFTA, is not limited to the AFTA but also addresses other aspects of economic

[1] Ministerial Understanding on ASEAN Cooperation in Finance.
[2] Ministerial Understanding on ASEAN Cooperation in Finance, art. 3.
[3] Ministerial Understanding on ASEAN Cooperation in Finance, art. 4.
[4] Ministerial Understanding on ASEAN Cooperation in Finance, art. 5.
[5] www.aseansec.org/12374.htm.

cooperation among ASEAN member states.[6] Therefore, there is doubt as to whether or not it is an international treaty.[7]

In the meantime, the economic ministers of all ASEAN member states signed the Agreement on the Common Effective Preferential Tariff Scheme for AFTA (CEPT),[8] as the main legal document of the AFTA, eliminating tariffs and non-tariff-barriers within the ASEAN area. In the fifth ASEAN Summit Meeting held in Bangkok, Thailand, in 1995, the Protocol to Amend the Framework Agreement on Enhancing ASEAN Economic Cooperation was reached, accelerating the integration process to ten years from the original fifteen years. Notwithstanding the Asian financial crisis, the integration of ASEAN member states developed at a faster space. In the sixth ASEAN Summit Meeting held in Hanoi, Vietnam in 1998, the free trade area plan was moved forward to 2002. In January 2002, a milestone for ASEAN development appeared. The six founding member states of ASEAN, i.e. Brunei, Indonesia, Malaysia, the Philippines, Singapore and Thailand, had generally achieved the target stipulated in the Paragraph 7 of Clause 2 of CEPT – they had reduced inter-tariffs of most goods to anywhere between 0 and 5 per cent.[9] The new target is to eliminate all inter-tariffs in 2010.[10]

3. AFAS financial services commitments

On 15 December 1995, ASEAN Economic Ministers concluded the ASEAN Framework Agreement on Services (AFAS) in order to reduce service trade barriers among ASEAN countries.[11] According to Article IV of the AFAS, ASEAN States shall enter into negotiations on measures affecting trade in specific service sectors which should be beyond their GATS/WTO commitments. On 6 April 2002, the ASEAN States concluded the Protocol to Implement the Second Package of Commitments of Financial Services under the ASEAN Framework Agreement

6 The Framework Agreement on Enhancing ASEAN Economic Cooperation includes 15 clauses, but only para. A, cl. 2 is specifically concerned with AFTA.

7 J. Pelkmans, 'ASEAN and APEC, A triumph of the "Asian Way"'?, in P. Demaret, J-F. Bellis and G. Jimenez (eds.), *Regionalism and Multilateralism after the Uruguay Round: Convergence, Divergence and Interaction* (Brussels: European Inter-university Press, 1997), p. 211.

8 www.aseansec.org/12375.htm.

9 Speech by George Yeo, Minister for Trade & Industry for Singapore, at the AFTA Seminar, Jakarta, 31 January 2002.

10 The six new member states including Cambodia, Laos, Burma and Vietnam are allowed to clear their tariffs before 2015.

11 The AFAS was slightly amended on 2 September 2003.

on Services.[12] In the Annexes to this Protocol, there are specific commitments in financial services made by the ASEAN States, which are an integral part of the AFAS.[13] In addition to horizontal commitments which apply to all service sectors, ASEAN States made specific financial commitments, which are inscribed in the Schedule of Specific Commitments (for the Second Package of Commitments).[14] For the convenience of analysis, summarized in Table 13.1, we choose two columns of the Schedule, that is, sector or sub-sector column, and limitations on market access column. Among the four modes of supply of service, we choose the most important one, i.e., commercial presence.

Compared to ASEAN members' specific financial services commitments under the WTO framework, the specific financial commitments under the ASEAN/AFTA are not significantly broader, and the scope of sector or sub-sectors opened are not much wider. For example, under the WTO, Indonesia also made the same commitment that all market access limitations in the Non Banking Financial Services Sub-sector will be eliminated by the year 2020 subject to similar commitments by other Members.[15] Indonesia only repeated this WTO commitment in its ASEAN/AFTA Schedule. Cambodia's specific financial commitment under the ASEAN/AFTA are identical to its WTO commitments with respect to market access limitation.[16] As for Brunei Darussalam, it only made one more opening of a sub-sector, that is, advisory and other auxiliary financial services under the ASEAN/AFTA, compared with its WTO Schedule.[17]

Overall, while AFAS commitments to date are not significantly greater than those under the WTO financial services framework, the potential involvement of China could effect notable change. Essentially, China as part of WTO accession made significant commitments in financial services liberalization – much greater than are typically the case for a developing country, especially in the context of banking and insurance. If, at some point in future, China were to argue that other ASEAN/ASEAN+3 members were to make similar commitments in the context of AFAS and not in the context of WTO negotiations, this would provide an important liberalization of trade in financial services in ASEAN+3 and lay the groundwork for a more liberalized ASEAN+3 market in

[12] Second Package of Commitments of Financial Services under the ASEAN Framework Agreement on Services.

[13] Second Package of Commitments of Financial Services under the ASEAN Framework Agreement on Services, paras. 3 and 4.

[14] The Schedule of Specific Commitments in the Financial Area.

[15] GATS/SC/43/Suppl.3. [16] WT/ACC/KHM/21/Add.2. [17] GATS/SC/95.

Table 13.1 *ASEAN Financial Service Commitments (Commercial Presence)*

ASEAN State	Financial Sector Opened	Limitations on Market Access
Brunei Darussalam	Advisory and other auxiliary financial services.	Ministry of Finance approval is required and subject to existing domestic laws
Cambodia	Lending of all types; Acceptance of deposits;	Only permitted through licensed financial institutions as banks
Indonesia	Not specifically identified	Non-banking financial service limitations will be eliminated by the year 2020; Banking limitations will be eliminated by the year 2010; Foreign banks may establish or acquire domestic banks. Foreign bank branches and joint ventures are subject to economic needs test.
Lao PDR	Acceptance of deposits; Lending of all types; Guarantees and commitments; Provision and transfer of financial information;	Foreign bank branches allowed to establish only in Vientiane (capital of Laos)
Malaysia	Direct insurance companies	Foreign shareholding not exceeding 30%
Myanmar	Average and loss adjustment services	No limitations
The Philippines	(1) Life and non-life insurance and reinsurance/ retrocession (2) Insurance auxiliary services	(1) Acquisition of and investing in up to 60% of the voting stock of an existing domestic or locally incorporated insurance company; Non-Filipino on board of directors is limited to one-third. (2) Foreign equity limitation of 40%; one-third membership of non-Filipino on board of directors.

Singapore	(1) Life and non-life insurance services (2) Insurance intermediation (3) Services auxiliary to insurance	(1) Foreign parties can only acquire equity stakes of up to 49% in locally owned insurance companies; Unbound for issuance of new insurance licences and new representative offices; (2) No limitation except that direct and reinsurance brokers must be established as subsidiaries (3) No limitation.
Thailand	Acceptance of deposits; Lending of all types; Financial leasing; Payment and money transmission services; Guarantees and commitments; Trading for own account or for account of customers; Participation in issues of all kinds of securities; Asset management; Advisory, intermediation and other auxiliary financial services; Provision and transfer of financial information.	No limitation for representative offices; Market access limited to share acquisition of existing companies only; Unbound for new licences; Maximum foreign equity participation is allowed up to 100% of paid-up capital; For a securities company with foreign equity not exceeding 50% capital, one-half of the directors must be Thai nationals; For a securities company with foreign equity exceeding 50% capital, foreign managing directors and executive directors must be present in Thailand for not less than 60 days per year.
Vietnam	Guarantee	Foreign bank branches, joint-venture banks shall only be permitted to conduct following banking guarantee operations:

Table 13.1 (*cont.*)

ASEAN State	Financial Sector Opened	Limitations on Market Access
		(1) Providing banking guarantee in local currency to specific persons and legal entities, such as foreign citizens in Vietnam, diplomatic corps, foreign-funded companies in Vietnam. (2) Providing banking guarantee in foreign currency to some specific persons and legal entities in borrowing and payment relations with foreign counterparts; (3) Providing guarantees and re-guarantee in foreign currency to borrowing and payment of commercial banks of Vietnam, foreign bank branches and joint-venture banks in Vietnam.

financial services (especially banking and insurance) than that available under the WTO framework.

4. APEC

APEC has had a limited involvement in trade in financial services development among its members (which are, considerably broader than the East Asia region) in addition to those adopted in the context of ASEAN and AFTA (especially the AFAS).

APEC began in 1989 with its first Ministerial meeting in Canberra. In APEC's policy formation, the hesitation against rapid institutionalization, avoidance of rigid binding rules, and preference for informality are preserved in its process, and at the same time have hindered its potential as an institution of regional economic integration.

In the economic sphere, APEC had some success in relation to financial issues prior to the Asian financial crisis but has been relatively less successful thereafter, with emphasis shifting to multilateral organizations such as the WTO and the IMF, as well as to ASEAN/ASEAN+3. The fifth Ministerial Meeting and the first Leaders' Meeting at Seattle in 1993 decided to hold regular Finance Ministers' Meetings. Before the Seattle meetings, the US and Japan had been generally reluctant to discuss financial matters. They claimed that economic policy coordination should be made by existing frameworks, such as the Group of Seven Industrialized Nations (G-7) and the Organization for Economic Cooperation and Development (OECD).

Even after the Seattle meeting, financial authorities in the US and Japan continued to oppose economic policy coordination. In 1994, the first APEC Finance Ministers Meeting only called for Regional Consultations on Banking Sector and Securities Market Supervision and Regulation. In the investment area, APEC Non-Binding Investment Principles (NBIP) were proposed at the Seattle meeting and completed at the Bogor, Indonesia meeting in 1994. The NBIP set out basic principles for regional investment based upon liberalization and fairness. The third APEC Finance Ministers Meeting in 1996 endorsed the objective of achieving prudential supervision and regulation of financial markets in conformity with international standards and encouraged the deepening of cooperation among regulators in the region concerning the development of regulatory principles and practices, and enhanced market surveillance. Under the APEC Finance Ministers' Findings, the finance ministers declared that they would contribute to stable capital flows and would foster domestic financial and capital market development.

The fourth APEC Finance Ministers' Meeting focused on international efforts to harmonize the financial sector. The meeting (i) discussed international efforts to promote financial stability; (ii) noted the on-going work of the Basel Committee on Banking Supervision (Basel Committee), the International Organization of Securities Commissions (IOSCO) and the International Association of Insurance Supervisors (IAIS) to strengthen supervision and regulation of internationally active financial institutions and to increase cooperation among regulators in order to reduce systemic risks in global financial markets; (iii) noted the efforts of the Working Party on Financial Stability in Emerging Economies, in which a number of APEC economies participated; and (iv) looked forward to receiving their conclusions and recommendations with a view to considering how the member countries might apply them.

B. Cooperation in monetary affairs

At present, cooperation in monetary affairs is primarily evidenced by a series of currency swap/credit line arrangements amongst ASEAN+3 members. Although discussions of an Asian Monetary Fund or AMF developed during the initial stages of the Asian financial crisis, as noted above, these discussions were effectively ended through US opposition and the overriding demands of crisis management. Nonetheless, these discussions continue amongst officials in the region, quietly at first but now increasing in profile, with such items being a key element of discussions at the April 2006 ASEAN+3 Finance Ministers Meeting in Siem Riep, Cambodia. In addition, there are now early discussions of the possibility of an eventual Asian monetary union, modelled on that of the EU.

In May 2000, ASEAN+3 agreed the Chiang Mai Initiative (CMI) to promote Asian monetary cooperation especially through bilateral foreign currency swap agreements, usually among participating central banks.[18] Since then, a swap arrangement within ASEAN and an increasing number of bilateral swap agreements between ASEAN members have been initiated or expanded. Interestingly, these arrangements are now (following their increase at the ADB meetings in Istanbul in 2005) being

[18] The initiative was first described in a ministerial press release, see Joint Ministerial Statement of the ASEAN+3 Finance Ministers Meeting, 6 May 2000, www.aseansec.org/635.htm.

labelled the Asian Monetary Facilities or AMF (but not to be confused with older acronyms).

ASEAN+3's current network of sovereign[19] bilateral credit lines has two roots: collaborative foreign exchange swap lines set up by ASEAN's original five members; and a series of securities repurchase (repo) lines begun among members of the Executives' Meeting of East Asia–Pacific central banks (EMEAP) (discussed in the context of section C below) as a precautionary reaction to the 1994 collapse of the Mexican peso.[20] These origins show distinct purposes: the first was political and sought to show the group's robustness while the second was intended to assist economic policy.

ASEAN's arrangement began in 1977 as a modest US$100 million set of foreign exchange swap lines, facilitating simultaneous spot sale and forward purchases of local currency for US dollars among the five participating central banks to assist a member in temporary need of external liquidity. Such lines are a form of credit that become loans in the event of non-payment at maturity. Conforming with commercial practice, swaps could extend for up to 90 days and be renewable once only, given counterparty consent and the absence of competing demand from a second member. The spirit of the arrangement was foreshadowed in fictional France, the group agreeing to pool commitments equally for any line usage.[21] The scheme was extended, expanded, and may have been utilized once each by Indonesia, Malaysia, the Philippines and Thailand between 1979 and 1981, and a second time by the Philippines in 1992, in each case for modest amounts.[22] The arrangement's limited size and conditionality account for its failure to be used at any time in 1997, when all the members' external positions were put most under pressure.

Alongside ASEAN's swap arrangements came a series of bilateral repurchase lines among EMEAP members, the first introduced in late

[19] Counterparty risk is taken here as sovereign. Whether the primary counterparty is a central bank or finance ministry is national practice that is not of concern in this discussion.

[20] Reported in by R. Moreno, 'Dealing with currency speculation in the Asian Pacific basin', *Federal Reserve Bank of San Francisco Economic Letter*, 97–10, 11 April 1997.

[21] '"And now, gentlemen," said d'Artgagnan,. "All for one – one for all, this is our motto is it not?"', Alexandre Dumas, *The Three Musketeers*, Ch. 9.

[22] See C. Randall, *East Asian Financial Cooperation* (Washington DC: Institute for International Economics, 2002), p. 14, citing unnamed Thai sources. A United Nations Economic and Social Commission for Asia and the Pacific (UNESCAP) report claims that the arrangement 'has been extensively used' but this is unsupported and implausible, see Wang Seok-dong and L. Andersen, 'Regional financial cooperation in East Asia: the Chiang Mai Initiative and Beyond' (2003/3) *Bulletin on Asia–Pacific Perspectives* (Bangkok: UNESCAP), p. 90.

1995. Japan was noticeably active in their creation, partly due to its interest in promoting regional building blocks distinct from those involving other G-7 members. These allowed a participant to raise major currency liquidity for intervention or other purposes by discounting with a counterparty member high-grade securities held as international reserves, most commonly US government securities. Market practice knows several contexts in which the use of repurchase lines is prolific, involving both the commercial sector and central banks, but EMEAP's repurchase lines are analogous to the conduct of money market operations by central banks seeking to influence domestic liquidity, including cases where a central bank becomes a lender of last resort for a regulated institution and accepts collateral in the form of prescribed securities. Usage of EMEAP lines has of itself no consequence for domestic credit expansion. The amounts of these lines were made public only for those involving Japan, each being of US$1.0 billion.[23]

Excluding those involving Australia and New Zealand, two sets of lines thus evolved into more complex agreements heralded by the ASEAN+3 2000 Chiang Mai Initiative.[24] Chiang Mai provided a spur for ASEAN members (by now a group of ten) to raise their total swap arrangements to US$1.0 billion (later US$2.0 billion) and for China, Japan and Korea each to pledge to maintain bilateral credit lines for foreign currency swaps and securities repurchases, both among themselves and with each ASEAN member.[25] The initiative is not an agreement but an expression of intent, making ASEAN+3 the catalyst to bilateral arrangements customary among developed economies.

The results of Chiang Mai blend purposeful display with practical confusion.[26] First, most of the sixteen bilateral lines established by China, Japan and Korea[27] entail a contractual conditions precedent that make IMF sanction mandatory for most swap usage, not merely the

[23] See Moreno, 'Dealing with currency speculation'.

[24] See Joint Ministerial Statement of the ASEAN+3 Finance Ministers Meeting, 6 May 2000, www.aseansec.org/635.htm. The initiative is subject to no public agreement to which all its adherents are party.

[25] ASEAN's Indochina members were included but their implementation of the agreement has to date been waived.

[26] This view has support in official circles in China and Japan (for example, Institute for International Monetary Affairs, 'Report summary of studies on toward (sic) a regional financial architecture for East Asia', 29 March 2004, Tokyo, www.mof.go.jp/jouhou/kokkin/ASEAN+3research.htm.

[27] Totalling US$39.5 billion equivalent as at end-April 2005. Source: Ministry of Finance (Japan), www.mof.go.jp/english/if/if.htm.

satisfaction of conditions identical to those of the IMF.[28] It would have been impossible for Chiang Mai's expanded lines to have been drawn in the Asian crisis prior to an applicant having agreed terms for IMF support, by which time the need would have become redundant. In a similar instance in mid-1997, Thailand may have used a precursor swap line with Japan.[29] If true, doing so failed to trouble markets intent on selling the baht: drawing from a finite source could only encourage the seller.

Second, although the post-Chiang Mai lines provided by China, Japan and Korea allow for securities repurchases, this is now seen by all participants as outmoded practice and is given little attention compared to the swap provisions. The largest non-cash component of EMEAP international reserves is held in US government securities, part of the world's archetypal broad and deep bond market. Critics suggest that the liquidity available through repurchases could not compete with so profound a source.[30] More attention is now paid to swap operations and availability, both by participants and commentators. However, this approach neglects shocks not focused on Asia as in October 1987, when for a week following sizeable stock market losses the US Treasury market was highly illiquid, frequently closed to foreign participants and employable only by primary dealers. Infra-Asian repurchase lines could have insulatory value in such circumstances by promoting non-domestic liquidity, even if the region's reserves are concentrated in US dollar assets. Prevailing conditions have changed markedly given the substantial accumulation of international reserves since 2000 in ASEAN+3 vaults. That the 1995–7 repurchase lines were barely used, if at all, in the 1997 crisis was due to a scarcity of collateral or to the participants simultaneously suffering similar problems not amenable to mutual resolution.

Chiang Mai's outcome is said by ASEAN+3 to be regional but its facilities are entirely bilateral in creation and use, despite involving a

[28] In May 2005 ASEAN+3 raised the portion available unconditionally under post-Chiang Mai Initiative swap lines from ten per cent to twenty per cent of the total 'in order to better cope with sudden market irregularities' but stressed this represented no contradiction that 'the international financial arrangements and other disciplined conditions would be firmly maintained' (see Joint Ministerial Statement of the ASEAN+3 Finance Ministers Meeting, 4 May 2005, www.aseansec.org/17448.htm. Thus it is arguable that IMF sanction would be demanded for usage even if the Fund had itself not then made credit commitments to a hopeful user.

[29] *The Economist*, 10 May 2001 (cited by Randall, *East Asian Financial Cooperation*).

[30] For example, see Randall, *East Asian Financial Cooperation*, p. 22.

gesture to harmonization and shared views of crisis avoidance. In ASEAN's words:

> ASEAN shall adopt a more proactive role at various international and regional fora to ensure that its interests and priorities are given due consideration in any proposal to reform the international financial architecture.[31]

Practitioners see the post-2000 Chiang Mai swap line framework as inconsequential, whatever its political importance. History suggests using central bank swap lines for purposes other than to lessen prevailing volatility will at most delay the impact of selling pressure and may give confidence to the seller. It is ironic that Chiang Mai's cooption of IMF conditions make credit line usage unlikely, as some participants perhaps intended, and that the older repurchase lines are neglected, despite their true crisis usefulness.

Overall, the Chiang Mai–AMF arrangement is a high profile initiative but one of little real impact in its current form and scale. However it may provide the basic potential institutional arrangement necessary to support the creation of an East Asian 'snake' arrangement for currencies similar to that adopted in Europe in the 1970s or the foundation on which an AMF (in the pre-1997 sense) can be formed.

C. *Finance: Asian capital market development*

This section examines the contribution towards finance in Asia of a series of initiatives focused on capital market development. At present, these initiatives are primarily directed towards Asian bond and money market reform; efforts to support development of equity markets have only just commenced through ASEAN and ASEAN+3.

The efforts relating to bond markets have two primary streams, both of which have shown limited tangible results, but their main value is largely political rather than financial or developmental, an anomaly explained by official reluctance to cede national authority to the creation of regional policy capital. This is most visible in the common supremacy of national currency policies over cooperative market reforms (which is also a key factor that has constrained the success of regional initiatives targeting trade in financial services and monetary cooperation). The two streams are a series of collaborative efforts (the ASEAN+3 Asian

[31] ASEAN Finance Ministers Joint Ministerial Statement, 20 March 1999, www.aseansec.org/742.htm.

Bond Market Initiative, the APEC securitization initiative and the Asia Cooperation Dialogue), and the pooling of modest international reserves to create the first and second Asian Bond Funds through EMEAP.

1. ASEAN+3, APEC and ACD

First, the APEC Regional Bond Market Development Initiative was launched at the tenth APEC Finance Ministers Meeting in September 2003, to develop regional bond markets, securitization and credit guarantee markets and new products.[32] APEC established three teams in 2003 to examine aspects of market development. Two were given exploratory and promotional briefs; the work of the third was more specific, seeking recommendations for securitization and credit enhancement mechanisms to improve the credit risk quality of Asian bonds.[33] APEC asked if securitization could provide a continuous fundraising mechanism in the region and further assist the recycling of non-performing financial assets. The work was led by Hong Kong, Korean and Thai officials, the first two having experience of promoting financial architecture and legislation to facilitate large-scale securitization to assist the recycling of non-performing assets or businesses or the refinancing of residential mortgage loans and public assets.

Second, as part of the 'Asian Bond Market Initiative' (ABMI) announced in 2003, ASEAN+3[34] began research in working teams similar in scope to APEC's and with six objectives:

- Promote asset securitization to increase the available supply of debt instruments. This has now been formalized as ASEAN+3 ABMI Working Group 1 – New securitized debt instruments.
- Enhance local currency credit quality through credit guarantees and other forms of transaction structuring. This has now been formalized as ASEAN+3 ABMI Working Group 2 – Credit guarantee and investment mechanisms.

[32] Tenth APEC Finance Ministers' Meeting Joint Ministerial Statement, 4–5 September 2003, Phuket, Thailand.

[33] Securitization is a tool of structured finance involving the irrevocable transfer of defined financial assets by their originator, with consideration funded by the simultaneous sale to third-party investors of new securities issued by the asset buyer. Neither the asset buyer nor investors have transactional recourse to the originator. The asset buyer is most frequently an insubstantive vehicle taking the form of a company or trust.

[34] Six ASEAN+3 teams worked on specific topics for the group's Asian bond market initiative.

- Improve national clearing, custody and settlement systems. This has now been formalized as ASEAN+3 ABMI Working Group 3 – Foreign exchange transactions and settlement issues.
- Develop domestic credit rating agencies and promote information dissemination. This has now been formalized as ASEAN+3 ABMI Working Group 4 – Rating systems.
- Eliminate legal and regulatory impediments to cross-border bond investment. This group was initially formed to address issuance of bonds denominated in local currencies by multilateral development banks, foreign government agencies and Asian multinational corporations. However, under the chairmanship of China, the group only focused on local currency issuance by multilateral development banks. Following a few successful issues in China and Thailand among others by the ADB and IFC, this group concluded that it had successfully met its mandate and wound itself up in 2004.
- Harmonize market regulations to international best practice.

In addition to the above, a committee was formed to coordinate technical assistance.

The efforts of the ABMI and its associated working groups are now housed at the ADB as a sort of ABMI secretariat and are being provided financial support both in terms of research and implementation through ADB resources.

Third, Thailand initiated the ACD in 2002 to explore regional cooperation to encourage capital market activity. The ACD is ASEAN+3, India and fourteen other states east and south of the Caucasus. This group has assumed a lesser role in the projects sponsored by other groups and has sought instead to promote awareness of their work and to raise political encouragement. Following the end of Thailand APEC chairmanship in 2004, this group has dropped considerably in visibility. It is quite possible that the role of the ACD will be superseded by the created of the Asian Economic Summit (AES).

2. EMEAP and the Asian bond funds

EMEAP comprises ASEAN's founding five members and Australia, China, Hong Kong, Japan, Korea and New Zealand. EMEAP was used in 2003–5 to implement collaborative ideas first mooted in APEC by Hong Kong and Thailand. These are the first and second Asian Bond Funds, the former (ABF1) a US$1.0 billion pooling of core currency Asian bonds held by EMEAP's Asian member governments. The plan had two roots: criticism of massing reserves held in non-Asian risk assets, and the proposition that active capital markets could provide a stabilizing resource in times of heightened volatility. The project has technical assistance from the Bank for International Settlements (BIS), which is politically important given Asia's absence of regional or shared infrastructure in this regard, but both funds are indexed and managed passively. The project's ceiling is modest; now representing less than 0.2 per cent of the subscribers' aggregate reserves but it is innovatory in several respects. While the fund cannot directly contribute to liquidity it departs from traditional central bank reserve management practice by including sub-investment grade EMEAP sovereign risks.[35]

The second US$2.0 billion scheme (ABF2) begun in 2005 involves local currency risks. Families of single currency exchange traded funds and regional index funds will eventually each acquire and hold sovereign and quasi-sovereign Asian securities. Hitherto, proposals to create regional bodies have been ambitious and not easily implemented,[36] so if the more complex ABF2 is successful it may become a platform for cooperation on financial structure. So far, ABF2 has prompted the introduction of the first bond-related exchange-traded fund in Asia, arranging for two Asian domestic markets to allow the creation of local currency exchange-traded funds, and opening dealing in China's domestic inter-bank bond market to approved foreign investors.[37]

ABF2's single currency and regional index funds provide a means to lessen problems associated with direct investment in local currency instruments by most offshore investors and certain domestic investors, including problems relating to custody, enforcement of rights, reliability of transfer, and taxation.[38] If the plan succeeds, it will do so not overtly, but by forcing the removal of legal and regulatory constraints that currently make its objectives impossible to achieve. The test of the project must be whether it will generate greater liquidity and induce new participants to issue, invest or trade. This scheme is demanding because it effectively seeks to circumvent the problems of investor access,

[35] Many central banks actively trade liquid foreign currency debt securities but the assets held by ABF1 are generally illiquid and represent the fund's feasible investment universe.

[36] For example, currency cooperation pacts discussed at intervals by APEC and ASEAN.

[37] See Speech by Joseph Yam, Chief Executive of Hong Kong Monetary Authority at a conference on The Euro, Lessons for European and Asian Financial Markets, co-sponsored by the European Commission and the Hong Kong Monetary Authority, Hong Kong, 24 February 2006.

[38] Detailed in P. Lejot, D. Arner and Q. Liu, 'Missing links: Regional reforms for Asia's bond markets' (2006) 12(3) *Asia Pacific Business Review* 309.

custody, enforcement, transfer and taxation that exist for non-bank investors throughout the region (except largely in Hong Kong and Singapore) but in so doing will be self-limiting as to its external impact on market development. Indeed, pre-establishment announcements in 2004 suggested this might be intentional in that ABF2 would 'accelerate market reform', but no commitments to this effect have been disclosed and the examples used by the promoters to illustrate how this had begun are selective.[39]

D. *Institutional arrangements and the role of the ADB*

For several reasons, APEC and ASEAN have been unable to provide significant institutional resources in terms of arrangements assisting East Asian financial cooperation and integration. Furthermore, discussions for the creation of new institutions (such as an Asian Monetary Fund) have faltered. Increasingly, however, the Asian Development Bank (ADB) is giving support in the form of a secretariat and resource provision for financial cooperation and integration initiatives in East Asia (and perhaps eventually elsewhere).

The ADB is a multilateral development finance organization established in 1966 to reduce poverty in Asia and the Pacific.[40] As of 1 January 2006, the ADB had sixty-four members from within and outside the Asia–Pacific region. For the purpose of reducing poverty, regional cooperation to promote regional economic growth is an important ADB activity.

With respect to initiatives supporting Asian financial cooperation and integration, the ADB has been actively participating in East Asia's regional financial initiatives. In relation to monetary cooperation, the ADB has become a secretariat of sorts for the Chiang Mai/AMF swap/credit arrangements following a decision taken at the ADB annual meeting in Istanbul in 2005.

Further, as noted above, the ADB has become the secretariat for the various elements of the ABMI. Specifically, in December 2002, the ASEAN+3 meeting in Chiang Mai endorsed the ABMI and six working groups were established to coordinate bond market policy efforts among the member countries. In support of the six groups, the ADB also established six working groups internally to support the development

[39] EMEAP press release 16 December 2004, www.emeap.org.
[40] See www.adb.org.

of the Asian bond market,[41] including loans, technical assistance and bond issuance. The ADB also supported the transparency of both the various ABM initiatives and of Asian bond markets generally through the creation of an electronic resource called Asian Bonds Online.[42] In addition, the ADB has supported a series of related studies supported through technical assistance funding, issued local currency bond transactions in a number of economies and is considering investments in related projects.

In a potentially significant decision, following the appointment of its new President Haruhiko Kuroda, in April 2005 the ADB established the Office of Regional Economic Integration (OREI) to promote economic cooperation and integration of the developing members of the ADB, as well as to contribute to the 'harmonious economic growth of the region as a whole'.[43] Kuroda has determined the Asian regional integration, including financial integration, will be a key aspect of the ADB's role during his term. In support of this, in addition to the establishment of the OREI (with board support and approval), the ADB has also embarked on hiring of internal expertise to support regional economic and financial integration initiatives as well as funding technical assistance and investments for related research, initiatives and projects.

Overall, this reflects the situation that the ADB has found itself in recently: somewhat without a role despite being in the world's most dynamic economic region. Focusing efforts on regional matters differentiates it from the World Bank (which essentially only focuses on domestic financial market development initiatives) as well as from the private sector. In addition, because of weaknesses in the ASEAN and APEC institutional frameworks, East Asian policymakers have been supportive of its efforts.

IV. The European experience: Lessons for East Asia?

The EU's efforts in promoting regional financial integration are by far the most developed of all those around the world, though there have also been useful experiences in North America with NAFTA (North

[41] Speech of Khempheng Pholsena, ADB Vice-President, at the Seminar on Local Currency Bond Issuance by Foreign Multinational Corporations, Shanghai, 5 August 2004.

[42] Available at http://asianbondsonline.adb.org.

[43] Speech by Haruhiko Kuroda, ADB President, at the Governors' Seminar on a Roadmap for Asia's Economic Cooperation and Integration, Istanbul, Turkey, 3 May 2005.

American Free Trade Agreement), South America with Mercosur, and Africa with SADC (Southern African Development Community). Of these, the experiences of the EU are probably the most relevant to East Asia's next steps.

The treaty framework of the EU provides for free movement of goods, services, workers and capital, as well as freedom of establishment. As a consequence not least of the rulings of the European Court of Justice (ECJ), a very high level of integration has been achieved. Thus, at least in theory, investments may take place freely across borders and workers may move freely within the Union. There is also a relatively high degree of harmonization;[44] in a number of areas national legislation reflects developments at EU level. Decisions may be taken and legislative measures passed at EU level, which directly affect citizens of the EU as Member States are legally bound to adhere to certain types of EU legislation and may be fined if failing to do so. Also, Member States have been found liable for damages if failing to implement EU legislation to the detriment of citizens of Member States.

The idea of supranational authority was embraced in theory early on by the Member States. For many years paying little more than lip-service to the concept, however, Member States were eventually ushered into practical acceptance of at least a measure of supranationality. The importance of the ECJ in this respect cannot be overestimated.

The experience of the EU shows that regional integration can play a role in promoting the adoption of sound principles and practices in economies and in supporting their implementation. The fundamental principle of mutual recognition and a system of a single licence ensure that the framework of EU directives provide a set of minimum norms while at the same time avoiding the creation of obstacles to competition among financial institutions.

A. Creation of the internal market and single market for financial services

As a general matter, the EU has attempted to deal with trade and financial services and financial development (along with related financial regulation) in tandem. These efforts have to a large extent now created a

[44] See Speech by Elemer Tertak, Director of European Commission/DG MARKT, at the Conference on EURO: Lessons for European and Asian Financial Markets, Hong Kong, 24 February 2006.

common internal economic market and a single market for financial services, at least at the wholesale level (retail remains quite fragmented). However, these efforts have taken a significant amount of time, effort and trial-and-error dating back to at least the 1960s.

A study of capital markets by the European Economic Community (EEC) in 1966 addressed impediments to the effective functioning of national markets and their availability to foreign borrowers. The Segré Report[45] found that national markets in Europe discriminated in favour of domestic borrowers, especially national governments, as against foreign, primarily through regulations governing the investment of funds of savings banks and insurance companies. In addition, few European securities were listed on stock exchanges outside the domicile of the issuing company. As a result of practical governmental needs (combined with the forces of harmonization, access deregulation, and prudential re-regulation inherent in the process of market opening developed the 'Maastricht' objective of free movement of capital), national financial regulation in Europe has developed significantly in recent years.

The EU framework for financial services provides minimum standards for banks and other financial institutions, securities regulation, accounting and auditing, company law, and regulation of institutional investors, all based on the premise of universal banking and an open internal market. It should be borne in mind, however, that this framework is not complete. Since its purpose is to ensure the harmonization of the laws of the Member States to common minimum standards, insofar as this is necessary for the achievement of a single market, and to fill gaps relating to cross-border activities, it builds on the existing national systems of laws, rather than trying to replace them with a complete new system. The purpose of this chapter is not to evaluate the specific provisions of the EU framework; however, a general appreciation of the key elements of the EU framework is necessary to understand the development of European financial market regulation and the way in which it seeks to facilitate financial integration through integration liberalization and regulation (as well as monetary arrangements – discussed in the next section).

The EU legislative framework for financial markets seems to be grounded in a concept that can be thought of as a search for equivalence

[45] European Economic Community (EEC), 'The development of a European capital market' (1966) ('Segre Report'). See C. Kindleberger, *A Financial History of Western Europe*, 2nd edn (New York: Oxford University Press, 1993), pp. 438–9.

among disparate regulatory and legal systems, while taking into account the continuing reality of separate and distinct national legal and regulatory regimes as the basis of any overall EU initiatives.[46] Initially, efforts focused on harmonization of rules across Member States, however, this proved impossible in many areas and in the 1980s, efforts moved to the development of mutual recognition based upon common minimum standards. The key principles were outlined in the European Commission's 1985 White Paper[47] and enshrined in the 1986 Single European Act[48], implementing the common internal market on the basis of 'mutual recognition', based on common minimum standards applicable in all Member States through European Directives and implemented through domestic legislation.[49] According to this methodology, all Member States agree to recognize the validity of one another's laws, regulations and standards, thereby facilitating free trade in goods and services without the need for prior harmonization[50], while limiting the scope for competition among rules by mandating Member State conformity with a 'floor' of essential minimum European requirements. As such, financial services regulation in the EU seeks to avoid the problem of competitive deregulation and regulatory arbitrage that may undermine the legitimacy and efficiency of financial markets.

The single market is rooted in basic tenets of the Treaty of Rome respecting the free movement of capital, establishment and services, and is manifested in the various single 'passport' directives.[51] Under the concept of the 'single' passport, an EU firm authorized in one Member State (its 'home state') and wishing to operate in other Member States ('host states') will generally be able to choose to supply services through branches or to supply services on a cross-border basis without having a

[46] See B. Steil, *The European Equity Markets: The State of the Union and an Agenda for the Millennium* (London: Royal Institute of International Affairs, 1996), p. 113.

[47] European Commission, 'Completing the internal market', White Paper from the European Commission to the European Council, Com (85) 310 final (1985).

[48] Single European Act, 1987 OJ (L 169) 1 (1987), 1 July 1987.

[49] Single European Act. [50] See Steil, *The European Equity Markets.*

[51] The passport directives in the financial services area include: (1) the First and Second Banking Coordination Directives (1BCD and 2BCD) (banking); (2) the Investment Services Directive (ISD) (investment firms and securities markets); (3) the UCITS Directive (collective investment schemes); (4) the First, Second and Third Life Assurance Directives (life assurance); (5) the First, Second and Third Non-Life Insurance Directives (non-life insurance); and (6) the proposed First Pension Funds Directive (pension funds).

permanent physical presence in the host state.[52] The intended benefit of the passport is that it should increase competition by opening markets to a wider range of participants and by allowing firms to choose the most cost-effective means of supplying services to a particular market.[53] The passport directives in the financial services area have a number of common aspects: each defines its scope in terms of the type of institution and the activities that it will carry out (though perhaps with reference to particular instruments); each requires firms to be authorized and sets out the conditions a firm must satisfy for initial and continuing authorization; each sets the division of responsibility between the home state and the host state in various areas;[54] and each addresses the issue of relations with non-EU Member States.[55]

B. European Economic and Monetary Union

In relation to monetary cooperation (which to some extent has been driven by the goals of creating a common internal market and a single financial market), the EU has progressed to the most extreme form: monetary union – the adoption of a common currency across participating Member States.

On 1 January 1999, the individual currencies of the eleven EU Member States that met the relevant criteria and accepted the relevant obligations of the Maastricht Treaty (Austria, Belgium, Denmark, France, Germany, Ireland, Italy, Luxembourg, the Netherlands, Portugal, and Spain) became permanently fixed in exchange rate and ceased to exist, thereby creating a single European currency, the 'euro', and European Economic and Monetary Union (EMU). From 1 January 2001, the twelve (Greece had since been added) different sets of notes and coins were quickly replaced by a single physical currency. While significant differences still exist between domestic European financial markets, especially as they affect individual consumers and savers, the introduction of the euro has begun to make economic information more

52 See I. Fraser and P. Mortimer-Lee, 'The EC single market in financial services' (1993) 3(1) *Bank of England Quarterly Bulletin* 92.

53 Fraser and Mortimer-Lee, 'The EC single market'.

54 As a general rule, the home state will have responsibility for the prudential supervision of a firm and all its branches as well as the 'fitness and properness' of its managers and major shareholders, while the host state will be responsible for the conduct of a firm's business with its customers in the host state. See Fraser and Mortimer-Lee, 'The EC single market', 93.

55 Fraser and Mortimer-Lee, 'The EC single market', 93.

directly comparable. When combined with the painfully developed financial regulatory framework discussed in the previous sections, this shift is beginning to produce the development of a unified European financial market for the first time.

Prior to the signing of the Maastricht Treaty in 1992, there existed little impetus for Member States to actively implement the various financial services directives. However, with the entry into force of the Treaty in 1994, and its requirements for adoption and implementation of the framework supporting freedom of capital movements necessary to underpin EMU, Continental Member States adopted and implemented legislation quite foreign to the financial markets of their domestic systems. The result has been an increased awareness of the use of financial markets and the realization that the legislative changes, when combined with the advent of the single currency, will change (and have already changed) the nature of finance throughout the EU, but most especially in the Euro-12 members.

While the ultimate result is yet to be seen, significant movements have already taken place with the significant and continuing development of domestic financial markets in the EU. Further, new initiatives are coming rapidly, seeking to take advantage of new opportunities and to place competitors at an advantage in the European markets that are, in all likelihood, to arrive in short order. Although numerous impediments to such developments remain (most notably in the area of taxation), activity is set to continue increasing at a rapid pace, putting pressure on the barriers that remain. Other issues related to the need to differentiate between wholesale and retail financial services.[56] One example of the recognition of continuing impediments and the pressure to remove them is the establishment of financial services committees to review aspects of EU financial markets and to develop proposals to remove remaining barriers to the creation of a single European financial market.

V. Moving forward: Implications for governance?

It is this 'real world' experience of the countries of the EU and their moves to develop a single regional financial market that indicates the real challenges that may lie ahead for East Asian financial integration.

[56] C. Jordan and G. Majnoni, 'Financial regulatory harmonization and the globalization of finance', World Bank Policy Research Working Paper 2919 (October 2002), at p. 9.

At the same time, the development of European financial markets has provided some impetus to the process in East Asia.

Jordan and Majnoni suggest that two lessons can be drawn from the European experience with financial integration:[57]

> First, the principle of minimum harmonization together with mutual recognition principles underlines the potential for leaving integration to market forces once national legal and regulatory frameworks share common minimum standards. Secondarily, in a financially integrated world, size matters both for regulated entities and for the regulators and the same set of rules may not be efficient and equitable for both large and small players.

At the same time, the EU experience also highlights the possible implications for and challenges posed by financial integration to governance in East Asia. In looking at governance, the ADB defines governance as 'the manner in which power is exercised in the management of a country's economic and social resources for development'.[58] In the context of this definition, the ADB also identifies four of the basic elements of good governance as accountability, predictability, participation and transparency.

While the EU experience is definitely instructive, the reality is that the EU process will not be politically acceptable in the environment of East Asia due to its impact on sovereignty. At the same time however certain elements (mutual recognition, harmonization to minimum standards, formal commitments) may serve as elements of a possible course for future East Asian financial cooperation and development. Likewise, the initiatives so far all have the potential to increase accountability, participation and transparency, if not so far predictability, in ways which should be generally beneficial to economic development in East Asia.

To date, Asian financial integration has been slowly developing through shared efforts at the levels of APEC, ASEAN, ASEAN+3, AFTA or EMEAP, and with ADB interest and participation. At the same time, Asian financial integration is part of the on-going process of Asian economic integration, although the former lags far behind the latter.[59]

The groups engage at various levels in relation to occasion and task, the most visible being annual meetings of ASEAN or APEC heads of

[57] Jordan and Majnoni, 'Financial regulatory harmonization', pp. 9–10.

[58] ADB, 'Improving Governance and Fighting Corruption: Implementing the Governance and Anticorruption Policies of the Asian Development Bank', Summary Report, February 2006).

[59] Speech by Joseph Yam, see above note 37.

government and of ASEAN finance ministers. ASEAN is the oldest, dating from 1967; APEC was constituted twenty-two years later. All are discussion forums that since inception have functioned consensually and with particular respect for national sovereignty. Three of the principles of conduct described in the most comprehensive treaty emanating from ASEAN cite mutual respect for national independence, sovereignty and disdain for external interference in any member's internal affairs.[60]

While ASEAN identifies finance as one of its thirteen fields of economic cooperation it devotes no permanent resources to the sector. Unsurprisingly, the five groups boast only two institutional examples of collective financial policymaking, each being arrangements implemented separately by national governments and functioning bilaterally among member states.[61] The older is a web of credit lines for short-term foreign exchange swaps and repurchases among ASEAN+3 central banks; the more recent are two Asian Bond Funds, conceived separately although established under EMEAP's umbrella.

The 1997–8 financial crisis has been subjected to extended analysis within Asia's five intergovernmental groups with similar agendas but limited results as to practical reforms. Surges of public policy interest since late 2001 focused on reviewing structural changes but have generally yet to lead to greater market usage. All the main groups have worked, and it is not yet clear that the results will be more substantial than those of past undertakings. Successful outcomes would be novel: Asia's regional bodies are unused to collaborative financial policy. In other circles, capital market reform initiatives attract scant interest among regional trade negotiators, perhaps because financial services liberalization has been a low WTO priority. The most valuable single result of the post-crisis attention directed by APEC and ASEAN to bond market development may be the web-based portal established at ASEAN+3's suggestion by the ADB, which collects and promotes market information more comprehensively than any commercial or national source.[62]

The official attention given since the mid-1990s to market development has thus led to two tangible results. The first, a repurchase line

[60] Treaty of Amity and Cooperation in Southeast Asia, ch. 1, art 2. (24 February 1976, www.aseansec.org/1217.htm. The treaty has since been acceded to by Australia, China, India, Japan, Korea, Mongolia, New Zealand, Pakistan, Papua New Guinea and Russia as non-ASEAN members.

[61] In contrast, EU policy initiatives are first made substantive by a regional body and followed where necessary with national legislation.

[62] See http://asianbondsonline.adb.org.

construct, is discounted; the second, ABF2, is presently constrained from directly affecting liquidity. Yet that these steps have been attempted suggests that practical objectives could be employed to guide all national and regional reforms (ignoring corporate disclosure standards, which are beyond the scope of this chapter[63]).

Deliberate cooperation in financial policy among Asia's newly industrialized and developing economies has a short history and slender results, even though Asia's need for market reforms may be identified with substantial tasks in national and multilateral policymaking. Past regional initiatives on financial issues have lacked practicality, or foundered when confronted by competing interests, for example in recent years from China, Japan or the United States[64] leading to doubts as to the effective influence in financial policy formation of Asia's multiplicity of regional bodies.[65] To the extent that material results now exist, their value may rest more in the fact of completion than any practical effect. At the same time, there have been long-standing examples of the adoption by national authorities of like external financial policies, most clearly seen in currency management in the five years prior to 1997.

From the perspective of law, the whole integration process should be based on a stable legal framework, or in other words, a legal mechanism, so as to guarantee the normal and continuous operations of such integration. However, from the above description and analysis, we find that the Asian economic and financial integration process lacks a developed institutional and legal framework. In contrast to the rule-oriented WTO

[63] 'Asymmetric information [..] appears always to have limited the scope and use of financial markets'. F. Baskin, 'The development of corporate financial markets in Britain and the United States, 1600–1914: Overcoming asymmetric information' (1988) 62(2) *Business History Review* 199 (reviewing 300 years of market evolution).

[64] See notably J. Baker, *The Politics of Diplomacy: Revolution, War, and Peace, 1989–1992* (New York: G. P. Putnam's Sons, 1995), pp. 609–11. The former US Secretary of State notes his determination while in office that 'any move towards economic integration in East Asia include the United States', such that notably in 1991 he did his 'best to kill' an East Asian Economic Group then proposed among APEC's East Asian members.

[65] Typical sceptics are N. Bisley, 'The end of East Asian regionalism?' (2003) 17(1) *Journal of East Asian Affairs* 148, and J. Ravenhill, 'APEC adrift: Implications for economic regionalism in Asia and the Pacific' (2000) 13(2) *Pacific Review* 319. Others see policy success in the creation of bilateral central bank repurchase and credit lines, especially their expansion after 2000. See N. Thomas, 'An East Asian economic community: multilateralism beyond APEC', presentation to Asia–Pacific Economies: Multilateral vs. Bilateral Relationships conference, City University of Hong Kong, May 2004; S. Yamakage, 'The construction of an East Asian order and the limitations of the ASEAN model' (2005) 12(2) *Asia–Pacific Review* 1, suggests that Asia's regional model body may inherently conflict with collective policy initiatives.

or the EU, Asian regional economic institutions are relation-oriented and highly adverse to any impact upon sovereignty.

References

ADB, 'Improving governance and fighting corruption: Implementing the governance and anticorruption policies of the Asian Development Bank', Summary Report, February 2006)

Baker, J., *The Politics of Diplomacy: Revolution, War, and Peace, 1989–1992* (New York: G. P. Putnam's Sons, 1995)

Baskin, F., 'The development of corporate financial markets in Britain and the United States, 1600–1914: Overcoming asymmetric information' (1988) 62(2) *Business History Review* 199

Bisley, N., 'The end of East Asian regionalism?' (2003) 17(1) *Journal of East Asian Affairs* 148

European Economic Community (EEC), 'The development of a European capital market' (1966)

Fraser, I., and Mortimer-Lee, P., 'The EC single market in financial services' (1993) 3(1) *Bank of England Quarterly Bulletin* 92

Institute for International Monetary Affairs, 'Report summary of studies on toward (sic) a regional financial architecture for East Asia', 29 March 2004, Tokyo, www.mof.go.jp/jouhou/kokkin/ASEAN±3research.htm

Joint Ministerial Statement of the ASEAN+3 Finance Ministers Meeting, 6 May 2000, www.aseansec.org/635.htm

Jordan, C. and Majnoni, G., 'Financial regulatory harmonization and the globalization of finance', World Bank Policy Research Working Paper 2919 (October 2002)

Kindleberger, C., *A Financial History of Western Europe*, 2nd edn (New York: Oxford University Press, 1993)

Kuroda, Haruhiko, ADB President, at the Governors' Seminar on a Roadmap for Asia's Economic Cooperation and Integration, Istanbul, Turkey, 3 May 2005

Lejot, P., Arner, D. and Liu, Q., 'Missing links: Regional reforms for Asia's bond markets' (2006) 12(3) *Asia Pacific Business Review* 309

Moreno, R., 'Dealing with currency speculation in the Asian Pacific basin', *Federal Reserve Bank of San Francisco Economic Letter*, 97–10, 11 April 1997

Pelkmans, J., 'ASEAN and APEC, A triumph of the "Asian Way"'?, in P. Demaret, J-F. Bellis and G. Jimenez (eds.), *Regionalism and Multilateralism after the Uruguay Round: Convergence, Divergence and Interaction* (Brussels: European Inter-university Press, 1997)

Pholsena, Khempheng, ADB Vice-President, at the Seminar on Local Currency Bond Issuance by Foreign Multinational Corporations, Shanghai, 5 August 2004

Randall, C., *East Asian Financial Cooperation* (Washington DC: Institute for International Economics, 2002)

Ravenhill, J., 'APEC adrift: Implications for economic regionalism in Asia and the Pacific' (2000) 13(2) *Pacific Review* 319

Steil, B., *The European Equity Markets: The State of the Union and an Agenda for the Millennium* (London: Royal Institute of International Affairs, 1996)

Tertak, Elemer, Director of European Commission/DG MARKT, at the Conference on EURO: Lessons for European and Asian Financial Markets, Hong Kong, 24 February 2006

Thomas, N., 'An East Asian economic community: Multilateralism beyond APEC', presentation to Asia–Pacific Economies: Multilateral vs. Bilateral Relationships conference, City University of Hong Kong, May 2004

Wang, Seok-dong and Andersen, L., 'Regional financial cooperation in East Asia: the Chiang Mai Initiative and Beyond' (2002/3) *Bulletin on Asia–Pacific Perspectives* (Bangkok:ESCAP)

Yam, Joseph, Chief Executive of Hong Kong Monetary Authority at a conference on The Euro, Lessons for European and Asian Financial Markets, co-sponsored by the European Commission and the Hong Kong Monetary Authority, Hong Kong, 24 February 2006

Yamakage, S., 'The construction of an East Asian order and the limitations of the ASEAN model' (2005) 12(2) *Asia–Pacific Review* 1

Yeo, George, Minister for Trade & Industry for Singapore, at the AFTA Seminar, Jakarta, 31 January 2002

PART III

Law and development in China and India: Domestic issues

14

Law and development in China and India

RANDALL PEERENBOOM

At first glance, China and India seem to contradict the basic premise of the law and development movement that law plays a key causal role in economic growth. According to the standard view, China has enjoyed high growth rates despite weak legal institutions and the lack of rule of law, while India's growth rates have lagged far behind China's despite a reputation for rule of law and stronger legal institutions.[1] Closer examination however reveals that the experiences of China and India are not as inconsistent with the prevailing wisdom regarding the relationship between law and development as is often suggested.

I. General law and development lessons

At the risk of reiterating the obvious, let us begin with some general lessons of the new law and development movement.[2] First, "rule of law" and a functional legal system are necessary but not sufficient for

The paper was first presented at the National University of Singapore in June 2006 at the International Symposium on China, India and the International Economic Order.

[1] On the relationship between law and economic development in general and in China, see generally, Dani Rodrik (ed.), "Introduction," to *In Search of Prosperity: Analytic Narratives on Economic Growth* (Princeton University Press, 2003), pp. 8–15; Kenneth Dam, *The Law–Growth Nexus: The Rule of Law and Economic Development* (Washington DC: Brookings Institution, 2006). Michael Trebilcock and Jing Leng, "The role of formal contract law and enforcement in economic development," (2006) 92 *Virginia Law Review* 1519; Donald Clarke, Peter Murrell, Susan Whiting, "The role of law in China's economic development", available at http://ssrn.com/abstract=878672; Randall Peerenboom, *China's Long March Toward Rule of Law* (Cambridge University Press, 2002); Donald Clarke, "Economic development and the rights hypothesis: The China problem," (2003) 51 *American Journal of Comparative Law* 89.

[2] See Thomas Carothers, "The problem of knowledge," in *Promoting the Rule of Law Abroad: In Search of Knowledge* (Washington, DC: Carnegie Endowment for Int'l. Peace, 2003). Carothers notes that the lessons learned about the relationship between law and development are often too general and superficial. At the same time, he also points out that they are often ignored in practice. Thus, there may still be some value in setting out some of the basic principles.

sustained growth. The empirical evidence is surprisingly consistent about this general relationship.[3]

Second, the relationship between rule of law and economic growth is non-linear.[4] Legal institutions are costly. There is less need for formal legal institutions in predominantly rural economies where contracting parties are bound together in tight social networks and there are informal mechanisms for enforcing contracts.

Third, informal mechanisms may provide a useful supplement, but they are not adequate substitutes for functional formal institutions in a reasonably developed economy. Informal mechanisms operate against a background of formal institutions, and often could not function without the possibility of ultimately turning to the courts should other means for resolving the dispute fail. As economies develop and become more complex and diversified, the need for rule of law and formal legal institutions increases. Economic growth provides the resources to support institutional development. Not surprisingly, there is a high correlation between wealth and rule of law and other good governance indicators.[5]

[3] The literature on this topic is vast. See Rodrik (ed.), "Introduction," to *In Search of Prosperity*; Dam, *The Law–Growth Nexus*. For some of the empirical surveys that support this general proposition, see the literature survey in Randall Peerenboom, *China's Long March Toward Rule of Law* (Cambridge University Press, 2002). See also Sergio Godoy and Joseph Stiglitz, "Growth, initial conditions, law and speed of privatization in transition countries: 11 years later" (2006) NBER Working Paper No. W11992.

[4] Robert Barro, *Determinants of Economic Growth* (Cambridge MA: MIT Press, 1997).

[5] See Randall Peerenboom, "Show me the money: The dominance of wealth in determining rights performance in Asia" (2004) 15 Duke J. Comp. & Int'l. L. 148 (using World Bank data for rule of law and good governance, the correlation between GDP and rule of law is r=.82; government effectiveness r=.77; control of corruption r=.76; voice and accountability r=.62). "Rule of law" measures the extent to which people have confidence in and abide by the rules of society, how fair and predictable the rules are, and how well property rights are protected. The indicators include perceptions of incidence of crime, the effectiveness and predictability of the judiciary, and the enforceability of contracts. "Government effectiveness" measures the provision of public services, the quality of the bureaucracy, the competence and independence of civil servants and the credibility of the government's policy commitments. Whereas government effectiveness focuses on the institutional inputs required to implement policies effectively, "regulatory quality" focuses on the policies themselves. It includes measures of market-unfriendly policies such as price controls or inadequate bank supervision, as well as perceptions of excessive regulation of foreign trade and business development, reflecting a bias toward neoliberal economic policies. "Control of corruption" measures perceptions of corruption, the effects of corruption on business, and "grand corruption" in the political arena. The "Voice and Accountability" index is another measure of civil and political rights. "Political stability and absence of violence" combines several indicators that measure the likelihood that the government will be overthrown or destabilized by unconstitutional or violent means, including terrorism. It is included as a good governance measure

Fourth, the relationship between law and development is not unidirectional.[6] There is a push and pull mechanism at work. Market reforms and economic policies create a demand for legal reforms. At the same time, legal reforms support economic growth by facilitating commercial transactions and creating the conditions for doing business.

Fifth, the relationship between law and development is broader than just reliance on courts to enforce property rights. Dispute resolution is only one of the economic functions of a legal system, and litigation only one of many ways of resolving disputes. The legal system also performs an enabling function by creating the basic infrastructure for transactions, including markets, security exchanges, mortgage systems, accounting practices and so on. A wide range of institutions and actors are involved: central and local legislatures and administrative agencies, the legal profession, arbitrators and mediators, public notaries, accountants, police, prosecutors, anti-corruption bodies and ombudsmen, as well as others. Also not surprisingly, the World Bank and other key actors in the new law and development movement have emphasized not only rule of law but good governance, including both sound economic policies and the institutions that make and implement them.

Sixth, the relationship between law and development is also nonlinear in the sense that development does not move along a smooth upward trajectory. Many countries experience the middle-income blues. They are able to make some initial progress and show improvement in terms of economic growth, institutional development and good governance given low starting points. However, once they reach the middle-income level, they get bogged down. Powerful interest groups capture the reform

because political instability and violence not only affect the ability of the ruling regime to govern but deprive citizens of the ability to peacefully select and replace those in power. Daniel Kaufmann *et al.*, *Governance Matters III: Governance Indicators for 1996–2004* (2005), available at www.worldbank.org/wbi/governance/pdf/govmatters3.pdf.

6 Using time series data, Chang and Calderon find that the causal relationship between institutions and economic growth runs in both directions, although the impact of growth on institutional development is stronger than the impact of institutions on growth. Alberto Chang and Cesar Calderon, "Causality and feedback between institutional measures and economic growth" (2000) 12 *Economics and Politics* 69. See also Roberto Rigobon and Dani Rodrik, "Rule of law, democracy, openness, and income: Estimating the interrelationships" (2005) 13 *Economics of Transition* 533. Kaufmann *et al.* agree that wealth matters to some extent but claim that the causal impact of income on governance is small and that "most of the correlation between governance and per capita incomes reflects causation from the former to the latter." Daniel Kaufmann *et al.*, *Governance Matters III: Governance Indicators for 1996–2004* (Washington DC: World Bank, 2007) at 38.

agenda, opposing further reforms or pushing for reforms that do not benefit the broad public. Economic growth slows or reverses. The reform momentum is dissipated. Some states settle into a stable but dysfunctional holding pattern, while others sink into chaos and become failed states.[7]

Despite large sums of money and the best efforts of international and domestic actors, the results of the original law and development movement in the 1960s and 1970s and its current reincarnation under the banner of rule of law and good governance have been on the whole rather poor. In 2005, the authors of the World Bank's ongoing study of good governance cautiously concluded that there is no evidence of "any significant improvement in governance worldwide, and if anything the evidence is suggestive of a deterioration, at the very least in key dimensions such as rule of law, control of corruption, political stability and government effectiveness."[8]

East Asian countries are the one notable regional exception. Singapore, Japan, Hong Kong, Taiwan and South Korea all rank in the top quartile on the World Bank's rule of law index. Apart from North American and Western European countries, Australia and Israel, the only other countries in the top quartile are Chile and French Guiana from Latin America, Slovenia as the lone (non)representative from Eastern Europe, and a handful of small island states and oil-rich Arab countries.[9]

Seventh, the "East Asian Model" (EAM) involves the sequencing of economic growth, legal reforms, democratization and constitutionalism,

[7] There has been considerable attention to the problems of failed states, as well as many attempts to export the institutions of advanced states to developing countries. However, international donor agencies are only beginning to focus on the particular problems of middle-income countries. In 2006, the World Bank, for instance, issued its third strategy paper in six years, reflecting the difficulty the Bank has had grappling with the complex issues confronting middle-income countries. See, World Bank, Projects, "Middle-Income Countries (MICs)," available at http://web.worldbank.org/WBSITE/EXTERNAL/PROJECTS/0,,contentMDK:20976054~pagePK:41367~piPK:51533~theSitePK:40941,00.html; for East Asia, see World Bank, "Ten Years after the Crisis," April 2007, available at http://siteresources.worldbank.org/INTEAPHALFYEARLYUPDATE/Resources/550192–1175629375615/EAP-Update-April2007-fullreport.pdf.

[8] Daniel Kaufmann *et al.*, *Governance Matters III*, at 14.

[9] These include Antigua and Barbuda, Barbados, the Bahamas, Bermuda, the Cayman Islands, Malta, Martinique, Mauritius, Puerto Rico, and Samoa, in addition to Oman, Qatar, Bahrain, Kuwait and the United Arab Emirates. Several of the island states rely heavily on tourism and the provision of financial services to companies looking for tax havens for economic development. Most have populations between 50,000 and 500,000.

with different rights being taken seriously at different times in the process.[10] More specifically, the EAM involves:

(i) an emphasis on economic growth rather than civil and especially political rights during the initial stages of development, with a period of rapid economic growth occurring under authoritarian regimes;
(ii) a pragmatic approach to reforms, with governments following some aspects of the Washington Consensus and rejecting or modifying others; in particular, with governments adopting most of the basic macroeconomic principles of the Washington Consensus for the domestic economy; rejecting or modifying the neoliberal aspects that would greatly reduce the role of the state through rapid privatization and deregulation, with the state also more active in reducing poverty and in ensuring minimal material standards to compete in a more competitive global economy;[11] and modifying the prescribed relationship between the domestic and global economy by gradually exposing the domestic economy to international competition while offering some protection to key sectors and some support to infant industries;
(iii) as the economy grows and wealth is generated, the government invests in human capital and in institutions, including reforms to

[10] The scare quotes reflect reservations about whether there is a single model. The main reservations are that the common features are stated at a high level of abstraction; there is considerable diversity with respect to specific issues and policies; and the essence of the East Asian approach has been pragmatism – which emphasizes flexibility and adaptation rather than dogmatic adherence to specific guidelines. That said, there are significant "family resemblances" (to borrow Wittengstein's phrase) or patterns among East Asian states. Thus, the World Bank, while denying that there is a single model or recipe for success, then turns around and summarizes a number of principles and lessons for other developing countries. World Bank, *The East Asian Miracle: Economic Growth and Public Policy* (New York: Oxford University Press, 1993). In the end, not much hinges on whether these principles, lessons and patterns are referred to as a "model" or "suggestive guidelines that must be interpreted and adapted to fit local circumstances." Given the absence of any methodological or substantive standards for distinguishing between a "model" and "suggestive guidelines," I will continue to refer to the East Asian Model (EAM) or the model – without quotes. For a more extensive discussion of the East Asian Model, see Randall Peerenboom, *China Modernizes: Threat to the West or Model for the Rest* (Oxford University Press, 2007).

[11] China has learned this lesson the hard way. While China has done reasonably well in addressing poverty, the focus on aggregate economic growth has led to rising inequality. In addition, the relatively low amount of public spending on education and health, combined with a turn toward market forces in the health sector, have increased social tensions. In recent years, however, the government has begun to increase public spending on education, health and welfare services.

establish a legal system that meets the basic Fullerian requirements of a procedural or thin rule of law; over time, as the legal system becomes more efficient, professionalized and autonomous, it comes to play a greater role in the economy and society more generally;

(iv) democratization in the sense of freely contested multiple party elections for the highest level of office is postponed until a relatively high level of wealth is attained;

(v) constitutionalism begins to emerge during the authoritarian period, including the development of constitutional norms and the strengthening of institutions; social organizations start to emerge and "civil society" begins to develop, albeit often a civil society with a different nature and political orientation than in Western liberal democracies, and with organizations with a political agenda subject to limitations; citizens enjoy economic liberties, rising living standards for the vast majority, and some civil and political rights although with limitations especially on rights that involve political issues and affect the control of the regime; judicial independence remains limited, with the protection of the full range of human rights and in particular civil and political rights suffering accordingly;

(vi) there is greater protection of civil and political rights after democratization, including rights that involve sensitive political issues, although with ongoing abuses of rights in some cases and with rights frequently given a communitarian or collectivist interpretation rather than a liberal interpretation.

II. Lessons from China and India

Law has played a greater role in China's development than is often suggested.[12] As expected, the legal system has improved over time as gross domestic product (GDP) increased and the economy became more complex and diversified. China ranked in the 41st percentile in 2004 on the World Bank *Rule of Law Index*; had the *Index* existed in 1976, at the end of the Cultural Revolution, China would have ranked at or near the bottom.[13] Given the high correlation between rule of law and wealth, comparing China's performance with the performance of the average

[12] See generally Peerenboom, *China's Long March Toward Rule of Law*, chapter 10; see also Clarke, Murrell, Whiting, "The role of law in China's economic development."

[13] Daniel Kaufmann *et al.*, *Governance Matters III: Governance Indicators for 1996–2004.*

country in its income class may be more informative than its percentile ranking. In light of the frequent complaint that "China lacks the rule of law," it may come as a surprise that China actually outperforms the average in its lower-middle income class.

The push and pull mechanism has also clearly been at work in China. Economic reforms began in 1978, as did legal reforms. However, legal institutions were relatively weak. The regulatory framework was still fairly restrictive and undeveloped. Officials working in government and administrative agencies often were not very pro-business. However, over time, investor demands have led to changes in the regulatory framework and in formal legal institutions.[14] Foreign investors have been lobbying the government aggressively to address their concerns, arguing generally that reforms are in China's own national interests.[15] Lobbying by the business community is frequently combined with bilateral and multilateral pressure, although administrative litigation and other mechanisms also provide disgruntled parties avenues for challenging government acts. Tying the promotions of government officials to economic performance has also contributed to a considerably more pro-business regulatory environment, albeit at times one in which government officials ignore central laws in their headlong pursuit of economic growth. As a result, China ranked 34th out of 131 countries in the 2007–8 World Economic Forum's *Global Competitiveness Index*, and 57th out of 127 countries on the *Business Competitiveness*

[14] See Clarke, Murrell, Whiting, "The role of law in China's economic development"; Peerenboom, *China's Long March Toward Rule of Law*, chapter 10; Peerenboom, *China Modernizes*, chapter 3.

[15] According to one survey, 71% of foreign companies have in-country staff dedicated to lobbying the government. The main tasks are management relationship; advocacy for specific projects; advocacy for regulatory and policy changes; followed by business development, image management, corporate social responsibility and regulatory compliance. Only one-third of respondents were working on foreign corrupt practices compliance issues or environmental, health and safety compliance issues. USCBC, "Conducting government affairs in China," October 30, 2007, www.uschina.org/public/documents/2007/10/survey-gov-affairs.pdf. See also Scott Kennedy, *The Business of Lobbying in China* (Cambridge MA: Harvard University Press, 2005). Looking at lobbying by both foreign and domestic companies, Kennedy found that business–government relations varied by sector in terms of the relative usefulness of business associations, the amount of direct contact with the government, the extent to which businesses adopted a cooperative or confrontational approach, and the transparency of the political process. In general, size matters: larger companies that account for a bigger share of the market or economy have more influence on the policy process. Moreover, size matters regardless of ownership form (state-owned snterprise (SOE) or private) or nationality (domestic or foreign).

Index.[16] In 2008, the World Bank ranked China 92nd out of 178 countries for doing business overall.[17]

As the general law and development literature predicts, informal institutions have been a useful supplement to the formal legal system, but they are not an adequate substitute. As elsewhere, informal institutions themselves often require formal institutions as a backstop.[18] Reliance on *guanxi* – social networks and personal connections – has decreased.[19] Parties are entering into written contracts more often. There has been a marked increase in litigation, and a marked decrease in mediation.[20] When disputes do go to court, there are fewer court-mediated settlements and more final judgments.[21] While arbitration is a popular choice for foreign investors, the total number of disputes settled through arbitration is small relative to the number of cases settled through litigation.[22]

Much of what seems puzzling about the relationship between law and development in China and East Asia more broadly is the result of reducing the relationship between law and development to the role of courts in enforcing property rights. To be sure, it is important to sort out the role of courts in enforcing different types of rights such as property rights (government takings) and contract rights (horizontal transactions).[23] However, the so-called rights thesis is too narrow to capture the complex and multi-faceted relationship between law and development.

[16] The index is based on twelve pillars: institutions; infrastructure; macro economy; health and primary education; higher education and training; goods market efficiency; technological readiness; labor market efficiency; financial market sophistication; innovation; market size; business sophistication; and innovation.

[17] China fared better on some indicators than others, including enforcing contracts (20), registering property (28), trading across borders (31), closing a business (76), and protecting investors (86). Problem areas include the time and difficulties involved in starting a business (128), dealing with licenses (175), and the amount and administrative burden of paying taxes (173).

[18] The informal sector itself needs legal protection. For example, Wenzhou's informal commodities markets were eventually closed by the authorities. See Clarke, Murrell, Whiting, "The role of law in China's economic development."

[19] Douglas Guthrie, "The declining significance of guanxi in China's economic transition" (1998) 154 *The China Quarterly* 255.

[20] Zhu, Jingwen (ed.), *Zhongguo falü fazhan paogao(1979–2004)* [=*China Legal Development Report (1979–2004)*] (Beijing: Zhongguo renmin daxue chubanshe [=People's University Press], 2007).

[21] Clarke, Murrell, Whiting, "The role of law in China's economic development."

[22] Zhu (ed.), *Zhongguo falü fazhan paogao(1979–2004)* [=*China Legal Development Report (1979–2004)*]. Arbitration, of course, requires a contractual relation between the parties. But many disputes involve third parties or non-contractual disputes, as in tort cases.

[23] See Clarke, "Economic development and the rights hypothesis."

The experiences of China and India confirm that both policies and institutions matter. Good policies alone are not enough, as China demonstrates: while growth has been high, it most likely would have been even higher had there been stronger institutions. Conversely, good institutions alone are not enough, as India demonstrates: India has had a reasonably functional legal system, at least as measured by the World Bank *Rule of Law Index*, and yet has adopted policies that have impeded growth.

Both China and India were command economies from the late 1940s to the late 1970s.[24] However, during that period, China outperformed the average developing country in growth and human development while India's performance was below average.[25] Both countries began reforms around 1980. Both have adopted a gradual approach, rejecting the big bang approach favored in Eastern Europe and elsewhere. China, however, opened its economy more rapidly and extensively. India began to accelerate the pace of market reforms only in 1991, at which point growth rates rose.

There are other policy differences, as well as some similarities. Whereas China began with agricultural reforms before turning to manufacturing, India focused more on industrial reforms. China has invested more in infrastructure, and more aggressively sought (foreign direct investment) FDI through various tax policies, the creation of special economic zones and two-track legal reforms that offered a number of advantages to foreign parties such as greater freedom in contracting and special standing rules that allowed foreign investors to bring suits in higher level courts. China has also adopted stringent birth control policies.

Both China and India rejected aspects of the Washington Consensus, especially rapid privatization and financial liberalization. Both escaped relatively unscathed from the Asian financial crisis. However, China has emphasized growth at the expense of equality, at least until recently when the government has renewed its commitment to achieving social justice and a harmonious society. India more firmly rejected trickle down economics – in part because democratic leaders were forced to take into account populist objections to policies that would have accelerated growth but disadvantaged influential constituencies.[26]

[24] Roderick MacFarquhar, "Introduction," in Edward Friedman and Bruce Gilley (eds.), *Asia's Giants* (New York: Palgrave, 2005), p. 12.

[25] Bruce Gilley, "Two passages to modernity," in Friedman and Gilley (eds.), *Asia's Giants*, at 26.

[26] James Manor, "India's reform strengths," in Friedman and Gilley (eds.), *Asia's Giants*, at 99–104.

In terms of institutional development and capacity, China and India are roughly comparable. Using World Bank indicators, China fares slightly better on government effectiveness and regulatory quality, while India performs slightly better on rule of law and control of corruption.[27] Other surveys have reached similar results, or given the edge to China. A World Economic Forum survey ranked India higher on judicial independence and protection of property rights, but gave the edge to China in public trust of politicians and less favoritism in officials' decisions.[28] In contrast, China fared better in a World Bank survey of private enterprises regarding business constraints. China outperformed India on six of eight measures, including government efficiency, corruption, the judiciary, policy stability, taxes and regulations, and economic and social constraints (i.e., inflation, exchange rate issues, street crime and organized crime). India had the edge in financing and tax compliance.[29]

These results must be interpreted with caution. The World Bank for example, aggregates a number of surveys that rely on subjective impressions. Biases are possible, and in the case of a comparison between a democratic state and a single party socialist one, likely. India benefits from the *perception* of better rule of law because of a better record on civil and political rights, greater judicial independence, the familiarity with the legal system that comes from a history of British colonialism, and higher quality judges especially at the Supreme Court level, where many of the justices, some of them trained in the United Kingdom, publish impressively erudite judgments in English.

In contrast, China's poor record on human rights has tarnished the image of the courts.[30] Critics of the legal system often assume that if the courts lack the independence to handle politically sensitive cases fairly, then they also lack the independence to handle other cases fairly. Yet the leap across the chasm from the highly unusual case of the regime-challenging Falun Gong to a broad generalization that Chinese courts

[27] However, India does much better relative to the average country in its income class on government effectiveness (55.8% to 21.5%), rule of law (50.7% to 23%), and control of corruption (47.3% to 23.5%), but just average on political stability (24%). China does much better relative to the average country in its higher income class on government effectiveness (60.1% to 40.2%) and political stability (46.6% to 36.5%), and does slightly better or about average for the other indicators.

[28] Tony Saich, "Development and choice," in Friedman and Gilley (eds.), *Asia's Giants*, at 235.

[29] Yasheng Huang and Tarun Khanna, "Indigeneous versus foreign business models," in Friedman and Gilley (eds.), *Asia's Giants*, at 169.

[30] See generally Randall Peerenboom, "Assessing human rights in China: Why the double standard?" (2005) 38 *Cornell International Law Journal* 71–172.

lack the independence and authority needed for a fair trial in run-of-the-mill commercial, criminal or administrative litigation cases is worthy of Evil Knievel.

There is no more reason to believe that problems in politically sensitive cases in China undermine the adequacy of Chinese courts as a forum for commercial cases than to believe that the use of military courts, the allegations of torture or the treatment of "unlawful combatants" in the US undermine the adequacy of US courts for commercial disputes.[31]

While the legal systems of several Asian countries handle civil and political cases differently than Western liberal democracies, they still rank highly in their handling of commercial cases. Singapore, for instance, is generally ranked as one of the best legal systems in the world by investors, even though human rights groups claim Singapore lacks the rule of law because opposition figures have lost in defamation suits and because of other limitations on the democratic process and civil and political rights.[32]

Some aspects of the legal system that fall under the broad rubric of rule of law are more relevant to economic growth than others. India's courts are no doubt more independent when it comes to handling politically sensitive cases. But the role of the Indian Supreme Court in protecting civil and political rights may not contribute much, if anything, to growth. Investors may be more worried about judicial corruption and long delays. Plagued by corruption and a lack of resources, India's legal system is overburdened. As of July 2002, there were 13 million cases pending in lower courts, and 3.5 million cases in high courts.[33]

In contrast, China's courts are much more efficient in handling commercial disputes. In response to the rapid rise in commercial cases over the last twenty years, the Supreme People's Court (SPC) has

[31] In the past, the US legal system provided an adequate forum for commercial cases even though there were many restrictions on rights for minorities, women, laborers and criminals. While judicial reforms were fueled in part by the desire to deal with the slavery in the wake of the Civil War, economic nationalism was the main impetus behind a stronger federal judiciary in the last half of the nineteenth century. See Howard Gillman, "How political parties can use the courts to advance their agendas: Federal courts in the United States, 1875–1891," in Tom Ginsburg & Robert Kagan (eds.), *Institutions & Public Law: Comparative Approaches* (New York: Peter Lang, 2005).

[32] East Asian countries in general score lower than the average country at their income level on civil and political rights while outperforming the average on most other measures of human rights, good governance and human well-being. See Peerenboom, *China Modernizes.*

[33] US State Department Country Reports on Human Rights Practices, India—2003 (2004), available at www.state.gov/g/drl/rls/hrrpt/2003/27947.htm.

encouraged greater use of simplified and summary procedures to enhance efficiency.[34] The SPC has also issued regulations that clarify the time limits for disposing cases and various stages in the litigation process.[35] Judges who fail to complete cases on time are subject to sanctions. The overwhelming majority of cases are completed within the time limits.[36] China has also implemented a variety of reforms to reduce judicial corruption, deal with local protectionism and increase the authority and independence of the courts.[37]

Aggregate indicators of rule of law serve a useful purpose in facilitating broad comparisons between countries, and in providing a basis for measuring the impact of legal institutions on economic development. However, China and India are huge countries. There is wide variation in legal development in China and in India. In China, different areas of law are progressing at different rates, with the commercial law area among the strongest and criminal law among the weakest. The quality of the judiciary varies by level of the court, the region, the division within the court and the type of case. Problems such as judicial competence, local protectionism and corruption mainly affect basic level courts.[38] The general relationship between wealth and the quality of the legal system is also found within China, where some provinces are as wealthy as upper middle income countries while other provinces are as poor as low income countries. In richer areas, there are more and better judges, lawyers and law schools. Overall, people have fewer complaints than their counterparts in poorer areas. But when they have a dispute, they are more likely to resort to litigation to resolve them, and significantly more likely to be satisfied with the result.[39] Accordingly,

[34] In 2006, simplified and summary procedures were used in 39% of first instance criminal, and 71.26 of first instance civil cases. SPC 2007 Work Report, available at http://news.sina.com.cn/pc/2007–03–13/326/152.html. The SPC's Second Five-year Agenda reiterates the need to improve, and make greater use of, such procedures. It also recommends the establishment of small claims courts to further enhance efficiency.

[35] Several Regulations on the Strict Implementation of the System of Deadlines in Trying Cases, issued by the Supreme People's Court, and effective as of Sept. 28, 2000.

[36] In 2006, 95% of all first instances cases were completed within the time limits. SPC 2007 Work Report.

[37] See Randall Peerenboom, "Judicial independence in China: Common myths and unfounded assumptions," in Randall Peerenboom (ed.), *Judicial Independence in China* (forthcoming 2009).

[38] The President of the Supreme Court, Xiao Yang, has stated that 80% of problems occur in basic level courts. Peerenboom, *China's Long March Toward Rule of Law.*

[39] See Randall Peerenboom and He Xin, "Dispute resolution in China: Patterns, causes and prognosis," in Randall Peerenboom (ed.), *Dispute Resolution in China* (Oxford Foundation for Law, Justice and Society, 2008), available at www.fljs.org/section.aspx?id=1931.

an adequate assessment of legal reforms requires that the broad notion of rule of law be disaggregated.[40]

Whatever their differences, China and India are both showing signs of the middle-income blues. Despite China's rapid progress in improving the legal system and good governance *appears* to be slowing, if not reversing. As indicated by the World Bank's database on Worldwide Governance Indicators, China's rule of law and good governance rankings are all lower in 2004 than in 1998.[41]

Such evidence has led to dire predictions for China's future. It is now commonplace to suggest that the rapid pace of economic reforms combined with more modest political reforms have created a mismatch that threatens China's development. Minxin Pei has concluded dramatically that China is trapped in transition.[42] Although lower-middle income China generally outperforms low income India on most economic and human development indicators, commentators have begun to challenge the standard account of a successful China and a failed, or less successful, India.[43] In this revisionist story, India, having struggled to establish democratic institutions, is now poised for growth, while China has backloaded the costs of transition to a sustainable form of government. The most plausible result, we are told, is that India will soar while China will crash, at which point "the true costs of dictatorship in China" will be plain for all to see, demolishing the myth of China as a success story among developing countries.[44]

40 Fu Hualing, "Putting China's judiciary into perspective: Is it independent, competent and fair, in beyond common knowledge," in Eric G. Jensen and Thomas C. Heller (eds.), *Empirical Approaches to the Rule of Law* (Stanford University Press, 2003).

41 "PRC good governance indicators 1998 and 2004," generated from the World Bank, *Worldwide Governance Indicators* (at http://info.worldbank.org/governance/wgi/sc_country.asp).

42 Minxin Pei, *China's Trapped Transition: The Limits of Developmental Autocracy* (Cambridge MA: Harvard University Press. 2006). However, others have suggested that in focusing so much on the negative aspects, Pei has presented a misleadingly gloomy one-sided view. See, e.g., Andrew J. Nathan, 'Present at the stagnation', *Foreign Affairs*, July/August 2006, (www.foreignaffairs.org/20060701fareviewessay85414/andrew-j-nathan/present-at-the-stagnation.html. At a recent conference, all three legal specialists took issue with Pei's conclusion that legal reforms are stalled, as did Barry Naughton with regard to economic reforms, Joseph Fewsmith with respect to political reforms, and Dali Yang with respect to governance reforms. See Randall Peerenboom (ed.), *Is China Trapped in Transition?* (Oxford Foundation for Law, Justice and Society 2007) available at www.fljs.org/section.aspx?id=1939.

43 See Gilley, "Two passages to modernity," at 19–54; Edward Friedman, "Why democracy matters," in Friedman and Gilley (eds.), *Asia's Giants*, at 183–210. Supporters of this view also note that growth has been more equitable in India, and that India has avoided disasters like the Great Leap Forward and the Cultural Revolution.

44 Gilley, "Two passages to modernity," at 21.

There are several problems with this story. First, although there are some signs of reform fatigue and diminishing returns in China, the view that China's legal system as a whole deteriorated between 1998 and 2004 is incorrect.[45]

Second, while it is true that India has recently experienced high growth, attracted more FDI than in the past and shown improvements in human development, India is starting from a much lower base than China in terms of GDP, FDI and human development as measured by the Human Development Index (HDI).[46] It will be some time before India catches up with China.

Third, it is much too early to conclude that China is trapped in transition. China is currently following the East Asian model, adapted slightly in light of the realities of the twenty-first century. Only time will tell if it will be as successful as Japan, Taiwan, South Korea, Singapore and Hong Kong. However, given the successful experiences of these other countries, there are grounds for optimism.

Fourth, sustaining growth and the momentum for institutional reforms will become increasingly difficult in India, just as it is for other middle-income countries. India is still a low-income country, but its high growth rates in recent years are pushing it toward the lower-middle income category. India is also beginning to show signs of the middle-income blues. Like China, India's World Bank rule of law and good

[45] Kaufmann *et al.*, concede the difficulties of assessing trends in a particular country indicator given the large margins of error. The decreases may be attributable to the addition of new data sets and more importantly large margins of error (standard deviation of .12 for rule of law). After new data sets were added, China's scores from earlier years were lower than reported previously. For example, China's 2002 rule of law ranking is now listed as the 48.5 percentile rather than the 51.5 percentile previously given when the data came out in 2003. Other indicators for 2002 are also anywhere from 2 to 4.5 percentage points lower now than when reported in 2003. The World Bank index aggregates results from several other data sets that rely on subjective judgments by business people and others familiar to one degree or another with China. Thus, there is also the possibility that subjective impressions are out of line with objective circumstances, particularly when it comes to a technical area such as legal reforms. Non-specialists in particular might have been disappointed that China's accession to the World Trade Organization did not miraculously lead to a rule of law compliant legal system overnight. For an overview of legal reforms in China in recent years and a more detailed discussion of why critics may be so quick to find fault with China, see the policy briefs by Peerenboom, deLisle and Dowdle in *Is China Trapped in Transition?*.

[46] Much also depends on the baseline. India's improvement in HDI has accelerated since 1990 at a higher rate than China's. However, China posted a 55% improvement in the HDI for the period 1975–2002, compared to India's more modest 42% improvement. Gilley, "Two passages to modernity," at 31.

governance indicators are down from 1998. India scored lower on five of the six indicators in 2004 than it did in 1998.[47]

Progress on human development is also slowing in both countries. The UNDP claims that economic growth has outstripped social progress, noting that China advanced thirty-two places on global wealth rankings but just twenty places on the Human Development Index. While the rate of child mortality continued to decline, the rate of progress slowed in the 1990s, although much depends on what reference years are used. Yet India has experienced a similar pattern of a declining rate of progress in the 1990s on child mortality and other human development indicators.[48]

Fifth, at the heart of the revisionist story is the assumption that India's early move to democratize will give India the long-term advantage. To be sure, a common view attributes many of India's problems to its being a democracy.[49] Even India's prime minister claimed in 1997 that Indians have had to "to pay the economic price for political democracy."[50] In contrast, one of the striking features of the successful transition in Taiwan and South Korea is that the transition to democratization has come only after economic growth reached relatively high levels. In East Asia and elsewhere, countries that democratized at lower levels of wealth tend to be unstable.[51] India remains a puzzling exception.[52]

[47] "India's good governance indicators 1998 and 2004," generated from the World Bank, *Worldwide Governance Indicators*, available at http://info.worldbank.org/governance/wgi/sc_country.asp.

[48] UNDP Human Development Report 2005, available at http://hdr.undp.org/reports/global/2005/pdf/HDR05_complete.pdf), pp. 22, 29.

[49] This was, at least until recently, the dominant view in China. Huang Jinxin, "China rethinks India," in Friedman and Gilley (eds.), *Asia's Giants*.

[50] Quoted in Friedman, "Why democracy matters," at 196.

[51] Przeworski *et al.* found that democracies have a life expectancy of just eight years when their per capita income is less than US$1,000, and that twelve democracies with a per capita income less than US$2,000 fell within a year after experiencing declines in growth. See also Robert J. Barro, "Democracy: A recipe for growth?" in Muhammad G. Quibria and J. Malcolm Dowling (eds.), *Current Issues in Economic Development: An Asian Perspective* (New York: Oxford University Press, 1996). Adam Przeworski *et al. Democracy and Development: Political Institutions and Well-being in the World, 1950–1990* (Cambridge University Press, 2000). For the experiences of Asian countries, see Peerenboom, *China Modernizes*.

[52] Gilley, "Two passages to modernity," at 33, "explains" the mystery of why low-income India has remained democratic while so many low-income democracies have failed and reverted to authoritarianism as due to the value "the poor" place on freedoms. But then what explains why democracies have failed elsewhere, given that in his view the poor everywhere place such a high value on freedom, even over increased material benefits? India has been able to sustain democracy in part because the state is too weak to overcome the various centers of power and no single group is sufficiently powerful to dominate the others. Lele and Quadir offer another

Empirical studies have yet to sort out the complicated causal ways in which democracy, rule of law and wealth interact to support each other.[53] All else being equal, authoritarian regimes tend to outperform democratic regimes at relatively low levels of economic development.[54] However, in general, regime type is a poor predictor of economic growth. Regime type is not as important as the stability of the regime and variations within regimes. Not all democracies are alike, and neither are all authoritarian regimes. Regimes are more likely to be successful if they are market-oriented, dominated by technocrats, and relatively free from corruption, and they invest in human capital and institutional development.

China and other East Asian states including Singapore, South Korea and Taiwan have implemented reforms that have benefited the broad public, including institution-building measures, and investment in education and human resources.[55] In contrast, in Latin America and Africa, reform efforts have largely been undermined by patronage systems in which state leaders divert state assets into the hands of a few and elites block reform efforts aimed at benefiting the majority of citizens. The problems have continued even after democratization. The public good nature of legal reforms has been a barrier to reforms in democracies: even though reforms would be welfare enhancing overall, the benefits are widely dispersed, leading to collective action problems.[56] Individual beneficiaries of reforms may not have the incentive to become

plausible explanation: "The literature on democracy and development . . . rarely mentions the most obvious and perhaps the only necessary condition for the survival of formal democracy. It can survive and thrive anywhere as long as it protects the interests of the entrenched and dominant classes and as long as they hold can hold economic, political and ideological sway over the subaltern classes." Jayant Lele and Fahimjul Quadir, "Introduction: Democracy and development in Asia in the 21st century: In search of popular democratic alternatives," in Lele and Quadir (eds.), *Democracy and Civil Society in Asia* (New York: Palgrave Macmillan, 2004).

53 Rigobon and Rodrik, "Rule of law, democracy, openness, and income," found that while democracy and rule of law are both related to higher GDP levels, the impact of rule of law is much stronger.

54 See Barro, "Democracy: A recipe for growth?."

55 The correlation between wealth and civil and political rights, economic rights, rule of law and other good governance indicators is lower in Latin America and Africa than in East Asia, indicating that government leaders in Latin America and Africa are not utilizing economic resources for the benefit of the broad public to the same extent as in East Asia. See Peerenboom, *China Modernizes*, at 41.

56 *Cf.* Ronald J. Daniels and Michael J. Trebilcock, "The political economy of rule of law reform in developing countries," available at www.wdi.bus.umich.edu/global_conf/papers/revised/Trebilcock_Michael.pdf.

politically active. However, those with a vested interest in maintaining the *status quo* inside or outside the government are motivated to block reforms or to undermine reforms at the implementation stage.

In China, the government has been able to push through welfare-enhancing legal reforms despite opposition from certain sectors. To be sure, even in China, the policy-making process is contested, and compromises are frequently required to get reforms passed. Nevertheless, the Party generally retains the authority to resolve disputes between different state organs when necessary.

Democratic India has been unable to pursue the same policies as authoritarian China because of its political structure.[57] As noted, India has largely avoided neoliberal trickle down economics and opted for slower but more equitable growth. Manor notes that the Congress Party, United Front and Bharatiya Janata Party (BJP) all avoided politically tough decisions such as reductions in subsidies and curtailment of financial support to loss-making public enterprises. The result has been slower growth but less social dislocation than in China, where many state-owned enterprises (SOEs) have been privatized and workers have been laid off in large numbers.[58] Apparently, many Indian citizens prefer this approach (as do many Chinese, as reflected in rising discontent over inequality, a sharp increase in protests and demands for social justice). The BJP was voted out of office despite overseeing a period of rapid economic growth. The vote reflected a deep dissatisfaction with growing income disparities and widespread poverty amidst the growing wealth of some segments of society. The BJP's campaign slogan of India Shining only highlighted the discrepancies between the haves and the have-nots.

Similarly, some commentators have attributed India's lower level of investment in infrastructure to its democratic nature, and the need to appease different interest groups.[59] Mukherji, for instance, points out that India is no exception to the general problem that democracies are

[57] Gilley, "Two passages to modernity," acknowledges that China outperformed the average developing country in terms of human development from 1950–73 while India lagged behind the average. He claims, however, that the fast gains in China did not depend on authoritarianism, while average (actually below average) gains in India are not attributable to democracy. Yet he then argues, inconsistently, that India's fragile democracy lacked the state capacity of China to push radical poverty alleviation. Friedman, "Why democracy matters," at 204, also argues that regime type is not determinative: what matters are political institutions, policy, leadership, identity and will.

[58] Manor, "India's reform strengths."

[59] Joydeep Mukherji, "The causes of differential development: Beyond regime dichotomies," in Friedman and Gilley (eds.), *Asia's Giants.*

more likely to give in to populist protectionist pressures. He notes China's pragmatic approach to reforms that favored certain groups and regions would not be not politically feasible in India, and that powerful private sector companies in India have slowed the pace of liberalization in India. China's economic success is also due in part to much-criticized one-child policies that are possible only in an authoritarian state. India's inability to control population growth so rigorously may make sustained increases in per capita income difficult to achieve. Legal scholars have also noted that vested interest groups – including judges – have been able to resist legal reforms, including reforms to the judiciary in India.[60]

Although differences between China's particular type of authoritarian regime and India's democracy may be one factor in explaining the differences between China and India, such differences are only part of the story. China's relative success and India's relatively poor performance cannot be attributed simply to regime type. In any event, only time will tell whether the revisionists are correct. Much will depend on how well both China and India respond to the challenges facing middle-income countries. Much will also depend on how and when China democratizes, assuming, as seems likely, that it will eventually democratize.[61] Will the transition be gradual, or the result of regime collapse?

III. Conclusion

Comparisons between India and China are inevitable. Both are large developing countries of geopolitical importance. Both started off in roughly similar places in the late 1940s. One is a long-standing democracy; the other a single party socialist state. It is also tempting to use China and India to test general theories of law and development.

[60] Upendra Baxi, "Rule of law in India: Theory and practice," in Randall Peerenboom (ed.), *Asian Discourses of Rule of Law* (New York: Routledge, 2004).

[61] Some commentators believe that China is on the verge of collapse – again. Gordon Chang, *The Coming Collapse of China* (New York: Random House, 2001). Other commentators have pointed out the resiliency of the current regime. See Andrew J. Nathan, "Authoritarian resilience" (2003) 14(1) *Journal of Democracy*; Barry J. Naughton and Dali L. Yang (eds.), *Holding China Together: Diversity and National Integration in the Post-Deng Era* (Cambridge University Press, 2004). Some have questioned whether China is moving toward democracy. James Mann, *China Fantasy: How Our Leaders Explain Away Chinese Repression* (New York: Viking, 2007). I have argued that the future is likely to be one of authoritarian resilience with ongoing reforms leading eventually to a communitarian or other nonliberal variant of democracy. Peerenboom, *China Modernizes.* Others have argued that a gradual transition to democracy is not likely. Bruce J. Dickson, *Red Capitalists in China: The Party, Private Entrepreneurs and Prospects for Political Change* (Cambridge University Press, 2003).

Any theory unable to account for half of the world's population would seem to be in trouble.

However, such comparisons are risky and fraught with methodological problems. China and India are very different than other developing countries. In any event, the experiences of a single country, even such a large one as India or China, do not undermine general relationships across a range of countries.

Direct comparisons between China and India are also problematic. Data are often unreliable, available for different years or collected in different ways. There is also considerable regional variation within both countries. Moreover, each country does better in some respects than others. By selecting particular measures, one can present either a positive or negative image of either. Accordingly, across the board generalizations about the superiority of one or the other are dubious. Generalizations are difficult even within a particular area such as rule of law or economic development.

Nevertheless, some general observations are possible: China does better in terms of economic measures, poverty reduction, and most measures of human development. India does better in terms of political freedoms and income equality. Both have poor environmental records, low public health spending and repress minorities with secessionist tendencies. Both do relatively well compared to the average in their income class on good governance measures.

The normative conclusions to be drawn from these results are even less clear, and more contested. Is it better or worse to suffer from hunger than to not be able to advocate the overthrow of the government through peaceful or even violent means? Is there a necessary tradeoff between freedom and growth, or between faster growth and more equitable growth? Do people everywhere value freedom over economic growth and a higher standard of living?[62]

The revisionist view sees India's democracy as a great asset in overcoming the middle-income blues. Conversely, although China is also experiencing the middle-income blues, it is following the path of other East Asian countries that were able to make the transition from middle to upper income countries, from weak institutions and rule of law to strong institutions and rule of law, and from authoritarianism

62 Gilley, "Two passages to modernity," at 33, claims people in China and everywhere value freedom over economic growth and higher standard of living. Yet polls suggest otherwise. See Peerenboom, *China Modernizes*, at 254–56.

to democracy.[63] At this point, however, the jury is still out as to whether China and India will join the ranks of upper income countries whose citizens enjoy rule of law, good governance and high standards of living and human development (and in China's case, democracy).

[63] Saich, "Development and choice," at 237, claims that few, if any, socialist states have managed a peaceful transition from authoritarianism. But then China is already unique among socialist states in the degree to which it has endorsed market, legal and even political reforms. The pragmatic nature of Chinese leaders as well as experiences to date suggest that China may be able to follow the path of other East Asian states.

References

Barro, Robert J., "Democracy: A recipe for growth?" in Muhammad G. Quibria and J. Malcolm Dowling (eds.), *Current Issues in Economic Development: An Asian Perspective* (New York: Oxford University Press, 1996)

Determinants of Economic Growth (Cambridge MA: MIT Press, 1997)

Baxi, Upendra, "Rule of law in India: Theory and practice," in Randall Peerenboom (ed.), *Asian Discourses of Rule of Law* (New York: Routledge, 2004)

Carothers, Thomas, "The problem of knowledge," in *Promoting the Rule of Law Abroad: In Search of Knowledge* (Washington DC: Carnegie Endowment for Int'l. Peace, 2003)

Chang, Alberto and Calderon, Cesar, "Causality and feedback between institutional measures and economic growth" (2000) *Economics and Politics* 12

Chang, Gordon, *The Coming Collapse of China* (New York: Random House, 2001)

Clarke, Donald, "Economic development and the rights hypothesis: The China problem" (2003) 51 *American Journal of Comparative Law* 89

Clarke, Donald, Murrell, Peter and Whiting, Susan, "The role of law in China's economic development," available at http://ssrn.com/abstract=878672

Dam, Kenneth W., *The Law–Growth Nexus: The Rule of Law and Economic Development* (Washington DC: The Brookings Institution, 2006)

Daniels, Ronald J. and Trebilcock, Michael J., "The political economy of rule of law reform in developing countries," available at www.wdi.bus.umich.edu/global_conf/papers/revised/Trebilcock_Michael.pdf

Dickson, Bruce J., *Red Capitalists in China: The Party, Private Entrepreneurs and Prospects for Political Change* (Cambridge University Press, 2003)

Friedman, Edward and Gilley, Bruce (eds.), in *Asia's Giants* (New York: Palgrave, 2005)

Gilley, Bruce, "Two passages to modernity," in Friedman and Gilley (eds.), *Asia's Giants*

Gillman, Howard, "How political parties can use the courts to advance their agendas: Federal courts in the United States, 1875–1891," in Tom Ginsburg and Robert Kagan (eds.), *Institutions & Public Law: Comparative Approaches* (New York: Peter Lang, 2005)

Godoy, Sergio and Stiglitz, Joseph, "Growth, initial conditions, law and speed of privatization in transition countries: 11 years later" (2006) NBER Working Paper No. W11992

Guthrie, Douglas, "The declining significance of guanxi in China's economic transition" (1998) *The China Quarterly* 154

Hualing, Fu, "Putting China's judiciary into perspective: Is it independent, competent and fair, in beyond common knowledge?" in Eric G. Jensen and Thomas C. Heller (eds.), *Empirical Approaches to the Rule of Law* (Stanford University Press, 2003)

Jinxin, Huang, "China rethinks India," in Friedman and Gilley (eds.), *Asia's Giants.*

Kaufmann, Daniel *et al.*, *Governance Matters III: Governance Indicators for 1996–2004* (Washington DC: World Bank, 2005), available at www.worldbank.org/wbi/governance/pdf/govmatters3.pdf

Kennedy, Scott, *The Business of Lobbying in China* (Cambridge MA: Harvard University Press, 2005)

Lele, Jayant and Quadir, Fahimjul, "Introduction: Democracy and Development in Asia in the 21st Century: In Search of Popular Democratic Alternatives," in Lele and Quadir (eds.), *Democracy and Civil Society in Asia* (New York: Palgrave Macmillan, 2004)

MacFarquhar, Roderick, "Introduction," in Friedman and Gilley (eds.), *Asia's Giants*

Mann, James, *China Fantasy: How Our Leaders Explain Away Chinese Repression* (New York: Viking, 2007)

Manor, James, "India's reform strengths," in Friedman and Gilley (eds.), *Asia's Giants*

Mukherji, Joydeep, "The causes of differential development: Beyond regime dichotomies," in Friedman and Gilley (eds.), *Asia's Giants*

Nathan, Andrew J., "Authoritarian resilience" (2003) 14(1) *Journal of Democracy*

"Present at the stagnation"*Foreign Affairs*, July/August 2006, available at www.foreignaffairs.org/20060701fareviewessay85414/andrew-j-nathan/present-at-the-stagnation.html

Naughton, Barry J. and Yang, Dali L. (eds.), *Holding China Together: Diversity and National Integration in the Post-Deng Era* (Cambridge University Press, 2004).

Peerenboom, Randall, "Assessing human rights in China: Why the double standard?" (2005) 38 *Cornell International Law Journal* 71–172

China's Long March toward Rule of Law (Cambridge University Press, 2002)

China Modernizes: Threat to the West or Model for the Rest (Oxford University Press, 2007)

Is China Trapped in Transition? (Oxford Foundation for LawJustice and Society 2007) available at www.fljs.org/section.aspx?id=1939

"Judicial Independence in China: Common Myths and Unfounded Assumptions"in Randall Peerenboom (ed.), *Judicial Independence in China* (forthcoming)

"Show me the money: The dominance of wealth in determining rights performance in Asia" (2004) 15 Duke J. Comp. & Int'l. L.

Peerenboom, Randall and Xin, He, "Dispute resolution in China: Patterns, causes and prognosis," in Randall Peerenboom (ed.), *Dispute Resolution in China* (Oxford Foundation for Law, Justice and Society, 2008), available at www.fljs.org/section.aspx?id=1931

Pei, Minxin, *China's Trapped Transition: The Limits of Developmental Autocracy.* (Cambridge MA: Harvard University Press, 2006)

Przeworski, Adam *et al.*, *Democracy and Development: Political Institutions and Well-being in the World, 1950–1990* (Cambridge University Press, 2000)

Rigobon, Roberto and Rodrik, Dani, "Rule of law, democracy, openness, and income: Estimating the interrelationships" (2005) **13** *Economics of Transition*

Rodrik, Dani (ed.), "Introduction," to *In Search of Prosperity: Analytic Narratives on Economic Growth* (Princeton University Press, 2003)

Saich, Tony, "Development and choice," in Friedman and Gilley (eds.), *Asia's Giants*

SPC 2007 Work Report, available at http://news.sina.com.cn/pc/2007–03–13/326/152.html

Trebilcock, Michael and Leng, Jing, "The role of formal contract law and enforcement in economic development" (2006) **92** *Virginia Law Review*

US State Department Country Reports on Human Rights Practices, India–2003 (2004), available at www.state.gov/g/drl/rls/hrrpt/2003/27947.htm

World Bank, *The East Asian Miracle: Economic Growth and Public Policy* (New York: Oxford University Press, 1993)

"India's good governance indicators 1998 and 2004," generated from the World Bank, *Worldwide Governance Indicators*, available at http://info.worldbank.org/governance/wgi/sc_country.asp

"PRC good governance indicators 1998 and 2004," generated from the World Bank, *Worldwide Governance Indicators*, available at http://info.worldbank.org/governance/wgi/sc_country.asp

"Ten Years After the Crisis," April 2007, available at http://siteresources.worldbank.org/INTEAPHALFYEARLYUPDATE/Resources/550192–1175629375615/EAP-Update-April2007-fullreport.pdf

World Bank, Projects, "Middle-income countries (MICs)," available at http://web.worldbank.org/WBSITE/EXTERNAL/PROJECTS/0,,contentMDK:20976054~pagePK:41367~piPK:51533~theSitePK:40941,00.html

Yasheng Huang and Tarun Khanna, "Indigeneous versus foreign business models," in Friedman and Gilley (eds.), *Asia's Giants*

Zhu Jingwen (ed.), *Zhongguo falü fazhan paogao(1979–2004)* [*China Legal Development Report (1979–2004)*] (Beijing: Zhongguo renmin daxue chubanshe [People's University Press], 2007)

15

The development of modern corporate governance in China and India

NICHOLAS CALCINA HOWSON
AND VIKRAMADITYA S. KHANNA

I. Introduction

Corporate governance reform has become a topic of considerable debate both in the US and in many emerging markets. Indeed, the discussion is important because these reforms may have potentially long-standing effects upon the global allocation of capital, and in understanding the ways in which governance norms are communicated across markets and nations in an ever-globalizing world. In this chapter we examine the corporate governance reform efforts of the world's two biggest and fastest growing emerging markets, the People's Republic of China (PRC or China) and India. In the process we find that our understanding of how and why corporate governance reform comes about, where it leads, and what value it has can vary significantly, but still shares some commonalities that are of considerable theoretical and practical importance.

The inquiry commenced in this chapter is inspired by certain key facts. First, China and India are growing at a remarkable and unprecedented pace and seem to have survived the 2008–9 Global Financial Crisis better than most other economies. Second, China and India are *not* Western countries, but have been heavily influenced by "globalized" Anglo-American notions of corporate law, corporate governance norms, and securities regulation. Third, China and India are presently two of the most popular destinations for foreign capital in the world – whether via foreign direct investment (FDI) in essentially private (or pre-public) transactions or public capital markets transactions. Fourth, both India and China have undergone, and are progressing through, incredibly important (indeed world-changing) programs of economic reform and restructuring. At the same time they are increasingly – in the Chinese phrase – "opening to the outside world." These are the shared "facts" of our inquiry, which of course are met by many deep differences, in particular relating to the history, internal organization and political and economic structures of the two great nation-civilizations. However, we believe that the common "facts" recited above – rapid economic development, significant private and public foreign investment, economic, structural and legal/regulatory reform, speedy recovery from the Global Financial Crisis, and a shared interest in (if not implementation of) in essentially Anglo-American corporate law norms – provide an interesting and rich platform for consideration of popular or contested corporate governance and corporate governance reform precepts.

To engage in this exploration, we approach the task in several sections. Section II provides the background for examining the development of corporate governance reform in China and India. We examine in skeletal form the political, economic, legal and other features animating the environments in both countries. Section III examines the development of modern corporate governance reform in India which, unlike many other emerging markets, was largely initiated by industry (rather than being, for example, scandal driven). Section IV begins with detailed discussion of the modern effort at corporate business organization in China, and the program of reform applied to the corporate governance implemented subsequently. In particular, we examine how the advent of "corporatization" (a strategy to finance underperforming state-owned enterprises (SOEs)), along with certain central government agencies and reform-oriented individuals in China, helped further the development and reform of modern Chinese corporate governance. Section V explores what the Indian and Chinese experiences can tell us about broader theoretical issues animating the corporate governance literature. In particular, we examine what we can learn about the impact of "legal origins" (common law or civil law) as compared to "politics" on the development of stock markets in the two countries. In addition, we discuss whether India and China provide evidence for some kind of convergence in corporate law. We find that the support for the "legal origins" view is not strong, but that the "politics" account seems more relevant in explaining stock market development in India and China. Further, while there is a good deal of evidence of partial formal convergence in corporate law, we cannot identify the same or expected convergence in ownership or corporate structure. This creates an odd fit between corporate and securities law and the corporations they shape and regulate, suggesting some path dependence. Section VI concludes.

II. Background environments in China and India

Before discussing the development of corporate governance reform in China and India it seems useful to provide some context for the discussion. Although there is presently great enthusiasm about the prospects for both countries, it is important to note the similarities and differences between them.

In terms of similarities, both countries are geographically vast with very large populations.[1] They both also have huge urban populations, but still sizeable rural areas. Further, China and India possess large and highly successful diasporas throughout the world, which are involved in varying degrees with the growth and success in their countries of origin. Moreover, both countries started their lives in modern times as post-colonial independent or newly autonomous nations at roughly the same time (1947 and 1949), with both initially adopting less market-oriented policies. Nevertheless, over the last three decades both countries have implemented market-oriented reforms that have led to phenomenal growth rates and nearly geometric expansion in international trade connections and access to global capital markets. Indeed, they have become the most attractive destinations for foreign direct investment, and now routinely record the world's largest initial public offerings and capital markets corporate finance transactions. Finally, although both countries are generating significant growth, they are still plagued by some of the familiar problems of emerging markets: slow (and sometimes ill-prepared and politically compromised) judiciaries, corruption at various levels, and acute infrastructure problems (e.g., electricity, roads).

This, however, is where most of the similarities end. In terms of political structure the two countries are quite different.[2] India is a functioning democracy with many political parties and active elections, whereas China remains a one Party state, whereby the state is ruled absolutely by the Communist Party of China.[3] In addition to this,

[1] Many of the facts noted in this paragraph come from a variety of sources. See, e.g.: Yasheng Huang and Tarun Khanna, "Can India overtake China?" *Foreign Policy*, July–August 2003; *The Economist* (2006); and *Business Week* (2005) (article on China–India).

[2] Huang and Khanna, "Can India overtake China?".

[3] China's political and governance structure is theoretically divided between: the Party (under the Politburo), the state (under the executive (State Council and its ministries)), the legislature (the National People's Congress) and the military (the People's Liberation Army, under the Central Military Commission, the Chairman of which is a Party appointee). The state (executive and legislature) and military are in fact controlled by the Party through Party appointments to what appear to be state or military institutions.

although both countries have populations including different groups of people, the heterogeneity in India is quite broad relative to that in China. There are many official languages in India (over 20), no clear majority group (except arguably "Hindus"), and the presence of parallel legal systems operating simultaneously throughout the country. These factors simply underscore the heterogeneity reflected in India's population. The population's heterogeneity, absence of a clear majority group, and democracy in India mean that it is considerably more difficult to pass orders from the "top" and expect them to be followed at the grass roots.[4] Indeed, India's policies have tended to flow from the grass roots upwards. While China proclaims its more than 50 "national minorities," it is a far more homogeneous polity in ethnic and language terms. China's political and institutional culture is a work in progress, and certainly the significant contest between central and regional (or local) authority has been exacerbated by the devolution of political and economic decision making in the Reform era. Notwithstanding, China is still formally a unitary state, and its governance and reform experience has long been more "top down" than that made necessary and possible by India's historical and political development.[5]

Nowhere are these political differences seen more than in the approach toward economic development and the financing of it. China commenced its domestic economic reforms concurrent with a financing strategy that focused on raising FDI – initially private foreign investment and in the last 15 years foreign equity participation in public capital markets. Only recently has it turned to domestic capital. India, on the other hand, began by attempting to develop local talent and only then focused on the attraction of FDI. This was not only a result of historical aversion in India to foreign investment post-colonization, but also

[4] When there is no clear majority in a democracy, coalitions become necessary. Moreover, when there are many different groups (i.e., high heterogeneity) one cannot simply ignore some groups because one may have to enter into coalitions with them later. This suggests more consensus-oriented decision-making.

[5] Note, this is not to suggest that China has no need for consensus decision making – it is simply a relative statement compared to India. Moreover, China does have divisions: horizontally between the various regions in China, and vertically between the central and local levels. Many of these tensions have become exacerbated in recent years as different areas of China develop at radically different speeds, and the gap between rich and productive coastal (and in some cases interior) urban areas and the countryside widens. At this time, the central government is attempting to address this widening disparity, often relying upon a difficult-to-implement re-centralization to effect it.

because consensus decision-making would have made it difficult to follow a path of simply encouraging foreign investment in India.

The result, at least at this point in history, is that while China's growth has outpaced India's there are few truly indigenous Chinese firms (and only a handful not built on a pre-existing SOE or local government-promoted enterprise) that are considered internationally competitive, whereas many completely indigenous and non-state owned Indian firms compete internationally in many of the highest growth fields (high tech, pharmaceuticals, biotech). Indeed, in the early stages of China's capital markets development, China placed restrictions on the ability of non-SOE firms to raise capital largely to reduce the competitive threat they would pose to China's then cash-hungry and increasingly corporatized SOEs.[6]

However, FDI is only one small part of the reform programs that both countries have put into effect. We simply note that both countries have moved away from the communist (China) or somewhat socialist (India) visions they possessed and toward more mixed market economies. China has in fact moved to a kind of "wild west" autocratic capitalism, where control and often ownership remain vested in state or state-tied actors, limited duopolies flourish, and the state does not provide any real social support for broader society.

In China this has involved, amongst other things, the "corporatization" process (described in greater detail in Section IV) wherein a number of SOEs are being, or have been, reorganized as corporations in law, but not *privatized* in any real sense. Although there were exceptions for sensitive areas (e.g., national security and major infrastructure or energy), most non-sensitive previously state owned assets have been devolved to local level government actors (which function at differing levels of entrepreneurialism) or into private, entrepreneurial, hands. The relations between the enterprises and other economic actors have become increasingly subject to a marketplace where prices are not controlled, and value-creating transactions (including finance transactions) are described and normatively enforced "under law."[7]

[6] Although the Chinese Communist Party has, since 1979, engaged in an aggressive program of economic reform, it has been far more cautious about anything that might relate to, or trigger, *political* reform.

[7] Indeed, growth has been stimulated by local level enterprises (many originally permitted "collective" enterprises), foreign funded enterprises (which have been the lynchpin of China's export-led growth), and private enterprises (especially in "new" sectors where neither SOEs nor collectives were present, for example in the Internet-related sector).

In India, SOEs are being privatized on a case-by-case basis. Although the process has been erratic at times, it appears to be on somewhat more solid footing now. The newly privatized entities have been revamped and some are considered very profitable and are market leaders.[8]

These reforms, among other factors, have led to tremendous growth in both countries. We will not rehearse the numbers here except to note that in most numerical categories China has outperformed India (e.g., gross domestic product (GDP) growth around 9% compared to 5% to 6% for India), but in the last few years the gap has narrowed considerably.[9]

Clearly, economic growth is important for both countries. In China, it may be most important, as it may be the last and only way that the Communist Party can maintain the support and affection of Chinese citizens. At the same time, there is a sense in which India's growth – although by no means evenly distributed – is less skewed than China's. The broader base of growth in India implies somewhat greater political stability and support. In China if growth were to slow significantly then some fear that those who have not benefited from growth might react to weakening economic conditions and add to China's already roiling social discontent. This scenario only highlights how important sustained growth in China is – politically – for the Chinese Communist Party and its continuing hold on power. Good governance at the enterprise level, and the resulting efficiency gains, are thus of paramount importance in the political–economic calculations of China's leadership.

In light of the sheer speed of China's economic growth and its political importance, it seems surprising that China's stock markets languished for the five year period between 2000 and 2005, while India's boomed over the same period. One set of reasons for this difference, other than the structures of the respective financial sector, was the situation regarding corporate governance at the enterprise level and general rule of law concerns in China. Before briefly touching on those it is perhaps noteworthy that

[8] An example would be Industrial Credit and Investment Corporation of India (ICICI) Bank.

[9] For the past twenty-five years China has seen average annual GDP growth rates of more than 9% (except for two years); since 1999, the PRC has seen steadily ascending percentage increases in GDP growth on the year earlier from 7.5% (1999) to just under 10% (2005). The economy has other strengths too: national revenue growth has averaged 18% since 1994, the current deficit is only 1.6% of GDP, and public debt is less than a quarter of GDP; and China currently has almost US$850 billion in foreign exchange reserves, and one of the world's highest savings rates (approximately 40% of GDP). Much of the information contained in this paragraph is taken from James Miles' excellent China Survey in *The Economist*, 25 March 2006, p. 12. Also for greater comparative discussion of India and China see Huang and Khanna, "Can India overtake China?".

India and China came at the problem of corporate governance from different perspectives. In India corporate governance reform was built on a pre-existing corporate landscape and started with the private sector and only later became an issue for the public sector as well, whereas in China it worked the other way round.[10] This is not surprising given that in China there were initially few, if any, truly private enterprises with a large appetite for capital, only newly corporatized SOEs. Accordingly, corporate governance concerns in China focused first on what we might think of as public sector firms. Nonetheless, the starting point for corporate governance reform – although not surprising in each country – is likely to have important implications for the shape of how that reform occurred and is likely to proceed.

Having begun discussion of some corporate governance differences between the countries, we proceed now to briefly sketch out some other legal differences of note.[11] Legislation in India is seen as being more transparent and shaped more by the rule of law than in China where there appears to be considerable opacity in determining who is drafting laws, with what degree of technical expertise, and in the service of what policies. Moreover, various state departments and agencies in China are able to issue regulations which often have greater specificity, and force, than "law" promulgated by the legislature. Additionally, in India, although the judiciary operates on a somewhat glacial time frame, it is considered more experienced with commercial matters. Chinese courts are generally considered less technically competent and not nearly as autonomous or politically independent as their Indian counterparts.

Some may attribute these distinctions to somewhat artificial assignments of legal system affiliation/origins: between common law (India) and civil law (China). We explore this issue more fully in sub-section V.A, but suffice to say for now that these labels are somewhat misleading. In particular, China's developing legal system is a more mixed bag of different legal systems and regimes than the obscuring "civil law" designation conveys.[12]

10 Governance concerns emanated first from the SOEs and that is where most of the legislation has been. However, governance reform is now happening in China's foreign-funded enterprises, reformed collectives, and newly established private enterprises.

11 Huang and Khanna, "Can India overtake China?"

12 Many PRC scholars will articulate easy assurances that the PRC has established a "civil law" system (*dalu faxi*). Although one can examine why this view became common, we avoid that and instead simply note that China's modern, post-Reform, legal system was based on an imperfectly understood Stalinist Soviet system (itself channeling prior Alexandrine reforms from the nineteenth century). That system was attached to a prior tradition of law which has existed in China for more than 2,000 years (what Qu Tongzu

With this background we now examine the development of corporate governance reform in India and in China. Although we have noted some differences between the countries, we want to re-emphasize that there remain many commonalities too – rapid economic development, significant private and public foreign investment, economic and structural reform, and a shared interest in (if not implementation of) Anglo-American corporate law norms – which we will argue provide an interesting and rich platform for consideration of popular or contested corporate governance and corporate governance reform precepts.

III. The development of corporate governance in India

The reform of corporate governance is a worldwide phenomenon. In the last decade India has engaged in an ambitious series of reforms. In order to better understand the context of these reforms, we briefly discuss the corporate governance situation in India prior to these reforms.

Modern corporate governance in India dates back to the later half of the 1800s under the British Raj. By the time of Independence in 1947 India had functioning stock markets and a comparatively well-developed model of corporate governance. Following Independence the Indian government pursued socialist policies that led to the growth of the state owned sector and a greater role for the state as the primary provider of debt and equity capital. The results included a decline in corporate governance. By 1991 the financial position of the Indian government was quite precarious. This led it to embark on a series of market oriented reforms involving a retraction of the state from the corporate sector and a general liberalization of the economy. By the mid 1990s Indian industry began to search for capital to expand into the competitive spaces being left open by the liberalization policies. The need for capital, amongst other things, led to the first forays into corporate governance reform in India starting with the Confederation of Indian Industry's

called "the Confucianization of Law"), and then a German-influenced system (mediated through Meiji Japan) implemented by the late Qing and then Guomindang Republican governments of the 1920s and 1930s. After 1979, and the advent of "legal construction," and always based on the pre-existing Soviet-inspired system, China has been subject to a number of strong influences, depending upon the specific sector of "law" implicated. For instance, in the corporate and securities law spheres, the influence of US-style corporate law and securities law – notwithstanding the adjacency of British law haven Hong Kong – has been near overwhelming. This no doubt is a result of the pervasive influence of US ideas and structures communicated through the US-directed globalized capital markets.

Code for Corporate Governance in 1998 which was quickly followed by the government enhancing corporate governance via listing requirements (in 2000) and amendments to the Company Law.

In many respects the saga of modern corporate governance in India is the story of the prodigal son – a promising start followed by a decline with much more recent attempts at enhancing governance. The details of how this happened are briefly described in the next few paragraphs.

A. Origins of modern corporate governance in India (1866 to 1947)

India, unlike a number of emerging markets, has had functioning stock markets since 1875 where much of the activity was organized in the form of joint-stock limited liability companies. In light of the early presence of corporations in India it is not surprising that the regulation of corporate governance started relatively early. From 1866 onwards there were many pieces of legislation governing corporate governance, trust activity, banking activity and securities regulation.[13] Moreover, it appears that Indian industry grew considerably during World War II because the Chinese and Japanese economies, which were in some sense competitors, were damaged by the war and by wartime activities on their territories.[14] Thus, by the time of Independence (1947), India appeared to have well-functioning stock markets, an active manufacturing sector, a large corpus of corporate and securities laws, and a well-developed banking

[13] Amiya Kumar Bagchi, *Private Investment in India, 1900–1939* (Cambridge University Press, 1972); Radhe Shyam Rungta, *The Rise of Business Corporations in India, 1851–1900* (Cambridge University Press, 1970). See the Indian Companies Act 1866; Indian Companies Act 1882; Indian Trusts Act 1882; Indian Companies Act 1913; Reserve Bank of India Act 1934; 1956 Indian Companies Act (in the process of being re-written); 1956 Securities Contracts (Regulation) Act (defines powers and conduct for stock exchanges); 1985 Sick Industrial Companies (Special Provisions) Act (bankruptcy provisions for financially distressed companies – also being re-written); 1992 Securities and Exchange Bureau of India (SEBI) Act (sets up SEBI – regulator of stock markets). For more discussion of the growth of Indian Industry since the beginning of the twentieth century see M. D. Morris, "The growth of large scale industry up to 1947," in D. Kumar (ed.), *Cambridge Economic History of India*, vol. II (Cambridge University Press, 1983), pp. 553–676. Note that even prior to the 1866 Act there were corporations in India, primarily in the Bengal (Calcutta) area.

[14] See Sir Purshotamdas Thakurdas, J. R. D. Tata, G. D. Birla, Sir Ardeshir Dalal, Sir Shri Ram, Kasturbhai Lalbhai, A. D. Shroff and John Matthai, *The "Bombay Plan" for India's Economic Development* (Bombay: Printed by S. Ramu, at the Commercial Printing Press, 1944).

establishment.[15] Although there were certainly corporate governance abuses, the general state of corporate governance and the overall economy in India placed it in an enviable position amongst many decolonized countries.[16] This position was, however, about to receive some serious setbacks.

B. From Independence to liberalization (1947 to 1991)

Following Independence the Indian government put into place a number of policies that had the effect of weakening corporate governance in India. This started with a series of Industrial Policy Resolutions which entrusted the state with much greater responsibility for managing the economy.[17] The changes wrought by these resolutions included a much expanded state-owned sector.[18] The government was to become the sole provider of many goods and services.[19] This led to the nationalization of certain industries (in particular financial institutions such as banks and insurance companies) and the removal of private firms and competition from large sectors of the economy. This would have reduced the competitive pressure to be efficient. Moreover, Indian SOEs were not simply

[15] Rajesh Chakrabarti, *The Financial Sector in India: Emerging Issues* (New Delhi; New York: Oxford University Press, 2006); Omkar Goswami, "India: The tide rises gradually," in Charles P. Oman (ed.), *Corporate Governance in Development: The Experiences of Brazil, Chile, India, and South Africa* (Issy-les-Moulineaux: OECD Development Center; Washington DC: Center for International Private Enterprise, 2003).

[16] Many corporations in India during this time frame were operated under the managing agent system. This provided an impetus to dispersed ownership and a separation of ownership from control. Although the use of the corporate law statutes helped to contain the agency costs that arose from this situation, it was hardly perfect and many instances of abuses by managing agents are documented in the modern business history of India. See Rungta, *The Rise of Business Corporations*, pp. 219–55.

[17] Rakesh Mohan and Vandana Aggarwal, "Commands and controls: Planning for industrial development in India, 1951–1990" (1990) 14 *Journal of Comparative Economics* 681.

[18] Some of these changes bear considerable similarity to the suggestions laid out by the leading Indian Industrialists in the 1944 Bombay Plan. The Plan was to be a blueprint for economic growth in India and many of its suggestions seem to have been adopted by the first few Indian governments.

[19] There were also some industries where only the state could start new firms. See Goswami, "India: The tide." There appeared to be a belief that the private sector, domestic and foreign, could not be relied upon to provide these goods and services and that they may have incentives that do not enhance social welfare. See Chakrabati, *Financial Sector*; Thakurdas *et al.*, *The "Bombay Plan."* One expects the suspicion of private enterprise may have deep historical roots as the growth of the British Empire was tied to the success of the East India Company which had some very serious negative consequences for India.

being run to maximize profits, but for a variety of additional reasons as well.[20] In light of this, it is unsurprising that such firms would not focus on efficiency as the aim of corporate governance.

This was accompanied by a series of enactments that worked as entry barriers to certain markets and to investment. First, there was a series of enactments that required industrial enterprises to obtain a number of licenses from various government agencies to conduct business or to expand capacity (commonly known as the "license raj").[21] The requirement to obtain the government's approval provided opportunities for rent-seeking and corruption that likely led to a less competitive environment for many Indian businesses. The lack of competition would have benefited incumbents, but would also have hindered further improvement in corporate governance by reducing the competitive pressure to be efficient.

Second, the government erected barriers to both foreign investment in India and to foreign competition. There were large trade barriers and tariffs accompanied by limits on how much stock a foreign entity could own in an Indian enterprise and requirements for firms to purchase their goods from primarily indigenous producers.[22] This insulated domestic firms from foreign competition and, when combined with the extensive licensing requirements, insulated domestic firms from much further domestic competition.

This was compounded by how private sector firms were capitalized and the incentives of the various capital providers to monitor management. The primary source of capital for many Indian firms was debt capital. This was made available by the state through a variety of state-owned and -operated development finance institutions (DFIs).[23] The performance of DFI employees was not assessed based on whether the firms they provided funding to made a profit, but rather on the total amount of loans that had been made. This, of course, created an incentive to maximize the amount of loans rather than providing loans to businesses with viable business plans. DFIs then had little incentive

[20] Goswami, "India: The tide."

[21] Goswami, "India: The tide."

[22] Mohan and Aggrawal, "Commands and Controls"; Goswami, "India: The tide."

[23] World Bank, *India: Role of Institutional Investors in the Corporate Governance of their Portfolio Companies*, World Bank Report (2005); Chakrabarti, *Financial Sector*; Omkar Goswami, *Corporate Bankruptcy in India: A Comparative Perspective*, Development Centre Studies (Paris: Development Centre, Organisation for Economic Co-operation and Development; Washington DC: OECD Publications and Information Center, 1996).

to monitor management. Indeed, the DFIs often favored management due to a variety of reasons including corruption and political gain.

Although the DFIs were often the primary credit providers, other creditors did exist and would have had some incentive to monitor management. This was, however, hampered by the glacial speed of India's bankruptcy process. There were inordinate delays in the process of restructuring and liquidating a firm (e.g., it could easily take 10 years to liquidate a firm) and this would have placed these non-DFI creditors in an unenviable situation.[24] Indeed, it was not very common for private creditors to provide credit to anyone but blue chip companies or companies backed by government guarantees. Thus, these creditors were unlikely to exercise real oversight over management.

Even if creditors could not or did not monitor management, perhaps shareholders could. Here also there were problems. First, the primary providers of equity capital were the DFIs. Although most DFIs would provide finance primarily in the form of debt, they might also invest in the form of equity when their internal debt ratios would prohibit them from funding any more amounts as creditors. Indeed, for many companies the DFIs had collectively well over 50% of the equity stock. However, the DFIs had, as before, little incentive to act as careful monitors of management and used to routinely appoint nominee directors to the boards of these corporations that would rubber stamp the decisions of management[25]

If the DFIs did not exercise oversight, then what about other minority (non-management) shareholders – they might be able to exercise oversight. There was certainly provision in the Companies Laws for minority shareholders to raise oppression and mismanagement concerns at various adjudicative fora.[26] However, they were unlikely to have their grievances redressed for the following reasons:[27]

First, the Indian judicial system was full of delays and years could pass before such litigation would be adjudicated. Second, there appeared to be many irregularities in the share transfer and registration process which would have further delayed minority shareholders in bringing their cases. Third, the disclosure of ownership structure and related

[24] T. C. A. Anant and Omkar Goswami, "Getting everything wrong: India's policies regarding 'sick' firms," in Dilip Mookherjee (ed.), *Indian Industry: Policies and Performance* (Delhi: Oxford University Press, 1995); Goswami, *Corporate Bankruptcy in India.*

[25] World Bank, *India: Role of Institutional Investors*; Goswami, "India: The tide."

[26] See Sections 397 and 408, Indian Companies Act 1956.

[27] Goswami, "India: The tide."

party transactions was very opaque in India making it even harder for minority shareholders to achieve redress. This was exacerbated by the very high tax rates for corporations and individuals, which led to a tremendous amount of tax evasion achieved by devising highly complicated cross-holding structures. Although this aided tax evasion, it had the by-product of making ownership structure even more opaque to minority shareholders. Finally, even if someone tried to buy up shares in the corporation from the DFIs the government could block share transfers that might result in a change in the board that the government considered "prejudicial to the interest of the company or the public interest." Given that government (via the DFIs) tended to vote with management one can easily see how this would lead to entrenchment of management and little scope for effective oversight by other shareholders.

Of course, even if non-management shareholders and creditors exercise little oversight it may be that management has incentives aligned with maximizing wealth as most managements were the promoters and initial investors in the company. Here, too, capital structure played an invidious role. Because the ultimately passive DFIs provided so much of the capital (both debt and equity), the more active and interested promoters could maintain control with as little as 15 percent of the equity of a firm and, given the amount of funding they received in the form of debt, the promoters could have maintained control of a firm by providing only 3 percent of its capital.[28] With such excessive leverage the promoters could recover their initial investment very early on. Moreover, with so little invested in the firm the promoters and management would face incentives that might diverge quite widely from the rest of the shareholders, including the inattentive DFIs. The prospect for self-dealing and moral hazard would loom large in this environment.

Of course, such a system should have led to considerable looting by management and many failed companies. Although the looting did occur, the system was insulated from some of the consequences of failed companies both by the slow bankruptcy process and by the fact that the state could take over failing businesses and keep them afloat to maintain employment. The employment dislocation that would otherwise follow such policies did not eventuate, but at the cost of increasing the effective debt burden for the state.[29]

[28] Chakrabarti, *Financial Sector*; Goswami, "India: The tide."
[29] Anant and Goswami, "Getting everything wrong."

Thus, by 1991 the Indian corporate scene had changed considerably from its pre-Independence situation, leading India to become a laggard in healthy corporate governance. For state owned enterprises the familiar story of lack of competition and little profit incentive contributed to the inefficiency of the enterprise and its atrophied corporate governance. For private firms corporate governance was ineffective for a number of reasons. First, the DFIs as large shareholders and creditors played little to no monitoring role given the structuring of their incentives and the political context in which they acted. Second, the non-DFI creditors could exercise only limited oversight given the very slow pace of bankruptcy proceedings in India. Third, minority shareholders (non-DFI shareholders) faced considerable obstacles in enforcing their rights. There were lengthy judicial delays, little information about related party transactions, opacity in ownership structure (largely motivated by tax evasion) and irregularities in transferring shares. Fourth, promoters could start firms by putting up only the smallest sliver of their own capital. When this was combined with the ineffective oversight by other parties the potential for mismanagement and fraud becomes quite large. Moreover, these private firms faced little competitive pressure to improve their efficiency because of the "license raj" system, which limited domestic competition, and the high trade and other barriers limiting foreign competition. Finally, the employment dislocation that might have been caused by very inefficient management leading to failed firms was not felt in its entirety because the state could take over failing firms and keep their work force employed. This would have reduced the political cost of supporting inefficient management.

This is a recipe for dysfunctional corporate governance and that is precisely what India had. In formal terms, India had the laws and the legal system to enforce good corporate governance practices, but the functioning of the system, the inconsistent disclosure requirements, and largely ineffective boards of directors created instead a failing governance system. Indeed, Indian firms that were looking for capital were forced to look primarily to internal sources or the capital provided by the DFIs.[30]

[30] Asish K. Bhattacharyya and Sadhalaxmi Vivek Rao, "Economic impact of 'regulation on corporate governance': evidence from India," Indian Institute of Management Calcutta Working Paper No. 486/2004, January 17, 2004, available at Indian Institute of Management Calcutta Working Paper No. 486/2004, January 17, 2004 (2005), available at http://129.3.20.41/eps/fin/papers/0504/0504002.pdf; World Bank, *India: Role of Institutional Investors*.

C. Liberalization and corporate governance reform (From 1991 to the present)

The sheer weight and cost of this system came crashing down on the Indian economy in 1991 when the Indian government, in response to a financial crisis, embarked upon a general program of liberalization. It was the advent of these 1991 reforms that would lead to the corporate governance reforms that are examined in this paper. Liberalization was to take the form of selling off some of the SOEs and beginning to sell off or rationalize the state's interests in other firms. Further, the DFIs were now to be assessed on "bottom line" measures (i.e., return on assets) rather than the amount of loans sanctioned or "assets" created.[31] Moreover, trade barriers were to be reduced, foreign investment permitted (and even encouraged) and the "license raj" to be eased thereby permitting increased domestic and foreign competition.[32] Thus, post-1991 India would have new competitive spaces opening up (where the SOEs would no longer be the sole provider of goods or services), old industries becoming more competitive with the inflow of foreign competition and new domestic competition, and government institutions more motivated by efficiency than before. Following this the government created the securities market regulator – the Securities & Exchange Board of India (SEBI) – in 1992 and slowly granted it increasing powers and the mandate to regulate the many domestic stock markets in India.[33] This was significant because SEBI could take on an adjudicatory role and thereby relieve some pressure on the court system and provide more timely resolution of disputes insofar as they had publicly traded equity.[34]

It is against this backdrop that corporate governance reform would develop in India. Indeed, one of the more unique things about Indian corporate governance reform is that it was initiated and initially pushed by industry. Although there were scandals in the Indian stock markets

[31] Indeed, the DFIs were no longer provided the kind of subsidized access to funds they had in the past and they were sometimes merged with private entities (World Bank, *India: Role of Institutional Investors in the Corporate Governance of their Portfolio Companies*, World Bank Report (2005)). The primary DFIs before 1991 were: – IFCI, ICICI, IDBI, UTI, LIC, GIC and Public Sector Banks. Now there are 3 sets of Institutional Investors – the DFIs, new private sector Mutual Funds, and Foreign Institutional Investors.

[32] Anne Krueger (ed.), *Economic Policy Reforms and the Indian Economy* (University of Chicago Press, 2002); Goswami, "India: The tide."

[33] The Securities and Exchange Board of India Act, 1992.

[34] Delays in the Indian Judicial system are well known. See Bibek Debroy, "Some issues in law reform in India," in J.J. Dethier (ed.), *Governance, Decentralization, and Reform in China, India, and Russia* (Boston MA: Kluwer, 2000), pp. 339–68.

following liberalization (and even before it), it was when industry got involved that reform moved forward quickly.[35] The Confederation of Indian Industry (CII) drafted the first corporate governance code in India in 1998 and it was that code that formed the basis for Clause 49 of the Stock Exchange Listing Agreement.[36] Indian industry pushed governance reform because access to capital was necessary to take advantage of the opportunities created by liberalization and to stay ahead of (or at least with) the competition.[37] However, given the generally poor level of governance Indian corporations could not seriously expect domestic and foreign investors to provide capital without some greater assurance.[38] Indeed, some outside enforcement (e.g., via SEBI or the exchanges) might be needed to bolster the credibility of any governance reform. Thus, the corporate governance reform movement in many respects was motivated by a desire to access capital markets to fund investment in new business opportunities or to enhance chances in current endeavors. Reform was also supported by the increasing presence of foreign investors, the Indian financial press being quite active, and the desire to access US and developed world capital markets.[39]

Following the 1998 CII code, SEBI decided to form the Kumarmangalam Birla Committee (KMBC) and commission a report on corporate governance reform leading to changes in the listing agreement of the stock exchanges. The KMBC's draft set of recommendations came out on 1 October 1999 and became effective as Clause 49 of the listing agreement with the exchanges on 21 February 2000 – a stunning 5 months later. Firms failing to meet the requirements of Clause 49 could be delisted.[40] The details of Clause 49 are provided in Appendix 15.1, but a quick overview is provided below.

Clause 49 had both mandatory and non-mandatory requirements. In the mandatory portion were a number of reforms designed to require greater independence on boards. This involved prescribing minimum percentages of independent directors (50% or 33% depending on whether the Chairman was an executive director) and significantly tightening up the definition of "independence." In addition, Clause 49 mandated

35 Goswami, "India: The tide."

36 See Confederation of Indian Industry, *Desirable Corporate Governance: A Code* (1998).

37 See Goswami, "India: The tide"; Chakrabarti, *Financial Sector.*

38 See Vikramaditya Khanna, "Corporate governance in India: Past, present and future?"(2009) 1 *Jindal Global Law Review* 171–95.

39 Goswami, "India: The tide."

40 Now there is the possibility of financial penalties from Section 23 E of 2004 Act. See Securities Laws (Amendment) Act, 2004, S.11.

the number of meetings per year, expected boards to develop a code of conduct and imposed limits on the number of directorships a director could simultaneously hold. Clause 49 also enhanced the power of the audit committee both by requiring financial literacy, experience and independence, and by expanding the scope of activities on which the audit committee had oversight. Executives were also expected to be more personally involved in corporate affairs as seen by the requirements for certification by the Chief Executive Officer (CEO) and Chief Financial Officer (CFO) of financials and overall responsibility for internal controls. This was combined with considerably enhanced disclosure obligations (on many things including accounting treatment and related party transactions) and enhanced requirements for holding companies when overseeing their subsidiaries. These series of changes appear aimed at making boards and audit committees more independent, powerful and focused monitors of management. Moreover, the enhanced disclosure would aid institutional and foreign investors in exercising oversight as well.

A number of further committees were formed which made a series of recommendations (e.g., Naresh Chandra Committee, Department of Company Affairs Report, Malegam Committee, and the Narayana Murthy Committee) leading to further changes in the listing requirements.[41] Additionally, amendments were made to the Companies Law and some proposals are still under consideration. Moreover, the corporate governance of banks was reformed at this time as well.[42]

Although there were some changes to the statutory law during this period, most of the changes were in the listing requirements. This is not too surprising. Changes in listing agreements carry the penalty of de-listing, which although significant, is less personally painful for executives than violations of the statutory law which could involve direct financial penalties and jail time. Moreover, listing requirements are generally enforceable only through SEBI and the exchanges which can utilize enforcement discretion thereby softening the impact of the changes. This would have dulled opposition to the reforms because the cost of non-compliance looks less severe. Indeed, a strategy of first changing listing requirements looks very much like an attempt to first

[41] See Murthy Committee (2003); Chandra Committee (2002); Malegam Committee (1995).

[42] Chakrabarti, *Financial Sector*. In banks the system of nominee directors is being phased out and the banks use the CAMELS system (Capital Adequacy, Asset Quality, Management, Earnings Liquidity and Systems and Controls). See Murthy Committee (2003); Chandra Committee (2002); Malegam Committee (1995).

"test the waters" in a relatively low cost way, so that if the change "sticks" regulators can proceed with statutory changes thereby providing firms with sufficient time to adapt before penalties became more significant. Such a strategy is less likely to encounter political opposition and may still provide enough assurances to encourage the investment of capital in India. This is certainly a plausible way to describe the reforms that have occurred in India.

Indeed, consistent with this the next series of important reforms are statutory changes which are to be tabled in front of Parliament soon (based on the J. J. Irani Committee's (2005) recommendations).[43] The changes will apply to all firms in India (not just those listed on the exchanges). The proposed changes are summarized in Appendix 15.1 and compared to the changes wrought by Clause 49.

From our perspective a number of things are noteworthy about the Irani Committee's recommendations. Although they tighten up certain things and loosen others relative to Clause 49, the overall thrust of the recommendations is that the statutory law will permit greater customization and self-regulation (e.g., requiring shareholder approvals for executive compensation) for all companies. Moreover, this will be accompanied by greater protection for smaller shareholders, especially in merger transactions. Finally, the process of enforcement is to be streamlined, the bankruptcy system upgraded, and the actual legal provisions rationalized and simplified (eliminating redundancies and so forth). These changes are not inconsistent *per se* with Clause 49. This is because Clause 49 is specifically targeted at listed companies and one might expect tighter regulation for these kinds of companies (as they raise capital from the general public) compared to all firms (listed or not) which may raise capital from smaller and perhaps better informed sets of people.

One could, of course, view the Irani Committee as taking a more cautious approach to governance reform than Clause 49. This is perhaps not that surprising given that India attracts much more capital now than it did before the enactment of Clause 49 (indicating that the marginal gain from governance reform now may not be as large). In addition, there are many firms who have had difficulty in complying in a timely manner with Clause 49, indicating that further reform may be fairly costly on top of the reforms in Clause 49.

[43] See "Cabinet approves Companies Bill," *The Times of India*, August 30, 2008. There is also some further movement on disclosures as per the Parekh Sub-Committee Report (2008).

Although these governance reforms are important, there are many others one could also examine and reform: voting rights, bankruptcy reform, and perhaps shareholders suits. Indeed, one might view the above-described changes and proposed changes as just parts of a broader package of reforms that make capital investment or lending more attractive in India.

IV. The development of corporate governance in China

Any discussion about corporate governance – and more recently *improved* corporate governance – in China must be prefaced by background on the broader reform of China's post-1949 centrally planned, state-owned, economic system and the subsequent formal corporatization of state-owned asset groupings. In a word – before there could be "corporate" governance or corporate governance "reform," there had to be corporations. In the initial stages of Chinese reform, corporatization was the repositioning of line-Ministry operated factories and other state-owned assets under the umbrella of independent legal persons established under law.[44] Only in the last decade and a half – and after the growth of domestic capital markets, the creation of a distinct private and public shareholder class (Chinese and foreign), and the appearance of more independent (and themselves corporatized and profit-seeking) providers of credit – have these re-organized asset groupings and their new corporate identities become the focus of what Chinese participants and academic observers theorize as corporate governance "reform." Thus, we begin our analysis of corporate governance reform in China by addressing (i) how the industrial enterprise system was organized in the PRC prior to reform, (ii) the actual process of corporatization (not "privatization") which commenced in the mid-1980s and continues today, and (iii) the shifting policy goals over two and a half decades which have animated adoption of the corporate form generally in reform-era China.

If, as we posit above, the story of modern corporate governance in India calls to mind the tale of the "prodigal son," then China's encounter with the corporate form is something more alarming to the receiving

[44] As will be alluded to below, this process should not be called "privatization" as such newly established legal entities continued to be largely owned, and controlled, by state administrative departments, themselves reorganized as "holding companies" or "controlling groups."

parents – the arrival on the family doorstep of a fully formed, overseas-adopted (or at least foreign-educated) child one had no expectation of ever meeting, much less letting onto the premises to race around the house freely!

A. *From the Communist Revolution to the start of the reform era (1949 to the mid-1980s) – Policy reforms*

The post-1949 Chinese economic system was characterized by an overwhelming reliance on two key mechanisms: (i) central planning and (ii) direct bureaucratic-administrative control of the industrial economy's productive instruments.[45] Productive assets in China were organized as SOEs (usually as part of coterminous "work units") under "line Ministries" reporting to the State Council. These Ministries and their subordinate bureaus acted as agents of the state in operating the SOEs under their charge, with the state in turn deemed to be the representative of the ultimate owners – "all the people."[46] This structure was consistent with orthodox Marxist ideology, and the requirement that ownership of the means of industrial production be vested in a certain very large group of politically privileged citizens.[47] That ideological characterization dovetailed nicely with the Chinese leadership's perceived requirements – especially after the destruction and dislocation of the

[45] The summary provided here is an over-generalization. In truth, the organization of the Chinese industrial economy even pre-reform was far more complex and highly differentiated. See Barry Naughton, *Growing Out of the Plan: Chinese Economic Reform, 1978–1993* (Cambridge University Press, 1995). However, our summary description in this article should prove useful as a template to understand the (under-performing if not failing) system in place prior to generalized reform and then implementation of the specific remedy directed at failing SOEs, corporatization.

[46] The term "state-owned enterprises" in English is in fact a translation of the Chinese term more literally rendered "owned by all the people-system enterprises" (*quanminsuoyouzhi qiye*). Chinese Communist Party (CCP) organizational structure closely shadowed the governance structure of SOEs and in fact possessed far more power than formally designated enterprise "managers." Even after corporatization and global public offerings by transformed SOEs, Communist Party cells or committees continue to have huge governance power over Chinese firms, usually more power than the formal board of directors, independent directors, or senior management. With respect to the corporatized commercial banks alone, see Nicholas Calcina Howson, "China's restructured commercial banks: The old nomenklatura system serving new corporate governance structures?" in M. Avery, M. Zhu and J. Cai (eds.), *China's Emerging Financial Markets: Challenges and Global Impact* (Singapore: John Wiley and Sons, 2009).

[47] Under the Chinese revolutionary scheme, a wider group than merely the "proletariat," and thus inclusive of workers, peasants, military – but excluding those declared to be *without* political rights (class enemies, criminals, etc.)

Anti-Japanese War, World War II, the Chinese Civil War and eventual Liberation (in 1949) – for strict central control and planning of the industrial economy. At the lowest reaches of this system was the "work unit" or *danwei*, often coterminous with specifically identified SOEs but also sometimes subordinate units aggregated into a larger SOE. These work units operated at the instruction of the planning bureaucracy and had little autonomy. In theory, work units/SOEs were allocated inputs or other necessary resources by government bureaucratic actors and then closely instructed on production requirements (usually set as quotas or directed production levels). The SOEs then distributed product through mandated channels to specified buyers, and collected revenues determined according to state-controlled pricing. Gross cash in-flows to SOEs were immediately remitted, *in toto*, to the SOE's planning or administrative superior (i.e., a bureaucratic actor in the line Ministry system), with that superior body subsequently re-allocating cash back down to the SOE/unit to fund the next temporal cycle of productive activity. Importantly, these SOEs/work units also bore the very significant burden of certain "social" or non-economic tasks – delivering housing, medical care, education, day care, retirement support and even entertainment for members of the unit or SOE (including their non-employee family members).

At least until the early 1980s then, SOEs and the SOE system were strangers to common aspects of corporate structuring or corporate law. For example, SOEs did not have distinct legal personality, did not contract as independent legal persons, and did not formally "own" assets they operated or controlled. Instead, SOEs were essentially arms of the state bureaucracy and as such were not separate from the political or administrative authorities. They merely "operated" but did not "own" the assets assigned to their charge. The SOE structure, when set against the background of the Communist Party-ruled state, resulted in SOEs managed almost entirely by planning and political authorities. This in turn had important effects on how these entities were governed:

First, there were no identified owners of the SOEs (only the political fiction of "all the people"), and thus no specific or human actor interested in the performance or growth of the assets collected under the umbrella of a given SOE. Monitoring by "all the people" was impossible, even if sincerely intended, because of the most severe kind of collective action problem. The only authority which could monitor the SOEs and their managers were the state-bureaucratic organs to which management of these enterprises was formally delegated. In any case, at this time SOEs were not tasked with pursuing profitable activity – instead, they were responsible for fulfilling the commands of centralized planning authorities, using centrally allocated funds to manufacture goods, and sell products to stipulated buyers at state-controlled prices. Thus, "monitoring" of SOEs consisted of passive acceptance by higher administrative authorities of annual confirmations by subordinate SOE groupings with respect to whether these instruments of the planned economy (and indirectly their managers) had fulfilled quota production or distribution targets. Likewise, because the aim of such SOEs was not to create profits or grow value but to fulfill commands. There was no requirement for profit accounting, merely cost accounting to track mandated inputs and directed outputs. Similarily, because growth of the enterprise *qua* SOE was entirely irrelevant, there was no need for a balance sheet to understand the changing value of the SOE firm. Thus, even if there was a party interested in monitoring the firm, the measurement of performance and value on an enterprise basis would have been near impossible.

Second, the sole provider of credit to significant SOEs was the state-owned and controlled banking system (excepting direct cash allocations by government and planning authorities). In effect, banks were merely an alternative mechanism for planned allocations of capital by the state directly to SOEs. The banking system itself, and the instruments of that system, were equally unconcerned with profitability, efficiency or return on assets. As a result, there was no inquiry by these credit providers as to the creditworthiness or profitability of the "borrower" SOEs, and scant concern or expectation that such borrowers would pay interest or even principal. In this context, the state banking system had little incentive to monitor SOEs (or their managers') performance. These difficulties were only intensified by the lack of any hard budget constraint at the SOE enterprise level, even a notional bankruptcy threat, or a legal structure for security interests and exercise of the same by the providers of credit. In short, under the pre-reform structure, even the providers of credit to productive SOEs had no monitoring interest or incentive whatsoever.

Thus, the historical SOE system was characterized by an absence of any monitors of enterprise profitability, much less methods to assess the performance of those individuals entrusted with operating the SOEs. Instead, performance evaluation focused on conformity with top-down bureaucratic commands, with little or no connection to the most efficient or productive utilization of state assets. Indeed, performance evaluations for SOEs may well be termed almost entirely political (or bureaucratic) and opaque to any external actors.

After the end of the Great Proletarian Cultural Revolution and the death of Mao Zedong in 1976 it was widely recognized that the SOE system, in large part because there was no effective monitoring, furthered widespread inefficiency, low factor productivity, and wastage in key capital intensive industrial sectors.[48] Accordingly, and starting in the late 1970s, China began far-reaching *policy* reforms of the SOE system to attack widely acknowledged SOE inefficiency.[49] In particular, the PRC allowed substantial liberalization of so-called "collective enterprises" (not SOEs) and permitted the establishment of foreign-invested enterprises – primarily project-specific joint ventures between inefficient SOEs and foreign investors matching cheap labor with foreign capital and technology to produce exported consumer goods.[50] Moreover, for SOEs, new measures were implemented that provided key managers with personal incentives to be concerned with SOE asset productivity, and provided

[48] Nicholas R. Lardy, *China's Unfinished Economic Revolution* (Washington DC: Brookings Institution Press, 1998).

[49] See Stoyan Tenev and Chunlin Zhang, with Loup Brefort, *Corporate Governance and Enterprise Reform in China: Building the Institutions of Modern Markets* (Washington DC: World Bank; International Finance Corporation, 2002), pp. 10–16; Naughton, *Growing Out of the Plan*, pp. 57–170; Lardy, *China's Unfinished Economic Revolution*, pp. 21–58. Some of these policy reforms were subsequently codified in what was presented as "law," as the PRC's parallel "legal construction" program gathered steam and substance.

[50] There were smaller scale enterprises (collectively owned enterprises and some truly "privately"-owned enterprises) in some areas. "Collectively owned" refers to the idea that these were "owned" by a local level collective – often a local-level government body and employee workers – and not fully nationalized or state-owned, at least not by *central* state authorities. However, this formal "ownership" by the collective did not imply any kind of governance power over the collectively held assets, or profit participation in the collective's revenues, made clear only in subsequent laws applicable to such collectively owned entities. In fact, many of the successful collectives were corporatized after the 1994 Company Law was passed, as much to get governance and profit-sharing benefits as to prepare for public listings. Chinese-*foreign* joint ventures allowed SOEs to contribute state-owned assets already entrusted to the SOEs into new, independent, "legal persons" (these foreign-invested enterprises became China's first post-1949 corporate entities). It has become clear that these Chinese-foreign joint ventures contributed mightily to fueling China's exploding export sector. But at least one study suggests that the initial program of attracting direct foreign investment had detrimental effects because it kept bankrupt SOEs afloat and diverted foreign capital investment away from more efficient and entrepreneurial, but less politically favored, enterprises. See Yasheng Huang, *Selling China: Foreign Direct Investment During the Reform Era* (Cambridge University Press, 2003). Finally, SOEs could also at this time re-position state-owned assets under "joint enterprises" (*lianying qiye*), which were permitted to operate more autonomously than SOEs. These gained a formal basis in law only with the General Principles of the Civil Law 1986. See *Zhonghua Renmin Gongheguo Minfa Tongze* (The General Principles of the Civil Law of the People's Republic of China), Articles 51–3.

institutional incentives to force the SOEs themselves to operate more efficiently by tying the amount of resources the SOEs could retain at the enterprise level (or not submit to the government directly) to their economic performance.[51] Thus, the "better" the SOE performed, the more cash assets (as retainable revenues) it could maintain under its control – something of considerable benefit to the SOE and SOE management. Although not quite the same as a profit mechanism, this key reform was designed to provide enterprise management with incentives to boost performance at the SOE level.

At the same time, there were very early stage changes to the banking system,[52] whereby banks were made notionally more credit-oriented in continuing to dole out planned capital allocations in the form of "bank loans." Moreover, 1986 saw the promulgation of an "experimental" Bankruptcy Law applicable only to SOEs. This was an important (future) marker for the legal consequences and creditor's rights arising after the imposition of a real hard budget constraint on enterprises. Although important from the perspective of putting these issues on the table, these developments had little real bite as there was – in these early days – no true hard budget constraint at the enterprise level, a notional bankruptcy constraint which was rarely applied, and bank loans distributed according to political signals rather than credit signals, even by purportedly "commercial" lenders.

By the end of this initial – primarily *policy*-based – period of reform, enterprise governance had improved somewhat as SOE management had slightly better internal incentives to operate more efficiently. However, the system still left very much to be desired in terms of external monitoring of PRC firms – the kind of external firm monitoring needed to significantly enhance efficiency.[53]

[51] This included the use of dual track pricing (designed to introduce market incentives and re-orient SOE production) and liberalization of the labor markets thereby allowing for the possibility of dismissing certain workers.

[52] The People's Bank of China, China's sole domestic lender, spawned three new banks – People's Construction Bank, Industrial and Commercial Bank, and Agricultural Bank of China – to exist alongside China's pre-Liberation foreign exchange banking institution, the Bank of China. For a more detailed treatment of the full banking reform agenda, from the mid-1980s to 2009, see Howson, "China's restructured commercial banks."

[53] Chinese policy makers apparently sincerely believed that net changes in the way SOEs were managed – when matched with increased marketization of the external economy within which such firms acted – would lead to corresponding productivity and efficiency gains from the SOEs themselves. Notwithstanding a great deal of rhetoric, policy pronouncements, and promulgation (if not implementation) of "laws" and "regulations" and other "normative documents," many of the external and internal incentives (or disincentives) shaping enterprise performance remained very weak.

It is also important to note that these changes were not implemented (i) through formal corporatization of the firms or (ii) *under law.* This policy-inspired reform approach can be seen clearly in the PRC Law on Enterprises Owned by All of The People (SOE Law).[54] That "law" is in fact a catalogue of reform policy choices and aspirations rather than an enforceable statute.[55]

B. Formal reorganization of the industrial economy and corporatization (from early/middle 1980s to date)

Formal corporatization of Chinese assets really began in the early 1980s, as part of self-declared "experimental" programs undertaken at local (sub-national) level government initiative.[56] In large part, these efforts were directed at the corporatization of (or in the accepted Chinese idiom, use of the "share system" (*gufenzhi*) by) smaller, and locally promoted, collectively owned enterprises. As an example, local governments made a practice of foregoing collection of an array of fees or taxes from pre-existing collectives, either for a recognized profit participation

[54] *Quanminsuoyouzhi Gongyeqiye Fa* (Law on Industrial Enterprises Owned by All of the People), adopted at the First Session of the Seventh National People's Congress and promulgated by Order No. 3 of the President of the PRC on April 13, 1988, and effective on August 1, 1988.

[55] Thus, while the SOE Law does provide one of the initial confirmations, in law, of legal personality, hard(er) budget constraints, and independent accounting for SOEs, the SOE Law is really only a strong policy statement dressed up as a "law" designed to express the increased responsibilities and powers of factory/SOE managers, and the uneasy balance between state planned activity and the productive ambitions of SOEs themselves. Article 2 of the SOE Law says it quite well:

> [the SOE is] a socialist commodity production and operation unit that shall, in accordance with law, make its own management decisions, take full responsibility for its profits and losses, and practice independent accounting. The property of the enterprise shall be operated and managed by the enterprise with the authorization of the state in line with the principle of separation of ownership and management authority. The enterprise shall enjoy the right to possess, utilize and dispose of, according to the law, the property that the state has authorized it to operate and manage.

Perhaps the most interesting question about the promulgation of the SOE Law pertains to why the Chinese government saw the need to promulgate it. Was it merely something deemed consistent with the appearance of the legal construction program then moving into high gear, or was it a political/institutional marker to establish basic, and presumably irreversible, policy choices for all actors in Chinese society?

[56] These initiatives were undertaken first without any basis in national law or local-level or administrative regulation.

in the collective's future earnings, or something like "founders equity" in a formally re-organized, or even subsequently corporatized, collective.[57] In those very early days, one of the primary perceived benefits of corporatization – at this very local level – was the relatively painless and cost-free creation of non-transferable "equity" interests in China-domiciled firms, which were used (oppressively in some cases) in *lieu* of unavailable cash compensation for employees.

The great impetus for wide-scale corporatization of China's SOEs and eventually transformed collectively owned enterprises was capital-raising. As early as 1984, eleven SOEs became "shareholding system enterprises," with a number of other corporatizations of SOEs completed before the end of that decade.[58] The almost premature establishment of Chinese stock exchanges at Shanghai and Shenzhen in 1990–1, and the speculative frenzies resulting immediately, only heightened the attractive pull of the corporatization idea.[59] Above all, corporatization reform at this stage was animated by what must have appeared to be an easy bargain for Chinese enterprises and their bureaucratic (central or local) masters: the ability to attract financing (Chinese and, almost immediately, foreign)[60] for poorly performing SOEs, but without any dilution of the state's near absolute control in the resulting corporate entities.[61] That being said, it is also clear that many reformist policy makers in China understood corporatization and the listing of shares on public exchanges – domestic or foreign – as a useful first step to increased monitoring of Chinese enterprises by public markets (both via market valuation and participation by shareholders in governance), even if that would come at some time in the very distant future.

In November 1993, the Chinese Communist Party officially unveiled and provided political sanction for the "modern enterprise

57 See, eg., background to the formation of Stone, China Legend (now "Lenovo"), Hai'er, etc.

58 See Tenev and Zhang with Brefort, *Corporate Governance and Enterprise Reform*, p. 16.

59 The frenzies, and in one August 1992 case surrounding the distribution of subscription forms for the Shenzhen Development Bank where riots resulted, led directly to the creation of China's powerful securities regulator, the China Securities Regulatory Commission (CSRC).

60 We note that the first public offerings on the Shanghai and Shenzhen Stock Exchanges were for the equity in transformed Chinese-foreign equity joint ventures ("transformed into what?" lawyers might ask in the absence of a company statute) and directed to *foreign* purchasers of "B" shares.

61 The fact that many participants saw the bargain as "easy" in the late 1980s and early 1990s does not refute the reality of the Faustian bargain struck in fact, as real governance constraints began to bite ten to fifteen years later.

system."[62] This signaled the introduction and acceptance into China of the corporate mechanism and its attendant structural (legal), governance and management norms. Perhaps most important in the PRC context was the acceptance by the ruling Party of separation of the state's continued ownership rights (in the corporate legal person) on one hand, and the corporate legal person's exercise of ownership rights over the assets it now "owned," on the other. This political (note, not yet *legal*) pronouncement was the culminating policy-ideological expression of the long effort to maintain state "ownership" of the means of production, while at the same time creating real incentives for management autonomy (and property rights) at the enterprise level.[63]

Although a considerable move forward, the declaration of the age of "modern enterprise" in China did not enhance the governance situation at firms appreciably. The state remained the largest shareholder (in the 70–80% range) and was still essentially "absent" as a shareholder interested in enterprise profitability. That "absent" but formal shareholder was also still far distant from insider (cadre) managers who more often than not fell prey to the temptations of opportunistic behavior with regard to the corporate assets left in their charge. Credit providers remained state-owned and run by Communist Party cadres, and were often captured by local-level government-dominated branches with interests closely aligned to the same local level government insider managers. Finally, even as China's "legal construction" program continued apace, there was little corporate or securities law designed to protect the interests and monitoring rights of those who provided real capital, and the weak courts did not have the competence, political strength or will to enforce what law and regulation there was.

C. *Company law and China (1993–2006)*

In 1993, in line with the simultaneous policy confirmation of the "modern enterprise system," China's legislature promulgated China's first, and deeply flawed, post-Revolution Company Law – which law

[62] See Third Plenum of the Fourteenth Congress of the Chinese Communist Party, "Decision on Issues Concerning The Establishment of a Socialist Market Economic Structure."

[63] This same Decision from the Third Plenum of the Fourteenth Party Congress also ratified, and made ideologically "safe," a development already far advanced – the rise of so-called "diversified forms of enterprise ownership": individually owned, privately owned and foreign-owned enterprises.

became effective on July 1, 1994.[64] That law (along with China's Securities Law 1999) was subject to wholesale and rather significant amendments in late 2005, which came into effect on January 1, 2006. Yet, even with the 2005 amendment of these basic statutes, the *corpus* of corporate or company law in China today is by no means limited to a single statute which is called the "Company Law" or, with respect to listed companies, the "Securities Law." A great deal of China's corporate law-making and regulation, and many would argue corporate law that is more readily enforced, is found elsewhere. The great source of this regulation in modern China is the China Securities Regulatory Commission (CSRC), the administrative agency specifically charged with governing public (listed) company activity and all securities trading.

Since 1994, China's central government, the legislature, and the CSRC have accepted – with some pronounced and rather awkward exceptions – the rhetoric of the "standard shareholder-oriented" model of corporate law and governance.[65] At the same time, it was quite clear that until 2005

[64] The history of corporate law in China actually stretches a full ninety years before the enactment of the 1994 Company Law: on January 21, 1904, the then newly created Ministry of Commerce under the declining Manchu Qing Dynasty promulgated a Company Law (*Gongsilu*). See Wellington K. K. Chan, *Merchants, Mandarins and Modern Enterprise in Late Ch'ing China* (Cambridge MA: East Asian Research Center; Harvard University Press, 1977). Chinese scholars trace the first corporate (albeit experimental) establishment to 1873, with the promotion of the *Lunchuan Zhaoshangju* (China Steam Merchants Company) and some go even farther back in time to the 1700s and invoke the formation of Sichuan's "contracting stock system" (*qiyue gufenzhi*) enterprises and their essential corporate characteristics. See Jiusong Peng, *Zhongguo Qiyue Gufenshi* (*China's Contracting Stock System*) (1994). China's efforts at company law between 1904 and 1948 were directed towards several clear aims: creating a tool for China's industrial development (especially in competition with foreign companies making their presence increasingly felt on Chinese soil); attaining perceived "Western" or "modern" standards of law (with the hope that this would lead to the abolition of "extraterritoriality" imposed upon China after the Opium Wars); and, perhaps most importantly, but never explicitly, strengthening central government power. See William C. Kirby, "China unincorporated: Company law and business enterprise in twentieth century China" (1995) 54(1) *Journal of Asian Studies* 43. Many of the same things motivate the creation and implementation of a corporate law for China in the present age. On the US and UK influence, and the use of "modern" corporate law as the price of winning freedom from the burden of "extraterritoriality," see Lanxin Xiang, *Recasting the Imperial Far East: Britain and America in China, 1945–1950* (Armonk, NY: M. E. Sharpe, 1995).

[65] This suggests a high degree of formal convergence. See Henry Hansmann and Reinier H. Kraakman, "The end of history for corporate law" (2001) 89 *Georgetown Law Journal* 439. At the same time, PRC corporate law evidences some continuing loyalty to other models, including the "manager-oriented" and "state-oriented" models (conflated into one) or the "labor-oriented" model. For instance, a separate and inconsistent chapter was inserted into the Company Law to address a sub-species of the limited liability company form: the so-called "wholly state-owned company" (*guoyou duzi gongsi*): state

various institutions in China were not deemed sufficiently ready to bear the full burden of corporate law duties and adjudication.[66] Indeed, as Black and Kraakman note about emerging markets generally, and which is wholly applicable to China even thirty years after the start of "legal construction": "[a] company law that depends on fast and reliable judicial decisions is simply out of the question."[67] So it was that the Chinese corporate and securities law system – at least in form – initially had many features of the "self-enforcing" model, including enforcement of norms by voting rules and transactional rights granted to direct participants, reliance on procedural protections and even prohibitions of disfavored transactions, attempts to invoke bright-line rules, a rhetoric (if not always the reality) that privileges the protection of "minority shareholders," and some expression of legal remedies (administrative and criminal) in formal law and regulation. Notwithstanding the understandable initial orientation toward a "self-enforcing" system, Chinese law academics, drafters and officials have focused more recent efforts in the service of corporate governance mechanisms requiring *ex post* judicial interpretation (e.g., fiduciary duties, piercing the corporate veil, derivative actions, etc.), as expressed in the 2005 Company Law effective January 1, 2006,[68] while maintaining a good number of

administrative department-*invested and -established* legal person entities, which have *no* shareholders' meeting, but which do have boards of directors which delegate management to an executive group. There seems little doubt that this section was inserted into the Company Law as a sop to certain political and economic actors in China who saw corporatization as the prelude to real privatization. Fealty to the European style of "labor-oriented" corporate entities is revealed in China's corporate structures wherein a "supervisory board" is required of such companies. The truth in today's China is, however, that such supervisory boards are established in formal terms, but ignored or misunderstood over the life of the company.

66 See Chunying Xin, 'What kind of judicial power does China need?' (2003) 1(1) *International Journal of Consititutional Law* 58; Randall Peerenboom, *China's Long March Toward Rule of Law* (Cambridge University Press, 2002), Chapter VII; Donald C. Clarke, "Power and politics in the Chinese court system: The enforcement of civil judgments" (1996) 10 *Columbia Journal of Asian Law* 1.

67 See Bernard S. Black and Reinier H. Kraakman, "A self-enforcing model of corporate law" (1996) 109 *Harvard Law Review* 1911. Black and Kraakman include the 1994 PRC Company Law in their chart Survey of Company Law in Emerging Markets at the end of the article, with China deservedly scoring well from a purely formal standpoint.

68 For one recent study which indicates pre-2005 convergence over *ex post* corporate governance mechanisms by China's much-maligned courts – at least with respect to traditional Anglo-American fiduciary duties. See Nicholas Calcina Howson "The doctrine that dared not speak its name: Anglo-American fiduciary duties in China's 2005 company law and case law intimations of prior convergence," in H. Kanda, K. Kim and C. Milhaupt (eds.), *Transforming Corporate Governance in East Asia* (Abingdon: Routledge, 2008).

self-enforcing mechanisms (mostly super-majority and recused shareholder votes).

D. Focus on corporate governance reform in China (late 1990s to 2006)

Even with the arrival of a new machine – the corporate entity – and attendant legal and regulatory norms, the varied and ingenious abuses or simple dysfunctions quickly seen at China's new corporations, especially those publicly listing a portion of their capital, almost beggar comprehensive description. As Stephen Green wrote in 2003 with respect to PRC companies listed on China's domestic stock exchanges:

> China's stock market, ... was not a vehicle for privatization: whenever companies were listed the state retained large controlling stakes. As a result, the market has evolved into a dysfunctional halfway house, where neither public officials nor private shareholders enjoy effective control over most listed firms, and few in management have incentives to help their firms create value ... The poor quality of listed companies is the cause of the market's most serious problems, and until corporate performance and governance standards improve, there will be no significant improvement in the market as a whole.[69]

Green echoes an observation that we make above: a significant problem for China's new companies is not that there is an oppressive principal shareholder (the state or local governments), but that there is *no* principal, or an "absent principal." The formal owner of the corporatized firm (just like the "all the people" deemed owners of the predecessor SOEs) is too amorphous and attenuated to do anything but cede control to opportunistic, or just incompetent, insider managers.[70] It takes no great imagination to understand some of the ways in which Chinese companies have been misgoverned and abused by other actors in the new corporate scheme.[71] Indeed, with the rise of the "modern enterprise system", public listings of firms, and widely reported abuses, a virtual

[69] Stephen Paul Green, *China's Stock Market: A Guide to its Progress, Players and Prospects* (London: Profile, 2003), p. 118.

[70] See also Donald C. Clarke, "Corporate governance in China: An overview" (2003) 14 *China Economic Review* 494.

[71] Examples abound and include: blatant self-dealing and overcompensation of insider managers; political interference in operations; disregard of minority shareholder interests and accounting problems. Moreover, due to the absent principal problem, sometimes even the controlling shareholder (the state or local government-backed shareholder) will cede effective control to either (i) large holders of "legal person shares" (*farengu*) (often local government or local level identities of present or former line

obsession about "corporate governance" (*gongsi zhili*) has arisen inside China – among both the professionals, investors and analysts who seek to understand China's progress,[72] and the retail "punters" who seem willing to participate in what prominent reformer Wu Jinglian has called "a casino." Although this obsession has focused, mistakenly we assert, on aspirations for traditional Berle and Means separation of ownership and management (and the remedying of related agency problems),[73] the general movement has also been concerned with the growth, and overall health, of liquid and deep stock markets.

Whether or not China's domestic stock markets are what Professor Wu decries as a "casino," real and perceived weaknesses in the governance of China's listed companies have had a decidedly negative impact on the overall value of China's capital markets. Indeed, the result to 2005 and then after Spring Festival 2008 appeared to be a nightmare vision that Bernie Black borrows from the insurance sector – a "death spiral," where information asymmetry and adverse selection "combine to drive almost all honest issuers out of the market, and ... drive share prices to zero."[74] While Chinese stock prices have not been driven to "zero," and politically privileged issuers continue to seek listings or follow-on

Ministries), or (ii) politically qualified (or local-government backed) managers or insiders.

[72] It is important to note that this focus and enthusiasm pre-dated corporate governance scandals and headlines in North America and Europe, and was inspired by an active, reformist and very learned cadre of officials working at the CSRC in the periods 1992–5 and then 1999–2003. The power and influence of these individuals, many trained in the United States and Commonwealth countries with experience at international law firms, global accountancies and banks, was very seriously compromised by revelations about Enron, WorldCom, Arthur Andersen, etc because these individuals had vouched for a securities regulation and corporate governance system based on US models. These failures, which occurred under the watch of the then-recommended public disclosure (and independent accountancy) system, were used by opposing political forces to remove those same officials from the commanding heights of China's corporate and securities regulatory structures.

[73] The focus has been almost entirely on (i) Chinese SOEs, most often once formal separation of ownership and management is effected and they are transformed into companies limited by shares under the PRC Company Law, and (ii) *listed* companies (regardless of where they list their stock), which are necessarily companies limited by shares. See Clarke, 'Corporate governance in China'. This focus is unfortunate because there are many governance issues for other legal and spontaneous forms as well as private (non-listed entities). See for instance, Dehua Tang (ed.), *Qita Gongsi Zuzhi Xingshi Yu Gufen Hezuo Qiye Falu Shiwu* (*Legal Treatise on Other Firms of Corporate Organization and the Stock Cooperative Enterprise*) (1998), p. 219.

[74] Bernard S. Black, "The core institutions that support strong securities markets" (2000) 55 *Business Lawyer* 7.

offerings, the trend over the past ten years (with the intermediate surge resulting from initial announcement of the "stock rights reallocation initiative" (*guquan fenzhi*) and rather blind foreign interest in public Chinese equities suddenly accessiable via a Qualified Foreign Institutional Investor (QFII) program) has been volatile. This situation had made the Chinese domestic exchanges a potentially unattractive place to raise money, both for the large reformed SOEs, which are permitted to issue and list shares on such exchanges, and the smaller, sometimes truly private, entities which have not generally been allowed wide access to the same markets.[75]

In recent years, along with revision of China's corporate and securities law statutes in 2006,[76] the PRC has taken important steps to reform (rather than merely establish) corporate governance. For instance, the 2006 Company Law finally establishes that companies limited by shares (*gufenyouxianzeren gongsi*)[77] possess the five basic features of Anglo-American corporations, which are: (i) full legal personality for the firm, (ii) limited liability for shareholders; (iii) shared ownership in the firm by investors; (iv) formal separation between ownership and management, with management being delegated by the owners (shareholders) to a board of directors, and then to a management group; and (v) transferable share interests (transferability is a very complex question in the Chinese context; a multitude of restrictions work on the proposed transfer of share capital in China, listed or not, in most cases depending upon who or what owns and is seeking to transfer shares). Numerous other legal and regulatory changes have been implemented in the same period, many of which are invoked below. Overall, the changes effected in the last half decade or so have led to (i) changes in the expectations (and hence demands) of investors, (ii) an increase in the efforts of the CSRC, and indirectly the courts and the media, to enhance governance,

[75] As a result, they are forced to rely upon foreign investment, bank intermediaries (which are undergoing their own liberalization), intra-group financing, or the insufficient drip of retained earnings.

[76] Some of the changes – not dealt with in depth here – impact upon the symbolic or rhetorical nature of the Law. For instance, literally hundreds of allusions to the "state's" role in corporate formation, governance and business decision making has been washed out of the new law's text.

[77] The PRC Company Law allows for two basic corporate forms, both of which confer limited liability for shareholders: companies limited by shares (*gufenyouxianzeren gongsi*) and limited liability companies (*youxian zeren gongsi*). The former is similar to what in American parlance is called a joint stock company; the latter is more like a closed corporation or corporate partnership.

(iii) greater, or more clearly specified, legal obligations on management and controlling shareholders, (iv) better access to court enforcement of governance via permitted shareholder suit mechanisms, and (v) the potential for increased monitoring by credit-evaluating financial institution lenders. These changes suggest that we might begin to see greater monitoring by the primary credit and equity providers in China (due to their increasing presence and greater incentives than before) which, when supplemented by law that is technically better and potentially greater enforcement, provides a more promising future for governance. We summarize only the most important steps below.

1. Investor expectations

Investor expectations in China have begun to change for a number of reasons. First, China continued to corporatize SOEs and collective enterprises or township and village enterprises (TVEs). The increasing issuance of equity interests to the public and other independent and commercially concerned (if often local government-backed) entities has introduced new owner-shareholders who have had a very significant impact on the way such enterprises are operated, and in whose interest.

Second, and relatedly, corporatization of wholly domestic firms was preceded by the introduction of *foreign* equity investors in or alongside PRC enterprises. Indeed, this program commenced with private FDI from the first moments of China's Reform and Opening to the Outside World policy.[78] Since the early 1990s, the PRC has pursued a very successful program to attract foreign investment to finance Chinese corporatized state-owned assets through both the private and public equity capital markets. Although this has been accomplished through a series of important (and often quite creative) moves,[79] we will focus on

78 This process also attracted early governance norms and pressures, not to mention more profound and significant notions of contract, enforcement of contract and law, and property rights holders' "rights."

79 The "public" and offshore side of this was achieved in four ways. First, China-domiciled issuers offered shares in newly corporatized entities to foreign, *public*, investors – starting with "H" (for Hong Kong) share offerings. For example, Shanghai Petrochemical's "H" shares IPO in 1993. This was followed by expanding to "N" (for New York) share offerings (Shandong Huaneng Power Development Company completed an initial public offering of ADSs on the New York Stock Exchange in August 1994), "L" (for London) share, "S" (for Singapore) shares, and so on. Second, and following from this, were the so-called "indirect" overseas listings, whereby PRC-dominated issuers were domiciled in Hong Kong or other offshore jurisdictions and issued shares on foreign markets. For example, China Telecom (which became China Mobile), CNOOC, etc., – which have issuers that are Hong Kong companies, issuing shares in the foreign (or Hong Kong)

the net effects of these efforts. The biggest effect was to induce foreign venture capital, private equity, retail and institutional shareholders to invest in PRC-domiciled or PRC-controlled foreign (including Hong Kong and foreign tax haven-domiciled) firms.

In order to attract foreign, public equity, investors the PRC made a series of statutory, regulatory and governance changes to serve the perceived specific interests of foreign shareholders. These ranged from special statutes applicable only to foreign-invested or PRC-domiciled issuers listing overseas, to mandatory corporate constitutions for overseas-listing entities which introduced shareholder-friendly minority voting or class rights into Chinese law. As noted below, many of these items were later picked up and made applicable to *all* Chinese companies and purely Chinese public shareholders. In addition, so-called overseas listings brought Chinese issuers (and their shareholders, governing departments and advisers) into close contact with foreign legal and regulatory regimes – whether it was Hong Kong, New York or London. Thus, the introduction of foreign capital not only effected indigenous legal change – and brought about the first encounter with sophisticated and highly regulated foreign regimes – but also made foreign investors active in Chinese companies of every stripe, bringing along with that participation their more sophisticated governance expectations.

2. Regulatory efforts

Although the PRC legislature has made changes reflected in so-called "basic" laws – like the Company Law and the Securities Law – the CSRC has been the undisputed leader in reforming corporate governance more broadly. These reforms have conformed with the CSRC's authority to regulate the public markets and Chinese exchanges, and thus their work has concentrated on the corporatized SOEs permitted to list in China or abroad, and the kind of Chinese company which we identify above as the focus of China's corporate governance obsession. The efforts of the CSRC have gone some way in bringing governance to the fore and

capital markets after taking title to in-country PRC assets. Third, foreign investment was permitted in the previously walled-off "A" share markets (RMB yuan denominated shares traded among PRC citizen retail investors through China's domestic exchanges) via a Qualified Foreign Institutional Investor (QFII) program. Finally, foreign, private "strategic" investment (with board designations accompanying) was permitted alongside foreign public investment, explicitly so as to introduce strong, and relatively concentrated foreign shareholder participation in business decision-making and internal firm governance.

providing benchmarks against which investors and firms can measure themselves. This, in and of itself, is invaluable.

For example, the CSRC has: promulgated a coherent statement of Corporate Governance Principles; "recommended" (but in reality mandated) articles of association for purely domestic issuers with important elaborations of corporate governance; mandated a compulsory independent director system (requiring listed company boards to have at least a one-third "independent" board); established a veto right for "public shareholders" with respect to certain significant transactions (later incorporated into the amended Company and Securities Laws); issued rules requiring approval by disinterested persons for certain transactions; and set out qualifications for who could serve as a director of a Chinese company.

In addition, the CSRC has worked to increase the amount and relevance of mandatory disclosure by PRC companies seeking capital on the Chinese domestic markets. This served to not only make markets more transparent for shareholders, but also provided additional information for China's muckracking financial media, which revels in its relative freedom to expose continuing governance difficulties or fraud. And the CSRC has had a significant role in creating rules and transactional imperatives for public company mergers and acquisitions, going some way to creating a necessary market for corporate control in China, with attendant governance and monitoring benefits.

Finally, the CSRC has built an impressive and sophisticated enforcement bureaucracy which maintains some objectivity because the CSRC (and its local departments) are independently, and centrally, funded. (China started regulating its embryonic exchanges and securities trading via local branches of the central bank, the People's Bank of China, which were quickly co-opted by local powers or proved technically incompetent.) No doubt, the CSRC does not have the massive resources required to monitor corporate activity through China's vast hinterland. This is one reason why the CSRC above all other departments has pushed the private right of action for shareholders in China's courts so strongly. However, the enforcement function has performed admirably in the context of China's political, commercial and geographical context.

In addition to the CSRC's efforts, several years ago China ended the long-standing "quota" system governing access to listings. Regional governments used to be given a "quota" of firms they could select to list on the Chinese exchanges or on overseas exchanges. This also meant that local governments would select affiliated firms for listing and bar other, often more entrepreneurial, firms from accessing capital. Now, however, the opportunity to list may be available more broadly. These simple, if incremental, changes not only reduced the cronyism that persisted before, but also brought a new kind of corporation to the attention of public investors: issuers which did not have the support, or protection, of state or political actors, and who might seriously attend to profitability and performance to continue raising capital and appealing to the markets. This also would have further focused attention on firm profitability and how proclaimed and demonstrated governance might enhance it.

3. Legal duties and obligations

Not only has the mix of investors and the regulatory environment changed, so has the law. The radically amended Company and Securities Laws 2006 now provide, in the most explicit terms desirable, the following: (i) directors' and officers' fiduciary duties – including Anglo-American style duty of care and duty of loyalty; (ii) joint and several liability for directors, officers and supervisory board members for a broad range of violations or breaches of "law" (including the duties described in (i) above); (iii) liability of "controlling shareholders" who abuse the corporate form, or prefer their own interests to the disadvantage of minority interests;[80] and (iv) increased protection for minority shareholders.[81] Although many of these measures will need to rely on court enforcement (which is problematic due to lack of political power and experience with such matters), they were in many cases absent from prior "basic" enactments and are critically useful continuing steps in enhancing governance. There is in fact evidence that the People's Courts have greater competence and political power in identifying and

[80] The heightened obligations include: greater disclosure requirements for controllers, new legal duties governing their actions, and liability for misdeeds nominally attributed to their dominated subsidiaries. It should be noted that the Company Law 2006 also introduces "veil piercing" protection for third parties dealing with PRC corporations. While not entirely workable in the short term (given the lack of sophistication and power of the judiciary), the mechanism stands as an additional warning to "tyrannical" controlling shareholders. In the context of this writing, this development is also of interest because it, once again, throws a good deal of work to the Chinese courts for articulation and resolution.

[81] Protection for minority shareholders now includes cumulative voting for the election of directors (Company Law 2006, Article 106), the ability for 10% or more of the shareholders to call a shareholders' meeting (Article 102) or a board meeting (Article 111), the ability of 3% or more of the shareholders to propose shareholders' resolutions (Article 103), mandatory shareholders meetings to approve large asset or external guaranty transactions (Article 105) (and supermajority approval for the same) (Article 122), and the ability of 10% or more of the shareholders to trigger liquidation (Article 83).

enforcing against breaches of these key governance duties, even before the duties were finally set forth in law.[82]

Moreover, when this is coupled with the now completed effort to sell down the state's (or legal person's) interest in Chinese corporations which have publicly listed stock via the "stock rights allocation" (*guquan fenzhi*) program we can see important changes afoot. Indeed, the desire to rid the Chinese capital markets of a burdensome "overhang" of illiquid shareholdings (and thus move closer to market valuation) is only one of the purposes of this incremental sell-down. A perhaps equally important goal is to create the potential for improved governance at China's listed firms, and allow greater power or at least input for private (retail or institutional) shareholders when faced with unresponsive, conflicted or corrupt holders of non-tradeable shares.

4. Enforcement

The Company Law 2006 establishes the first private right of action for shareholders in Chinese companies to sue on a wide range of corporate malfeasance or breach of corporate law duties. Since China's Supreme People's Court – in response to CSRC, popular and media pressure – first allowed a limited shareholders private right of action with respect to false or misleading securities disclosure in January and December 2002, this has been an issue of surpassing importance in China. Now, the Company Law 2006 provides a private right of action for shareholders to sue directors, officers and supervisory board members, directly or derivatively, and the Securities Law 2006 expands the class of potential defendants by creating joint and several liability for "controlling shareholders" or "actual control shareholders"[83] where there is false or misleading disclosure in issuance-related disclosure, or continuing disclosure and reporting.[84] Granted, the utility of these new rights of action remain unproven, as China awaits definitive rules from the court bureaucracy as to how litigants can actually bring such cases. However, as the creation of the all-important legal basis for private enforcement of corporate law and securities regulation, these new rights represent a huge step forward which will have much meaning in the decades to come. Of course, in the short to medium term, the crafting of these rights in law represents a keen challenge to the PRC court system, although one that is

82 Howson, "The doctrine that dared not speak its name."
83 Company Law 2006, Article 217.
84 Securities Law 2006, Article 69 (amending the Securities Law 1999, Article 63).

almost certain to be taken up over time under pressure from aggrieved owners of Chinese firms.

5. Credit providers and bankruptcy constraints

Finally, the context for external monitoring of firms by providers of credit is changing rapidly. There is a significant change under way in the way third party providers of credit – China's commercial banks – are established, capitalized, corporatized, operated, and how they monitor the use of the capital they lend. Because of these changes it is most likely that banks – over time – will become far more effective monitors of Chinese corporate performance even as they become better monitored by their owners and the public markets generally. In formal terms, the bankruptcy or hard budget constraint on Chinese firm performance has been strengthened, with the promulgation of a PRC Bankruptcy Law, which greatly empowers and protects creditors at least in formal terms. As with the private right of action to sue for corporate law and disclosure breaches, it is still too early to understand how this new Law and its attendant monitoring powers will play out over time. However that unfolds, it is important to note once again the legal basis in Chinese law for this very significant and useful mechanism for the monitoring of Chinese firms into the future.

The series of changes detailed above provide the seeds for the development of improved and more effective corporate governance in China. We also note, importantly, that these changes have not come about in isolation, but in the context of rapid and impressive institutional change and reform which comprehends: deepening involvement by non-trade foreign investors (e.g., venture capital, private equity and institutional investors rather than multinational product investors); an expanded and increasingly autonomous role for the courts (and better trained, less conflicted, politically more powerful personnel); the rise of an independent bar; and a media that has obtained some significant freedom insofar as they limit their exhortations to the financial, commercial or economic sectors. These contextual changes are necessary if some of the corporate governance changes noted above are to become anything more than merely formal, or empty and unapplied, changes in law.

E. What remains to be done in China (short term)

The short-term requirements for China's continuing corporate governance reform seem obvious, but will be constrained given political, institutional and resource limitations. We enumerate here some of these possible developments to further illuminate the scope of the challenge facing China's policy makers and legislators in the next decade.

It perhaps goes without saying that China's legislation and regulation will need on-going substantive elaboration and clarity. To give one narrow but critically important example, while the new declarations of "duty of care" and "duty of loyalty" in Chinese company law are laudable, it is far from clear what those concepts really mean in China, how they can be reliably described, and whether or not they will be enforceable in any real way, or even actionable given parallel systems of regulation which might prohibit actions on breach of fiduciary duties (as the Supreme People's Court presently asserts).

Consider another example. One option to solve the "absent principal" problem in Chinese firms controlled by state or state-delegated entities is to set up intermediate shareholding entities which are interested in, and operate, the enterprises they are invested in. In the financial sector, the PRC made headway in this regard by recapitalizing its technically insolvent SOE commercial banks via a new entity established by the Ministry of Finance and the PRC central bank and known as *Huijin* which became the dominant and controlling shareholder in China's commercial banks. Real personnel were suddenly involved in *Huijin*'s monitoring of commercial banks and more importantly the often conflicted insider management at the same banks. (*Huijin* has since been absorbed into China's main sovereign wealth investor, China Investment Corporation (CIC), and it is open to question whether CIC will – with its far more diffuse investment portfolio in China and abroad – be able to match *Huijin*'s record of close monitoring.) In the non-financial state assets sector, 2003 saw the establishment of something billed as a *Huijin*-like entity, the State-owned Assets Supervision and Administration Committee (SASAC). However, the jury is still out on the extent to which the SASAC can and will act as a real principal, or whether its monitoring capacities will be overcome by the very large number of enterprises it now controls (as compared to the four commercial banks controlled by *Huijin*) and it will revert to the status of another "absent" principal which has dominated the history of China SOE corporatizations.

For external monitoring, it is clear that the commercial banking industry must continue to be reformed and modernized before it will be able to resist providing capital to Chinese firms on a political rather than commercial basis. In this regard, the agreement and implementation of a complete, and sophisticated, bankruptcy regime, and a court or decisional system sophisticated enough to handle bankruptcy matters, is of signal importance. If *ex post* standards are to be applied to, and articulated for, the key actors in any governance inquiry, then the courts must find some way to increase their sophistication, political power, and enforcement capabilities prior to that part of the corporate governance system becoming workable. This is the great task of China's overall "legal construction" program.

In the institutional sphere, and especially in the absence of a strong or competent judiciary, the CSRC must continue to be supported (financially and politically) so that it can continue its unique legislative, investigative and enforcement functions. Notwithstanding that reality, those concerned with institutional reform and empowerment must continue to pay close attention to procedural changes which – one day – will allow courts to be a viable instrument in the application and enforcement of a reforming corporate governance system. For instance, the Supreme People's Court will be required to accept the broad shareholders' (or company's) right of action set forth in the Company Law 2006. It remains to be seen if the Supreme People's Court will resist – by its own administrative rules and explanations (such as the Rules on Private Shareholders Suits for False or Misleading Disclosure of December 2002) – what is now plainly authorized in a national statute promulgated by the PRC legislature. Likewise, the PRC will need to come to terms with the notion of class action litigation coupled with lawyers' contingency fee arrangements. (Note that the problem in the PRC at this point is not too many frivolous suits, but too little monitoring of the firm by shareholders and others as well as resource constraints on the CSRC limiting its ability to monitor on the shareholders' behalf.) However, the class action is relevant to the prosecution of actions in areas more sensitive than firm governance – i.e., land confiscations, labor unrest, environmental outrages, and official malfeasance in connection with health disasters. Accordingly, it may be some time before the Chinese authorities write into law a useful class action mechanism.

V. Insights on corporate governance from China and India

The accounts of the development of corporate governance reform in China and India may also provide insights on topical debates in corporate law scholarship. In particular, the experiences of China and India help us to examine how certain theories operate in the world's two largest emerging markets and fastest growing economies.

A. Stock market development and "legal origins"

The question of how law might help to create better governed companies and thereby develop stock markets has captured the imagination of the academy. In their now seminal articles, La Porta, La Silanes, Schleifer and Vishny find that countries with a common law legal system tend to have more developed stock markets than countries with a civil law legal system (the "legal origins" perspective).[85] They suggest at least two reasons for this. First, they argue that the common law is more protective of property rights, specifically the interests of smaller shareholders, than a civil law system. This, they assert, is because the common law expects judges to use application of flexible fiduciary duties principles in regulating behavior whereas the civil law is more rigid. The greater latitude granted to judges permits them to police opportunistic behavior and outright fraud more effectively than civil law courts and this is something small investors (the likely victims of such fraud and opportunism) value. Consequently, one would expect to find that jurisdictions that are part of the common law system have more developed stock markets because the common law is more protective of small shareholders and this motivates and encourages small shareholders to participate in capital markets regulated in such jurisdictions.

Another reason why "legal origins" may matter is that the civil law is said to over-regulate relative to the common law. This is important because the lighter regulatory orientation of the common law is said to facilitate private ordering (i.e., market based transactions) whereas the civil law tends to discourage such private ordering because outcomes (or perhaps processes) are determined by regulation. The more private-ordering-friendly approach of the common law is

[85] Rafael La Porta, Florencio Lopez-de-Silanes, Andrei Shleifer and Robert Vishny, "Legal determinants of external finance" (1997) 52 *Journal of Finance* 1131; Rafael La Porta, Florencio Lopez-de-Silanes, Andrei Shleifer and Robert Vishny, "Law and finance" (1998) 106 *Journal of Political Economy* 1113. Later papers have suggested that common law systems tended to outperform civil law systems both in their countries of origin (i.e., European civil law countries tended to perform worse than Anglo-American common law countries) and even in countries where they had adopted one of these approaches (i.e., the former German and French colonies performed worse on stock market development compared to former English colonies). Further studies also suggested that it was securities laws in particular that seemed to make a substantial difference in the outcomes. See Rafael La Porta, Florencio Lopez-de-Silanes and Andrei Shleifer, "What works in securities laws" (2006) 61(1) *Journal of Finance* 1–32.

important because securities markets tend to thrive in such market-friendly environments.[86]

Although these papers have been highly influential, there has been considerable discussion of alternative views. In particular, a series of papers from both economists and legal academics suggest that "legal origin" is not the primary explanation for why we tend to see common law countries with better governed firms and thus more developed stock markets.[87]

These other papers first suggest that the descriptions of common law and civil law oversimplify reality and that in many instances so-called common law countries have even more regulation bias than civil law countries.[88] Indeed, both systems – as seen in developed economies – seem quite adept at being able to use (or borrow) tools and techniques from the other. Second, these papers suggest that the growth of stock markets is better explained by three other factors. First, that there is demand for what stock markets can provide – external capital. This has tended to be the case when economic or technological changes require the aggregation of capital from many sources and there is no really good alternative to stock markets. Second, the institutions that support stock markets are in place or are being put in place by legislators or private ordering. Such institutions and practices include such staples as functioning (and independent) courts, adequate disclosure requirements, and effective methods of containing self-dealing.[89] Third, the general

[86] One might also interpret the "over-regulation" in the civil law as being regulation that benefits incumbents by making entry into domestic markets more difficult. This serves to weaken one of the other primary constraints on managers (and factors pushing toward better governance) – product market competition – because when firms face less competition then the consequences of their inefficient governance choices take longer to be visited upon them. By weakening the impetus for better governance from the product markets, civil law might tend to reinforce inefficiencies in governance and thereby also be a less attractive place for small shareholders to invest.

[87] Raghuram G. Rajan and Luigi Zingales, "The great reversals: The politics of financial development in the twentieth century" (2003) 69 *Journal of Financial Economics* 5; Mark J. Roe, "Legal origins and stock markets in the twentieth century" (2006) 120(2) *Harvard Law Review* 460–527. Even some papers in the "legal origins" literature seem to suggest it is statutory securities laws (rather than judicially enforced common law) that seems to spur stock market development. This suggests "legal origins" are not after all determinative. See La Porta, *et al.*, "What works in securities laws."

[88] Roe, "Legal origins and stock markets."

[89] Black, "The core institutions"; John C. Coffee, Jr., "The future as history: The prospects for global convergence in corporate governance and its implications" (1998–9) 93 *Northwestern University Law Review* 641; John C. Coffee, Jr., "Racing towards the top?: The impact of cross-listings and stock market competition on international corporate governance" (2002) 102 *Columbia Law Review* 1757.

political environment of a particular jurisdiction is deemed conducive to (or, at least, will not thwart) the growth of stock markets.[90]

Although the latter account summarized immediately above is more complex than the "legal origins" account, its adherents suggest that it better explains the actual development of stock markets over the last 100 years or so. Indeed, it appears that the asserted connection between common law structures and stock market development is of relatively recent origin. In the early 1900s civil law countries had at least as well developed, if not better developed, stock markets than common law countries. Moreover, in terms of stock market development, it was only after World War II that common law countries seemed to climb above civil law countries and even that trend seems somewhat short lived as the gap between civil and common law countries has diminished in recent times. This suggests, as Rajan and Zingales point out, that time-invariant structural explanations (e.g., "legal origins") cannot explain what we have seen over the last hundred years.

The question then becomes: what does explain the experience with corporate governance and stock market development over the last hundred years? Although clearly the absence of certain critical institutions (e.g., functioning courts) would retard progress in improved corporate governance and developing stock markets, many commentators focus on whether there is the political will to create responsibly governed corporate entities and develop healthy capital markets. The implicit (and sometimes explicit) assertion is that if there is the national political will then there is a political (and economic, legal and institutional) way.

Rajan and Zingales suggest that, normally, incumbents will oppose stock market development because it provides easier access to capital for new entrants and hence enhances competition for those incumbent firms. However, incumbents may be willing to support such development if they also need access to external capital to take advantage of perceived business opportunities and there is no other viable source of such external capital besides functioning securities markets. Thus, Rajan and Zingales suggest that stock markets may obtain popular support once incumbents also have a desire to access external capital. This is, of course, more likely in an expanding trade and investment environment, or when trade and investment is more open. Trade was indeed more

[90] Rajan and Zingales, "The great reversal"; Roe, "Legal origins and stock markets."

open before World War II and after the 1980s, and that is precisely when we see stock markets growing in many different jurisdictions.[91]

Although trade policy is important, Roe suggests another important historical factor: that the economic and political devastation wrought on many countries by World War II may have led their polities to become less "friendly" to stock markets in the aftermath of such destruction. He argues that after World War II in Europe many nations had few resources, and the citizenry had few savings. In such an environment the polity is more likely to focus on labor rather than investment interests, as few people have any savings to invest. Moreover, in much of Europe there was an on-going political and ideological battle against the ideological and material attractions of Communism. In order to maintain the support of the citizenry for market-oriented economies, national legislatures may have tended to favor labor. The consequence for not doing so might have triggered political reversal and a move towards Communism. This, Roe suggests, provides a better explanation for why so many countries in Continental Europe adopted less shareholder-friendly laws and tended to favor labor in the early post-War years. Indeed, this provides a good explanation for why these countries may have been averse to free trade and preferred more "protectionist" policies. On the other hand, countries that were not as badly devastated in World War II and that were further away from the front-line ideological battle over Communism (the US, Switzerland, UK) were in a better position to support stock markets oriented away from labor and toward investors. The polity in these countries had relatively more savings and thus investment resources and, one might imagine, would have been keen to pursue investment policies and probably more open trade. Once the polities in Continental Europe had savings and investment capacity, a change in the approach to stock markets might be seen, with their becoming more favored.[92]

Adherents to this account (we call it the "politics" account) suggest their explanations gel better with the experience of the last hundred years.

[91] Rajan and Zingales, "The great reversal." Rajan and Zingales do not fully reject the "legal origins" account. Rather they suggest that the "politics" account and the "origins" account may work together in some ways, In particular, they suggest that in the civil law, being more centralized than the common law, it may be easier for private interests to have their agenda enacted (they need only convince the legislature not courts and so forth). If so, then when the political will is present for change it may occur more quickly in civil law countries than common law. They find evidence of this in how quickly the civil law was able to slow down its stock markets and how quickly it was able to speed up the development of its stock markets later as compared to common law countries.

[92] Roe, "Legal Origins and Stock Markets."

The policy prescriptions emanating from this account are more contextual. In the case of a given country one would need to understand whether the polity was supportive of stock markets and then devise legal policy in light of that to help build the institutions needed for well functioning stock markets. If the polity was not supportive then widespread reform could not proceed without first having measures to obtain support from the polity.

Both the "legal origins" and "politics" accounts provide predictions for what will lead to stock market development, but neither has been applied in significant detail to the experiences in either of the two largest emerging markets – India and China. What does our discussion of corporate governance reform and the establishment of functioning capital markets in India and China suggest?

On a quick glance the different experiences of India and China appear to provide some support to both accounts, but looks can be deceiving.

First, let us examine the "legal origins" account. Most observers will understand India as a nation firmly in the common law tradition, and China in the twentieth and twenty-first centuries closer to a civil law jurisdiction. Further, the growth of India's stock markets over the long term has been more positive and less volatile than China's, even though China has, for much of the last twenty years, experienced a higher economic growth rate than India. This, on cursory inspection, provides some support to the "legal origins" account. However, one needs to look more closely before coming to firm conclusions.

Although, India does have a common law system, for most of the period following independence (1947–91) it followed a socialist development path with policies that significantly impeded the growth of its stock markets. Many people would have easily described India as being over-regulated (the "license raj" epithet comes to mind),[93] which is one of the major supposed vices of the civil law.

Moreover, the description provided in subsection III.B suggests that the background law – while apparently protective of small shareholders as it was based on English Law – was not, in reality, very protective of smaller shareholders. India's judiciary, although independent and arguably one of the most powerful in the world, did not appear to be active,

[93] See Tarun Khanna and Krishna Palepu "The evolution of concentrated ownership in India: Broad patterns and a history of the Indian software industry," in Randall K. Morck (ed.), *A History of Corporate Governance around the World* (University of Chicago Press, 2005), pp. 283–324; Goswami, "India: The tide."

prompt and flexible in protecting shareholders interests.[94] Thus, India, while nominally a "common law" country, was performing like a civil law country on the dimensions that matter most under the "legal origins" account – protecting small shareholders and being less regulated than civil law.

One might respond by saying that we should then categorize India as something closer to a civil law-family nation (although this is contrary to how the "legal origins" literature normally categorizes). But what then explains the considerably better performance of Indian stock markets over the long term? Perhaps the answer is that India is now adopting a more common law style in terms of protecting small investors and regulating less. This is only partially true. India is certainly protecting small investors more than it has before. However, it is not necessarily regulating less, it is just changing its domain of regulation away from a direct mechanism – licenses to enter business – to indirect regulation featuring mandated disclosure and corporate governance features.

China's legal system is a different case because it partakes of different traditions or "origins" – all at the same time – in different sectors of application (e.g., Soviet and European civil law heritage in criminal law and procedure, German civil law (via Japan and Taiwan) in commercial and contract law, and the Anglo-American tradition in recent corporate and securities law (with an occasional entanglement with an inflexible "business regulation" orientation). Thus, divining a connection between legal origin, corporate governance and stock market growth in China is not a straightforward exercise. In China's reform experience, corporatization and domestic exchanges were permitted first as a politically attractive and relatively costless method of financing state-owned (and controlled) assets[95] and as a substitute for direct state allocations of capital. As a result, China's enactments cleaved very closely to a business regulation orientation, or one that enabled the creation of viable financing vehicles, with little regard for the rights and interests of

[94] See Debroy, "Some issues in law reform in India"; C. D. Cunningham, "The world's most powerful court: Finding the roots of India's public interest litigation revolution in the Hussainara Khatoon prisoners case," in S. P. Sathe and S. Narayan (eds.), *Liberty, Equality and Justice: Struggles for a New Social Order* (Lucknow, India: Eastern Book Company, 2003), pp. 83–96; Susan Thomas, "How the financial sector in India was reformed," in S. Narayan (ed.), *Documenting Reforms: Case Studies from India* (New Delhi: Macmillan, 2006).

[95] Although China had some history with the corporate form from the end of the Qing Dynasty (to 1911), and even domestic exchanges in the Shanghai International Concession and other places before World War II, the reappearance of these norms and institutions in the late 1980s and early 1990s was in the context of *no* related legal tradition.

minority shareholders. Indeed, China initially rejected the Anglo-American model in formal terms. The current interest in protection of minority rights, and more broadly good corporate governance, has come from the sometimes bitter diet of fraud, oppression and opportunism forced onto such rights holders. This in turn has spurred concerns for political stability and the general viability, reputation and health of China's domestic capital markets. It is these concerns that have caused China's policy and lawmakers, and regulators, to look to the Anglo-American models for a pre-packaged aid menu.[96]

One can also examine the "politics" account. Recall that according to this account stock market development starts with demand for external capital, the presence of supportive institutions and the political will to have strong stock markets (which is less likely after a devastating war or when the country is having an ideological battle with Communism). Here we obtain some greater traction.

In the case of China it is fairly clear that by 1949, after the Anti-Japanese War, World War II and the Chinese Civil War, its domestic economy was devastated. It seems unsurprising therefore that China's new Communist rulers would, apart from ideological reasons, implement a centralized, planned, and state-owned economy rhetorically committed to the interests of "labor" and protective against imperialist economic powers. This much seems consistent with the "politics" account. However, very serious disruption continued in China for quite some time – through the Anti-Rightist Campaign, the Great Leap Forward and the start of the Great Proletarian Cultural Revolution – until greater stability (and legitimacy for the Party) arose after the winding down of the most violent period of the Cultural Revolution in the late 1970s. After this level of chaos one might have expected a greater

[96] The story behind the absorption of fiduciary duties into China's Company Law 2006 is illustrative of this: China's first national Company Law (1994) was very heavy on business regulation and aspirational commands; more importantly, the statute contained only very oblique references to what might be construed as fiduciary duties for directors, managers and supervisory board members. When queried on this, most Chinese academics, regulators and practitioners, justified the rejection of Anglo-American concepts with ringing calls about China's adherence to the Japanese (and incidentally Taiwanese), "Asian" and even "Confucian" traditions. Some of the abuses described, caused Chinese lawmakers to import, via direct translation, specific duties of care, loyalty and good faith into the Company Law 2006, even without any strong notion as to the viability of court articulation of enforcement of the same (and absolutely no thought that such courts were acting or would be acting in a "common" or "civil" law tradition). See Howson, "The doctrine that dared not speak its name."

focus on labor, rather than capital. Somewhat surprisingly then, China's policy makers adopted a new strategy of economic revitalization (through experimental and ideologically incorrect marketization strategies) and the attraction of foreign capital and trade. Moreover, when the demand for external capital became great enough we witnessed a thaw in the attitude towards some notions of property and enforceable rule of law. When that same interest in capital attraction – Chinese and foreign – grew in the 1980s, there became only increasing awareness of the need to protect shareholders interests so as to attract equity investors in newly corporatized Chinese entities, and then develop strong stock markets. This account seems somewhat conflicted from a "politics" perspective. Economic reconstruction and post-trauma social instability *and* a desire to favor capital. However, it seems clear that in China the ability to bring about economic growth (which required capital) was one of the critical elements the Party needed to maintain political power. Thus, here we see a polity interested in economic growth (after a long period of economically poor performance) – albeit to serve political ends – that led to reforms specifically designed to attract capital.

The broader point is that the "politics" perspective – and in particular the changing political, reconstruction and stabilization needs of China over time – do seem to explain increasing awareness and implementation of new corporate governance solutions and the development of stock markets. In short, this might lead us to conclude that modern corporate governance reform in China is not only desired and delivered to serve investor expectations (and an ever more useful capital markets), but is "permitted" by a developing historical-political circumstance.[97]

In the case of India, World War II did not wreak the same level of domestic devastation. However English colonial rule, the difficult process of Independence and the tragedy of Partition of the Sub-Continent, among other things, seriously weakened the economic base within India. The effects of this devastation, although not identical to those of a war, likely had a somewhat similar effect on savings. Moreover, the political

[97] We should note that the Chinese system has not completely abandoned the rhetoric of the first solutions required by politics, history and ideology. This can be seen in the ongoing debate about the extent to which the law should protect private property or Socialist property, the real nervousness surrounding selling down the state's interest in newly corporatized entities, and "social" or "labor" model aspects of China's corporate statutes. (On the latter issue, we point to the quickly atrophying "supervisory board" mandated at Chinese companies – now given a new lease on life under the Company Law 2006 as the recipient of shareholders' demands in the event of proposed derivative suits.)

movement in India that led to the withdrawal/removal of the British Raj relied on obtaining something like consensus within India's vast and highly heterogenous population. This frequently involved the use of strikes and other measures that unified labor. This, one might imagine, led to the perception (accurate or not) that the polity was more favorable towards labor than capital.

However, once there was liberalization, greater international trade, and competitive spaces opened up, the demand for external capital was high. Indeed, in India industry pushed for corporate governance reform in order to attract external capital. The response was as described in subsection III.C and was embodied in a rather quick reform effort. This seems broadly consistent with the "politics" account: start with labor-oriented policies after a severe economic weakening and then as the economy grows and external capital becomes more attractive we see changes toward a more capital-friendly environment.

The experiences of India and China, however, also suggest a broadening of the "politics" account. First, the experience of India suggests that it need not only be war that leads to a change (e.g., capital-friendly to labor-friendly). Any kind of devastation of the economy (e.g., colonial policies) is likely to lead to such a change. Second, the experience of China suggests that change following devastation depends on what the *status quo* was before the change.[98] In the case of most Continental European nations and India the devastation occurred under governments that were generally more market-friendly. In this situation the change was away from market-friendly to more labor-friendly policies. In China, however, the devastation culminated during the rule of a government that, in theory, favored labor and was actively hostile to capital investors. In this context, the final post-devastation approach (if we see the devastation as something lasting to 1976 and the death of Mao) was the opposite – more capital-friendly. This suggests, tentatively, that the change around the time of devastation may not be simply towards labor, but depends on what kind of regime preceded the devastation, and, perhaps most importantly, the political goals of the post-devastation regime.

[98] In India one might view the 1991 financial crisis as the turning point for reforms. Although no doubt true, one can hardly describe the 1991 financial crisis as a "devastation." Moreover, India's growth post-Independence has not been stellar, but it can hardly be described as being analogous to what happened in China between the mid-1930s and the late 1970s.

B. *Convergence and to what?*

Another important and related debate in corporate law academia is whether corporate law will eventually converge onto a particular model (e.g., the Anglo-American model based on dispersed ownership, the separation of ownership and control, application of flexible legal standards *ex post*). Views differ considerably on whether convergence is likely to happen and, if it does, whether it will be formal convergence (the laws look very similar) or functional convergence (the laws are different but achieve the same functions) or some intermediate point.

The formal convergence argument was most recently articulated by Hansmann and Kraakman where they argue that formal convergence is likely (or already happening) because (i) the shareholder primacy view of corporate law (i.e., managers owe duties to maximize shareholder wealth) has trumped other views, (ii) the competition of the global market place – in particular the global competition for capital, but also product markets competition – will lead firms and nations to choose the Anglo-American model of corporate governance, and (iii) that there is now a shift of interest groups in favor of an emerging class of shareholders. Although all three parts are important to the formal convergence argument, many commentators have focused on prong (iv) because of the perception that competition in the product and capital markets will force firms with different governance structures to compete with each other.[99]

The implication is that Darwinian competition will lead to the success of the Anglo-American model as it is more suited to capital-raising than other models, and because access to capital may be a significant factor in obtaining success in product and other markets. This is especially significant for newer firms and industries, not to mention new entrants from emerging markets. Moreover, as the speed of innovation increases we might expect the newer firms to become more important and dominant in each country.

[99] There is debate over whether the shareholder primacy account has truly won out. See Lynn Stout, "Bad and not-so-bad arguments for shareholder primacy" (2002) 85 *Southern California Law Review* 1189; Kraakman and Hansmann. "The end of history for corporate law". However, for purposes of analysis we assume that it has won out to examine how competition in product and capital markets might influence the selection of corporate laws and institutions. Further, the interest groups supporting the shareholder class are interesting because often these groups are pension plans and unions which represent labor. Labor and capital are then interlinked, rather than opposing, forces in this account.

The primary alternative to the formal convergence account is the "path dependent" account. Under this view, corporate laws are much less likely to converge onto a single model because aspects like ownership structure and corporate rules are much less amenable to change than one might think. Bebchuk and Roe argue that rules can be path dependent for both efficiency reasons, as well as rent-seeking (i.e., inefficient) reasons.[100]

Rules can be *efficiently* path dependent because the background institutional structure may be too costly to change and hence only some rules (i.e., the path dependent ones) are worth pursuing. If so, then the fact that the rules are not the same as the Anglo-American model may not be inefficient given the costs of institutional change in a particular country. Rules can also be *inefficiently* path dependent because parties who benefit (i.e., incumbents) under the pre-existing structure may lobby effectively to block change, even when it is efficient overall, because it reduces their gains. Such rent-seeking may lead to inefficient and path dependent results. Regardless of the source of path dependent rules, their presence (and the difficulty and cost of changing the background institutional structure) is likely to impede convergence.

Of course, neither side is suggesting clearly defined outcomes. The path dependency advocates would probably accept that if the advantages of change are sufficiently (and perhaps overwhelmingly) large then even the costs associated with change can be overcome. Further, the convergence advocates do not predict that governance rules will converge overnight. Thus, one could view the convergence and path dependent camps as occupying two points on a continuum assessing how fast, and how much, change might occur: the convergence advocates would suggest quickly and the path dependent advocates would suggest slowly, if at all. Moreover, if convergence will take time then it is possible that even the countries currently using the Anglo-American model may not be using it in fifty years (e.g., serious economic downturn in that country leading to the adoption of more socialist policies). Thus, by the time one country has adopted the Anglo-American model it is possible that countries that used to employ it do not any more – making it difficult to describe this process as convergence. The critical matter then is whether the forces for convergence (e.g., product and capital market

100 Lucian A. Bebchuk and Mark J. Roe, "A theory of path dependence in corporate ownership and governance" (1999) 52 *Stanford Law Review* 127.

competition) will move quickly enough to overcome the forces of path dependency (e.g., entrenched interests and institutions, high costs associated with change).

Finally, some have suggested intermediate accounts of legal change in the corporate arena. Gilson suggests that corporate law rules may tend towards functional convergence rather than formal convergence. The competitive forces that make the Anglo-American model attractive may lead many firms and countries to want the advantages this brings (e.g., more capital, better products), but the cost to changing all the institutions may be too high or take too long.[101] So instead of changing all institutions to mimic the Anglo-American model, countries and firms may make changes that have the same effects as the Anglo-American model (e.g., protecting minority shareholders, enhanced disclosure), but in form are still similar to the pre-existing rules which were not in conformity with the Anglo-American model. This provides, Gilson argues, most of the benefits of the Anglo-American model while not implicating the huge costs of formal change. This might be termed the "path of least resistance" or "path of greatest convenience" approach.

Coffee also suggests an intermediate account where a firm can specifically enhance its capital raising abilities by simply listing on, and meeting the requirements of, a foreign securities exchange.[102] In some respects the firm is borrowing the apparently better disclosure, accounting and governance requirements of the foreign securities exchange to enhance its image in the eyes of potential investors, whether from the same country or abroad. Of course, this is a partial solution as some elements of the regulatory regime imposed by virtue of the foreign exchange listing may not be credible in the country from which the firm emanates. Nonetheless, such listings may help individual firms.

In light of these differing theories on convergence, what can we learn by examining India and China? The experiences of India and China throw light on the issue of convergence because both countries face intense product and capital market competition (sometimes with each other), but they have long histories with strong interests and powerful, pre-existing, institutions. The countervailing forces – competition for convergence and institutional strength behind path dependence – provide an interesting testing ground for the convergence debate.

[101] Ronald J. Gilson, "Globalizing corporate governance: Convergence of form or function" (2001) 49 *American Journal of Comparative Law* 329.

[102] Coffee, "The future as history"; Coffee, "Racing towards the top?"

Overall, we do see some trends toward convergence, but it is unclear how fast they will develop and the extent to which they will mimic the Anglo-American model or something else. For example, in India and China over the last decade we see greater protections for minority shareholders, increased customization, independence requirements, enhanced disclosure, more expectations of the board and audit committee for monitoring and increased obligations on executives. These all seem consistent with the Anglo-American model for dispersedly held corporations.

However, controlled (not dispersedly held) firms are still the most important and frequent players on the major Indian and Chinese exchanges. This is true even though many of the top corporations on the exchanges are relatively new players in the field. This suggests only partial convergence has occurred so far. The law is converging, but the corporations are still largely controlled not widely held.

Further, the reforms in the Indian equity markets have progressed much faster than similar reforms in the Indian debt markets. Even now, the Indian corporate bonds markets are weak and insolvency laws painfully slow.[103] This reflects the political balance in India as it relates to debt and insolvency where labor interests are much more likely to block significant reforms in this sphere than in the equity sphere.[104] This suggests that – at least on the debt side – there are serious path dependencies at work. What impact this will have on convergence in governance reforms on the equity side is still to be seen.

In China, we witness a rather complex set of developments. There seems little doubt that a kind of "convergence" can be identified with respect to China's corporate governance and securities regulation norms. China's earliest incursions into corporate governance reform occurred under the protection of (then) Vice Premier Zhu Rongji and were in large part driven by a unique generation of "returned from abroad" (*haigui*) individuals who had received graduate-level law training in the United States and to a lesser extent the UK and Commonwealth countries. Once corporatization and the establishment of stock exchanges became politically more palatable, these individuals implemented a

[103] See Jennifer Asuncion-Mund, "India's capital markets: Unlocking the door to future growth," Deutsche Bank Research Paper, February 14, 2007.

[104] See Madhukar R. Umarji, "Trends and developments in insolvency systems and risk management: The experience of India," working paper (2004); Vijay Joshi and I. M. D. Little, *India's Economic Reforms 1991–2001* (Oxford: Clarendon Press, 1996); S. Thomas, "How the financial sector in India was reformed."

system closely patterned on what they had seen in more developed, foreign markets or, where they were unable to, they adjusted the laws to suit the specific needs of overseas investors.[105] Some of this initial convergence was frustrated or even reversed when both the Company Law 1994 and to a much lesser extent the Securities Law 1999 were captured by more conservative drafting groups and superseded earlier regulations.[106] Perhaps more pernicious in the frustration of convergence was the stubborn capital structure of SOEs corporatized as companies limited by shares. As has been noted widely, China's new corporations continued to be owned at a level of 70–80% by former state bureaus or local government actors. Thus, we have witnessed adoption of legal forms suitable to the Anglo-American model of the dispersedly held firm, but the actual firms still remain controlled rather than widely dispersed. We do not at this stage speculate as to why the PRC adopted a formally (not functionally) convergent corporate law, aside from the obvious reason that they could do it and still attract vast infusions of capital – foreign and domestic – to prop up and then expand failing SOEs.

Yet an important fact is the on-going, and far more realistic functional, corporate governance reform in China (e.g., substantive changes in the Company Law, provision for shareholder suits on corporate breaches, establishment of an independent directors system, an increasingly activist and independent financial media, and diluting the state/legal person dominance at PRC issuers to create more widely dispersed capital structures). Some might ascribe the impetus for these changes to the requirements of foreign investors and foreign regulatory systems, but that is a simplistic view.[107] It disregards the purely indigenous aspect of

[105] The 1993 promise by the now defunct Commission for Reform of the Economic System to the Hong Kong Stock Exchange that a form of words in the 1992 Opinion on Standards for Companies Limited by Shares governing PRC issuers to Hong Kong had the same meaning (and presumably effect) as the entire jurisprudence of "fiduciary duty" under Hong Kong law is a remarkable demonstration of this fact.

[106] For instance, the Company Law 1994 contained a nonsensical Article 4 which maintained that state shareholders continued to own, *directly*, state assets contributed to the corporation, effectively looking right through the intervening corporate entity. By the same token, the Company Law 1994 was replete with special provisions for what were SOEs, in all but name, including the troublesome creation of a "wholly state owned corporation" with no shareholders, no shareholders' meeting, but a board of directors appointed by the state department "owning" the company.

[107] It would also disregard the surprising fact that many purportedly sophisticated investors and portfolio managers continue to throw money at China's newly corporatized issuers regardless of the form or function of corporate governance, or the listing domicile, seemingly unable to miss a ride on the China "growth story."

the push for corporatization and better corporate governance at China's enterprises: *Chinese* forces which want better governed and more efficient firms, policy makers who want healthier capital markets, regulators who want better markets and a "just" result for participants damaged by fraud, shareholders who want remedies or compensation, and the legal reform constituency which has a long-term "rule of law" agenda which it thinks can be implemented first in the corporate and commercial sector. The point is that China may now be moving past a period of formal-not-functional convergence into functional (and sometimes formal) convergence, and for reasons not directly related to the assumed requirements of foreign external finance. This in turn may cause us to query why the PRC has consistently chosen the "shareholder oriented" model of business organization, a disclosure-based securities regulatory structure, and the beginnings of a private enforcement mechanism (as an adjunct to outright business regulation) – all in a world where everyone seems to admit that property rights are weak, the business regulation tradition is weak, the courts are still deficient, and China has no experience with (or interest in allowing for) enterprises with widely dispersed shareholding.

Indeed, when looking at both India and China one question constantly occurs: why have both countries adopted Anglo-American style corporate and securities law reforms – generally thought to be most suitable for widely held (Berle and Means described) firms – when neither country has seemed enthusiastic about encouraging such widely held firms in either new or old industrial sectors? Rather, both countries continue with largely controlled firms (though there are more new dispersedly held Indian firms than before), and even some re-consolidation of previously devolved entities (e.g., in China's aviation and power generation sectors). Even the firms from India and China that list on foreign exchanges are generally controlled firms. Moreover, at least for Indian firms these foreign securities exchanges are not their primary source of capital; for China, this is also becoming true, as even many of the solely offshore-listed (including Hong Kong SAR-listed) firms are returning to the Shanghai Exchange for large, follow-on, RMB yuan financings. Rather, such cross-listings appear more and more designed to provide comfort to the likely "products markets" customers of the Indian and Chinese firms – US and European firms.

One explanation may be that convergence is in the early stages in both countries. It may simply be that the laws are relatively new and that it will take some time for dispersed shareholdings to become more common or politically palatable. However, both countries have been engaged in corporate governance reforms for more than a decade and one wonders why newer firms have not sought more dispersed capital structures under the umbrella of legal and regulatory systems which would seem to lead them to the same. Of course, there is yet a broader question – why have adopted reforms aimed at one type of firm (widely held) been fairly successful at raising capital for different kinds of firms (controlled)? One could speculate that this is because the market is not responding as one might expect or the reforms are simply signals to investors about what to expect (i.e., better governance) or that some elements of laws designed for widely held firms also help to reduce problems with controlled firms.

VI. Conclusion

China and India are the new economic juggernauts. Both countries have experienced phenomenal growth and dramatic interest from foreign investors. Both have survived the Global Financial Crisis 2008–9 in far better shape than most of their developed-world competitors. Indeed, the efforts of both countries to reform their corporate and securities laws to attract foreign and domestic investors and develop stock markets have been front page news. In this chapter we have explored how these reforms have come about and what we might learn from them. Although both countries have many differences, we suggest that the similarities – rapid economic development, significant private and public foreign investment, economic and structural reform, booming stock markets and a shared interest (if not implementation) in "formal" Anglo-American corporate law norms – provide an interesting and rich platform for consideration of contested corporate governance and corporate governance reform issues.

In order to explore these issues we began by briefly providing some political, economic and legal background for both China and India and then discussing their corporate governance reform efforts. Both countries have emerged from less market-oriented economic and regulatory systems to world-shaking economic reform programs, resulting in huge growth, the development of domestic capital markets and dominant participation in the global capital and product markets. And, in the case of each nation, this change has been matched by widely proclaimed corporate governance reform. Our central question revolves around the connection between the obvious developments in China and India, and the corporate governance reforms in both countries. When we evaluate the experiences of these two economic juggernauts and try to apply them to corporate governance theories, we can gain interesting insights. In particular, both countries' experiences suggest that the "legal origins" account does not provide the best explanation for the development of their respective corporate governance templates or domestic capital markets. Rather, a nuanced politics "account" provides greater explanatory power, especially when we try to understand the true effects of difficult and ultimately dislocating historical circumstances like India's Independence, English Colonial Rule and the trauma of Partition, and China's very difficult twentieth century at least to the end of Maoist rule in 1976. As noted in this chapter, both countries appear to have adopted, or are adopting, Anglo-American style corporate governance forms and reforms, yet most of the significant firms domiciled inside these nations (listed or not) remain stubbornly controlled. Thus, more than a decade after radical reform, the capital structure of China and India's corporations remains as it was: subject to overwhelming control by one or a group of connected and often politically powerful shareholders. Thus, perhaps the greatest puzzle raised by this initial inquiry is the fate and future of these corporate establishments – will they change to meet the structures assumed under the received Anglo-American models of corporate governance and securities regulation? If they do not change, how is it that a legal and regulatory strategy designed for different kinds of corporate entities and investor populations can continue to benefit the development of viable stock markets? These questions become increasingly important, not just for corporate governance specialists, as the world watches the rise of India and China in the global capital and product markets.

Appendix 15.1 *Comparing clause 49 and the J. J. Irani Committee recommendations*

Characteristic	Clause 49	J. J. Irani Committee
Independence	• *Requirement* – 50% independent directors if Chairman is executive director or 33% if Chairman is not. • *Definition* – not related to Board or one level below Board and audit partners must have no prior relationship with the Company for the last 3 years. • *"Material"* – There is no requirement for the relationship to be "material." • *Financial institutions* – are considered independent.	• *Requirement* – 33% for companies with public interest. • *Definition* – not related to employees of the Company and no prior relationship with the Company for one year. • *"Material"* – board to review what is "material" on an on-going basis. • *Financial institutions* – not considered independent.
Board requirements & limitations	• Meet 4 times a year (maximum gap of 3 months between meetings). • Limits on number of committees a director can be on (10), but only 5 for which director can be Chair of committee • Develop Code of Conduct.	• Meet 4 times a year (maximum gap of 4 months between meetings). • Limits of number of directorships (15).
Audit Committee composition	• At least 3 directors (two-thirds must be independent). • All financially literate. • At least one having accounting or financial management experience.	• No minimum number of directors (majority need to be independent). • No requirements for financial literacy. • At least one should have accounting/financial management knowledge.

Audit Committee role and powers	• Audit Committee Meetings – 4 meetings (gap between meetings not exceed 4 months). • Audit Committee role is broad – review statutory and internal auditors as well as internal audit function.	• Audit Committee Meetings – number not specified.
Disclosures	• Related party transactions • Accounting treatments and departures • Risk management • Proceeds from offerings • Compensation for directors (including non-executives and obtain shareholders' approval) • Details of compliance history for last 3 years • Corporate governance reports (and disclose adoption, if any, of mandatory and non-mandatory requirements)	• Related party transactions • Executive compensation • Unusual transactions • Director's background

Certifications	• *CEO & CFO:*
	  • financial statements
	  • effectiveness of internal controls
	  • legal transactions
	  • inform audit committee of any significant changes in the above.
	• *Auditor or Company Secretary:*
	  • Compliance with corporate governance
		• *CEO, CFO & Company Secretary*
		  • financials
		• *CEO and CFO:*
		  • internal controls (with audit committee approval)

Subsidiary Companies	• At least one Independent director of Holding Company should sit as a director on Board of material non-listed Indian subsidiary.	

Appendix 15.1 (*cont.*)

Characteristic	Clause 49	J. J. Irani Committee
	• Significant transactions report to Holding company Board (along with subsidiary board's minutes).	
Other	• Whistleblower policy is optional. • Independent directors lose status as "independent" if served 9 years at company. • Training board members. • Evaluate non-executive board performance.	• Whistleblower policy and protection for whistleblower is encouraged.

References

Anant, T. C. A. and Goswami, Omkar, "Getting everything wrong: India's policies regarding 'sick' firms," in Dilip Mookherjee (ed.), *Indian Industries: Policies and Performance* (Delhi: Oxford University Press, 1995)

Asuncion-Mund, Jennifer "India's capital markets: Unlocking the door to future growth," *Deutsche Bank Research Paper*, February 14, 2007

Bagchi, A. K., *Private Investment in India: 1900–1939* (Cambridge University Press, 1972)

Bebchuk, Lucian A. and Mark J. Roe, "A theory of path dependence in corporate ownership and governance" (1999) 52 *Stanford Law Review*

Bhattacharyya, Asish K. and Rao, Sadhalaxmi Vivek, "Economic impact of 'regulation on corporate governance': Evidence from India," Indian Institute of Management Calcutta Working Paper No. 486/2004, January 17, 2004 (2005), available at http://129.3.20.41/eps/fin/papers/0504/0504002.pdf

Birla, Shri Kumar Mangala, Report of the Committee Appointed by the SEBI on Corporate Governance under the Chairmanship of Shri Kumar Mangala Birla (1999)

Black, Bernard S., "The core institutions that support strong securities markets" (2000) 55 *Business Lawyer* 7

Black, Bernard S. and Kraakman, Reinier H., "A self-enforcing model of corporate law" (1996) 109 *Harvard Law Review* 1911

Chakrabarti, Rajesh, *The Finacial Sector in India: Emerging Issues* (New Delhi; New York: Oxford University Press, 2006)

Chunying, Xin, "What kind of judicial power does China need?" (2003) 1(1) *International Journal of Constitutional Law* 58

Clarke, Donald C., "Power and politics in the Chinese court system: The enforcement of civil judgments" (1996) 10 *Columbia Journal of Asian Law* 1

"Corporate governance in China: An overview" (2003) 14 *China Economic Review* 494

Chan, Wellington K. K., *Merchants, Mandarins and Modern Enterprise in Late Ch'ing China* (Cambridge MA: East Asian Research Center; Harvard University Press, 1997)

Coffee, John C., Jr., "The future as history: The prospects for global convergence in corporate governance and its implications" (1999) 93 *Northwestern University Law Review* 641

"Racing towards the top?: The impact of cross-listings and stock market competition on international corporate governance" (2002) 102 *Columbia Law Review* 1757

Confederation of Indian Industry, *Desirable Corporate Governance: A Code* (1998)

Cunningham, C. D., "The world's most powerful court: Finding the roots of India's public interest litigation revolution in the Hussainara Khatoon prisoners case," in S. P. Sathe and S. Narayan (eds.), *Liberty, Equality and Justice: Struggles for a New Social Order* (Lucknow, India: Eastern Book Company, 2003)

Debroy, Bibek, "Some issues in law reform in India," in J. J. Dethier (ed.), *Governance, Decentralization, and Reform in China, India and Russia* (Boston MA: Kluwer, 2000)

Dehua, Tang (ed.), *Qita Gongsi Zuzhi Xingshi Yu Gufen Hezuo Qiye Falu Shiwu (= Legal Treaties on Other Firms of Corporate Organization and the Stock Cooperative Enterprise)* (1998)

Durnev, Artyom, and Kim, E. Han, "To steal or not to steal: Firm attributes, legal environment, and valuation" (2005) 60 *Journal of Finance*

Gilson, Ronald J., "Globalizing corporate governance: Convergence of form or function" (2001) 49 *American Journal of Comparative Law*

Goswami, Omkar, *Corporate Bankruptcy in India: A Comparative Perspective*, Development Centre Studies (Paris: OECD, 1996)

"India: The tide rises gradually," in Charles P. Oman (ed.), *Corporate Governance in Development: The Experiences of Brazil, Chile, India, and South Africa* (Issy-les-Moulineaux: OECD Development Center; Washington DC: Center for International Private Enterprise, 2003)

Government of India (1997), *Report of Working Group on the Companies Act*

Green, Stephen Paul, *China's Stock Market: A Guide to its Progress, Players and Prospects* (London: Profile, 2003)

Hansmann, Henry and Kraakman, Reinier H., "The end of history for corporate law" (2001) 89 *Georgetown Law Journal* 439

Howson, Nicholas Calcina, "China's restructured commercial banks: The old nomenklatura system serving new corporate governance structures?" in M. Avery, M. Zhu and J. Cai (eds.), *China's Emerging Financial Markets: Challenges and Global Impact* (Singapore: John Wiley and Sons, 2009)

"The doctrine that dared not speak its name: Anglo-American fiduciary duties in China's 2005 company law and case law intimations of prior convergence," in H. Kanda, K. Kim and C. Milhaupt (eds.), *Transforming Corporate Governance in East Asia* (Abingdon: Routledge, 2008)

Huang, Yasheng, *Selling China: Foreign Direct Investments During the Reform Era* (Cambridge University Press, 2003)

Huang, Yasheng and Khanna, Tarun, "Can India overtake China?" (2003: July–August) *Foreign Policy*

Johnson, Simon, Peter Boone, Alasdair Breach, and Eric Friedman, "Corporate governance in the Asian financial crisis" (2000) 58 *Journal of Financial Economics*

Joshi, Vijay and Little, I. M. D., *India's Economic Reforms 1991–2001* (Oxford: Clarendon Press, 1996)

Khanna, Tarun and Krishna Palepu, "The evolution of concentrated ownership in India: Broad patterns and a history of the Indian software industry," in

Randall K. Morck (ed.), *A History of Corporate Governance around the World* (University of Chicago Press, 2005)

"Is group affiliation profitable for in emerging markets? An analysis of diversified business groups" (2000) 55 *Journal of Finance*

"Policy shocks, market intermediaries, and corporate strategy: The evidence from Chile and India" (June 1999) 8(2) *Journal of Economics & Management Strategy* 271–310

Khanna, Vikramaditya S., "Corporate crime legislation: A political economy analysis" (2004) 82(1) *Washington University Law Quarterly*

"Corporate governance in India: Past, present and future?" (2009) 1 *Jindal Global Law Review*

Kirby, William C., "China unincorporated: Company law and business enterprise in twentieth century China" (1995) 54(1) *Journal of Asian Studies* 43

Klapper, Leora F. and Love, Inessa, "Corporate governance, investor protection and performance in emerging markets" (2003) *Journal of Corporate Finance*, forthcoming, available at http://ssrn.com/abstract=303979

Krueger, Anne (ed.), *Economic Policy Reforms and the Indian Economy* (University of Chicago Press, 2002)

La Porta, Rafael, Florencio Lopez-de-Silanes, Andrei Shleifer, and Robert Vishny, "Investor protection and corporate valuation" (2002) 57 *Journal of Finance*

"Law and finance" (1998) 106 *Journal of Political Economy*

"Legal determinants of external finance" (1997) 52 *Journal of Finance*

"What works in securities laws" (2006) 61 *Journal of Finance*

Lardy, Nicholas R., *China's Unfinished Economic Revolution* (Washington DC: Brookings Institution Press, 1998)

Malegam, Shri Y. H., Report of the Sebi Committee on Disclosure Requirements in Offer Documents under the Chairmanship of Shri Y. H. Malegam (1995)

Miles, James, "China Survey," *The Economist* (25 March 2006)

Mohan, R. and Aggrawal, V., "Commands and controls: Planning for industrial development in India, 1951–1990," (1990) 14 *Journal of Comparative Economics* 681

Morris, M. D., "The growth of large scale industry up to 1947," in D. Kumar (ed.), *Cambridge Economic History of India*, vol. II (Cambridge University Press, 1983), pp. 553–676

Murthy, Shri N. R. Narayana, Report of the Committee Appointed by the Sebi on Corporate Governance Under the Chairmanship of Shri N. R. Narayana Murthy (2003)

Naresh Chandra Committee, Report of the Naresh Chandra Committee on Corporate Audit and Governance (December 23, 2002)

Naresh Chandra Committee, Report of the Committee on Regulations of Private Companies and Partnership (Naresh Chandra Committee – II, July 31, 2003)

Naughton, Barry, *Growing Out of the Plan: Chinese Economic Reform 1978–1993* (Cambridge University Press, 1995)

Parekh, Shri Sandeep P., Report of the SEBI Sub-committee on Integrated Disclosures under the Chairmanship of Shri Sandeep P. Parekh (2008)

Peerenboom, Randall, *China's Long March Toward Rule of Law* (Cambridge University Press, 2002)

Peng, Jiusong, *Zhongguo Qiyue Gufenshi* (*China's Contracting Stock System*) (1994)

Rajan, Raghuram G. and Luigi Zingales, "The great reversals: The politics of financial development in the twentieth century" (2003) 69 *Journal of Financial Economics*

Roe, Mark J., "Legal origins and stock markets in the twentieth century" (2006) 120(2) *Harvard Law Review*

Romano, Roberta, "The Sarbanes-Oxley Act and the making of quack corporate governance" (2005) 114(7) *Yale Law Journal*

Rungta, Radhe Shyam, *The Rise of Business Corporations in India, 1851 – 1900* (Cambridge University Press, 1970)

Stout, Lynn, "Bad and not-so-bad arguments for shareholders primacy" (2002) 85 *Southern California Law Review*

Tenev, Stoyan and Zhang, Chunlin, with Brefort, Loup, *Corporate Governance and Enterprise Reform in China: Building the Institutions of Modern Markets* (Washington DC: World Bank; International Finance Corporation, 2002)

Thakurdas, Sir Purshotamdas, Tata, J. R. D., Birla, G. D., Dalal, Sir Ardeshir, Ram, Sir Shri, Lalbhai, Kastrubhai, Shroff, A. D. and Matthai, John, *The "Bombay Plan" for India's Economic Development* (Bombay: Printed by S. Ramu, at the Commercial Printing Press, 1944)

Thomas, Susan, "How the financial sector in India was reformed," in S. Narayan (ed.), *Documenting Reforms: Case Studies from India* (New Delhi: Macmillan, 2006)

Umarji, Madhukar R., "Trends and developments in insolvency systems and risk management: The experience of India," paper presented at OECD's Forum on Asian Insolvency Reform (2004)

World Bank, *India: Role of Institutional Investors in the Corporate Governance of their Portfolio Companies*, World Bank Report (2005)

World Bank, *Doing Business in South Asia in 2007*, country profile of India (2007)

Xiang, Lanxin, *Recasting the Imperial Far East: Britain and America in China, 1945–1950* (Armonk NY: M. E. Sharpe, 1995)

16

An institutional race

A comparative study of the competition law regimes in India and China

ZHANG XIAN-CHU

The rise of China and India in the twenty-first century has attracted a great deal of international attention.[1] Even in his recent State of the Union Address, President Bush of the United States specifically named India and China as the strong challengers to the American competitiveness in the world economy.[2] Indeed, the two nations share many similarities, such as being giant developing countries with long glorious civilizations and colonial histories; but at the same time they have equally many differences, particularly on their completely different political, social and legal systems.[3]

This chapter is developed from a conference paper presented at the Conference on China, India and the International Economic Order at the National University of Singapore in June 2006. The law and the legislative information stated are based on the materials available as of May 2007. The author would like to thank Professor Aditya Bhattacharjea of University of Delhi, India for important research materials he kindly provided.

[1] For example, in the Annual Meeting 2006 of the World Economic Forum held in Davos, Switzerland, it was projected that by 2050 China and India would occupy two of the places among the world's top three largest economies. Mark Landler, "India mounts a charm offensive," *International Herald Tribune*, January 27, 2006, p. 9.

[2] See the report "Bush warns against isolation," *International Herald Tribune*, February 2, 2006, p. 6.

[3] For some selected readings in this regard, see Sanjukta Banerji Bhattacharya (ed.), *India at the End of the Twentieth Century: Essays on Politics, Society, and the Economy* (New Delhi: Lancer's Books, 2001); Manju Saxena and Harish Chandra, *Law and Changing Society* (New Delhi: Deep & Deep Publishers, 1999); Freshfields (ed.), *Doing Business in China* (New York: Juris Publishing Inc., 2006); *China Business Law Guide* (Singapore: CCH Asia Pte Ltd, 2004); Kuan-I Chen and J. S. Uppal, *Comparative Development of India and China* (New Delhi: Free Press, 1971); Jean-Jacques Dethier (ed.), *Governance, Decentralization and Reform in China, India and Russia* (Boston: Kluwer Academic Publishers, 2000).

Despite the sharp discrepancies, the unsettled territory dispute and the recent international political uneasiness,[4] the tide of globalization has more and more rung the two giants on the arena of international competition. The trade between China and India between 2000 and 2004 rose by more than 350 percent to record nearly US$14 billion and the governments' joint efforts are expected to push the trading volume to reach US$20 billion in 2008 and US$30 billion in 2010.[5] The two countries have also agreed in 2006 to set up six joint task forces to explore the feasibility of a China–India Regional Trade Agreement.[6] In the course of trade development, the concerns with the competition of the two countries have also been raised. For example, in the period of 1995–June 2005, India initiated 412 anti-dumping petitions, of which 81 were made against imports from China. Since 2000, China has also initiated at least two anti-dumping investigations against products from India.[7] In this context, it has been predicted by some renowned scholars that despite the friendly will of the two governments the lack of balanced complementarity and the political sensitivity would make the conclusion of the bilateral regional trade agreement difficult.[8]

Fueled with the race of the two countries' economic development, comparative studies on the institutional advantages and development strategies of China and India have been gaining momentum in recent years. Although these studies approach and examine the issues from different perspectives and disciplines, there seems a consensus among

[4] For some general comments, see Francine R. Frankel and Harry Harding (eds.), *The India–China Relationship: What the United States Needs to Know* (New York: Columbia University Press, 2004); and Zia Mian, "The United States, China and India: A story of leaders, partners and clients," *Economic and Political Weekly*, September 10, 2005. For some recent developments, see Manik Mehta, "United States seeks closer ties with India to counter China's hegemonic ambitions," *Taiwan Journal*, October 28, 2005, available at http://taiwanjournal.nat.gov.tw/ct.asp?xItem=21618&CtNode=122 (visited on May 16, 2007); and the report "U.S.–India nuclear deal on course ahead of President Bush visit," *Online NewsHour*, February 24, 2006, www.pbs.org/newshour/updates/india_02–24–06.html (visited on May 16, 2007), which stated that the deal was seen as "a backdoor attempt to build an alliance against China's emerging domination in Asia."

[5] Accenture Policy and Corporate Affairs Practice, 'China and India: Partners in competition' (2005), available at www.accenture.com/NR/rdonlyres/4D8920BC-4590–4868-B9DB-94DC58EA3B34/0/pca_china_india.pdf (visited on May 16, 2007).

[6] See the report 'India and China agree to study regional trade agreement', The *Hindu Business Section*, March 17, 2006.

[7] See the statistics of the WTO, available at www.wto.org/english/tratop_e/adp_e/adp_e.htm (visited on May 16, 2007).

[8] Aditya Bhattacharjea, "India's trade relations with China and Russia in the context of the WTO" (2005) 41(4) *China Report* 432.

scholars and experts that the development and competition of the two countries are measured not only by the statistical numbers, but more fundamentally by their institutional advantages.[9] According to some commentators, although a superficial look at China and India argues in China's favor in the race of rise, India's competitive entrepreneurship, demographic trends, and commitment to capitalism will allow India to make more impressive developments than China within twenty years from now.[10] Professor Huang of Massachusetts Institute of Technology and Professor Khanna of Harvard University further pointed out that India's strong infrastructure to support the private sector, including its legal system is considerably more advanced as compared with China's.[11]

Against this background, this article compares the developments of anti-monopoly law in the two countries as a reflection of the different concerns and paths to their modernization. Section I highlights the main features of the anti-monopoly regime in India and the current developments; section II examines the history of the anti-monopoly legislation, the main provisions of the recent draft and certain unsettled issues in China; section III compares the anti-monopoly laws of the two countries and identifies some key similarities and divergences; and finally, section IV draws some preliminary conclusions.

As shown in many writings, issues concerning competition can be analyzed from both policy and legal perspectives. As Mr. Vinod Dhall, Member of the Competition Commission of India (CCI) pointed out recently, the former includes "liberalized trade policy, industrial licensing policy, relaxed foreign investment and ownership requirements, economic deregulation, privatization, etc." and the latter focuses on the competition law. "Merely having a competition law by itself cannot

[9] Some recent publications include Yasheng Huang and Tarun Khanna, "Can India overtake China?" (July–August 2003) *Foreign Policy* 74–81; Bhattacharjea, "India's trade relations with China and Russia," 427–35; Jinxin Huang, "A new Chinese discourse of India" (Nov 2005) 14 *Journal of Contemporary China* 631–41; Accenture Policy, "China and India"; Valerie Cerra, Sandra A. Rivera and Sweta Chaman Saxena, "Crouching tiger, hidden dragon: What are the consequences of China's WTO entry for India's trade?" (2005) International Monetary Fund Working Paper WP/05/101, available at www.imf.org/external/pubs/ft/wp/2005/ wp05101.pdf (visited on May 16, 2007); Hugo Restall, "India's coming eclipse of China," *Far Eastern Economic Review*, March 11, 2006, pp. 12–17; Sriharsha Pappu and Saurabh Kumar, "Impact of China's entry into the WTO on India" (2001), available at http://papers.ssrn.com/sol3/papers.cfm?abstract_id=303439 (visited on May 16, 2007).

[10] William Pesek Jr, "Surprise! India will pull ahead," *International Herald Tribune*, January 31, 2006, p. 15; and Restall, "India's coming eclipse of China."

[11] Huang and Khanna, "Can India overtake China?" 75.

produce or ensure competition in the market unless this is facilitated by appropriate government policy. On the other hand, government policies without law to enforce such policies and prevent competition malpractice would also be incomplete."[12] Given the existence of such a close relationship between the competition law and policy, this article does not intend to define the precise boundary of the two, but just develop its discussion on a general proposition that competition policy is principally composed of competition law and competition advocacy.[13]

I. An overview of the competition law regime in India

India's competition legislation can be traced back to 1969 when the Monopolies and Restrictive Trade Practice (MRTP) Act was adopted. Today it is generally agreed that the first generation enactment in the era of licenses, permits and control of the government was based on consumers' welfare as part of public interest, rather than market economy disciplines of free competition. Moreover, although a state commission was established to oversee the implementation of the Act, it was apparently not powerful enough to deal with violations. For example, it could not impose any penalty for breach of the law, except issuing an order to direct the party concerned to "cease and desist" from the alleged monopolistic or other unfair trade practice.[14]

The 1969 Act was amended several times and subjected to some extensive reviews in the 1980s and the 1990s in the course of India's socio-economic development, which reflected the path of competition law development in India. For instance, adding the Unfair Trade Practice (UTP) Enquiries to the Act, empowering the Commission headed by a judge to award compensation, and providing the CCI with powers of independent investigation were all the important milestones in this period.[15]

[12] Vinod Dhall, "Competition policy and multilateral trading," speech made on WTO/UNESCAP/ASCI Regional Seminar for Asia and Pacific Economies at Hyderabad on 6 October 2004, p. 5, available at http://competition-commission-india.nic.in (visited on January 23, 2006).

[13] Douglas H. Brooks, "Competition policy and development" (October 2005) Economics and Research Department (ERD) Policy Brief No. 39, p. 2, available at www.asiandevbank.org/Documents/EDRC/ Policy_Briefs/PB039.pdf (visited on May 16, 2007).

[14] Competition Commission of India, "Public awareness on competition law and policy" (2003), pp. 2–3, available at http://competition-commission-india.nic.in (visited on 23 January 2006).

[15] Competition Commission of India, "Public awareness," 3–4.

In 2002 the new Competition Act was promulgated by the Parliament to replace the 1969 Act with the intention of modernizing the competition law "in line with international practice and to suit the Indian conditions."[16] The 2002 Act has included important features of the new generation of competition law which can be found in most of the competition law regimes of the market economies, such as prohibition of anti-competition agreements and abuse of dominant market position, regulations of combination, promotion of competition advocacy and international cooperation.

As a general principle, s. 3 of the 2002 Act prohibits and invalidates any agreement entered into by either enterprises or individuals in respect of production, supply, distribution, storage, acquisitions or control of goods or provision of services, which causes or is likely to cause an appreciable adverse effect on competition within India.[17] More specifically, both horizontal agreements, including cartel, on price fixing, limiting or controlling production, supply, markets, technical development, investment or provision of services, sharing the market or sources and direct or indirect bid rigging,[18] and vertical agreements, such as tie-in agreements, exclusive supply agreements, exclusive distribution agreements, refusal to deal and resale price maintenance, are disallowed.[19]

The 2002 Act defines a "dominant position" as a position of strength, enjoyed by an enterprise in the relevant market in India, which enables it to operate independently of competitive forces prevailing in the market or affect its competitors or consumers or the relevant market in its favor.[20] According to the law, the dominant position itself is not a violation *per se*, but abuse of such a position is unlawful, which includes directly or indirectly unfair or discriminating prices (such as predatory prices), limiting or restricting production of goods, provision of services or technical development, denial of market access, conclusion of contracts subject to unrelated supplementary obligations, and use of the dominant position in one market to enter into or protect other relevant markets.[21]

Under s. 5, "combination" is defined quite broadly to include not only mergers and acquisitions, but also acquisition of control and amalgamations. However, the high thresholds may limit the application of the rules to a small number of cases. According to the section, only

16 Dhall, "Competition policy and multilateral trading," 4–5.

17 ss. 3 (1) and (2) of the 2002 Act.

18 2002 Act, s. 3 (3).

19 2002 Act, s. 3 (4). Certain exceptions are also provided.

20 2002 Act, s. 4, Explanation.

21 2002 Act, ss. 4 (1) and (2).

mergers or amalgamations that either involve assets value of more than rupees one thousand crores or turnover of more than rupees three thousand crores, or in India or outside India in aggregate the assets of value of more than US$500 million or turnover of more than US$1.5 billion would be subject to the jurisdiction of the Act.[22]

The regulation on combination includes a voluntary notification scheme. Any person or enterprise to a proposed combination may voluntarily give notice to the Commission disclosing the details of the combination within seven days of its board approval or the execution of the relevant agreement.[23]

Upon receiving the notice, the Commission shall deal with the matter according to its implication of the appreciable adverse effect and the specific circumstance. It may issue a notice to the parties concerned to show cause in order to avoid further investigation of the CCI; it may direct the parties concerned to publish further details of the proposed combination for providing the public and parties affected with the knowledge or information; it may invite any person affected or likely to be affected by the proposed combination to file his written objection, or it may just require a party concerned to submit more information.[24] In making an inquiry into a proposed combination on its possible appreciable adverse effect on competition in India, many factors that are listed in s. 20 (4) shall be taken into consideration.

On the basis of the necessary investigation, the Commission may by order approve or disapprove a proposed combination, or it may propose appropriate modification to the proposed combination.[25] Section 31(11) of the Act stipulates that if the Commission does not pass an order or issue any direction to effect any procedure within ninety working days, the combination shall be deemed to have been approved by the Commission.

The voluntary notification regime, however, does not apply to share subscription, financing facility or any acquisition by a public financial institution, foreign institutional investor, bank or venture capital fund, pursuant to any covenant of a loan agreement or investment agreement. All such acquisitions must be filed with the Commission with detailed information within seven days of the acquisition.[26]

[22] 2002 Act, ss. 5 (a) (i) (A) and (B); and (b)(ii) (C).
[23] 2002 Act, s. 6 (2). [24] 2002 Act, s. 6 (3) and s. 29.
[25] 2002 Act, ss. 31 (1), (2) and (3). [26] 2002 Act, s. 6 (4) and (5).

Competition advocacy is another important feature of the 2002 Act and a Commission's major responsibility. Under s. 49 (1) and (2) the Central Government of India in formulating a policy on competition may make a reference to the Commission for its opinion, although not binding, on the possible effect of such a policy. In addition to the Central Government, any statutory authority may have to make reference to the Commission if any party raises an issue in the course of a proceeding before the authority that its decision is or will be contrary to any provision of the 2002 Act and shall pass its order after receiving the Commission's opinion within 60 days on the issue to the extent as it deems fit.[27] The 2002 Act also mandates the Commission to take suitable measures for the promotion of competition advocacy, creating awareness and imparting training about competition issues.[28] In this regard, certain fields of capacity building have been identified by the Commission as its working focus, such as promoting the culture of competition and public awareness of competition issues, better defining governing policy and laws and regularly publishing enforcement decisions, provision of educational and training programs, and close cooperation with other state branches, professional organizations and competition authorities outside India.[29]

In the era of globalization, the 2002 Act has equipped the Commission with extended powers to deal with cross-border concerns. Notwithstanding that an agreement is concluded outside India, any party to such agreement is outside India, any party abusing its dominant position is outside India, a combination has taken place outside India, or any other matter, practice or action is outside India, the Commission shall have the power to make its inquiry into such an agreement or matter if it has, or is likely to have, an appreciable adverse effect on competition in the relevant market in India.[30] In order to discharge its duty to protect the domestic market and consumers, the Commission may with the approval of the Central Government enter into a memorandum or arrangement with any agency of any foreign country.[31]

The modernization under the 2002 Act reflects a new level playing field where the government business undertakings are also subject to the provisions of the Act. According to the definition of s. 2 (h), "enterprise" in the Act includes not only a commercial entity or natural person, but also any department of the Government which is or has been engaged in

[27] 2002 Act, s. 21. [28] 2002 Act, s. 49 (3).

[29] Dhall, "Competition policy and multilateral trading," 7–11; and Competition Commission of India, "Public awareness," 14–16.

[30] 2002 Act, s. 32. [31] 2002 Act, s. 18.

any business activity, investment, or other undertakings, either directly or through its units or divisions, except the activities relatable to the sovereign function of the Government.

As far as its legal status is concerned, the CCI under the 2002 Act is a body corporate which may sue or be sued.[32] All the members of the Commission shall function on a full-time basis and are required to be of ability, integrity and standing with qualification as a judge of a High Court, or special knowledge and professional experience of no less than fifteen years.[33] A member of the Commission may be removed for a cause, including personal insolvency, taking other paid employment, conviction of an offence involving moral turpitude, potential conflict of interest, abuse of power, or physical or mental incapacity.[34]

In addition to the updated legislation, the judiciary of India further enhances the competition regime with its accumulated experience on competition case adjudication and the institutional checks and balances under the rule of law. For example, in a well-known case, the Supreme Court of India denied the challenge to a merger of Hindustan Level Ltd. as a multinational company, with an Indian firm, TOMCO based on the necessary government approval and the public interest. The court held that no government approval was needed under the MRTP as amended in 1991, which specifically intended to allow foreign firms to do business in India more easily.[35]

Another telling example of Indian's legal tradition and the institutional checks and balances is the recent case of *Brahm Dutt v. Union of India*, where the constitutionality of certain provisions of the 2002 Act was challenged. According to Rule 3 of the "Competition Commission of India Rules 2003," the Central Government would constitute the Commission consisting of a retired judge from the Supreme Court or a High Court or a retired chairperson or a bureaucrat or a distinguished jurist or a senior advocate or senior specialist and expert. The Government would nominate the members of the Commission and the chairperson. According to the legislation, the Competition Commission would have adjudicatory power over enquiries relating to monopolistic practice and the judicial and executive members work in tandem in the process. But as compared with the earlier practice in India where

[32] 2002 Act, s. 7 (1). [33] 2002 Act, ss. 8 (2) and (3). [34] 2002 Act, ss. 11 (2).

[35] *Hindustan Level Employees' Union v. Hindustan Level and Others* [1995] SCC 499, paras. 71–3; quoted from Aditya Bhattacharjea, "Trade, investment, and competition policy: An Indian perspective" in Aaditya Mattoo and Robert M. Stern (eds.), *India and the WTO* (Oxford University Press, 2002), pp. 206–7.

tribunals were composed of a mix of judicial and non-judicial members, the CCI is considered "a different ball game altogether." Although it is more regulatory in nature than adjudicatory, its adjudicatory function should be manned best by persons trained in law.[36] Thus, after the Central Government appointed Mr. Dipak Chatterji as the Chairperson of the CCI for a term of five years on October 14, 2003, a petition was filed with the Supreme Court to challenge the appointment on the ground that, *inter alia*, Mr. Chatterji as a senior bureaucrat should not sit in judgment over retired judges of the High Court and the Supreme Court.

Despite the Government's argument that the Commission, also being an expert body, needed more than judicial expertise, the Supreme Court stood firm on the judicial independence and the doctrine of separation of powers guaranteed by the Constitution of India. In January 2005 during the pendency of petition, the Government by a submission, promised to amend the Act to enable the Chairperson and the members of the CCI to be selected by the committee presided over by the Chief Justice or his nominee. On this basis the Supreme Court disposed of the petition leaving open the issues concerned to be decided after the promised amendment.[37] In its decision, the Supreme Court suggested an approach to create two separate bodies: one with expertise that is advisory and regulatory and the other adjudicatory. In addition, there may be an appellate body to sit in appeal over the decision of such an adjudicatory body.[38]

Pursuant to the decision of the Supreme Court, the Government introduced the "Competition (Amendment) Bill 2006" to the Parliament on March 9, 2006,[39] which brought in some significant changes by amending most of the sections of the original Act and introducing more than twenty new sections.[40] The new Bill proposed to split the Competition Commission of India and the Competition Appellate Tribunal (CAT). The former will be composed of a chairperson and no more

[36] Anurag K Agarwal, "Competition law in India: Need to go slow and steady" (October 2005) Working Paper no. 2005–10–05 of India Institute of Management, at 6, available at www.iimahd.ernet.in/publications/data/2005-10-05anurag.pdf (visited on May 16, 2007).

[37] *Brahum Dutt v. Union of India*, Case No. Writ Petition (civil) 490 of 2003, 20 January 2005 as the date of judgment.

[38] *Brahum Dutt v. Union of India*, para. 6.

[39] See the report: "Competition Act Amendment Bill introduced in Lok Sabha," *The Hindu Business Line*, available at www.thehindubusinessline.com/2006/03/10/stories/2006031003300800.htm (visited on March 28, 2006).

[40] Aditya Bhattacharjea, "Amending India's Competition Act," *The Economic and Political Weekly*, October 14, 2006.

than six other members to be appointed by the Government.[41] Although the selection procedure has not been set out and administration experience has been removed from the qualifying criteria for the members of the CCI, the Bill still suggests sixty-five as the age limit for the posts and transfers of all the current MRTP Commission to the CCI. The Selection Committee both for the CCI and the CAT will be headed by the Chief Justice of India or his nominee and two other members who are the Secretary in the Ministry of Company Affairs and the Secretary in the Ministry of Law and Justice respectively.[42] According to the Bill, the CAT is empowered to hear appeals against the orders of the CCI and to adjudicate compensation claims. The chairperson of the CAT shall be a person who is, or has been, a judge of the Supreme Court, or the Chief Justice of a High Court; and the members of CAT shall be persons of ability, integrity, and standing having special knowledge of, and professional experience of not less than twenty-five years in competition, business, law, public affairs or in any other matters which in the opinion of the Central Government, may be useful to the Tribunal.[43] Moreover, s. 49 of the new Bill extends consultation to the CCI on formulating a competition policy by the Central Government to local state governments and under s. 46, a leniency scheme is created where the penalty on the first firm to disclose vital information on its participation in a cartel may be reduced if such disclosure was made prior to the CCI investigation.

However, the proposed amendments may not bring the battle to an end. Thus far, no procedure for identifying candidates of the Commission has been outlined. The age limit of sixty-five is still considered liable to lead to the CCI becoming a parking space for retired/retiring bureaucrats.[44] As such, the controversy may continue in the near future.

After the powers of the Commission are divided, with the adjudicatory power being reserved to the CAT, it is worried that the Commission may become a toothless tiger.[45] Moreover, the jurisdictions of different authorities/regulators over certain matters need to be further clarified in

[41] The Competition (Amendment) Bill 2006, art. 4.

[42] The Competition (Amendment) Bill 2006, art. 5.

[43] The Competition (Amendment) Bill 2006, Chapter VIIIA.

[44] CUTS (Customer Unity and Trust Society) International, "The Competition (Amendment) Bill 2006: What needs to be done?" (2006) 2 *Bill Blowup* 2, available at www.cuts-international.org (visited on April 30, 2006).

[45] Pradeep S. Mehta, "Competition Bill: Still too many flaws," *Business Standard*, January 7, 2006, available at www.rediff.com/money/2006/jan/07guest1.htm (visited on February 4, 2006).

order to avoid confusion. For instance, prevention of market access through unfair practice currently may be subject to the jurisdiction of both the competition and consumer protection authorities.[46] It is also proposed that the CCI should be granted the prime or at least the concurrent responsibility of acting on sectors concerned and the consultation and advocacy between sector regulations and the competition authority should be mandatory.[47] Further, as a major drawback, the power to deal with competition issues in certain regulated sectors, such as telecommunications and public utility is not given to the Commission. This limit would make the Indian regime different from other countries' practice to create a competition authority with powers to deal with all relevant issues on the market.[48] In particular, there may be certain potential conflict on anti-monopoly rules concerning mergers and acquisitions between the Competition Act 2002 which is based on some capital and turnover benchmarks and the government guideline to ensure that there are at least three market operators on a given intra-circle.[49] Given the overlap in the functions assigned to sectoral regulators and the CCI, it is held that a common appellate tribunal should be established to avoid inconsistent decisions.[50] The effective function of the Commission may be further limited after the proposal to establish regional benches of the Competition Commission would be dropped due to its lack of adjudicatory power.[51]

Despite the existing uncertainties, Shri Gupta, the Minister of Company Affairs of India, expressed his optimistic view recently that the amendment to the Competition Act 2002 would be completed soon and the CCI would be fully functional in a few months.[52]

[46] Pradeep S Mehta, "Defanging the Competition Act," *Business Standard*, August 1, 2005, available at www.business-standard.com (visited on March 13, 2006); Mehta, "Competition Bill: Still too many flaws"; and the report, "Competition Panel can't rule on legal issues," *Economic Times News Network*, March 10, 2006, available at http://economictimes.indiatimes.com/ articleshow/1444854.cms (visited on March 13, 2006).

[47] CUTS International, "The Competition (Amendment) Bill 2006" (2006) 2 *Bill Blowup* 2–3.

[48] CUTS International, "The Competition (Amendment) Bill 2006" (2006) 2 *Bill Blowup* 3.

[49] Pradeep S. Mehta, "Competition vs Regulation: The best way forward," *The Hindu Business Line*, September 16, 2005, pp. 2–3, available at www.thehindubusinessline.com/2005/09/16/stories/2005091600401000.htm (visited on February 4, 2006).

[50] CUTS International, "The Competition (Amendment) Bill 2006," (2006) 2 *Bill Blowup* 3.

[51] Mehta, "Competition vs Regulation," 3.

[52] See the report entitled "Shri Prem Chand Gupta hopes competition commission would be functional in a few months," available at www.indlawnews.com/38015ad8fc90dc27e781af47f5446e2d (visited on 4 January 2007).

II. Development of competition law in China

As compared with the legal regime in India, China's anti-monopoly legislation and practice lags far behind. As early as 1987 a drafting group of anti-monopoly law was formed within the Legislative Department of the State Council; however, it only produced a draft of "Anti-Unfair Competition Law" as a half-done effort in 1993.[53] The further legislative process was not resumed until 1994 when a working group was established by the State Council to further study competition policy.[54] After more than ten years' effort the "Draft Anti-Monopoly Law" was finally submitted to the Standing Committee of the National People's Congress for "the first reading" on June 24, 2006 (the 2006 Draft) and the second reading in the first half of 2007.[55] The PRC Anti-Monopoly Law was officially promulgated on 30 August 2007 and would take effect on 1 August 2008.

It should be noted that China embarked on its undertaking to establish an anti-monopoly regime with social, political, economic and legal conditions quite different from those of India. Being a socialist country ruled by the totalitarian government of the Communist Party with a history of planned economy for over thirty years the short reform experience has not allowed the market disciplines and competition culture to really take their roots in the country.[56] Lack of independence and experience in dealing with market monopoly has thus far limited the role the judiciary has to play in developing the legal framework. As such, it is ironic that the reluctance of the governments at all the levels to give up their powers in the market reform and the local firms' heavy reliance on the local government protection in a market without a fair level playing field have made the administrative power in the market even stronger in certain sectors, although such practice is supposed to be weakened and eventually eliminated in the course of reform. The local protectionism

[53] Junjing Liu (ed.), *A Study on Implementation Systems of Anti-Monopoly Law in China and Foreign Countries* (Beijing University Press, 2005), pp. 313–14 (in Chinese).

[54] Mark Williams, *Competition Policy and Law in China, Hong Kong and Taiwan* (Cambridge University Press, 2005), at pp. 172–3.

[55] See the report entitled "Anti-monopoly draft provokes debates," *China Economic Net*, November 15, 2006, available at http://en.ce.cn/national/Law/ 200611/15/t20061115_9428909.shtml (visited on January 4, 2007).

[56] Lucian W. Pye, "An overview of 50 years of the People's Republic of China: Some progress, but big problems remain" (1999) 159 *The China Quarterly* 569–83; and William C. Jones, "Trying to understand the current Chinese legal system," in C. Stephen Hsu (ed.), *Understanding China's Legal System: Essays in Honor of Jerome A. Cohen* (New York: New York University Press, 2003), pp. 7–45.

and administrative monopoly have been considered the most serious obstacles to the development of an anti-monopoly regime in China.[57]

The long delay of adopting the anti-monopoly law, however, does not mean that there is no enactment in this regard at all. Thus far, quite a few national laws and administrative regulations as well as government policies have been adopted to address anti-monopoly concerns in different perspectives. For example, the "Anti-Unfair Competition Law of 1993," the "Consumer Protection Law of 1993," the "Advertising Law of 1994," the "Price Law of 1997," the "Bidding Law of 1999," the "Government Procurement Law of 2002," the "Harbor Law of 2003" and the "Foreign Trade Law of 2004" all include some provisions to deal with monopoly or related practices. In addition, numerous administrative decrees have been promulgated by different government authorities in different business areas in the past two decades.[58] In order to deal with some urgent tensions between local governments on market accession and distribution, the Central Government has issued several policy directions.[59]

Despite the notable rule-making efforts, all these administrative measures, since their first adoption, have suffered fundamental and intrinsic defects. Firstly, the piece-meal approach fails to develop a coherent competition policy and legal system; secondly, the vague and general provisions have made the application of the regulations ineffective. In many decrees, a one sentence provision to prohibit monopolist or anti-unfair competition conduct looks more like an empty policy statement

[57] There are many comments in this regard. For one in English, see Chaowu Jin and Wei Luo, *Competition Law in China* (Buffalo NY: William S. Hein & Co. Inc., 2002), p. 208, stating that in today's China the administrative monopoly disturbs the market economy more than economic monopoly does. A series of rules adopted by the Central Government against administrative monopoly have never been put into practice effectively.

[58] To name some as examples here: "Certain Provisions on Prohibition of Restriction on Competition by Public Enterprises" issued by the State Administration of Industry and Commerce in 1993, "Provisions on Curbing Dumping of Industrial Products at Predatory Price" jointly adopted by the State Planning Commission and the State Commission of Economy and Trade in 1998, "Provisions on Prohibition of Regional Blockade on Market Activities" stipulated by the State Council in 2001, "Interim Provisions on Curbing Monopolistic Pricing" issued by the State Commission of Development and Reform in 2003, "Provisions on Penalizing Price Violations" promulgated by the State Council in 2005.

[59] These policy directions of the State Council include "The Interim Provisions on Developing and Protection of Socialist Competition of 1980"; "The Decisions on Prohibition of Local Blockage on Market Activities of 2001"; "The Decision on Consolidation and Streamlining Market Order of 2001"; "The Key Points of Consolidation and Streamlining the Market Order of 2004"; and "The Key Points of Consolidation and Streamlining the Market Order of 2005."

than a legal rule with real teeth. Most of them include neither definition, nor handling procedures and penalties.[60] Thirdly, certain such provisions themselves actually restrict, rather than promote, healthy competition on the market. For instance, the State Planning Commission and the State Commission of Economy and Trade in their "Provisions to Curb Dumping Industrial Products at Predatory Price of 1998" required the state authorities in different trades to first decide the average cost of the trade as the admonitory line of self-discipline and then use it to determine the existence of dumping at a predatory price and the basis on which to penalize the enterprises concerned.[61] As Professor Xiaoye Wang of the Chinese Academy of Social Science pointed out, this practice to determine the trade price and efficiency of a market by the state authority without consideration of competition conditions and business autonomy well illustrated the continuing influence of the old ideology of the planned economy.[62]

Even the State Administration of Industry and Commerce (SAIC) as the state authority responsible for the market supervision has openly admitted the existence of serious problems concerning market competition, including lack of specific legislation and definitions applicable to monopolistic practices, weak control of administrative monopoly, state monopoly in different sectors, lack of professional services and support, ineffective enforcement and penalties, and overlapping government authorities in regulating the market.[63]

Despite the pressing challenges to the healthy development of a market economy in China, the introduction of an anti-monopoly law has been very controversial. From the very beginning, the enactment was opposed by some scholars on the ground that such legislation would be unnecessary and unworkable as the proposed law was riddled with uncertainties and anomalies.[64] Such opposition was echoed by some

[60] For example, art. 21 of the "Advertising Law of 1994" reads that "No advertisement owner, operator, or publisher shall engage in unlawful competition in any form." Art. 29 of the "Harbor Law of 2003" states that "the state encourages and protects fair competition in harbor operation. No harbor operator shall carry out monopolistic and unfair competition conducts and shall not provide service with coercing means".

[61] Arts. 8, 10 and 12 of the Provisions.

[62] Xiaoye Wang, "Regulating conduct to restrict competition by multi-nationals under anti-monopoly law," in Xiaoye Wang (ed.), *New Developments of Competition Law under Globalization* (Beijing: Social Science Academy Press, 2005), pp. 248–9 (in Chinese).

[63] Presentation made by Mr. Xue-zheng Wang of SAIC, China to OECD Global Forum on Competition on October 17–18, 2001, CCNM/GF/COMP/WC (2001).

[64] Williams, *Competition Policy and Law*, p. 162.

government officials who claimed that the current market conditions in China were still premature to the legislation.[65] Although the debate has been open and frank, much of the opposition is associated with the policy and the mentality of the Government to maintain its strong position or influence on the market. Even long after the start of the legislative process, some scholars still questioned the seriousness of the Government's commitment. It is said that the real test for the Government in the anti-monopoly enactment is whether it will give up its monopolistic restriction on market access; otherwise, promulgation of any code or law will not eliminate state monopoly in the market.[66]

Another interesting aspect that reflects the Government's commitment to the introduction of an anti-monopoly law into China is its serious reference to the foreign experience and advice, and good cooperation with foreign governments and organizations. In the course of drafting, several international conferences supported by foreign governments with the participation of international experts were held on Chinese competition legislation.[67] China participated in the OECD Global Forum on Competition in as early as 2001 and made some frank submissions.[68] A couple of drafts of the law were passed to foreign governments and professional organizations for comments. For example, the government branches of the European Union and Japan and the three sections of the American Bar Association all submitted their detailed comments on, and proposals to, the draft of the legislation.[69]

65 Williams, *Competition Policy and Law*, p. 162.

66 Zhaofeng Xue, "What monopoly the government should fight against," *Southern Weekend*, 20 January 2004, available at www.nanfangdaily.com.cn (visited on March 21, 2006) (in Chinese).

67 In 2005 alone two such international conferences were held in China in April and October with Japan and the EU respectively on competition policy and law; also see Williams, *Competition Policy and Law*, p. 175.

68 The submission in recent years included Xuezheng Wang, "Challenges/obstacles faced by competition authorities in achieving greater economic development through the promotion of competition" (2004) 16 CCNM/GF/COMP/WD made on 9 January 2004 and Wang, "The relationship between competition authorities and sectoral regulators" (2005) 9 DAF/COMP/GF/WD made on 12 January 2005.

69 John Yong Ren and Ning Yang, "The imminent release of China's anti-monopoly law: What to expect" (Septemer 2005) *China Law & Practice* 26; the Joint Submission of the American Bar Association's Sections of Antitrust Law, Intellectual Property Law and International Law on the Proposed Anti-Monopoly Law of the People's Republic of China dated August 5, 2005 is available at www.han-wen.com (visited on March 21, 2006).

The decade long legislative efforts, thus far, have produced several versions of drafts, which reflect the progress made, unsettled issues, and the on-going debates at different stages. The brief discussion in this article will primarily focus on the "2006 Draft Law" dated June 22, 2006, which was developed from a draft of 2005 and comments of foreign institutions and professionals. The 2006 Draft includes eight chapters and fifty-six articles. At the very beginning the legislative purposes are stated to prohibit monopolistic conduct, to safeguard fair competition, to protect legitimate rights of consumers and the public interest, and to ensure the healthy development of the socialist market economy in China.[70]

On its surface, the 2006 Draft does not provide any clear definition of "monopolistic conduct," but only sets out three categories of such conduct: (1) any agreement, decision, or other concerted action among undertakings; (2) abuse of dominant market positions by undertakings; and (3) concentration of enterprises that eliminates or restricts competition.[71] Since "undertakings" are only defined to include legal persons, other organizations or natural persons that engage in commodities and services trades,[72] the applicable scope of the law seems to indicate the Government's unwillingness to directly subject the state organs and their monopolized businesses to the jurisdiction of the Law. In the "2005 Draft," the abuse of administrative power by government agencies and their subordinate departments that eliminates or restricts competition was listed in the monopolistic conduct. In the "2006 Draft," administrative monopoly by abusing government powers was deleted from the monopolistic conduct list. Instead, a general statement was added that administrative agencies shall not abuse their powers to eliminate and restrict competition. Thus, on the one hand, abuse of government powers by administrative agencies may not be considered monopolistic conduct as such; on the other hand, the Draft attempts to deal with administrative monopoly with a different approach with separate rules. Chapter 5 of the "2006 Draft" sets out more detailed rules against abuse of their administrative powers, including forced purchase, regional blockage, forced restriction on competition, and eliminating or restricting competition by enactments in violation of the national laws and administrative regulations.[73]

[70] Art. 1 of the Draft Anti-Monopoly Law of the People's Republic of China (2006), on file with the author.

[71] Draft Anti-Monopoly Law, art. 3.

[72] Draft Anti-Monopoly Lawa art. 4.

[73] Draft Anti-Monopoly Law, arts. 26–31.

Any agreement to eliminate or restrict competition among undertakings is prohibited. According to the "2006 Draft," such agreements include those to fix, maintain or change the prices of products; to limit the output or sales of the products; to allocate sale markets or raw material purchasing markets; to limit purchase of new technology or new facilities, or the development of new products or new technology; to jointly boycott transactions;[74] to limit resale prices;[75] or to rig bids.[76] Like the legislation in other jurisdictions, such prohibition is subject to some important exceptions, such as agreements for quality upgrading or efficiency improvement, agreements to deal with economic depression, or agreements to develop new products.[77] However, certain exceptions may not be familiar to some other market economies. For instance, art. 10(5) exempts agreements to safeguard rightful interests of undertakings in foreign trade and economic cooperation. The unclearly defined interests may not only create different treatment of domestic firms in the domestic market depending on whether they can link their otherwise unlawful agreement with export to the international market, but also lead to potential conflict of laws by allowing domestic undertakings to use such prohibitive agreements in China with impacts on the international market.

Abuse of dominant market position is another focus of the proposed legislation. Article 12 of the "2006 Draft" defines "dominant market position" as the market power of one or several undertakings to control the price, quantity or other trading conditions of relevant products so as to eliminate or affect competition within the relevant market. According to the Draft, such a position can be established by the proof of certain key factors, including market share and status of the undertakings concerned as well as the relevant market conditions.[78] A dominant market position may be assumed if a single undertaking's market share accounts for one half or more, or two undertakings that jointly account for two-thirds of the market share or more; or three undertakings that jointly account for three-quarters of the market share or more. In these calculations, undertakings with a market share of less than one-tenth shall be excluded.[79] Once a market dominant position is established, abuse of such a position will be found through trading at a monopolistic high price, predatory pricing, discriminatory treatment,

74 Draft Anti-Monopoly Law, art. 7.
75 Draft Anti-Monopoly Law, art. 8.
76 Draft Anti-Monopoly Law, art. 9.
77 Draft Anti-Monopoly Law, art. 10.
78 Draft Anti-Monopoly Law, art. 13.
79 Draft Anti-Monopoly Law, art. 14.

refusal to deal, exclusive or forced transactions, tie-in schemes, or refusal of access to network.[80]

The "2006 Draft Law" also sets out rules governing market concentration, which arises in the situations of merger or acquisition of substantial assets with, or direct or indirect transfer of control of, other undertaking(s). In the case of market concentration, a mandatory notification by the parties concerned in advance shall be filed with the anti-monopoly authority if the sales of all the undertakings concerned worldwide in the previous year exceed RMB 12 billion and the worldwide sales of any undertaking in the concentration concerned in the preceding year within China exceed RMB 800 million.[81] The concentration that meets the statutory threshold shall not be carried out unless the filing is made subject to the approval of the state anti-monopoly authority.[82]

The proposed concentration shall not be carried forward until the decision of the preliminary examination not to do further review or the final no-objection decision of the anti-monopoly authority is granted. Where no decision of further review is made by the authority within thirty days of receipt of all the filed documents, the proposed concentration may be implemented on the basis of no objection. If the anti-monopoly authority decides it necessary to further examine the proposed concentration, it shall inform the parties concerned and carry out the scrutiny within 90 days of the decision made. In special circumstances, the examination period may be extended by up to 150 days.[83] The major considerations in the government scrutiny include the control and concentration of the undertakings concerned in the market, the possible impacts on market access, consumers, innovation of the technology, the national economic development, the social public interests and other factors that the state authority thinks it necessary to consider.[84] The state anti-monopoly authority may allow certain concentrations on a balance test of positive and negative factors in proposed transactions, or on public interest considerations, although the concept is not defined at all.[85]

The "2006 Draft Law" sets out the rules to establish the Anti-Monopoly Commission under the State Council composed of state ministries and agencies as well as experts.[86] However, in terms of implementation of an anti-monopoly regime in China the powers are apparently divided among the different state organs. Different state enforcement agencies

[80] Draft Anti-Monopoly Law, arts. 15.
[81] Draft Anti-Monopoly Law, art. 24.
[82] Draft Anti-Monopoly Law, art. 17.
[83] Draft Anti-Monopoly Law, arts. 21–2.
[84] Draft Anti-Monopoly Law, art. 23.
[85] Draft Anti-Monopoly Law, art. 24.
[86] Draft Anti-Monopoly Law, art. 32.

may enjoy their powers to formulate anti-monopoly guidelines, and measures, and deal with violations and notification of market concentration in their own jurisdictions.[87] As a result, the authority of the national Anti-Monopoly Commission is limited to adopting relevant competition policies, carrying out research and studies, supervising and coordinating anti-monopoly enforcement.[88]

The "Draft Law" spells out three types of legal liabilities against violations of the law, including criminal liability, administrative penalties ranging from a fine of up to RMB 5 million to compulsory correction of the wrongdoings, and civil compensation to the victims.[89] If an interested undertaking disagrees with the decision of the anti-monopoly authority, the People's Court may conduct judicial review upon the party's petition as the legal remedy.[90] It is noted, however, that the penalties in the "2006 Draft" are much more lenient as compared with the "2005 Draft." For example, the maximum fine is reduced from RMB 10 million to the current RMB 5 million and the civil compensation up to twice the actual loss suffered by the victim is deleted.

Presently, the two most controversial issues on the way to introduce an anti-monopoly law into China are how to establish the anti-monopoly authority in China's government structure and how to develop a consistent legal regime equally applicable to monopolistic practice of both domestic and foreign undertakings. For a long time, different state authorities have claimed their jurisdiction over competition-related matters. Among them the State Administration of Industry and Commerce (SAIC) and the Ministry of Commerce (MOFCOM) are two major players in the power struggle. Although both of them have agreed that the anti-monopoly authority should be formed under the State Council, they have been trying to reserve as much as possible of their own power in the anti-monopoly regime that is to be established. The MOFCOM established its Anti-Monopoly Office responsible "for upsetting market monopoly and regional blockage, preventing monopolistic activities, and promoting the establishment of a unified, open, competitive, and orderly market system."[91] At the same time the SAIC claims that as a government agency directly under the State Council,

[87] Draft Anti-Monopoly Law, art. 34. [88] Draft Anti-Monopoly Law, art. 33.

[89] Draft Anti-Monopoly Law, Chapter 7 entitled Legal Liabilities.

[90] Draft Anti-Monopoly Law, arts. 45–51.

[91] Interview with Mr. Ming Shang, the Director of the Anti-Monopoly Office of the MOFCOM on November 26, 2004, available at http://search.mofcom.gov.cn (visited on February 17, 2006) (in Chinese).

its duties include, *inter alia*, supervising market competition and dealing with violations, such as monopoly and unfair competition.[92] According to the SAIC, currently it has a market supervision team of more than 30,000 officers who have performed their duties on the front line of the market on a daily basis, and thus, is more capable than any other state authorities of performing the regulatory duties.[93]

The "2006 Draft" apparently tries to compromise the heated power struggle by allowing the regulatory and enforcement authority to be shared by different state agencies. However, this approach is strongly opposed by all the scholars involved in the legislation. According to Professor Xiaoye Wang, "No country in the world appoints so many administrative departments to enforce a law to protect market competition. Without a unified and authoritative law enforcement system, the anti-monopoly law will be difficult to be enforced."[94]

Another serious test to the effectiveness of the anti-monopoly law in China is whether the future legislation will ensure a fair level playing field. Given the present strong position of the Government and administrative monopoly in the market and the aggressive expansion of foreign investors in China, the equal application of the anti-monopoly rules to be adopted has been a very sensitive concern of all the market players. In fact, in dealing with the wave of foreign mergers and acquisitions (M&As) after China's accession to the WTO, some state authorities jointly issued the "Interim Provisions on Acquisition of Domestic Enterprises by Foreign Investors" in 2003.[95] In addition to the requirement for compliance with the state industrial and investment policy, the Provisions subject foreign investors to mandatory filing with the MOFCOM and the SAIC for anti-monopoly clearance before the transactions can be proceeded.[96] Although the Provisions are considered not sophisticated

[92] The duty statement of the SAIC, available at www.saic.gov.cn/zhzjg/zhin.html (visited on March 21, 2006).

[93] Presentation of Professor Jiemin Sheng of Peking University at the 7th Annual Conference of Peking University-Hong Kong University Legal Research Centre on December 21, 2005 at the University of Hong Kong.

[94] Quoted from the report entitled "Anti-monopoly draft provokes debates," *China Economic Net*, November 15, 2006; available at http://en.ce.cn/national/ Law/200611/15/t20061115_9428909.shrml (visited on December 20, 2006).

[95] For a general discussion, see Xian Chu Zhang, "New landscape of foreign mergers and acquisitions in China after its WTO accession" (2003) 2 *Journal of Chinese and Comparative Law* 229–55.

[96] Arts. 19 and 20 of the Provisions jointly issued by the MOFCOM, the SAIC, the State Administration of Foreign Exchange and the State Administration of Taxation on March 7, 2003.

enough,[97] some scholars have criticized them for their biased protection of domestic enterprises.[98]

In May 2004 the SAIC published an investigation report entitled "Multinationals' Activities to Restrict Competition in China and the Counter-Measures" to support the acceleration of the anti-monopoly legislation. According to the report, some multinationals have obtained their dominant market position in China with monopolistic tendencies in several business sectors. Large multinationals, such as Eastman Kodak, Microsoft, and Tetra Pak were named in the SAIC's investigation and accusation list. Some other unnamed transnational companies were also found to build up their dominant positions in China with their technological, capital and managerial advantages. According to the report, the multinationals' aggressive expansion has constituted a threat to the safety of the national economy.[99] In 2005 before the "Draft Law" was submitted to the State Council for review, the Commission of State Assets Management made an open and high profile statement that in the transitional period the state authority ought to be more involved in the development of state-owned enterprises to prevent any shaking-up of the leading position of the public ownership in China. Mr. Rong-Rong Li, the Director of the State Commission, even warned that irresponsible withdrawal of the public economy from the market will not only prevent the state sector from playing its major role in the national economy, but cause more troubles.[100]

The MOFCOM, however, apparently disagrees with such a radical position. In a research paper published later by the Research Institute of the MOFCOM, it argued that foreign investment that had made an important contribution to China's economic development, neither threatened the economic safety of China nor controlled the technology market and any sensitive business sector. Thus, the expansion of foreign investment should not be frightened by the anti-monopoly legislation in China.[101] Mr. Ming

[97] Emma Davies and Cheng Li Yow, "China's anti-trust regime" (April 2005) *China Law & Practice* 24.

[98] Ling Ping, "Anti-Monopoly control on enterprise mergers and acquisitions in China" in Xiaoye Wang (ed.), *New Developments of Competition Law under Globalization* (Beijing: Social Science Academy Press, 2005), pp. 33–8 and 282 (in Chinese).

[99] The report was printed in *Journal of State Administration of Industry and Commerce*, vol. 5 (May 2004) (in Chinese).

[100] See the report of the speech of Mr. Rong-Rong Li, available at http://finance.qianlong.com/26/2005/01/21/206@2483110.htm (visited on January 22, 2005) (in Chinese).

[101] Hua Lin, "Are multinationals really practicing monopoly?" (2005) 1 *Foreign Investment in China*, available at http://search.mofcom.gov.cn (visited on February 17, 2006) (in Chinese).

Shang, the Head of the Treaty and Law Department and the Director of the Anti-Monopoly Investigation Office of the MOFCOM, further pointed out that the anti-monopoly law should be equally applied to both domestic and foreign enterprises. The anti-monopoly enactment should aim at promoting and safeguarding fair competition of all kinds of enterprises on the market while preventing monopolistic activities.[102]

The divergence in the drafting of the anti-monopoly law seems to have escalated and led to a further twist in 2006. In early 2006, in an interview Mr. Deshui Li, the Director General of the National Bureau of Statistics, warned that foreign "malicious" M&As in China would threaten the economic security and national sovereignty and called for action to curb the multinationals in China.[103] Against this background, the State Assets Management Commission revealed its plan to make 30–50 huge state-owned enterprise groups as the national champions by 2020 through M&As and state support.[104] On the other hand, Mr. Jingyan Hu, the Director of Foreign Investment Department of the MOFCOM, continued to openly refute the proposition against the expansion of foreign businesses in China. According to him, in no business sector with material national interests have foreign market percentages exceeded 3 percent. As such, currently there is neither emerging foreign monopoly in any region or business sector, nor any foreign control of economic lifeline in China.[105]

Despite the obvious disagreement, the "Provisions on Mergers and Acquisitions of Domestic Enterprises by Foreign Investors" was jointly promulgated by the MOFCOM, the SAIC, the Commission of State Assets Management, the State Taxation Administration, the China Securities Regulatory Commission and the State Foreign Exchange Administration on August 8, 2006. According to the "Provisions," foreign M&As shall not be allowed if they cause over-concentration, eliminating or restricting competition, disturbing the social and economic

[102] Interview with Mr. Ming Shang.

[103] Mure Dickie, "Chinese official demands curbs on 'Malicious' buying by multinationals," *The Financial Express*, March 12, 2006, available at www.financialexpress-bd.com (visited on May 9, 2006).

[104] See the report on Chinainfobank entitled "Centrally controlled enterprises entering into a big leap forward period" dated May 8, 2006, available at www.chinainfobank.com (visited on May 9, 2005); and the report on the MOFCOM website entitled "30 Large-sized enterprise groups to be fostered by 2020" dated November 18, 2005; available at http://search.mofcom.gov.cn (visited on May 9, 2006) (in Chinese).

[105] See the report of Xinhua News Agency dated January 17, 2006, available at www.sccwto.net:7000/wto/content.jsp?id=12385 (visited on March 23, 2006) (in Chinese).

order as well as social public interests, or loss of state assets.[106] For this purpose, a compulsory application procedure is created for foreign M&As that lead to *de facto* control in key industries and may affect the national economic safety or transfer control over well-known trademarks or enterprises of China.[107] Moreover, a foreign M&A must be reported to the MOFCOM and the SAIC if the foreign investor's annual sales in China exceed RMB 150 million, the number of domestic enterprises in the relevant business it has taken over within a year exceed ten, the foreign party's market share in China has reached 20 percent, and the proposed M&A would result in a 25 percent market share of the foreign party in China. Even if these thresholds are not met, any competing domestic enterprise in a given industry, government department or business association may still petition the MOFCOM and the SAIC to require the foreign party to submit a report on the ground that the proposed M&A involves a huge market share, or would seriously affect the market competition.[108] The proposed M&A shall be disapproved if the hearing involving relevant parties finds that the transaction would lead to over-concentration, hinder rightful competition, or damage consumers' interests.[109] Furthermore, for the first time, some rules on overseas foreign M&As with impacts in China are stipulated in the "Provisions."[110] As such, as compared with the provisions of the "2006 Draft Law" the "Provisions" seem to set out some different rules with tougher standards specifically applicable to foreign M&As in China.

At the same time, to what extent the anti-monopoly legislation will eliminate administrative monopoly in the market also provoked further controversy. It was reported that the draft version at the end of 2005 deleted all the provisions against administrative monopoly, except one empty policy declaration that abuse of administrative power by the government branches to eliminate or restrict competition would be prohibited. As a result, the "Draft Law" would merely deal with monopoly concerning business entities. According to some insiders, the deletion was made after a heated debate in December 2005 and represented the victory of the so-called "elimination by reform" school. It believes that the problem of administrative monopoly cannot be effectively dealt with by the anti-monopoly law, but further institutional reform, which

[106] Art. 3 of the Provisions dated August 8, 2006.

[107] Provisions dated August 8, 2006, art. 12.

[108] Provisions dated August 8, 2006, art. 51.

[109] Provisions dated August 8, 2006, art. 52. Art. 54 sets out certain grounds for exemption.

[110] Provisions dated August 8, 2006, art. 53.

may not have any definite timetable. Hence, it may not be appropriate to assign the political task to this single legislation.[111]

Although the deletion may make the legislation on its face look more like the enactments in other market economies with their focus on market monopolistic activities, the crucial concerns with the administrative monopoly in China are completely left out and thus the value of the legislation will be significantly diminished. As a result, the characteristic of the so-called socialist market economy in China will continue to be deeply concerned with other market players. In this context, the Draft has been criticized by domestic experts. According to them, the current version, that authorizes a government authority to correct abuse of power of other government departments that hampers market competition, would simply mean the anti-monopoly law enforcement organ may have limited authority to curb administrative monopoly.[112] Multinationals, although praising the government's continuing effort to improve the "Draft Law," do not hide their worries about more market barriers in the market created by the new draft. Some foreign experts even believe that there is a danger that the anti-monopoly law may become an instrument to protect the state monopoly.[113]

III. A brief comparison of the competition law regimes in India and China

A complete comparison of the anti-monopoly regimes in the two countries is certainly beyond the scope of this short piece, but some preliminary observations may be made on the basis of the review above.

The experience of the two countries in developing an anti-monopoly legal regime shares some important similarities. Both India and China have recognized an anti-monopoly regime as a crucial institution to support the efficiency of their market development and have realized the urgency to develop such a regime as part of their competitive edge in the global economy. As stated by Mr. Chidambaram, the Finance

[111] See the report of Hong Kong *Commercial Daily*, January 12, 2006, available at www.fayhoo.com/servlet/info.infolanmuxx?lmid=20100104&id=20060112:1515128 (visited on March 21, 2006) (in Chinese); also Williams, *Competition Policy and Law*, pp. 158–9.

[112] "Shri Prem Chand Gupta hopes competition commission would be functional."

[113] See the MOFCOM report entitled "The Draft Anti-Monopoly Law causes worries in the West," available at http://search.mofcom.gov.cn (visited on February 17, 2006) (in Chinese); and Peter A. Neumann and Tony Zhang, "China's new foreign-funded M&A provisions: Greater legal protection or legalized protectionism?," (Oct. 2006) *China Law & Practice* 21–9.

Minister of India, "a world class legal system is absolutely essential to support an economy that aims to be a world class. India needs to take a hard look at commercial laws and the system of dispensing justice in commercial matters."[114] Given that competition law and competition authorities have been established in over ninety countries in the world, competition and liberalization are considered essential to unleash the entrepreneurial force in the economy and to stimulate innovation and the optimum allocation of resources.[115]

Such enthusiasm has been echoed in China. According to Mr. Shang Ming of the MOFCOM, the importance of introducing an anti-monopoly law into China links up with the establishment of a market economy in China, the enhancement of the Chinese enterprises' competitiveness, and compliance with international market disciplines.[116] In the "2005 Reform Plan," the State Council has specifically required the acceleration of the promulgation of the anti-monopoly law.[117] Recently, the long delay of the enactment has also raised concerns among deputies of the National People's Congress.[118]

Establishment of an effective competition and anti-monopoly regime in both India and China may also have profound political implications where political democracy needs to be further developed. As an economic level playing field is being built up for more equal competition, the model of totalitarian governance will inevitably be challenged. As such, it would be a daunting question to be answered in both countries as to whether political democracy and judicial activism can support economic growth. In this regard, although the people in India may have more opportunities to express their will through the ballot box as compared with the people in China, the process of liberalization to promote private investment and the privatization of profitable state

[114] P. Chidambaram, "Law and commerce: And the twain shall meet," *Sunday Express* (Ahmedabad, October 26, 2003).

[115] Speech of Mr. Shri Vinor Dhall as member of the Competition Commission of India on January 15, 2005 at Indian Paint Industry Conference, available at http://competition-commission-india.nic.in (visited on March 2, 2006).

[116] Shang Ming, "The present conditions of anti-monopoly legislation in China," in Xiaoye Wang (ed.), *New Developments of Competition Law under Globalization* (Beijing: Social Science Academy Press, 2005), pp. 4–5.

[117] s. 6 of the "Opinions of the State Council on deepening economic system reform in 2005" dated April 19, 2005, available at http://search.mofcom.gov.cn (visited on January 25, 2006).

[118] See the report on the website of the MOFCOM dated March 8, 2006, available at http://search.mofcom.gov.cn (visited on April 5, 2006) (in Chinese).

enterprises has been and will be slow.[119] In the context of China, the enactment has been viewed as a catalyst to accelerate political reform,[120] and has raised the expectations of the private sector for the law to fight for fair market access and environment.[121]

Moreover, both China and India, although having paid close attention to the experiences of the European Union and the United States in developing their anti-monopoly legal regimes, have insisted that the models of such developed economies may not be entirely suitable to the needs of developing countries with very different social-political and economic conditions.[122] In China, some experts argue that in a developing country like China, its current economic conditions should be adequately considered in formulating its competition law and policy. As a result, the promotion of the domestic economic efficiency should be the primary goal of anti-monopoly legislation. Thus, the "national champion" approach should be carefully considered from the viewpoint of China's needs.[123]

Both India and China as two giant developing countries have been facing infrastructural and resource difficulties in developing their anti-monopoly regimes. For example in India, the primary dependence of the CCI on the government resource for funding may negatively affect the institutional independence and credibility of the agent and the inadequate budget could seriously impair the effectiveness of the Commission. One recent study found that the budget allocation to the Commission was just about 0.0009 percent of the total government budget, which was even lower than a small and poor country like Zambia with 0.005 percent of the national budget allocated to its Competition Commission. This may even be taken as evidence to show the Government's failure to take the regime seriously.[124] Moreover, it may be difficult with the salaries provided by the Government to attract and

[119] Hilary K. Josephs, "Legal institutions and their 'proper' place in economic development: India and China compared" (2004), available at http://ssrn.com/abstract=572165; also see Editorial, "Coming down to earth," *The Economist*, May 29, 2004, p. 25.

[120] Xiaoye Wang, "Accelerating the adoption of China's Anti-monopoly Law with its WTO accession," at 2, available at www.iolaw.org.cn/ shownews.asp?id=242 (visited on June 7, 2005) (in Chinese).

[121] See the report of the website of the Ministry of Commerce dated April 22, 2005, available at http://search.mofcom.gov.cn (visited on May 4,2006) (in Chinese).

[122] Agarwal, "Competition law in India," 4–5.

[123] Yong Huang and Zhiqiang Li, "Conflict of laws and international cooperation in antitrust enforcement," in Xiaoye Wang (ed.), *New Developments of Competition Law under Globalization* (Beijing: Social Science Academy Press, 2005), pp. 224–5 (in Chinese).

[124] See CUTS (Customer Unity and Trust Society) International, "Pulling up our stocks: A study of competition regime of seven developing countries of Africa and Asia under

retain a very small number of capable professionals with the knowledge and skills needed. As a result, capacity building will be a long-lasting task in India.[125]

In China, the market reforms have trimmed the oversized Government dramatically. Since the late 1990s, the number of government staff has been cut by 1.15 million and the number of ministerial units under the Central Government has been reduced from 40 to 29.[126] Recently, an unprecedented document entitled the "Key Working Points of the State Council of 2006" was issued with the emphasis on improving efficiency and the rationalization of resource allocation.[127] Against this background, some scholars consider that it would be difficult for the Central Government to establish a high-level anti-monopoly agency with a sufficient number of staff and resources to support its full authority and function.[128] The lack of expertise in China will further challenge the function of the anti-monopoly regime to be established. In this regard, a recent study found that there are few officials with professional qualification and specialized knowledge capable of carrying out their duties of competition law enforcement.[129]

The two countries also offer different experiences in the course of developing their competition legal regimes. First of all, in developing such a regime and a sound competition policy, China has lagged far behind India. This is reflected not only in the accumulated experience in the enactment and practice of the past four decades, but also in the different level of democratic development and depth of research support. In this context, India's contribution to the discussion on trade and competition policy issues within the WTO and the close attention to competition advocacy in formulating its anti-monopoly law and competition policy are two telling examples.

India actively participated in the discussion of the so-called "Singapore Issues" and the Doha Round Negotiation, which originally

the 7-up project" (2003), at 14–15, available at www.cuts-international.org/pulling.pdf (visited on April 12, 2006).

125 Dhall, "Competition policy and multilateral trading," 9–10.

126 See the report dated October 30, 2002 at the Chinainfobank, available at www.chinainfobank.com (visited on March 23, 2006) (in Chinese).

127 See the report of *Outlook Weekly*, April 3, 2006 (in Chinese).

128 Presentation of Professor Jiemin Sheng of Peking University at the 7th Annual Conference of the Legal Research Centre of Peking University and the University of Hong Kong on December 21, 2005.

129 Liu Ningyuan (ed.), *Study on Antitrust Law Enforcement System in China and Foreign Countries* (Beijing: Beijing University Press, 2005), p. 318.

included a negotiation agenda on trade and competition policy until 2004 when it was deleted.[130] In this course, India took a bifurcate approach. On the one hand, being supported by other developing countries, the Indian Government insisted that the negotiation could not be taken up until developing countries' concerns about the implementation of existing WTO agreements were addressed. The Government further held that the competition policy should be implemented to safeguard the public interest with the emphasis on cost minimization, profit maximization and the optimal use of resources;[131] at the same time, it took a position against the European Union's (EU) proposal to extend the "national treatment" principle automatically to the competition policies of WTO members.[132] Under the Doha mandate, India insists that a sustainable competition regime should be maintained by different countries by either integrating public interest considerations into their laws, or by creating exceptions or by enforcing their laws in a particular way.[133] On the other hand, the cautious position and the failure of the negotiation on this issue in the WTO did not prevent India from further developing its own competition legal regime. In the course of the Doha Round Negotiation, India modernized its regime by adopting the new "Competition Act 2002," which has been praised by Western countries as "WTO-plus-plus."[134] The Indian approach that refuses a non-discriminatory competition regime in developing its domestic institution against aggressive operations of international cartels has been recognized as a proactive industry policy dealing with the negative effects of the globalization within the WTO network.[135]

[130] In July 2004 the General Council of the WTO decided that the interaction between trade and competition policy would no longer form part of the Doha Round Negotiation. The WTO decision is available at www.wto.org.

[131] The Ministry of Commerce of the Government of India, "Report of the Expert Group on interaction between trade and competition policy" (1999), para. 1.4.12.

[132] See WTO document: *Communication from India*, WT/WGTCP/W/216, September 26, 2002.

[133] Markus W. Gehring, "Sustainable competition law for the 2003 Fifth Session of the Ministerial Conference of the WTO in Cancun" (September 10–14, 2003), available at www.cisdl.org/pdf/Cancun_WTO_LegalBrief2.pdf (visited on May 16, 2007).

[134] See the report, "FDI behind India's stance: Larmy," *Business Standard*, March 15–16, 2003, p. 2.

[135] Aditya Bhattacharjea, "India's competition policy: An assessment" (August 23, 2003) 34 *Economic and Policy Weekly* 3561–74; and Josef Drexl, "International competition policy after Cancún: Placing a Singapore issue on the Doha Development agenda," in Xiaoye Wang (ed.), *New Developments of Competition Law under Globalization* (Beijing: Social Science Academy Press, 2005), pp. 188–9 (quoted from the Chinese translation).

Another important aspect of the competition law development in India is its close attention to competition advocacy, which is particularly recognized by a research study of the Asian Development Bank (ADB). Some specific provisions of the "Competition Act 2002" seek to form a direct relationship between competition advocacy and competition law enforcement in order to foster conditions that will lead to a more competitive market structure and business behavior, thus avoiding the need for intervention and enforcement by the competition agency.[136] In this course, building public awareness of the competition policy, fostering a competition culture, and providing professional training are all identified as formidable tasks.[137]

As compared with India, China's short WTO membership has not allowed her to develop any sophisticated theories and positions to deal with the Doha Negotiation of the WTO. A recent search on the website of the Ministry of Commerce does not reveal any official policy statement or submission in this regard.[138] However, according to Professor Xiaoye Wang, a leading expert on competition law in China,[139] the proposal of the EU to establish a uniform competition regime within the WTO framework was widely supported and China should take a proactive attitude to participate in the multilateral negotiation. She further believed that such an agreement would restrain the multinationals' unfair competition in China and thus, China should accept the non-discriminatory application of national treatment as proposed by the EU.[140] This position appears quite different from the one insisted on by the Indian Government and scholars.[141]

136 Asian Development Bank, *Asian Development Outlook 2005* (Chapter III: Competitive Policy Regime), available at www.adb.org/documents/books/ado/2005/ado2005.pdf (visited on May 16, 2007).

137 Competition Commission of India, "Public awareness on competition law and policy," 14–16.

138 The search was conducted by the author on May 1, 2006 at www.mofcom.org.cn.

139 For a brief introduction of Professor Wang, see Williams, *Competition Policy and Law*, p. 156.

140 Wang, "Regulating conduct to restrict competition," pp. 306–10.

141 In addition to the official documents quoted above, some scholars' works also deserve mentioning. Professor A. Bhattacharjea of the University of Delhi, for example, argued that developing countries should not allow themselves to be enticed into an agreement unilaterally in favor of developed countries and thus, India should resist a multilateral agreement on competition. Bhattacharjea, "India's competition policy," 3570–3. Also see R. Basant and S. Morris, *Competition Policy in India: Issues for a Globalising Economy* (Ahmedabad: Indian Institute of Management, 2000), p. 157; Aditya Bhattacharjea, "Export cartel: A developing country perspective" (April 2004) 38(2) *Journal of World Trade* 331–59.

Beyond the policy concerns, the role of the judiciary in the two countries in enforcing the relevant laws may also demonstrate different landscapes. In India, although the Constitution of India does not formally provide the doctrine of separation of powers in its absolute rigidity, the Supreme Court has held that it is one of the basic features of the Constitution. Judicial review has been used as a powerful weapon to restrain any unconstitutional act of the Government. In recent years, the traditional judicial passive role is being shifted to judicial creative activism to address the changing needs of the society.[142] In this regard, the Supreme Court's decision on the challenge to the "Competition Act 2002" and its consequence leading to the division of powers in different natures into the CCI and the CAT may serve as the best examples of the high independence and the full constitutional guarantee of the judicial function in India.

By contrast, in China the checks and balances principle has not been recognized and thus, the judiciary may have limited independence and is subject to the budgetary and personnel control of the Government as well as its policy influence. As a result, despite the continuing reform in the last decade, the quality of the judiciary and judicial independence and impartiality still face some serious problems.[143] Thus, it is said that the legal system in India as part of its strong infrastructure, while not without substantial flaws, is considerably more advanced than that in China.[144]

Such an infrastructure gap may be illustrated by an interesting case in China where a patient in Sichuan Province found there was no medicine's name on her prescription issued by a local hospital, but only some unreadable code so that the medicine could only be purchased from the hospital. She filed her complaint with the local office of the SAIC. The investigation found that the hospital was selling some outdated drugs and the unreadable code violated the patient's right to information as stipulated in the "Anti-Unfair Competition Law." However, the hospital filed an action against the local SAIC for unlawful enforcement. The People's Court ruled in favor of the hospital on the ground that the hospital was only subject to the supervision of the public health department and thus, the SAIC had no authority to carry out its enforcement

142 Subhash C. Jain, *The Constitution of India: Select Issues & Perceptions* (New Delhi: Taxmann, 2000), pp. 157–9.

143 Albert Hongyi Chan, *An Introduction to the Legal System of the People's Republic of China*, 3rd edn (Hong Kong: LexisNexis, 2004), pp. 131–59.

144 Huang and Khanna, "Can India overtake China?" 75.

measures. The appeal of the SAIC put the People's Court in a very difficult position between two state authorities. Finally, the case ended with a conciliation of the parties involved for the sake of both sides saving face. The judges, when being interviewed, indicated that in such a tough situation, the Court may not be able to firmly support the implementation of anti-monopoly/unfair competition rules.[145]

A closely related concern in this context is the independence of the competition authority. In India, even after the "Competition (Amendment) Bill 2006" was introduced, the provision of funding by the Government to the CCI and the binding force of the directions of the Government on CCI continue to worry practitioners for their negative impacts on the CCI's independence. CUTS International has further proposed establishing a committee under Parliament as the authority responsible for the CCI's accountability.[146] But in China, under the current draft the anti-monopoly authority will be subordinate to the Central Government with the administrative personnel and budgetary control; as a result, the independence and impartiality of such an authority can hardly be guaranteed. Moreover, assignment of the anti-monopoly function to a government branch against, *inter alia*, administrative monopoly would lead to potential conflict of interest and weakening of its authority. As such, the authority under the current designs is not able to effectively carry out its duties.[147] According to a recent report of the SAIC, since 1993, over 5,600 monopoly cases have been dealt with; among them administrative monopoly counted for only 519. The reason provided is not because there are not many such violations, but because the SAIC is not able to effectively deal with this kind of case.[148]

Indeed, both India and China have to deal with administrative monopoly problems in developing their economies. However, the conditions in the two countries are quite different. In India, the so-called "natural monopoly" still exists in infrastructure fields such as airports, railway lines, roads, electricity, oil, gas, power and telecommunications with the government's strong ownership and the ambivalent attitude on many

[145] Chuanhui Wang, *Economic Analysis of Anti-Monopoly Law* (China: People's University Press of China, 2004), pp. 277–90 (in Chinese).

[146] CUTS International, "The Competition (Amendment) Bill 2006" (2006) 2 *Bill Blowup* 4.

[147] Bingsheng Zhang, "On design of anti-monopoly enforcement authority in China: Questions to the current plans" (2005) 2 *Legal Science (Journal of Northwestern College of Political Science and Law)* 117–19 (in Chinese).

[148] See the report of *Commercial Daily* (Hong Kong), January 12, 2006 (in Chinese).

aspects of competition under a kind of softer brand of socialism. However, the new "Competition Act" has developed the regime to a new stage which encourages competition and where more private service providers have been allowed, despite the slow pace, to access the infrastructure sectors.[149] Although some anti-competitive activities are still rampant at the state level,[150] the current Government has been seriously committed to improving competition conditions in the market and has carried out some profound reforms. For instance, in the past thirty years, almost all business sectors, except three, have been open to private investors; the ownership limit on foreign direct investment in high priority industries has been raised from 40% to 51% and further to 74%; the government's additional approval for large or dominant enterprises under the old "Monopolies and Restrictive Trade Practice Act" was abolished; in many industries, approval for foreign controlling ownership may be automatically granted. The securities market has become pretty competitive and transparent.[151] The President of India in his Address to the Parliament on June 7, 2004 stated that "Competition, both domestic and external, will be deepened across industry with professionally run regulatory institutions in place to ensure that competition is free and fair. . . . My government will devolve full managerial and commercial autonomy to successful, profit-making companies operating in a competitive environment."[152] As such, despite the existing defects, India has developed a preliminary level playing field for all market players.

By contrast, in China, the implementation of a foreign-direct-investment-driven and export-orientated manufacturing approach for over twenty-five years has inevitably led to the accumulation and domination of foreign investment in some areas and the Government's ferocious protection of the state sector from competition has created even further market concentration with dominating powers.[153] Thus, although both China and India as developing countries have been supporting a strategy of promoting "national champions," the potential abuse and impairing impacts on private sector development are much more serious in China. As Professor

[149] S. L. Rao, "Competition in infrastructure," available at www.cuts-international.org (visited on April 23, 2006).

[150] Pradeep S. Mehta, *Towards a Functional Competition Policy for India: An Overview* (New Delhi: Academic Foundation, 2005), p. 9.

[151] Bhattacharjea, "Trade, investment, and competition policy," pp. 204–5; Linda S. Spedding, *Trade and Investment in India: Economic Development and Environmental Issues* (London: Cameron May, 1997), pp. 18–20 and 66–7.

[152] Quoted from Mehta, *Towards a Functional Competition Policy*, p. 2.

[153] Huang and Khanna, "Can India overtake China?" 75–6.

Yasheng Huang of MIT pointed out, excessively relying on foreign investment is a reflection of the irrational domestic financial and legal system, which will inevitably lead to aggressive expansion of multinationals in China. Moreover, the development under this model is made at the cost of the development of the domestic sectors. As such, the crucial problem facing China is not excessively opening to foreign investors, but seriously insufficient opening to the domestic private sector.[154] In this regard the economic and institutional liberalization in China is much more difficult because not only may the private sector bring in more competition to the market, particularly to the state enterprises, but also privatization has been highly sensitive in China as a socialist country.[155]

The contradictory approach of the Chinese Government has been openly criticized. According to some scholars, the biased anti-monopoly enactment on the ground of national economic safety with the different standards applicable to domestic administrative monopoly and foreign expansion respectively would deprive the essence of the law and further hurt the domestic consumers who have suffered from the callous administrative monopoly for a long time. In this sense, the foreign M&As in China, which have subjected the Government and the public sector to competitive pressure and accelerated the anti-monopoly legislation, are even thought of as a catalyst from the perspective of the rule of law development in China.[156] Moreover, it is predicted that the biased competition legislation will have much vitality.[157]

As compared with the disparities in the institutional infrastructure, political ideology and market orientation of India and China, the technical differences of the current competition regimes of the two countries seem to become less important. As reflected above, the regimes of the two countries differ in their basic philosophy, objectives, application

[154] An interview with Professor Yasheng Huang of MIT dated February 16, 2006: "2006, the year of India or the year of China?", available at http://www2.chinesenewsnet.com, (in Chinese); for a more detailed analysis, see Yasheng Huang, *Selling China: Foreign Direct Investment during the Reform Era* (Cambridge: Cambridge University Press, 2003).

[155] Even after the reform of over two decades, privatization is still a dirty world in China. See the Editorial, "China's coming recession," *The Economist*, May 2, 1998, p. 11; Toshiki Kanamori and Zhijun Zhao, *Private Sector Development in the People's Republic of China* (Tokyo: Asian Development Bank Institute, 2004), particularly Chapter 4 discussing lack of a level playing field and the biased policy, pp. 43–57; and Asian Development Bank, *Private Sector Assessment: The People's Republic of China* (Philippines: Asian Development Bank, 2003), particularly on policy bias and legal environment, pp. 32–40.

[156] Qiu Feng, "The logical disarray of anti-monopoly," *Southern Municipal Daily*, March 16, 2006, p. A3 (in Chinese).

[157] Wang, "Regulating conduct to restrict competition," p. 282.

scope, legal status of the anti-monopoly authority and function design, legal standards to determine monopolistic conducts, investigation procedures and legal remedies. The competition law in India as the second generation framework is apparently more advanced with further government commitment, better market environment, stronger institutional support, particularly the rule of law and more flexible common law approach, and a fair and transparent level playing field. In China, the current enactment of the anti-monopoly law is considered just a first step toward a credible competition policy.[158]

IV. Conclusion

In the course of dynamic economic taking-off, both China and India are taking active measures to establish and modernize their competition regimes as an important institution to support the national development. Although the two developing giants share in some aspects common concerns and face similar challenges, the different political, legal and market conditions seem to reflect more disparities in their breaking paths, which will be valuable experiences to the world. On the international level, the latest Global Competitiveness Report of the World Economic Forum ranked China and India 49th and 50th respectively.[159] This reality will not only shed more light on the two giants' economic competition, but also raise the importance of their learning from each other. As such, a recent article published in an influential journal in China on a comparative study of the capital markets of China and India concluded with a call for China to learn from, in addition to developed countries, India for its experience to develop a more open and advanced market.[160]

[158] Nathan Bush, "Chinese competition policy: It takes more than a law" (May–June 2005) *The China Business Review* 30.

[159] See the Xinhua News Agency report dated 10 December 2005, available at www.southcn.com/news/china/zgkx/200512100126.htm (visited on March 10, 2006).

[160] Shu Mei, "The capital market of China should learn from India," *Southern Weekend*, March 2, 2006, p. C23.

References

Accenture Policy and Corporate Affairs Practice, "China and India: Partners in competition" (2005), available at www.accenture.com/NR/rdonlyres/4D8920BC-4590–4868-B9DB-94DC58EA3B34/0/pca_china_india.pdf (visited on May 16, 2007)

Agarwal, Anurag K., "Competition law in India: Need to go slow and steady" (October 2005) Working Paper no. 2005-10-05 of India Institute of Management, at 6, available at www.iimahd.ernet.in/publications/data/2005–10–05anurag.pdf (visited on May 16, 2007)

American Bar Association, Joint Submission of the American Bar Association's Sections of Antitrust Law, Intellectual Property Law and International Law on the Proposed Anti-Monopoly Law of the People's Republic of China dated August 5, 2005 is available at www.han-wen.com (visited on March 21, 2006)

American Bar Association, "Anti-monopoly draft provokes debates," *China Economic Net*, November 15, 2006, available at http://en.ce.cn/national/Law/200611/15/t20061115_9428909.shtml (visited on January 4, 2007)

"Anti-monopoly draft provokes debates," *Chinese Economic Net*, November 15, 2006, available at http://en.ce.cn/national/Law/200611/15/t20061115_9428909.shtml (visited on January 4, 2007)

Asian Development Bank, *Asian Development Outlook 2005* (Chapter III: Competitive Policy Regime), available at www.adb.org/documents/books/ado/2005/ado2005.pdf (visited on May 16, 2007)

Private Sector Assessment: The People's Republic of China (Philippines: Asian Development Bank, 2003)

Basant, R. and Morris, S., *Competition Policy in India: Issues for a Globalising Economy* (Ahmedabad: Indian Institute of Management, 2000)

Bhattacharjea, Aditya, "Amending India's Competition Act," *The Economic and Political Weekly*, October 14, 2006

"Exportcartel: A developing country perspective" (April 2004) 38(2) *Journal of World Trade*

"India's competition policy: An assessment" (August 23, 2003) 34 *Economic and Policy Weekly* 3561–7

"India's trade relations with China and Russia in the context of the WTO" (2005) 41(4) *China Report* 432

"Trade, investment, and competition policy: An Indian perspective," in Aaditya Mattoo and Robert M. Stern (eds.), *India and the WTO* (Oxford University Press, 2002)

Bhattacharya, Sanjukta Banerji (ed.), *India at the End of the Twentieth Century: Essays on Politics, Society, and the Economy* (New Delhi: Lancer's Books, 2001)

Brooks, Douglas H., "Competition policy and development" (October 2005) Economics and Research Department (ERD) Policy Brief No. 39, at 2, available at www.asiandevbank.org/Documents/EDRC/Policy_Briefs/PB039.pdf (visited on May 16, 2007)

"Bush warns against isolation," *International Herald Tribune*, February 2, 2006

Bush, Nathan, "Chinese competition policy: It takes more than a law" (May–June 2005) *The China Business Review* 30

Cerra, Valerie, Rivera, Sandra A., and Saxena, Sweta Chaman, "Crouching tiger, hidden dragon: What are the consequences of China's WTO entry for India's trade?" (2005) *International Monetary Fund Working Paper* WP/05/101, available at www.imf.org/external/ pubs/ft/wp/2005/wp05101.pdf (visited on May 16, 2007)

Chan, Albert Hongyi, *An Introduction to the Legal System of the People's Republic of China*, 3rd edn (Hong Kong: LexisNexis, 2004)

Chen, Kuan-I and Uppal, J. S., *Comparative Development of India and China* (New Delhi: Free Press, 1971)

Chidambaram, P., "Law and commerce: And the twain shall meet," *Sunday Express* (Ahmedabad), October 26, 2003)

China Business Law Guide (Singapore: CCH Asia Pte Ltd, 2004)

Chinainfobank, "Centrally controlled enterprises entering into a big leap forward period" dated May 8, 2006, available at www.chinainfobank.com (visited on May 9, 2005)

"Competition Act Amendment Bill introduced in Lok Sabha," *The Hindu Business Line*, available at www.thehindubusinessline.com/2006/03/10/stories/2006031003300800.htm (visited on March 28, 2006)

Competition Commission of India, "Public awareness on competition law and policy" (2003), at 2–3, available at http://competition-commission-india.nic.in (visited on January 23, 2006)

"Competition panel can't rule on legal issues," *Economic Times News Network*, March 10, 2006, available at http://economictimes.indiatimes.com/ articleshow/1444854.cms (visited on March 13, 2006)

CUTS (Customer Unity and Trust Society) International, "The Competition (Amendment) Bill 2006: What needs to be done?" (2006) 2 *Bill Blowup*, available at www.cuts-international.org (visited on April 30, 2006)

"Pulling up our stocks: A study of competition regime of seven developing countries of Africa and Asia under the 7-up project" (2003), available at www.cuts-international.org/pulling.pdf (visited on April 12, 2006)

Davies, Emma and Yow, Cheng Li, "China's anti-trust regime" (April 2005) *China Law & Practice* 24

Dethier, Jean-Jacques (ed.), *Governance, Decentralization and Reform in China, India, and Russia* (Boston MA: Kluwer Academic Publishers, 2000)

Dhall, Shri Vinor, Speech of Mr. Shri Vinor Dhall as member of the Competition Commission of India on January 15, 2005 at Indian Paint Industry Conference, available at http://competition-commission-india.nic.in (visited on March 2, 2006)

Dhall, Vinod, "Competition policy and multilateral trading," speech made on WTO/UNESCAP/ASCI Regional Seminar for Asia and Pacific Economies at Hyderabad on October 6, 2004, p. 5, available at http://competition-commission-india.nic.in (visited on January 23, 2006)

Dickie, Mure, "Chinese official demands curbs on 'Malicious' buying by multinationals," *The Financial Express*, March 12, 2006, available at www.financialexpress-bd.com (visited on May 9, 2006)

Drexl, Josef, "International competition policy after Cancun: Placing a Singapore issue on the Doha Development agenda," in Xiaoye Wang (ed.), *New Developments of Competition Law under Globalization* (Beijing: Social Science Academy Press, 2005) (quoted from the Chinese translation)

Editorial, "China's coming recession," *The Economist*, May 2, 1998

Editorial, "Coming down to earth," *The Economist*, May 29, 2004

"FDI behind India's stance: Larmy," *Business Standard*, March 15–16, 2003

Feng, Qiu, "The logical disarray of anti-monopoly," *Southern Municipal Daily*, March 16, 2006 (in Chinese)

Frankel, Francine R. and Harding, Harry (eds.), *The India–China Relationship: What the United States Needs to Know* (New York: Columbia University Press, 2004)

Freshfields (ed.), *Doing Business in China* (New York: Juris Publishing Inc., 2006)

Gehring, Markus W., "Sustainable competition law for the 2003 Fifth Session of the Ministerial Conference of the WTO in Cancun" (September 10–14, 2003), available at www.cisdl.org/pdf/Cancun_WTO_LegalBrief2.pdf (visited on May 16, 2007)

Huang, Jinxin, "A new Chinese discourse of India" (Nov 2005) 14 *Journal of Contemporary China*

Huang, Yasheng, "2006, the year of India or the year of China?," interview dated February 16, 2006 available at http://www2.chinesenewsnet.com, (in Chinese)

Selling China: Foreign Direct Investment during the Reform Era (Cambridge University Press, 2003)

Huang, Yasheng and Khanna, Tarun, "Can India overtake China?" (July–August 2003) *Foreign Policy*

Huang, Yong and Li, Zhiqiang, "Conflict of laws and international cooperation in antitrust enforcement," in Xiaoye Wang (ed.), *New Developments of Competition Law under Globalization* (Beijing: Social Science Academy Press, 2005) (in Chinese)

"India and China agree to study regional trade agreement," *The Hindu Business Section*, March 17, 2006

Jain, Subhash C., *The Constitution of India: Select Issues & Perceptions* (New Delhi: Taxmann, 2000)

Jin, Chaowu and Luo, Wei, *Competition Law in China* (Buffalo NY: William S. Hein & Co. Inc., 2002)

Jones, William C., "Trying to understand the current Chinese legal system," in C. Stephen Hsu (ed.), *Understanding China's Legal System: Essays in Honor of Jerome A. Cohen* (New York: New York University Press, 2003)

Josephs, Hilary K., "Legal institutions and their 'proper' place in economic development: India and China compared" (2004), available at http://ssrn.com/abstract=572165

Kanamori, Toshiki and Zhao, Zhijun, *Private Sector Development in the People's Republic of China* (Tokyo: Asian Development Bank Institute, 2004)

Landler, Mark, "India mounts a charm offensive," *International Herald Tribune*, January 27, 2006

Li, Rong-Rong, The report of the speech of Mr. Rong-Rong Li, available at http://finance.qianlong.com/26/2005/01/21/206@2483110.htm (visited on January 22, 2005) (in Chinese)

Lin, Hua, "Are multinationals really practicing monopoly?" (2005) 1 *Foreign Investment in China*, available at http://search.mofcom.gov.cn (visited on February 17, 2006) (in Chinese)

Liu, Junjing (ed.), *A Study on Implementation Systems of Anti-Monopoly Law in China and Foreign Countries* (Beijing University Press, 2005) (in Chinese)

Mehta, Manik, "United States seeks closer ties with India to counter China's hegemonic ambitions," *Taiwan Journal*, October 28, 2005, available at http://taiwanjournal.nat.gov.tw/ct.asp?xItem=21618&CtNode=122 (visited on May 16, 2007)

Mehta, Pradeep S., "Competition Bill: Still too many flaws," *Business Standard*, January 7, 2006, available at www.rediff.com/money/2006/jan/07guest1.htm (visited on February 4, 2006)

"Competition vs Regulation: The best way forward," *The Hindu Business Line*, September 16, 2005, pp. 2–3, available at www.thehindubusinessline.com/2005/09/16/stories/2005091600401000.htm (visited on February 4, 2006)

"Defanging the Competition Act," *Business Standard*, August 1, 2005, available at www.business-standard.com (visited on March 13, 2006)

Towards a Functional Competition Policy for India: An Overview (New Delhi: Academic Foundation, 2005)

Mei, Shu, "The capital market of China should learn from India," *Southern Weekend*, March 2, 2006

Mian, Zia, "The United States, China and India: A story of leaders, partners and clients," *Economic and Political Weekly*, September 10, 2005

Ming, Shang, "The present conditions of anti-monopoly legislation in China," in Xiaoye Wang (ed.), *New Developments of Competition Law under Globalization* (Beijing: Social Science Academy Press, 2005)

The Ministry of Commerce of the Government of India, "Report of the Expert Group on interaction between trade and competition policy" (1999), para. 1.4.12

MOFCOM, "30 large-sized enterprise groups to be fostered by 2020" dated November 18, 2005, available at http://search.mofcom.gov.cn (visited on May 9, 2006) (in Chinese)

"The Draft Anti-Monopoly Law causes worries in the West," available at http://search.mofcom.gov.cn (visited on February 17, 2006) (in Chinese)

Report dated March 8, 2006, available at http://search.mofcom.gov.cn (visited on April 5, 2006) (in Chinese)

Neumann, Peter A. and Zhang, Tony, "China's new foreign-funded M&A provisions: Greater legal protection or legalized protectionism?," (October 2006) *China Law & Practice* 21–9

Ningyuan, Liu (ed.), *Study on Antitrust Law Enforcement System in China and Foreign Countries* (Beijing University Press, 2005)

"Opinions of the State Council on deepening economic system reform in 2005" dated April 19, 2005, available at http://search.mofcom.gov.cn (visited on January 25, 2006)

Pappu, Sriharsha and Kumar, Saurabh, "Impact of China's entry into the WTO on India" (2001), available at http://papers.ssrn.com/sol3/papers.cfm?abstract_ id=303439 (visited on May 16, 2007)

Pesek, William Jr, "Surprise! India Will Pull Ahead," *International Herald Tribune*, January 31, 2006

Ping, Ling, "Anti-monopoly control on enterprise mergers and acquisitions in China," in Xiaoye Wang (ed.), *New Developments of Competition Law under Globalization* (Beijing: Social Science Academy Press, 2005), pp. 33–8 and 282 (in Chinese)

Pye, Lucian W., "An overview of 50 years of the People's Republic of China: Some progress, but big problems remain" (1999) 159 *The China Quarterly* 569

Rao, S. L., "Competition in infrastructure," available at www.cuts-international.org (visited on April 23, 2006)

Ren, John Yong and Yang, Ning, "The imminent release of China's Anti-Monopoly Law: What to expect" (September 2005) *China Law & Practice* 26

Report of *Commercial Daily* (Hong Kong), January 12, 2006, available at www.fayhoo.-com/servlet/info.infolanmuxx?lmid=20100104&id=20060112:1515128 (visited on March 21, 2006) (in Chinese)

Reportof the website of the Ministry of Commerce dated April 22, 2005, available at http://search.mofcom.gov.cn (visited on May 4, 2006) (in Chinese)

Report of Xinhua News Agency dated January 17, 2006, available at www.sccwto.net:7000/wto/content.jsp?id=12385 (visited on March 23, 2006) (in Chinese)

Restall, Hugo, "India's coming eclipse of China," *Far Eastern Economic Review*, March 11, 2006

SAIC, The duty statement, available at www.saic.gov.cn/ zhzjg/zhin.html (visited on March 21, 2006)

Saxena, Manju and Chandra, Harish, *Law and Changing Society* (New Delhi: Deep & Deep Publishers, 1999)

SHANG Ming, Interview with Mr. Shang Ming, the Director of the Anti-Monopoly Office of the MOFCOM on November 26, 2004, available at http://search.mofcom.gov.cn (visited on February 17, 2006) (in Chinese)

Sheng, Jiemin, Presentation of Professor Jiemin Sheng of Peking University at the 7th Annual Conference of Peking University–Hong Kong University Legal Research Centre on December 21, 2005 at the University of Hong Kong

"Shri Prem Chand Gupta hopes competition commission would be functional in a few months," available at www.indlawnews.com/38015ad8fc90dc27e781af47f5446e2d (visited on January 4, 2007)

Spedding, Linda S., *Trade and Investment in India: Economic Development and Environmental Issues* (London: Cameron May, 1997)

"U.S.–India nuclear deal on course ahead of President Bush visit," *Online NewsHour*, February 24, 2006, www.pbs.org/newshour/ updates/india_02–24–06.html (visited on May 16, 2007)

Wang, Chuanhui, *Economic Analysis of Anti-Monopoly Law*(People's University Press of China, 2004)

Wang, Xiaoye, "Accelerating the adoption of China's Anti-monopoly Law with its WTO accession," at 2, available at www.iolaw.org.cn/shownews.asp?id=242 (visited on June 7, 2005) (in Chinese)

"Regulating conduct to restrict competition by multi-nationals under anti-monopoly law," in Xiaoye Wang (ed.), *New Developments of Competition Law under Globalization* (Beijing: Social Science Academy Press, 2005) (in Chinese)

Wang, Xuezheng, "Challenges/obstacles faced by competition authorities in achieving greater economic development through the promotion of competition" (2004) 16 CCNM/GF/COMP/WD made on January 9, 2004

Presentation made by Mr. Xue-zheng Wang of SAIC, China, to OECD Global Forum on Competition on October 17–18, 2001, CCNM/GF/COMP/WC (2001)

Wang, "The relationship between competition authorities and sectoral regulators," OECD document: DAF/COMP/GF/WD (2005)9, January 12, 2005

Williams, Mark, *Competition Policy and Law in China, Hong Kong and Taiwan* (Cambridge University Press, 2005)

WTO, Statistics, available at www.wto.org/english/tratop_e/ adp_e/adp_e.htm (visited on May 16, 2007)

Xinhua News Agency report dated December 10, 2005, available at www.southcn.com/news/china/zgkx/200512100126.htm (visited on March 10, 2006)

Xue, Zhaofeng, "What monopoly the government should fight against," *Southern Weekend*, January 20, 2004, available at www.nanfangdaily.com.cn (visited on March 21, 2006) (in Chinese)

Zhang, Bingsheng, "On design of anti-monopoly enforcement authority in China: Questions to the current plans" (2005) 2 *Legal Science* (*Journal of Northwestern College of Political Science and Law*) 117–19 (in Chinese)

ZHANG Xian Chu, "New landscape of foreign mergers and acquisitions in China after its WTO accession" (2003) 2 *Journal of Chinese and Comparative Law* 229–55

INDEX